Little pilgrimages among the men who have written famous books : second series

E F. b. 1872 Harkins

Nabu Public Domain Reprints:

You are holding a reproduction of an original work published before 1923 that is in the public domain in the United States of America, and possibly other countries. You may freely copy and distribute this work as no entity (individual or corporate) has a copyright on the body of the work. This book may contain prior copyright references, and library stamps (as most of these works were scanned from library copies). These have been scanned and retained as part of the historical artifact.

This book may have occasional imperfections such as missing or blurred pages, poor pictures, errant marks, etc. that were either part of the original artifact, or were introduced by the scanning process. We believe this work is culturally important, and despite the imperfections, have elected to bring it back into print as part of our continuing commitment to the preservation of printed works worldwide. We appreciate your understanding of the imperfections in the preservation process, and hope you enjoy this valuable book.

Photo Bradshaw, Hastings

H. N. Pillsbury

THE HASTINGS
CHESS TOURNAMENT

1895

CONTAINING THE

AUTHORISED ACCOUNT OF THE 230 GAMES
PLAYED AUG.–SEPT. 1895

WITH ANNOTATIONS BY PILLSBURY, LASKER, TARRASCH, STEINITZ
SCHIFFERS, TEICHMANN, BARDELEBEN, BLACKBURNE
GUNSBERG, TINSLEY, MASON, AND ALBIN

AND BIOGRAPHICAL SKETCHES OF THE CHESS MASTERS

EDITED BY HORACE F. CHESHIRE

WITH TWENTY-TWO PORTRAITS

NEW YORK . G P. PUTNAM'S SONS
LONDON CHATTO & WINDUS, PICCADILLY
1896

GV
1455
H35
1895

~~6695 D 57~~

A.152958
COPYRIGHT, 1896
BY
G P PUTNAM'S SONS

Gift. C. S. Northrup

PREFACE

No excuse should be necessary for adding this volume to the long list of chess works now before the public. One of the advantages of a tournament such as that held at Hastings is, that it helps to advance the theory of the game, and a book is necessary as a permanent record. It is also hoped that we may recall the keen enjoyment felt by those who were fortunate enough to attend, as well as be able to somewhat recompense those who were unable to do so.

In arranging the matter at our disposal we have endeavoured to avoid dryness, by giving it chronologically with running comments.

Some of the games have already received the light of publication, and their general excellence should be a sufficient guarantee of the merits of the whole

A few matters not strictly belonging to a record have been lightly touched upon in the Appendix, which, however, it is believed will also be found sufficiently interesting.

In conclusion we beg to thank players who furnished notes for their biographies, Mr Hoffer for filling a few gaps, also the annotators, and all friends local and otherwise who proved so ready to assist.

HORACE F. CHESHIRE.

St. Leonards, *June* 1896.

vii

CONTENTS

The following table gives at a glance both the page on which each game will be found and the first moves, the pages being entered opposite the name of the player who had the move in each case:

Name	Country Represented	ALBIN	BARDELEBEN	BIRD	BLACKBURNE	BURN	GUNSBERG	JANOWSKI	LASKER	MARCO	MASON	MIESES	PILLSBURY	POLLOCK	SCHIFFERS	SCHLECHTER	STEINITZ	TARRASCH	TCHIGORIN	TEICHMANN	TINSLEY	VERGANI	WALBRODT
ALBIN, A.	America	—	32	22, 55		319		172, 248	235, 73, 77		226	183, 108		135, 148	210, 280	98		187, 236	227, 165	306, 287		143, 86	36
BARDELEBEN, C. VON	Germany		—		64		271						229		300	83	47	150, 90	118	293	331	110	149
BIRO, H. E.	England	115	174	—	14, 315	150		84	332	239	292	323, 240, 127	199	175, 232	48	68, 295	87, 273			224, 251	169, 50, 211, 76	272	
BLACKBURNE, J. H.	England	276	13, 296	201, 308	—	40	241, 171, 108	96		202, 24	253, 105		151, 185	38, 189	245, 88	145, 299	111	230, 19	30, 54, 275			207, 297	176, 134
BURN, A.	England	332		102, 180		—	325	66	264, 166		288	140	104	62		250, 321		34, 213	291, 71, 334		302		232
GUNSBERG, I.	France				39	259	—	150, 220	115, 256, 52	307, 55	164				330	285	173	178, 310		82, 44, 107		46	
JANOWSKI, D.	Austria	165	338, 100	239	281		26	—		196		270	132	16, 93	261						279	242	312
LASKER, E.	England			153, 130	94	171, 218		284, 320	—	182	70	203, 195, 57	20		113	42	209		79	162, 98	246, 262	27, 327	60, 187
MARCO, G.	Germany	78	261		259		141	124	304	—	336	25	179	314	147, 156	223	244	133	254	69		172	17
MASON, J.	England			267	121, 190	95	205			139	—												
MIESES, J.	Germany			197	233	283	194, 58	41, 278		128, 268	80	—	309, 238	258		161, 328					114		92
PILLSBURY, H. N.	America	255	126, 157										—										
POLLOCK, W. H. K.	Canada													—									
SCHIFFERS, E.	Russia	266								182					—								
SCHLECHTER, C.	Austria															—							
STEINITZ, W.	America	53	257														—						
TARRASCH, Dr. S.	Germany	72																—					
TCHIGORIN, M.	Russia																		—				
TEICHMANN, R.	England		212																	—			
TINSLEY, S.	England	290																			—		
VERGANI, B.	Italy																					—	
WALBRODT, A.	Germany																						—

PORTRAITS

H N PILLSBURY		*Frontispiece*
AMOS BURN	*To face page*	13
JAMES MASON	,,	19
SAMUEL TINSLEY	,,	29
W. H. K. POLLOCK	,,	46
E SCHIFFERS	,,	48
DR. TARRASCH	,,	60
GEORG MARCO	,,	76
I GUNSBERG	,,	90
D. JANOWSKI	,,	105
M TCHIGORIN	,,	121
R TEICHMANN	,,	139
B. VERGANI	,,	156
E. LASKER	,,	171
J. H. BLACKBURNE	,,	199
W. STEINITZ	,,	218
A ALBIN	,,	235
H E. BIRD	,,	248
CARL SCHLECHTER	,,	261
J MIESES	,,	275
A WALBRODT	,,	290
C. VON BARDELEBEN	,,	306

INTERNATIONAL CHESS CONGRESS

HASTINGS 1895

Royal Patron—H.R.H. THE DUKE OF YORK, K.G.

PATRONS.

PRINCE DEMIDOFF DE SON DONATO (Attaché Russian Embassy).
EARL OF DARTREY, K.P. (President of the St. George's Chess Club).
EARL OF ASHBURNHAM.
VISCOUNT CANTELUPE
LORD BRASSEY, K C B.
HON. T. A. BRASSEY.
SIR GEORGE NEWNES, BART. (President of the British Chess Club).
THE LORD MAYOR OF LONDON (President of the Metropolitan Chess Club).
THE MAYOR OF HASTINGS (MAJOR WESTON).
THE DEPUTY-MAYOR OF HASTINGS (B. H W. TREE, ESQ.).
SIR ISRAEL HART (President of the Leicester Chess Club).
A. MOCATTA, ESQ. (President of the City of London Chess Club).
CANON DEANE (Chairman of the Southern Counties Chess Union).
DR HUNT (Vice-Chairman of the Southern Counties Chess Union)
JAMES WHITE, ESQ. (President of the Leeds Chess Club).
G E BARBIER, ESQ (President of the Glasgow Chess Club).
W. H. JACKSON, ESQ (President of the Wilts Chess Club).
REV. F. J. SUGDEN (President of the Battersea Chess Club).
PLAYER ISAAC, ESQ. (President of the Brighton Chess Club).
E. J. BRADFIELD, ESQ. (President of the Warminster Chess Club).
H. S. LEONARD, ESQ (President of the Guildford Chess Club).
F. FREMLIN, ESQ. (President of the Maidstone Chess Club).
W. NICHOLLS, ESQ. (President of the Jersey Chess Club).
J. E. HALL, ESQ. (President of the Henfield Chess Club).
CAPTAIN BEAUMONT (President of the South Norwood Chess Club).
D. POWELL, ESQ. (President of the Liverpool Chess Club)
WM. KIRKLAND, ESQ. (President of the Cyprus Chess Club).
L. RAYMOND, ESQ. (President of the Southsea Chess Club)
H HAYWARD, ESQ., J P. (President of the Dover Chess Club).
R. CHIPPERFIELD, ESQ., J.P. (President of the Southampton Chess Club)
W. LUCAS SHADWELL, ESQ., M.P.
COLONEL BROOKFIELD, M.P.
C. J. FLEMING, ESQ , Q C., M P.
L. A. ATHERLEY JONES, ESQ., M.P.

PATRONS (continued).

W. J. EVELYN, ESQ.
JOSEPH COOKE, ESQ.
CHARLES ANTHONY, ESQ.
EDWYN ANTHONY, ESQ.
REV. C. E. RANKEN.
ROBERT STEEL, ESQ.

WILSON NOBLE, ESQ.
REV. W. SAYER-MILWARD.
I. M. BROWN, ESQ.
J. W. ABBOTT, ESQ.
LIEUT. A. E. STUDD.
W. LEUCHARS, ESQ.

G. HEYWOOD, ESQ. (President of the Newcastle Arts).

COMMITTEE OF MANAGEMENT.

President: J. WATNEY, ESQ. | *Vice-President*: H. CHAPMAN, ESQ.

Chairman: T. COLE, ESQ.

Joint Trustees: { A. H. HALL, ESQ.
                   { J. COLBORNE, ESQ.

COMMITTEE.

(Including those added for executive purposes.)

A. ALOOF, ESQ.
G. BRADSHAW, ESQ.
H. CHAPMAN, ESQ.
H. CHESHIRE, ESQ.
H. COLBORNE, ESQ.
J. COLBORNE, ESQ.
T. COLE, ESQ.
REV. E. CROSSE

H. E. DOBELL, ESQ.
A. EARL, ESQ.
J. ELSDEN, ESQ.
A. HALL, ESQ.
J. HALLAWAY, ESQ.
G. HERINGTON, ESQ.
E. JUKES, ESQ.
H. KING, ESQ.

F. KUHN, ESQ.
C. LOCOCK, ESQ.
E. MCCORMICK, ESQ.
H. TRENCHARD, ESQ.
F. TUDDENHAM, ESQ.
J. WATNEY, ESQ.
F. WOMERSLEY, ESQ.

Hon. Treasurer: A. H. HALL, ESQ. | *Hon. Secretary*: H. E. DOBELL, ESQ.

LIST OF COMPETITORS.

A. ALBIN (America)
H. E. BIRD (England)
A. BURN (England)
D. JANOWSKI (France)
J. MIESES (Germany)
G. MARCO (Austria)
W. H. K. POLLOCK (Canada)
C. SCHLECHTER (Austria)
DR. TARRASCH (Germany)
S. TINSLEY (England)
B. VERGANI (Italy)

C. VON BARDELEBEN (Germany)
J. H. BLACKBURNE (England)
I. GUNSBERG (England)
E. LASKER (England)
J. MASON (England)
H. N. PILLSBURY (America)
E. SCHIFFERS (Russia)
W. STEINITZ (America)
M. TCHIGORIN (Russia)
R. TEICHMANN (England)
A. WALBRODT (Germany)

Reserve: N. W. VAN LENNEP (Holland).

THE

HASTINGS CHESS TOURNAMENT

THE
HASTINGS CHESS TOURNAMENT
1895

INTRODUCTION.

DURING parts of August and September an event of no little importance in chess history occurred in the holding of an International Tournament at Hastings.

It is our pleasant, if laborious, duty to lay before our readers an account of its rise, progress, and close, with a copy of the games and a brief summary of the social proceedings. In doing so we have left the beaten track somewhat, and tried to present the whole matter in a narrative form in chronological order. We have also expunged many details commonly given, and utilised the space at our disposal for matters interesting to the votaries of chess.

It has been rather freely said by the press, and, may we say, we hope with justice, that this Tournament has been the most successful ever held. At any rate, that it was to be at least successful was quite evident from the very first week. It perhaps was due to many favouring factors, including fortuity of time, presence of an experienced local master, magnanimous help of friends, and cautious originality of committee with an almost alarming independence of action, with considerable experience in managing club chess festivals, and last, but not least, the generous assistance of the press.

Some of the advice received from friends and would-be friends was eccentric, but most was useful, and it all was carefully considered in the spirit in which it was offered, and much of it adopted with benefit.

The games will be found arranged in order of date, and also as nearly as possible to bring the notes into view at the same time as the score. The annotations are all by competitors and mostly by the prize winners, though some of these, through pressure of time, &c., could not undertake many of them, and thirty games was made a maximum number. The games were distributed so as to give as great a variety of opinion on the various openings and styles of play as possible, and so that no one should annotate his own games. The notes will be found to vary in style also: from the ponderous to the light and chatty, from the historical to the strictly analytical, with many intermediate grades.

The play has produced many surprises. It was curious to watch the varying predictions as to the winner; in the early days few, if any, were right, though the secretary was in possession of a letter which said, 'Young Pillsbury will not be far out at the finish.'

Four Dutch papers were represented, besides five French and numberless German and British. The full reports in the press necessarily helped considerably. There were, of course, a few funny slips, due to the essential hurry and bustle, such as a player sacrificing his King for the opposing Rook's Pawn, but it was noticeable how very much more correct chess reports are now than they were a few years ago when they were left too much to non experts.

Well-known players from all parts of England were recognised—in fact, from all parts of the world; and a very remarkable feature was the large number of ladies who graced the meeting with their presence, and the interest they took in the games. There were several minor tournaments held, as (i.) Problem-solving Tournament. A. E. Studd, Esq., the well-known problemist, had offered prizes for a solving tournament, and the Committee asked him to carry out the arrangements for them, which he did in the most able and generous manner. He provided three prizes, 3*l.*, 2*l.*, and 1*l.*, and some elaborately got up solving papers with full instructions and beautifully printed diagrams. He was good enough also to conduct the competition in person, and we beg on behalf of the Committee to tender him our most heartfelt thanks. The problems and other particulars will be found under their proper date, and the solutions at the end of the book. (ii.) An Amateur Tournament. One difficulty of all large tournaments is the apparent necessity of some sort of minor tournament. After negotiations, a second committee of British Amateurs was formed, which, however, quickly took the matter out of our hands, and we had little to do with its success except supplying funds and hiring rooms for it to be played in ; the Committee secured the Newnes Cup, and making an entrance fee of 1*l.* provided prizes to the value of 20*l.*, 15*l.*, 10*l.*, and 5*l.*, and four consolation prizes of 5*l.*, 4*l.*, 3*l.*, and 2*l.* The entries received were so numerous that they were thinned down to thirty-two, and divided into eight sections. The chief prizes were won by Géza Maroczy, H. M. Atkins and R. Loman equal, and Dr. Cohn, whilst the consolation prizes were won by F. Hollins, R. P. Michell, Dr. Smith, and Rev. J. Owen in the order named. The thanks of our Committee are due to the Amateur Committee and to their hon. secretary, Mr. Grantham Williams, who conducted the Tournament. (iii.) Then there was a Ladies' Tournament, which was kindly managed by a Ladies' Committee, consisting of Mrs. Gunsberg, London, and Mrs. Baird, Brighton, with Miss Watson, Hastings, and Mrs. Bowles, London. The entrance fee was 5*s.*, and the competitors had the choice of a Major and a Minor Tournament. The first prize was a handsome set of ivory chess men and board, presented by the 'Lady's Pictorial,' and was won by Lady Thomas, lady of the Manor of Marston ; second prize, Miss Field ; third prize, Miss Fox ; fourth prize, Miss Finn. The Minor section was won by Mrs. Ridpath.

Amongst the non-competitive experts Mr. Hoffer was especially conspicuous by the assistance he rendered to the success of the Hastings International Tournament, and amongst the competitors Mr. Gunsberg holds a similar position, but all, including Messrs. Blackburne, Lasker, Tinsley, Van Vliet, Mason, Guest, I. M. Brown, &c., were ever ready, and are also most sincerely thanked.

The thanks of the Committee are also tendered to Patrons, Donors, the Press, and helpers generally, not forgetting the Secretaries of the London and other Clubs, and to the competitors for the ready way in which they acquiesced in all arrangements, and showed appreciation of the efforts made on their behalf.

Now, as it is said that chess tournaments and chess history are synonymous, we will proceed to the origin and early history of ours.

ORIGIN AND EARLY HISTORY.

IMAGINE some years ago a London expert and three local enthusiasts wandering along some of the quiet roads of Hastings when the sun is giving us a holiday, after one of our chess events, and these four conspirators discussing the possibilities of the future, when lo! at the witching hour of night, near the fairy dell of St. Andrew's Arch, the plot is hatched to expand the Chess Festivals to something which should startle the world

This nocturnal perambulation seems at least to have given definite direction to the somewhat vague longings which had perhaps existed for some time, and have gradually reached so desirable a consummation

Mr. Dobell has since that memorable occasion never let the matter slip, though as a good chess-player he was not going to be premature. His hobby has always been in mind and it has largely framed our club history

At last he saw a favourable combination of the pieces and at once seized upon the opportunity to make the most of the position. Steinitz, the long-time champion, had been beaten, and his return challenge remained unmet, whilst Lasker, though scarcely yet robust, would probably be sufficiently recovered from his exhausting illness to try conclusions in a masters' tournament. Dr. Tarrasch had done wonders in smaller tournaments, but there were many in the foremost rank with whom he had found no opportunity to cross Pawns. Again there were several rising stars throwing their bright, if fitful, rays across the horizon, and anxious to test their brilliancies against the steadier lights of the luminaries of greater altitude.

Tchigorin also had not played in an international tournament for some years, and would doubtless be pleased to again try conclusions with his peers. And it was felt that if these four could be secured success was certain.

Our energetic—we were nearly saying ambitious—secretary approached our president, Mr. Watney, and one of our vice-presidents, Mr. Horace Chapman, who both fell in with the idea

INTRODUCTION

and generously promised 50*l.* each. A small committee was at once formed, nearly identical with our club committee, and although some seemed rather scared at the magnitude of the scheme and responsibilities, unity became strength, and they guaranteed that the club members' subscriptions should not reach less than 150*l.* A few special desires in the way of competitors were approached, as well as some British experts, and when everything was ripe, public announcement was made, further subscriptions were invited, advice was requested and promised full consideration.

The Committee had preliminarily determined on sixteen places, but when entries were invited thirty-eight were actually received! And then the process of selection had to be undertaken, in doing which the first consideration was strength as shown by performances, and a minor one that of nationality, but young players on the up grade were shown some preference to older ones on the down, as they were probably a little better than their reputation. It was remarked in committee : 'Who knows? We may bring a new genius to light,' and it is evident that these new experts cannot have the history of the older ones. At length twenty-two were selected and one reserve man, whose services were however never required One strong player wished to enter *incog.*, but the condition was declined and the entry lost.

We had now fairly entered on our arduous labours. Special arrangements were made with the Queen's Hotel, and many of the masters availed themselves of them. The town authorities lent the large room of the Brassey Institute, which is close to the sea front, and several smaller rooms in it free of all charges, and some special tasks were delegated to individual members. Mr. Womersley, for example, undertook the heavy duty of the arrangement of the room, and getting out scoring cards, &c. Mr. King looked after the distinguishing badges, and so on, all under the eagle eye of our general. Thus everything was soon in readiness for the new battle of Hastings. It will therefore be seen that the Tournament was largely a simple outgrowth of the constant activity of the flourishing Hastings and St. Leonards Chess Club which, fortunately situated in the most picturesque part of our South Coast, has from a small beginning gradually but surely grown to its present prominent position. It might almost be said that it was the natural development of their annual events, at which the 'master' element was always a feature.

We will now introduce our competitors and give the regulations, &c. under which they played, and when they have finished we will give a short account of their history.

REGULATIONS
OF THE INTERNATIONAL TOURNAMENT.

Place and Date.—The Tournament will be held in the Brassey Institute, Hastings, and will commence on Monday, August 5, 1895.

PRIZES.

First Prize	150*l.*	Fifth Prize	40*l.*
Second Prize	115*l.*	Sixth Prize	30*l.*
Third Prize	85*l.*	Seventh Prize	20*l.*
Fourth Prize	60*l.*		

Total 500*l.*, and consolation money in addition.

SPECIAL PRIZES.

The player who wins most Evans' Gambits (accepted), either as White or Black, will be presented by Joseph Cooke, Esq., of Knockgraffon, with a handsome ring, and in addition with 'The Theory and Practice of Chess' (in four octavo volumes), by Carlo Salvioli, of the value of forty lire. In the event of a tie, the preference would be given to the player in whose games the normal position occurred most frequently.

The first winner of seven games will be presented by Mr. Bradshaw, of Hastings, with an enlarged photograph, value 4*l.* 4*s.*

A special prize of 5*l.* will be presented by the Committee to the non-prize winner who makes the highest score (including drawn games) against the seven prize winners. This will not exclude him from consolation money.

Consolation.—Each non-prize winner will receive as consolation 1*l.* for each game that he wins, and in the event of his winning a game from the 1st, 2nd, or 3rd prize winner, he will receive for such game the sum of 2*l.* instead of 1*l.*

Entrance Fee.—All entries must be received on or before July 5, accompanied by an entrance fee of 5*l.*

Order of Play.—Each player must play one game with every other competitor. The order of play and pairing will be decided by the president drawing lots publicly immediately before the commencement of the Tournament. The future pairing will depend on this, but will not be known until the morning of each day.

INTRODUCTION

Score.—The winner of a game scores 1, the loser 0, and in a drawn game each player scores ½.

Days of Play.—Monday, Tuesday, Wednesday, Friday, Saturday. Thursday will be a by-day for playing off unfinished games.

Hours of Play.—From 1 P.M. to 5 P.M., and from 7 P.M. to 10 P.M., but no game may be adjourned in the evening until sixty moves have been recorded on each side.

Time Limit.—Thirty moves for the first two hours, and fifteen moves per hour afterwards. The player who exceeds the time limit will forfeit his game, which will be scored as won by his opponent.

Differences between Players.—All questions between players shall be decided by the official in charge, and on questions of fact such decision shall be final; in other cases the players shall have the right of appeal to the Committee.

Absentees.—The official in charge will see that all the clocks are started at the time fixed for play, and if a player is an hour late in arriving, his game is lost. Should neither player be present within an hour, the game will not be scored.

Adjournments.—At the time fixed for adjournment the player whose turn it is to move must deliver his next move in writing, in a closed envelope, to the official in charge. Such envelope will be opened after the adjournment by the official then in charge, in the presence of both competitors, and he will make on the board the move as written down. Analysing of moves on a chess-board during the adjournment, and consultation with anyone, is strictly prohibited. Any player proved guilty of an infringement of this rule will be expelled from the Tournament, and will forfeit his right to a prize or to consolation money.

Scores of the Games.—All the games are the property of the Committee. The winner of a game, or the first player in a drawn game, is bound to deliver at the conclusion of the same a correct and legible score to the member of the Committee in charge. Until this is done, the result will not be entered on the score-sheet.

Arrangements between Players.—All arrangements between players which will affect the result of the Tournament are illegal, unless sanctioned by the Committee. Each competitor is bound in honour to play all his games with his full strength, and in behalf of the other competitors no player is allowed to waive any exaction of a penalty, either under the rules of the Tournament or the general laws of chess. All parties proved guilty of violating this rule will be expelled from the Tournament, with a forfeit of prizes or consolation money.

Withdrawing.—In case of any player withdrawing from the Tournament before its conclusion, his unplayed games will be forfeited to his opponents, and he will forfeit his entrance fee and any consolation money.

Tie among Prize Winners.— In case of a tie between two players for the first prize, they shall play a match for the first winner of three games, drawn games not counting. If three or more players should tie for the first prize, a match between those players will be arranged by the Committee ; the winner of this match to be declared the winner of the Tournament. In case of a tie for another than the first prize, the players shall divide their prizes.

Modification of Regulations.—The Committee will reserve to themselves the absolute power to modify any of the above rules in special cases.

NOTE.—To the prizes were afterwards added two for the player who should win a game by the greatest display of sound brilliancy.— 1st prize, 5*l.*, given by H. Chapman, Esq., and Anon., 2nd prize, 3*l.*, given by W. Leuchars, Esq. And to the consolation money the Committee added after the conclusion of the play 10*s.* for every draw by a non-prize winner against a prize winner.

Also, the words 'in the presence of both competitors' were struck out of the regulation for adjournments, as it was found better to open the envelope, make the move, and set the clocks going, whether the competitors were present or not.

Rules (Revised International Code).

I. If a player notices before his fourth move that either the board or Pieces have been misplaced, he has the right to demand that the game shall be re-commenced.

II. Before the beginning of the first game, the first move and choice of colour are determined by lot. The first move changes alternately in match play.

III. If a player desires to adjust the position of a Piece or Pawn on the board, he must say *J'adoube*, before touching it, otherwise—

IV. If a player touches a Piece or Pawn of his own he must move it. If he touches one of his adversary's he must take it if it can be taken. If he touches a plurality of Pieces or Pawns of the same colour, in either of these instances his adversary may elect which such Piece or Pawn he will call upon him to play or take, as the case may be. If the rules governing the moves of Pieces do not admit of the adversary exacting penalty as above, the player must move his King, but may not castle. If the King cannot be moved without exposure to check, no penalty can then be exacted.

N.B.—The adversary must claim a penalty under this rule before he makes his own next move. While he is considering the penalty his own time must run, and not that of his adversary.

V. A move is not completed until the player's hand has quitted the Piece or Pawn played.

VI. 'Check' is announced to the King only ; it is not absolutely necessary to call it. If a player, on attacking his adversary's King, omits to call check, penalties under Rule 4 cannot be enforced. The player whose King is attacked must move out of check, or cover, or capture the attacking Piece so soon as his attention is called to the fact , and if any moves have been made by either party while a King has remained exposed to attack, they must be cancelled.

VII. If the same position occurs thrice during a game, it being on each occasion the turn for the same player to move, the game is drawn.

VIII A player may at any time call upon his adversary to mate him within fifty moves (move and reply being counted as one). If, by the expiration of such fifty moves, no Piece or Pawn has been captured, nor Pawn moved, nor mate given, a draw can then be obtained.

IX. The King cannot be castled out of check nor cross an attacked square. In the act of castling, the King must be moved first, or else must be touched before the Rook is quitted.

X A Pawn reaching the eighth square must be named as a Queen or Piece, at the option of player, independent of the number of Pieces on the board The created Queen or Piece acts immediately in its new capacity. Until the Pawn has been so named the move is incomplete

XI. Time runs until a move is completed, as under these Rules.

XII. If, on the resumption of an adjourned game, the position is wrongly set up, all subsequent moves are void, and the position must, if possible, be correctly replaced, and the game then played from the point of adjournment.

XIII. In the event of proof that a clock or glass has recorded incorrect time, the umpire shall be empowered to make such adjustment in the record of the time as he shall consider equitable in view of the circumstances disclosed, provided that he shall make no allowance in the case of actual stoppage of a clock, it being the duty of a player to see that his adversary's clock is set going.

SOCIAL ARRANGEMENTS.

Thursday, August 8.—Drive to, and inspection of Battle Abbey (by kind permission of the Duchess of Cleveland), and of Normanhurst Court (by kindness of Lord Brassey). The masters as guests. On that evening a performance in the Gaiety Theatre, and Concert on Hastings Pier, under the patronage of the Chess Congress.

Thursday, August 15.—Reception in the evening by the president and vice-president. There will be music.

Thursday, August 22.—Problem-solving Tournament, from 3 to 5 P.M. ; Prizes, value 3*l*., 2*l*, 1*l*., having been given by A. E. Studd, Esq., of Brighton. No entrance fee for solvers Banquet in the Queen's Hotel in the evening, the masters as guests.

Tuesday to Thursday, August 27 *to* 29.—Carnival Week in Hastings : Military Tournament, Floral Fête and Procession, National Fire Brigades Review and Demonstration, Fireworks, &c. The Carnival Committee will present a ticket to each of the masters, admitting them to all of these exhibitions.

THE OPENING DAY.

The opening ceremony was held before a numerous assembly in the Tournament Room at 12.30, August 5. The president, Mr. Watney, as chairman, welcomed the masters (who were all seated on the platform) ; he spoke in high praise of Mr. Dobell, and wished the Tournament all the success it deserved.

The Mayor, Major Weston, welcomed them on behalf of the townspeople and Corporation to the beautiful watering-place, and hoped the masters would find time to enjoy the beauties of the district.

Mr. Lucas Shadwell, M.P., spoke of the Tournament as being unique in the history of Hastings, and especially welcomed the foreign competitors to England, and hoped they would not be able to grumble at the climate of sunny Hastings.

The president then made the draw of the names to match with the numbers with which the pairings had been arranged, and as the names were called the players were cheered, Blackburne, of Hastings, naturally coming in for the chief ovation : this draw determined the first moves and the pairings of all the rounds, but not the order in which the rounds were to be played. The draw was then made for the round for the day, and the president explained that he, or in his absence the director in charge, would

INTRODUCTION

make this draw each day before play commenced. By 1.15 all were at work with eleven clocks ticking away, and not a single competitor absent or late. Mr. Van Lennep, the reserve man, was also present, but as there was no vacancy he was constrained to play the *rôle* of an onlooker

The pairing of the opening day gave promise of some fine games, and the spectators were not disappointed. Imagine a very large room covered with red baize and the walls hung with pictures by the best artists; eleven tables in two rows of four and one of three, whilst rows of chairs cause about 100 spectators to keep a sufficient distance from the players.

Then twenty-two players, sitting with knitted brows, making intellectual war with each other, many of them not by any means looking physically powerful men—in fact, expert chessists are as a rule rather diminutive; the spectators moving gently about trying to find the most interesting game and endeavouring to swallow as much as possible, and some writing diagrams as if their life depended on it; the numerous press men of all nations—busy-looking people generally—moving more rapidly and gathering information for their papers, and the officials of the Tournament well-nigh overwhelmed with the numerous details that have to be looked after, and anxious that even in their first day no hitch should occur. The day wears on and all is going smoothly. Lasker is moving with such extreme slowness that some of his friends begin to fidget about his time; but presently his plans are mature, he moves quickly, and scores the first win of the Tournament. One game is over, there is now a hurrying of feet, the official rubber stamp is brought into requisition, the various score cards are marked, the score of the game is secured and taken to the official at the desk, who commences his investigations as to accuracy and supplies the press copies to those who crowd round him. Presently another game is finished, and the same process is gone through, though with more familiarity. Soon the 5 o'clock adjournment is approaching, diagram forms are got ready, and when the bell rings there is a great registering of positions and sealed moves. The precious envelopes and the unfinished scores are put under lock and key, to be brought out again at the 7 o'clock resumption. At 7, clocks are set going, positions set up, sealed moves made, and all goes on merrily if busily. During the day all the present favourites win except Tarrasch, who lets his clock beat him; Bird shows some of his brilliancies in a fine game against Albin, and Pillsbury gives Tchigorin plenty of trouble, and thereby begins to draw attention to his chances.

ORDER OF PAIRING.

Ballot No.	Name	August 5	August 6	August 7	August 9	August 10	August 12	August 13	August 14	August 16	August 17	August 19	August 20	August 21	August 23	August 24	August 26	August 27	August 28	August 30	August 31	September 2
1	Burn, A.	22	13	10	15	2	9	6	5	18	21	20	3	16	11	14	17	12	19	4	7	8
2	Janowski, D.	21	12	9	14	1	8	5	4	17	20	19	22	15	10	13	16	11	18	3	6	7
3	Schlechter, C.	20	11	8	13	21	7	4	22	16	19	18	1	14	9	12	15	10	17	2	5	6
4	Teichmann, R.	19	10	7	12	20	6	3	2	15	18	17	21	13	8	11	14	9	16	1	22	5
5	Mason, J.	18	9	6	11	19	22	2	1	14	17	16	20	12	7	10	13	8	15	21	3	4
6	Tchigorin, M.	17	8	5	10	18	4	1	21	13	16	15	19	11	22	9	12	7	14	20	2	3
7	Albin, A.	16	22	4	9	17	3	21	20	12	15	14	18	10	5	8	11	6	13	19	1	2
8	Lasker, E.	15	6	3	22	16	2	20	19	11	14	13	17	9	4	7	10	5	12	18	21	1
9	Tinsley, S.	14	5	2	7	15	1	19	18	10	13	12	16	8	3	6	22	4	11	17	20	21
10	Schiffers, E.	13	4	1	6	14	21	18	17	9	12	11	15	7	2	5	8	3	22	16	19	20
11	Steinitz, W.	12	3	21	5	13	20	17	16	8	22	10	14	6	1	4	7	2	9	15	18	19
12	Vergani, B.	11	2	20	4	22	19	16	15	7	10	9	13	5	21	3	6	1	8	14	17	18
13	Gunsberg, I.	10	1	19	3	11	18	15	14	6	9	8	12	4	20	2	5	21	7	22	16	17
14	Mieses, J.	9	21	18	2	10	17	22	13	5	8	7	11	3	19	1	4	20	6	12	15	16
15	Marco, G.	8	20	17	1	9	16	13	12	4	7	6	10	2	18	21	3	19	5	11	14	22
16	Bird, H. E.	7	19	22	21	8	15	12	11	3	6	5	9	1	17	20	2	18	4	10	13	14
17	Pillsbury, H. N.	6	18	15	20	7	14	11	10	—	5	4	8	21	16	19	1	22	3	9	12	13
18	Tarrasch, Dr.	5	17	14	19	6	13	10	9	1	4	3	7	20	15	22	21	15	2	8	11	12
19	Walbrodt, A.	4	16	13	18	5	12	9	8	21	3	2	6	22	14	17	20	14	1	7	10	11
20	Pollock, W. H. K.	3	15	12	17	4	11	8	7	22	2	1	5	18	13	16	19	13	21	6	9	10
21	Blackburne, J. H.	2	14	11	16	3	10	7	6	19	1	22	4	17	12	15	18	17	20	5	8	9
22	Bardeleben, C. von	1	7	16	8	12	5	14	3	20	11	21	2	19	6	18	9	16	10	13	4	15

Photo., Bradshaw, Hastings

Amos Burn

THE PLAY

AUGUST 5.

A. Burn *v.* C. von Bardeleben.

WHITE	BLACK
1 P to Q 4	P to Q 4
2 P to Q B 4	P to K 3
3 Kt to Q B 3	Kt to K B 3
4 Kt to K B 3	B to K 2
5 P to K 3	Castles
6 B to K 2 [1]	P × P
7 Castles	P to Q B 4
8 P × P	B × P
9 B × P	P to Q R 3
10 Q to K 2	P to Q Kt 4
11 B to Q Kt 3	B to Q Kt 2
12 B to Q 2 [2]	Q Kt to Q 2
13 K R to Q sq	Q to K 2
14 B to K sq	P to Kt 5
15 Kt to Q R 4 [3]	B to Q 3
16 Q to Q 3 [4]	B to Kt sq
17 Q R to Q B sq	
	B × Kt [5]
18 P × B	Kt to K 4
19 Q to K 2	P to Kt 4
20 R to Q 4	P to Q R 4
21 P to B 4	P × P
22 R × P	K to R sq
23 P to K B 3 [6]	Kt to R 4
24 R to Q 4	B to R 2
25 B to R 4	Q to Kt 2
26 R to K 4	P to B 4 [7]
27 R × Kt	Q to Kt 2, ch
28 K to R sq	Q × R

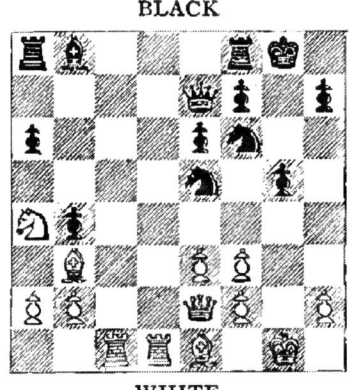

White to make his 20th move.

WHITE	BLACK
29 R to B 6	Kt to Kt 2
30 B to K B 2	Q R to Q sq
31 Kt to Kt 6	B × Kt
32 R × B	Q to B 4
33 P to K 4 [8]	Q to B 8, ch
34 B to K sq	P × P
35 Q × P	R to B 5
36 Q to K 2	Q R to K B sq
37 K to Kt 2	R × P
38 Q to K 5	P to R 5 [9]
39 B × R P	Q to B 5
40 B to Kt 5	Q to Kt 5, ch

White resigns.[10]

Notes by S. Tinsley.

[1] In a very similar position recently (Steinitz v. Lásker, St. Petersburg, January 9, 1896) the first player proceeds with P to B 5, which is doubtless generally regarded with distrust. It is curious that White seems to have no better move than the text, which appears to amount to nothing if the Bishop has to take the Pawn subsequently. Kt to K 5 has points, supported later by P to K B 4, and that may eventually turn out to be the strongest continuation

[2] R to Q sq suggests itself at once as a more vigorous line of play. P to K 4 would be good now, but for the reply P to Q Kt 5.

[3] The question naturally occurs, what is the future of this Piece? Kt to Q Kt sq was probably superior, notwithstanding appearances to the contrary. Afterwards Q Kt to Q 2, and then to Q B 4, or K B sq, as circumstances suggest.

[4] By first playing B to B 2, a good deal might be threatened later, and the disagreeable counter-attack by Black would have been at least deferred.

[5] The exchange, not generally favourable in such positions, is here evidently in Black's favour. He makes a doubled Pawn at once, and has many good prospects of a King's side attack.

[6] White has already drifted into a most unsatisfactory position, and this is one of the best of a number of poor defences. It will be noted that White's Rook is in a line with Black's King's Bishop, and that some means must be found to prevent a fatal attack by Black's Q to R 5, &c. later

[7] A very charming resource, the point of which is not at first sight apparent, but is disclosed in the following moves.

[8] We have indicated a few weak points in White's play in our 2nd, 3rd, and 4th notes. We are informed, and the game bears out the statement, that White was short of time at one or two points. In such a difficult game it is no wonder White went astray under those circumstances. In the latter part of this game we can suggest no variation satisfactory to him. On the other hand, Herr Bardeleben, if by no means enterprising, conducts his attack with deadly accuracy and force

[9] Leading up to a very pretty winning move, Q to B 5.

[10] If 41. B to Kt 3, R to B 7, ch ; 42. K to R sq or Kt sq ; 43. Q to Q 8, ch, &c. Or if K to R sq at once, then R to B 8, ch, and mate next move.

D. Janowski v. J. H. Blackburne.

	WHITE	BLACK		WHITE	BLACK
1	P to K 4	P to K 3	7	B × Kt	Kt to B 3
2	P to Q 4	P to Q 4	8	B to Q 3	B to Q 3 [3]
3	Kt to Q B 3	P × P [1]	9	Castles	Castles
4	Kt × P	Kt to K B 3	10	B to K Kt 5	P to K R 3
5	B to Q 3 [2]	Q Kt to Q 2	11	B to R 4	B to K 2
6	Kt to K B 3	Kt × Kt	12	Q to K 2	Kt to Q 4

AUGUST 5

	WHITE	BLACK		WHITE	BLACK
13	B to Kt 3	B to Q 3	31	P to B 5	K P × P
14	P to B 4	B × B	32	Q to B 4 [8]	Kt to Kt 5
15	R P × B [4]	Kt to B 3	33	B to Kt 3	R to Q 2
16	Q R to Q sq	B to Q 2	34	R to K sq	R to K 2 [9]
17	Kt to K 5	B to B 3	35	R to K B sq	B to Kt 4
18	B to B 2	Q to Q 3	36	Q × Kt [10]	P × Q
19	P to B 4	B to K sq	37	R × Q	K × R
20	P to K Kt 4	P to K Kt 3	38	R × P	P to K Kt 4
21	Q to B 2	K to Kt 2	39	P to Q 5	R to K 8, ch
22	P to Kt 5	Kt to Kt sq	40	K to R 2	R to Q B 8 [11]
23	Q to R 4	P to K B 3 [5]	41	P to R 4	B to R 3
24	P × B P, ch	Kt × P	42	P to Q 6	R × P
25	R to B 3	Kt to Kt sq [6]	43	P to Q 7	K to K 2
26	R to K Kt 3	R to B 3	44	R to Q 4	K to Q sq
27	K to R sq	R to Q sq	45	B to K 6	R to K 4
28	P to Q B 5	Q to B sq	46	B to B 7	P to Kt 3
			47	B to Q 5	R to K 2
			48	B to B 6	R to K 3
			49	B to B 3	R to Q 3
			50	R to K 4	R × P
			51	R to K 5	R to Q 3
			52	P to Q Kt 4	B to B sq
			53	P to Kt 5	B to Q 2
			54	B to Q 5	R to K B 3
			55	R to K 2	P to B 3
			56	P × P	B × P
			57	B × B	R × B
			58	R to K 4	K to Q 2
			59	K to Kt 3	P to K R 4
			60	K to B 3	R to B 6, ch
			61	K to B 2	K to Q 3
			62	K to K 2	R to Q R 6
			63	K to B 2	P to R 4
				White resigns. [12]	

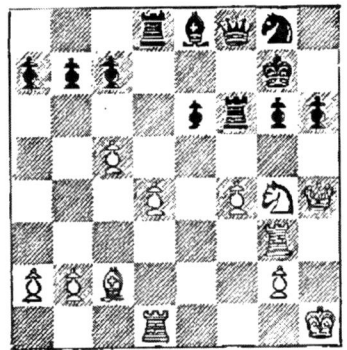

BLACK

WHITE

Black to make his 29th move.

29	Kt to Kt 4 [7]	R to Q 4
30	Kt × R	Kt × Kt

NOTES BY S. TINSLEY.

[1] There appears to be no real objection to this. I played it, probably for the first time in my life, against Lasker in this Tournament, and one leading critic remarked that it was my favourite variation!

[2] The thin trap, the Queen's Pawn left apparently undefended, occurs in many similar positions.

[3] We may point out that Black has here an excellent development, worthy of imitation by less experienced players.

[4] Rather preferable, possibly, is 15. P × Kt, B to Q 3; 16. P × P,

B or P × P; 17. Q to K 4, P to Kt 3, White having, at all events, a good game.

⁵ A somewhat unexpected move, which improves in appearance the more it is examined. One effect is to give Black a good deal more freedom for his King and other Pieces.

⁶ White intended evidently to capture the Kt P with B or Kt. If now 25. B × P, B × B; 26. R to Kt 3, R to B 3, and Black can defend by Kt to K 2, &c.

⁷ This gains the exchange at once, but White is afterwards soon in difficulties. Sounder play was first B to K 4 or to Kt 3.

⁸ With an attack on the Q B P. Black, it may be noted, threatened P to K Kt 4, then P to B 5, &c., and White's danger is Queen and King in line.

⁹ An uncommonly clever offer of the exchange of Pieces. If now 34. R × R, ch, Q × R, and mate is threatened. In fact, Black would win a Rook by the check at R 5, or gain a winning position after the exchange.

¹⁰ At first sight curious; but White presumably considered it the least of several evils. Black's Knight is the difficulty, being so strongly posted, and he must win something sooner or later. If now 36. R × Kt, B × R, and that is worse. But the text move speedily loses the game.

¹¹ There is nothing but plain sailing for Black after the exchanges about move 36. But it was M. Janowski's custom to 'play it out to the bitter end' in every case, and this principle he carries out here to the fullest extent.

¹² A curious, but not a brilliant game. White should have done better. Black's genius is observable at critical points.

C. SCHLECHTER v. W. H. K. POLLOCK.

	WHITE	BLACK
1	P to K 4	P to K 4
2	Kt to K B 3	Kt to Q B 3
3	B to Kt 5	P to Q R 3
4	B to R 4	Kt to B 3
5	Kt to B 3	B to Kt 5 ¹
6	Kt to Q 5	B to B 4 ²
7	P to Q 3 ³	P to R 3
8	B to K 3	B × B
9	P × B ⁴	P to Q 3
10	Castles	B to K 3 ⁵
11	Kt × Kt, ch	Q × Kt
12	Kt to Q 4	Q to Kt 4
13	Kt × Kt ⁶	Q × K P, ch
14	K to R sq	B to Q 2
15	Kt × P ⁷	B × B
16	Kt × B P	Castles (!)

White to make his 13th move.

	WHITE	BLACK
17	Q to R 5	B to K sq

Opposite F
Missing in P
and Bind

Best Ima
Availab

Page
Printing
ding

age
ble

Photo., Bradshaw, Hastings

Jas Mason

[10] To exchange the Queens in that critical position is the same as if he had resigned.

[11] Played for a trap: the last resource for White.

[12] This game illustrates the proverb that 'Expectations are better than realisations.' Pretty things are promised but never given.

J. MASON v. DR. TARRASCH.

	WHITE	BLACK		WHITE	BLACK
1	P to K 4	P to K 4	16	B to K 3	Kt to Kt sq
2	Kt to K B 3	Kt to Q B 3	17	Kt to K 2	P to B 4 [4]
3	B to B 4	B to B 4	18	P × P	B × P
4	Kt to B 3	Kt to B 3	19	Kt to R 2	K B to Kt 3
5	P to Q 3	P to Q 3	20	Kt to Kt 3	B to B sq [5]
6	B to K 3	B to Kt 3	21	Q to Q sq	R to Kt 2
7	Q to Q 2	B to K 3	22	Q to R 5	Q R to K B 2
8	B to Q Kt 5 [1]	Castles	23	R to K B sq [6]	Q to B 2
9	B × Kt	P × B	24	P to Q B 4 [7]	Kt to K 2
10	B to Kt 5 [2]	B to R 4	25	Q to K 2	Kt to Kt 3
11	P to Q R 3	P to B 4	26	Q to Q 2	Kt to B 5
12	Castles	R to Kt sq	27	P to B 3	P to Q 4
13	K R to Kt sq	P to B 3	28	B × Kt	P × B
14	P to R 3	K to R sq	29	Kt to K 2	R to Q sq
15	Q to B sq [3]	P to K R 3	30	Q to B 3	Time expired [8]

NOTES BY R. TEICHMANN.

[1] Entirely against the spirit of the Giuoco Piano; the exchange of the King's Bishop for the Black Queen's Knight is itself ill-judged, and besides strengthens the Black centre Pawns.

[2] Losing another move

[3] White's play is somewhat eccentric and without any set plan Q to K 2 followed by B to Q 2 appears to be preferable.

[4] Black has now an excellent development, and with this move inaugurates a strong attack.

[5] He prefers this to B to K 3 in order to be able to play P to Q 4 in answer to Kt to K 4, viz: 21 Kt to K 4, P to Q 4; 22. Kt × P (?), P to Q 5, winning a Piece which would not have been feasible with the Bishop at K 3

[6] White has lost much time with his Queen and Rook, which has been used by Black for a very favourable disposition of his forces on the King's side.

[7] This makes the Queen's Pawn fixed and weak; but it is difficult to suggest a satisfactory line of play for White.

[8] In this position Dr. Tarrasch, under the impression that he had made his 30th move already, exceeded his time, and the game was claimed by Mason. There can be no doubt that, on the merits of the position, Dr. Tarrasch ought to have won the game. The simplest

plan seems to be to double the Rooks on the King's file, after which White's position seems quite hopeless; the scope of his Knights being very limited and a defence of the weak Queen's Pawn in the long run impossible.

[Mr. Mason drew his opponent's attention to his clock more than once, and informed him that he had only made twenty-nine moves; but unfortunately the doctor had written his name at move one, and was sure he had made thirty moves.—ED.]

M. TCHIGORIN v. H. N. PILLSBURY.

	WHITE	BLACK		WHITE	BLACK
1	P to K 4	P to K 4	19	Q to K R 5	Kt to Kt 3 [5]
2	P to K B 4	B to B 4	20	B to Q 5	P to Q R 3
3	Kt to K B 3	P to Q 3	21	K to Q 2	Kt × B
4	B to Q B 4	Kt to Q B 3	22	Kt × Kt	R to K Kt sq
5	Kt to Q B 3	Kt to B 3	23	P to K Kt 4	B to Kt 5, ch [6]
6	P to Q 3	B to K Kt 5	24	Kt × B	Q to Q 5
7	P to K R 3	B × Kt [1]	25	Kt to B 2	Kt × Kt
8	Q × B	Kt to Q 5	26	K × Kt	R to Kt 3
9	Q to Kt 3 [2]	Kt × P, ch	27	B to Q 2	R to Q 3
10	K to Q sq	Kt × R	28	R to B 3	Q to R 5, ch
11	Q × Kt P	K to Q 2 [3]	29	K to B sq [7]	Q × R P
12	P × P	P × P	30	B to B 3	R to Q B 3
13	R to B sq	B to K 2	31	Q × P	P to Kt 4
			32	Q to K 7	Q to Kt 6
			33	K to Q 2	P to R 4
			34	R to B 5	K to Kt 2
			35	R to B 5	Q R to R 3
			36	P to Kt 5	R × R
			37	Q × R	R to Q B 3
			38	Q to Q 5	Q to R 5
			39	P to Kt 6	P to Kt 5
			40	P to Kt 7 [8]	P × B, ch
			41	P × P	Q to R 6
			42	P to Kt 8 (Q)	Q × P, ch
			43	K to K 2	Q to B 7, ch
			44	K to B 3	Q to Q 8, ch
			45	K to Kt 3	Q to Kt 8, ch
			46	K to R 4	Q to B 7, ch
			47	K to R 5	Q to B 6, ch
			48	Q to K Kt 4	Q to B 3
			49	Q (Kt 4) to B 5	
					Q to R 3, ch
			50	K to Kt 4	Q to Kt 2, ch
			51	Q to Kt 5	Resigns [9]

BLACK

WHITE

White to make his 14th move.

14	Q × B P [4]	K to B sq
15	B to K Kt 5	R to K B sq
16	Q to K 6, ch	K to Kt sq
17	Q B to R 6	R to K sq
18	Q × P	Kt to Q 2

AUGUST 5

Notes by E. Lasker

[1] An early exchange of Bishop for Knight being as a rule objectionable, some of the best players prefer to remove this Bishop to K 3, relying on the speedy development of their Pieces, which, in their opinion, forms a compensation for the double Pawn (after B × B, &c.)

[2] To remove Q to Q sq is hardly advisable. Although there might be no vital objection against it, yet it would seem that after 9. Q to Q sq, Kt to Q 2, Black will obtain a free and open game with many good chances, for no sacrifice in material or position whatever.

[3] The only possible move in this position, as proved by 'book' long ago; the reply to 11 R to B sq, for instance, might be

WHITE	BLACK	WHITE	BLACK
12 P × P	P × P	15 B × P, ch	K to Q 2
13 R to B sq	B to K 2	16 Q × K P	
14 Q B to Kt 5	Kt to R 4		

when obviously Black's game must fall to pieces.

[4] Although Mr. Tchigorin must have had his reasons why he should prefer this capture to the apparently stronger and more natural continuation by B to K Kt 5, we fail to see what Black could have replied to such an attack. To corroborate our opinion we give the following variations:—

14 B to K Kt 5	R to K Kt sq	21 Q to B 5, ch, and wins Q or checkmates in two.	
15 Q × B P	R × B (a, b, c)		
16 Q to K 6, ch	K to K sq	(c) 15	K to B sq
17 R × Kt (threatening mate in two by R to B 8, ch, &c.)	R to Kt 2	16 B × Kt	R to B sq
		17 B × B	R Q
18 Kt to Q 5	P to Q B 3	18 R × R, speedily regaining the Queen.	
(or 18. Q to Q 3; 19. Kt × P, ch, Q × Kt, 20. B to Kt 5, ch, K to Q sq; 21. R to B 8, ch, B × R; 22. Q to K 8, mate)		If—	
		14	Q to B or Kt sq,
		then—	
19 Q × K P	R to B sq	15 B × Kt will follow, and the exchange of Queens will turn out to the advantage of White, as the Black Knight at Q R 8 is virtually lost	
20 Kt × B	R × Kt		
21 R to B 8, ch, and should win.			
		If finally—	
(a) 15	Q to K B sq	14	K to B sq
16 Q to K 6, ch	K moves	15 B × Kt	B × B
17 R × Kt		16 R × B	R to K Kt sq
		17 Q × R P	R × P
(b) 15	R to K B sq	18 Q to B 5, ch	K to K Kt sq
16 Q to K 6, ch	K to K sq	(or Q to Q 2; 19 B to K 6)	
17 Kt to Q 5	Kt × Kt	19 R × P	R to K Kt sq
18 R × R, ch	K × R	20 Q × P, and Black is quite helpless.	
19 B × Kt	K to K sq		
20 Q to B 7, ch	K to Q 2		

[5] So far Black's defensive manœuvres have been perfect. Although

he is a Rook ahead, the strong position of all of the White men and Pawns, the blocked positions of the King and Queen's Rook, and finally, the exposure of the Knight at Q R 8, place it beyond doubt that White must be in the advantage. Black ought, therefore, not to disdain a possible draw. His best course seems to be—

	WHITE	BLACK		WHITE	BLACK
19		B to B sq	23	K to Q 2	Kt to K 4
20	B to K Kt 5	B to K 2		or—	
21	B to R 6	B to B sq	23	Q × P	B × Kt [B 3
22	B to K 3	B to Kt 2	24	P × B	Kt to K 4, or to

when Black has a great many chances for a successful counter-attack. The move actually made makes it impossible for him to bring his Rook at Bishop's square speedily into play, as now 20. B to B sq would be answered by 21. Q × R, Q × Q; 22 R × B, &c.

" An ingenious manœuvre, whose outcome is that the Bishop is exchanged for the Knight. Pretty though it is, it appears doubtful whether it was now the opportune moment to exchange anything which only makes the White Pawns so much stronger and his King safer. The right play seems to be—

	WHITE	BLACK		WHITE	BLACK
23		B to B 4	26	R to B sq	K to R 2
24	R × Kt	P to B 3		leaving him with	
25	B to B 4, ch	K to R 2	27	Q × B	Q × Q
26	Kt to B 7	Q to Q 5	28	B to K 3	Q × B, ch
	or—		29	K × Q	Q R to K B sq
25	Kt to B 3	Q to Q 5		Good chances for the ending.	

[7] Of course not 39. K to Kt sq, on account of Q to Q 8, ch.

[8] The decisive manœuvre. Nothing can stop that Pawn, nor has the Black Queen any checks for the present.

[9] At last the moment has arrived —which by necessity had to arrive sooner or later, the Black Rook being pinned where the checks have exhausted themselves, and Black therefore resigns the hopeless fight.

A. ALBIN v H. E. BIRD.

	WHITE	BLACK		WHITE	BLACK
1	Kt to K B 3	P to K B 4	12	Kt to K 5	Kt to B 2
2	P to Q Kt 3	Kt to K B 3	13	B to K 2	B × Kt [2]
3	B to Kt 2	P to K 3	14	P × B	Kt to K 5
4	P to K 3	B to K 2 [1]	15	P to B 3	Kt to B 4
5	Kt to Q B 3	P to Q Kt 3	16	P to Q Kt 4	Kt to Q R 3
6	P to Q 4	B to Kt 2	17	Q to Q 2	Q to K 2
7	B to Q 3	Castles	18	P to Q R 3	P to B 4
8	Castles	Q to K sq	19	Q R to Q sq	K R to Q sq
9	Kt to K 2	Kt to Q B 3	20	P to Kt 5	Kt to B 2
10	P to Q B 4	Kt to Q sq	21	Q to B 3	Kt to R sq [3]
11	Kt to B 4	B to Q 3	22	K to R sq [4]	Kt to Kt 3

AUGUST 5

	WHITE	BLACK
23	K R to Kt sq	R to K B sq
24	R to Q 2	R to B 2
25	K R to Q sq	R to Q sq
26	R to Q 6	Kt × Kt [5]
27	P × Kt	Kt to K sq
28	Q R (6) to Q 2	P to Kt 3 [6]
29	P to Q R 4 (!)	Kt to Kt 2
30	P to R 5	Q to R 5
31	P to Kt 3 [7]	Q to R 3
32	P × P	P × P
33	R to Q 6	P to Kt 4
34	R × Kt P [8]	P × P (!)
35	Q B to B sq [9]	Kt to R 4 (!)
36	R to Kt sq [10]	R to Kt sq (!)
37	R to Q 6	R to Kt 2
38	R to Kt 2 [11]	K to R sq
39	Q to K sq	R (Kt sq) to Kt [sq
40	K to Kt sq	P × P [12]
41	B × Q	P × P, ch
42	K × P	R × R, ch
43	K to R 3 [13]	R (7) to Kt 3
44	B to K 3 [14]	P to B 5

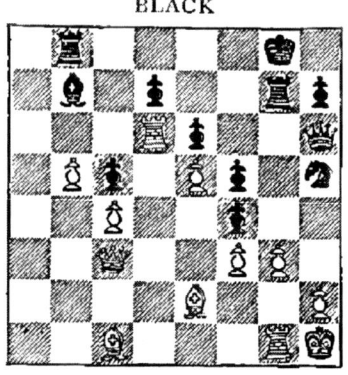

White to make his 38th move.

	WHITE	BLACK
45	B to B 2	R to R 3
46	B to R 4	Kt to Kt 6
47	R × Q P	Kt × B
48	R to Q 8 [15]	R × R
49	K to Kt 2	R to Kt sq, ch
50	K to B 2	R × B
51	K × Kt	R to R 6
52	Q to R 5	B × P, ch
	White resigns.	

NOTES BY E. SCHIFFERS.

[1] Here B to Q 3 can also be played; see move 11.

[2] I think this move is not advantageous for Black, but that P to Q B 4 followed by B to Q B 2 would be better.

[3] P to Q 3; 22. P × P, Kt × P is better.

[4] In this and the following move White prepares for P to K Kt 4, but afterwards changes his mind; the position of the White King on K R sq with Black's Bishop at Q Kt 2 is fraught with danger. It would have been better at once to double the Rooks on the Queen's file.

[5] Not Kt to K sq on account of 27. Kt × P, Kt × R; 28. Kt × R, &c.

[6] Perhaps P to Q 3 is better, or even P to Q 4.

[7] B to Q B sq could have been played; the actual move weakens the P at K B 3.

[8] He ought to have played P × P, Q × P; 35. Q B to B sq, &c.

[9] R × B will not do on account of P × P.

[10] If B × P then Kt × B; 37. P × Kt, R to Kt 2; 38. R to Kt sq, K to R sq, with a strong attack; White has not time to capture the B at Q Kt 2.

[11] Q to K sq was better; Black could now force the win by

38. Kt × P, ch , 39. R × Kt (if K to Kt sq, Kt × B, &c.), R × R ; 40 B × P, R × P ; 41. B × R (if B × Q, R to B 8, mate [1]), Q takes B , 42. K to Kt 2, K to R sq and wins (see diagram).

[12] A pretty but not altogether sound continuation . 40 Q to Kt 3 decided the game immediately

[13] If K to R sq, then R × B.

[14] He should have played Q to Q B sq, then if R to Kt 6, ch ; 45. K to R 4, R to Kt 7 , 46 Q to K R sq (or B to B 4), R × B, 47 R × Q P, B - K B P ; 48. B to Kt 7, ch, R × B ; 49. R to Q 8, ch, R to Kt sq ; 50. R × R, ch, K × R ; 51 Q × B, &c.

[15] If R × B, then Kt to Kt 8, ch, wins.

E. LASKER *v.* G. MARCO.

	WHITE	BLACK		WHITE	BLACK
1	P to Q 4	P to Q 4	15	Castles	Q to Q 2 [11]
2	Kt to K B 3	P to K 3	16	B to K 2	K R to Q sq
3	P to Q B 4	Kt to K B 3	17	K R to Q sq	Kt to K 5 [12]
4	Kt to B 3	B to K 2	18	Kt to B 3	Kt × Kt
5	B to B 4	Castles	19	Q × Kt	P to Q 5 [13]
6	Q to B 2 [1]	P to B 3 [2]	20	Q to B 2	Kt to R 4
7	P to K 3	P to Q Kt 3 [3]	21	Kt to K 5	Q to K 3
8	P to Q R 3 [4]	B to Kt 2	22	Q to R 4	B to K B 3 [14]
9	P × P [5]	K P × P	23	B to Kt 4	Q to Kt 3
10	B to Q 3	P to B 4	24	B × R	B × B
11	Kt to Q Kt 5 [6]		25	P to Q Kt 4	B × Kt
		Kt to B 3	26	B × B	Kt to B 3
12	B to B 5 [7]	P to K Kt 3	27	Kt P × P	Q × P
13	B to Q 3 [8]	R to B sq [9]	28	B × P	Kt × B
14	P × P	P × P [10]	29	R × Kt	Resigns

NOTES BY DR. TARRASCH.

[1] P to K 3 was preferable. The Queen has seldom a favourable position on the Queen's Bishop's file in the Queen's Gambit, besides which the development of the King's side was more opportune.

[2] To move the Pawn first one step and a few moves later another step is no proof of a well-considered plan. He might play at once P to B 4, and continue with 7. Q P × P, Q P × P ; 8. R to Q sq, Q to R 4

[3] Black is cramped through his sixth move, and has hardly another way of development, although the Bishop on Kt 2 is locked up by two Pawns.

[4] Unnecessary.

[5] This Pawn exchange facilitates Black's game.

[6] White should here and in the next move exchange the Pawns, and not leave his opponent a majority of Pawns on the Queen's side The text move and the consequent attack should lead to a general retreat

[7] Probably in order to play 13. B to B 7, Q to K sq ; 14. Kt to Q 6.

[8] White ought at least to keep to his plan with B to R 3.
[9] Black could here drive back White's Pieces with P to B 5, P to R 3, and P to Kt 4, obtaining a far superior game.
[10] I consider B × P better. Black had then an isolated Queen's Pawn, it is true, but it was not so weak as the two connected Pawns. He would provide the Knight with a strong square at K 5, and the Pawn would have advanced sooner or later to K 5 by the exchange of this Knight, the usual fate of the isolated Queen's Pawn.
[11] The Queen was safer on Kt 3.
[12] Even with other moves Black's position is no longer a good one.
[13] Black has no moves with any prospect of success.
[14] A grievous mistake; Q to Kt 3 was forced.

S. Tinsley v. J. Mieses.

	WHITE	BLACK		WHITE	BLACK
1	P to Q 4	P to Q 4	26	B to B sq	P to B 5 [8]
2	P to K 3	Kt to K B 3			
3	B to Q 3	P to K 3			
4	Kt to K B 3	P to Q Kt 3			
5	Castles	B to Kt 2			
6	Kt to K 5	P to K Kt 3 [1]			
7	Q Kt to Q 2	B to Kt 2			
8	P to Q Kt 3 [2]	Kt to K 5			
9	P to K B 4 [3]	P to K B 3			
10	Kt to Kt 4	P to K B 4			
11	Kt to K 5	Q Kt to Q 2			
12	Q Kt to B 3	Kt × Kt			
13	Kt × Kt	B × Kt			
14	B P × B [4]	Q to K 2			
15	P to Q R 4	P to K R 4 (!)			
16	P to R 5	P to K R 5			
17	B × Kt	Q P × B			
18	Q to K 2	P to K Kt 4	27	P × P	P × P
19	P to Q B 4	Castles Q R [5]	28	B × P	P to K 6
20	P × P	R P × P	29	Q to Q B 4	R to Q 7
21	R to Q R 2	K R to Kt sq	30	R × R	P × R
22	B to R 3	Q to K R 2	31	R to Q sq	R × P, ch
23	P to B 5	P × P	32	K to B sq	Q to B 3
24	P × P [6]	R to Q 6	33	Q to Q 3	B to R 3
25	Q to Q B 2	Q to Q 2 [7]		White resigns.	

White to make his 27th move.

NOTES BY C. VON BARDELEBEN.

[1] The usual continuation; B to K 2 is preferable.
[2] 8. P to Q B 3 would be better, to be followed by Q to B 2 and P to K 4.

³ This move weakens the King's Pawn; 9. P to K B 3, Kt × Kt; 10. B × Kt, Castles; 11. B to B 3, &c, would be better.

⁴ Preferable would be 14. Q P × B. After 14. B P × P has been done, Black is enabled to advance his King's Knight's and his King's Rook's Pawns, and to establish by this line of play a strong attack against the White King.

⁵ Very well played. The attack of White is not so violent as it seems, but it is very difficult to foresee that.

⁶ A mistake, which opens the Black Queen's Rook file. He should have played 24 B × P.

⁷ White threatened 26. P to B 5.

⁸ Decisive, for, if White answers 27. R to K sq, there follows Q to Q 4.

E. SCHIFFERS v. I. GUNSBERG.

	WHITE	BLACK
1	P to K 4	P to K 4
2	K Kt to B 3	Q Kt to B 3
3	Kt to B 3	P to Q R 3 ¹
4	P to Q 4	P × P
5	Kt × P	K Kt to K 2
6	K B to B 4 ²	Kt × Kt
7	Q × Kt	P to Q Kt 4
8	B to Kt 3	P to Q 3
9	Q to K 3	B to Kt 2
10	Q to B 3 ³	P to K B 3
11	B to K B 4	Kt to Kt 3
12	Castles Q R	Q to Q 2
13	B to Kt 3	Castles
14	Q to K 3 ⁴	R to K sq
15	Q to R 7 ⁵	Kt to K 2
16	K R to K sq ⁶	Kt to B 3
17	Q to K 3	P to K R 4
18	P to K B 4	P to R 5 ⁷
19	B to B 2	P to K Kt 3
20	Kt to Q 5	B to Kt 2
21	P to K R 3	P to B 4
22	Q to Q 3	P × P
23	R × P	R × R
24	Q × R	Q to B 4
25	Q to K 3	K to Kt sq ⁸
26	K to Kt sq ⁹	Q to R 4

	WHITE	BLACK
27	P to B 3	B to R 3
28	P to R 4	P to Kt 4
29	R P × P	Kt P × P
30	Q to Q 3	P × P ¹⁰

BLACK

WHITE

White to make his 31st move.

31	Kt × B P (!)	R to Q sq
32	Kt × P	B to R 3
33	B to Q 5	Q to K sq
34	P to B 4	B × Kt
35	P × B	Kt to Kt 5
36	B to R 7, ch	Resigns ¹¹

NOTES BY J. H. BLACKBURNE.

¹ A move not to be commended for second player, although Mr. Gunsberg has frequently played it with success when first player.

[2] The other B to B 4 is perhaps the stronger continuation.
[3] Castling or P to K B 4 is better. The Queen is not well posted on this square.
[4] This and the next few moves of the Queen does not advance White's game. Q to R 5, followed by P to B 4 or K R to K sq according to Black's move, would have been a stronger line of play.
[5] This is a useless move.
[6] P to B 4, so as to enable the Queen when attacked to retire to K B 2, was preferable.
[7] Kt to R 4, getting rid of the White Bishop, would have given Black some chances of a win.
[8] To avoid Kt to K 7, ch, and B to K 6, ch, winning the Queen.
[9] There is no meaning in this move. P to B 3 at once is more forcible.
[10] There is nothing better, for if Kt to R 4, then Q to Q 4, winning easily (see diagram).
[11] For if K × B, mate follows in three moves, and if K to B sq or B 2, then R to Q B 1, ch, and mates in a few more moves. The finish is neatly played by White.

W. Steinitz v. B. Vergani.

	WHITE	BLACK
1	P to K 4	P to K 3
2	P to Q 4	P to Q 4
3	Q Kt to B 3	K Kt to B 3
4	P to K 5	K Kt to Q 2
5	Q Kt to K 2	P to Q B 4
6	P to Q B 3	P × P [1]
7	P × P	Q Kt to B 3
8	P to B 4	B to Kt 5, ch [2]
9	Q Kt to B 3	Castles
10	Kt to B 3	P to B 3
11	P to Q R 3	B × Kt
12	P × B	P to Q R 3
13	P to Q R 4	Kt to R 4
14	B to Q 3	Q to B 2
15	Q to B 2	P to B 4
16	P to Kt 4 [3]	P to Kt 3
17	P × P	K P × P
18	P to R 4	Kt to Kt 3
19	P to R 5 [4]	K to Kt 2
20	P × P	P to R 3 [5]
21	Q to R 2	R to R sq [6]
22	Q to R 4	Q to Q sq
23	B to R 3	Kt to B 3

White to make his 16th move.

	WHITE	BLACK
24	Q to R 5	Kt to B 5
25	Kt to R 4	Kt × B
26	Kt × P, ch [7]	B × Kt
27	Q × B	Q to K B sq [8]
28	Q to Q 7, ch	Q to K 2
29	Q × Q P [9]	Q R to Q sq
30	Q to Kt 3	K R to B sq
31	Q × Kt	Q × Q

WHITE	BLACK		WHITE	BLACK
32 R × Q	R × B P		37 P × Kt	R (Q 5) × Q P
33 K to K 2	Kt to K 2		38 R × P	R × B
34 R to Q Kt sq	R to Q 2		39 P to K 6	R to Q 7, ch
35 Q R to Kt 3	Kt to Q 4		40 K to K sq	R to Q 8, ch
36 P to B 4	R × P [10]		41 R × R	Resigns.

NOTES BY H. N. PILLSBURY.

[1] A premature exchange. Black obtains a very good game by Q to Kt 3 ; 7. P to K B 4, Q Kt to B 3 ; 8 Kt to B 3, P to K B 3, in fact, White seems unable to develop his game so as to obtain any attack.

[2] B to K 2 was preferable.

[3] This powerful advance gives White a tremendous attack (see diagram).

[4] Pursuing the attack with precision and vigour.

[5] If P × P, 21 Q to R 2, with a winning position.

[6] If Q × P, ch, 22 K to K 2, R to R sq ; 23. B to Q 2, winning a clear Piece

[7] R × Kt would have won the second Pawn, and keep the attack well in hand.

[8] 27 R to K B sq would, of course, be met by 28. Q to R 5, &c But the correct play was Q to K 2 ; 28. Q to B 6, ch, Q × Q ; 29. P × Q, ch, K × P , 30 R × Kt, Q R to K sq ch, with a very good chance of resistance White could not in the foregoing continue 28. R × Kt on account of Q R to K B sq, followed by Q × R. After this point the game is lost for Black.

[9] White is bound to win the imprisoned Knight, and increases his Pawn force before doing so.

[10] A last desperate attempt, and leading to rather an amusing finish

Photo., Bradshaw, Hastings

Saml. Tinsley

AUGUST 6.

This round is quite as good as the first; Lasker is to play Tchigorin! and Bird is to meet another of the brilliant order in Walbrodt. Steinitz also is to play the brilliant Austrian Schlechter. The round is particularly fatal to the favourites: Tarrasch loses to Pillsbury in a magnificent game, which attracts a great deal of attention and spots Pillsbury as a dangerous competitor; Steinitz only draws, and Lasker loses. Mieses wins a fine game from Blackburne.

Marco and Pollock also distinguish themselves by finishing a lively game in seventy minutes.

S. TINSLEY v. J. MASON.

	WHITE	BLACK		WHITE	BLACK
1	P to Q 4	P to Q 4	22	B to B 3	B × Kt
2	P to K 3	Kt to K B 3	23	Q × B	R to Q 3 [2]
3	B to Q 3	P to B 4	24	B to R 5 [3]	Kt to B 5
4	P to Q B 3	P to K 3	25	B × Kt	P × B
5	Kt to B 3	P to B 5	26	P to B 3	B to Q 4
6	B to B 2	Kt to B 3	27	Q × P (B 4)	Q to K Kt 2 [1]
7	Q Kt to Q 2	B to Q 3	28	R to Kt 8, ch (!)	
8	Castles	P to Q Kt 4			K × R
9	R to K sq	B to Kt 2	29	Q × R, ch	K to R 2
10	P to K 4	P × P	30	R to K 2	Q to Kt 2
11	Kt × P	Kt to K 2	31	K to B 2	Q to Kt 2
12	Q to K 2	Kt × Kt	32	P to Kt 4	R to Kt sq
13	B × Kt	Kt to Q 4	33	Q to B 5, ch	K to R sq
14	B to Q 2	Q to B 2	34	Q to Q 6	K to R 2
15	R to Kt sq	P to Q R 3	35	P to Q R 4 [5]	Q to B 3
16	P to K R 3	P to K R 3	36	Q to K 5	Q to R 5, ch
17	Q R to B sq	P to Kt 4	37	Q to Kt 3	Q × Q, ch [6]
18	P to Q Kt 3	Castles Q R	38	K × Q	P to B 5, ch
19	P × P	P × P	39	K × P	R to B sq, ch
20	R to Kt sq	K R to Kt sq [1]	40	K to K 5	R × P
21	Kt to K 5	P to B 4	41	P to Kt 5	R to B 4, ch

	WHITE	BLACK		WHITE	BLACK
42	K to Q 6	P × P	47	P to Q 6	K to B 3
43	B to Kt 4	R to B 8	48	R to K 4	R × B P
44	B × P	B × B	49	P to Q 7	R to Q 6
45	K × B	R to B 6	50	R × P, ch	K to Kt 2
46	P to Q 5	K to Kt 3	51	R to B 8	Resigns.

NOTES BY A. ALBIN.

[1] P to B 4, and if White does not take the Knight, P to Kt 5 was a strong continuation.

[2] Q × Q was the proper move, and afterwards P to Kt 5, with the chances at least of a draw by Bishops of different colours in case B × Kt.

[3] Doubling the Rook on the Knight's file is better.

[4] R to B 3 in order to exchange the Queens, and after that R to Kt 4 would have been better.

[5] With 35. P × P, White could get the open file for his Rook, for if R to Kt 8, then B to Kt 6, with a winning position.

[6] Black should not exchange the Queens.

E. LASKER v. M. TCHIGORIN.

	WHITE	BLACK		WHITE	BLACK
1	P to Q 4	P to Q 4	21	B to R 3	R to Q B 3
2	K Kt to B 3	B to Kt 5	22	B to B 5	R to R 3
3	P to B 4	B × Kt	23	P to Q R 4	Kt to B 3
4	Kt P × B	Kt to Q B 3	24	R to Q Kt sq	R to Q 2
5	Kt to B 3	P to K 3	25	K R to K Kt sq	
6	P to K 3	B to Kt 5			Kt (Kt 3) to K 2
7	P × P	Q × P	26	R to Q Kt 2	Kt to Q 4
8	B to Q 2	B × Kt	27	K to Q 2	R to R 4 [8]
9	P × B [1]	K Kt to K 2	28	R (Kt sq) to Kt sq	
10	K R to Kt sq [2]				P to Q Kt 3
		Q to K R 4	29	B to R 3	P to Kt 3
11	Q to Kt 3 [3]	Kt to Q sq [4]	30	R to Kt 5	R to R 3
12	Q to Kt 5, ch [5]		31	B to B sq	Kt to Q sq
		Q × Q	32	R to R sq	Kt to K B 2
13	B × Q, ch	P to B 3	33	R (Kt 5) to Kt sq	
14	B to Q 3	Kt to Kt 3			Kt to Q 3 [9]
15	P to K B 4 [6]	Castles	34	P to B 3	Kt to K B 2
16	K to K 2	R to B sq	35	R to R 3	P to K Kt 4 [10]
17	R to Kt 3	P to Q B 4	36	K to K 2	P × P
18	Q R to K Kt sq		37	P to K 4	Kt to B 3
		P to B 5	38	B × P [11]	Kt to R 4
19	B to B 2	P to B 4 [7]	39	B to K 3	P to B 5
20	B to B sq	R to K B 2	40	B to B 2	R to R 4

AUGUST 6

	WHITE	BLACK
41	R to Kt sq, ch	K to B sq
42	Q R to R sq	P to K 4
43	Q R to Q Kt sq	
		Kt to Kt 2
44	R to Q Kt 4	R to B 2
45	B to Kt sq	Kt to K 3
46	R to Q sq	Kt (K 3) to Q sq
47	R to Q 2 [12]	Kt to B 3
48	R to Kt 5 [13]	R × P
49	P × P	Kt (B 2) × P
50	B to R 4	R to K Kt 2
51	K to B 2	R to Kt 3
52	R (Q 2) to Q 5	R to R 8 [14]
53	B to Q 8	Kt to Q 6, ch [15]
54	B × Kt	P × B [Kt 8 [17]
55	R × Q P [16]	R (R 8) to K
56	R to B 5, ch	K to K sq

White resigns.

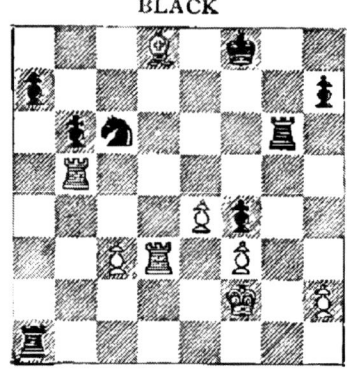

Black to make his 55th move.

NOTES BY W. STEINITZ.

[1] Tchigorin's practical genius is almost privileged to defy theoretical modern principles, but I must consistently dissent. Black's game is inferior; White's two Bishops and his compact centre will more than neutralise the drawback of the doubled King's Bishop's Pawn, and the two open Knights' files for the Rooks ought also to outweigh the isolation of the two Rooks' Pawns, which are practically inaccessible to Black's attack. With little alterations, chiefly of a transposing character, White has copied the lines of attack first adopted by Steinitz in his second Havanna match against Tchigorin, 1891-92.

[2] Not good, if only because 10. P to K 4 was so much better, for if, then, 10. Q to K R 4; 11. Q R to Kt sq, threatening R to Kt 5. White had also no reason to abandon so soon his option of Castling King's side and bringing Rooks into communication. His menace against the adverse King's wing amounted to nought.

[3] If 11. R × P, Kt to Kt 3, followed soon by K to B sq, winning.

[4] If 11. P to Q Kt 3; 12. Q to R 4, and Black dare not capture the Bishop's Pawn on account of 13. B to Kt 2. Nor would 12. Q × R P; 13. R × P be favourable to Black's game.

[5] Good enough probably; yet a more lively line of play like 12. R to Kt 3, Q × R P; 13. P to K 4, Q to R 4; 14. P to Q B 4 was, I believe, worth the chances of the attack against a Pawn.

[6] If he intended in the near future to dissolve the doubled Pawn by P to B 5, then this was all right. But events show that he does not, and no good cause can be given why five of his centre Pawns should all have been placed on black squares and on diagonals where they exercise little command, when 15. P to K 4, with the view perhaps of proceeding with P to Q B 4 later, would have grouped a

strong front of Pawns abreast. 15. P to K 4, which perhaps he feared, would have been no good on account of simply 16. P × P, Kt × P ; 17. B to K 2.

[7] Black's tactical skill has been assisted by weak strategical disposition on the other side, and the force of White's two Bishops and of his centre Pawns is at least neutralised. White has neglected to dissolve his doubled Pawn, which is now fixed for good until it will be convenient for the opponent to make it the mark of attack. The useless assertion of the Rooks on the King's Knight's file are retracted by Lasker himself from the 24th to the 28th move.

[8] The manner in which this Rook is shut out later on must create doubts whether this Piece could not have been better employed.

[9] Now, and not two moves later, was the time for breaking in by 33. P to K Kt 4, with the continuation 34. P × P, Kt × Kt P; 35. R to R 3, Kt to K 5, ch (not 35 Kt to B 6, ch ; 36. K to K 2, Kt × R P ; 37. P to B 3, &c.) ; 36. B × Kt, P × B, followed soon by R to K Kt 2, with a winning attack

[10] He has given the adversary time to prepare a cunning device which renders his onslaught ineffectual now.

[11] Much better than 38. P × P, P × P ; 39. K B × P, R to K 2, ch, 40. K to B 2, Kt to Q 3, and accordingly as the Bishop retreats, Black protects his Pawn by Kt to Q 4 or Kt to R 4.

[12] White's Rooks have been moved about thoughtlessly for the most part without sufficient reason or inflicting harm, but this loses a Pawn, which might have been avoided by 47. B to R 2, P to Kt 4; 48. R × Kt P, R × P ; 49. R to Kt 2, &c.

[13] If 48 R × B P, Kt × P, ch, winning the exchange.

[14] Hardly as reliable as 52. R to K R 3, 53. B to Kt 5, R × P, ch ; 54. K to B sq, R to Q R 8 ; 55. B × P, R × B, ch, followed by R to R 8, ch, and after the exchanges Black's Queen's side will win, especially as White's Queen's Bishop's Pawn will also fall soon.

[15] Compulsory now, as White threatens B to B 7.

[16] A blunder, which loses at once a hard fought game. After 55. B to B 7, R to R 7, ch ; 56. K to B sq, R (Kt 3) to Kt 7 (it 56 P to Q 7; 57. R to Kt sq, followed by R to Q sq); 57. R × Q P, best (not 57. B × P, R (R 7) to B 7, ch ; 58. K to K sq, R × B P, threatening R to K 7, ch, and wins) ; 57. R × P ; 58. K to Kt sq, and it is not clear that Black can win.

[17] See diagram of this remarkable position. White cannot save the mate excepting at the cost of a Piece by R to Kt 5 or B to Kt 5.

A. ALBIN v. C. VON BARDELEBEN.

	WHITE	BLACK		WHITE	BLACK
1	P to K 4	P to K 4	6	P to K R 3[1]	B to K 3
2	Kt to K B 3	Kt to Q B 3	7	B to Q Kt 5	P to Q R 3
3	B to B 4	Kt to B 3	8	B × Kt, ch	P × B
4	P to Q 3	B to B 4	9	Kt to Q R 4	B to R 2
5	Kt to B 3	P to Q 3	10	Q to K 2	P to B 4

AUGUST 6

	WHITE	BLACK
11	P to B 4	P to R 3
12	B to K 3	Kt to Q 2 [2]
13	P to K Kt 4	Kt to Kt sq
14	Kt to B 3	Kt to B 3
15	Q to Q sq [3]	Kt to Q 5
16	B × Kt	B P × B
17	Kt to K 2	B to Q B 4
18	K to B sq	Q to Q 2
19	K to Kt 2	R to Q Kt sq
20	R to Q Kt sq	P to Kt 3
21	Kt to Kt 3	Q to B 3
22	K to R 2 (?)	Q to Q 2
23	K to Kt 2	P to Q R 4
24	P to Kt 3	Q to Q sq
25	Kt to R 2	Q to R 5 (?)
26	Kt to B 3	Q to Q sq
27	Q to Q 2	B to Kt 5
28	Q to B sq	P to Q B 3
29	P to B 5	R to Kt 4
30	P × P	Q × P
31	Q to Q sq	B to Q 2
32	Kt to Q 2	B × Kt
33	Q × B	Q to Kt 5
34	Q to K 2	P to R 5
35	Q to B 3	K to K 2
36	P to R 4	P × P
37	P × P	R to R sq
38	P to R 5	P to Kt 4
39	Kt to B 5, ch	B × Kt
40	Q × B	Q to Q 3 [Kt sq
41	R to R sq	R (R sq) to Q
42	R to R 7, ch	R (Kt 4) to Kt 2
43	K R to R sq	Q to K 3
44	Q to B 3	K to B sq
45	Q R to R 6	R × P
46	R to Q B sq	R (Kt 6) to Kt 3
47	R to R 7	K to Kt 2 [2 [4]
48	R to B 5	R (Kt sq) to Kt
49	R to R 8	R to Kt 4
50	R to B 4	R to Kt sq
51	R to R 7	R (Kt 4) to Kt 2
52	R to R 6	R to B 2
53	Q to Kt 3 [5]	R to Kt 6 [6]
54	R to R 5	P to B 3

	WHITE	BLACK
55	R × Q P	P to Q B 4
56	R to Q 8	P to B 5
57	R (R 5) to Q 5	P to B 6
58	R (Q 5) to Q 6	Q to B 2
59	Q to B 3	P to B 7
60	Q to B 5	R (Kt 6) to Kt 2 [7]

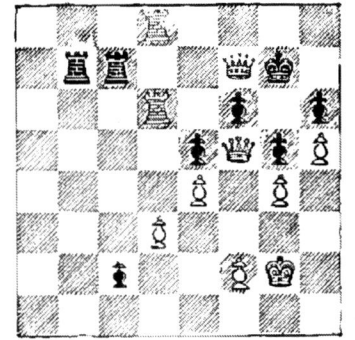

White to make his 61st move.

	WHITE	BLACK
61	P to Q 4 [8]	R to K 2 [9]
62	R to Q B 8	R (Kt 2) to B 2
63	P × P	R × P
64	R × R	R × Q
65	R × Q, ch	K × R
66	R to B 6	R to K 4
67	P to B 3	R to R 4
68	R × Q B P	R to R 6
69	K to B 2	R to Kt 6
70	K to K 2	R to R 6
71	R to B 7, ch	K to Kt sq
72	R to Q 7	R to Kt 6
73	R to Q 3	R × R
74	K × R	K to B 2
75	K to Q 4	K to K 3
76	P to K 5	P × P, ch
77	K to K 4	K to B 3
78	K to Q 5	K to B 2
79	K × P	K to K 2
80	K to Q 5	K to Q 2

Drawn game.

Notes by E. Schiffers.

[1] The move B to Kt 5, before Castling, is not dangerous. Here Mason would probably have played B to K 3.

[2] Black's Knight starts immediately for Q 5.

[3] In order to give the Knight room at K 2.

[4] White threatened R × P.

[5] Threatening R × Q P, P × R, Q × R, &c.

[6] In order to take Q P, after the above-mentioned moves.

[7] After Q to Q B 8 or P to B 8 (Q) would follow: 61. R to Q 7, R × R; 62. R × R, Q × R (otherwise Q to K Kt 6, ch, &c.); and 63. Q × R, ch, and after a few moves R to Q Kt 3, remaining with a Pawn ahead and better position.

[8] Cleverly played.

[9] If P to Q B 8 (Q), then 62. P × P, Q to Q R 8 (Q Kt 7); 63. P × P, ch, Q × P; 64. R × Q, Q · R; 65. R to K Kt 8, ch, &c.

H. N. Pillsbury v. Dr Tarrasch.

	WHITE	BLACK		WHITE	BLACK
1	P to Q 4	P to Q 4	28	Kt to K 2	Q to R 5
2	P to Q B 4	P to K 3	29	Kt to Kt 4 [8]	Kt to Q 2
3	Kt to Q B 3	Kt to K B 3	30	R (B 4) to B 2 [9]	
4	B to Kt 5 [1]	B to K 2			K to Kt sq [10]
5	Kt to B 3	Q Kt to Q 2	31	Kt to Q B sq [11]	
6	R to B sq	Castles			P to B 6
7	P to K 3	P to Q Kt 3	32	P to Q Kt 3	Q to B 3
8	P × P	P × P	33	P to K R 3	P to Q R 4
9	B to Q 3	B to Kt 2	34	Kt to R 2	P to R 5
10	Castles	P to B 4	35	P to Kt 4 [12]	P × P
11	R to K sq [2]	P to B 5 [3]	36	P × P	R to Q R sq [13]
12	B to Kt sq	P to Q R 3	37	P to Kt 5	R to R 6
13	Kt to K 5 [4]	P to Kt 4			
14	P to B 4	R to K sq			
15	Q to B 3	Kt to B sq [5]			
16	Kt to K 2	Kt to K 5			
17	B × B	R × B			
18	B × Kt	P × B			
19	Q to Kt 3	P to B 3 [6]			
20	Kt to Kt 4	K to R sq			
21	P to B 5	Q to Q 2			
22	R to B sq	Q R to Q sq			
23	R to B 4	Q to Q 3			
24	Q to R 4	Q R to K sq			
25	Kt to B 3	B to Q 4			
26	Kt to B 2	Q to B 3			
27	R to B sq	P to Kt 5 [7]			

BLACK

WHITE

White to make his 44th move.

AUGUST 6

WHITE	BLACK		WHITE	BLACK
38 Kt to Kt 4	B × P		45 K to R sq	Q to Q 4
39 R to K Kt 2	K to R sq		46 R to K Kt sq	Q × B P
40 P × P	P × P		47 Q to R 4, ch	Q to R 4
41 Kt × B [14]	R × Kt		48 Q to B 4, ch	Q to Kt 4
42 Kt to R 6	R to Kt 2		49 R × Q	P × R
43 R × R	K × R		50 Q to Q 6, ch	K to R 4
44 Q to Kt 3, ch [15]			51 Q × Kt	P to B 7
	K × Kt		52 Q × R P, mate.	

NOTES BY I. GUNSBERG.

[1] No good results from this early sortie of the Bishop. The attack, or, perhaps better speaking, would-be attack, differs from similar play in the French defence, inasmuch as White has not P to K 5 at his command. Generally speaking, both the first and the second player in this opening require their Queen's Bishop on the Queen's side.

[2] If White had had his Queen's Bishop posted on Q Kt 2 with his Pawn on Q Kt 3, we should then certainly have recommended the exchange of Black's Pawn. The Bishop would then prevent P to Q 5, and the two Black Pawns on Q 4 and B 4 unable to advance, are for White a convenient object of attack, as has frequently been proved by experience.

[3] This move places a premium on White's move of P to K 4. So that if Black in the ending wishes to reap the advantage of the superior Pawn position on the Queen's side, he must do everything possible in his power to meet the impending King's side advance.

[4] Played in accordance with the plan of action indicated in the previous note. White's idea being to clear away the Knight which guards the Black Rook's Pawn as well as the Queen's Pawn, so as to be able to play Q to R 5 The weakness of the Queen's Pawn may also be pointed out here, as having a prejudicial reflex effect on the King's side. Black, for instance, could not play Kt × Kt on account of 14. P × Kt, Kt to K sq ; 15. B × B, Q × B ; 16 Kt × P.

[5] This move will always be found a useful defensive resource when a King's side attack is threatened.

[6] It was to be foreseen that White would seek to continue the attack by means of Kt to Kt 4 and P to B 5. Black could have forestalled both these moves by playing B to B sq before playing P to B 3, and exchanging the Knight if it plays to Kt 4.

[7] Now the position affords an object lesson as to the effect of White's early move of 4. B to Kt 5. The attack on the King's side, which this move was intended to promote, has apparently been met, and therefore Black begins to advance from the Queen's side, where White's Pawns are insufficiently supported.

[8] Quite right. It was useless to attempt to defend the compromised Queen's side, White was, therefore, justified in abandoning it, and making up his mind to either do or die on the King's side. He now threatens Kt × P, and if P × Kt, then Q × B P, ch, R to Kt 2, R to Kt 4, &c. Therefore Black cannot take the Rook's Pawn just yet

[9] To make room for Kt to B 4, which, besides attacking the Bishop, would threaten Kt to Kt 6, ch. The move also serves this important object, that it brings the Rook in a line with his Queen's side Pawns.

[10] It is dangerous at any time to capture a far-away Pawn, and in this particular instance Black was well advised in not doing so, for if Q × P, the following would be a likely, though not altogether forced, line of play:

WHITE	BLACK	WHITE	BLACK
31 Kt to B 4	B to B 2	38 Q to R 8, ch	R to Kt sq
32 Kt to Kt 6, ch	B × Kt	39 R × P, ch	K to K 2
33 P × B	P to R 3	40 Q to R 7, ch	K to Q sq
34 Kt × R P	P × Kt	41 R to Q 5	Q to R 5
35 Q × R P, ch	K to Kt sq	42 P to Q Kt 3	P × P
36 R to B 5	R to Kt 2	43 R to B 7, and White should win.	
37 R to R 5	K to B sq		

[11] As no useful object would now be served by Kt to B 4, White defends his Queen's side.

[12] Both players proceed consistently, with the same strategy, though they are often compelled to change their tactics. Black with P to R 5 follows up the Queen's side attack, whereas White with P to K Kt 4 pursues the King's side attack, on which his existence depends.

[13] It might have been worth while for Black to stay his Queen's side operations for a moment, in order to play P to R 3, which move, though not without its dangers, would have gained some little time by compelling White to play Q to Kt 3, P to R 4, &c.

[14] Of course it must always remain a matter of judgment whether or not Black would have done better to take a little more care of his King's side before proceeding on the Queen's wing. In any case both players have treated us to magnificent specimens of play in their own particular way, and White played Kt × B in furtherance of the beautiful idea which he will presently develop, it being important that the Black Rook should not be able to retire to Rook's square for the protection of the King.

[15] Played with desperate ingenuity, and producing a combination far out of the common run, which forces the game in a few moves. The more we think over the position, specially in connection with White's preparatory move of 41. Kt × B, and the waiting move which White is bound to make on his next move, the greater our admiration will be. Of course K to B sq was impossible on account of Q to Kt 8, ch, winning the Rook.

H. E. BIRD v. A. WALBRODT.

WHITE	BLACK	WHITE	BLACK
1 P to K B 4 [1]	P to Q 4 [2]	6 Kt to Q B 3	B to K 2 [4]
2 Kt to K B 3	P to K 3	7 Kt to K 2	Kt to K R 4 [5]
3 P to K 3	P to Q B 4	8 Kt to K Kt 3	Kt to K B 3
4 P to Q Kt 3 [3]	Kt to Q B 3	9 P to Q R 3	Q to Q Kt 3 [6]
5 B to Q Kt 2	Kt to K B 3	10 R to Q Kt sq	B to Q 2

AUGUST 6

	WHITE	BLACK
11	B to Q 3	P to K R 3
12	Castles	P to K Kt 3 [7]
13	Kt to K 5	R to K Kt sq
14	Q to K B 3	Q to Q B 2
15	R to K B 2	Kt to Q sq [8]
16	P to Q B 4	B to Q B 3
17	P × P	Kt × P
18	Q to K 2	B to Q 3
19	Kt to K 4	P to K B 4
20	Kt × B, ch	Q × Kt
21	R to Q B sq	Kt to K 2 [9]
22	Kt to B 4	Q to Q 2
23	P to K 4 [10]	Kt to B 2
24	Kt to Q R 5 [11]	
		P × P
25	B × P	B × B
26	Q × B	Kt to Q 3 [12]
27	Q to Q B 2	P to Kt 3
28	Kt to B 4	Kt × Kt
29	Q × Kt	Q to Q 4
30	R to K sq [13]	Q × Q
31	P × Q	K to Q 2

White to make his 24th move.

	WHITE	BLACK
32	R (B 2) to K 2	
		Kt to B 3
33	R × P	Q R to K B sq
34	P to Kt 3	R to B 2
35	B to B 3	R to K 2
36	R × R, ch	Kt × R
37	K to Kt 2	And drew.

NOTES BY S. TINSLEY.

[1] This has often been quoted as 'Bird's Opening.' It is Mr. Bird's by adoption only. In early issues of the 'Chess Player's Chronicle,' before Mr. Bird's playing days, there are questions relating to this P to K B 4 (White) opening. But a writer in the 'B.C.M.' goes much further back and shows conclusively that this, like a good many other 'Chess Novelties,' belongs to the sixteenth century! It, in fact, appears in one of the Polerio MSS. 1590 (*vide* 'British Chess Magazine,' vol. xv. p. 463, November 1895). Mr. Bird deserves the credit of demonstrating again and again that the opening may be productive of highly interesting games, of which this present *partie* is a case in point.

[2] This is often said to be the best reply. I am reminded of what was said to me once by a player in the North. I adopted something very irregular, and he played Herr Walbrodt's move, remarking 'When I have to meet anything about which I know nothing, I always play P to Q 4 and trust to Providence.' This example is a good one for the inexperienced to imitate. The From Gambit 1. P to K B 4, P to K 4; 2. P × P, P to Q 3; 3. P × P, B × P, &c. (another ancient game), is also an effective defence for Black here.

[3] This is the point to which attention should be directed, for in this Queen's side development (B to Kt 2, &c., to follow) lies the whole secret of White's attack, Black usually Castling King's Rook.

⁴ Instead of the text move B to Q 3 is preferable. Players are sometimes advised to play for Black about this period P to K Kt 3, and develop the Bishop at K Kt 2, meeting White in that way by his own tactics. But very likely a sort of Fianchetto on the Queen's wing is better: P to Q Kt 3, P to Q R 3, if necessary; B to Q Kt 2, &c.

⁵ Apparently recognised as a wasted move later. But Black has already a poor game.

⁶ With a view to P to B 5, &c. He is apparently afraid to Castle.

⁷ To prevent P to K B 5. His game is, however, still further compromised.

⁸ In the absence of anything very threatening he could perhaps do better by some little Queen's side attack—say P to Q R 3, followed by P to Q Kt 4. He cannot Castle because of Kt × B P.

⁹ There seems no harm in Kt to B 2 now. If 21. Kt × Kt, K × Kt, and 22. B to K 5, though embarrassing is not very serious.

¹⁰ This is the true line of attack, and if properly followed up should break down the defences. The point is, it opens a file to the King and the weak King's Pawn.

¹¹ The Knight was excellently posted. R to K sq seems effective and obvious. P × P is then threatened; B to B 6 and other good openings are in prospect, and I think White should win.

¹² Shattering at a blow or two every winning prospect of White, and mainly as result of White's weak 24th move. Now everything is exchanged and there is nothing left in the game.

¹³ A good many moves too late, as we have shown. Furthermore, it allows the exchange of Queens as well as the other Pieces, and a Pawn becomes isolated. The ending is as poorly played by White as the opening and middle game are well conducted. Except that Herr Walbrodt takes advantage at the end, this game shows little of his true genius.

G. Marco v. W. H. K. Pollock.

	WHITE	BLACK
1	P to K 4	P to K 4
2	Kt to K B 3	Kt to Q B 3
3	B to Kt 5	P to Q 3
4	P to Q 4	B to Q 2
5	Kt to B 3 ¹	K Kt to K 2
6	P to Q 5 ²	Q Kt to Q Kt [sq
7	Kt to Kt 5 ³	Kt to Kt 3
8	Q to R 5	B × B
9	Kt × B	P to Q R 3
10	Kt to Q B 3	P to R 3 ⁴
11	Kt to K 6 ⁵	Q to K 2
12	Castles	K to Q 2 ⁶
13	P to B 4	P × P
14	B × P	Kt × B

BLACK

White to make his 11th move.

AUGUST 6

	WHITE	BLACK		WHITE	BLACK
15	R × Kt	P × Kt [7]	21	Kt to K 2	B to K 2
16	R to B 7	P to K 4	22	Kt to Kt 3	Kt to Q 2
17	QR to KB sq	K to Q sq	23	Kt to R 5	P to K Kt 3
18	R × Q	B × R	24	Q × Kt P	R to K B sq
19	R to B 7	B to B 3	25	Q to Kt 7	R × R
20	Q to B 5	R to K sq	26	Q × R	Resigns.[8]

NOTES BY R. TEICHMANN.

[1] At this juncture P to Q B 3 is preferable; it has been played very successfully in this Tournament against the Steinitz defence to the Ruy Lopez.

[2] We do not like this early advance of the Queen's Pawn, but White seems to have had a preconceived plan of a very early attack.

[3] This in connection with the somewhat adventurous-looking sally of the Queen next move forms a novel kind of attack in this opening, which even if not quite correct certainly makes the defence very difficult.

[4] But this is a strange mistake, which loses the game very soon. The natural move Kt to Q 2 and to B 3 would have enabled Black to drive the White Pieces back with a good development of his own. White could not, of course, capture the King's Rook's Pawn, e.g Kt to Q 2; 11. Kt × R P, B to K 2; 12. Q Kt to B sq, winning a Piece.

[5] White takes immediate advantage of Black's weak move and finishes the game with a few powerful strokes.

[6] A futile attempt to save the game. But P × Kt; 13. Q × Kt, ch, Q to B 2; 14. Q × P, ch, would also have left him with a bad game and a Pawn minus.

[7] If P to B 3, then 16. Kt to K 2 and to Q 4, to B 5, or almost anything, all the Black Pieces being blocked in

[8] For he is quite helpless against the threatened Kt to Kt 7 or Kt to B 6, if the Black Knight should move.

J. MIESES v. J. H. BLACKBURNE.

	WHITE	BLACK		WHITE	BLACK
1	P to K 4	P to K 4	12	Castles	B × Kt
2	Kt to K B 3	Kt to Q B 3	13	P × B	Q to B 3
3	P to Q 4	P × P	14	B to Kt 5 ([1])	P to B 3 [3]
4	Kt × P	B to B 4	15	P × P	Q × Q P
5	B to K 3	Q to B 3	16	B to B sq ([1])	B to Kt 2
6	P to Q B 3	K Kt to K 2	17	P to B 3	Q to R 4
7	B to Q Kt 5	P to Q R 3 [1]	18	R to K sq [4]	K to Q 2
8	B to R 4	P to Q Kt 4	19	P to Q B 4 ([1])	Q R to K sq
9	B to B 2	Kt × Kt [2]	20	P × P	P × P
10	P × Kt	B to Kt 5, ch	21	P to Q R 4	Kt to Q 4
11	Kt to B 3	P to Q 4	22	B to Q 2	P to Kt 5

WHITE	BLACK	WHITE	BLACK
23 R to Kt sq	B to R 3	28 Q to Q 5, ch	K to B 2
24 B to K 4	Kt to Kt 3	29 B to B 4, ch	K to Kt 3
25 Q to B 2 [5]	P to Q B 4	30 Q to B 5, ch	K to Kt 2
26 B to B 5, ch	K to Q sq	31 B to B 8, ch	R × B
27 Q × P	Kt to B 5	32 Q × Q [6]	Resigns.

NOTES BY DR. TARRASCH.

[1] A very poor move; this and the following one drive the Bishop to his best square. The most natural and the best play is Castling.

[2] How many such Scotch games has Blackburne won when he had the first move! and chiefly because the opponents committed this mistake, which strengthens the centre, frees the best square for the Bishop, and costs a move.

[3] After P × P, B × Kt follows, and then B × K P. Black has already a very bad game, a consequence of the erratic opening.

[4] White prevents Castling and opens a decisive attack, no matter whether the King moves to the Queen's side or the King's side.

[5] White continually makes the best and strongest moves.

[6] More precise was mate with R to K 7, ch, &c.

I. GUNSBERG v. A. BURN.

WHITE.	BLACK.	WHITE	BLACK
1 P to K 4	P to K 3	22 Kt to K 7, ch [6]	
2 P to Q 4	P to Q 4		R × Kt
3 P × P	P × P	23 B × R	Q × B
4 K Kt to B 3	K Kt to B 3	24 Q × P, ch	K to R 2
5 B to Q 3	B to Q 3		
6 Castles	Castles		
7 Kt to B 3	P to B 3		
8 Kt to K 2	Q Kt to Q 2		
9 Kt to Kt 3	R to K sq		
10 Kt to B 5	B to B 2		
11 B to K Kt 5 [1]	Kt to B sq		
12 Q to Q 2	B × Kt		
13 B × B	Q to Q 3 (!) [2]		
14 B to R 4	Kt to K 5		
15 Q to Q 3	P to K Kt 3		
16 B to R 3	P to K B 4		
17 B to Kt 3	P to B 5		
18 B to R 4	P to K R 3		
19 Kt to K 5	B to Kt 3 [3]		
20 K to R sq [4]	B × P (!) [5]		
21 Kt × B P	B to Kt 2		

Black to make his 25th move.

25 P to K B 3	Kt to Kt 4 [7]
26 Q R to K sq	Q to Q B 2

AUGUST 6

	WHITE	BLACK		WHITE	BLACK
27	R to K 2	R to Q sq	41	R to B 2	B to Q 5
28	Q to Kt 3	Kt × B	42	R to Q 2	B × P [10]
29	P × Kt	R to Q 3	43	R to Q 7, ch	Kt to K 2
30	R (B sq) to K sq	R to Q 2	44	R (K 8) × Kt, ch	K to Kt 3
31	R to K 8	Q to Q 3	45	R to K 6, ch	K to R 4
32	P to B 4	Q to K B 3	46	R to R 7	B to B sq
33	P to B 5	Q to R 5 [8]	47	P to Q R 4	R to Q 4
34	Q to Kt 4	R to K B 2	48	R to K B 6	R to Q sq
35	Q to Kt 3	Q to B 3	49	K to Kt 2	P to Kt 3
36	Q to Q 5	P to K Kt 4	50	K to B sq	R to K sq
37	P to Kt 4	Kt to Kt 3	51	R to R 8	B to Kt 2
38	P to Kt 5	Q to B 4	52	R (B 6) × P, ch	B × R
39	Q × Q	R × Q	53	R × R	Resigns.
40	R to Q B sq	B to Kt 7 [9]			

NOTES BY C. VON BARDELEBEN.

[1] I prefer, 11. K Kt to R 4, Kt to B sq ; 12. Q to B 3.
[2] By this move Black obtains the attack.
[3] If P to K Kt 4, White answers, 20 P to K B 3.
[4] White cannot avoid material loss. Bad would be, 20. P to Q B 3, because of P to Kt 4 ; 21. P to B 3, P × B ; 22. P × Kt, Q × Kt, winning a Piece.
[5] Now would P to Kt 4 be inefficacious, on account of 21. P to K B 3.
[6] White cannot save the Piece, for if he plays 22 Kt to R 5, there follows, Kt to B 4 (¹) ; 23. Q to K B 3, P to K Kt 4 ; 24 Q R to Q sq, Kt to K 5 , 25. Kt × P, Q to Q B 3 ; 26 Kt to R 5, Q to Kt 4, and Black wins a Piece.
[7] Black should have played Kt to B 3 ; 26 Q to Kt 3, R to K sq ; or 26 Q to Q 2, R to Q sq , 27 Q to B 2, Q to Kt 5 ; 28. P to B 3, Q to B 5 , again, 25. Kt to Kt 4 is not good, because White with his following move occupies the King's file.
[8] Q to B 3 was much better.
[9] Instead of B to Kt 7 he ought to have played R to B 2 ; 41. R to Q B 8, B to K 4 ; 42. P to B 6, P × P ; 43. P × P, Kt to K 2 ; 44. R to Q R 8, Kt to Q 4.
[10] Disastrous ; the best move was B to Kt 2.

B. VERGANI v. D. JANOWSKI.

	WHITE	BLACK		WHITE	BLACK
1	P to Q 4	P to Q 4	5	Castles	Castles
2	P to K 3	Kt to K B 3	6	P to Q B 4	P to Q B 3 [1]
3	Kt to K B 3	P to K 3	7	P to B 5 [2]	B to B 2
4	B to K 2	B to Q 3	8	P to Q Kt 4	P to Q R 4

	WHITE	BLACK		WHITE	BLACK
9	P to Kt 5	P × P	21	Kt to Q 2	B to Q 2
10	B × P	Kt to Q B 3	22	K R to Q B sq	
11	Kt to Q B 3	B to Q 2			Q to K 2 [sq [7]
12	Q to Kt 3 [3]	R to K sq	23	R to R sq	R (B sq) to Kt
13	B to Q Kt 2 [4]	R to Q Kt sq	24	R to R 2	Kt to Kt 5
14	Q R to Kt sq	Q to K 2	25	Kt to B 3	B × K R P
15	P to Q R 3	P to Q Kt 3	26	Kt to Q sq	Q to B 3
16	Q to R 4	K R to Q B sq	27	Kt × B	Q to R 5
17	K to R sq [5]	Q to K sq	28	Q to B 7	P to K 4 [8]
18	P × P	R × P	29	K to Kt sq	Q × Kt, ch
19	B × Kt	B × B		White resigns.	
20	Q to Q B 2 [6]	B to Q 3			

NOTES BY J. H. BLACKBURNE.

[1] This move, in all openings on the Queen's side, was condemned by the old masters, but is frequently adopted by many players of the present day. The object of the move is to break up the centre later on by P to K 4.

[2] Premature. Kt to Q B 3 or Q to Kt 3 was the correct play.

[3] R to Q Kt sq is stronger

[4] Again a weak move. B to R 3 or Kt to Q R 4, and White's game is all right

[5] Of course White could not win the Knight, on account of B × P, ch, winning the Queen, but P to Kt 3 would have been stronger than the move made.

[6] White's game is now very bad

[7] This is necessary before playing Kt to Kt 5, for suppose 23. Kt to Kt 5 ; 24. Kt × P, P × Kt ; 25. Q × R, ch, B × Q ; 26 R × B, ch, and White wins a Pawn.

[8] Black finishes off the game in fine style.

W. STEINITZ v. C. SCHLECHTER.

	WHITE	BLACK		WHITE	BLACK
1	P to K 4	P to K 4	12	B × Kt, ch	P × B
2	K Kt to B 3	Q Kt to B 3	13	Kt to K 5	Castles
3	B to B 4	B to B 4	14	Kt × Q B P	Q to B 3 [3]
4	P to B 3	Kt to B 3	15	Q R to Kt sq	B to B 4
5	P to Q 4	P × P	16	R to Kt 3 [4]	B to Q 2
6	P × P	B to Kt 5, ch	17	Kt to Kt 4	B to R 5
7	Kt to B 3	K Kt × P	18	Kt × P	Q to Q sq
8	Castles	B × Kt	19	Q to Q 3	B × R
9	P × B	P to Q 4	20	P × B	R to K sq
10	B to R 3 [1]	B to K 3 [2]	21	P to Q B 4	P to Q B 3
11	B to Kt 5	Kt to Q 3	22	Kt to K 3	Q to Q 2

AUGUST 6

	WHITE	BLACK
23	P to Q 5	Q R to Q sq
24	B to Kt 2	P to K B 3
25	B to Q 4 [5]	Kt to B sq
26	R to Q sq	Kt to Kt 3

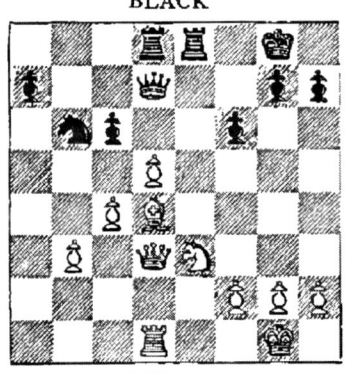

BLACK

WHITE

White to make his 27th move.

| 27 | P to Q 6 [6] | Q × P |
| 28 | P to B 5 | Q to K 3 |

	WHITE	BLACK
29	P × Kt	P to Q B 4
30	P × P	R × B
31	Q to B 2	R × R, ch
32	Q × R	Q to B 2
33	P to R 4	Q × R P
34	P to R 5	P to R 3
35	Kt to B 5	Q to Q B 2
36	P to Kt 3	Q to B 3
37	K to R 2	K to R sq
38	Q to Kt 4	Q to Q 2
39	Q to B 3	R to K 4
40	Kt to R 4	K to Kt sq
41	Kt to Kt 6	R to K sq
42	Kt to B 4	R to Kt sq
43	Q to K 4	Q to K B 2
44	Q to B 5	Q × Kt P
45	Q × Q B P	Q to Kt 4
46	Q to B 7	R to K sq
47	K to Kt 2	R to Kt sq
48	K to R 2	R to K sq
49	K to Kt 2	

Drawn game.

NOTES BY E. LASKER.

[1] A novelty by the leader of the White forces. White intends to give up the Piece in order to prevent Black from Castling into safety.

[2] Black declines the acceptance of the sacrifice with doubtful judgment. If 10. P × B, the consequence might be—

11	R to K sq	P to K B 4
12	Kt to Q 2	K to B 2
13	Kt × Kt	P × Kt
14	R × P	Q to B 3

This appears to be the only possible move, as R to K sq would be answered by Q to R 5, ch, and B to B 4 by R to B 4.

15	Q to K 2	B to K 3 (?) (a, b)
16	Q R to K sq	K R to K sq
17	P to Q 5, and wins.

(a) 15 | B to Q 2 (?)
16 Q × P, ch | K to Kt 3

17	P to Q 5	Kt to K 4
18	Q × B P	K R to K sq
19	Q × Kt P, with three Pawns for the Piece.

(b) 15 | B to B 4 (!)
16 R to B 4 | P to K R 4
17 Q × B P, ch | K to Kt 3
18 P to Q 5 | Kt to K 4
19 Q × P | K R to K sq

and although Black is two Pawns behind for the Piece, and may lose a third, his attack is excellent.

[3] Black plays exceedingly well for position. It is with best judgment that he allows White the opportunity of doubling his Queen's

Pawn, and White is wise to abstain from it, as by doing so he would involve both his Knight and his Queen's Bishop's Pawn in difficulties.

⁴ The Rook ought to have left the open file, as R to Kt 4 would be answered by P to Q R 4; and the move actually made loses the exchange for a Pawn.

⁵ A poor place for the Bishop. It seems as though B to R 3 would give him better prospects of fixing his Pawns far ahead in the camp of his adversary.

⁶ A faulty combination, which by opening up all lines to the Rooks endangers White's game to a considerable extent. White probably expected to win a Piece in case the Pawn was captured, but overlooked the retort of Black's 29th move regaining the Piece immediately.

E. SCHIFFERS v. R. TEICHMANN.

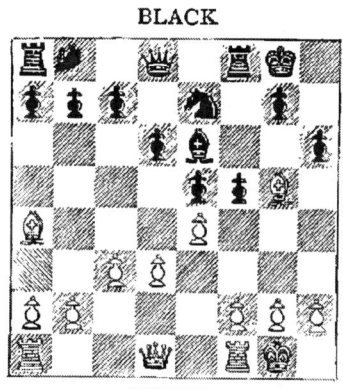

White to make his 15th move.

	WHITE	BLACK
1	P to K 4	P to K 4
2	Kt to K B 3	Kt to Q B 3
3	Kt to B 3	Kt to B 3
4	B to Kt 5	B to Kt 5
5	Kt to Q 5 [1]	B to K 2 [2]
6	P to Q 3	P to Q 3
7	Castles	Castles
8	Kt × Kt, ch [3]	B × Kt
9	P to Q B 3	Kt to K 2
10	B to R 4	B to K 3
11	Kt to Kt 5	B × Kt
12	B × B	P to K B 3
13	B to K 3	P to K B 4
14	B to K Kt 5	P to K R 3 [1]
15	B to Kt 3 [5]	B × B [6]
16	Q × B, ch	K to R 2
17	B × Kt	Q × B
18	P × P [7]	P to B 3
19	P to K B 4	R × P [8]
20	P × P	R × P
21	Q to B 7	R to K sq
22	Q × Q	Q R × Q
23	P to Q 4	R to K 7
24	R to B 2	K to Kt 3
25	K to B sq	R (K 7) to K 5
26	P to K Kt 3	P to Q R 4
27	K to Kt 2	R to K 8
28	R × R	R × R
29	K to B 3 [9]	K to B 4
30	P to K R 3	P to K R 4
31	P to Q R 3	P to K Kt 3
32	P to K R 4	P to Q Kt 4
33	K to Kt 2, ch	K to K 3
34	K to B 3	

Drawn game.[10]

NOTES BY H. N. PILLSBURY.

¹ Formerly considered a strong move, but now proven premature.

² Far better is the following continuation—viz.: 5. Kt × Kt; 6. P × Kt, P to K 5; 7. P × Kt, Q P × P; 8. B to K 2, P × Kt; 9. B × P, Castles; 10. Castles. (See Schiffers and Steinitz's game.)

AUGUST 6

³ 8. B × Kt, P × B, 9. Kt × B, ch, Q × Kt; 10. B to Kt 5, would appear to give White a slight superiority; Black would find it difficult to dissolve the doubled Pawn, nor would he obtain a satisf‍‍‍‍‍‍ory position by B to Kt 5; 11. P to K R 3, B × Kt; 12. Q × B, Q to K 3; 13 B × Kt, Q × B; 14. Q × Q, P × Q; 15. P to K B 4, with the better position for the end game.

⁴ 14. P to B 3 was the correct move to maintain the Pawn.

⁵ An ingenious move, which should have given White a superiority in material. (See diagram.)

⁶ If Q to Q 2; 16 B × B, ch, Q × B; 17 B × Kt, Q × B; 18. Q to Kt 3, ch, winning the Knight's Pawn.

⁷ Just why White does not take the Pawn with Queen is incomprehensible. After 18. Q × P, P to B 5 (there seems nothing more promising); 19. P to B 3, Q R to Kt sq; 20. Q × R P, R × P; 21. R to B 2, White appears to have a decided superiority.

⁸ If P × P, White obtains the better position by 20. Q R to K sq, &c.

⁹ A bad move; White could have formed an easy drawing position by 29 P to K R 3 and moving the King alternately to R 2 and Kt 2; his position warranted no more than a draw. He should not have allowed the adverse King to cross to the Queen's side.

¹⁰ Black has certainly the far better position, and the last move of White has given him a clear winning position. After K to Q 4; 35 K to B 4, R to K 5, ch; 36. K to B 3, R to K 3, White will be unable to prevent the adverse King reaching the Q Kt 6th square, and by the timely advance P to Q B 4 Black will be enabled to attack the Pawns on the Queen's side with the Rook, which will obtain attacking entrance through the then opened files. For instance,

WHITE	BLACK	WHITE	BLACK
37 K to Kt 2 (if 37. P to Kt 3, R to K 8 and attacking the Pawns in the rear)		Kt 3, and will win)	
	K to B 5		R to K 4
38 K to B sq	K to Kt 6	42 K to B sq	P to B 5
39 R to Q 2	P to B 4	43 K to B 2	P to R 5
40 P × P	P × P	44 K to B sq	R to K 6
41 K to B 2 (if 41. R to Q 5, K × P; 42. R × B P, R to		45 K to B 2	R to Q 6
		46 R to K 2	R to Q 8, with an easily won game.

Other variations also appear to win for Black.

AUGUST 7.

Two rounds have been so exciting that perhaps it is fortunate that this is quieter. Tarrasch begins to score himself and spoils Mieses's clean run by drawing a good game with him, and the Bishop's Gambit by Blackburne v. Steinitz attracts a large audience; at one time the former looks like winning, and beads of perspiration are seen on Steinitz's forehead. These two are old opponents, and Steinitz is to be congratulated on his chivalry in always accepting any opening offered.

W. H. K. POLLOCK v. B. VERGANI.

	WHITE	BLACK		WHITE	BLACK
1	P to K 4	P to Q B 4	13	K × B	Q × Q
2	P to Q 4	P × P	14	B × Q	R to Q sq
3	Kt to K B 3	P to K 4[1]	15	R to Q sq	P to B 4
4	K B to B 4	P to K R 3[2]	16	P × P	Kt to B 3
5	Castles	Kt to Q B 3	17	B to Q 5	Kt to Kt 5
6	P to B 3	B to B 4	18	Kt to B 3	Kt × B
7	P to Q Kt 4	B to Q 3[3]	19	P × Kt	B to Q 2
8	P × P	P × P	20	Q R to Kt sq	
9	Kt × P	K Kt to K 2			B to B sq
10	Kt × Kt	Q P × Kt	21	R to K sq	K to B sq
11	B to Kt 2	Castles[4]	22	P to Q 6	R to Q 2
12	Q to Q 4	B × P, ch	23	Kt to Q 5	Resigns

NOTES BY C. VON BARDELEBEN.

[1] This move is not to be recommended, since it does not further Black's development. The book-move is P to K 3.

[2] Obviously with the intention of preparing Kt to K B 3 or K 2; but the move P to K R 3 loses too much time, and therefore gives the opponent the advantage of by far quicker development. Better would be B to K 2, 5. Castles, P to Q 3, &c.

[3] A weak move. Preferable would be B to Kt 3.

[4] Black would defend himself for a longer time by R to K Kt sq, although Black's game at length could not be sufficiently defended.

Photo. Bradshaw, Hastings

W H K Pollock

AUGUST 7

J. H. Blackburne *v.* W. Steinitz.

WHITE	BLACK
1 P to K 4	P to K 4
2 P to K B 4	P × P
3 B to B 4	Kt to K B 3 [1]
4 Kt to Q B 3	Kt to B 3
5 P to Q 4 [2]	B to Kt 5
6 Q to Q 3	Castles
7 Kt to K 2	P to Q 4 [3]
8 P × P	K Kt × P
9 Castles	B × Kt
10 P × B	Q Kt to K 2
11 Kt × P	B to B 4
12 Q to B 3	P to Q B 3 [4]
13 B to R 3	Kt × Kt
14 Q × Kt	B to K 3 [5]
15 B to Kt 3 [6]	Q to Q 2
16 Q to B 3 [7]	P to Q R 4
17 Q to K 2	K R to K sq
18 B × B	P × B
19 R to B 3	R to K B sq
20 R × R, ch [8]	R × R
21 R to K sq	R to B 3
22 Q to K 5	Kt to Q 4
23 Q to Kt 3 [9]	P to R 3
24 B to Q 6	P to Q Kt 4
25 B to K 5	R to B 4
26 P to K R 4	P to R 5
27 R to K 4	P to R 4

WHITE	BLACK
28 Q to K sq	Q to K B 2
29 B to Q 6 [10]	R to B 3
30 B to K 5	R to Kt 3

BLACK

White to make his 31st move.

31 R to K 2	Q to B 6 [11]
32 R to B 2	Q × B P
33 Q × Q	Kt × Q
34 P to R 3	R to Kt 5
35 P to Kt 3	R to K 5
36 K to B sq	Kt to Kt 8
37 B to Q 6	R × Q P

White resigns.

Notes by I. Gunsberg.

[1] An unobjectionable defence. A remark which applies to the same move when played as a defence in the Scotch Gambit. In both cases, however, we think there is a more fearless and likewise a more profitable way of dealing with the attack, in a manner calculated to benefit Black.

[2] Kt to B 3 seems preferable here, as White's move of P to Q 4 admits of the rather favourable development of Black King's Bishop.

[3] This move breaks up White's centre and enables Black to get all his Pieces into play.

[4] Kt × Kt; 13. Q × Kt, B × P; 14. B × P, ch, would not be favourable for Black.

[5] A peculiar move requiring considerable courage, but supposing we consider the move in its bearing on an end game, we may easily see the idea underlying it. For instance, if B × B, P × B; Q × R, ch, Q × Q; R × Q, ch, K × R; B × Kt, ch, K × B; now Black will have a

chance of either playing P to Q B 4, or P to K 4, thereby breaking up White's Pawns.

[6] As White has made up his mind to resist the exchange of Bishops he should have played B to Q 3, which would threaten B × R P, ch, K × B ; Q to R 4, ch, winning the exchange.

[7] There was no harm in Black's threat of Kt to Q 4, for then White could have retired his Queen to Q 2, therefore Q to B 3 was a lost move. P to B 4 might have been played, followed, or even preceded, by K R to K sq, or Q R to Q sq, threatening B × Kt, and P to Q 5, &c. The combination thus indicated would have given White good chances. In fact it was easily to be foreseen that unless White advances his Queen's Bishop's Pawns they sooner or later would become weak.

[8] This exchange is unfavourable to White, who ought to have fore seen that a reduction of Pieces renders Black's isolated King's Pawn all the more secure. Q R to K B sq could have been played, or B × Kt, followed by P to B 4, so as to prevent Black pressing on the advance on the Queen's side. The omission to take the Knight proved fatal

[9] Black has succeeded in placing his Knight on Q 4, threatening White's weak Pawns White would not have gained anything by Q to Kt 8, ch, K to B 2, Q to B 8, ch, K to Kt 3. On account of the check with the Queen, Black cannot play R to Kt 3 now. Still we should have preferred P to B 4, so as to prevent by all means in our power the Pawns becoming weak.

[10] White in the last few moves has further compromised his position. His best plan would have been to mark time by R to K 2, and not move the Bishop at all, though even then Black by Kt to Kt 3, and Kt to B 5, would effect his purpose in a different way.

[11] A substantial gain will now be the reward of Black's clever play, which was made possible chiefly owing to White's omission to prevent his Queen's Bishop's Pawn being weakened by Black in the manner shown.

A. Burn v. E. Schiffers.

	WHITE	BLACK		WHITE	BLACK
1	P to Q 4	P to Q 4	15	P × Kt P	P × P
2	P to Q B 4	P to K 3	16	P to Q R 4 (¹)	P × P
3	Kt to Q B 3	Kt to K B 3	17	Q × R P	Q to Kt 3 [11]
4	Kt to K B 3	B to K 2	18	P to B 4 (¹)	B to Q 2
5	P to K 3 [1]	Castles	19	Q to R 2	Q to Kt 7
6	B to K 2 [2]	P to Q B 3 [3]	20	R to Q 2	Q × Q
7	Castles	Q Kt to Q 2	21	R × Q	P × P (!)
8	B to Q 2 [4]	B to Q 3	22	B × P	K R to B sq
9	Q to Q Kt 3 [5]	Kt to K 5 [6]	23	B to Q 3	R to Kt 6 [12]
10	B to K sq [7]	P to K B 4	24	R to R 6	R to B 8 [13]
11	Kt to Q 2	Q Kt to B 3	25	B to Q 2	R × R, ch
12	Q R to Q sq	Kt × Q Kt [8]	26	K × R	Kt to K 5 [14]
13	Kt P × Kt	R to Kt sq	27	B to B 4 (!)	R to Kt 8, ch
14	Kt to K B 3 [9]	P to Q Kt 4 [10]	28	K to K 2	P to Kt 4 [15]

Photo, Bradshaw, Hastings

E. Schyffer

AUGUST 7

	WHITE	BLACK
29	R × R P	B to Kt 4
30	B × B	R × B
31	R to R 2 [16]	P to Kt 5
32	Kt to K sq	B × R P
33	P to Kt 3	P to K R 4
34	Kt to Q 3	R to Kt 8
35	Kt to B 5	Kt × P, ch
36	P × Kt	B × P [17]
37	B to B 3	P to R 5
38	R to R sq [18]	R × R
39	B × R	P to R 6
40	K to B sq	K to B 2
41	Kt to Q 3	K to K 2
42	B to B 3	K to Q 3
43	Kt to B 4	B × Kt
44	P × B	K to Q 4
45	K to B 2	K to K 5
46	B to Q 2	K × P
47	K to Kt 3	K to Q 6 [19]
48	B to R 5	K to K 7
49	B to Kt 6	K to Q 6
50	B to B 7	K to K 7

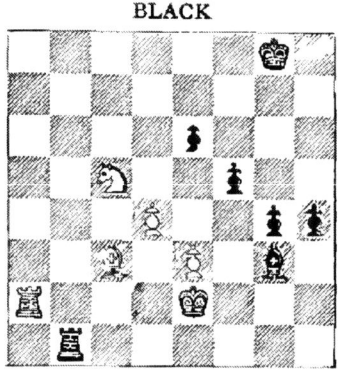

White to make his 38th move.

	WHITE	BLACK
51	B to K 5	K to B 8
52	B to Q 4	K to K 7
53	B to Kt sq	K to B 8
54	B to Q 4	K to K 7
55	B to K 5	K to B sq
56	B to Q 6	K to K 7

Drawn game.

NOTES BY DR. TARRASCH.

[1] I consider it more advantageous first to develop the Queen's Bishop, leaving the King's wing.

[2] There can scarcely be any doubt that in the Queen's game the post at Q 3 for the King's Bishop is in every respect better.

[3] Here P to B 4, together with Kt to B 3, would be correct. The move P to B 3 cramps Black, though Black will develop his game with P × B P and P to K 4, or Q B 4, as Tchigorin did against the same opponent.

[4] Here Mr. Burn blocks his Queen's file. I don't agree with this method of development.

[5] With Q to B 2 White would not only have prepared against his opponent's following attacking move, but would also have had the opportunity of forcing forward his opponent's King's flank Pawns, which he could have done long ago if he had brought his King's Bishop into his proper place at Q 3.

[6] With this Black succeeds in getting a good game.

[7] This idea belongs to Mr. Burn's system, which, however, was originated by Steinitz.

[8] There was time for this when White played P to K B 3.

[9] For what reason? A good plan was to push forward the King's Pawn after the preliminary moves have been made.

[10] Rather risky; Kt to K 5 was better, in order to prepare an attack upon the King, either with Q to B 3 and P to K Kt 4, or with R to B 3 and R 3, with the threat of R × R P and Q to R 5.

[11] Black is in trouble now with his isolated Rook's Pawn; he defends it nevertheless in the future very cleverly, though indirectly, by counter-attacks

[12] Black is now, on account of his better development (White's Queen's Bishop and King's Rook are still undeveloped), and through the command of the open files, in a good position, in spite of the isolated Rook's Pawn.

[13] This is not good, for it leads only the change of the active Rook against the undeveloped one at Bishop's sq. Black had two promising methods of attack, first B to Kt sq, and second R × B, followed by B to Kt 4. There was then still an advantage, while now the disadvantage of the weak Rook's Pawn and King's Pawn again count for something.

[14] The Knight cannot be taken on account of Bishop checks, but R × B; 27 R × B, B to Kt 4, is certainly preferable.

[15] Black could only guard the Queen's Rook's Pawn by considerably damaging his own position, and therefore he sacrifices it in order to continue his attack. After 29 Kt × P, might follow, B to Q B sq; 30. B × P, ch, B × B; 31. Kt × B, R to Kt 7.

[16] With this White prevents the dangerous move of R to Kt 7.

[17] After the sacrifice of the Knight the game looks to give the best chance for Black. It is very dangerous for White, as the Rook's Pawn seems likely to go straight for a Queen.

[18] This move leads to a draw Instead of this an attack of the three Pieces against the King seemed to be very promising, and might easily lead to a mate, as the combinations of Rook, Bishop and Knight against the King standing on the last file frequently bring a mate about. The game might assume the following form : 38. R to R 7, P to R 6 ; 39 Kt × P, P to R 7 , 40 R to Kt 7, ch, K to R sq; 41. P to Q 5, P to R 8 (Q) (?); 42. R to Kt 6, ch, K to R 2 ; 43. Kt to B 8, mate. One would think now that White must win, but Black's counter-moves are very clever. Even at the last moment Black might have given perpetual check by 41. R to K 8, ch , 42 K to Q 2, R to Q 8, ch ; 43. K to K 2 (¹). There is also 38. R to R 7, P to R 6 ; 39. P to Q 5, P to R 7 , 40. R to Kt 7, ch, K to B sq (!) ; 41. Kt × P, ch, K to K sq ; 42. B to B 6, R to K 8, ch, or B to Q 6, and Black could escape mate.

[19] With P to K 4 ; 48. P × P, K × P ; 49. B to B 4, ch, K to K 5; 50 B to B 7, P to B 4, ch ; 51. B × P, P to R 7 ; 52. K × P, K × B; 53. K to Kt 2, the game again becomes a draw.

D. JANOWSKI v. S. TINSLEY.

WHITE	BLACK	WHITE	BLACK
1 P to K 4	P to Q 4	4 P to Q 4	B to K Kt 5
2 P × P	Kt to K B 3	5 P to Q B 4	Kt to K B 3
3 Kt to K B 3	Kt × P	6 B to K 3	P to K 3

AUGUST 7

	WHITE	BLACK
7	Q to Kt 3	P to Q Kt 3
8	Kt to K 5	P to Q B 3 [1]
9	Kt to Q B 3	B to Q 3
10	B to K Kt 5	B to K B 4
11	B to K 2	Q to B 2
12	Kt to B 3	Q Kt to Q 2
13	B to R 4	Castles K R
14	B to Kt 3	P to Q R 3
15	Kt to K R 4	B to Kt 3
16	Kt × B	R P × Kt
17	R to Q sq	K R to Q sq
18	B to B 3	Q R to B sq
19	Castles	K to B sq [2]
20	K R to K sq	B × B
21	R P × B	K to Kt sq
22	Q to R 3	P to R 4
23	Q to R 4	Kt to B sq
24	P to Q R 3	Kt(B sq) to R 2
25	Q to B 2	Kt to Kt 4
26	Q to B sq	Kt (Kt 4) to R [2] [3]
27	P to Q Kt 4	P × P
28	P × P	Q to Q 3
29	P to B 5	Q to B 2
30	Kt to R 4	P to Q Kt 4
31	Kt to Kt 6	R to Kt sq
32	Q to K B 4 [4]	Q to Kt 2
33	P to K Kt 4	Kt to Q 2
34	Kt × Kt	Q × Kt
35	P to Kt 3	P to B 3 [5]
36	Q to K 4 [6]	Kt to Kt 4
37	Q × B P [7]	Q R to B sq
38	Q × Q	Kt × B, ch
39	K to B sq	R × Q
40	R × P	R × Q P
41	R to Q R sq	R × Q Kt P

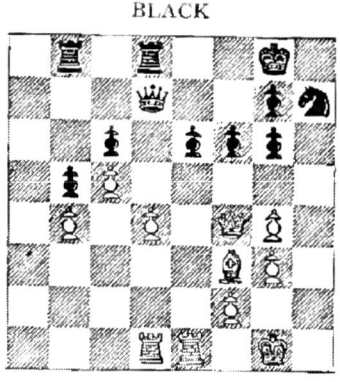

White to make his 36th move.

	WHITE	BLACK
42	R (R sq) to R 7	R to K 5
43	R to Kt 6	R to R 5
44	R to K 7	K to R 2
45	K to Kt 2	Kt to K 4
46	P to Kt 5	Kt to B 3
47	R to Q 7	P × P
48	R (Kt 6) to Kt 7	R to K Kt sq
49	R × P	R to Q Kt 5
50	R × R	Kt × R
51	R to Q 4	R to Q Kt sq
52	K to B 3	R to Kt 4
53	K to K 4	Kt to R 3
54	P to B 6	R to Q B 4
55	R to Q 5	R × P
56	R × P	R to B 4
57	R × R	Kt × R, ch

White resigns.

NOTES BY R. TEICHMANN.

[1] Black treats the opening in a novel manner; but these Pawn moves weaken his Queen's side.

[2] I fail to see the object of this move; Black is entirely on the defensive and cannot undertake anything.

[3] Of course if Kt × B, then White would get an attack on the King's Rook's file.

[4] White is playing very well, and with this move brings the Queen

into action. Black dare not exchange Queens because after Q × Q; 33. P × Q, Kt to Q 4; 34. B × Kt, K P × B; 35. R to K 7, White would have an easily won end game.

[5] One of Mr. Tinsley's wily traps.

[6] It is unaccountable that such an ingenious player as Mr. Janowski should not have seen Black's design. B to Kt 2 was his move now, and there can be no doubt that the weakness of all the Black Pawns would have led to loss of material sooner or later (see diagram).

[7] Losing a Piece and the game. The rest is silence.

C. Schlechter v. E. Lasker.

	WHITE	BLACK
1	P to K 4	P to Q B 4
2	Kt to K B 3	Kt to Q B 3
3	P to Q 4	P × P
4	Kt × P	P to K Kt 3
5	Kt × Kt [1]	Kt P × Kt [2]
6	Q to Q 4	P to K B 3
7	B to Q B 4	P to K 3
8	Castles	Kt to R 3
9	Kt to B 3	Kt to B 2
10	B to K 3	B to K Kt 2
11	Q R to Q sq	Castles
12	Q to Q 2	P to K B 4
13	P × P [3]	Kt P × P
14	B to Q 4 [4]	P to Q 4
15	B × B	K × B
16	B to K 2	P to K 4
17	Kt to R 4	Q to B 3
18	Kt to B 5	P to B 5
19	P to K B 3	B to K B 4
20	B to Q 3	Q R to K sq
21	Q R to K sq	Q R to K 2
22	R to B 2	Kt to Q 3
23	Q to B 3	B to Kt 3
24	R (B 2) to K 2	R (B) to K sq
25	B × B	P × B
26	Kt to Q 3	Kt to B 5
27	Kt to B 2	Kt to K 6
28	Kt to Q sq	P to Q 5
29	Q to Q 3	P to K 5
30	P × P	R × P
31	Kt × Kt	B P × Kt
32	R to K B sq	R to B 5
33	R × R	Q × R [5]

White to make his 34th move.

	WHITE	BLACK
34	Q to Q sq	P to Q B 4
35	P to Q Kt 3	P to Q R 4
36	Q to K sq	P to R 5
37	Q to R 5	R to K B sq
38	Q to K sq	R to K B 4
39	Q to Q sq	K to B 3
40	Q to K sq	K to K 3
41	Q to Q sq	K to Q 4
42	P to K R 3 [6]	Q to K 5
43	Q to K sq	Q to B 5
44	Q to Q sq	K to K 4
45	Q to K sq	K to B 3
46	Q to Q sq	K to Kt 2
47	Q to K sq	R to B 3
48	Q to Q sq	Q to Kt 6
49	Q to Q 3	R to B 7
50	Q to K 4 [7]	Q to K B 5
51	Q to K 7, ch	K to R 3

White resigns.[8]

NOTES BY H. N. PILLSBURY.

¹ Although this line of play has been adopted by Lasker himself with considerable success, it is probably premature, owing to the strengthening of Black's centre Pawns.   5. B to K 3 is more usual and more correct.

² In an exhibition game, played in New York, Lasker, as second player, re-took here with the Queen's Pawn, allowing the exchange of Queens, and relied upon his end game ability to outplay his opponent, and was successful. It is not, however, as good as the text.

³ This still more strengthens Black's already formidable centre. Probably best now was 13. P to B 3, P to Q 4 ; 14 P × Q P, B P × P, 15. B to Kt 3, B to Q R 3 ; 16 K R to K sq, retaining a pressure on the centre Pawns.

⁴ Premature at least. 14. P to B 4, P to Q 4 ; 15. B to K 2, threatening R to B 3 and Kt 3, was far superior.

⁵ Black has managed his centre attack in capital style, and obtained a theoretical winning position. White is unable to stir, and although the game lasts for some time, the issue can hardly be doubtful.

⁶ This hastens the end, as Black, after judiciously retreating the King to avoid danger of perpetual check arising from Q to Q 3, &c., is enabled to put his Queen at K Kt 6, and then the game is over.

⁷ An ingenious attempt to draw by perpetual check, which would succeed if Black took the Rook.

⁸ For if R to K sq, Black wins by either R × P, ch, Q to B 7, ch, &c., or by the simpler P to K 7.

R. TEICHMANN v A. ALBIN.

	WHITE	BLACK		WHITE	BLACK
1	P to K 4	P to K 4	12	P × B ²	Q × P, ch
2	Kt to K B 3	Kt to Q B 3	13	B to Q 2	Q × K B
3	B to Kt 5	P to Q R 3	14	Q × P	Q to K 5, ch
4	B to R 4	Kt to B 3	15	B to K 3 ³	P to Q Kt 3
5	Kt to B 3	B to B 4	16	Q to R 3	B to Kt 2
6	Kt × P ¹	Kt × Kt	17	P to K B 3	Q × K P
7	P to Q 4	B to Kt 5	18	Castles	Q to K 2
8	P × Kt	Kt × P	19	Q × Q	K × Q
9	Q to Q 4	Kt × Kt	20	B × P	P to K B 3
10	P × Kt	P to Q B 4		Drawn game	
11	Q to K 3	Q to R 4			

NOTES BY J H. BLACKBURNE.

¹ Castling gives a more lasting attack. The text move leads to a rapid exchange of Pieces, and leaves nothing to combine with.

² Some lively variations arise from P to K 6, but with the best defence the result is a draw.

³ K to Q sq might also be played with perfect safety, for if Q × Kt P, White replies with B to Kt 4, and ought to win

J. Mason v. M. Tchigorin.

	WHITE	BLACK
1	P to K 4	P to K 4
2	Kt to K B 3	Kt to Q B 3
3	B to B 4	Kt to B 3
4	P to Q 3	B to B 4
5	B to K 3	B × B [1]
6	P × B	Castles
7	Kt to B 3	P to Q 3
8	Castles [2]	Kt to Q R 4
9	B to Kt 3	P to B 3
10	Q to K sq	Kt × B
11	R P × Kt	Kt to Kt 5
12	P to R 3	Kt to R 3
13	P to K Kt 4 [3]	K to R sq
14	Q to Kt 3	B to K 3
15	K to R 2	P to B 3
16	R to B 2	Q to K 2
17	R to K Kt sq	P to K Kt 4
18	K to R sq	R to K Kt sq
19	Q R to K B sq	
		R to Kt 3
20	Kt to R 2	Kt to Kt sq
21	Q to B 3 [4]	R to K B sq [5]
22	Kt to K 2	P to K R 4
23	P × P	R to R 3
24	K to Kt 2	Q to Q 2
25	R to K R sq	P to Q 4
26	Kt to Kt 4 [6]	R × P

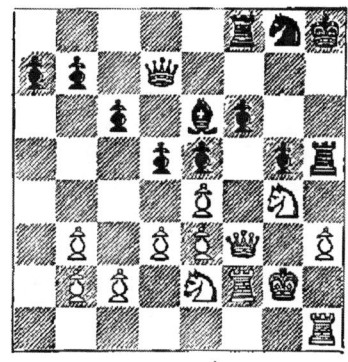

White to make his 27th move.

	WHITE	BLACK
27	Kt to Kt 3 [7]	P × P
28	P × P	B × Kt
29	P × B	R × R
30	K × R	R to Q sq
31	R to R 2, ch	K to Kt 2
32	Kt to B 5, ch	K to B sq
33	Q to B 2 [8]	Q to Q 8, ch
34	K to Kt 2	R to Q 7
	White resigns.	

NOTES BY E. SCHIFFERS.

[1] Apparently better than B to Q Kt 3 ; anyhow, Black loses no time in developing his game. The open file does not prove dangerous.

[2] Here White should have played P to Q R 3, as then Black would have no advantage in moving Kt to R 4, and if B to K 3, then Bishop takes, with perfectly even game. In the present instance it would be more advantageous to allow the exchange of Bishops than to give up the Bishop for the Knight. P to Q 4 is bad, as it completely weakens White's centre.

[3] Evidently to prevent P to K B 4.

[4] This move makes a place for the Knight at K Kt 3, but does not prevent the advance to R 4.

[5] Tchigorin remarks that it would be better to play at once P to K R 4.

[6] White has no better move, the Rook's Pawn cannot be retained Upon Kt to B sq may follow P to K Kt 5

[7] Here Kt × K P could have been played The best reply was Q to R 2; 28. P × P, P × P. White is a Pawn ahead, but Black threatens R to Q R sq, and gets an attacking position. But if 27. Q to R 2; 28. P × P, P to K Kt 5 (?), then 29 Kt × P, B × Kt; 30. Q × B, R to Kt 4; 31. Q × R, P × Q, 32. R × R, and wins, having two Rooks and two Pawns for the Queen, with a better position.

[8] If 33. R to R 8, then Q to Q 7, and upon 34. Kt to R 6, Q to K 8, ch; 35. King moves, R to Q 7, ch; 36. K to R 3, Q to R 5, mate.

C. BARDELEBEN v H. E. BIRD

	WHITE	BLACK		WHITE	BLACK
1	P to K 4	P to K 3	14	Kt to Q Kt 3	Kt to Q sq
2	P to Q 4	P to Q 4	15	Kt to Q B sq	B to Q 3
3	B to K 3[1]	Kt to K B 3	16	Kt to K 5	B to K sq
4	P to K 5	K Kt to Q 2	17	Q Kt to Q 3	Kt to K 5
5	Kt to K B 3[2]	P to Q B 4	18	B to K R 5	B to Q Kt 4
6	P to Q B 3	Kt to Q B 3	19	R to K sq	Q to B 2
7	Q Kt to Q 2	Q to Q Kt 3	20	R to Q B sq	Q to K 2
8	Q R to Q Kt sq		21	B to B 3	Kt to Kt 4
		P × Q P	22	B to Kt 4	Q B × Kt
9	P × P	B to K 2	23	Q × B	Kt to K 5
10	B to K 2	Castles	24	B to K B 3	Kt to Kt 4
11	Castles	P to K B 4	25	B × Kt	Q × B
12	P × P *en passant*		26	R to Q B 2[3]	
		Kt × P		Drawn game.	
13	P to K R 3	B to Q 2			

NOTES BY R. TEICHMANN.

[1] Alapin's idea. The sacrifice of the Pawn seems to be correct, for after P × P; 4. Kt to Q 2, Black would get a very difficult game to defend, if he tried to keep the Pawn with P to K B 4, whilst, after Kt to K B 3; 5. P to Q B 3, followed by Q to B 2, would recover the Pawn with a good game.

[2] P to K B 4 appears to be preferable.

[3] The play in this game was tame, and featureless to a degree, and does not require any comment. Apparently both players were satisfied with the result.

H. N. PILLSBURY v. G. MARCO.

	WHITE	BLACK		WHITE	BLACK
1	P to Q 4	P × Q 4	6	R to B sq	P to Q B 3[1]
2	P to Q B 4	P to K 3	7	P to K 3	P to Q Kt 3
3	Kt to Q B 3	Kt to K B 3	8	B to Q 3	B to Kt 2
4	Kt to B 3	B to K 2	9	Castles	Q Kt to Q 2[2]
5	B to B 4	Castles	10	P to K 4[3]	P × K P

56 THE HASTINGS CHESS TOURNAMENT

WHITE	BLACK
11 Kt × P	Kt × Kt
12 B × Kt	Kt to K B 3
13 B to Q Kt sq [4]	
	P to B 4 (!)
14 P × P	Q × Q [5]
15 K R × Q	B × P [6]
16 P to Q R 3 [7]	K R to Q sq [8]
17 P to Q Kt 4	B to K 2
18 Kt to Q 4	Kt to K sq
19 B to R 2	P to Q R 4 [9]
20 P to B 5	R P × P
21 P to B 6	B to Q B sq [10]
22 P to B 7	R to Q 2
23 Kt to B 6	B to B 3
24 Kt × P [11]	R × R, ch
25 R × R	B to Kt 2
26 R to Q 7	K to B sq
27 B to Q B 4	B to K 2 [12]
28 P to K R 3 [13]	R to B sq

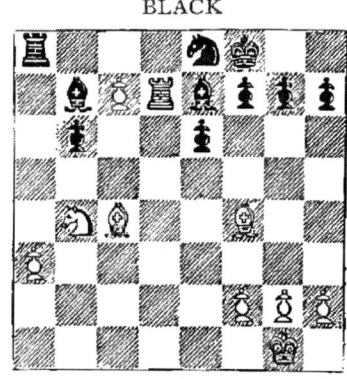

WHITE
White to make his 28th move.

WHITE	BLACK
29 B to R 6	B × B
30 Kt × B	Kt to B 3
31 R to Q 3 [14]	Kt to Q 4
32 B to K 3	K to K sq
Drawn game. [15]	

NOTES BY DR. TARRASCH.

[1] This move is not good, first, because it shuts in the Queen's wing, and, secondly, because it loses an opportunity, for the Pawn is destined to advance to B 4, and it might be done at once without preparation.

[2] Black is ready now for a big disaster, while White possesses a well-ordered game. Black's position is bad in the abstract, he has only one Piece, viz. the King's Knight, as well placed as the corresponding one on the other side, while the Queen, Queen's Knight, and the two Bishops are shut in.

[3] This, in my opinion, opens the game too early; Q to K 2 followed by R to Q sq would assist.

[4] Here Q to K 2, to prevent the advance of the Black Queen's Bishop's Pawn, was decidedly stronger. The Bishop plays no great part in the sequel. Black has now almost an equal game.

[5] By the exchange Black develops the White Rook, but if he does not take, White plays Q to K 2, followed by R to Q sq, and then pins the Knight by B to Kt 5 in an unpleasant way.

[6] Here and also in the following moves Black ought to spoil White's Pawn position by B × Kt, which would have been disadvantageous for White in spite of the two remaining White Bishops. That White did not prevent this in the following moves is astonishing—he could not promise himself any advantage by this exchange.

[7] The game is now nearly equal, but White has the majority of Pawns on the Queen's side, and is two moves ahead in the development, viz. the Rook's moves.

AUGUST 7

[8] If Black tries to prevent the advance of the Knight's Pawn by P to Q R 4, there follows 17. B to Q 6, B × B ; 18. R × B, with an attack on the Knight's Pawn.

[9] R to B sq would be better, in order, if possible, to prevent the advance of the Bishop's Pawn.

[10] Even with B to R 3, together with R to B sq, Black still could not avoid being placed at disadvantage.

[11] With 24. R × R, B × R ; 25. Kt to Kt 8 (!), B to B sq ; 26. R to Q sq and Q 8 White must have won.

[12] Rook cannot take the Rook's Pawn on account of the reply R to Q 8.

[13] B to R 6 would be stronger, and when B × B ; 29. Kt × B (threatening Kt to Kt 8), R to B sq ; 30. B to K 5 (to prevent Kt to B 3), giving White another chance of attacking combinations. If Black replies P to B 3, then 31. B to Q 4, P to Kt 4 ; 32. B to Kt 6, followed by K to B sq, and R to Q 8 ; or if 30. Kt to B 3 ; 31. B × Kt, B × B ; 32. P to Q R 4, K to K sq ; 33. Kt to Kt 8, and Black's play is full of difficulty. For example, 33. B to K 4 ; 34. R to Q 8, ch, R × R ; 35. P × R (Q), K × Q ; 36. Kt to B 6, ch, and wins the Bishop ; in any other case the White King enters the play with effect (see diagram).

[14] Now 31. Kt to Kt 8 does not help on account of K to K sq. (Not Kt × R on account of Kt × Kt, ch, followed by Kt × P.)

[15] If Black takes the Bishop's Pawn, White wins the Knight's Pawn.

Dr. Tarrasch v. J. Mieses.

	WHITE	BLACK
1	P to Q 4	P to Q 4
2	Kt to K B 3	Kt to K B 3
3	P to B 4	P × P [1]
4	P to K 3	P to K 3
5	B × P	P to B 4
6	Castles	P × P
7	Kt × P [2]	Kt to B 3
8	Kt × Kt	Q × Q
9	R × Q	P × Kt
10	P to Q Kt 3	B to K 2
11	B to Kt 2	Castles
12	Kt to Q 2	B to Kt 2
13	B to K 2	P to B 4
14	Kt to B 4	Q R to Q sq [3]
15	Kt to R 5	B to R sq
16	B to Kt 5	Kt to Q 4
17	B to Q B 6	R to Q 3 [4]
18	B × B	R × B
19	P to K 4	Kt to Kt 3
20	R × R	B × R
21	R to Q sq	B to B sq
22	K to B sq	P to B 3
23	K to K 2	K to B 2
24	R to Q 3	R to B sq

BLACK

WHITE

White to make his 25th move.

25	R to R 3 [5]	P to B 5
26	P × P	B to Kt 5
27	B to B 3	B × Kt

	WHITE	BLACK		WHITE	BLACK
28	B × B	R × P	41	P to Kt 4	R to Q 6
29	B × Kt	P × B	42	R to R 5	R to Q 4
30	R to Q Kt 3	R × P, ch	43	R to R 6	K to K 4
31	K to B 3	R to R 5	44	R to R sq	R to B 4
32	R × P	R × P	45	R to Q sq	K to K 5
33	R to Kt 7, ch	K to Kt 3	46	R to K sq, ch	K to Q 4
34	P to Kt 3	P to B 4	47	R to K R sq	R to Kt 4
35	R to Kt 6	K to B 3	48	R to R 6	R to Kt 8
36	P to R 4	P to R 3	49	R to Kt 6	P to K 4
37	R to B 6	R to R 6, ch	50	R × P	K to K 5
38	K to Kt 2	P to Kt 4	51	R to B 5	R to Kt 6
39	P × P, ch	P × P	52	R to B 8	
40	R to B 5	P to B 5		Drawn game.	

NOTES BY JAMES MASON.

[1] As good as anything else, to avoid complications, and with the first object of a draw.

[2] Exchanges ensuing upon this are not sufficiently favourable to the first player. He keeps the draw in hand; but the chances of a win become few indeed. It would be perfectly safe to take otherwise, the bogy of the isolated Pawn notwithstanding.

[3] All of which goes to show that Herr Mieses simply desires to get the matter over without losing. In the nature of things he easily holds his ground, the position even now being sufficiently rigid to exclude any but the most commonplace proceedings on either side.

[4] It is worthy of note that B × B would not be good, or, rather, why it would not. And he does not want to admit of White's later R to Q 7. Black is on the defensive, of course, and a little care is necessary; but, beyond this, there is no real difficulty.

[5] Not promising anything, except risk. But, in the resulting Rook and Pawn ending, the extra Pawn does not matter. Only White himself has to play to draw.

A. WALBRODT v. I. GUNSBERG.

	WHITE	BLACK		WHITE	BLACK
1	P to K 4	P to K 4	12	Q to Q 2	P to Q B 3
2	K Kt to B 3	Q Kt to B 3	13	B to R 4	Kt to K 3 [3]
3	P to Q 4	P × P	14	B to Kt 3	Q to Q sq
4	Kt × P	B to B 4	15	Q R to K sq	K to R sq
5	B to K 3	Q to B 3	16	P × P [4]	Kt (K 2) × P
6	P to Q B 3	K Kt to K 2	17	Kt × Kt	P × Kt
7	B to Q Kt 5	Castles	18	P to B 4	P to B 4
8	Castles	B × Kt	19	B to K B 2	Q to Q 3
9	P × B	P to Q 4	20	R to K 5	Kt to B 2
10	P to B 3 (!) [1]	Kt to Q sq [2]	21	R to B sq	B to Q 2
11	Kt to B 3	Q to Q Kt 3	22	Q to B 3	Q R to B sq

AUGUST 7

	WHITE	BLACK
23	Q to Kt 3	B to B 3
24	Q to R 3	B to Q 2
25	R (B sq) to K sq	
		B to K 3
26	Q to R 5	Q to Q 2
27	R (K sq) to K 3	
		R to B 3
28	Q to K 2	P to K R 3
29	B to Q sq	R to K sq
30	B to K R 4	R (B 3) to B sq
31	Q to K sq	B to B 2
32	R to K 7	R × R
33	R × R	Q to B 3
	Drawn game.[5]	

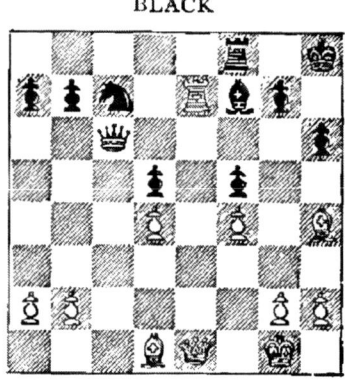

Position at the end.

NOTES BY C. VON BARDELEBEN.

[1] Much better than P to K 5.

[2] This and the following move give the second player a cramped game. B to K 3 would be better.

[3] Black has no other square for the Knight, but the latter now prevents the Bishop being developed.

[4] White had an excellent game, but his last move gives up all his advantage. If White had played 16. B to Q B 2, to be followed by 17. P to K 5, he would have had the superior game.

[5] White agrees very early to a draw, and my opinion is that he still has a somewhat better chance. The game might proceed with: 34. Q to B 3, Q × Q; 35. P × Q, Kt to Kt 4; 36. B to K sq, R to K sq; 37. R × R, ch, B × R; 38. K to B 2, and the ending is a little in favour of White.

AUGUST 8.

TO-DAY the masters are taken to Battle in waggonettes, and by the kind permission of the Duchess of Cleveland and Lord Brassey visit Battle Abbey and Normanhurst Court.

A party of fifty-five, including all the masters (except Lasker and Burn) and many press-men, start in splendid weather, which keeps up all day. They drive to the Abbey, where they are photographed, go over Normanhurst Court, which is much admired, and, driving back, arrive at six o'clock, having thoroughly enjoyed the day. In the evening the masters are taken to a special concert on the pier, and the enjoyment manifested proved the oft-made assertion that chess-players are generally musicians. The masters had the option also of seats at the theatre to see *Charley's Aunt*, but *all* chose the music.

AUGUST 9.

To DAY Tarrasch scores his first win by a magnificent ending against Walbrodt, and at the same time wins the second brilliancy prize. Lasker makes his second loss, and Tchigorin's career is checked by losing to his compatriot Schiffers. Steinitz, too, delights his admirers by the way in which he won an apparently even position; the game is well worthy of its author.

Bird *v.* Blackburne attracts a fair share of attention, as the former is so peculiarly fatal to the latter in tournaments.

DR. TARRASCH *v.* A. WALBRODT.

	WHITE	BLACK		WHITE	BLACK
1	P to K 4	P to K 4	23	Q to Q 3	K to R sq[6]
2	Kt to K B 3	Kt to Q B 3	24	Q to Kt 3	R to R 2
3	B to Kt 5	P to Q R 3	25	Kt (R 5) to B 4	
4	B to R 4	Kt to B 3			R to Kt sq
5	Kt to B 3	P to Q 3	26	Q R to K sq	P to Kt 4
6	P to Q 4	B to Q 2	27	R to K 2	B to Q sq
7	B × Kt[1]	B × B	28	Q to Q 3	Q R to K Kt 2
8	Q to K 2[2]	P × P	29	P to Kt 3	P × P[7]
9	Kt × P	B to Q 2			
10	Castles	B to K 2			
11	P to Q Kt 3	Castles			
12	B to Kt 2	P to Q Kt 4[3]			
13	P to Q R 4	P to Kt 5			
14	Kt to Q sq	P to B 4			
15	Kt to K B 3	B to B 3			
16	Kt to Q 2	P to Q 4			
17	P to K 5	Kt to K sq			
18	Kt to K 3	Q to Q 2[4]			
19	Q R to Q sq	P to Q 5			
20	Kt (K 3) to B 4				
		Q to K 3			
21	P to B 4	P to B 4[5]			
22	Kt to R 5	B to Q 4			

Black to make his 32nd move.

Photo., Bradshaw, Hastings

AUGUST 9

WHITE	BLACK	WHITE	BLACK
30 R × P	R to Kt 4	34 R × P [11]	Kt × P
31 R (K 2) to B 2		35 Kt × Kt	R × Kt, ch
	Kt to Kt 2	36 P × R	R × P, ch
32 Kt to Q 6 [8]	Q × P [9]	37 K to B sq	R × Q
33 Kt × P	Kt to R 4 [10]	38 R to Kt 4 [12]	Resigns

NOTES BY H. N. PILLSBURY.

[1] In the same variation where the Black Pawn has not driven the Bishop back to Q R 4, this exchange of Bishop for Knight has been found very advantageous for White, but here the position of Black's Queen's Rook's Pawn makes a considerable difference in his favour, as he is soon able to advance all the Queen's wing Pawns, and form an early counter-attack on that side; therefore it would seem that 7. Castles, and if P to Q Kt 4; 8. P × P, P × P; 9. B to Kt 3, was preferable.

[2] Q to Q 3 seems somewhat better.

[3] See the first note. Black now threatens to win the exchange by P to Q B 4, P to Kt 5, and B to Q Kt 4; if the Queen were at Q 3, the Knight at Q 4 could cross to K Kt 3 *via* K 2, with a better position than it actually obtains; then the other Knight, which afterwards becomes posted at K 3, would in conjunction threaten Kt to K B 5.

[4] To keep the Knight from B 5 before continuing P to Q 5.

[5] White's attack is now brought to a standstill, and his Pieces are unable to break into the Black position, and although he has a passed King's Pawn it benefits him nothing.

[6] Preparing to attack directly on the King; the strength of the Bishop at Q 4 becomes more and more apparent.

[7] Black has prepared his counter-attack with admirable force, but before opening matters he should have posted his King's Bishop at Q B 2 to prevent the subsequent entry of the adverse Knight at Q 6. Had he taken this precaution it is difficult to see how White could avoid decisive loss.

[8] Owing to Black's lack of precaution at move 29, the attack has in reality changed hands, and the King's Bishop's Pawn has become the focus of a powerful attack. (See diagram.)

[9] The position admits of beautiful possibilities, and Black permits himself to be out-generalled by his more experienced opponent. It was not wise to take this Pawn, and is a violation of principle to put King and Queen on the same diagonal with an adverse Bishop, and Black pays dearly therefor. It has been suggested that 32. R to B sq was the correct move, but it will not answer, e.g.:

32	R to B sq	34 Kt × Q B P	Q × P
33 Kt (Q 2) to K 4 (the winning move)		35 Kt × B P	R (R 4) × Kt, (best; if Kt × Kt—36. R × Kt, R (R 4) × R, 37. B × P, R × R; 38. B × Q, ch, K to Kt sq; 39. Q × B, ch, and wins.)
	R to R 4 (best; if B × Kt—34. Kt × B, R to R 4; 35 Kt × P, Q × P, 36. Kt to Q 7, and wins.)		

WHITE	BLACK		WHITE	BLACK
36 B × P	R × R		33 Kt × P	B × K P
37 B × Q	R × R		34 Kt × Kt	R (Kt 4) × Kt,
38 Q × B, threatening Kt to K 6, and should win as Black's scattered Pawns would soon fall, and he can hardly save the exchange also.			with a fine game ; or if	
			33 Kt (Q 2) to B 4	K B × Kt
			34 Kt × B	Q × P
			35 Kt × P	Kt × Kt
			36 R × Kt	R × R
			37 R × R	Q to K 8, ch
But the correct play for Black was			38 R to B sq	Q to K 5, with at least a draw.
32	B to B 2, and if			

[10] Not seeing the beautiful countermine of White, as Kt to K 3 still gave Black a good game, for if then 34. R to R 4, R × P, ch ; followed by B × R, leaves White in a hopeless position.

[Dr. Tarrasch has since given the following as the probable continuation if Black had played 33. Kt to K 3 (!) :—34. R to K 4, B × R ; 35. Q × B, Q × Q ; 36. Kt × Q, and now although the exchange behind White has a strong attack which might be continued : 37. Kt × P and B × P, ch ; or if, as best, Black replied 36. R to Kt 3, then 37. Kt (K 4) to Q 6, R to B sq ; 38. R to K 2, Kt to B 5 ; 39. R to K 5, B to Kt 3 ; 40. R to K 7, still with a strong attack.—ED.]

[11] A very fine sacrifice, which forces absolute mate in a few moves.
[12] A fine finish.

H. N. Pillsbury v. W. H. K. Pollock.

WHITE	BLACK		WHITE	BLACK
1 P to K 4	P to K 4		20 Q R × B	Q to R 5 [4]
2 Kt to K B 3	Kt to Q B 3			
3 B to Kt 5	P to Q R 3			
4 B to R 4	Kt to B 3			
5 Castles	Kt × P			
6 P to Q 4	P to Q Kt 4			
7 B to Kt 3	P to Q 4			
8 P × P	B to K 3			
9 P to Q B 3	B to K 2			
10 R to K sq	Castles			
11 Kt to Q 4	Kt × Kt [1]			
12 P × Kt	P to Q B 3 [2]			
13 P to B 3	Kt to Kt 4			
14 Kt to B 3 [3]	B to K B 4			
15 P to Kt 4	B to B sq			
16 P to B 4	P to Kt 5		White to make his 21st move.	
17 Kt to R 4	Kt to K 5			
18 P to B 5	B to Kt 4		21 R to K 2	Kt to Kt 4
19 Q to B 3	B × B		22 Q to Kt 3 [5]	Q × Q, ch

AUGUST 9

	WHITE	BLACK		WHITE	BLACK
23	P × Q	Kt to B 6, ch	40	Kt × P	R to B 4
24	K to B 2	Kt × Q P	41	Kt × R P	R to Kt 4
25	R to Q 2	Kt × B	42	K to K 3 [10]	R × P, ch
26	P × Kt [6]	B to Kt 2 [7]	43	K to Q 4	R × K Kt P
27	Kt to B 5	B to B sq	44	Kt to B 5 [11]	P to R 5
28	K to K 3	P to K R 4	45	P to Kt 4	P to R 6
29	K to B 4	P to Kt 3	46	R to Q R 2	K to Kt sq
30	K to Kt 5 [8]	K to Kt 2	47	R to R 8, ch	K to R 2
31	P to B 6, ch	K to R 2	48	P to K 6	P × P
32	Kt to Q 3	B × P	49	Kt × B	P × Kt
33	R × P	K R to K sq	50	P to B 7	R to K B 6
34	R to B 7	K to Kt sq	51	P Queens	R × Q
35	K to R 6	B to B 6	52	R × R	P to Kt 4
36	R to K 7	K to B sq	53	K × P	P to Kt 5
37	R × R, ch	R × R	54	R to B sq	P to K 4
38	K to Kt 5	B to K 5	55	P to Kt 5	P to Kt 6
39	K to B 4	R to B sq [9]	56	R to K R sq	Resigns. [12]

NOTES BY S. TINSLEY.

[1] With slight transpositions we arrive here at precisely the same position and by the same moves as those made in the memorable games by Tarrasch *v.* Zukertort, 1887, and Gunsberg, 1890, in Frankfort and Manchester respectively. If now 11. Q to Q 2 ; 12. Kt × B and wins a Piece and the game, for whether Q or P takes the Kt, R × Kt, wins. Kt × K P is also out of the question, as White replies P to B 3

[2] A bolder course is P to Q B 4, but the text move strengthens Black's Pawn position.

[3] Attempts to win the Kt by P to K R 4 would with an undeveloped Queen's side probably prove dangerous, but it is noticeable that P to K R 4 is possible at this stage.

[4] The game suddenly reaches a critical point. Except for the presence of Black's Queen White might safely dispose of the strongly posted Knight. But 21. R × Kt, P × R ; 22. Q × P, P to K R 4, would break up White's game on the King's side completely.

[5] The consequences are evidently foreseen They give Black a momentary advantage.

[6] And Black is a Pawn to the good in an end game. It will be seen however that White's turn is yet to come, and that he must speedily regain lost material.

[7] Not B to Q 2, because of Kt to Kt 6, &c., regaining at least a Pawn.

[8] We assume that White, having established his position, and being able *pro tem.* to keep Black confined closely, is playing for a mating position with his Rooks. Supposing, for instance, Black plays here P × Kt P, then P to B 6, followed soon by R to R 2, &c.

[9] Another critical point of a very interesting game is here reached.

Black scarcely rises to the occasion. He might as well have gone on with P to Q R 4, or perhaps better 39. P to Kt 4, ch ; 40. K × P (best), B × Kt ; 41. R × B, R × P, ch ; 42. K to B 4, R to K 3 ; 43. K to Kt 5, R to K 4, ch, and would apparently either draw or win.

[10] The charming audacity of this bold bid for a win is very noticeable. It is probably safe to say that there is no other way to win and that this is the only chance left.

[11] Necessary to prevent Black winning by giving up a Piece by R to Q 6, ch, &c. later; also to capture the Bishop presently, and furthermore to guard the outlet of the Black King at his Q 2. See his 46th move. R to Q Kt 6 is also now guarded against.

[12] I have found this game, and especially the ending, exceptionally difficult. One gains the impression gradually as it proceeds that Black should have won, but where is not easy to detect in a brief space of time. Of its absorbing interest after about move 26 there can be no question. Those addicted to analyses will here find a rare opportunity.

H. E. Bird v. J. H. Blackburne.

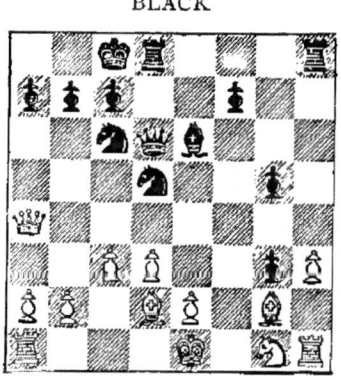

White to make his 14th move.

	WHITE	BLACK
1	P to K B 4	P to K 4
2	P × P	P to Q 3
3	P × P	B × P
4	P to K Kt 3 [1]	P to K R 4 [2]
5	B to Kt 2	Kt to Q B 3 [3]
6	Kt to Q B 3	P to R 5
7	Kt to K 4	P × P
8	P to K R 3	Kt to B 3
9	Kt × B, ch	Q × Kt
10	P to Q 3	B to K 3
11	P to B 3	Castles Q R
12	Q to R 4	Kt to Q 4
13	B to Q 2	P to K Kt 4 [4]
14	B × P	Kt × B P
15	Q to K B 4 [5]	Q × Q
16	B × Q	Kt to Q 4
17	B × Kt P	Q R to Kt sq
18	K to B 2	R to R 3
19	B × Kt	B × B
20	Kt to B 3	Kt to Kt 5
21	B to K 5	R to R 4
22	P to Q 4	Kt to Q 6, ch
23	K to K 3 [6]	Kt × P
24	Q R to K Kt sq	
		R × R
25	R × R	R × P
26	K to B 4	Kt to Q 6, ch
27	K to B 5	B × Kt
28	P × Kt	B to Q 4
29	K to B 6	K to Q 2
30	R to Q B sq	R to R 3, ch
31	K to Kt 7	R to Kt 3, ch
32	K to R 7	R to Q B 3
33	R to Q Kt sq	
		R to B 7
34	R to Kt 5	K to B 3

AUGUST 9

WHITE	BLACK	WHITE	BLACK
35 R to R 5	P to R 3	54 K × P	P to Q B 4
36 P to R 3	B to Kt 6	55 B to K 3	R to Q B 5
37 B to B 4	K to Q 2	56 K to Kt 6	K × P
38 K to Kt 7	R to Kt 7, ch	57 P to R 5	B to K 5
39 K to B 6	B to K 3	58 P to R 6	R to B 6
40 P to Q 5	R to Kt 3, ch	59 R to Q 2, ch	R to Q 6
41 K to K 5	B to R 6	60 B × P, ch	K to K 4
42 R to B 5	B to Kt 7	61 R to K 2	R to Q sq
43 K to Q 4	P to Q B 3	62 P to R 7	P to Kt 6
44 P to Q 6	B to Q 4	63 K to Kt 5	K to B 4
45 R to B 2	R to Kt 5	64 K to Kt 4	B to B 7
46 R to B 2	P to Kt 4	65 K to R 3	R to Q R sq
47 K to B 5	P to R 4	66 R to K 7	K to Kt 3
48 P to Q 4	R to Kt sq	67 R to Kt 7	B to K 5
49 R to K 2	R to K sq	68 R × Kt P	P to B 4
50 R to K R 2	P to Kt 5	69 K to Kt 4	K to B 2
51 P to R 4 [7]	R to K Kt sq	70 K to B 3	K to K 3
52 K to Kt 6	R to Kt 5	71 R to Kt 8	K to K 4
53 B to Q 2	R × P		Drawn game.

NOTES BY E. SCHIFFERS.

[1] The line of defence adopted by Zukertort commences: 4. Kt to K B 3, Kt to K R 3; 5. P to Q 4, Kt to K Kt 5; 6. B to K Kt 5, P to K B 3; 7. B to R 4, &c.

[2] Here Lasker played P to K B 4 against Bird.

[3] Apparently P to K R 5 would be stronger.

[4] The beginning of a pretty combination.

[5] After P × Kt would follow 15. ... Q to Q B 4, with a triple attack on Q B 6, K Kt 4, and K B 7.

[6] If 23. P × Kt, then R to K B 4, regaining a Piece, with a strong attack.

[7] If 51. P × P (?), then R to Q Kt sq, and mate next move.

G. MARCO v. A. BURN.

WHITE	BLACK	WHITE	BLACK
1 P to K 4	P to K 3	10 B to Q Kt 5	Q to Q Kt 3
2 P to Q 4	P to Q 4	11 B × Kt, ch [4]	P × B
3 Kt to Q B 3	Kt to K B 3	12 Castles	P to K R 4 [5]
4 B to Kt 5	P × P [1]	13 Q to Q 2	P to K R 5
5 Kt × P	B to K 2	14 Kt to K 2	B to Q R 3
6 B × Kt	P × B [2]	15 K R to K sq [6]	Castles Q R
7 P to Q B 3 [3]	P to K B 4	16 P to Q R 3	R to R 2
8 Kt to Kt 3	P to Q B 4	17 P to Q Kt 4	P to Q B 5
9 Kt to K B 3	Kt to Q B 3	18 P to Q R 4	R to K Kt 2

	WHITE	BLACK
19	K R to Q Kt sq	
		Q R to Kt sq
20	Kt to K sq	B to Kt 2
21	P to K B 3	Q to Q sq
22	P to Kt 5 [7]	P to Q B 4
23	Q to K 3	Q to Q B 2
24	P to R 5	B to Kt 4 [8]
25	P to K B 4	B to K 2
26	P to Kt 3	Q to Q 2 [9]
27	P × P	P × P
28	P × P	Q to Q 4
29	P to B 6	B to B 4
30	P × B, ch	K × P
31	Kt to Q 4	R × P, ch
	White resigns.	

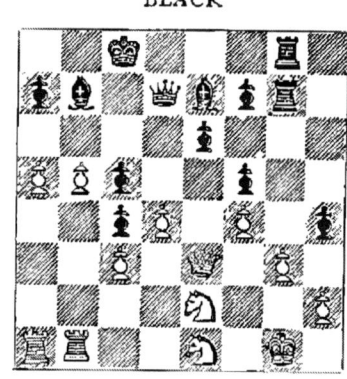

White to make his 27th move.

NOTES BY J. H. BLACKBURNE.

[1] Recommended by Lasker.

[2] Mr. Burn is of opinion that this is the best way of taking the Bishop, and probably he is right.

[3] Unnecessary at present; therefore better to develop by B to Q 3.

[4] This gives Black the better game; stronger would have been Q to K 2.

[5] Better than taking the Queen's Knight's Pawn, as White might, in that case, have obtained some attack by Kt to K 5 followed by Q to K R 5.

[6] Timidly played. Castling on the Queen's side must be prevented at all hazards, therefore P × P, followed by P to Q Kt 4, was more to the purpose.

[7] A bad move; Q to R 2 attacking Queen's Bishop's Pawn would have given a little relief.

[8] Well played, forcing P to K B 4, thereby weakening White's position.

[9] This also is the right move. The latter part of this game is a good specimen of Mr. Burn's play.

J. MIESES v. D. JANOWSKI.

	WHITE	BLACK		WHITE	BLACK
1	P to K 4	P to K 4	9	B to Kt 5	B to K 2
2	K Kt to B 3	Kt to Q B 3	10	B to R 6	P to Q 3
3	P to Q 4	P × P	11	Q to Kt 3	B to K 3
4	Kt × P	Kt to B 3	12	Kt to B 3	B to R 5
5	Kt × Kt	Kt P × Kt	13	Q to B 3	B to Kt 4
6	P to K 5 [1]	Kt to Q 4 [2]	14	B × B	Q × B
7	B to Q 3	B to B 4	15	P × P	P × P
8	Q to Kt 4	P to Kt 3	16	B to K 4 [3]	Castles K R

AUGUST 9

WHITE	BLACK
17 B × Kt	P × B
18 Castles K R	Q R to Kt sq
19 P to Q Kt 3	R to Kt 5
20 P to K Kt 3	R to B sq
21 K R to K sq	Q to Q 7
22 R to K 3	P to Q 5
23 Kt to K 4	Q × Q B P
24 R to K 2	Q to B 2
25 Q to B 4	P to Q 6
26 Q to R 6 [4]	P to B 4 [5]
27 Kt to B 6, ch	K to B 2
28 Kt to R 5 [6]	P × Kt
29 Q × P (R 7), ch [7]	
	K to B sq
30 Q to R 8, ch	K to B 2
31 Q × P, ch	K to K 2
32 Q to R 7, ch	K to Q sq
33 Q to R 8, ch	K to Q 2
34 Q to Kt 7, ch	K to B 3
35 Q × Q, ch [8]	R × Q
36 R × B	K to Q 4
37 K R to K sq	R to K 5
38 R × R	P × R
39 K to B sq	K to K 4
40 P to K R 4	P to Q 4

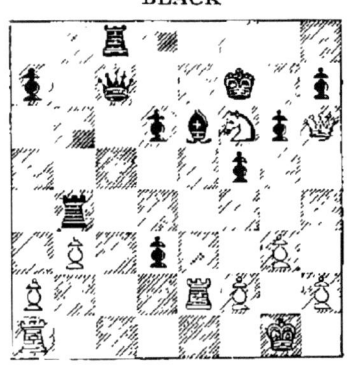

White to make his 28th move.

WHITE	BLACK
41 R to Q sq	P to Q 5
42 P to R 5	R to R 2
43 P to B 3	R × P
44 K to Kt 2	P to K 6 [9]
45 P to Kt 4	P to K 7
46 R to K sq	R to R sq
47 K to B 2	K to B 5
48 R to K Kt sq	
	R to R 7, ch

White resigns.

NOTES BY R. TEICHMANN.

[1] Mieses has the credit of having revived this good variation of the Scotch game by adopting it several times in this Tournament with success

[2] Doubtless best, and preferable to Kt to Kt sq as played by Lasker, or Q to K 2 as played by myself against Mieses.

[3] White has played this opening in a very spirited manner, and with this move gets a decisive advantage in position.

[4] A pretty combination.

[5] This move ought to lose   He had a valid defence in Q to K 2, if then 27. Kt to Kt 5, Q to B 3, with the better game   He could also have sacrificed the exchange by R × Kt, which would have enabled him to draw the game, the advanced passed Pawn then becoming very strong.

[6] Extremely fine, and the key move to the whole combination. Black must take the Knight, for if P × R, then 29. Q to Kt 7, ch, K to K sq ; 30. Kt to B 6, ch, K to Q sq ; 31. Q to B 8, mate   (See diagram.)

[7] With this, however, he throws away a well-deserved victory.

The obvious move R × B would have forced the game in a few moves, e.g. 29. R × B, Q to B 6, best; 30. R to Q sq (!) (not R to K sq on account of 30 ... R to K 5). 30 ... R to K 5 (there is nothing better), 31. R × R, P × R; 32. Q × R P (R 7), ch, K moves; 33. Q × K P and wins easily.

⁸ A fatal mistake. He could still have drawn with Q to B 3, ch, because Black must play his King back to Q 2 and cannot avoid the perpetual check.

⁹ If 35. R × P, then of course R to R 8 (!); 36. K × R, P to K 7, winning.

I. Gunsberg v. C. Schlechter.

	WHITE	BLACK		WHITE	BLACK
1	K Kt to B 3 [1]	P to Q 4	11	Kt × Kt	B × Kt
2	P to Q 4	K Kt to B 3	12	R to B sq	P × P
3	P to B 4	P to K 3	13	P × P [6]	R to B sq
4	P to K 3	P to Q Kt 3 [2]	14	Q to Q 3	B to Q 3
5	B to K 2	B to Kt 2	15	R × R	Q × R
6	Castles [3]	B to K 2	16	Kt to K 5	Q to Kt 2
7	P to Q Kt 3	Castles	17	Kt × Kt	Q × Kt
8	B to Kt 2	Q Kt to Q 2 [4]	18	R to B sq	R to B sq
9	Kt to B 3	P to B 4	19	R × R	Q × R
10	B P × Q P [5]	Kt × P		Drawn game.	

Note by A. Albin.

The development of the game into similar positions and the exchange of the Pieces with admirable precision show that neither player had aspirations higher than a draw. Any notes would be superfluous.

[¹ This preliminary move prevents Black accepting the Queen's Gambit and following it up with P to K 4, a course which is thought by some to be favourable to him.

² It is better not to be in too much hurry to advance this Pawn.

³ Proceeding on safe lines, another course is to develop the Queen's Pieces to make use of the Queen's Bishop's file and, if possible, to prevent Black's P to Q B 4.

⁴ Contemplating Kt to K 5 and possibly Q Kt to B 3. Also supporting the advance of the Queen's Bishop's Pawn.

⁵ Modern ideas are leaning towards the exchange of these centre Pawns in such positions.

⁶ Kt × P avoids the isolation of the Pawn and keeps the Bishop diagonal open. There are also possibilities at B 6 and perhaps at Kt 5.

The text move, on the other hand, will support the K Kt at K 5 presently, and it keeps out the adverse Knight for a time.—Ed.]

AUGUST 9

B. Vergani v. R. Teichmann.

	WHITE	BLACK
1	P to Q 4	P to K B 4 [1]
2	P to K 3	P to K 3
3	P to Q B 4	Kt to K B 3
4	Kt to K B 3	P to Q Kt 3
5	B to K 2	B to Kt 2
6	Castles	B to Q 3 [2]
7	P to K R 3 [3]	Castles
8	P to Q Kt 3	Kt to K 5
9	B to Kt 2	Kt to Q B 3
10	Kt to Q B 3	P to Q R 3
11	P to Q 5	Kt × Kt
12	B × Kt	Kt to R 2
13	P × P	P × P
14	Q to Q 4 [4]	Q to K 2
15	K R to Q sq	B to K 5
16	Q to Q 2	Q R to Q sq
17	Q to K sq [5]	B to Kt 2
18	R to Q 2	P to K 4
19	Q R to Q sq	P to K 5
20	Kt to R 2	Kt to Q B 3
21	Kt to K B sq	Kt to K 4
22	Kt to K Kt 3 [6]	Q R to K sq
23	Kt to B sq	Kt to B 6, ch (!)
24	B × Kt [7]	P × B
25	P to K Kt 3	P to B 5 (!)
26	R × B [8]	P × R
27	K P × P	Q to Q 2
28	Kt to K 3	Q × R P

White to make his 24th move.

	WHITE	BLACK
29	Q to B sq	Q to R 4
30	R × P	R × Kt [9] (!)
31	P × R	P to B 7, ch
32	K × P	Q to B 6, ch
33	K to K sq	Q × P, ch
34	Q to K 2	Q × B, ch
35	K to B 2	P to Q Kt 4
36	R to Q 7	B to R sq
37	R to Q 3	Q to B 3
38	P × P	P × P
39	R to Q 2	Q to B 3
40	Q to K 3	R to K sq

White resigns.

Notes by E. Schiffers.

[1] Many of those who took part in the Hastings Tournament were completely opposed to this move. Tarrasch attributed his possible defeat by Steinitz chiefly to the weakness of this opening. Tchigorin did not altogether agree with this view, but nevertheless admitted that the move P to K B 4 was feeble. Morphy chose this opening in three of the games in his match with Harrwitz and played it with success. Everything depends upon the line of play Black adopts eventually. Besides Morphy's games and the actual one, compare the game Janowski-Albin, in which the latter conducted this opening with remarkable correctness.

[2] This good continuation is generally adopted by Bird. Albin, after B to K 2 and P to Q 3, endeavours to prepare the advance P to

K 4, which can also be recommended. In confirmation of the above opinion, we may remark that scarcely anyone would censure a similar line of development for White in the opening 1. P to K B 4, P to Q 4, &c., with the Bishops advanced to Q Kt 2 and Q 3.

[3] A weak move, only proper when the Black Knight goes to K Kt 5. The move should be 7 Kt to Q B 3.

[4] Feeble; he should have played 14. Kt to K 5 (or Q 4), and if Q to K Kt 4, then 15 B to K B 3, or if Q to K B 3, then 15. P to K B 4. White has for the moment a slight superiority, owing to the temporary retirement of the Black Knight

[5] The White Queen is badly placed now, and Black can advance his Pawn centre

[6] If B × Kt, then Q × B, threatening B to Q Kt 5.

[7] In reply to 24. P × Kt; there might follow P × P; 25. B to Q 3, Q to Kt 4, ch, 26. Kt to K Kt 3, P to K B 5, &c. (see diagram).

[8] Comparatively best move.

[9] Black reduces his opponent in a few powerful strokes.

W. STEINITZ v. J. MASON.

	WHITE	BLACK		WHITE	BLACK
1	P to K 4	P to K 4	18	B × B	Kt to Kt 3
2	Kt to K B 3	P to Q 3	19	Castles Q R [8]	Q R to Q sq
3	B to B 4	B to K 2	20	P to K R 4	R × R, ch
4	P to B 3	Kt to K B 3	21	R × R	R to K sq [9]
5	P to Q 3	Castles	22	P to R 5	Kt to B sq
6	Q Kt to Q 2	Kt to B 3	23	P to R 6	P to K Kt 3
7	B to Kt 3 [1]	B to K 3	24	P to Kt 5	Kt (B 3) to Q 2
8	B to B 2	P to Q 4 [2]	25	B to Q 5 [10]	Q to R 5
9	Q to K 2	B to Q 3 [3]	26	B × Kt P	Q × R P
10	Kt to B sq	P to Q R 3 [4]	27	Q × P	Q to Kt 6
11	Kt to Kt 5	Q to Q 2 [5]	28	B to Q 5 [11]	Q to Kt sq
12	Kt to K 3	P × P [6]	29	Q to R 2	R to K 2
13	P × P	Kt to K 2	30	Q to R 8	Q × Q [12]
14	P to B 3	B to Q B 4	31	B × Q	Kt to K 3
15	Kt × B	Q × Kt	32	B to Q 5	Kt to B 5 [13]
16	B to Kt 3	Q to B 3	33	B to B 6	Kt to B sq
17	P to Kt 4	B × Kt [7]	34	B to B 5	Resigns

NOTES BY DR. TARRASCH.

[1] To prevent the exchange of the King's Bishop after Kt to Q R 4

[2] In consequence of the two Bishop's moves on the part of White, Black gets now the initiative, but does not know how to make use of it.

[3] Much stronger was Kt to Q 2 and P to K B 4.

[4] Black shows clearly that he does not know what to do with his good position; Steinitz, on the other hand, true to his method, tries

to obtain one advantage after another. This game offers a good example of his method of play.

[5] Black should not allow the exchange of the Bishop, but should withdraw it to Q 2. Perhaps he was afraid of the continuation 12 P × P, Kt × P ; 13. Kt × R P (K × Kt [?] ; 14. Q to K 4, ch, and Q × Kt), but after 13. . . . R to K sq, White would have been very much embarrassed by the threat of Kt to B 5.

[6] It is again evident that Black has no definite plan.

[7] So that the Knight should not establish itself at B 5.

[8] White has now with his Bishops a far superior game.

[9] Kt × R P would be wrong on account of giving possession of the open file to the Queen and Rook

[10] The advance of the Pawns has prepared this move, and White now wins a Pawn and with it the game.

[11] The Bishop is indefatigable.

[12] After Q to Kt 4 might follow 31. B to B 6, Q to K 7 ; 32. B to B 5, Kt × B ; 33 Q × Kt, ch, &c.

[13] This hastens the end.

E. SCHIFFERS v. M. TCHIGORIN

	WHITE	BLACK		WHITE	BLACK
1	P to K 4	P to K 4	11	R × Kt	Q to B sq
2	Kt to K B 3	Kt to Q B 3	12	B to Kt 5	P to B 3 [3]
3	B to B 4	Kt to B 3	13	Q to K 2 [4]	B to Q B 4 [5]
4	P to Q 4	P × P	14	Q to Kt 5, ch	P to B 3
5	Castles	Kt × P	15	Q × B	P × B
6	R to K sq	P to Q 4	16	R to K sq	P to Q Kt 3
7	B × P	Q × B	17	Q to K 5 [6]	K to B 2
8	Kt to B 3	Q to Q sq [1]	18	Kt to K 4	Q to K Kt sq
9	R × Kt, ch	B to K 3 [2]	19	Kt × P, ch	K to Kt 3
10	Kt × P	Kt × Kt	20	Kt × B	Resigns.

NOTES BY H. N. PILLSBURY

Q to K B 4 , 9. Kt × Kt, B to K 2, 10. B to Kt 5, Castles, 11. Kt × P, Q to Kt 3, leads to an equal game If for White 9. R × Kt, ch, B to K 2 ; 10 Kt × P, Kt × Kt , 11. Q × Kt, B to K 3, and White dare not capture the proffered Pawn on account of the following 12. Q × Kt P, B to B 3 , 13. Q to Kt 3, Castles (Q R) ; 14. R to K sq, K R to Kt sq ; 15. Q to B 4, R × P, ch ; 16. K × R, Q to R 6, ch , 17. K to R sq, B × Kt, and wins.

[2] Very much inferior to B to K 2 ; 10 Kt × P, P to B 4 ; 11 R to B 4, Castles , 12. Kt × Kt, Q × Q, ch ; 13. Kt × Q, P × Kt, &c. Black's two Bishops should prove ample compensation for the doubled Pawn

[3] This move should have cost Black the game at once. B to K 2 was the only resource.

[4] The following variation (first pointed out by Mr. Lipschuetz, of New York) forces a winning attack:

WHITE	BLACK	WHITE	BLACK
13 B × P	P × B		Q × Kt
14 Q to R 5, ch	B to B 2 (best)	18 Q × B P	Castles
15 R to K sq, ch	B to K 2	19 R to Kt 4, ch	B to Kt 3
16 Q to R 6	Q to B 4 (best)	20 R × B, ch	P × R
17 Kt to Kt 5 (not R [Q 4] to K 4, which allows Black to Castle Q R)		21 Q × P, ch	K to R sq
		22 R × B and wins.	

[5] An oversight which loses in a few moves. 13 K to B 2; 14. R to K sq, B to Q 3 (if P × B, 15. R to Q 8, and wins), left Black with a fairly good game.

[6] Q to B 5 was more direct and decisive.

S. TINSLEY v. A. ALBIN.

WHITE	BLACK	WHITE	BLACK
1 P to Q 4	P to K B 4	13 B × Kt	Kt P × B (!)
2 P to Q B 4	P to K 3	14 Kt P × P	B P × B
3 Kt to Q B 3	B to Kt 5 [1]	15 Kt to K 5	B to Q 2
4 P to K 3	Kt to K B 3	16 Q to Kt 2	Q to K 2
5 B to Q 3	Castles	17 P to K B 4	R to R 3
6 B to Q 2 [2]	B × Kt	18 K to Q 2 [7]	R to Kt 3
7 B × B	P to Q 4	19 Q to R 2	Q to R 5
8 Kt to B 3 [3]	Kt to B 3	20 P to Kt 3	Q to R 6
9 Q to B 2	Kt to K 5	21 K R to K sq	Q R to R 3 (!) [8]
10 Castles Q R [4]	P to Q R 4 [5]	22 Q to Kt 3 [9]	B to R 5
11 P to Q R 3	Kt to Kt 5 [6]	23 Q × P	R to Kt 3
		24 R to Q Kt sq	R × Q
		25 R × R	Q × R P, ch
		26 R to K 2	Q to Kt 8
		27 R to K sq	Q to B 7, ch
		28 R to K 2	Q × Kt P
		29 P × P	P × P
		30 P to B 4	P × P
		31 Kt × P	Q to Kt 8
		32 Kt to Kt 2	B to Q 2
		33 R to K sq	Q to B 7, ch
		34 R to K 2	Q to Kt 6
		35 R to K sq	B to Kt 5
		36 Kt to Q sq	R to Q R sq
		37 R to Kt 2	P to R 4
		38 Kt to B 3	Q to B 7, ch
		39 Kt to K 2	R to R 6
		White resigns.	

BLACK

WHITE

White to make his 12th move.

12 P × Kt   P × P

AUGUST 9

NOTES BY C. VON BARDELEBEN.

[1] The usual move is Kt to K B 3.

[2] 6. Kt to K 2 would be better.

[3] This move is bad, because later on the Black King's Knight can be posted on K 5, and White then cannot play P to B 3. Preferable would therefore be 8. Kt to K 2.

[4] Too dangerous! He ought to have Castled King's Rook.

[5] Black rightly assumes the attack at once.

[6] A brilliant combination, which gives the second player the superior game. White cannot play 12. Q to K 2 because of Kt to R 7, ch; 13. K to B 2, Q Kt × B; 14. P × Kt, B to Q 2; 15. K to Kt 2, R to Kt sq, and Black has a very strong attack.

[7] Necessary, for Black threatened K R to R sq.

[8] The winning move. Q × P, ch, would be bad, because of 22. R to K 2.

[9] The alternative would be: 22. Q to Kt 2, K R to R sq; 23. Q R to R sq, R × R; 24. R × R, Q × P, ch, and Black wins easily.

C. VON BARDELEBEN v. E. LASKER.

	WHITE	BLACK
1	P to Q 4	P to Q 4
2	P to Q B 4	P to K 3
3	Kt to Q B 3	Kt to K B 3
4	B to B 4 [1]	B to K 2
5	P to K 3	Castles
6	Kt to B 3	P to Q Kt 3
7	B to Q 3	P to Q B 4
8	Q P × P	Kt P × P
9	Castles	Kt to B 3
10	P × P [2]	P × P
11	R to B sq	B to K 3
12	Kt to K 2	Q to Kt 3
13	Kt to K 5 [3]	Kt × Kt
14	B × Kt	Kt to Kt 5
15	B to B 3	Q to Q 3
16	P to K Kt 3	B to Q 2
17	Kt to B 4	Q to K R 3 [4]
18	P to K R 3	Kt to B 3
19	B × Kt	B × B
20	Kt × P [5]	B × R P
21	Kt × B, ch	Q × Kt
22	Q to R 5 [6]	Q to K R 3
23	Q × Q	P × Q
24	K R to Q sq	Q R to B sq
25	R to B 3	K R to Q sq

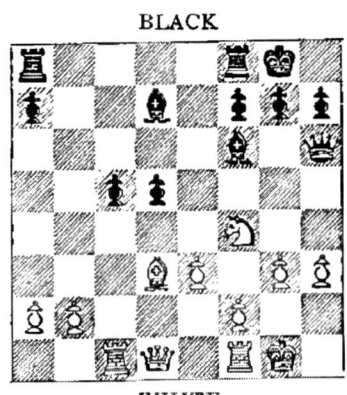

White to make his 20th move.

	WHITE	BLACK
26	K R to Q B sq	
		R to B 3
27	B to K 4	R to R 3
28	R × P	R × P
29	R to Q Kt 5 [7]	
		B to K 3 [8]
30	R to B 7	P to Q R 4
31	B to B 5	R to R 8, ch
32	K to Kt 2	B to R 7 [9]
33	P to Kt 3 [10]	P to R 5 [11]

WHITE	BLACK	WHITE	BLACK
34 P × P	R to Q 7	48 R (Kt 5) to Q B 5	
35 P to Q R 5	P to R 4 [12]		R to K 3, ch
36 P to R 6	B to Q 4, ch	49 K to B 2	R to B 3, ch
37 P to K 4	R (R 8) to R 7 [13]	50 K to Kt 2	R to Q 3
38 K to B 3 [14]	R to R 6, ch	51 R (B 8) to B 7	
39 K to B 4	R × P, ch		R to Q 7, ch
40 K to K 5	B × P	52 K to R 3	R to Q 3
41 B × B	R × R P	53 R (B 5) to B 6	
42 K to Q 4	R to R 3 [15]		R to Q 4
43 K to K 3	R to B 8	54 R to B 2	R to K B 4
44 K to K 2	R (B 8) to B 3 [16]	55 K to Kt 2	P to K Kt 4
45 R to B 8, ch	K to Kt 2	56 R to B 2	R × R, ch
46 R to Kt 5, ch	R (R 3) to Kt 3	57 K × R	K to Kt 3
47 B × R	R P × B	58 K to B 3	Resigns

NOTES BY I. GUNSBERG.

[1] We consider this move of doubtful value.

[2] We quite approve of this exchange of Pawns, though with the Bishop placed on K B 4 it is not quite as effective as with the Bishop placed on Q Kt 2.

[3] A clever way of defending the Queen's Knight's Pawn.

[4] Black has obtained a promising attack, but he is so placed that unless he succeeds with it he will suffer loss on the Queen's side.

[5] A bold course, and showing that White must have seen a long way ahead, and satisfied himself as to his future safety (see diagram).

[6] A fine move, and the key to the whole combination, which has evidently taken Black by surprise

[7] This move not only protects the Pawn, but also enables White to make better use of his Rooks.

[8] Black might have been first in the field by playing R to Q 7. If he was afraid of R to K R 5, he ought to have adopted different play on his 27th move.

[9] Curiously enough this was the only square available for the Bishop If he had played B × B, and 33. R × B, R to B sq , 34. R to R 7; P to R 5 , 35. R to B 4, R to R 7 ; 36 R to Q Kt 4, &c.

[10] Again cleverly played. White could not have taken the Rook's Pawn, as Black would have replied with B to Q 4, ch. P to Kt 3 was played to cut out the Bishop.

[11] This is best, as R to R sq would have been answered by B to K 4, followed by B to Q 5, &c. Black, by giving up the Pawn, liberates his Bishop, and plans a very ingenious counter-demonstration.

[12] An important factor in Black's plan, directed against the White King

[13] Black's carefully prepared plan has now matured,

[14] A courageous reply, and the only move to win the game, for if either Pawn takes Bishop or Rook takes Bishop, Black will obtain a draw by perpetual check.

[15] Black's object was, if possible, to play P to R 5.

[16] It seemed necessary to keep the Rook on this file, as otherwise White plays R to Kt 5, ch, followed by B to Q 5. But it admits of White pursuing his advantage even more forcibly in a different way.

AUGUST 10.

To-day (Saturday) is to complete the first week, and Tarrasch is to meet Tchigorin. Burn, who has not hitherto been doing well, plays very finely. Gunsberg also plays a spirited Evans' against Steinitz. An immense concourse of people witness the play, and the greatest care has to be taken to provide for the comforts of the gladiators.

G. Marco v. S. Tinsley.

	WHITE	BLACK		WHITE	BLACK
1	P to K 4	P to K 4	14	R × B	Q to Kt 3 (!) [7]
2	Kt to K B 3	Kt to K B 3	15	Q to Q B sq	P to K B 5
3	Kt × P	P to Q 3	16	P × Kt	P × R
4	Kt to K B 3	Kt × P	17	P to B 5	Q to B 2
5	P to B 4 [1]	B to K 2	18	P × P	Q × P
6	P to Q 4 [2]	Castles	19	Kt to B 3	P × P
7	B to Q 3	P to K B 4 [3]	20	Kt × P	P to K 7
8	Castles [4]	P to Q B 3 (!) [5]	21	Kt to K 3	B to Q 2
9	R to K sq	P to Q 4	22	B × P	Q R to K sq
10	Kt to K 5	Kt to Q 2	23	B to B 4, ch	K to R sq
11	P to K B 3 (?) [6]		24	Kt to B sq	Q × B P, ch
		Kt × Kt	25	K to R sq	B to B 3
12	Q P × Kt	B to B 4, ch		White resigns. [8]	
13	B to K 3	B × B, ch			

NOTES BY C. VON BARDELEBEN.

[1] The usual move at this juncture is P to Q 4 at once.

[2] Now White has by a transposition of moves adopted the usual line of play.

[3] I prefer Kt to K B 3.

[4] White should have played, 8 Q to B 2, R to K sq; 9. Castles, with an excellent game.

[5] The right answer of Black, for, if now 9 Q to B 2, then P to Q 4.

[6] A blunder which renders his game hopeless. If White played 11. Kt × Kt, B × Kt; 12. P × P, P × P; 13. Kt to B 3, B to Q B 3; 14. B to K B 4, the game would be equal.

Phot., Bradshaw, Hastings

[7] Black promptly takes advantage of the adversary's weak play. This at least wins the exchange.

[b] White has no defence against the threatening R or Q to B 7.

H. E. BIRD v. E. LASKER.

	WHITE	BLACK
1	P to K B 4	P to K 4
2	P × P	P to Q 3
3	P × P	B × P
4	P to K Kt 3 [1]	P to K B 4 [2]
5	P to Q 3	Kt to K B 3
6	P to Q B 3	Kt to B 3
7	B to Kt 2	Kt to K 4
8	Kt to Q 2	Q to K 2
9	Kt to B sq	B to Q 2
10	B to B 4 [3]	Castles K R
11	B × Kt	B × B
12	Q to B 2	K to R sq
13	B to B 3 [4]	Q R to Q Kt sq
14	Q to Q 2	K R to K sq
15	P to K R 3 [5]	Q to Q 3
16	K to B 2	P to Q B 4
17	P to K 3	B to Kt 4 [6]
18	Q R to Q sq	Q R to Q sq
19	P to Q B 4	B to B 3
20	Q to K 2	P to Q Kt 4
21	P to Kt 3	P × P
22	Kt P × P	B to R 5
23	R to Kt sq	R to Q Kt sq
24	Kt to Q 2 [7]	B × P, ch
25	K to Kt 2	B to R 5

BLACK

White to make his 18th move.

	WHITE	BLACK
26	R to R 2	B to Q B 7
27	R × R	R × R
28	P to Q 4	P × P
29	P × P	R to K sq
30	Q to K B sq	R to K 8
31	P to B 5	Q × Q P
32	Q × R	B × Q
33	Kt to Kt 3	B × Kt
34	P × B	Q × B P

White resigns.

NOTES BY J. H. BLACKBURNE.

[1] One of Bird's innovations, but not so strong as the usual move Kt to K B 3.

[2] P to K R 4 may also be played with advantage.

[3] Perhaps White is right in not taking the Queen's Knight's Pawn, as it would lose time, and still further weaken his position.

[4] Castling would certainly have been better, but even then his position would not be easy.

[5] White's last two moves have not in any way improved his position; if anything, the reverse.

[6] An awkward move to parry, and there does not appear any better defence than the one selected (see diagram).

[7] White's position is now hopeless. Mr. Lasker's play throughout

the whole of this game is characterised by his usual correctness and force, but who would recognise Mr. Bird's play? He evidently was out of form this day, or it may be this opening is not suited to his attacking style.

H. N. Pillsbury v. A. Albin.

	WHITE	BLACK
1	P to K 4	P to K 4
2	Kt to K B 3	Kt to Q B 3
3	B to Kt 5	P to Q R 3
4	B to R 4	Kt to K B 3
5	Castles	Kt × P
6	P to Q 4	P to Q Kt 4
7	B to Kt 3	P to Q 4
8	P to Q R 4 [1]	R to Q Kt sq
9	Q P × P	B to K 3
10	P × P	P × P
11	P to B 3	B to Q B 4
12	Q Kt to Q 2	Castles
13	B to B 2	Kt × Kt
14	Q × Kt	R to K sq
15	P to Q Kt 4 [2]	B to Kt 3
16	Q to B 4	Kt to K 2
17	P to R 4 [3]	Q to Q 2
18	Kt to Kt 5	Kt to Kt 3 [4]
19	Q to B 3 [5]	B to Kt 5
20	P to K 6 [6]	B × K P [7]
21	P to R 5	B to Kt 5 (?) [8]
22	P × Kt (!) [9]	B × Q
23	P × B P, ch	Q × P [10]
24	Kt × Q	K × Kt [11]
25	P × B	K to B 3
26	B to Q 3	P to K Kt 4
27	B × Q Kt P	B × P, ch
28	K × B	R × B
29	R to R 6, ch	K to B 4
30	R to K Kt sq	R to K Kt sq

White to make his 22nd move.

	WHITE	BLACK
31	B to K 3	P to R 4
32	B to Q 4	R to K Kt 3
33	R × R	K × R
34	B to K 3	P to Q 5
35	B × Q P	R to K B 4
36	K to K 3	R to K B sq
37	R to Q R sq	P to R 5
38	R to R 6, ch	K to B 4
39	R to K R 6	R to K sq, ch
40	K to B 2	R to K B sq
41	P to Kt 5	P to Kt 5
42	R to B 6, ch	R × R
43	P × P, ch	K to Kt 3, ch
44	B × R	K × B
45	P to B 4	Resigns.

Notes by Dr. Tarrasch.

[1] This move was first played in the London Tournament of 1883 by Tchigorin against Rosenthal. The opening of that game proceeded as follows:—

| 8 | P to Q R 4 | P to Kt 5 (?) | 10 | Kt × Kt | P × Kt |
| 9 | P to R 5 | Kt × Q P | 11 | Q × P | P to Q B 3 |

AUGUST 10

WHITE	BLACK		WHITE	BLACK
12 Kt to Q 2	Q to B 3		16 Q × B	Q to K 2
13 Q to Kt 6	Kt × Kt		17 Q to B 3	Castles
14 B × Kt	B to K 2		18 Q × B P, with one Pawn more.	
15 B × Kt P	B × B			

[2] White intends to drive the King's Bishop from the King's side preparatory to the coming attack on the King.

[3] In order to drive away the Knight, in case it should be played to Kt 3.

[4] Not B to K B 4, on account of 19. P to Kt 4, B × B ; 20. Q × P, ch, K to R sq ; 21. Kt to K 6, R to Kt sq ; 22. B to R 6, and wins.

[5] After Q to Kt 3, Black gets an advantage with B to K B 4.

[6] It is evident now that the attack 18. Kt to Kt 5 was wrong. White must lose the King's Pawn, and tries with this move to dispose of it more advantageously.

[7] The correct move is to take the Pawn with the Queen, in which case Black has a slight advantage.

[8] A great mistake, which leads to an immediate loss ; Kt to B sq ought to have been played now.

[9] White perceives his chance at once ; he gets a Rook and two minor Pieces for the Queen (see diagram).

[10] Black has now one Piece less—sufficient reason for resigning.

[11] Rather better is B to K 7. The remainder is merely a matter of routine.

Dr. Tarrasch v. M. Tchigorin.

WHITE	BLACK		WHITE	BLACK
1 P to Q 4	P to Q 4		20 P × P	R × P
2 P to K 3	Kt to K B 3		21 B to Kt 4	B to B 4
3 B to Q 3	Kt to B 3[1]		22 B × B	P × B
4 P to K B 4[2]	Kt to Q Kt 5		23 Q to Q 2	Q to Q 3
5 Kt to K B 3[3]	Kt × B			
6 P × Kt	P to K 3			
7 Castles	B to K 2			
8 Q Kt to Q 2[4]	Castles			
9 Q to B 2	B to Q 2			
10 Kt to Kt 3	B to R 5			
11 Q to B 3	P to Q Kt 3			
12 Q to K sq	P to B 4			
13 B to Q 2	B to Kt 4			
14 Kt to K 5	Kt to Q 2			
15 Kt to B sq	Kt × Kt			
16 Q P × Kt	R to B sq			
17 R to B 2	P to B 3			
18 B to B 3	P to Q 5			
19 P × Q P	P × Q P			

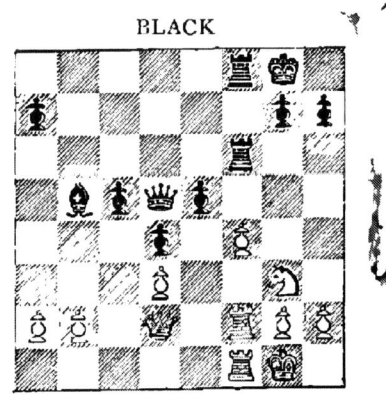

White to make his 27th move.

WHITE	BLACK	WHITE	BLACK
24 Kt to K 2	Q R to K B sq	31 R to B 8, ch	K to R 2
25 Q R to K B sq	Q to Q 4	32 Q to Kt 4	B to B 3
26 Kt to Kt 3	P to K 4 [5]	33 Q to Kt 8 [7]	R × P
27 P to B 5 [6]	P to B 5	34 R to R 8, ch	K to Kt 3
28 Kt to K 4	P × P	35 R to K B 8	R to Kt 5
29 Kt × R, ch	R × Kt	36 R (B 8) to B 3	P to Q 7
30 R to Q B sq	P to K R 3	White resigns.	

NOTES BY H. N. PILLSBURY.

[1] A favourite idea of the Russian master, who aims to secure an open game in this and similar variations of the Queen's side openings by advancing P to K 4 at the earliest possible moment.

[2] Kt to K B 3 would be met by 4. B to Kt 5, and if 5. B to K 2, B × Kt; 6. B × B, P to K 4, &c.

[3] 5. B to K 2, B to B 4, 6. Kt to Q R 3, P to K 3; 7. P to B 3, Kt to B 3, 8. Kt to B 2, Kt to K 5; 9. Kt to B 3, B to Q 3, &c, was probably a better method of procedure in this position than the text continuation. Black's two Bishops come strongly in evidence later on, and the opened Queen's Bishop's file White is not able to utilise

[4] 8. Kt to B 3 seems preferable

[5] White has laboured under a disadvantage since the opening owing to the weak Pawn at Q 3, but Black up to this point has been unable to make much out of it. With the text move he prepares a deep trap involving the sacrifice of the exchange, but obtains a winning superiority in Pawn position.

[6] White could not afford this continuation. Better would be 27. Kt to K 4, R × P; 28. R × R, P × R; 29. R × P, R × R; 30. Q × R (threatening the check at Kt 8), with fully an equal game (see diagram).

[7] R to K B 8 was better, but would not save the game either.

A. WALBRODT v. J. MASON.

WHITE	BLACK	WHITE	BLACK
1 P to K 4	P to K 3	13 Castles	P to Q Kt 4
2 P to Q 4	P to Q 4	14 B to Q 3	P to Kt 5
3 Kt to Q B 3	Kt to K B 3	15 Kt to K 2	B to Q 2
4 B to K Kt 5 [1]	B to K 2 [2]	16 Kt (K 2) to Q 4	
5 P to K 5	K Kt to Q 2		Kt × Kt
6 B × B	Q × B	17 Kt × Kt	R to Q Kt sq
7 Q to Kt 4 [3]	P to K Kt 3	18 Q to B 3	Kt × B, ch [4]
8 P to B 4	P to Q R 3	19 R × Kt	P to R 4
9 Kt to B 3	P to Q B 4	20 K R to R 3 [5]	B to Kt 4
10 P × P	Kt to Q B 3	21 R to Q 2	P to R 5
11 P to K R 4	P to K R 4	22 K to Kt sq	Q to B 4
12 Q to Kt 3	Kt × B P	23 P to Kt 4	P × P [6]

AUGUST 10

	WHITE	BLACK
24	Q × Kt P	B to Q 2 [7]
25	P to R 5	R × P
26	R × R	P × R
27	Q × R P	Q to K B sq [8]
28	P to B 5	K to Q sq
29	Q to R 7	K to B 2 [9]
30	P × P	Q to R sq [10]
31	Q × Q	R × Q
32	P to R 3	B P × P
33	P × P	R to R 8, ch
34	K to R 2	R to R 4
35	R to K 2	R to R 5
36	P to B 3	R to R sq
37	K to R 3	K to Kt 3
38	R to Kt 2	R to R 8
39	P to Kt 3	P × P
40	R to Kt 6 [11]	R to K 8
41	Kt × K P	B to K sq
42	R to R 6	R × P
43	K × P	K to R 2
44	Kt to Q 4	K to Kt 2
45	P to Kt 5	R to K 2
46	Kt to B 6 [12]	B × Kt
47	R × B	R to Q 2
48	K to B 2	P to Q 5
49	P to B 4	P to Q 6, ch
50	K to Q 2 [13]	R to Q 5
51	P to B 5	R to Q 4
52	R to Kt 6, ch	K to B 2

BLACK

WHITE

White to make his 40th move.

	WHITE	BLACK
53	R to B 6, ch	K to Kt 2
54	R to Kt 6, ch	K to B 2
55	R to B 6, ch	K to Kt 2 [14]
56	K to K sq	R to K 4, ch
57	K to Q sq	R to R 4
58	K to B sq	R to Kt 4
59	K to Kt 2	R to Q 4
60	K to B sq	R to R 4
61	K to Q sq	R to Kt 4
62	R to Kt 6, ch	K to B 2
63	K to Q 2	R × P
64	R to B 6, ch	R × R
65	P × R	K × P

Drawn game.

NOTES BY J. H. BLACKBURNE.

[1] P to K 5 is now considered the stronger line of attack.

[2] P × P as recommended by Lasker is now usually played.

[3] This has recently taken the place of the good old-fashioned move of Q to Q 2.

[4] This was unwise. White now remains with a Knight against Bishop; rather have continued the attack by P to Q R 4.

[5] It is difficult to see the object of this move; it certainly is perfectly safe, and may, if necessary, be brought over to the Queen's side; still P to K Kt 4 at once was more to the purpose.

[6] Black's attack is at an end, and he must now adopt defensive measures; this move, however, is not the best at his disposal, B to Q 2 was stronger.

[7] Of course the King's Pawn must be further defended, otherwise

Kt × K P would win easily, but preferable to this would have been Q to K 2 or even R to Kt 3.

[8] This and the next few moves are the only ones to prevent immediate destruction.

[9] If P × P, then P to K 6, followed by R to Kt 2 if B × P.

[10] An ingenious but somewhat lucky resource; nevertheless it loses a Pawn.

[11] R to Kt 7 wins, for Black must move his Bishop, either to B sq or K sq; in the former case the following variation is likely to occur (see diagram):—

	WHITE	BLACK		WHITE	BLACK
40	R to Kt 7	B to B sq	48	K to B 5	R to K 6
41	R to Kt 6	R to K 8	49	K to Kt 6	R to K sq
42	Kt × K P	R × P	50	Kt to B 6	R to K 3
43	Kt to Q 4, disc. ch		51	R to Kt 8, ch	B to K sq
		K to Kt 2	52	K to B 5	R to K 6
44	P to Kt 5	B to Q 2	53	K to Q 4	R to K 8
45	K × P	R to R 4	54	Kt to K 5	K to Q sq
46	K to Kt 4	R to K 4	55	K × P	
47	R to Kt 7	K to B sq			

and there ought to be no trouble in winning. If, on the other hand, he plays B to K sq, then 40. R to K 7.

[12] This leads to a certain draw. K to Kt 4 might still have won.

[13] He might also have played K to Q sq, tempting Black to push on the Pawn, in which case R to Q R 6 would win.

[14] This position having occurred three times, the game is drawn, according to the rules.

W. H. K. POLLOCK v. R. TEICHMANN.

	WHITE	BLACK		WHITE	BLACK
1	P to K 4	P to K 4	18	B to Q 4	Kt to Q 3
2	Kt to K B 3	Kt to Q B 3	19	Kt to K 5	B to K sq
3	P to B 3	P to Q 4			
4	B to Kt 5	P × P [1]			
5	Kt × P	Q to Q 4			
6	Q to R 4	Kt to K 2			
7	P to K B 4 [2]	P × P *en passant*			
8	Kt × P	B to K 3 [3]			
9	Castles	P to Q R 3			
10	P to B 4	Q to Q sq			
11	B × Kt	Kt × B			
12	P to Q 4	B to Q 2			
13	Q to Kt 3	B to K 2			
14	P to Q 5 [4]	Kt to R 2			
15	B to K 3	P to Q Kt 3			
16	Kt to B 3	Castles			
17	Q R to K sq	Kt to B sq			

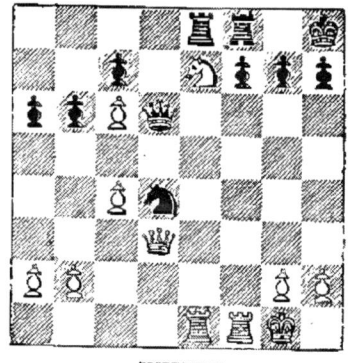

BLACK

WHITE

White to make his 26th move.

	WHITE	BLACK		WHITE	BLACK
20	Kt to B 6	B × Kt	27	Q × Kt	R × R
21	P × B	Kt to B 4	28	Kt to Kt 6, ch	
22	Kt to Q 5 [5]	Kt × B			P × Kt
23	Kt × B, ch	K to R sq	29	Q × R, ch	R to B sq
24	Q to Q B 3 (?)		30	Q to Q 7	Q to B 4, ch
		Q to Q 3	31	K to R sq	Q × P (B 5)
25	Q to Q 3 [6]	Q R to K sq	32	P to K R 3	
26	R × B P [7]	Kt to K 7, ch [8]			Drawn game.[9]

NOTES BY E SCHIFFERS.

[1] Here the move recommended by Steinitz, P to B 3, is more frequently played, or Kt to K 2, followed by P to B 3 if 5. Q to R 4.

[2] To 7. Kt × Kt the correct answer would be 7. ... Kt × Kt and not P × Kt (8. B to K 2).

[3] B to Q 2 can be played here; after 8. ... P to R 3 might follow 9. B to K 2, but not 9 B to B 4, Q to K R 4, and Black threatening P to Kt 4 gains time If 9. B to B 4, Q to K 5, ch (?), then 10 K to B 2, B to K 3; 11. P to Q 3, with a good game.

[4] Here and in the succeeding move White can apparently take the Knight's Pawn with impunity.

[5] Here White could play B × Q Kt P although the P at B 6 cannot be maintained, still White obtains the attack afterwards by Kt to Q 5.

[6] Defending the Pawn at B 6.

[7] Prettily conceived. (See diagram.)

[8] If R × R; 27. Kt to Kt 6, ch, P × Kt; 28. R × R, ch, R to B sq (!) (K to R 2; 29 Q mates); 29. R × R, ch, Q × R; 30. Q × Kt, with a Pawn ahead.

[9] 32 ... R to B 8, ch; 33. R × R, Q × R, ch; 34. K to R 2, Q to B 5, ch, &c.

J. H. BLACKBURNE v. C. SCHLECHTER.

	WHITE	BLACK		WHITE	BLACK
1	P to Q 3 [1]	P to Q 4	12	B to K 3	B to B 4
2	P to K Kt 3	P to K 4	13	B × B	Kt × B
3	B to Kt 2	P to Q B 3	14	P to K B 3	K to K 2
4	Kt to Q B 3	B to K 3	15	K to B 2	K R to Q sq
5	P to K 4	P × P	16	K to K 3	R × R
6	Kt × P	Kt to B 3	17	R × R	R to Q sq
7	Kt to K 2	Kt × Kt	18	R × R	K × R
8	B × Kt	B to Q 4	19	Kt to B sq	K to K 2
9	Castles	B × B	20	Kt to Q 3	Kt to Q 2
10	P × B	Q × Q			Drawn game.[2]
11	R × Q	Kt to R 3			

NOTES BY R. TEICHMANN.

[1] An inferior opening, which gives the advantage of the first move away. Mr. Blackburne tried several of these obsolete openings in the beginning of the Tournament (compare his game with Walbrodt).

[2] If the two players meant to solve the problem how to exchange as many Pieces as possible in the shortest number of moves they certainly could not have played better. It is time that such games, if games they can be called, should no longer make their appearance in tournaments. In this case the onus lies with the second player, who during the first part of the Tournament tried to force a draw whenever he possibly could; and it seems that Mr. Blackburne having chosen an inferior opening could not avoid it without loss of position, which he did not like to risk.

[It was to reduce such games to a minimum that the Committee adopted their system of consolation money, and they seemed to have succeeded fairly well. They, subsequent to the conclusion of the play, paid for drawn games against prize winners, but such games have their value. Herr Schlechter was unfortunate in the matter of draws, securing 12 out of 58 played, but was it not rather an outcome of the Viennese school of play, sound and cautious to a fault, and rather drawing than running any risk?—ED.]

A. BURN *v.* D. JANOWSKI.

	WHITE	BLACK
1	P to Q 4	P to Q 4
2	P to Q B 4	P to K 3
3	Kt to Q B 3	Kt to K B 3
4	Kt to B 3	B to K 2
5	P to K 3	Castles
6	B to K 2	P to Q Kt 3
7	Castles	B to Kt 2
8	B to Q 2 [1]	P to Q B 4
9	B P × P	K P × P
10	R to B sq	Kt to B 3 [2]
11	Q to R 4	P to Q R 3 [3]
12	P × P	P × P
13	K R to Q sq	Q to Kt 3
14	Q to B 2	Q to B 2
15	Kt to Q R 4	Kt to K 5
16	B to K sq	K R to Q sq
17	P to Q R 3	Kt to K 4
18	P to Q Kt 4	P to B 5 [4]
19	Kt to Q 4	P to Kt 3
20	P to B 3	Kt to K B 3
21	Kt to Kt 3	B to B 3
22	Kt to Q 4	B to K sq
23	Kt to B 3	P to Q R 4
24	R to Kt sq	P × P
25	P × P	Q to Kt 3

White to make his 29th move.

AUGUST 10

	WHITE	BLACK		WHITE	BLACK
26	P to Kt 5	R to R 6	45	R to Q 4	B to B 3
27	B to Q 2	R (Q sq) to R sq	46	K to B 2	K to Kt 2
28	B to Q B sq [5]	R (R 6) to R 2	47	P to Kt 3	K to B 3
29	P to B 4 [6]	Kt (K 4) to Q 2	48	R to B 4	B to Q 2
30	Kt to B 6	B to B 4 [7]	49	R to B 5	B to K 3
31	Kt × R	B × P, ch	50	K to K 2	P to R 4
32	K to R sq	B × B	51	R to Kt 5	P to K R 5
33	Kt to B 6	B to R 6	52	K to Q 3	P × P
34	B to B 3	Q to K 6	53	P × P	K to Kt 4
35	Kt × P [8]	Kt × Kt	54	K to Q 4	K to Kt 5
36	B × Kt	Kt to Kt 3	55	R × Kt	B × R
37	R to K sq	Q × P	56	K × B	K × P
38	Kt to K 7, ch	B × Kt	57	K to K 5	P to B 4
39	B × R	Kt × B	58	R × P, ch	K to Kt 5
40	R × B	B × P	59	R to B 4, ch	K to Kt 6
41	Q to K 4	Q × Q	60	R to Q R 4	K to B 6
42	R × Q	Kt to B 2	61	K to B 6	K to Kt 6
43	K to Kt sq	P to B 6	62	K to Kt 5	K to B 6
44	R to Q B sq	Kt to Q 4	63	K × P	Resigns

NOTES BY I. GUNSBERG

[1] We prefer to develop this Bishop on Q Kt 2.

[2] We have a theory, also expressed elsewhere, that the two Pawns on the Queen's file and Queen's Bishop's file, if standing by themselves are conveniently placed for attack. Black, therefore, should not have waited quietly till it suited White to take off the Pawns, but should have forestalled that intention. Moreover, why does Black play P to Q B 4 at all? Surely it must be for the purpose of further advance. If, therefore, as has been done in this game, White does not stop the further advance of the Pawn, by P to Q Kt 3 and B to Kt 2, then the spirit of the opening requires P to B 5 to be played, which would place both White Bishops in a wretchedly confined position. White's move of P to Q Kt 3 need not be feared in the least, as the Pawn could be taken off, and we consider that in that case Black's isolated Queen's Pawn would not be weak. In the great majority of cases Q Kt to Q 2 is a much stronger move than Q Kt to B 3. It leaves the Bishop's file open for the action of the Rook, and it offers good defensive resources in case of a King's side attack, when Black could play R to K sq and Kt to B sq in defence of the King's Rook's Pawn.

[3] We still consider P to B 5 a stronger move.

[4] White having got his chance adopts the right line of play, and attempts to weaken the advanced Pawns. Black cannot help himself, but must perforce provide the White Knight with a commanding

square on Q 5. If Black had played Kt × Kt first, then 19. B × Kt, P to B 5 ; 20 B × Kt, wins a Pawn

[5] No better proof in support of the opinion expressed in Note 1 can be cited than is afforded by the fact that this Bishop has to play back to its original square in defence of the Queen's side.

[6] White is adopting a vigorous policy. This move which looks dangerous on the surface is really very good play, as the Black Knight on K 4 has not a good square to play to. If Kt (K 4) to Kt 5, White replies B × Kt, followed by Kt × Q P. There can be no doubt that the task of defending these two Pawns involves the player who possesses them in difficulties of position and development. (See diagram.)

[7] There was no better way of giving up the exchange.

[8] This move marks the final consummation of White's plans against Black's centre Pawns, and henceforward further resistance is hopeless.

C. von Bardeleben v. B. Vergani.

	WHITE	BLACK		WHITE	BLACK
1	P to Q 4	P to Q 4	20	K to Kt sq	B to Q 3
2	P to Q B 4	P to K 3	21	Q to K B 2	P to B 3
3	Kt to Q B 3	Kt to K B 3	22	Kt to B 3	Q to Q 2
4	B to B 4	P to Q B 3	23	P to B 5	R to K 2
5	P to K 3	B to Q 3	24	Q R to Kt sq	Q R to K sq
6	B to Kt 3	Castles	25	Kt to Q sq	Q to B 2
7	Kt to B 3	P to Q Kt 3 [1]	26	P to Kt 4	R to Q B sq
8	B to Q 3	B to Kt 2	27	P to Kt 5	K to R sq
9	Q to B 2	Q to K 2 [2]	28	P to R 5	Kt to Q 2
10	Kt to K 5	Q Kt to Q 2	29	P to R 6	R to K Kt sq
11	P to B 4 [3]	K R to K sq [4]	30	P × P, ch	R (K 2) × P
12	B to R 4	Kt to B sq	31	R to R 6	Q to Q sq
13	Kt to Kt 4	Kt to Kt 3	32	P to Kt 6	Q to K 2
14	B to Kt 5	Q to Q sq	33	Q R to R sq	Kt to B sq
15	P to K R 4	B to K 2	34	Kt to Kt 5	P × Kt
16	Kt to K 5	Kt to B sq	35	P to B 6	Q to Q B 2
17	B × Kt	B × B	36	P × P	R to Q 2
18	Castles Q R	B to K 2	37	P × R(Q), ch	K × Q
19	P × P	K P × P	38	Q to B 3	Resigns

Notes by A. Albin.

[1] This weakens the Queen's Pawns. P × P and B to Kt 5, followed by Kt to Q 4 is stronger ; the text move is very weak.

[2] There was time yet for P × P, and Black could with that get the better position.

[3] Now White gets the best of it, and the attack is irresistible.

[4] Black gets now a cramped position, and whatever he may do the game is lost.

AUGUST 10

I. Gunsberg v. W. Steinitz.

	WHITE	BLACK		WHITE	BLACK
1	P to K 4	P to K 4	23	P × P	Q to Q sq
2	K Kt to B 3	Q Kt to B 3	24	R × R, ch	Kt × R
3	B to B 4	B to B 4	25	Q to R 5 [5]	Kt to K 4 (¹)
4	P to Q Kt 4	B × Kt P	26	B to Kt 2	Kt to K B 3
5	P to B 3	B to R 4	27	Q to Kt 5	P to K R 3
6	P to Q 4	P × P	28	Q to Q 2	P to Q R 4
7	Castles	P to Q 3	29	P to Q R 3	P to R 5
8	P × P	B to Kt 3	30	B to R 2	Q to B 2
9	B to Kt 2 [1]	Kt to B 3	31	P to B 4	Q to B 4
10	P to Q 5	Kt to K 2 [2]	32	K to R 2	Kt to B 5
11	Kt to B 3	Castles	33	B × Kt	P × B
12	Q to B 2	Kt to Kt 3	34	Q to B 3	Kt to K sq
13	Kt to K 2	B to Q 2	35	Kt to R 5 [6]	P to B 3
14	Q R to Q sq	R to K sq	36	R to K 4	Q × Q P
15	Kt to Kt 3	Q R to B sq (¹)	37	R × Kt, ch	B × R
16	P to K R 3	Q to K 2	38	Kt × Kt P	B to B 3 (¹)
17	K R to K sq	Kt to K 4	39	Q to Kt 3	K to B 2
18	Kt to Q 4 [3]	B × Kt	40	P to B 5	Q × P, ch [7]
19	R × B	P to B 3 [4]	41	Q × Q	B × Q
20	B to Kt 3	P × P	42	Kt to K 6	B to K 5
21	Q to Q sq (¹)	Kt to B 5 (¹)	43	Kt to Q 4	R to K Kt sq (¹)
22	B to B 3	P to Q Kt 4		White resigns.	

Notes by J Mason.

[1] By 7. P to Q 3 (in lieu of 7. P × P), and forthwith retiring his Bishop, Black sets up the 'normal defence' to the Evans'; as distinguished from the 'compromised defence,' whose characteristic is the capture of the second Pawn. There has long been diversity of opinion as to how the attack should proceed in these circumstances; but the move here chosen by Mr. Gunsberg has been less favoured, both in theory and practice, than 9. Kt to B 3 or 9 P to Q 5. Probably it is best to bring out the Knight, not obstructing the King's Bishop, and reserving employment of the other Bishop until there is some clearer indication of where it will do most good

[2] Much better than 10. Kt to Q R 4. White will not double any Pawn, opening up a dangerous line of invasion upon his own King.

[3] Already the first player has little or no advantage in position, and there is the solid Pawn against him looming in the future. Some very ingenious operations, with a view to attack, begin here, but they come to nothing.

[4] If 19 Kt × B; 20. R × Kt, all White's forces would be in excellent action. Besides, this advance is the natural complement of 19. Q R to B sq, leading on to counter-attack of considerable importance.

[5] It might be better to change off the Knight, and Rook if necessary. As it happens, this excursion of the Queen is in vain; and he has to take the Knight subsequently, on rather worse conditions.

[6] The sacrifice ventured here is somewhat puzzling, but it is unsound.

[7] As this very shortly and conclusively proves. A highly interesting Evans'.

J. Mieses v. E. Schiffers.

	WHITE	BLACK
1	P to K 4	P to K 4
2	Kt to Q B 3	Kt to K B 3
3	B to B 4	Kt to B 3
4	P to Q 3	B to Kt 5
5	K Kt to K 2	P to Q 4 [1]
6	P × P	Kt × P
7	P to Q R 3	B × Kt, ch
8	Kt × B [2]	Kt × Kt
9	P × Kt	Castles
10	Castles	Q to R 5 [3]
11	P to B 4	B to Kt 5
12	Q to Q 2	B to K 3
13	B to Kt 5 [4]	P × P
14	Q × P	Q to R 4 [5]
15	Q to Kt 5 [6]	Q to K 7
16	Q to Kt 3	Q × B P
17	B to Kt 5(!) [7]	K to R sq
18	P to Q 4	Q to Kt 3 [8]
19	B to Q 3	P to B 4
20	Q R to K sq	P to K R 3
21	B to K B 4	Q × Q
22	B × Q	Q R to K sq
23	B × Q B P	P to K Kt 3
24	P to B 4 [9]	B to Q 2
25	P to Q 5	Kt to Q sq
26	P to B 5	Kt to B 2
27	R to Kt sq	B to B sq
28	K R to K sq	P to R 3
29	P to Q 6	Kt to K 4
30	B to B 2	Kt to B 3
31	B to R 4	K to Kt sq
32	R × R	R × R
33	R to Kt 6	K to B 2 [10]
34	B × Kt	P × B
35	R × B P(?) [11]	R to K 8, ch
36	K to B 2	R to Q Kt 8

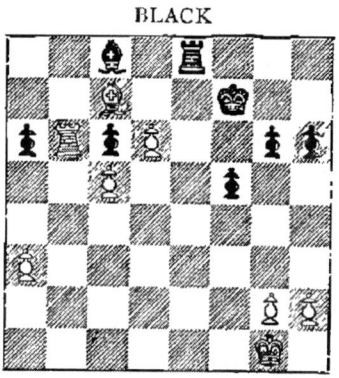

WHITE
White to make his 35th move.

	WHITE	BLACK
37	B to Kt 6	R to Kt 7, ch
38	K to K sq	B to Q 2
39	R to B 7	K to K 3
40	B to R 5 [12]	R to Q B 7
41	B to Kt 4	P to Kt 4
42	K to Q sq	B to R 5
43	R to K 7, ch	K to B 3
44	K to K sq	P to Q R 4
45	B × P	R × Q B P
46	B to Kt 4	R to K 4, ch
47	K to Q 2	R × R
48	P × R	P to B 5
49	K to B 3	B to B 3
50	K to B 4	K to B 2
51	P to Kt 3	P × P
52	P × P	P to R 4
53	K to B 5	B to R 5
54	K to Q 6	P to R 5
55	P × P	P × P

Drawn game.

AUGUST 10

NOTES BY C. VON BARDELEBEN.

[1] I prefer P to Q 3.

[2] It is better to retake with the Knight than with the Pawn, because the Black King's Knight is better posted than the White one, and retaking with the Knight, White manages to exchange the Knights.

[3] The attack introduced by this move is premature. Better would be Q to Q 3, followed by B to K 3, developing his Pieces by these moves.

[4] Well played. If

WHITE	BLACK	WHITE	BLACK
13 B × B, then	P × B	[17. Q × R (?),	R to K B sq]
14 P to Kt 3	Q to R 6	18 K to B 2	P to K 4 (!)
15 Q to K 3	P × P	19 P × P	R to B sq, ch
16 R × P	R × R	20 K to K sq	Kt × P (!) and
17 P × R	Q to Kt 5, ch	Black has the better game.	

[5] Black rightly avoids the exchange of the Queens as long as possible, since White by his two Bishops, in the ending, would have a slight advantage.

[6] If 15. B × Kt, P × B ; 16. Q × P, then Q to B 4, ch ; 17. K to R sq, Q × B P. Black has a good game.

[7] White makes this move with the intention to answer Q × B P by 18. B to B 6, Q to B 4, ch ; 19. P to Q 4.

[8] Black does not try to defend the Queen's Bishop's Pawn, which at length cannot be saved, White being able, by playing B to K B 4, to attack the Pawn for a second time and thus to secure it.

[9] White now has the superior game.

[10] R to K 8, ch ; 34. K to B 2, R to B 8, would be bad on account of 35. B × Kt, P × B ; 36. R to Kt 8.

[11] White should have played 35. K to B 2 in order to prevent the Black Rook from occupying the eighth rank of the board ; with 35. K to B 2 White would have an easily won game, the Black Queen's Bishop's Pawn being lost anyway (See diagram.)

[12] 40. P to B 6 would be bad on account of R × B ; 41. P × B, R × P.

The week has wound up with no adjourned games on hand.

The leading scores are : Steinitz 4½, Tchigorin and Bardeleben 4, Pillsbury and Schiffers 3½, Lasker, Tinsley, and Mieses 3, whilst Tarrasch is only 1½. Nobody has a clean score, and only Steinitz and Bardeleben are without a loss. Great disappointment is expressed at the bad scores of Lasker and Tarrasch, though both have shown some fine play.

AUGUST 12.

THE play of Monday, the 12th, loses Steinitz his lead and Tarrasch has another draw. Steinitz obtained a winning advantage on the Queen's side, but his ingenious opponent was too much for him on the other side of the board; the contest was thronged by spectators and proved a very fine one. In fact, this round was very productive of fine games, and gave Tchigorin his first nominal lead with four others close up, but Bardeleben had an adjourned game with Mason which he eventually wins, so that his position is really equal with Tchigorin.

I. GUNSBERG v. DR. TARRASCH.

	WHITE	BLACK		WHITE	BLACK
1	P to Q 4	P to Q 4	23	R to Q sq	Kt to R 5
2	Kt to K B 3	P to K 3	24	Q to Kt 4	Kt to Kt 3
3	P to K 3	B to Q 3	25	P to Kt 3 [8]	Kt to K 2
4	P to B 4 [1]	P to Q B 3 [2]	26	K to Kt 2	Kt to B 4
5	Kt to B 3	P to K B 4 [3]	27	Kt to Q 4	Q to B 3
6	P to B 5	B to B 2	28	K R to K sq	Kt × Kt
7	P to Q Kt 4	Kt to Q 2 [4]	29	B × Kt	Q to B 4
8	B to Kt 2	Q to K 2	30	Q × Q	R × Q
9	B to Q 3	Kt to R 3 [5]	31	R to K 7	R (B 4) to B 2
10	Q to Kt 3 [6]	P to K 4	32	Q R to K sq	B to Q sq
11	P × P	Kt × K P	33	R (K 7) to K 6	
12	Kt × Kt	B × Kt			B to B 3
13	Kt to K 2	B to B 2	34	B × B	R × B
14	B to Q 4	Castles	35	R to K 7	R (B 3) to B 2
15	P to K R 3	P to B 5	36	P to R 3	P to K Kt 3
16	P × P	R × P	37	R (K sq) to K 2	
17	Castles (K R)	R to B 2 [7]			K to Kt 2
18	Q R to K sq	Q to R 5	38	K to B 3	R to Q R sq
19	P to B 4	B to B 4	39	R to K 8	R × R
20	B × B	Kt × B	40	R × R	R to Q 2
21	B to B 2	Q to R 3	41	K to K 3	K to B 2
22	Q to B 3	Q R to K B sq	42	R to Q R 8	P to Q R 3

Photo., Bradshaw, Hastings

I Gunsberg

AUGUST 12

WHITE	BLACK		WHITE	BLACK
43 K to Q 3	R to K 2		46 R × R, ch	K × R
44 R to Q Kt 8	K to B 3		47 P to K Kt 4	K to K 2
45 R to K B 8, ch			48 K to K 3	K to Q 2
	R to B 2		Drawn game.[9]	

NOTES BY S. TINSLEY.

[1] This form of the Queen's Pawn game has sometimes been denominated the Stonewall opening. For a purely defensive game (not much to White's taste however) P to B 3 has attractions, but obviously it shuts up B 3 for the Knight. That Piece, however (Q Kt), can be developed to Q 2, and perhaps, *via* B sq, to the King's side later
[Is it not the K B P which forms the Stonewall?—ED.]

[2] Possibly P to Q Kt 3 is better at once. It gives the option of B to Kt 2, P to Q B 4, &c., later. The text move finds little favour. A similar opening, Tinsley *v.* Bird, was played on August 20.

[3] I do not remember seeing other recent games by Dr Tarrasch in which this move was adopted by him. At any rate the policy of advancing the King's Bishop's Pawn at this stage is doubtful. The centre Pawn be it observed is left with only one defence already, and is frequently in such cases a source of weakness in the course of the after-play.

[4] There is a want of enterprise here. Admittedly White's P to B 5 is bad, and Black could well afford to commence at once some little attack on the weak Queen's side Pawns. P to Q R 4 seems loudly called for. P to Q Kt 3 could follow with effect.

[5] He can go back to B 2 with a view to the important move aimed at by Q to K 2, &c, viz. P to K 4. It is an exceptional case where Kt to R 3 in preference to B 3 is at least not bad, especially as White's Queen's Bishop is at Kt 2.

[6] A very strong move, with plenty of chances of a good sacrifice of the Knight presently by Kt × Q P, &c., after P to K 4 by Black, especially after White has Castled King's side, and perhaps played P to Q Kt 3 or 4.

[7] It does not appear that any profitable attack could be obtained by R to R 5, as White in certain cases replies B × R P, ch, &c., the Queen being free then for King's side defence.

[8] The safe accomplishment of the very desirable object of defending the real weakness on the King's side, the King's Bishop's Pawn, is really meritorious and secures a fairly equal game at once.

[9] Apparently the ending is dead even, and as each has a passed Pawn or as good, attempts to win on either side might be dangerous. We have pointed out that apparently Black's true course was to attack early on the Queen's side Pawns, and that there was opportunity for such attack, as no advantage could be gained on the King's side, and several exchanges became necessary owing to the attempt on the King's side. White was, as it turned out, left with a very good and creditable draw.

B. Vergani v. A. Walbrodt.

	WHITE	BLACK		WHITE	BLACK
1	P to Q 4	P to K Kt 3	21	Q to Kt 2	Kt to Q 3
2	P to Q B 4[1]	B to Kt 2	22	P to Q R 3	Kt to B 3
3	P to K 3[2]	P to Q B 4	23	Q to B 2[11]	K R to Q B sq
4	Kt to K B 3[3]	P × P	24	Q to Q 3	Q × Q
5	P × P	P to Q 4	25	Kt × Q	Kt to Kt 4
6	Kt to B 3[4]	Kt to K B 3	26	P to Q R 4	Kt (Kt 4) × Q P
7	B to Q 3[5]	Castles	27	K to B sq	K to B sq
8	Castles	Kt to B 3	28	P to Q Kt 4[12]	P × P
9	B to K 3	B to Kt 5	29	Kt × P	Kt (B 3) × Kt
10	P to B 5	P to K 3[6]	30	R × R, ch	R × R
11	B to K 2	Kt to Q 2	31	R × Kt	Kt to B 7
12	Kt to K sq	B × B	32	R to Kt 3	R to R sq
13	Kt × B	P to Kt 3	33	B to B 5, ch	K to K sq
14	P × P[7]	Q × P[8]	34	Kt to B 3	R to B sq
15	P to Q Kt 3[9]	P to Q R 4	35	P to R 5	R × B
16	Kt to K B 3	K R to Q sq[10]	36	P to R 6	R to R 4
17	R to Kt sq	Kt to Kt 5	37	Kt to Kt 5	R to R 8, ch
18	Q to Q 2	Q to Q R 3	38	K to K 2	Kt to Q 5, ch
19	K R to Q B sq		39	Kt × Kt	B × Kt
		Kt to K B 3	40	R to Kt 8, ch	K to K 2
20	Kt to K sq	Kt to K 5		White resigns.	

Notes by J. H. Blackburne.

[1] It is better to play P to K 4 in reply to the 'King's Fianchetto,' and keep this Pawn in reserve to go one or two according to circumstances.

[2] Again he ought to play P to K 4

[3] Perhaps the other Kt to B 3 would have been preferable. White does not develop his game in accordance with the principles laid down by the great masters.

[4] Another weak move. In any case, White must remain with an isolated Pawn, but it was certainly better to take the Pawn, followed by Kt to Q B 3 and B to K 3.

[5] The Bishop is of very little use on this square; B to K 3, or even P to B 5, is preferable.

[6] This is safe and sure, but B × Kt followed by P to K 4 would have led to a more lively game

[7] This assists Black. Q to R 4, with the object of maintaining the Pawn on B 5 by Kt to Q 3 and P to Q Kt 4, would have given more chance of drawing.

[8] Taking with the Knight was stronger.

[9] Still Q to R 4 was the proper move.

[10] Why not K R to Q B sq at once? The same query applies to White's next move

AUGUST 12

[11] Only forcing Black to make a good move. Q to Q 2, intending Kt to Q 3 and B 5, and White's position is not hopeless.

[12] No doubt the game is gone, but this and the next few moves are recklessly played by White; he might still have given Black some trouble by B × Kt, trying to remain with Knight against Bishop.

W. STEINITZ v. W. H. K. POLLOCK.

	WHITE	BLACK
1	P to K 4	P to K 4
2	Kt to K B 3	Kt to Q B 3
3	B to B 4	B to B 4
4	P to Q B 3	Q to K 2 [1]
5	P to Q 4	B to Kt 3
6	P to Q R 4 [2]	P to Q R 4
7	Castles	P to Q 3
8	P to Q 5 [3]	Kt to Q sq
9	B to Q 3	K Kt to B 3 [4]
10	Kt to R 3	P to B 3
11	Kt to B 4	B to B 2
12	Kt to K 3	Kt to R 4
13	P to K Kt 3	P to K Kt 3
14	P to Q Kt 4	P to K B 4
15	Kt to Kt 2	P × Q P
16	P × Q P	Kt to B 2
17	R to K sq	Castles [5]
18	Kt to Q 4	Q to B 3
19	Kt to Kt 5	B to Kt 3
20	P × P [6]	B × R P
21	B to K 2	Kt to Kt 2
22	B to Q 2	B to Q 2
23	R to K B sq	Q R to B sq
24	P to Q B 4	B to Kt 3
25	B to K 3 [7]	B × B
26	P × B	Kt to Kt 4
27	Kt to B 3 [8]	P to B 5
28	Q to B 2	P to B 6
29	Kt to R 4	Kt to B 4 [9]
30	R × P	Kt × R, ch
31	Kt × Kt	Kt × K P
32	Q to Kt sq	Kt × Q B P
33	Kt to K 4	Q to Q sq
34	Q × Kt P	Kt to Q R 4
35	Q to Kt 4	B to Kt 5
36	R to K B sq	B to R 6
37	R to K sq	R to Q Kt sq

White to make his 27th move.

	WHITE	BLACK
38	Q × P	Q × Q
39	Kt × Q	R to Kt 7
40	B to Q sq	R to Kt 7, ch
41	K to R sq	R to K B 7
42	Kt to K 4	R (B 7) × Kt
43	B × R	R × B
44	P to Q 6	R to B 8, ch
45	R × R	B × R
46	K to Kt sq	B to Q 6
47	Kt to B 6, ch	K to B 2
48	Kt × P	K to K 3
49	K to B 2	K × P
50	K to K 3	B to B 7
51	P to R 4	Kt to B 5, ch
52	K to K 2	K to Q 4
53	P to Kt 4	K to Q 5
54	Kt to B 8	B to Q 6, ch
55	K to K sq	K to K 6
56	P to R 5	P × P
57	P × P	B to K 7
58	Kt to Q 7	Kt to R 6 [10]

White resigns.

NOTES BY H. N. PILLSBURY.

[1] Perhaps not so good as Kt to K B 3, but favoured by Dr. Pollock.

[2] Advances of this character so early seem premature, and only weaken the position later on. Although this includes a trap—viz. if in answer 6. P to Q 3 ; 7. P to R 5, winning two Pieces for Rook and Pawn, yet it is no exception to the foregoing rule. Any developing move, as 6. Castles, would be better.

[3] Rather than this advance, which allows Black later on to open the game at his leisure on the King's side, the lesser evil of the two, P to K R 3, would be preferable. Black could form no immediate assault upon this point, and his somewhat weakened Queen's wing would scarcely permit him to Castle on that side, with intent of a Pawn attack on the White King.

[4] The position would permit of a direct assault upon the Castled King, should Black desire, by 9. P to K B 3, followed soon by P to K Kt 4 and K R 4. In answer, 10. Kt to R 4 would be disastrous by 10 P to K Kt 4 ; 11. Q to R 5, ch, Kt to B 2 ; 12. Kt to B 3, B to Q 2 (!), followed by Castles Q R, now permissible owing to the displacement of the White Queen.

[5] With a fine position for attack ; a direct evidence of the weakness of White's 8th move.

[6] Only still further weakening his Pawns

[7] Q to Kt 3, with intent to force matters on the Queen's side, seems better

[8] A violation of an old-time principle 'that the Pieces should not be left loose and unguarded' Black takes advantage of this misplay with great precision, and from this point obtains a winning advantage. White should have played 27. Q to B 2, and if Kt to K 5 ; 28. Kt to B 3, Kt to B 4 ; 29. P to R 5, with a fair prospect of attack on the weak Queen's Knight's Pawn. (See diagram.)

[9] Perhaps B to R 6 was quicker, for if 30. R to B 2, B to Kt 7, wins without much trouble.

[10] Rather an amusing finish to a very interesting game.

E. SCHIFFERS v. J. H. BLACKBURNE.

	WHITE	BLACK		WHITE	BLACK
1	P to K 4	P to K 3	11	Q to K 2	Q × P
2	P to Q 4	P to Q 4	12	B to K Kt 5	Kt to Q 4
3	Kt to Q B 3	P × P [1]	13	B × B	Kt × B
4	Kt × P	Kt to Q 2	14	Q R to Q sq	P to B 3
5	B to Q 3	K Kt to B 3	15	Kt to B 4	Kt to B 3
6	Kt × Kt, ch [2]	Kt × Kt	16	P to Q B 3	P to B 4 (?) [3]
7	Kt to B 3	B to K 2	17	P to Q Kt 4 (!) [4]	
8	Castles	Castles			Q to K 2
9	Kt to K 5	P to B 4	18	P to Kt 5	Kt to Q sq
10	P × P	Q to B 2	19	Kt to K 5	Kt to B 2

AUGUST 12

	WHITE	BLACK
20	Kt × Kt	R × Kt
21	B to B 4	R to B 3
22	Q to K 5	P to K R 4 [5]
23	K R to K sq	K to R 2
24	R to Q 6	R to Kt 3
25	B × P	Q to Kt 4
26	B to Q 5	R × R
27	Q × R	P to R 5
28	P to K B 4	Q to R 4
29	P to K R 3	P to R 4
30	P to Q R 4	R to R 2
31	Q to B 8	P to Q Kt 3
32	Q × B	Resigns.

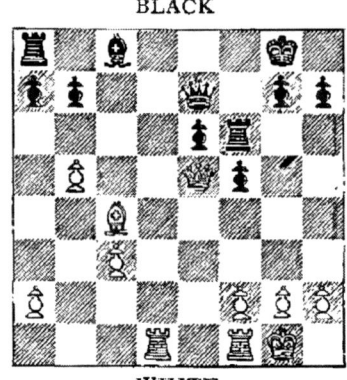

Black to make his 22nd move.

NOTES BY C. VON BARDELEBEN.

[1] I think the older move Kt to K B 3 is better. After Black's P × P he has a cramped game, because his Queen's Bishop remains shut in.

[2] Better than 6. Kt to K B 3, for if 6. Kt to K B 3, then Kt × Kt; 7. B × Kt, Kt to B 3, and Black gains time for his development.

[3] A great mistake. Now the King's Pawn becomes very weak. Preferable would be P to K 4.

[4] White takes advantage of the opponent's mistake very cleverly.

[5] This counter-attack has no chance and compromises Black's game, though other moves would hardly save him; for example, if B to Q 2, then 23. Q to B 7, or if P to Q Kt 3, then 23. K R to K sq, B to Kt 2; 24. B × P, ch, K to R sq; 25. R to Q 7, and White wins.

S. TINSLEY v. A. BURN.

	WHITE	BLACK		WHITE	BLACK
1	P to Q 4	P to Q 4	14	B × Kt	B P × B
2	P to K 3	P to K 3 [1]	15	B to Q 2	Kt to Q sq [4]
3	Kt to K B 3	Kt to K B 3	16	P to Q Kt 3	P to Q Kt 4
4	B to Q 3	B to K 2 [2]	17	P to Q R 4 [5]	B to Q 3
5	Castles	Castles	18	R P × P	B × Kt
6	Kt to K 5	P to B 4	19	Q P × B	R to Q Kt sq
7	P to B 3	Kt to Q B 3	20	P × P	Q × B P
8	P to K B 4	Kt to K 5	21	R × R P	Q × Kt P
9	Kt to Q 2	P to B 4	22	B to B sq [6]	Kt to B 3
10	Q Kt to B 3	P to B 5	23	R to R 2	Q to B 5
11	B to B 2	B to Q 2	24	Q to R 4 [7]	Kt × P
12	Kt × B [3]	Q × Kt	25	Q to R 6	Q R to K sq
13	Kt to K 5	Q to B 2	26	Q × Q	Kt × Q [8]

WHITE	BLACK	WHITE	BLACK
27 K to B 2	R to R sq	37 R × R	R × R
28 R to B 2	K R to Kt sq	38 B to K sq	K to Kt 4
29 B to Q 2	R to Kt 6	39 P to K R 4	K to R 5
30 K to K 2	K to B 2	40 B to Q 2	K to Kt 6
31 K R to Q B sq	K to K 2	41 R to B sq	R × R
32 B to K sq	K to Q 3	42 B × R	K to B 7 [11]
33 B to R 4	R to R 2 [9]	43 P to B 5	P × P
34 P to K Kt 4	K to B 4	44 P × P	K × P
35 B to K sq	R (Kt 6) to R 6	45 P to R 6	P to R 3
36 B to R 4 [10]	R to R 8	White resigns.	

NOTES BY E SCHIFFERS.

[1] Instead of this move we prefer to prepare the advance of P to K 4 by means of Kt to Q B 3 White can continue P to K B 4, and in course of time P to Q B 3 (Stonewall) ; B to Q Kt 5, with the exchange at B 6, does not give White any superiority. Black will rather be able to utilise his two Bishops. After Kt to Q B 3 ; 3. Kt to K B 3, might follow B to Kt 5

[2] Since, in the majority of cases, the Bishop eventually goes to Q 3, it is preferable to make this move at once.

[3] It would seem more advantageous either to take Kt at Q B 6, followed by Kt to K 5 or K to R sq, in conjunction with P to Kt 4 ; P to Kt 4 might even be played at once.

[4] Black wishes to retain the Knight against the Bishop and succeeds in this.

[5] This only weakens White's Queen's side.

[6] It would have been better to play Q to Kt 4 to force the exchange of Rook after R to Kt 2.

[7] A blunder. The continuation should have been 24. R to K B 2, followed by B to R 3 or P to B 4, according to circumstances. If 24. ... Q × P ; then 25 K to B 2.

[8] Black has now a considerable superiority in position. White's Bishop is completely hampered.

[9] To prevent B to K 7 and B to Kt 4.

[10] White has no moves.

[11] The Bishop is done for.

E. LASKER v. D. JANOWSKI.

WHITE	BLACK	WHITE	BLACK
1 P to Q 4	P to Q 4	7 R to B sq	B to Kt 2
2 P to Q B 4	P to K 3	8 P × P	P × P
3 Kt to Q B 3	Kt to K B 3	9 B to Q 3	P to Q B 4
4 B to K Kt 5	B to K 2	10 Castles	Q Kt to Q 2
5 Kt to B 3	Castles	11 P × P	Kt × P [1]
6 P to K 3	P to Q Kt 3	12 B to Kt sq	R to B sq

AUGUST 12

	WHITE	BLACK
13	B to B 5	Kt to K 3
14	B to R 4	K to R sq [2]
15	Kt to K 5	Q to K sq
16	Q to B 3 [3]	Kt to Kt sq
17	B to Kt 3	Kt to R 3
18	B to Kt sq	P to K B 3
19	Kt to Q 3	Q to Q 2
20	Q to Q sq	K R to Q sq
21	Kt to B 4	Kt × Kt [4]
22	B × Kt	P to K Kt 4 [5]
23	B to Kt 3	B to B sq
24	Q to Q 3	P to B 4 [6]
25	Kt to K 2	B to Kt 2
26	Kt to Q 4	R to B sq
27	R × R	Q × R
28	Q to Q 2 [7]	R to B 2
29	R to B sq	Q to K sq
30	P to K R 4	P × P
31	B × R P	B to Q B sq
32	B to Kt 3	Kt to Kt 5

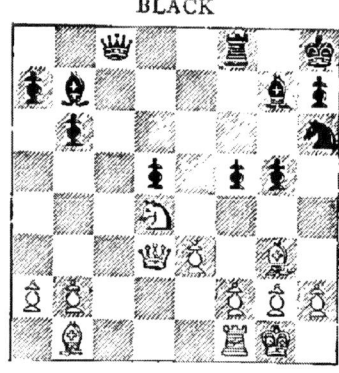

White to make his 28th move.

	WHITE	BLACK
33	Kt to Kt 5 [8]	R to B sq
34	Kt to Q 6	Q to K 3
35	R × B	R × R
36	B × P	Resigns.

NOTES BY R. TEICHMANN.

[1] Instead of this move, which leaves the Queen's Pawn isolated, I prefer P × P. The two Pawns can in this variation be sufficiently supported, and will form the basis of a counter-attack on the Queen's side.

[2] This is certainly a weakening move, but the position is very delicate and Black is at a loss what to do.

[3] Threatening now Q to R 3, followed by Kt × B P.

[4] This exchange is ill-judged and causes serious trouble. It would have been better to retire the Knight to B sq, where it would support K R 2, and then to try a counter-attack on the Queen's side, where his Rooks are in commanding positions.

[5] And this premature advance compromises his King's side irretrievably. An attack on the King's side is, on the face of it, without prospect.

[6] Creating another weakness. One of these two weak Pawns (Q 4 and K B 4) must fall in a few moves.

[7] Very subtle. The Queen is excellently posted here, and the Rook can now take possession of the important Queen's Bishop's file. (See diagram.)

[8] This powerful move leaves Black defenceless. The whole game was very well played by Mr. Lasker, and it is a good specimen of this variation of the Queen's Gambit, in which White maintains an advantage throughout by combining a direct attack on the King with a continuous pressure on the weak isolated Queen's Pawn.

A. Albin v. C. Schlechter.

	WHITE	BLACK		WHITE	BLACK
1	P to K 4	P to K 4	17	Kt to Q B 2	P to Q B 4 [5]
2	Kt to K B 3	Kt to K B 3	18	Castles Q R	B to Q B sq
3	B to B 4	Kt × P	19	Q R to K sq	B to B 4
4	Kt to B 3	Kt to B 3 [1]	20	P to Kt 3 [6]	B to Kt 3
5	Kt × Kt [2]	P to Q 4	21	B to B 3	Q R to K 2
6	B to Kt 5	P × Kt	22	K R to Kt sq [7]	
7	Kt × P	Q to Q 4			Q R to K B 2
8	B × Kt, ch	P × B	23	P to K Kt 4	B to K 2
9	Kt to Kt 4	B to R 3 [3]	24	P to Kt 5	B to Q 3
10	Kt to K 3	Q to K 3	25	P to K R 4	R to K 2
11	P to Q Kt 3	B to Q 3	26	R to R sq	B to R 4
12	B to Kt 2	Castles K R	27	K R to Kt sq	B to Kt 3 [8]
13	Q to Kt 4 [4]	Q × Q	28	R to R sq	B to R 4
14	Kt × Q	Q R to K sq	29	K R to Kt sq	B to Kt 3
15	P to Q B 4	P to K B 4	30	R to R sq	
16	Kt to K 3	P to K B 5		Drawn game.	

Notes by J. H. Blackburne.

[1] This brings about a drawish position of the Four Knights' Opening. Kt × Kt, and then defending Pawn by P to K B 3, is perfectly safe.

[2] B × P, ch, is sometimes played, but Black comes out with the superior game.

[3] This certainly prevents Castling on the King's side, but P to K B 4 would have been a stronger and more attacking line of play.

[4] Forcing the exchange of Queens, and thereby securing a draw.

[5] Unnecessary, because the Knight could not go to Q 4 with advantage.

[6] P to K Kt 4 would be more vigorous, because the Bishop could not take the Pawn on account of R to Kt sq.

[7] Again P to K Kt 4 is the proper play.

[8] Both players appear satisfied with the draw.

M. Tchigorin v. R. Teichmann.

	WHITE	BLACK		WHITE	BLACK
1	P to K 4	P to K 3	8	P × P	B to Q 3 [6]
2	Q to K 2	Kt to Q B 3 [1]	9	Q Kt to Q 2	Castles
3	Kt to K B 3	P to K 4 [2]	10	Kt to B 4	B to K 3
4	P to Q B 3	Kt to B 3	11	Castles	Kt to K sq [7]
5	P to Q 3	B to K 2 [3]	12	P to Q Kt 4 [8]	P to Q R 3
6	P to K Kt 3 [4]	P to Q 4	13	R to Q sq	Q to K 2
7	B to Kt 2	P × P [5]	14	P to Q R 4	P to K B 3

AUGUST 12

WHITE	BLACK
15 B to R 3	P to Q Kt 4 (?) [9]
16 P × P	P × P
17 Kt to K 3	R to Kt sq [10]
18 B to Q B sq [11]	
	Kt to Q sq [12]
19 R to R 7	Kt to B 3
20 R to R 6	Kt to Q sq
21 Kt to Q 5	Q to Q 2 [13]
22 Kt to K sq [14]	P to B 3
23 Kt to K 3	Q to Kt 2
24 R to R sq	B to Q B 2 [15]
25 Kt to K B 5 (!)	
	B to Kt 3 [16]
26 B to K 3 [17]	B × B
27 Q × B	R to B 2
28 Kt to Q 3 [18]	B to B sq [19]
29 Kt × K P	P × Kt

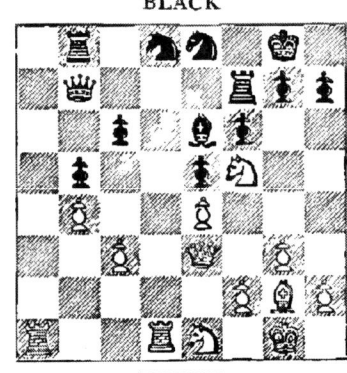

White to make his 28th move.

WHITE	BLACK
30 R × Kt	B to K 3 [20]
31 Kt to Q 6	Resigns [21]

NOTES BY DR. TARRASCH.

[1] I consider the best to be B to K 2. P to Q B 4 is also good.

[2] This gives an open game.

[3] P to Q 4 is stronger, with the development of the Queen's Bishop at Q 2, and Castles Queen's Rook.

[4] This development of the King's Bishop is the natural consequence of Q to K 2.

[5] With this Black plays the game in the centre, and fights for a chance to get an advantage there. B to K 3 was in every way stronger, followed by Q to Q 2, and Castles Queen's Rook. The Queen's file opened by the exchange of the Pawns is more serviceable to White than to Black.

[6] Unintelligible and at present certainly unnecessary.

[7] Black plays the whole game at least weakly, as is often the case when the other plays very strongly. The Knight becomes soon stifled here, and remains so to the end.

[8] Tchigorin gets points of attack for himself in a clever way.

[9] From this point Black gets into serious difficulties. He wishes to drive the threatening Knight, which he could have done before without disadvantage. The consequence of the text move is that the whole of Black's Queen's wing becomes weak, and White holds the sole control of the open Rook's file.

[10] The Knight's Pawn must be defended.

[11] In order to unmask the Rook.

[12] In order to move P to Q B 3, and then to develop with B to B 2 and Kt to Q 3, which White seeks to prevent.

[13] If Black takes the Knight, the Pawn re-takes, and the cleverly

isolated Pawn at Kt 4 is threatened with capture after R to R 5 and B to K B sq.

[14] In order to get possession of Q B 5.

[15] Black has temporarily driven back the White forces; but, nevertheless, he does not accomplish his planned development of the Kt at K sq.

[16] If B × Kt the diagonal of the White King's Bishop is opened, and therewith an attack on the Pawns. It would now be best to play P to Kt 3.

[17] In order to guarantee the Knight an entrance at Q B 5.

[18] The decisive, well-prepared move; Kt to B 5 is now threatened, followed by R × Kt and Kt × B. (See diagram.)

[19] R to R sq would be better, but White has then a particularly well-developed game.

[20] Here, if B × Kt; 31. R × R, Q × R; 32. P × B, and Black has a lost game.

[21] The game is an excellent example of the modern school of play.

J. Mason v. C. von Bardeleben.

	WHITE	BLACK		WHITE	BLACK
1	P to K 4	P to K 4	11	Kt to Kt 3	B to R 4
2	Kt to K B 3	Kt to Q B 3	12	P to B 3	Q to Q 2
3	B to B 4	Kt to B 3	13	P to Q 4	Castles K R
4	P to Q 3	B to B 4	14	P to K R 4 [2]	B × B
5	Kt to B 3	P to Q 3	15	P × B	B to B 2
6	B to K 3	B to Kt 3 [1]	16	P to R 5 [3]	Kt to K 2
7	P to K R 3	B to K 3	17	P × P	P × P
8	B to Kt 3	Kt to K 2	18	P to R 6 [4]	P to K Kt 3
9	Kt to K 2	Kt to Kt 3	19	Q × Q	Kt × Q
10	Q to Q 2	P to B 3	20	Castles Q R	K R to Q sq
			21	R to Q 2	P to B 3
			22	K R to Q sq	Kt to K B sq
			23	R × R	R × R
			24	R × R	B × R
			25	Kt to Q 2	B to B 2
			26	P to Kt 4 [5]	Kt to K 3
			27	K to Q sq	P to Kt 3
			28	Kt to B 3	K to B 2
			29	Kt to R 4	B to Q 3
			30	Kt to K 2	Kt to Kt sq
			31	P to K Kt 3	B to B sq [6]
			32	P to B 3	B × R P
			33	B × B	Kt × B
			34	K to Q 2	Kt to B 2
			35	K to Q 3	K to K 3

BLACK

WHITE

White to make his 14th move.

AUGUST 12

	WHITE	BLACK		WHITE	BLACK
36	Kt to Kt 2	Kt to Kt sq	61	Kt to B sq	P to Kt 5
37	Kt to Kt sq	P to K B 4	62	P × P, ch	K × P [8]
38	Kt to R 3	P to K R 3	63	Kt to Q 2	K to B 4
39	Kt to B 2	Kt to B 3	64	Kt to B 3	K to B 3
40	Kt to R 4	P × P, ch	65	P to B 4	P to Kt 4
41	Kt × K P	Kt × Kt	66	P × P [9]	P × P
42	K × Kt [7]	K to B 3	67	Kt to Q 2	K to B 4
43	Kt to Kt 2	Kt to K sq	68	Kt to B 3	K to K 3
44	Kt to K 3	Kt to Q 3, ch	69	Kt to Q 2	K to Q 4
45	K to Q 3	P to K R 4	70	Kt to Kt sq	P to K 5
46	K to K 2	Kt to B 4	71	Kt to B 3, ch	K to K 4
47	Kt to B sq	P to R 5	72	Kt to K 2	Kt to B 4, ch
48	P × P	Kt × P	73	K to B 2	Kt to Q 5
49	Kt to Q 2	K to K 3	74	Kt to B 3	P to R 3
50	K to Q 3	K to B 4	75	K to K 3	Kt to B 7, ch
51	K to K 3	Kt to Kt 7, ch	76	K to Q 2	Kt × P
52	K to B 2	Kt to B 5	77	Kt to K 2	Kt to Q 4
53	Kt to B 4	K to K 3	78	K to B 2	P to K 6
54	K to K 3	Kt to Q 4, ch	79	K to Q 3	Kt to B 5, ch
55	K to B 2	Kt to B 3	80	K × P	Kt × Kt
56	K to K 3	Kt to K sq	81	K × Kt	K to Q 5
57	Kt to Q 2	Kt to Q 3	82	K to Q 2	P to Kt 5
58	P to Kt 3	K to B 3	83	K to B 2	K to K 6
59	K to Q 3	K to B 4		White resigns.	
60	K to K 3	P to K Kt 4			

NOTES BY E. SCHIFFERS.

[1] Formerly this line of play was always adopted in similar cases; but latterly Steinitz and Tchigorin prefer to take the Bishop at K 3, doubling the Pawns. In a like position Tchigorin exchanged Bishops, and then exchanged the Knight by Kt to R 4 for the Bishop, obtaining a good game.

[2] A favourite attack of Mr. Mason's, which often, as in the present game, only leads to the loss of the Pawn. (See diagram)

[3] B to Kt 5 would have been better, with the ultimate view of placing the Knight at K B 5

[4] And now B to Kt 5 would be better.

[5] Evidently White cannot take the Pawn at R 7, on account of P to Kt 3, followed by Kt to B sq However, a move previously, after B × P, White would have lost the Bishop, but in exchange for three Pawns, and if B × R P, P to Kt 3, B to Kt 8, Kt to B sq, B × K P, &c.

[6] See note 2

[7] Taking with the Pawn would have been better, in spite of the isolated King's Knight's Pawn.

[8] Black has now a passed Pawn and some winning chances.

[9] If P to B 5, then Kt to B 2 (!), and in reply to K to K 4, P to R 3. Either the King or the Knight is obliged to retreat, and Black's Knight can occupy Q 4 or Q 5.

G. Marco v. H. E. Bird.

WHITE	BLACK	WHITE	BLACK
1 P to K 4	P to K 4	28 Q × P, ch	K to Kt sq
2 Kt to K B 3	Kt to Q B 3	29 B × P, ch	Kt × B
3 B to Kt 5	Kt to Q 5 [1]	30 Q × Kt, ch	K to Kt 2
4 Kt × Kt	P × Kt	31 Q to Q 4, ch	K to Kt sq
5 B to B 4	P to K R 4 [2]	32 Q to B 4, ch	K to Kt 2
6 P to Q 3	B to B 4		
7 Castles	P to Q 3		
8 P to B 4	P to Q B 3		
9 P to B 5 [3]	P to Q 4		
10 P × P	P × P		
11 B to Kt 3	P to B 3		
12 Q to B 3	Kt to K 2		
13 P to K R 3 [4]	P to R 4 [5]		
14 P to Q R 4	K to B sq		
15 P to Kt 4	P × P		
16 P × P	R to Q R 3		
17 B to K B 4	P to K Kt 3 [6]		
18 P × P	K to Kt 2		
19 Kt to Q 2	R to R 5		
20 P to Kt 5	R to Kt 5, ch		
21 K to R sq [7]	Q to R sq, ch		
22 B to R 2	R × P		
23 R to B 2	B to Kt 5		
24 Q to B 4	R to B 4		
25 Q to Kt 3	B to Q 3		
26 Q to Kt sq	R × R		
27 Q × R	P to B 4 [8]		

BLACK

WHITE

White to make his 33rd move.

33 Q to B 3, ch	K to Kt sq
34 Q to B 4, ch	K to Kt 2
35 Q to B 3, ch	K to Kt sq
36 Q to Kt 3, ch	K to Kt 2
37 Q to B 3, ch [9]	

Drawn game.

Notes by R. Teichmann.

[1] Mr. Bird's favourite defence to the Ruy Lopez, which gives a slight advantage to the first player on account of Black's doubled Queen's Pawn.

[2] Somewhat eccentric, and regardless of the established principles of development; but Mr. Bird likes to go his own way.

[3] White, however, attacks too hurriedly; he ought to develop his Knight first. This premature advance of the King's Bishop's Pawn forces him very soon to compromise his own King's position.

[4] Necessary, to be able to support the advanced Bishop's Pawn. Black cannot take it at once, because after 13. B × P, 14. R to K sq.

AUGUST 12

White would win the Queen's Pawn and open the diagonal again for his King's Bishop.

[5] Very well played. The Black Queen's Rook is thus brought into play without loss of time.

[6] This fine move initiates a powerful attack on the exposed White King's position, whilst the Black King will be perfectly safe at K Kt 2

[7] If 21. K to B 2, Kt × P, 22. B to Kt 3, P × P, winning in a few moves

[8] So far Black has played very well, but with this curious oversight he throws away what should have been an easily won game. The simplest way would have been to exchange Queens [by Q × B, ch], leaving him with a strong passed Pawn ahead for the end game

[9] The position (see diagram) being very difficult, Herr Marco tried to gain time by these checks, but he overlooked that with this move the same position occurred for the third time, which, according to the rules in force, permitted his opponent to claim a draw. White had a won game. It seems, however, difficult to force the game by the exchange of Queens, although White would be a Pawn ahead in the end game. But I think he could have won by the following interesting though difficult line of play:—

	WHITE	BLACK		WHITE	BLACK
33	Q to B 7, ch	K to R 3	41	K to B 2	P to K 8 (Q), ch
34	B × B	R × B		(if Q to B 4 ch, then 42 K	
35	K to Kt 2	Q to K 4 (best;		to K sq)	
	if Q to B 3, then 36. R to R		42	R × Q	Q to R 7, ch
	sq, ch, K to Kt 4, 37. Q to		43	K × B	Q to R 6, ch
	R 7, winning)		44	K to B 2	Q to R 7 (5), ch
36	R to R sq, ch	K to Kt 4	45	K to K 3 and the King gets out	
37	Kt to K 4, ch (otherwise he			of the checks. It is note-	
	cannot avoid the draw)			worthy, that in this variation	
		P × Kt (best)		White could even, instead of	
38	P to Kt 7	B to B 6, ch		40 K to B sq, play 40 K × B	
39	K to B 2	Q to B 4, ch (or a)		and still win, e.g.—	
40	K to B sq	B to Kt 7, ch	40	K × B	R to B 3, ch
41	K × B	Q × P, ch	41	K to K 2	R to B 7, ch
42	Q to B 2	Q × Q, ch	42	K to K sq	R × Q
43	K × Q and wins.		43	P to Kt 8 (Q), ch	
					R to Kt 2
(a)	39.	P to K 6, ch	44	R to Kt sq, ch	K to R 3
40	K to B sq	P to K 7, ch (best)	45	Q to R 8, ch, winning easily.	

[This game is a good illustration of Mr Bird's play—lively and original. He generally combines his 5. P to K R 4 with this defence, holding that his King is sufficiently safe on B sq without Castling.—ED]

J. Mieses v. H. N. Pillsbury.

	WHITE	BLACK
1	P to K 4	P to K 4
2	Kt to Q B 3	Kt to K B 3
3	B to B 4	B to Kt 5 [1]
4	P to K B 4	P to Q 3
5	Kt to B 3	Castles
6	Kt to Q 5 [2]	Kt × Kt
7	B × Kt	Kt to B 3 [3]
8	P to B 3 [4]	B to Q B 4
9	P to B 5	Kt to K 2
10	B to Kt 3	P to Q 4 (!)
11	P to Q 4	P × Q P
12	P to B 6	Kt P × P
13	Kt × Q P	Q P × P
14	B to R 6	Kt to Kt 3 (!) [5]
15	B × R	Q × B
16	R to K B sq [6]	Q to R 3 (!) [7]
17	Q to K 2	B × Kt
18	P × B	P to K B 4
19	P to K Kt 4 [8]	Kt to B 5 [9]

White to make his 15th move.

	WHITE	BLACK
20	Q to B 4	Kt to Q 6, ch
21	K to K 2	Q × R P, ch
22	K to K 3	P to B 5, ch
	White resigns.	

NOTES BY C. VON BARDELEBEN.

[1] I prefer B to B 4 or Kt to B 3.

[2] Unsound. White should have played 6. P × P, P × P; 7. Castles, and would have obtained a very good game by the open King's Bishop's file.

[3] Better would be B to Q B 4 to prevent White's Castling.

[4] White fails to take advantage of the opponent's mistake; instead of 8. P to B 3 he ought to have Castled.

[5] The sacrifice of the exchange is quite sound, Black being two Pawns ahead. Bad would be 14 ... R to K sq because of 15. Q to R 5, Kt to Kt 3; 16. Castles Q R, and White would have a strong attack. (See diagram.)

[6] Another weak move. If White played 16. Castles, his game was not so bad.

[7] Very cleverly played.

[8] Overlooking the simple reply of Black. Of course the right move was 19. P to Kt 3.

[9] Now it is plain sailing for Black.

Photo., Bradshaw, Hastings

AUGUST 13.

To-day Lasker is to meet Pollock, who so brilliantly defeated Steinitz, and he pays his adversary a compliment by declining his proffered Evans' Gambit; then Pillsbury and Steinitz are to meet.

Blackburne starts against Albin, and after many sittings, nearly 14 hours' play and 123 moves on each side, defeats him. The game Janowski *v.* Mason proves very entertaining also.

D. Janowski *v.* J. Mason.

	WHITE	BLACK
1	P to K 4	P to K 4
2	Kt to K B 3	Kt to K B 3
3	Kt × P	P to Q 3 [1]
4	Kt to K B 3	Kt × P
5	P to Q 4	P to Q 4 [2]
6	B to Q 3	B to K 2 [3]
7	Castles	Kt to Q 2
8	P to B 4	K Kt to B 3
9	P × P	Kt × P
10	Kt to B 3	Q Kt to B 3
11	R to K sq	P to B 3
12	B to K Kt 5	B to K 3
13	Kt to K 5	Castles
14	Kt × Kt [4]	B × Kt
15	B to B 2	R to K sq
16	Q to Q 3	P to K Kt 3
17	Q to K R 3	Kt to R 4
18	B to K 3 [5]	B to Kt 4
19	Q to Kt 4	B × B
20	P × B [6]	B to K 3
21	Q to K 2	Q to Kt 4
22	R to K B sq	Q R to Q sq
23	B to Kt 3 [7]	B × B
24	P × B	P to K B 3
25	Q to B 4, ch	R to Q 4 [8]

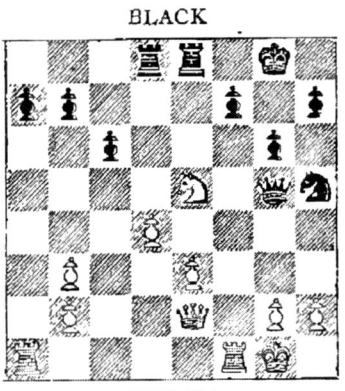

BLACK

WHITE

Black to make his 24th move.

	WHITE	BLACK
26	P to K 4	Q to K 6, ch
27	K to R sq	Q × K P
28	Q R to K sq	Q × Q P
29	Kt × Q B P	R × R [9]
30	Kt × Q	R × R, ch
31	Q × R	R × Kt
32	P to K Kt 3	R to Q 2
33	P to K Kt 4	Kt to Kt 2
34	Q × P	P to Q Kt 3
35	K to Kt 2	R to Q 7, ch

WHITE	BLACK	WHITE	BLACK
36 K to Kt 3	R to K 7	46 P × P	K to K 4
37 P to K R 3	R to K 3	47 K to Kt 5	Kt to Q 3
38 Q to B 4	P to Q R 4	48 Q to B 7	K to Q 4
39 K to R 4	P to R 4	49 K to B 4	R to B 3, ch
40 K to Kt 5	R to Q B 3	50 K to K 3	R to K 3, ch
41 Q to B 3	R to K 3	51 K to Q 3	Kt to K sq
42 K to R 6	P × P	52 Q to B 7	K to Q 3
43 Q to R 8, ch[10]	Kt to K sq	53 K to Q 4	Kt to B 2
44 Q to B 8	K to B 2	54 Q to B 4, ch	K to Q 2
45 Q to Q 7, ch	K to B 3	Drawn game.	

NOTES BY S. TINSLEY.

[1] Is it necessary—probably it is—to explain, for the benefit of the uninitiated, that White must not play Kt × P at once? The reply would be Q to K 2 with a very disagreeable attack, if not a winning game

[2] Sanctioned by many authorities recently But we have heard much about never moving a Piece twice in the opening It is necessary here, however, to play P to Q 4 to prevent White's Kt to Q 5, to support the Kt at K 5, and to bring B to K 3

[3] B to Q 3 has much in its favour

[4] The special point, if any, involved in a mere exchange of a minor Piece in such a position is difficult to discover. And there is this forcible objection to it, that the game soon tends to dulness and becomes unattractive to what is best described as the gallery

[5] The Bishop is retained in order to keep the Knight out By exchanging, a 'hole' would be open for that Piece at B 5.

[6] White's somewhat weak Queen's Pawn is now supported and the game seems quite even.

[7] Unless White saw the whole combination at starting this is surprising at first sight The White Bishop is valuable and is in excellent play, and a doubled Pawn is the result of the text move Moreover, his weak King's Pawn needed support, and the immediate effect of White's combination is unfavourable to him Or, possibly, White overlooked that after his P to K 4, Black could check at K 6 and capture that Pawn safely. The position is highly interesting at this point, which forms the crux of the game.

[8] It is necessary to interpose the Rook. Otherwise, 25. Q to B 7, ch, K to R sq ; 28. Q × R, ch, R × Q ; 29. Kt to B 7, ch, regaining the Queen and presumably winning easily

[9] One of the most exciting positions in the Tournament is now presented, Black's weakness of course being the unprotected Rook at King's square. Practically all this is forced. If Black play instead Q × Q, then 30. R × R, ch, K to B 2 ; 31. P × Q and wins.

[10] Whether on its merits White's game is a winning one is a moot point, anyhow the check is not opportune. The impression produced

AUGUST 13

by the latter part of the game is that White a little underestimated his opponent's splendid defensive powers with the material at his disposal. In one word, White probably expected an easy win.

C. Schlechter v. R. Teichmann.

	WHITE	BLACK		WHITE	BLACK
1	P to K 4	P to K 4	16	Q R to Q Kt sq [7]	
2	Kt to K B 3	Kt to Q B 3			B to B 3
3	B to Kt 5	P to Q R 3	17	Kt to Q 5	B × Kt
4	B to R 4	P to Q 3 [1]	18	P × B	Kt to Q 2
5	P to Q 4	P × P [2]	19	B × B	K × B
6	Kt × P	B to Q 2	20	Q R to K sq [8]	P to K B 4
7	Castles	Kt to K B 3	21	R × R [9]	Q × R
8	Kt to Q B 3	B to K 2	22	Q to Q 2	Q to B 2
9	B × Kt [3]	P × B	23	R to K sq	R to K sq
10	P to Q Kt 3	Castles	24	R × R	Q × R
11	B to Kt 2	R to K sq	25	P to Q B 4	Q to K 4
12	P to K B 3 [4]	K B to B sq	26	Kt to K 2	K to B 3
13	Kt (Q 4) to K 2		27	P to K Kt 3	Q to R 8, ch
		P to K Kt 3	28	K to Kt 2	Kt to K 4
14	Kt to Kt 3	B to Kt 2 [5]	29	P to B 4	Kt to B 2 [10]
15	Q to Q 3 [6]	P to Q B 4		Drawn game	

Notes by Dr. Tarrasch

[1] The originator of the defence 3. ... P to Q R 3; and 4. ... P to Q 3 is Alapin.

[2] B to Q 2 is better, in order to keep the point at K 4 as long as possible. The exchange of the Pawn facilitates White's attack.

[3] Preparing for the next move.

[4] White might better perhaps have waited with this and the following move till he was obliged; Q to Q 3, Q R to Q sq, and K R to K sq seem to be correct.

[5] Black has played admirably and nearly equalised matters, and especially paralyses the dangerous opposing Bishop.

[6] The Queen is well placed here; the Pawn at R 6 is attacked, and thus the Rook is kept at home.

[7] This protecting of the Bishop is unnecessary; he might have played at once and continued with 16. Kt to Q 5, and if Kt × Kt, 17. B × B, Kt to B 5 (?) or Kt to Kt 5 (?); 18. Q to B 3.

[8] White has still the better game, but too much has already been exchanged, and the game drifts gradually into a draw.

[9] Kt to K 2, B 4 and K 6 seems stronger.

[10] White could lock up the Queen with Kt to B 3, but would be obliged to set it free again on the next move.

C. von Bardeleben v. J. Mieses.

WHITE	BLACK	WHITE	BLACK
1 P to Q 4	P to Q 4	15 R to B 2	B to R 3
2 Kt to K B 3	Kt to K B 3	16 Q to Q 2	B × B
3 B to B 4	P to K 3	17 Q × B	R to K B sq
4 P to K 3	Kt to K 5[1]	18 Q Kt to Q 2	Castles
5 B to Q 3	Kt to Q 2[2]	19 P to B 4	P to K 4
6 B × Kt	P × B	20 P to Q 5	Q R to K sq
7 K Kt to Q 2	P to K B 4	21 Kt to K 4	Q to B 4
8 P to K B 3[3]	P to K Kt 4[4]	22 Q to R 3[6]	K to Kt 2
9 B to Kt 3	P to B 5	23 K Kt to Q 2	Q to Kt 5
10 K P × P	Kt P × P	24 P to R 3	Q to R 5
11 B × P	Q to B 3	25 R × R	R × R
12 B to K 3	P × P	26 Q to R 4	R to B 2
13 Castles[5]	P to Q Kt 3	27 P to B 5[7]	Kt to Kt sq
14 Kt × P	B to Q R 3	28 Kt to Q 6, ch	Resigns[8]

NOTES BY R. TEICHMANN.

[1] Premature; this move is only good when the Knight can be sufficiently supported on this square. To move a developed Piece twice is, besides, entirely against the minor principles.

[2] But now P to K B 4 would have been more consistent.

[3] Taking immediate advantage of Black's weak play.

[4] An extraordinary conception involving the sacrifice of a Pawn for the sake of a premature and compromising attacking manœuvre.

[5] Now White has a clear Pawn ahead with a splendid development.

[6] Making the most of his strong position and finishing the game in vigorous style.

[7] Against this there is nothing to be done, the loss of the Queen and at least one Piece being threatened at the same time.

[8] Herr Mieses played this and several other games in the Tournament certainly much below his usual strength, which he has shown elsewhere, and in his games with most of the other prize winners.

G. Marco v. I. Gunsberg.

WHITE	BLACK	WHITE	BLACK
1 P to K 4	P to K 4	9 P × P[6]	Kt to B 3[7]
2 K Kt to B 3	Q Kt to B 3	10 R to K sq, ch	B to K 2
3 B to Kt 5	Kt to B 3	11 B to Q B 4[8]	Castles
4 Castles	Kt × P	12 P to Q R 4[8]	P to B 3[9]
5 P to Q 4	P to Q R 3[1]	13 Q × P	Kt × P
6 B to Q 3[2]	P to Q 4	14 B × Kt	P × B
7 P to B 4[3]	Kt × Q P[4]	15 Kt to B 3	B to K 3
8 Kt × Kt[5]	P × Kt	16 B to B 4	Q to Q 2

AUGUST 13

WHITE	BLACK		WHITE	BLACK
17 B to K 5	P to B 3		31 P × P	P × P
18 B to Kt 3	B to B 2		32 Kt to K 4	B to Kt 6
19 Q R to Q sq	K R to Q sq		33 R to Q 2	P to Kt 5
20 P to R 4 [10]	Q R to B sq		34 B to Q 6	B to B 7
			35 B × B ch.	K × B
			36 R to Q 4	P to Kt 6
			37 K to Kt 3	R to R 3
			38 Kt to B 5	R to R 4
			39 Kt to R 4	K to K 3
			40 Kt to B 3	R to R 7
			41 Kt to R 4	K to K 4
			42 R to Kt 4	K to Q 3
			43 P to B 4	K to B 2
			44 P to B 5	K to Q 3
			45 K to R 4	P to Kt 3
			46 P × P	B × P
			47 R to Kt 6, ch	K to K 4
			48 Kt to B 5	R × P
			49 R × P	R × R
21 P to K R 5	B × P [11]		50 Kt × R	K to B 5
22 Q × P ch.	Q × Q		51 Kt to B 5	B to K sq
23 R × Q	B to B 2		52 Kt to K 6, ch	K to K 4
24 R × R	B × R		53 Kt to Kt 7	B to Kt 3
25 B to Q 6	P to R 3		54 K to Kt 3	K to Q 3
26 P to K Kt 4	R to B 3		55 K to B 4	K to K 2
27 B to Kt 3	K to B sq		56 Kt to B 5, ch	B × Kt
28 K to Kt 2	B to B 5		57 K × B	K to B 2
29 R to Q sq	B to K 2		58 K to K 4	
30 P to B 3	P to Q Kt 4		Drawn game.	

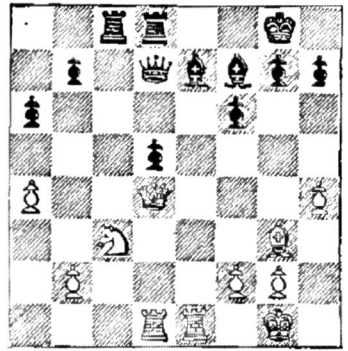

White to make his 21st move.

NOTES BY E. SCHIFFERS.

[1] A move frequently adopted by Morphy.

[2] If B to R 4, then P to Kt 4 and P to Q 4, leading to a known variation of the defence, 3..... P to R 3. 6. B × Kt, P × B, gives an even game.

[3] This line of attack was played by Zukertort in games with Rosenthal and with Winawer.

[4] Rosenthal, in one of the games of his match with Zukertort, played 7. B to K Kt 5. White wins if 7. B to K 3, because then 8. R to K sq.

[5] Stronger play would have been 8. P × P, and if Kt to K B 3; then 9. Kt × P (threatening Q to R 4, ch), Q × P ; 10. Kt to Q B 3, &c.

[6] 9. R to K sq might have been followed by B to K 2 ; 10. B × Kt

(P × P, Kt to B 3), P × B, 11 R × P, P to Q B 4, and Black is a Pawn ahead.

[7] It is evident that Q × P, B × Kt, &c., will not do.

[8] These moves clearly demonstrate the inconsistency of White's attack

[9] P to B 4 was stronger.

[10] White has already lost all attack.

[11] B to B 4 or P to K R 3 would have been better; the Pawn at R 5 remained weak, and Black would not have lost the important Queen's Pawn for it; eventually White very skilfully played for the draw.

H. E. Bird v. B. Vergani.

	WHITE	BLACK		WHITE	BLACK
1	P to K B 4	P to K 3	23	R to Q 2	B × Kt [5]
2	Kt to K B 3	Kt to Q B 3	24	Q P × B	R to B sq
3	P to K 3	P to Q 4	25	R to Q 6	Q to K Kt 3
4	B to Q Kt 5	B to Q 3	26	K R to Q sq	P to K R 3
5	P to Q Kt 3	Kt to K 2	27	Kt × K P	B × Kt
6	B to Kt 2	P to K B 3	28	Q × Q	Kt × Q
7	Castles	Castles	29	R × B	K to B 2
8	Kt to B 3	P to Q R 3	30	R (K 6) to Q 6	
9	B to K 2	B to B 4 [1]			K R to K sq
10	P to Q 4	B to R 2 [2]	31	R to Q 7, ch	R to K 2
11	Q to K sq	Kt to K B 4	32	B to R 3	Q R to K sq
12	Kt to Q sq	Q Kt to K 2	33	B × R	R × B
13	B to Q 3	Kt to Q 3	34	R × R, ch	K × R
14	Kt to K B 2 [3]	P to K B 4	35	K to Kt sq	Kt to B sq
15	P to B 4	Kt to K 5	36	K to B 2	Kt to K 3
16	Kt to R 3	P to Q B 3	37	P to Q Kt 4	P to K Kt 4
17	Kt to K 5	R to K B 3	38	P to K Kt 3	P to K Kt 5
18	R to Q sq [4]	Kt to K Kt 3	39	R to Q 6	P to K R 4
19	B × Kt	Q P × B	40	P to Q Kt 5	P × P
20	K to R sq	Kt to K 2	41	P × P	P × P
21	Q to K Kt 3	Q to K sq	42	R to Kt 6	Resigns.
22	Kt to Kt 5	B to Q Kt sq			

Notes by A. Albin.

[1] Not good; now P to K 4 was the correct move. He would with that obtain the better game.

[2] Again a bad move.

[3] Why not P to Q B 4?

[4] Instead of that P to K Kt 4 is stronger.

[5] Mr Vergani finds very early the only move that loses. Without that a draw would be the probable result.

AUGUST 13

H. N. Pillsbury v. W. Steinitz.

	WHITE	BLACK
1	P to Q 4	P to Q 4
2	P to Q B 4	P to K 3
3	Kt to Q B 3	Kt to K B 3
4	B to Kt 5	P to B 4 [1]
5	B P × P	K P × P
6	B × Kt	P × B [2]
7	P to K 3	B to K 3
8	K Kt to K 2 [3]	Kt to B 3
9	P to K Kt 3	P × P
10	P × P	B to Q Kt 5 [4]
11	B to Kt 2	Q to Kt 3
12	Castles	Castles Q R
13	Kt to R 4	Q to R 3 [5]
14	P to Q R 3	B to Q 3
15	P to Q Kt 4	B to Kt 5
16	Q Kt to B 3 [6]	Kt to K 2
17	P to Kt 5	Q to R 4
18	Q to Kt 3	K to Kt sq
19	P to K R 3	B to K 3
20	P to B 4	P to B 4
21	K R to Q sq	R to Q 2
22	Kt to R 4	R to Q B sq [7]
23	P to Kt 6 [8]	P to Q R 3
24	Kt (K 2) to B 3	R to B 3
25	B to B sq [9]	R to Q sq
26	Kt to R 2	B to Q 2
27	Kt to Kt 4	R (B 3) to B sq
28	Kt to B 3	R to Kt sq [10]
29	K to B 2	P to K R 4 [11]
30	P to K R 4	B × Kt
31	P × B	Q × P (Kt 3)
32	B to K 2 [12]	R to Kt 3
33	Kt × P	Q to K 3 [13]
34	B to B 3	B to B 3

BLACK

Black to make his 28th move.

	WHITE	BLACK
35	R to K sq	B × Kt [14]
36	R × Q	B × Q
37	R × Kt	R to B 7, ch
38	R to K 2	R to B 6
39	Q R to K sq	R to Q Kt 3
40	R to Q 2	R × P
41	P to Q 5	R to B 7
42	R × R	B × R
43	B × P	B to K 5
44	B × P	R to Q 5
45	B to K 6	R to Q 7, ch
46	R to K 2	R to Q 6
47	R to K 3	R to Q 7, ch
48	K to K sq	R to Q 5
49	P to R 5	B × P
50	B × P	B to B 2
51	P to R 6	R to Q sq
52	P to Kt 4	P to R 4
53	P to Kt 5	Resigns.

Notes by I. Gunsberg.

[1] B to K 2 is a preferable move. The text move may almost be described as an oversight.

[2] Black thus early handicaps himself with the most deplorable weakness, almost unpardonable in such an all-important game. We do not wish, however, to be misunderstood as inferring that this is the

necessary consequence of White's move of 4. B to Kt 5, of which we have not a favourable opinion.

[3] There are many delicate considerations which have prompted this move. Firstly, White wished to attack the Queen's Pawn by placing his Bishop on K Kt 2. Secondly, he wants to forestall the possibility of Black disorganising White's centre at any future time by the advance of P to K B 5. Thirdly, he wishes to some extent to support the Queen's side, rendered weak by the absence of the Queen's Bishop.

[4] Why not have followed White's example and played B to Kt 2? This would admit of Castling King's Rook, and of P to B 4, &c., at some future time.

[5] The play of the Queen on the Queen's side has been singularly unfortunate. This only further confirms our impression that Black should not have Castled on the Queen's side.

[6] White fences splendidly, and the text move is certainly preferable to P to B 3.

[7] If Black had played P to Kt 3, it was very difficult to see how he could ever hope to get his Queen into play.

[8] A fearless move which is admirably followed up.

[9] Part of a very interesting plan for manœuvring his Knights. He wants to prevent R to B 5.

[10] We must stop here a moment to examine what would be the line of play if Black had taken the Knight. We, however, must content ourselves with merely roughly indicating the likely course of events, which might be somewhat as follows: B × Kt; 29 P × B, Q × P (Kt 3); 30 P to Kt 5; now it is difficult to see any other move for Black than P × P, upon which follows (see diagram)—

WHITE	BLACK	WHITE	BLACK
31 Kt to R 4	Q to Kt 3	37 R (Q 3) to K 3	K R to K sq
32 Kt to B 5	B to B 3	38 Kt to B 5, ch	K to B 2
33 Q to R 3	R to Kt sq	39 Q to R 5, ch	K to Q 3
34 R to Q 3	K to B 2	40 Q to Kt 4	K to B 2
35 Kt × P	K to Q 2	41 B × P, and White should win	
36 R to K sq	Q to B 3		

[11] This move was ill-advised and helps to lose the game. The Pawn should have been let alone.

[12] White apparently did not, as we thought, place his trust on P to Kt 5, or perhaps it was owing to the fact that White has exposed his King too much to make that manœuvre feasible.

[13] If Black had played Kt × Kt; 34 Q × Kt, Q to Q 3 would have given him considerable defensive chances, even in spite of his luckless Pawn so ill-advisedly advanced to K R 4. Moral: an isolated Rook's Pawn is safest on R 2, and should not be moved except for a very special reason. Curiously enough, in the second game between Pillsbury and Lasker at St Petersburg, Lasker likewise moved an isolated Queen's Rook's Pawn against Pillsbury, and thereby contributed to the loss of the game.

AUGUST 13

[14] There is nothing else to do. And from this point it is all smooth sailing for White, though the tactics by which he scores a win are rather interesting.

Dr. Tarrasch v. E. Schiffers.

	WHITE	BLACK
1	P to K 4	P to K 4
2	Kt to Q B 3	Kt to K B 3
3	P to K B 4	P to Q 4
4	P × K P	Kt × P
5	Kt to B 3	Kt to Q B 3
6	B to Kt 5	B to Q Kt 5
7	Q to K 2	B × Kt
8	Q P × B	Castles
9	B to K B 4	Kt to K 2
10	P to K R 3	Kt to K B 4 [1]
11	R to K Kt sq	Kt (B 4) to Kt 6
12	Q to K 3	P to Q B 3
13	B to Q 3	Kt to K B 4
14	Q to K 2	Q to Kt 3
15	Castles	Kt to B 4
16	P to K Kt 4	Kt to K 2 [2]
17	Q to K sq [3]	Kt to Kt 3 [4]
18	B to K 3	Kt × B, ch
19	P × Kt	Q to R 4
20	K to Kt sq	B to K 3
21	P to Q 4	P to Q B 4
22	P to K R 4 [5]	P to Kt 4
23	P to R 5	Kt to K 2
24	P to R 6	K R to Kt sq [6]
25	R P × P	P to Kt 5
26	B to Q 2	Kt to B 3 [7]

BLACK

WHITE

White to make his 17th move.

	WHITE	BLACK
27	Kt to Kt 5	P to K R 3
28	Kt × B	P × Kt
29	B P × P	Kt × Kt P
30	P to R 3	Q to R 5
31	P × Kt	P × P
32	Q to K 3	P to Kt 6 [8]
33	B to B 3	R to Q B sq [9]
34	K to B sq	R to B 2
35	K to Q 2	Q R to Q B sq
36	Q × P	Resigns

Notes by H. N. Pillsbury.

[1] The manœuvres of the Black Knights on the King's wing lose time and assist the opponent to form his attack on the Black King. 10. P to Q B 3; 11. B to Q 3, Kt to Q B 4, was much better.

[2] If Kt to Q R 5; 17. P to Kt 3, Kt × P; 18. Q to Q 2, Kt × R; 19. P × Kt, Kt to B 7; 20. R × P, ch, K to R sq; 21. P to B 6, Kt to K 5; 22. Q to Kt 2, and mates in a few moves.

[3] Both to prevent Kt to R 5, and with ideas of attack via K R 4 later on. (See diagram.)

[4] To prevent B × P, ch, winning a pawn by Q to R 4, ch, &c. But Kt × B, ch; 18. P × Kt, Q to R 4; 19. K to Kt sq, B to K 3, gave

Black an equal position, with excellent prospects of attack by P to Q Kt 4, &c.

⁵ Both players have obtained formidable Pawn attacks against the adverse Kings, but the bad position of the Black Knight is much to his opponent's advantage; he gains time by attacking it, so that his attack breaks first.

⁶ Obviously if P to Kt 3, 25. Q to R 4, threatening Q to B 6

⁷ Black has no time for R to Kt 3, which is met by 27. P × Kt, P × Kt P; 28. Kt to Kt 5, and if R to R 3, 29. P to Q R 3, Kt to B 3; 30. Q to R 4, with a winning attack for White.

⁸ Nor would 32. R to Q B sq give Black any hope, since White wins by 33. P to Kt 3, Q to R 3 (best); 34. B × P, Q R to Kt sq; 35. Q × P and wins easily.

⁹ A last gasp, but White could even ignore the threat and continue 34. Q × P, Q to R 7, ch, 35. K to B sq, R × B, ch; 36. K to Q 2, Q × P, ch, 37 K to K sq, with an easily won game. Nevertheless, there is no necessity to permit even this.

A. WALBRODT v. S. TINSLEY.

	WHITE	BLACK		WHITE	BLACK
1	P to K 4	P to K 4	20	Q × Kt	B to B sq
2	Kt to K B 3	Kt to K B 3	21	P to Q B 3	P to Q R 4
3	Kt to B 3 ¹	P to Q 3 ²	22	P to Q R 3	Q to B 2
4	P to Q 4	P × P	23	Q to Q 2	R to R sq
5	Kt × P	B to K 2	24	Q to K 2	B to K 3
6	B to K 2	Castles	25	Kt × B	R × Kt
7	Castles	R to K sq	26	P to K Kt 4	P to Kt 3
8	B to Q 3	Kt to B 3	27	R to K Kt sq	P × P
9	Kt × Kt	P × Kt	28	Q × P	K to R sq
10	P to B 4	P to Q 4	29	P to B 5	P × P
11	P to K 5	B to B 4, ch	30	B × P	Q R to K sq
12	K to R sq	Kt to Kt 5	31	B × R	R × B
13	Q to K sq	P to B 4	32	B to K 3	P to R 4
14	Kt to R 4	B to B 7 ³	33	Q to B 4	Q to K 2
15	R × B	Q to R 5	34	Q to B 5	Q to K sq
16	P to Kt 3	Q to K 2	35	R to Kt 5	P to B 4
17	B to K 3	B to K 3	36	R × P, ch	K to Kt 2
18	B to Q 4	Q R to Kt sq	37	Q to R 7, ch	Resigns
19	Kt to B 5	Kt × R, ch			

NOTES BY R. TEICHMANN.

¹ P to Q 4, or Kt × P, gives White a slight advantage. With the text move White turns into quiet variations.

² Making a Philidor's Defence of it. Kt to B 3 is simpler and better.

³ This strange combination loses two Pieces for a Rook, and

AUGUST 13

leaves White with a won game He apparently overlooked White's simple rejoinder P to Kt 3. With B to B sq he would not have had a bad game, in spite of White's passed King's Pawn. The play afterwards is as easy as possible for White, and does not require any comment.

W. H. K. POLLOCK v. E. LASKER.

	WHITE	BLACK		WHITE	BLACK
1	P to K 4	P to K 4	13	Kt to R 3 [5]	P to Q 4 [6]
2	Kt to K B 3	Kt to Q B 3	14	Castles	Kt to Kt 3
3	B to B 4	B to B 4	15	P × P	Kt × P
4	P to Q Kt 4	B to Kt 3 [1]	16	Q to K sq [7]	Q to B 3
5	P to Q B 3	P to Q 3	17	B to Kt 5 [8]	Q to B 4
6	P to Q R 4	P to Q R 3	18	Kt to B 2 (?)	Kt × P
7	P to R 5	B to R 2	19	R × B [9]	B × Kt
8	P to Kt 5	P × P	20	Kt to K 3 [10]	Q × B
9	B × P	Kt to B 3 [2]	21	R × R	R × R
10	P to R 6 [3]	Castles [4]	22	Q × Kt	Kt to B 5
11	P to Q 3	Kt to K 2	23	R to R sq	Kt to K 7, ch
12	P × P	B × P		White resigns.	

NOTES BY DR. TARRASCH.

[1] It is noteworthy that Lasker usually declines the Evans' Gambit, although he has declared that he knows a winning defence.

[2] Kt to K 2 seems preferable.

[3] Instead of developing, White makes premature attempts at attack, which finally only facilitate and hasten the development of his opponent.

[4] Kt × P would be bad, on account of 11. Q to R 4, Kt to B 4; 12. P × P.

[5] B × P, ch, was threatened.

[6] Black is so far advanced in development that he can at once begin the attack.

[7] All of White's Pieces are in bad positions, with the exception of the King's Knight at B 3. White's game is thus no longer capable even of defence.

[8] With this and the mistake immediately following the Bishop gets also exposed. It would have been better to interrupt the file of the adverse Queen's Bishop with Kt to Kt 5 and K 4.

[9] He may well despair.

[10] After B to K 3, Q to Kt 5 wins.

J. H. BLACKBURNE v. A. ALBIN

	WHITE	BLACK		WHITE	BLACK
1	P to K 4	P to K 4	4	Castles	Kt to Q B 3 [2]
2	B to K 2 [1]	B to B 4	5	P to B 3	B to Kt 3 [3]
3	Kt to K B 3	P to Q 3	6	P to Q 4	Q to K 2

116 THE HASTINGS CHESS TOURNAMENT

WHITE	BLACK
7 Kt to R 3	Kt to B 3
8 P to Q 5	Kt to Q sq
9 Q to B 2	P to K R 3 [4]
10 Kt to B 4	Kt to R 2
11 P to Q R 4 (!)	
	P to Q B 3
12 Kt × B	P × Kt
13 B to K 3	P to Q B 4
14 Kt to Q 2	P to K Kt 4
15 Kt to B 4	Q to B 2
16 P to Q Kt 4	R to Q Kt sq
17 K R to Q Kt sq	
	Kt to K B 3
18 P to R 5	P to Kt 4 [5]
19 Kt to R 3	B to Q 2
20 Kt × P	B × Kt
21 B × B, ch	K to B sq
22 P × P	P × P
23 B to K 2	R to R sq
24 R to Kt 5	P to Kt 3
25 P to R 6	Kt to Q 2
26 Q to Kt 2	P to B 4

BLACK

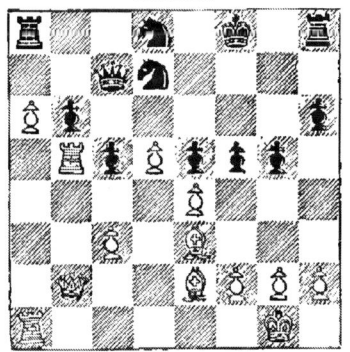

WHITE

White to make his 27th move.

27 P to B 3 [6]	P to K B 5
28 B to B 2	Kt to B 2
29 R to Kt 3	Kt to Q 3
30 K R to R 3	R to Q R 2
31 B to Kt 5	Kt × B

WHITE	BLACK
32 Q × Kt	K to K 2
33 Q to B 6	Q to Q 3
34 R to Kt 3	R to B 2
35 Q to Kt 5	R to Q R 2
36 K to B sq	P to R 4
37 K to K 2	P to R 5
38 P to R 3	R to Q B sq
39 R to Kt 2	K to B 2
40 K to Q 3	K to Kt 3
41 K to B 4	K to R 4
42 B to K sq	K R to B 2
43 Q R to Kt sq	R to B sq
44 B to B 2	K R to B 2
45 K to Q 3	Q to Kt 3
46 K to B 2	Q to Q 3
47 Q to K 2	K to R 3
48 K to B sq	R to B sq
49 Q to Kt 5	K to R 4
50 P to B 4	K R to B 2
51 B to K sq	R to R sq
52 B to B 3	Q R to R 2
53 R to Kt 3	R to B sq
54 Q to R 4	K R to B 2
55 Q to R sq	R to B sq
56 K to B 2	K R to Q R sq
57 R to R 3	Q to B 2
58 R to Kt 2	Q to B sq
59 Q R to R 2	Q to B 2
60 Q to Kt 2	Q to Q 3
61 R to Kt 3	R to Q B sq
62 R to R 4	R (B sq) to Q R [sq]
63 K to Q 2	R to K sq
64 R to R sq	R (K sq) to Q R [sq]
65 K to K 2	R to Q B sq
66 R to R 4	R (Q B sq) to Q R sq
67 K to Q sq	R to Q B sq
68 K to B sq	R (B sq) to Q R [sq]
69 K to Kt sq	R to Q B sq
70 K to B 2	R (B sq) to Q R [sq]
71 R (Kt 3) to R 3	R to Q B sq [7]
72 Q to Kt 5	K to Kt 3

AUGUST 13

	WHITE	BLACK
73	R to Kt 3	K to R 4
74	R to R sq	K to Kt 3
75	R (R sq) to Q Kt sq	
		K to R 4
76	Q to R 4	R (B sq) to B 2
77	R (Kt sq) to Kt 2	
		R to B sq [sq
78	Q to R sq	R (B sq) to Q R
79	R to R 2	R to Q Kt sq
80	Q to Kt 2	K to Kt 3
81	R to R sq	K to R 4
82	R to Q Kt sq	R (Kt sq) to Q [R sq (?) 8

BLACK

White to make his 83rd move.

83	R × P	Kt × R
84	Q × Kt	R × P
85	Q × Q	R × Q
86	R to Kt 5	R to R 7, ch
87	B to Kt 2	R (Q 3) to Q R 3
88	K to Kt 3	R (R 3) to R 4

	WHITE	BLACK
89	B × P	R (R 7) to R 6,
90	K to B 2	R to K 6 [ch
91	K to Q 2	R to R 5
92	R to Kt 6	R to R 7, ch
93	B to Kt 2	R (K 6) to R 6
94	K to B 2	R to R 3
95	R to Kt 5	R (R 7) to R 4
96	R to Kt 8	R to R sq
97	R to Kt 3	R (R 4) to R 3
98	P to K 5	K to Kt 3
99	R to Kt 5	R to Q B sq
100	R to Kt 7	R (B sq) to Q R
101	P to K 6	R to K sq [sq
102	R to Kt 5	R to Q B sq
103	K to Kt 3	K to B 4
104	B to R 3	R (B sq) to Q R
105	B to Kt 2	R to R 4 [sq
106	R to Kt 6	R (R 4) to R 3
107	R × R	R × R
108	B to R 3	R to R 4
109	P to K 7	R to R sq
110	B × P	K to B 3
111	P to Q 6	K to K 3
112	B to Kt 4	K to Q 2
113	P to B 5	K to B 3
114	K to B 4	R to Q Kt sq
115	B to R 3	R to Q R sq
116	K to Q 4	K to Q 2
117	B to Kt 4	R to Q Kt sq
118	K to Q 5	R to Kt 4
119	B to B 3	P to Kt 5
120	R P × P	P to R 6
121	P × P	R to Kt 8
122	P to B 6, ch	K to K sq
123	P to Q 7, ch	Resigns.

NOTES BY C. VON BARDELEBEN.

[1] This opening is irregular, and no chess-book as yet has analysed it. I think the best answer of Black is Kt to K B 3.

[2] If now Kt to K B 3, White plays 5. P to B 3 (!), and the King's Pawn cannot be taken because of 6. Q to R 4, ch.

[3] P to Q R 3 would be preferable, in order to preserve the important King's Bishop. Compare the 12th move.

[4] Now, again, he should have played P to Q R 3.

[5] If Q Kt P × P (?), White plays 19. P × Q B P, P × P ; 20. R to Kt 6, Q to K 2 ; 21. P to Q 6.

[6] A weak move, which enables Black to secure his position. White should have played 27. P × P, Kt to B 2 ; 28. R to Kt 3, Kt to Q 3 ; 29. P to Kt 4, and would have thus obtained the superior game.

[7] Obviously Albin does not know the English rule, that a game is drawn if the same move is made three times, otherwise he would not have continued this dull game.

[8] A blunder which throws away the game ; he ought to have played K to Kt 3, and then it was a clear draw.

[Albin was perfectly acquainted with the rule, which, however, requires that the same position should occur three times to secure a draw, and Blackburne took care that this should not happen. Blackburne, nevertheless, had his little joke, for, finding it necessary to repeat a position, he took care to reverse the Rooks, thus inventing a nice little puzzle for the Committee (in the event of its coming up a third time) as to whether the positions were the same in the meaning of the rule, though the King's Rook and Queen's Rook *had changed places.*

It is probable that the legitimate result of the end game was a draw, but as White, with a Pawn ahead, was contemplating several different winning sacrifices, it was difficult, even if possible, to avoid them all, and he may have thought the one made unsound.—ED.]

A. BURN *v.* M. TCHIGORIN.

	WHITE	BLACK
1	P to Q 4	P to Q 4
2	P to Q B 4	P to K 3
3	Kt to Q B 3	Kt to K B 3
4	Kt to B 3	P to B 3 [1]
5	P to K 3	B to Q 3
6	B to Q 3	Q Kt to Q 2
7	Castles	Castles
8	B to Q 2 [2]	R to K sq
9	Q to B 2	P to K R 3
10	Q R to Q sq [3]	Q to B 2
11	R to Q B sq	Q to Kt sq [4]
12	K R to K sq [5]	P × P
13	B × P	P to K 4
14	P to K Kt 3	Kt to Kt 3
15	B to B sq	B to K Kt 5
16	Kt to K R 4 [6]	P to K 5
17	B to K 2	Q to B sq
18	Q to Q sq	B × B
19	Q × B	P to K Kt 4
20	Kt to Kt 2	Q to R 6
21	P to B 3	P × P
22	Q × P	Kt to Kt 5

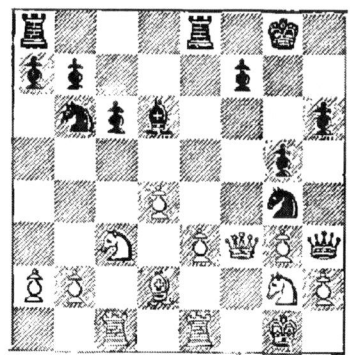

BLACK

WHITE

White to make his 23rd move.

AUGUST 13

WHITE	BLACK	WHITE	BLACK
23 Kt to K 4 [7]	R × Kt [8]	44 Q to R 3	P to Kt 5
24 Q × R	Q × P, ch [9]	45 Q to K 3	Q to Q 3
25 K to B sq	Q × P	46 P to Q 5 [13]	Q × Q P
26 K to K 2 [10]	Kt to B 7 [11]	47 Q to B 4	P to K R 4
27 Q to B 5	Q × Kt	48 R to K B sq	K to Kt 3
28 R to K Kt sq	Q to K 5	49 Q to Kt 8	R to Q sq
29 Q × Kt	Kt to Q 4	50 Q to B 4	R to K sq
30 K R to B sq	Q to Kt 3	51 R to Q B 2	Q to K 4
31 K to Q sq	R to K sq	52 Q to B sq	P to R 5
32 R to B 2	R to K 2	53 R to R sq	P to R 6
33 K to B sq	B to Kt 5	54 R to B 8	R × R
34 R to K sq	Q to K 5	55 Q × R	Kt to B 3
35 P to R 3	B × B, ch	56 Q to B 2	Q to K 5
36 R × B	P to K B 4	57 Q to R 2	P to B 5
37 Q R to K 2	K to Kt 2	58 R to K Kt sq	P to B 6
38 Q to R 2	Kt to B 3	59 Q to Kt 3 [14]	Q to K 7
39 K to Q 2	P to B 4	60 R to K sq	Q to Kt 7
40 K to B sq [12]	P × P	61 Q to Q 6	P to B 7
41 P × P	Q to B 3, ch	62 Q to Q 3, ch	Kt to K 5
42 K to Kt sq	Kt to K 5	63 R × Kt	P to B 8 (Q), ch
43 K to R sq	R to Q 2	White resigns.	

NOTES BY J. H. BLACKBURNE.

[1] A defence very often adopted at the present time, the idea being to break up the centre, later on, by P to K 4.

[2] The masters of fifty years ago or more considered the Bishop better posted here than on Q Kt 2, and a few of the present masters are inclined to agree with them

[3] This turns out a lost move. K R to K sq, intending P to K 4, is good, or perhaps better still is P × P, followed by R to Q B sq.

[4] To prevent P × Q P when Pawn plays to K 4.

[5] Better to have exchanged Pawns before this move

[6] Kt × P would have led to a perfectly even game. The move made allows Black to obtain the better, if not a winning, position.

[7] This is all very ingenious, but of no avail (see diagram).

[8] This is the winning move, but almost forced, as White threatened Q × Kt followed by Kt to B 6, ch, regaining the Queen, with a winning advantage.

[9] Here he does not take full advantage of his position. He ought to have played Kt to Q 4. For example . 24 Kt to Q 4 ; 25. B to B 3, Kt (Q 4) to B 3 ; 26. Q to B 3, Kt to R 4 ; 27. K R to Q sq, Kt × R P, 28. Q to B 2, B × P, and wins in a few more moves. White may also play : 25. K R to Q sq, Q × P, ch ; 26 K to B sq, Kt (Kt 5) to B 3, 27. Q to B 5, B × P ; 28. Kt to K sq, Kt to B 5, and mate follows in two or three moves.

[10] This ought to have lost right off, R to K 2 was the only possible chance of escaping.

[11] The play hereabout is of a most extraordinary character, and unaccountable; unless—which is very probable—both players were pressed for time. It will be seen that the simple move of Q to B 7, ch, and no matter where the King moves, Kt plays to B 3, winning at least a Piece.

[12] The reply to P × P would be Q to Q B 5.

[13] Doubtless the game is gone, but still this Pawn ought not to have been given up without a struggle.

[14] It is obvious that Q × P is useless on account of P to B 7.

Photo., Bradshaw, Hastings

M. Tchigorin

AUGUST 14.

The only exciting thing in the pairing to-day is at Board No. 1, for Tchigorin has five wins and a winning adjourned game, and if he can beat Blackburne he secures Mr. Bradshaw's special prize. But the play contains many surprises; Schlechter plays one of his phenomenal games, and sacrifices Pieces enough to please the most reckless. Vergani makes his first score against Marco, the pigmy against the giant, the most unequal-looking contest in the Tournament. Lasker again scored first win. Bardeleben by drawing gave Tchigorin his first real lead.

M. Tchigorin v. J. H. Blackburne.

	WHITE	BLACK		WHITE	BLACK
1	P to K 4	P to K 3	23	R to Q 2	P to Q R 4
2	Q to K 2 [1]	P to Q Kt 3 [2]	24	R to K sq	Q to B sq
3	P to K Kt 3	B to Kt 2	25	P to Q B 4 [7]	P to B 4
4	B to Kt 2	B to K 2	26	Q R to K 2	B to B 2
5	P to Q 3	P to K B 4	27	B to Q 2	Q R to B 2
6	Kt to K R 3	Kt to K B 3	28	B to B 3	R to B 4
7	Kt to B 3	Castles	29	R to K B sq [8]	Q to Q sq
8	Castles	P × P [3]			
9	Kt × P	Kt × Kt			
10	B × Kt	B × B			
11	Q × B	Kt to B 3			
12	Kt to B 4	B to Q 3 [4]			
13	Kt × P	P × Kt			
14	Q × Kt	Q to B 3			
15	Q to K 4	Q R to K sq			
16	P to Q B 3 [5]	P to K 4			
17	B to K 3	R to K 2			
18	Q R to K sq [6]	K to R sq			
19	K to Kt 2	Q to B 2			
20	P to Q R 3	Q to R 4			
21	P to R 3	Q to K sq			
22	R to K 2	Q to Q 2			

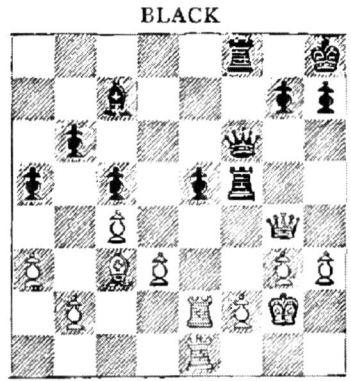

BLACK

WHITE

White to make his 32nd move.

	WHITE	BLACK		WHITE	BLACK
30	K R to K sq	Q to Kt 4		WHITE	BLACK
31	Q to Kt 4	Q to B 3 [9]	44	P to Kt 3	R to Q 5
32	P to B 4 [10]	Q to B 3, ch	45	K × P	P × P
33	Q to B 3	Q × Q, ch	46	K × P	P to Kt 7
34	K × Q	R to Q sq [11]	47	R to Kt 3	R to Q 6
35	B × K P [12]	B × B	48	R to Kt 7, ch	K to B 3
36	R × B	R × Q P, ch	49	R × Q Kt P	R × Kt P [14]
37	R (K sq) to K 3		50	P to Q R 4	R × P
		R × R, ch	51	P to R 5	R to Q R 6
38	K × R	R to B sq	52	K to Kt 6	P to R 4
39	R to K 6	R to Q Kt sq	53	P to Q B 5	K to K 2
40	K to K 4	K to Kt sq	54	P to B 6	K to Q sq
41	K to Q 5	K to B 2	55	K to Kt 7	R to Q B 6
42	R to K 3 [13]	P to R 5	56	P to R 6	Resigns.
43	K to B 6	R to Q sq			

NOTES BY W. STEINITZ.

[1] Mr. Tchigorin considers this the strongest continuation in the French defence. Having adopted it first in his match against Dr. Tarrasch, he has faithfully adhered to his innovation, and, especially in this Tournament, with great success. It is difficult to pass judgment on such a move, but I am inclined to believe that its first effect, namely, of delaying the advance of the adverse Queen's Pawn (in which case White gains a move by P × P, followed by Q Kt to B 3), is at least neutralised by the restriction placed on his King's Bishop.

[2] The order of development which I would select for Black would be P to Q B 4, Q Kt to B 3, P to Q 3, K Kt to B 3, B to K 2, and Castles, after which P to Q 4 will give the second player a strong attack.

[3] He is bound to unlock the position, for White threatens to do so by P × P with a slight advantage.

[4] White's Queen had a more free field, but this was not impressive, and altogether the game was even up to this blunder, which loses an important Pawn.

[5] Neglect on both sides. Black should have played P to Q B 4 or P to K 4 ere now, and White ought to have advanced P to Q 4 at this point, with the view of pushing it further to Q 5 if then attacked by P to K 4, thus establishing the majority of Pawns on the Queen's wing.

[6] White finds it difficult now to make his superiority of Pawns effective, and his shifting forces on the centre files turn out of no use. The better plan was anyhow, P to Q Kt 4, followed by P to Q R 4 and R 5, after which he could, according to circumstances, either press the attack further on the Queen's wing by Q to R 7, or else by doubling Rooks on the Queen's Rook file preliminary to exchanging Pawns.

[7] White is getting impatient and forms another plan, which is suffering from the drawback that his Queen's Pawn is left very weak,

⁸ The play on both sides, as well as the number of moves, indicate time pressure.

⁹ This looks feasible, but is fraught with disaster. Q to Q sq or Q to R 3 would have maintained the balance of positions in spite of the adverse Pawn ahead.

¹⁰ With keen insight White grasps the situation.

¹¹ Black perceives too late that if 34. ... P × P ; 35. R to K 7, P × P, ch ; 36. K to Kt 2, R to B 7, ch ; 37. K to Kt sq, B to Q sq ; 38. B × P, ch, K to Kt sq ; 39. B × R, and wins. However, the text move should also lose straight off.

¹² Of course good enough, but still better was evidently K to K 4, which gave him two clear Pawns ahead.

¹³ Time pressure may have influenced the play here. The retreat was unnecessary, while P to Q R 4 reduced chances of prolongation.

¹⁴ Certainly ill-judged. If he meant to go on at all the Rook's Pawn was the most dangerous and should have been captured. White was bound to lose another Pawn afterwards, and there was some more room for fight, though, no doubt, by proper play the result could not be altered.

J Mason v. A Burn

	WHITE	BLACK		WHITE	BLACK
1	P to Q B 4	P to K 3	18	B to Kt 5	B to K 2
2	P to K 3	P to Q 4	19	Q R to Q sq⁴	P to Q R 3
3	Kt to K B 3	Kt to K B 3	20	R to Q 3	R to Q B sq
4	Kt to Q B 3	B to K 2	21	R to B 3	Kt × Kt
5	P to Q 4	Castles	22	R × Q Kt (B 3)⁵	
6	B to Q 3	P to Q B 4			Q × P⁶
7	P × Q P	B P × P	23	Kt × B P	Kt to K 5
8	K P × P¹	Kt × P	24	B to K 3	R × R
9	Castles	Kt to Q B 3	25	Kt to R 6, ch	K to B sq
10	R to K sq	Q Kt to Kt 5²	26	Q × P	Q to Kt 2
11	B to Kt sq	Kt (Q 4) to B 3	27	P × R⁷	B to Q 3
12	P to Q R 3	Kt (Kt 5) to Q 4	28	Q to R 3	Kt × Q B P⁸
13	Q to Q 3	P to K Kt 3	29	B to Kt 3⁹	B to B 5
14	B to R 2	P to Kt 3	30	K to B sq¹⁰	P to R 4
15	Kt to K 5	B to Kt 2	31	B to Q B 4¹¹	P to Q Kt 4¹²
16	B to R 6	R to K sq	32	B to B 5, ch	Resigns.
17	Q to R 3³	B to K B sq			

NOTES BY H. N. PILLSBURY

¹ There is nothing to fear from isolating his Queen's Pawn, and moreover his Pieces are given increased freedom of action.

² The object of the Knight's moves is to keep the adverse Pawn isolated, and at the same time prevent any direct attack upon the King, but they permit the entrance of the White Knight at K 5, where it cannot be easily dislodged. Black could not play P to Q Kt 3

without loss by 11. Kt × Kt, Q × Kt (best) ; 12. B to K 4, Q to Q 3 ; 13. Q to B 2, Kt to Kt 5 ; 14. Q to Kt sq, winning a Pawn at least ; but 10. Kt × Kt ; 11. P × Kt, P to Q Kt 3 ; 12. Q to K 2, B to Kt 2 ; 13. Q to K 4, P to K Kt 3, was not very dangerous for Black, and preferable to the text, which allows too strong an attack.

[3] Threatening Kt × B P

[4] The sacrifice would not be sound at this point . e.g. 19. Kt × B P, K × Kt ; 20. Q × K P, ch, K to Kt 2 ; 21. Kt × Kt, Kt × Kt (best) ; 22. B × Kt, B × B ; 23. Q to K 5, ch, K to B 2, and will win.

[5] White can now win by 22 Kt × B P, K × Kt , 23. Q × K P, ch, K to Kt 2 , 24. Q to B 7, ch, K to R sq ; 25. R × B, and wins ; or if 22 Q × Q P ; 23. P × Kt, Q to K Kt 5 ; 24. Kt to R 6, ch, and wins.

[6] B to Q 4 was imperative now, and gave Black a good game.

[7] Kt to B 5 is met by R × B, and Black would win.

[8] B to Q B sq gave Black some hope , the text move should lose at once.

[9] 29. Kt to B 5 wins here in all variations.

[10] If now, 30. Kt to B 5, Kt to K 7, ch ; 31. K to R sq, P × Kt ; 32. B × B, Black obtains a winning superiority by B × P, ch, &c.

[11] Again Kt to B 5 wins, if in reply B to R 3, ch , 32. K to Kt sq, Kt to K 7, ch ; 33 K to R sq, P × Kt ; 34. Q × P, ch, K to K 2 ; 35. B × B, and must win ; and if Black in this variation 33. Queen moves anywhere ; 34. Q to R 6, ch, forcing mate in a few moves.

[12] Of course a frightful error, which loses at once.

R. Teichmann v D. Janowski.

	WHITE	BLACK		WHITE	BLACK
1	P to Q 4	P to Q 4	20	R to B 3	R to Q sq [7]
2	P to Q B 4	P to K 3	21	P to K R 3	Q to Q Kt 5
3	Kt to Q B 3	Kt to K B 3	22	R to B 2	Q to K 8, ch
4	B to B 4 [1]	B to K 2	23	K to R 2	Q to K 4, ch
5	P to K 3	Castles	24	P to Kt 3	P to K Kt 3
6	Kt to B 3	P to B 4 [2]	25	B to B 4	R to Q 2
7	P × B P	B × P [3]	26	R to K 2	Q to Q 5
8	P × P	P × P	27	R to B 2	K to Kt 2
9	B to Q 3	Kt to B 3	28	B to B sq	R to Q 4
10	Castles	B to K Kt 5	29	B to Kt 2	R to Q B 4 [8]
11	R to B sq	P to Q 5 [4]	30	Q to K 2	P to Kt 3
12	Kt to Q Kt 5 [5]	B to Kt 3	31	R to Q 2	R to K 4
13	Q Kt × Q P	Kt × Kt	32	Q to Q sq	Q to Q Kt 5
14	P × Kt	Q to Q 4 [6]	33	P to R 3	Q to K 2
15	B to K 5	Q R to B sq	34	Q to B 2	P to K R 4
16	Q to K 2	B × P	35	B to B 3	R to Q B 4
17	B × B	B × Kt	36	Q to Q 3	P to R 5 [9]
18	Q × B	R × R	37	K to Kt 2	R to K Kt 4
19	R × R	Q × B	38	Q to Q 4	P × P

WHITE	BLACK	WHITE	BLACK
39 P × P	Q to K 8	50 R × R	K × R
40 R to K B 2	R to K 4	51 K to Kt 5	Kt to K 5, ch
41 B to K 2	Q to R 4	52 K to B 4	Kt to B 4
42 B to B 4	R to K B 4	53 B to B 2	P to B 3
43 R to K 2	Q to B 4	54 P to Kt 4	Kt to K 3, ch
44 Q × Q	R × Q	55 K to K 4	K to Q 3
45 B to Kt 3	K to B sq	56 B to Kt 3	Kt to B 2
46 P to Kt 4	P to K Kt 4	57 B to B 4	K to K 2
47 K to Kt 3	R to B 2	58 K to Q 4	K to Q 3
48 P to K R 4 [10]	P × P, ch	59 K to K 4	Kt to K sq
49 K × P	R to K 2	Drawn game.	

Notes by I. Gunsberg.

[1] May we reiterate the fact that we look upon the Bishop's move with indifference?

[2] Circumstances alter cases. There is no reason why Black should rush on voluntarily to isolate his Pawn. He might play P to Q Kt 3 first, and we also think that when White has played B to B 4 some of the objections against the move of P to Q B 3 fall away, as a premium, so to speak, is placed on Black's chance of playing P to K 4, which, of course, is only possible in connection with P to Q B 3.

[3] P × P for Black does not look wholesome, though perhaps with careful play not much harm would result: e.g. P × P ; 8. B to Q 6, Kt to K sq ; 9. B × B, Q × B ; 10 Q to Q 4, &c.

[4] B to Kt 3 was requisite.

[5] A very effective move, which could not be met by Q to Kt 3, on account of B to B 7.

[6] B × P would not do, on account of White's reply, B × P, ch. If, however, Black had played B × Kt ; 15. Q × B, Q × P, White would be likely to get up a harassing attack with his Queen's Bishop and Rook somewhat as follows : 16. R to B 4, Q × Kt P ; 17. B to Kt 5, B to Q sq ; 18. R to K R 4, and so on. If in this variation Black on the fourteenth move, instead of Q × P, played B × P, he will likewise subject himself to the harassing action of the two Bishops, beginning with White's 16. B to Kt 5.

[7] Black has managed matters cleverly so far, having got rid of White's Bishops. R to Q sq is also a clever move, for if White plays Q × P, Black replies Kt to K 5.

[8] If R to K B 4, White plays 30. Q to K 3, though there would be no harm either in 30. Q × Kt P, or Q to K 2.

[9] A praiseworthy attempt to infuse some life into the game. If White had taken the Pawn Black did not stand to lose the draw, but he might possibly have obtained attacking chances.

[10] The game is gradually drifting towards the inevitable draw, though the conduct of play has been careful and sound on both sides If White plays 48. R to K 5, R to K 2 ; 49 R to K B 5, R to K 6, ch, &c.

C. Schlechter v. C. von Bardeleben.

	WHITE	BLACK		WHITE	BLACK
1	P to K 4	P to K 4	11	P × Kt	B × P
2	Kt to K B 3	Kt to Q B 3	12	P to Q 5[4]	P to Q B 4[5]
3	B to Kt 5	P to Q R 3	13	Kt to K 4	B × P
4	B to R 4	Kt to B 3	14	B × B	Kt × B
5	Kt to B 3[1]	B to B 4	15	Q to R 5	Kt × B
6	Kt × P[2]	Kt × Kt	16	P to B 5	P to K B 3
7	P to Q 4	B to Q 3	17	R to B 4	Q to K sq
8	Castles	Castles	18	Kt × K B P,ch	P × Kt
9	P to K B 4[3]	Q Kt to B 5	19	Q to Kt 4, ch	K to R sq
10	P to K 5	B to K 2	20	R to K 4	Q to B 2
			21	Q R to K sq	P to Q 3
			22	R to K 7	B to Q 2[6]
			23	R × Q	R × R
			24	R to K 6[7]	R to Kt 2
			25	Q to R 4	B × R
			26	Q P × B	Kt to Kt 3
			27	Q × B P	Kt to Q 4
			28	Q to Kt 2	K to Kt sq[8]
			29	P to B 6	Kt × P[9]
			30	Q × Kt	R to K B sq
			31	Q to R 4	R to K sq
			32	Q to B 6	R to K B sq
			33	Q to R 4	R to K sq
			34	Q to B 6	

BLACK

White to make his 12th move.

Drawn game.

NOTES BY E. LASKER.

[1] 5. Castles followed by 6. P to Q 4 seems to take better advantage of the useless advance of the Black Queen's Rook's Pawn.

[2] The only feasible continuation that promises attack. If, for instance, 6. Castles, P to Q 3 ; 7. P to Q 3, P to Q Kt 4 ; 8. B to Kt 3, B to K Kt 5, Black will certainly not have the worst of the position.

[3] This early advance strains the position to an extent which is not justified by the disposition of forces. It would have been simpler and far preferable to take the Knight immediately, and then to continue by Q to Q 3.

[4] White's game is now anything but comfortable. Black will be first to take the open King file with his Rooks in the ordinary course of events ; for instance :—

12	Kt to Q 5	P to Q Kt 4	15	B × Kt	P × B
13	B to Kt 3	B to Kt 2	16	B to K 3	K R to K sq
14	Kt × B, ch	Q × Kt	17	Q to Q 2	B to K 5, &c.

and will then, of course, have everything his own way, the advance of the King's Bishop's Pawn having left that file very weak. White therefore prefers to run great risks in order to be able to assume the attack.

⁵ He threatens now 13. ... B × Kt ; 14. P × B, P to Q Kt 4 ; 15. B to Kt 3, Kt to Kt 3, &c., and if 13. B to Kt 3, Kt to Q 3 ; 14. P to Q R 4, P to B 5 , 15. B to R 2, P to Q Kt 4.

⁶ Perfectly incomprehensible. So far he has correctly met the attack and need only remove his Queen to Kt sq to earn the reward for his circumspect play ; e.g. :—

	WHITE	BLACK		WHITE	BLACK
22		Q to Kt sq	25	Q R to K 7	R × R
23	Q × Kt	B × P	26	R × R	Q × P
24	R × P	Q R to K sq			

and should win ; or 23. Q to R 3, Kt to Kt 3, threatening Kt × P or Kt to Q 2 and K 4 with the same result. It must be admitted, however, that even in the text variation White's play to draw is exceedingly difficult to find.

⁷ A very interesting manœuvre. The Rook must eventually be taken, as otherwise the Queen's Pawn would fall. The passed Pawn at K 6 which White thus obtains is quite a compensation for the exchange sacrificed.

⁸ He has nothing else. 28. ... R to K B sq would have been answered by 29. P to K 7, Kt × P ; 30. P to B 6.

⁹ Of course the only alternative open to him, as otherwise he would have to lose one of his Rooks. The game is now perfectly equalised, and legitimately ends in a draw.

I. GUNSBERG *v.* J. MIESES.

	WHITE	BLACK		WHITE	BLACK
1	P to K 4	P to K 4	17	Castles Q R	P to Q R 4
2	P to K B 4	B to B 4	18	P to Q R 4	Q to R 6, ch [4]
3	Q Kt to B 3	P to Q 3	19	K to Kt sq	Kt to Kt 3
4	Kt to B 3	Q Kt to B 3	20	B to B sq	Q to Kt 5
5	B to Kt 5 [1]	B to K Kt 5 [2]	21	P to R 4	R to Kt sq
6	P × P	P × P	22	P to R 5	Kt to B 5
7	B × Kt, ch	P × B	23	B × Kt	P × B
8	Q to K 2	Kt to K 2	24	Q × P	B to B 4 [5]
9	P to K R 3	B × Kt	25	Q to K 5	B to K 2
10	Q × B	Castles	26	Q to Q 4	Q to R 6
11	P to K Kt 4	Kt to Kt 3	27	Q to Kt 2	Q to Q 3
12	Kt to K 2	Q to K 2	28	P to R 6	P × P
13	P to Q 3	Kt to R 5 [3]	29	Kt to Q 4	B to B 3
14	Q to Kt 3	Q R to Kt sq	30	Kt to B 5 [6]	B × Q
15	P to Kt 3	Q R to Q sq	31	Kt × Q	P × Kt
16	B to Q 2	B to Kt 3	32	K × B	K to Kt 2

BLACK

White to make his 30th move.

	WHITE	BLACK
33	R to R 5	R to Kt sq
34	R (Q sq) to K R sq	K to B 3
35	R × P, ch	R to Kt 3
36	R × P	R to K B sq
37	R (R7) to R 5	P to B 4
38	R to Q 5	K to K 3
39	P to Kt 5	R (B sq) to K Kt sq
40	R to R 6	R (Kt sq) to Kt 2
41	K to B 3	R to Kt sq
42	P to Q 4	R to Q B sq
43	P × P	P × P
44	K to B 4	K to K 2
45	R × R	P × R
46	R × P	Resigns.

NOTES BY R. TEICHMANN.

[1] This seems to be good enough; but Black can avoid this variation by developing his King's Knight first, after which White has no better move than B to B 4.

[2] Kt to K B 3 followed by Castling was better.

[3] Apparently with a view to preventing Kt to Kt 3 and B 5, and stopping the advance of the King's Rook's Pawn; but the Knight cannot be maintained in this awkward position.

[4] Entirely futile, the White King's position being impregnable. He had, however, no satisfactory defence against the threatened King's side attack and therefore counter-attack *à tout prix*.

[5] B to Q 5 would in my opinion have given him a better chance.

[6] White has played the whole game very well, and forces now an end game which must be won with ordinary care (see diagram).

B. VERGANI v. G. MARCO.

	WHITE	BLACK		WHITE	BLACK
1	P to K 4	P to K 4	11	B to Kt 3	Q to K 2
2	Kt to K B 3	Kt to Q B 3	12	Kt to Kt 5 [2]	P to R 3
3	B to B 4	B to B 4	13	Kt × B	P × Kt
4	P to Q 3	P to Q 3	14	Castles	K to R 2
5	B to K 3	B to K Kt 5 [1]	15	P to K B 4 [3]	K P × P
6	Q Kt to Q 2	B to Kt 3	16	R × P	P to Kt 3 (!)
7	P to Q B 3	Kt to B 3	17	Q to Q 2 [4]	Kt to K R 4
8	Kt to B sq	Castles	18	R × R	R × R
9	B × B	R P × B	19	Kt to Kt 4	Kt to B 5
10	Kt to K 3	B to K 3	20	K to R sq	Q to Kt 4

AUGUST 14

BLACK

WHITE

White to make his 21st move.

WHITE	BLACK
21 P to K Kt 3 [5]	Q × Kt
22 P × Kt	R × P
23 R to K Kt sq [6]	
	Q to B 6, ch
24 Q to Kt 2	Q × Q, ch
25 K × Q	R to Kt 5, ch
26 K to B 2	R × R
27 K × R	Kt to Q sq [7]
28 K to B 2	K to Kt 2
29 P to Q 4	K to B 3
30 K to Kt 3	P to Q Kt 4 [8]
31 B to B 2	P to Kt 5 (?) [9]
32 P × P	Kt to B 3
33 P to Kt 5	Kt × P

WHITE	BLACK
34 B to Q 3	K to K 4
35 P to Q R 4 (!)	
	P to B 4
36 P to R 5	K to B 3
37 K to B 4	P to K 4, ch
38 K to Kt 3	K to K 2
39 P to R 4	K to Q 2
40 B to B 4	K to B 2
41 K to Kt 4	K to Q 2
42 K to Kt 3	K to K 2
43 K to Kt 4	K to B 3
44 P to Kt 3	P to R 4, ch
45 K to Kt 3	P to Kt 4
46 P to R 6	P × Q R P
47 P × R P	Kt to B 3
48 B to Q 5	Kt to R 2
49 B to Kt 7	K to Kt 3
50 B to Q 5	K to B 3
51 B to R 8	K to Kt 3
52 B to Kt 7	K to B 3
53 B to Q 5	P × P, ch
54 K × P	K to K 2
55 K × P	K to Q 2
56 K to Kt 6	K to B 2
57 K to B 6	Kt to Kt 4
58 K to K 6	Kt to Q 5, ch
59 K to K 7	Kt to Kt 4
60 K to K 6	Kt to Q 5, ch
	Drawn game.[10]

NOTES BY C. VON BARDELEBEN.

[1] Premature; the tenth move of Black proves it to be useless to pin the Knight.

[2] White, by playing the opening very well, has obtained a good game. The 12th move, however, is not to be recommended; 12. P to K R 3 followed by 13. P to Kt 4 would be better.

[3] White dissolves Black's doubled Pawn because Black threatened to play P to K Kt 4.

[4] A weak move. White should have played 17. R to B sq; if then Kt to K R 4, White answers 18. Q to Kt 4, preventing Black from playing Kt to K B 5.

[5] White cannot save the game. If 21. Kt to K 3, then Kt × Kt P, or if 21. P to K R 3, then Kt × R P follows (see diagram).

[6] On 23. B × P, would follow Q to B 6, ch ; 24. K to Kt sq, Kt to K 4, with an excellent attack.

[7] Now Black has a won game ; but he throws away the victory by several mistakes. Instead of Kt to Q sq the proper move is P to K 4.

[8] The manœuvre introduced by this move is bad. The right move is P to K 4 at this juncture too ; after having played P to K 4, Black would be enabled to bring his Knight into play and to push the Pawns of the King's side protected by the Knight. By this line of play Black would win slowly but surely.

[9] The consequence of this move is, that White soon gets a strong passed Pawn on the Queen's Rook's file (see the 46th move of White) ; Black could still win the game if he played P to K 4.

[10] White has cleverly taken advantage of his opponent's weak play, and so succeeds in obtaining a draw.

Steinitz *v.* Bird.

	WHITE	BLACK
1	P to Q 4	P to Q 4
2	P to Q B 4	P to K 3
3	Q Kt to B 3	P to Q B 3 [1]
4	P to K 3 [2]	Q Kt to Q 2
5	Kt to B 3	B to Q 3
6	P to K 4 [3]	P × K P
7	Kt × P	B to Kt 5, ch [4]
8	Kt to B 3 [5]	Q Kt to B 3
9	B to Q 3	Q to R 4 [6]
10	B to Q 2	Kt to K 2
11	Castles	Castles
12	P to Q R 3	B × Kt
13	B × B	Q to B 2 [7]
14	Kt to K 5	R to Q sq
15	Q to K 2	P to Q Kt 3
16	P to Q Kt 4	B to Kt 2
17	P to K B 4 [8]	Kt to B 4
18	Q to K B 2 [9]	P to B 4 [10]
19	Q P × P	P × P
20	Q × P [11]	Q × Q, ch
21	P × Q	B to K 5
22	K R to Q sq	K R to Q B sq
23	P to B 6 [12]	B × B
24	R × B	Kt to K 5 [13]
25	B to Kt 4	P to Q R 4
26	Q R to Q sq	P × B
27	P to B 7	P to Kt 4 (!)

	WHITE	BLACK
28	R to Q 8, ch	K to Kt 2

Black to make his 29th move.

	WHITE	BLACK
29	Q R P × P	Kt to K 6 [14]
30	R × R	R × R
31	R to Q 4 [15]	P to B 4
32	R to Q 7, ch	K to R 3
33	P × P, ch	K × P
34	P to R 4, ch [16]	
		K to B 3
35	Kt to B 6	R to K Kt sq

White resigns. [17]

AUGUST 14

NOTES BY DR. TARRASCH.

[1] This defence of the Queen's Gambit is not worse than the usual one, but gives White for a long time the freer game.

[2] The Queen's Bishop's Pawn must now be protected at once; P to K 4 would be stronger.

[3] By this move White gets the freer game. To prevent the advance of this Pawn Black might play at the 4th move P to K B 4 (Stonewall for Black) as I played in this Tournament against Gunsberg and Burn.

[4] The more natural move is B to B 2

[5] I should have played B to Q 2, for Black could here (or in the following move) have doubled White's Pawns in a very disagreeable manner by exchanging the Bishop for Knight, and have prevented an advance by P to Q B 4 (besides playing eventually Q to Q R 4). Later on, Black after all does exchange, but under far less favourable circumstances.

[6] This move is not now good, for Black is forced to exchange his Bishop for the Knight in a few moves, and to retreat the Queen also.

[7] Now White has the better position.

[8] With this quite simple move White gives up his advantage, for the Knight at B 3 threatens to establish itself on K 5, and Black makes admirable use of his opponent's mistake.

[9] B × Kt is disadvantageous for White, on account of P × B and Kt to K 5.

[10] Exceedingly well played. With this fine Pawn sacrifice Black not only frees his game but obtains the better one White ought not to have accepted the gift, but should have advanced the Queen's Pawn.

[11] Also after 20. P × P, B to K 5, or if 20. P to Kt 5, still B to K 5, or even Kt to Q 5, and Black's position is a very good one.

[12] In order to make a trebled Pawn after B × P by 24 Kt × B; 25. Q B × Kt; and 26. K B × Kt.

[13] Black's Knights are now very menacing, besides which Black threatens to drive away the Knight by P to K B 3, and then to take, first, the Pawn at B 6, after which the second Pawn becomes weakened. Steinitz decides therefore to sacrifice a Piece, in order to utilise his Pawns. This truly beautiful plan of the old master is only wrecked by the circumstance that Black gets in the end game (thanks to the favourable position of his Knights) an attack which could not be foreseen.

[14] The decisive move; with it Black locks up White's King completely and forces the exchange of a Rook.

[15] After 31. R to Q 2, R to Q R sq wins at once.

[16] If White plays 34. Kt to Q B 6 in order to block the Rook file with 35. Kt to R 5, after R to R sq we get the following surprisingly beautiful termination · 34. Kt to B 6, K to B 3; 35. Kt to R 7, R to K Kt sq; 36. P to Kt 3, P to B 5; 37. B P queens, R × Q; 38 Kt × R, P to B 6, and wins.

[17] A true, genuine, master game, well played on both sides.

E. Schiffers v. H. N. Pillsbury.

	WHITE	BLACK
1	P to K 4	P to K 4
2	Kt to K B 3	Kt to Q B 3
3	B to B 4	B to B 4
4	P to Q Kt 4	B × P
5	P to B 3	B to Q 3 [1]
6	Castles [2]	Kt to K B 3
7	R to K sq [3]	B to K 2
8	P to Q 4	P to Q 3 [4]
9	Q to Kt 3 [5]	Castles
10	Kt to Kt 5	Q to K sq
11	Q to Q sq	P to K R 3
12	Kt to B 3	B to Kt 5
13	Kt to R 3	Kt to R 2
14	R to Q Kt sq	R to Kt sq [6]
15	Kt to B 2	Kt to Kt 4
16	K to R sq	K to R sq
17	Kt to K 3 [7]	B × Kt
18	P × B	Kt to R 6
19	R to Kt 2	B to Kt 4
20	Kt to B 5	Kt to K 2
21	B × B	P × B
22	B to Kt 5 [8]	Q × B [9]
23	P to K B 4 [10]	Kt × P, ch
24	R × Kt	Kt × Kt
25	Q to R 5, ch	K to Kt sq
26	P × Kt	K P × B P
27	Q × Kt P [11]	P to K B 3
28	Q × P (B 4)	Q R to K sq
29	R to K Kt sq [12]	
		Q to Q 4, ch

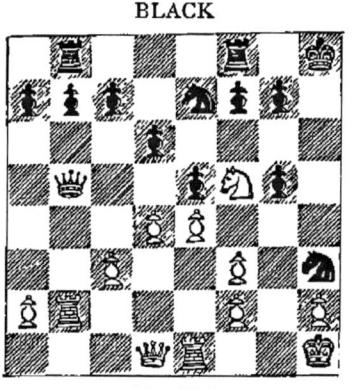

White to make his 23rd move.

	WHITE	BLACK
30	R (B 2) to Kt 2 [13]	
		R to B 2
31	Q to Kt 4	R to K 5
32	Q to R 5	R to K B 5 [14]
33	Q to K 2	R × B P
34	P to B 4	Q to B 6
35	Q to K 8, ch	R to B sq
36	Q to K 6, ch	K to R 2
37	Q to K 7	R to K Kt sq
38	Q × Q B P	R to K Kt 4
39	Q × Q P	R to K sq
40	P to K R 3	R to K 7
41	Q to R 2	R (Kt 4) × R
	White resigns.	

NOTES BY J. H. BLACKBURNE.

[1] In the early day of the Evans' Gambit this defence was considered perfectly sound by many of the well-known players, amongst them being the renowned Kieskeritzki. However, for many years past it has been abandoned in favour of the more natural-looking move of B to R 4. Some seven or eight years ago two Boston players, Messrs. Stone and Ware, reintroduced it, and for a long time it was all the rage at the Boston clubs. It became known as the 'Stoneware' defence. Mr. Pillsbury, who learnt his chess in Boston, and who, doubtless, is familiar with all its numerous and complicated phases, was, therefore, quite justified in adopting it against the European masters, many of whom probably knew nothing or very little about it.

AUGUST 14

² P to Q 4 is undoubtedly the stronger continuation.
³ Here, again, P to Q 4 might be played.
⁴ Black's game is all right now ; he has a Pawn more, and a safe position.
⁵ This attack is premature, as will presently be seen.
⁶ The best way of defending the Queen's Knight's Pawn.
⁷ B × Kt followed by Kt to K 3 was the correct play.
⁸ Either a great blunder or a miscalculation ; probably the former.
⁹ A 'bit of Morphy.' The game here becomes highly interesting. If R × Q, Black wins as follows . 23 R × Q, Kt × P, ch ; 24. K to Kt 2, Kt × Q ; 25 Kt × Kt, Kt × P ; 26. R to R 5, K R to K sq ; 27. Kt to B 5, P to K Kt 3 ; 28. Kt to R 6, K to Kt 2 ; 29. Kt to Kt 4, P × P, and the extra Pawns must win. (See diagram.)
¹⁰ Not without resource, threatening mate in two moves. It almost looks as if the previous move, B to Kt 5, was a deep-laid plot. Black has only one move to save the game, which, as a matter of course, he finds out
¹¹ There is nothing better ; P to B 6 is answered by K R to K sq, and P to K R 4 by Q × P.
¹² This Rook to K B sq would have maintained the King's Bishop's Pawn for a time, but ultimately Black would win with the extra Pawns on the Queen's side
¹³ The Rooks now are completely paralysed
¹⁴ Probably K R to K 2 would be more expeditious.

S Tinsley v. Dr. Tarrasch.

	WHITE	BLACK		WHITE	BLACK
1	P to Q 4	P to Q 4	20	B × Kt	B P × B
2	P to K 3	Kt to K B 3	21	K P × P ⁶	Q to Kt 2
3	B to Q 3 ¹	Kt to Q B 3	22	Kt to K 3	B × Kt
4	P to Q B 3	P to K 4 ²	23	Q × B	B to Kt 5
5	P × P	Kt × P	24	Q R to B sq	B to B 6, ch
6	B to K 2	B to Q 3	25	K to Kt sq	Q to Kt 5
7	Kt to K B 3	Castles	26	Q to B 2	P to K R 4 ⁷
8	Castles	Q to K 2	27	P to K R 4	P to B 4 (!)
9	Q Kt to Q 2	R to Q sq	28	K to R 2	P to Q 5
10	R to K sq	Kt to K 5	29	P × P	P × P
11	Kt × Q Kt	Q × Kt	30	B to Kt 4 ⁸	P to K 6
12	Kt to B sq ³	Q to Kt 4	31	Q to B 2	R to Q 2
13	P to K B 4	Q to R 5	32	Q to Q 3	R to K sq
14	P to K Kt 3	Q to K 2 ⁴	33	R to B 5	B to K 5
15	B to B 3	B to Q B 4	34	Q to Kt 5 (!)	P to R 3 ⁹
16	Q to K 2	P to K B 4	35	R to Kt 5, ch	K to R sq
17	B to Q 2	B to K 3	36	Q to Kt 6 ¹⁰	Q to K 3
18	Q R to Q sq	P to K Kt 4 ⁵	37	R × P, ch	B to R 2
19	K to R sq (!)	P × P	38	Q to B 5	P to Kt 3 (!)

WHITE	BLACK	WHITE	BLACK
39 Q to B sq	P to R 4	44 Q to B 8, ch	B to Kt sq
40 R to K 5	Q to B 2	45 P to K Kt 4	Q × B
41 R × R, ch	Q × R	46 K to Kt 3	R to K B 2
42 B to R 3	R to K Kt 2	White resigns.	
43 B to Q 6 [11]	Q to K Kt 3 (!)		

NOTES BY JAMES MASON.

[1] On general grounds, the King's Knight should be played in preference to the Bishop in this kind of game. Usually the Bishop has several courses open to him during the earlier stages; while, as a rule, the Knight has but one good post at the outset, viz. B 3. The inference seems obvious.

[2] Taking the initiative directly. But White appears content with assuming a more or less strictly defensive attitude; which he very ably maintains until driven to retaliatory measures by pressure of events.

[3] A surer protection than Kt to B 3 in this position.

[4] Little could be hoped for from Q to R 6, so she retires, satisfied for the moment with having induced the probably weakening advance of the Pawns.

[5] Clearly enough Black plays to win; and from that policy some risk is inseparable. It is found in the shape of serious danger to his own King later on.

[6] If 21. Kt P × P, then Q to R 5, &c. Profit from the open file would be all on the other side.

[7] Part of the general plan indicated at the 18th move. White does not want any closer acquaintance with this Pawn for the present.

[8] The contest increases in difficulty. The united passed Pawns are truly formidable. Yet White is not dismayed.

[9] Best, no doubt. Any exchange of Queens now would leave the passed Pawns good winning chances.

[10] This is a lost move with the Queen at a very critical period, and it helps to lose the game. Q to B 5 at once was better.

[11] A curious error, losing straight away, for the reply wins the Bishop of course. 43. P to Kt 3, with soon B to Kt 2, &c., might have at least drawn.

E. LASKER v. A. WALBRODT.

WHITE	BLACK	WHITE	BLACK
1 P to K 4	P to K 4	7 Kt × P	B to Q 2
2 Kt to K B 3	Kt to Q B 3	8 K Kt to K 2 [2]	Castles
3 B to Kt 5	Kt to K B 3	9 Kt to Kt 3	Kt to K 4 [3]
4 Castles	B to K 2 [1]	10 B × B	Q × B
5 Kt to B 3	P to Q 3	11 P to Kt 3	Q R to Q sq
6 P to Q 4	P × P	12 B to Kt 2	Kt to B 3

AUGUST 14

WHITE	BLACK
13 Kt to B 5	Q to K 3 [4]
14 R to K sq	Kt to K 4 [5]
15 P to K B 4 [6]	Kt to Kt 3
16 Kt to Q 5	P to B 3 [7]
17 Kt (B 5) × B, ch	
	Kt × Kt
18 P to B 5 [8]	Kt × B P
19 Kt × Kt, ch	P × Kt
20 P × Kt	Q × B P
21 R to K B sq	Q to K 5
22 B × P	Q R to K sq
23 R to B 3	P to K R 4
24 R to Kt 3, ch	Resigns.

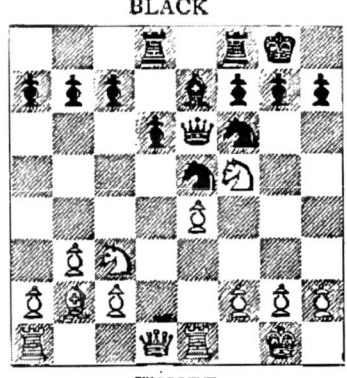

White to make his 15th move.

NOTES BY H. N. PILLSBURY.

[1] Most experts prefer the continuation Kt × P ; 5. P to Q 4, Kt to Q 3 ; 6. B × Kt, Q P × B ; 7. P × P, Kt to B 4, &c., as played between Tarrasch and Lasker in the present Tournament. The idea of allowing the exchange of Queens thus early is original with Dr. Tarrasch, and gives Black an even game.

[2] The usual continuation at this point 8. Kt × Kt, P × Kt ; 9. B to Q 3, seems inferior to the text.

[3] Certainly an ill-judged offer to exchange. He gives White command of a most important attacking square for the Knight. More satisfactory would be 9. R to K sq, followed soon by B to K B sq.

[4] If 13. Kt × P, White continues 14. Q to Kt 4, Kt to Kt 4 ; 15. Kt × B, ch, Q × Kt ; 16. Kt to Q 5, winning a Piece.

[5] 14. R to K sq still was the proper continuation. The text move allows White time to advance the King's Bishop's Pawn with crushing effect. Black has wasted valuable time with useless moves of this Piece, and the attack obtained by the first player is now almost irresistible.

[6] This and the following move have been well reserved by White, and the preparation for the final attack could not be improved upon.

[7] Nothing better ; if Kt × Kt ; 17. Kt × Kt P, Q to Q 2 ; 18. P × Kt, Kt × P ; 19. R × B, Q × R ; 20. Kt to B 5, Q to Kt 4 ; 21. Q to Kt 4, P to K B 3 ; 22. Q × Q, ch, P × Q ; 23. Kt to R 6, mate.

[8] The final stroke, and even the sacrifice of the Piece, does not enable Black to hold out long.

A. ALBIN v. W. H. K. POLLOCK.

WHITE	BLACK	WHITE	BLACK
1 P to K 4	P to K 4	4 P to Q 3	B to B 4
2 Kt to K B 3	Kt to Q B 3	5 Kt to B 3	P to Q 3
3 B to B 4	Kt to B 3	6 B to K Kt 5 [1]	P to K R 3

136   THE HASTINGS CHESS TOURNAMENT

	WHITE	BLACK
7	B to K 3	B to Kt 3
8	P to Q R 3 [2]	B to K 3
9	K B × B [3]	P × B
10	Q B × B	R P × B
11	Castles	Castles
12	P to R 3	Q to K sq [4]
13	Kt to K R 2	Kt to K R 4
14	K to R sq	Kt to Q 5
15	Kt to K 2	Kt × Kt
16	Q × Kt	Kt to B 5
17	Q to K 3	Q to Kt 3
18	Q to Kt 3 [5]	Q × Q
19	P × Q	Kt to K 7
20	R × R, ch	R × R
21	Kt to B sq [6]	R × Kt, ch [7]
22	R × R	Kt × P, ch
23	K to Kt sq	Kt × R
24	K × Kt	K to B 2
25	K to B 2	K to K 2
26	K to K 3	K to Q 2
27	K to B 3	K to B 3
28	K to K 2	K to B 4
29	K to Q 2	P to Q 4
30	K to K 3	P to Q Kt 4
31	P × P [8]	P × P
32	P to Q 4, ch	P × P, ch
33	K to Q 3	K to Q 3
34	K × P	P to B 4, ch
35	K to Q 3	K to K 4
36	K to K 3	P to Q 5, ch

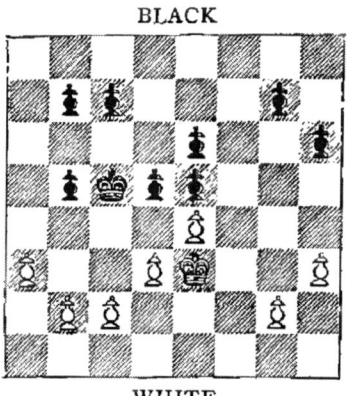

White to make his 31st move.

	WHITE	BLACK
37	K to B 3	P to B 5
38	P to K Kt 3	P to K Kt 4
39	P to K Kt 4	P to Q Kt 3
40	P to Q B 3	K to Q 4
41	P × P	K × P
42	K to K 2	P to B 6
43	P × P, ch	K × P
44	K to K 3	K to Kt 6
45	K to K 4	K × P
46	K to B 5	P to Kt 5
47	K to Kt 6	P to Kt 6
48	K × P	P to Kt 7
49	K × P	P to Kt 8 (Q)

White resigns.

NOTES BY R. TEICHMANN.

[1] To pin the Knights with the Bishops is, in the Giuoco Piano as a rule, bad, and this is proved again in this game.

[2] Another weak move, and loss of time.

[3] These ill-judged exchanges seem to be the consequence of his last bad move, as he could not now retire his B to Q Kt 3.

[4] A very good move, bringing his Queen into action, and enabling him to play Kt to R 4 and B 5.

[5] A decisive mistake, which ought to lose the game. But there was no more a defence against Black's powerful attack.

[6] If 21. P to K Kt 4, then R to B 7, threatening Kt to B 5, and winning at least a Pawn.

[7] Black is too eager to simplify the game and reduce it to what he

AUGUST 14

most likely thought an easily won Pawn ending. His two doubled Pawns on the Queen's side, however, ought to have given him some apprehensions about the possibility of winning. Kt to Q 5 followed by R to B 5 would have given Black a won game in a few moves.

[8] Suicidal; he could have forced the draw at once with P to Kt 4, ch, after which we fail to find a winning continuation for Black; e.g. 31. P to Kt 4, ch, K to Q 3; 32. K to K 2, P to Q Kt 3; 33 K to K 3, P to B 4; 34. K to K 2, P to B 5; 35 K to K 3. White only moves his King, and never exchanges any Pawns; we cannot see how Black can do anything. Clearly he gains nothing by playing the King over to the other side, as the White King is also free, and will always be able to keep the opposition or to block the Pawns. An interesting question arises whether Black, without the mistake on the 30th move, could have won this ending After a very careful analysis of the position I have come to the conclusion that, in spite of being a Pawn to the good and having the King well in play, Black cannot force a win against the best defence, as the two doubled Pawns can never be dissolved. The following variation shows the resources of the attack and the defence; e.g.—

	WHITE	BLACK		WHITE	BLACK
30		K to Kt 4	36.	P × P,	K to Kt 4, winning)
31	P to Kt 3	K to B 4			
32	P to B 3 (best)	P to Q Kt 4			K to Q 3
33	P to Kt 4, ch (best, Black threatened P to Q 5, ch;		34	K to B 3	P to Q Kt 3
	34. K to Q 2, P × P, ch;		35	K to K 3	P to B 4
	35. K × P, P to Kt 5, ch;		36	K to K 2	P to B 5
			37	K to Q 2	P to Q 5
			38	K to Q B 2	

and Black cannot win, because, as soon as he plays his King over to the King's side, White would force a passed Pawn on the other, and win

AUGUST 15.

This is truly an off day, not even an excursion; but Bardeleben finishes his adjourned game with Mason, and it wanted some very delicate handling, and so created considerable interest. In the evening is to be the reception by the president and vice-president in honour of the chess masters, but in Mr. Watney's absence Mr. Chapman and his daughter receive the guests in royal style. A large number have responded to the invitation, and the gathering is of the most enjoyable character. The steps are draped with red cloth and lined with foliage plants, producing a very pretty effect. The Museum is thrown open, and everyone seems well at ease, enjoying the picturesque effects and the charming music.

The musical programme, which was capitally executed under the direction of Mr. Val Marriott, was as follows:—

Song	'The Banks of Allan Water'		
	Mr. S Martin.		
Violin Solo	'2nd Dance'		*Nachez*
	Miss Constance Colborne.		
Song	'Molly Bawn'		*Lauer*
	Mr Edward Branscombe.		
Piano Solo			
	Mr. Lohman.		
'Cello Solos	(a) 'Lied'		*Schumann*
	(b) 'La Fileuse'		*Raff*
	Miss May Mukle.		
Song	'Love's Return'		*Tosti*
	Mlle. Marie Tietjens.		
Violin Duet	'Tola Novara'		*Sarasate*
	Mr. Val Marriott and Miss Constance Colborne.		
Song	'Take a Pair of Sparkling Eyes'		*Sullivan*
	Mr. Edward Branscombe.		
Song	'The Holy City'		*Step. Adams*
	Mlle. Marie Tietjens.		

Photo., Bradshaw, Hastings

R. Teichmann

AUGUST 16.

This morning the masters reassemble, but to work again. On the draw, the pairing shows that Lasker and Steinitz are to meet, and we do not know how to read the stars, but the room is teeming with combinations, board after board; all are complicated, and all are interesting. Early in the day of course the chief concern is centred in Lasker *v.* Steinitz. If we consider the circumstances, we may perhaps picture to ourselves the excitement of the players and spectators. Steinitz plays a sort of hedgehog defence, requiring most careful handling on the part of the opponent, but Lasker presently wins a Pawn, and eventually the game by a very fine combination. The Janowski-Pillsbury game also is equally fine, or better. Vergani at one time looks like winning against Albin; Tchigorin has a most complicated game, and that of Burn against Tarrasch is a curiosity.

R. Teichmann *v.* G. Marco.

	WHITE	BLACK
1	P to Q 4	P to Q 4
2	P to Q B 4	P to K 3
3	Kt to Q B 3	Kt to K B 3
4	B to B 4	B to K 2
5	Kt to K B 3	Castles
6	P to K 3	P to Q Kt 3
7	B to Q 3	B to Kt 2
8	R to Q B sq	P to Q B 4
9	P × Q P	K P × P
10	P × P	P × P
11	Castles	B to Q 3 [1]
12	B to K Kt 5	Q Kt to Q 2
13	B to B 5	Kt to Q Kt 3 [2]
14	Q to B 2	P to K Kt 3 [3]
15	B to Q 3	P to Q B 5 [4]
16	B to K 2	K to Kt 2
17	K R to Q sq	Q to Kt sq
18	P to Q R 4	P to Q R 4

	WHITE	BLACK
19	Q to Q 2	K Kt to Q 2

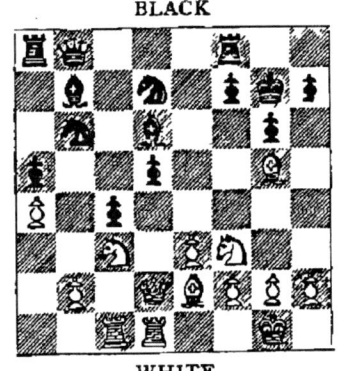

White to make his 20th move.

| 20 | P to K 4 (!) [5] | P × P |

140 THE HASTINGS CHESS TOURNAMENT

WHITE	BLACK		WHITE	BLACK
21 B to R 6, ch	K to Kt sq		27 B × P (!)	B × P, ch
22 Q to Q 4	P to K B 3		28 K to R sq	Kt × B
23 B × R	K × B		29 R × Kt	B to K 4
24 Kt × P	B × Kt		30 P to Q Kt 4	P × P
25 Q × Q B	Kt to K 4		31 R × P	Q to K sq
26 Kt × Kt	B × Kt		32 R to K sq	Resigns.

Notes by C. von Bardeleben.

[1] Kt to B 3 would be better.
[2] Preferable would be B to K 2, and if 14. Q to B 2, then P to K R 3.
[3] This move weakens the King's side; Black ought to have played P to K R 3; 15. B to R 4, B to K 2.
[4] Another bad move, which weakens the Queen's Pawn. The right move was B to K 2.
[5] White finishes the game very cleverly (see diagram).

J. Mason v. J. Mieses.

WHITE	BLACK
1 P to K 4	P to K 4
2 Kt to K B 3	Kt to Q B 3
3 B to Kt 5	P to Q R 3 [1]
4 B to R 4	P to Q 3
5 Kt to B 3	Kt to K 2 [2]
6 P to Q 4	B to Q 2
7 B to Kt 3	P to R 3 [3]
8 B to K 3	P to K Kt 3
9 P × P	P × P
10 Q to K 2	B to Kt 2
11 R to Q sq	Q to B sq [4]
12 Castles	B to Kt 5
13 P to K R 3	B × Kt
14 Q × B	Castles
15 B to B 5	P to Kt 3
16 B × Kt	Kt × B
17 R to Q 2	R to R 2
18 K R to Q sq	
	P to Q B 4
19 B to Q 5 [5]	K to R sq
20 Q to Kt 4	P to B 4
21 P × P	P × P
22 Q to R 5	P to K 5 [6]
23 Kt to K 2	Q to B 2

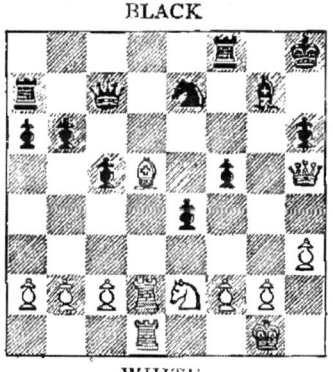

White to make his 24th move.

WHITE	BLACK
24 P to Q B 3 [7]	Q to K 4
25 B to Kt 3	Q R to R sq [8]
26 R to Q 7 [9]	P to Kt 4
27 R (Q sq) to Q 6	
	P to Q B 5
28 B to B 2	R to B 3
29 R × R	Q × R
30 Kt to B 4	Q to K 4 [10]
31 Q to R 4 [11]	B to B sq

AUGUST 16

	WHITE	BLACK
32	Q × Kt	Q × Q [12]
33	Kt to Kt 6, ch	
		K to Kt 2
34	Kt × Q	K to B 3
35	Kt to B 6	K to K 3
36	R to Q sq	R to B sq
37	Kt to Q 4, ch [13]	
		K to K 4
38	P to K Kt 3	B to B 4

	WHITE	BLACK
39	K to Kt 2	P to Q R 4
40	Kt × Kt P	P to B 5
41	R to K sq	P to K 6
42	P × P, ch	K × P
43	P × P, ch	B × P
44	R to B sq, ch	K to Kt 4
45	Kt to Q 6	R to B 3
46	R to B 5, ch	K to R 5
47	B to Q sq	Resigns.

NOTES BY J H BLACKBURNE.

[1] If the P to Q 3 defence is intended, then it is better not to make this move.

[2] B to Q 2 is considered the correct line of play, although Steinitz often adopts the text move.

[3] A stronger defence is Kt × P.

[4] It is difficult to say which is Black's best, but certainly Kt to Q 5 is preferable to this move.

[5] B × P, ch, looks tempting, but the answer would be K to R sq.

[6] This cannot be good, as it allows the Knight to come into powerful play on the King's side.

[7] Quite unnecessary, as the Knight's Pawn cannot be captured at present More forcible was P to K Kt 3, preventing P to K B 5 and also threatening Kt to B 4.

[8] Played without due consideration ; P to K B 5 would have given chances of a draw

[9] Probably R to Q 6 was slightly stronger

[10] Very ingenious, but of no avail. If White now takes Knight, the reply is Q × Kt, and would draw. Black could also play 30. K to Kt sq, in which case White would win as follows :—

30		K to Kt sq	34	Q × P, ch	Q to Kt 3
31	B × P	P × B	35	Q × R	Q to Kt 8, ch
32	Kt to Q 5	Kt × Kt	36	K to R 2	Q to B 4
33	Q × Kt, ch	K to R 2	37	Q to R 7, winning easily.	

[11] Decisive ; Black must lose a Piece whatever he does.

[12] The result is the same if he takes with the Bishop

[13] It is now only a matter of time. White has a Piece ahead and a safe game.

M. TCHIGORIN v. I. GUNSBERG.

	WHITE	BLACK
1	P to K 4	P to K 4
2	K Kt to B 3	Q Kt to B 3
3	B to B 4	B to B 4
4	P to Q Kt 4	B × Kt P

	WHITE	BLACK
5	P to B 3	B to B 4
6	Castles	P to Q 3
7	P to Q 4	P × P
8	P × P	B to Kt 3

	WHITE	BLACK		WHITE	BLACK
9	Kt to B 3	B to Kt 5	36	Q to R 5 (!)[19]	
10	B to Q Kt 5	K to B sq			Kt to Kt 3
11	B to K 3	K Kt to K 2[1]			
12	P to Q R 4	P to Q R 4[2]			
13	B to Q B 4[3]	B to R 4			
14	K to R sq[4]	Kt to Kt 5[5]			
15	P to Q 5 (!)	B × B[6]			
16	P × B	Kt to Kt 3			
17	B to K 2	K to Kt sq[7]			
18	R to B sq	P to R 3[8]			
19	Kt to Q 4	B × B			
20	Q × B	Kt to R 3[9]			
21	R to B 3	Kt to K 4			
22	R to Kt 3[10]	K to R 2			
23	R to B sq	Kt to B 4			
24	Q to R 5[11]	R to K Kt sq[12]			
25	Kt to B 5[13]	Q to K B sq			
26	R to R 3[14]	Kt (B 4) to	37	Kt × B P (!)[20]	
27	Kt to Kt 5	R to B sq [Q 2[15]			Kt × R
28	Q to K 2[16]	R to K R sq	38	P × Kt	Q to K B sq
29	Kt (Kt 5) to Q 4		39	Kt to Kt 5, ch	
		P to B 4[17]			K to Kt sq
30	Kt to Kt 5	R to R sq	40	Kt to K 6	Q to B 2
31	Kt (Kt 5) × P		41	Q to R 3	Kt to B sq
		R to R 3	42	Kt to Q 6	Q to Q 2
32	Kt to Kt 5	R to K Kt 3	43	P to K 5	R × Kt
33	R to R 4[18]	Q to Q sq	44	P × R	Q × P
34	R (R 4) to B 4		45	Q to Kt 3	Kt to Q 2
		P to Kt 3	46	R to K sq	Kt to B sq
35	Kt (B 5) to Q 6		47	P to B 5	Q to Q 2
		R to B 3	48	P to K 6	Resigns.

White to make his 37th move.

NOTES BY DR. TARRASCH.

[1] This position has often occurred before, and I am of opinion that White has a far superior game—complete freedom, and opportunity for attack on all sides. It is difficult for Black to develop or even to find a counter-attack; true, Black has one Pawn more, but it is of very little use or importance; with equal players six times out of ten White would win.

[2] One might suggest here or there some defensive move, but what is the good if one cannot recommend a complete plan of defence with any prospect of success?

[3] Threatens B × P, ch, followed by Kt to Kt 5, ch.

[4] With the intention of removing the Queen, and after B × Kt,

P × B, to occupy the open Knight's file with the Rook. White can allow himself such preparations, for his attack at present is not strong, but extraordinarily persisting.

⁵ This is what I call a defensive plan. Black wishes to break up the centre with P to Q 4, and to get the Knight there, using it as a basis for his operations. But what is the use of this pretty idea if it can be frustrated at once by the opponent?

⁶ The best chance for Black, though the Bishop's file is opened. If Black permits B × B, doubling the Pawns, it would only produce a fresh weakness, and the Steinitzian move of Kt to B sq would not assist.

⁷ Contemplating the exchange of Bishops, but the Pawns, the strong centre and the open file, are ready to keep up the attack. [White was threatening Kt to Q 4 and K 6.—ED.]

⁸ In order to play K to R 2 and free the Rook.

⁹ With Kt to K 4, which was better, Black could prevent the development of the coming attack; but White could attack the Knight at any time with Kt to K B 3, and eventually remove it.

¹⁰ White does not mind shutting in his Rook for a short time.

¹¹ This threatens R × B P, and Q to Kt 6, ch.

¹² This Rook plays a wretched part throughout the game.

¹³ Threatening R × Kt P, ch, and Q × R P.

¹⁴ To prevent P to K Kt 3.

¹⁵ He was threatened with R to B 4, R to R 4, and Q × R P (!).

¹⁶ To reply to Kt to K B 3 with Kt × R P and R × Kt.

¹⁷ Black does not know what to move, and I, in his place, would not know either. He makes another mistake—a psychological necessity in sad positions

¹⁸ White brings back the Rook at the right moment, and at the same time keeps the Black Rook from Kt 5.

¹⁹ Threatening R × R, and if Kt × R, then Q × Kt

²⁰ The end. Gunsberg, it is true, has played this game like a player of the second rank, but this shall be no blame to him, for after the first dozen moves there were no moves of the first rank left to be played.

[We have always defended this branch of the Evans' with 10. P to Q R 3, and if 11. B to R 4, then K to B sq, and we believe invariably won with Black. The driving back of the Bishop prevents it coming to the help of the King's side at K 2, and also stops P to Q R 4, which is an awkward move to parry Black can usually institute a strong counter-attack against the King after Kt to Kt 3, and perhaps P to K R 4.—ED.]

A. ALBIN v. B. VERGANI.

WHITE	BLACK	WHITE	BLACK
1 P to K 4	P to K 4	4 P to Q 4	Kt × K P
2 Kt to K B 3	Kt to Q B 3	5 P × P	Kt to B 4 ¹
3 B to Kt 5	Kt to B 3	6 Castles	B to K 2

144 THE HASTINGS CHESS TOURNAMENT

	WHITE	BLACK		WHITE	BLACK
7	Kt to B 3	Castles	30	P to R 6	P × P
8	Kt to Q 5	Kt to K 3	31	R × P	R to Kt 8, ch
9	B to Q 3	P to Q 3	32	K to Kt 2	R to Q R sq
10	Kt × B, ch	Q × Kt	33	P to K B 4	P to R 4
11	Q to K 2	P to K Kt 3 [2]	34	P to R 4	P to R 5
12	B to R 6	R to K sq	35	P to B 5	P × P
13	P to B 3 [3]	P × P	36	P to R 5	K to B sq
14	Kt × P	Kt to Kt 2	37	P to R 6	K to Kt sq
15	Kt × Kt	Q × Q	38	R to Kt 7, ch	K to R sq
16	B × Q	R × B	39	R to B 7	P to R 6
17	Kt to Q 4	R × Kt P	40	R to Q R 7	P to R 7
18	B × Kt	K × B	41	K to B 3	R to Q B 8
19	K R to K sq	K to B sq	42	R × P	R × P, ch
20	P to Q R 4	B to Q 2	43	K to B 4	R to K R 6
21	P to Q R 5	P to B 4	44	R to R 7	R × P
22	Kt to K B 3	P to B 3 (?) [4]	45	K × P	K to Kt sq
23	Q R to Q sq	B to Kt 5	46	P to B 4	R to R 2
24	R to Q 6 [5]	K to B 2	47	R to R 6	R to R 3
25	P to R 3	B × Kt [6]	48	R to B 6	K to B 2
			49	R to B 7, ch	K to B sq
			50	K to K 6	P to B 4, ch
			51	K × P	R to Q Kt 3
			52	K to Kt 5	P to B 5
			53	P to B 4	P to B 6
			54	R × P	R to Q 3
			55	K to B 4	K to B 2
			56	K to K 5	R to Q R 6
			57	R to B 7, ch	K to B sq
			58	R to Q 7	R to Q Kt 3
			59	R to K R 7	R to Q B 3
			60	K to Q 5	R to B 3
			61	K to K 5	R to Q Kt 3
			62	R to Q R 7	R to Q B 3
			63	K to K 4	R to B 3
			64	R to R 7	R to Q Kt 3
			65	K to B 4	R to K B 3
			66	K to K 5	R to Q Kt 3
			67	R to Q 7	R to Q R 3

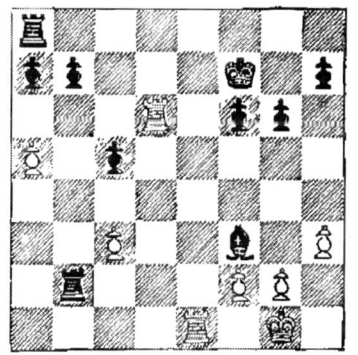

BLACK

WHITE

White to make his 26th move.

26	R to Q 7, ch	K to B sq
27	P × B [7]	R to K sq
28	R × R	K × R
29	R × R P	R to Kt 4

Drawn game.

NOTES BY E. SCHIFFERS.

[1] Better than B to K 2 at once, for after 6. B to K 3, Castles; 7. Q to K 2, Kt to B 4; 8. B × Kt, &c.

AUGUST 16

[2] Better play Kt to Q B 4 and exchange the dangerous Bishop.
[3] I prefer 13. P × P.
[4] Why not R to K sq (Kt to K 5, B to K 3)?
[5] The result of P to K B 3.
[6] Black has lost all superiority and the game must end in a draw.
[7] If K R to K 7, then B to Q 4.

E. Lasker v. W. Steinitz.

	WHITE	BLACK
1	P to K 4	P to K 4
2	Kt to K B 3	Kt to Q B 3
3	B to Kt 5	P to Q R 3
4	B to R 4	P to Q 3 [1]
5	Castles	K Kt to K 2
6	P to B 3	B to Q 2
7	P to Q 4	Kt to Kt 3
8	R to K sq	B to K 2
9	Q Kt to Q 2	Castles
10	Kt to B sq	Q to K sq [2]
11	B to B 2	K to R sq
12	Kt to Kt 3	B to Kt 5 [3]
13	P to Q 5	Kt to Kt sq
14	P to K R 3	B to B sq [4]
15	Kt to B 5	B to Q sq
16	P to K Kt 4	Kt to K 2
17	Kt to Kt 3	Kt to Kt sq [5]
18	K to Kt 2 [6]	Kt to Q 2
19	B to K 3	Kt to Kt 3
20	P to Kt 3	B to Q 2
21	P to B 4	Kt to B sq [7]
22	Q to Q 2	Q Kt to K 2
23	P to B 5	P to K Kt 3
24	Q to B 3	P to B 4 [8]
25	Kt × K P	P × Kt
26	Q × P, ch	Kt to B 3
27	B to Q 4 [9]	P × Kt P [10]
28	P × P	B × P [11]
29	Q to Kt 5	Q to Q 2
30	B × Kt, ch	K to Kt sq
31	B to Q sq	B to R 6, ch
32	K to Kt sq	Kt × P [12]
33	B × B	Kt to B 5
34	B to B 6	Q to Q 7
35	R to K 2 [13]	Kt × R, ch
36	B × Kt	Q to Q 2
37	R to Q sq	Q to B sq [14]
38	B to B 4, ch	B to K 3
39	P to K 5	B × B
40	Kt to B 5 [15]	Resigns.

White to make his 18th move.

Notes by I. Gunsberg.

[1] If a census were taken of the games played with the P to Q 3 defence as against any other defence to the Ruy Lopez, it would be found that this move has up to the present produced the worst proportionate results.

[2] Somehow or other we do not believe in the manœuvre of bringing the White Queen's Knight over on to the King's side; we think

too much time is lost thereby, and it is advisable for Black to adopt an aggressive policy before White has time to fully develop his Pieces. Suppose Black played P takes P instead of Q to K sq, and if 11. P × P, then P to Kt 4; 12. B to B 2, Kt to Kt 5; 13. B to Kt 3, P to Q B 4, 14. P to Q 5, P to B 5, 15. B to B 2, Kt × B, 16. Q × Kt, P to B 4. The point is to do something while the Knight is on B sq, and before it can get to Kt 3.

[3] We do not see what good can come from this move; anyway it would have been stronger if P × P had preceded it.

[4] The fact that the Bishop ought not to have gone to Kt 5 at all must now be clear. B × Kt would not have been an improvement, as that would bring White's Queen into play.

[5] Black has now completed his strategic movement towards the rear. If this is good strategy, then the modern theory of development must be all wrong. One fact, however, must be borne in mind. Black, having all his Pieces concentrated on his base, is certainly less assailable, and should White rashly advance against that formation, Black might probably be able to break up the White line with advantage to himself.

[6] Considering that Black's only hope lies in an advance of the King's Bishop's Pawn, we should have preferred to play K to R 2, so as to be able to occupy the King's Knight's file with the Rook, which would effectually prevent P to K B 4 at any future time. And, after developing his Rooks, White could take his own time about cautiously turning on the pressure. (See diagram.)

[7] There seems little prospect of Black being able to harass White by a flank attack on the Queen's side. Yet it is the only way at present that promises some relief.

[8] It was pointed out by Mr. Steinitz that he would have done much better if he had played P to R 3 first. In this we perfectly agree with him, as it would have given the King some elbow room, and would, therefore, have made the impending sacrifice less profitable, which by-the-by must have stared Black in the face in rather an obvious manner.

[9] White's play is extremely interesting. If he had simply contented himself with 27. P to Kt 5, Black might have replied in several ways: i.e. Kt × Q P; 28. B to Q 4, Kt to Kt 5; 29 B to Kt sq, K to Kt sq; 30 P × Kt, B × P; 31. Q × Q, Q R × Q, &c. Though these moves may be varied, we still think this line would have been profitable for Black.

[10] K to Kt sq would not have released the Knight, as White would, nevertheless, have played P to Kt 5, and the Knight could not move. P to B 5 also looks an enticing move, but then White would have replied with 28. P to Kt 5, and Black could not take the Knight.

[11] This was a deceptive move. It seemed no doubt advantageous to get rid of this Knight's Pawn, but it did not result favourably.

[12] Black played the following moves with desperate ingenuity. The move of R × B does not promise much, nor is P to R 3 any better, except that it would allow Black to play K to R 2 on the following move, which would give him more liberty of action.

[13] Though this is the only move on the board, yet it answers all practical purposes of defence.

[14] Black having failed in his counter-attack, there is little left for him to do. If he had played Q to K sq or Q to B 3 it would not have made much difference in the position.

[15] A neat finish to a brilliantly played game.

S. Tinsley v. E. Schiffers.

	WHITE	BLACK		WHITE	BLACK
1	P to Q 4	P to Q 4	21	Kt to B 5	Q × B P
2	P to K 3	Kt to K B 3	22	R to Kt sq	Q to B 7
3	B to Q 3	Kt to Q B 3[1]	23	R to K sq	Q to Q 8, ch
4	P to Q B 3[2]	P to K 4	24	R to B sq	Q to Kt 5
5	P × P	Kt × P	25	R to B 3	Q × Q
6	B to K 2[3]	B to Q 3	26	P × Q	Kt to K 5
7	P to K B 4[4]	Kt to Kt 3	27	B to R 3	P to K Kt 3
8	Kt to B 3	Castles	28	Kt to R 6, ch	K to Kt 2
9	Castles	R to K sq	29	Kt to Kt 4	P to K R 4
10	Q to Q 3	Q to K 2	30	Kt to K 5	P to B 3
11	Kt to Q 4	P to B 4	31	Kt to Q 7	Kt to Q 7[8]
12	Kt to B 5	B × Kt	32	R to Kt 3	B × P, ch
13	Q × B	P to Q R 3	33	K to R sq	B × B P
14	B to B 3	Kt to R 5	34	B to Kt 2	Kt to K 5[9]
15	Q to R 3	Kt × B, ch	35	R to K Kt 2	P to B 6
16	R × Kt[5]	P to B 5	36	Q R to K Kt sq	
17	Kt to Q 2	B to B 4			P to K Kt 4[10]
18	Kt to B sq	Q to K 5	37	B to R 3	P to Q Kt 4
19	P to Q Kt 4[6]	B to R 2	38	R to K B sq	Kt to Q 7
20	Kt to Kt 3	Q to B 7[7]	39	R to Q sq	Kt to B 5
			40	B to B sq	B × B
			41	R × B	P to Q 5
			42	P to K R 4	Kt to K 6
			43	P × P	Kt × R
			44	P × P, ch	K to B 2
			45	K × Kt	R to K 7, ch
			46	K to B 3	Q R to K sq
			47	R to K Kt sq	
					K R to K 6, ch
			48	K to B 4	R to K Kt sq
			49	R to Q B sq	K to K 3
			50	Kt to B 5, ch	K × P
			51	Kt to K 4, ch	K to K 3
			52	P to K R 3	R to K B sq, ch

White to make his 21st move.

White resigns.

NOTES BY H. N. PILLSBURY.

[1] Tchigorin's favourite idea, and apparently proving White's opening moves inferior.

[2] At any rate giving the lead to Black. Either 4. P to K B 4, Kt to Kt 5; 5. B to K 2, B to B 4; 6. Kt to Q R 3, or 4. Kt to K B 3, B to Kt 5; 5. B to Q Kt 5, were better continuations.

[3] For Black has now, as second player, the same position that the attack might obtain from the French defence, as follows: 1. P to K 4, P to K 3; 2. P to Q 4, P to Q 4; 3. Kt to Q B 3, P × P; 4. Kt × P, B to K 2; 5. Kt to K B 3, P to Q B 3.

[4] It is rarely advisable to advance P to K B 4 in positions of this nature, as the centre Pawn is left too weak, and this is no exception to the rule.

[5] In endeavouring to keep his King's Pawn and at the same time develop his Queen's wing, White has been obliged to place his Queen and King's Rook in very bad positions, especially the former, which is totally out of play.

[6] This weakens another Pawn without aiding his case. Perhaps P to K Kt 4, followed by Q to Kt 2, would have enabled his Queen's side Pieces to eventually come into play.

[7] Taking advantage of the opponent's weak 19th move, Black wins this Pawn easily, and the opponent's feints against his King are easily met.

[8] The second weak Pawn goes almost as easily as the first. After this the rest is not difficult for Black.

[9] Much better than B × R, to which White would answer Kt × P.

[10] He could take the Bishop safely, but almost anything will win.

C. VON BARDELEBEN v. W. H. K. POLLOCK.

	WHITE	BLACK
1	P to Q 4	P to Q B 4 [1]
2	P to Q 5	P to K Kt 3
3	P to K 4	B to Kt 2
4	B to Q 3	Kt to Q R 3 [2]
5	P to Q B 3	Kt to B 2
6	Kt to K 2	P to Q 3
7	Castles	Kt to K R 3
8	P to B 3	P to K 3 [3]
9	P to Q B 4	P to Q Kt 4 [4]
10	B P × P	K P × P
11	P × P	B to Q Kt 2
12	B to Q B 4	Kt to B 4
13	Q Kt to B 3	Castles
14	Q to Q 3	Q to K 2 [5]
15	B to Q 2	K R to K sq
16	Q R to K sq	Q to R 5
17	Kt to K 4	P to K R 3

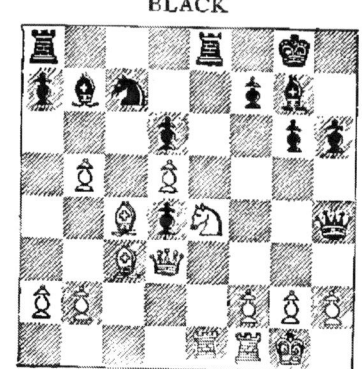

White to make his 20th move.

AUGUST 16

WHITE	BLACK		WHITE	BLACK
18 B to B 3	Kt to Q 5		23 Kt × P	R × R
19 Kt × Kt	P × Kt		24 R × R	Kt to Kt 5
20 P to K Kt 3 [6]	Q to R 4		25 Q to Q 4, ch [8]	
21 B × P	Kt × Q P [7]			K to R 2
22 B × B	K × B		26 Kt to K 8	Resigns.

NOTES BY J. H. BLACKBURNE.

[1] This bizarre defence is not to be commended.

[2] One of Pollock's favourite manœuvres; if B × Kt, then Queen checks and takes the Bishop with Queen.

[3] Black's scheme is evidently to advance the Pawns on the Queen's side; therefore it would, perhaps, have been advisable to play P to Q Kt 4 before attempting to break up the centre.

[4] This is far too elaborate; the simple move of P × P at once was the play.

[5] Lost time; R to K sq is better.

[6] He could play B × P at once with perfect safety; for instance, 20. B × P, P to B 4; 21. B × B, P × Kt; 22. Q to B 3, and White has two Pawns ahead. (See diagram.)

[7] Leading to still further loss, but his game is hopelessly gone.

[8] Stronger than winning the Knight by Q to B 3, ch.

J. H. BLACKBURNE v. A. WALBRODT.

WHITE	BLACK
1 P to K 4	P to K 4
2 B to K 2 [1]	Kt to Q B 3
3 Kt to K B 3	Kt to B 3
4 P to Q 3	P to Q 4
5 P × P	Kt × P
6 Castles	B to K 2
7 Kt to B 3	Castles
8 Kt to K sq [2]	P to B 4
9 Kt × Kt	Q × Kt
10 B to B 3	Q to K 3
11 B × Kt [3]	Q × B
12 Kt to B 3	B to B 3
13 B to Kt 5	P to K 5
14 B × B	R × B
15 Kt to K 5 [4]	Q to Kt 4
16 Kt to B 4	B to K 3
17 P to Q Kt 3 [5]	R to Q sq
18 Q to K 2	P × P
19 P × P	P to B 5
20 Kt to K 5	P to B 6

BLACK

WHITE

White to make his 21st move.

WHITE	BLACK
21 Q to K 3 [6]	P × P
22 K × P	R to R 3
23 K to R sq	R to R 4
24 Q R to K sq	B to R 6
25 R to K Kt sq	Q to Q 4, ch

150 THE HASTINGS CHESS TOURNAMENT

WHITE	BLACK		WHITE	BLACK
26 Kt to B 3 [7]	R to K B sq		32 R to K 7	Q to B 3
27 R to Kt 3	B to Q 2		33 Q to K sq	B to Q 4
28 Q to K 7 [8]	P to K Kt 3		34 R × B P	R × R P [9]
29 Q to K 4	B to B 3		35 P to B 3	Q to R 5
30 K to Kt sq	Q to B 2		White resigns.	
31 Q to Q Kt 4	B × Kt			

NOTES BY R. TEICHMANN.

[1] Giving the advantage of the first move away. It is strange that a player of such essentially aggressive style as Mr. Blackburne should choose such tame openings.

[2] A bad move, the idea of which is not discernible. R to K sq and B to B sq seems a good continuation.

[3] Showing the weakness of his second move, if he has nothing better, after about four wasted moves, than exchanging this Bishop for the Black Queen's Knight.

[4] If 15. P × P, P × P, Black would get a very strong attack.

[5] White is already in great difficulties, and there seems to be no satisfactory line of play.

[6] Of course if 21. Kt × P, then B to Kt 5, and if P × P, B to R 6, winning the exchange; for if the attacked Rook moves, then 22. ... R to Kt 3, ch; 23. Kt × R, Q to Kt 4, ch.

[7] This if forced, for if P to B 3, then R × Kt wins.

[8] There is no possibility of saving the Knight. If Q to K 4 or Q 4, then simply B to B 3, and the Knight will ultimately be lost.

[9] This obvious sacrifice finishes the game at once.

A. BURN v. DR. TARRASCH.

WHITE	BLACK
1 P to Q 4	P to Q 4
2 P to Q B 4	P to K 3
3 Kt to Q B 3	P to Q B 3
4 P to K 3	P to K B 4 [1]
5 Kt to K B 3	B to Q 3
6 P to B 5 [2]	B to B 2
7 P to Q Kt 4	Kt to Q 2
8 B to Q Kt 2	Q to K 2 [3]
9 P to Kt 5	Q to B 3
10 P to Q R 4	Kt to K 2
11 P to R 5	P to Q R 3
12 P × P	P × P
13 Q to Q 2 [4]	P to K 4 [5]
14 Kt to Q R 4	P to K 5
15 Kt to Kt sq	P to B 5
16 Kt to Kt 6	P × P

WHITE	BLACK
17 P × P	Castles

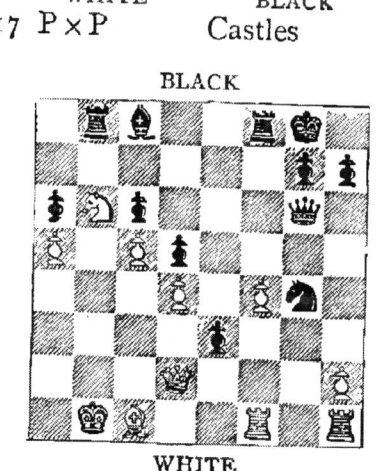

White to make his 28th move.

AUGUST 16

	WHITE	BLACK		WHITE	BLACK
18	Castles [6]	R to Kt sq	25	Kt to B 4	B × Kt (B 5)
19	Kt to K 2	Kt to B 4	26	P × B	Kt × B
20	K to B 2 [7]	Q to R 3	27	Q R × Kt	P to K 6, ch
21	B to B sq	Kt to B 3	28	P to B 5	P × Q
22	P to K Kt 3	Kt to Kt 5	29	P × Q	B to B 4, ch
23	R to K sq [8]	Kt (B 4) × P, ch	30	K to R 2	P × B (Q)
24	K to Kt sq	Q to Kt 3		White resigns.	

NOTES BY E. SCHIFFERS.

[1] Black has formed the so-called 'stone wall.' It is well known that formerly Dr. Tarrasch did not approve of this opening

[2] This is hardly ever good; on the approach of White's Pawns, Black blocks up the game on the Queen's side and generally obtains an opportunity for attacking on the other wing.

[3] Apparently loses time.

[4] In order to defend the Queen's Rook's Pawn after Kt to Q R 4, White should have first brought out his White Bishop and Castled on the King's side.

[5] Black had gradually prepared this move, and now obtains the attack.

[6] Dangerous, but necessary; Kt to K R 3 would be no better. White has made too many moves on the Queen's side, and thus left the King's side undeveloped. See note 2.

[7] Black threatened to capture the King's Pawn with the Knight if the White Knight leaves K 2.

[8] White cannot save the game; his forces are completely disorganised.

D. JANOWSKI v. H. N. PILLSBURY.

	WHITE	BLACK		WHITE	BLACK
1	P to Q 4	P to Q 4	17	Kt to Q 4	B to Kt 2
2	P to Q B 4	P to K 3	18	Kt to Kt 3 [7]	Q to R 5
3	Kt to Q B 3	Kt to K B 3	19	B × Kt [8]	P × B
4	Kt to B 3	B to K 2	20	Kt to B 3	Q to Q 2
5	B to B 4	Castles	21	Kt to Q 4	B to K B 3
6	P to K 3	P to B 4	22	Q to Q 3	Q R to Q B sq
7	B to Q 3	Kt to B 3 [1]	23	R (K B sq) to Q sq	
8	Castles [2]	Q P × P			K R to K sq
9	B × B P	Kt to K R 4	24	R to K sq	P to Kt 3
10	P × P [3]	Kt × B	25	R × R, ch	Q × R
11	P × Kt	B × P	26	R to Q sq [9]	Q to Q 2
12	Kt to K 4 [4]	B to K 2	27	Q to K 3	R to K sq
13	R to B sq	Q to R 4	28	Q to B 3	P to Q R 3
14	Q to B 2 [5]	Kt to Kt 5	29	Q to Q 3	P to Q Kt 4
15	Q to K 2	Kt to Q 4	30	P to Q R 3 [10]	Q to B 2
16	P to K Kt 3 [6]	P to Q Kt 3	31	Q to B 3	Q to B 5 [11]

WHITE	BLACK	WHITE	BLACK
32 Kt (B 3) to K 2 [12]	R to K 5 [13]	36 P to B 5	P to Q R 4
		37 P to Kt 4	P to Kt 5
		38 R P × P	R P × P
		39 Q to K Kt 3	B to K 4
		40 P to B 4	B to Kt 7
		41 Q to R 4	R to K sq
		42 P to B 6	B to K 5
		43 P to Kt 5	P to R 4
		44 Kt to Kt 3	P to B 6
		45 Kt × B	P to B 7
		46 Kt to Kt 3	P to B 8 (Q), ch
		47 K to Kt 2	Q to Q 7, ch
		48 K to R 3	R to K 7 [17]
		49 Kt × R	Q × Kt
		50 Q to Kt 3	B to Q 5
		51 P to B 5	Q to B 8, ch
		52 K to R 4 [18]	B to B 7
		53 P × P	P × P
		54 P to B 7, ch	K × P
			White resigns.

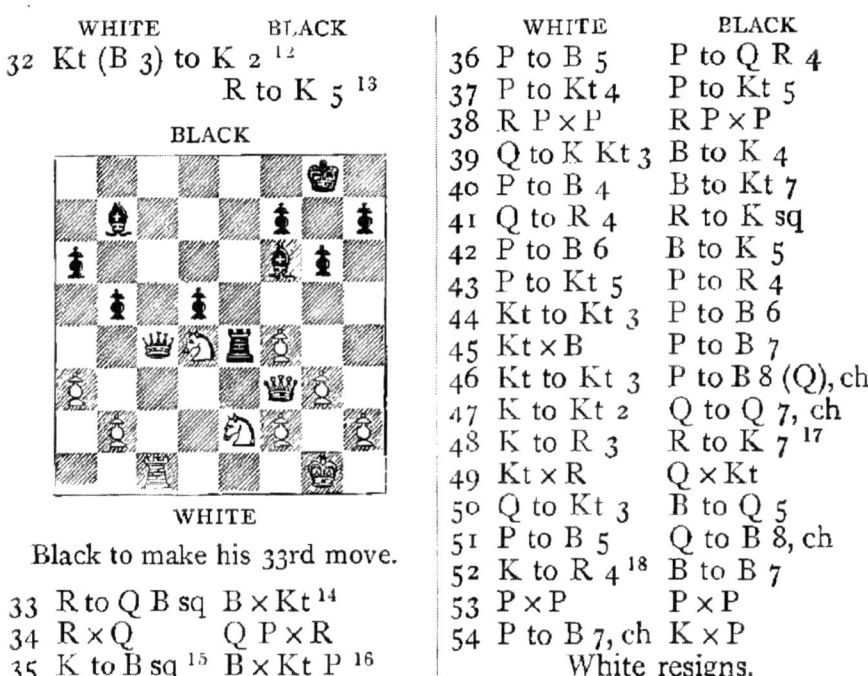

Black to make his 33rd move.

33 R to Q B sq	B × Kt [14]		
34 R × Q	Q P × R		
35 K to B sq [15]	B × Kt P [16]		

NOTES BY DR. TARRASCH.

[1] Black has managed this difficult opening with great care.

[2] Here P to K R 3 would be advisable, so as to secure the Bishop against exchange after Kt to R 4.

[3] It was better to withdraw the Bishop to Kt 3.

[4] The game up to this is tolerably even. Although White has the better development, he has a doubled Pawn, and Black has the advantage of two Bishops; as frequently happens, when positions are equal and no immediate attack is possible, the play begins to be without definite scheme.

[5] Q to K 2 at once would save time.

[6] The King's position is now somewhat weakened, and White must be careful that the possession of the long diagonal should not be ruinous to him.

[7] Here P to B 5 was very strong. Black by taking would yield White a good attack by Kt × P; if the Pawn advances Black's centre is blocked, and the action of White's Bishop would be strengthened; the Pawn also threatens a timely further advance.

[8] After this exchange White gets some disadvantage, by degrees, on account of the passed Queen's Pawn. It was still preferable to play P to B 5, for if then P × P; 20. B × Kt, B × B; 21. Kt to B 3, Q to Q 2; 22. R to Q sq, winning a Piece, or 22. Kt × B, Q × Kt; 23. Q × B.

[9] The Rook is not wanted on this file, since the chance of a

successful attack on the isolated Queen's Pawn is slight ; he should, on the contrary, rather try to occupy the King's file.

[10] This weakens the Queen's wing, but if White omits the move, P to Kt 5 drives the Knight from its attack on the Queen's Pawn and gives Black a greater choice of play

[11] Black has strengthened his position in the last few moves

[12] Evidently with the design of driving the Queen from her threatening position by R to Q B sq.

[13] Commencing a beautiful, well-considered sacrificial combination, which decides the game. Black has manifestly reckoned on the following move of his opponent

[14] This sacrifice is not compulsory, for Black can attack also by Q to R 7 ; 34. Kt to B 3, Q × Kt P , 35. R to Kt sq, Q to Q 7 ; 36. Kt × R, P × Kt ; 37. Kt to Kt 3, Q to R 7 ; 38 Q to Q sq, Q × R P, breaking in.

[15] The White Pieces are unpleasantly fettered ; if Kt × B, the Rook checks and wins the Queen. White could, however, apparently get an even game by Q × R, B × Q (Black must not play B × P, ch, gaining a Pawn, on account of its giving White two extra moves in a position where time is so important) , 36 Kt × B, &c., but even then Black, after bringing his K to Q B 4, will have the better game, as analysis has shown me, on account of the majority of Pawns on the Queen's side giving him an advantage.

[16] Pillsbury has now a won game, which he follows to the end with masterly precision.

[17] White could have resigned now Notice the energy with which Pillsbury plays, not simply to win, but for a mate

[18] If White interpose the Queen, mate follows by Q × P, ch, B to B 7, ch, and Q to Kt 5.

C. Schlechter v. H. E. Bird.

	WHITE	BLACK		WHITE	BLACK
1	P to K 4	P to K 3	15	K R to K sq	B to K sq
2	P to Q 4	P to Q 4	16	Q to B 2	Kt (K 2) to Q 4
3	Kt to Q B 3	Kt to K B 3	17	Kt to Kt 5	P to K Kt 3
4	B to K Kt 5	B to K 2	18	Kt (Kt 5) to K 4	
5	P × P [1]	Kt × P			Kt × Kt
6	B × B	Kt × B [2]	19	Kt × Kt	P to Q Kt 3
7	Kt to B 3	P to Q B 3	20	Q to Q B sq [5]	Q to K B 5
8	B to Q 3	Kt to Q 2	21	Q × Q	Kt × Q
9	Castles	Kt to B 3	22	B to B sq	K to Kt 2
10	Kt to K 2 [3]	Castles	23	P to K Kt 3	Kt to Q 4
11	P to Q B 3	Q to Kt 3	24	B to K Kt 2	P to K R 3
12	Q to Kt 3 [4]	Q to B 2	25	Kt to Q 2	Q R to Q B sq
13	Kt to Kt 3	R to Q sq	26	Kt to B 4	Q R to Q B 2
14	Q R to Q sq	B to Q 2	27	Kt to K 5	K R to Q B sq

THE HASTINGS CHESS TOURNAMENT

WHITE	BLACK		WHITE	BLACK
28 Kt to Q 3	Kt to K 2		39 Kt to K 2	B to R 4
29 B to K 4	P to Q B 4 [6]		40 R to K sq	B × Kt
			41 Q R × B	Kt to B 4 [10]
			42 R × P	R × P
			43 B to Q 5	Kt to Q 5
			44 R to K 8	P to B 4
			45 R to Kt 8, ch	K to R 2
			46 R (K sq) to K 8	
				P to Kt 5
			47 R to R 8, ch	K to Kt 3
			48 R (K 8) to Kt 8, ch	
				R to Kt 2
			49 R to Q 8	R to R 3
			50 P to R 3	P × P
			51 K to R 2	Kt × P
			52 K × P	Kt to Q 5
			53 R to Q B 8	Kt to Kt 6 [11]
			54 P to B 3	R to Q 3
30 P × P	P × P		55 P to Kt 4	K to Kt 4
31 Kt to K 5	B to Kt 4 [7]		56 K to Kt 3	P × P
32 B to Kt 2	R to Q Kt sq		57 P × P	R to K B 3
33 R to Q 2	R to Kt 3 [8]		58 R (B 8) to K 8	
34 K R to Q sq	R to R 3			Kt to Q 7 [12]
35 P to Q B 4	B to R 5		59 R to K 5, ch	K to Kt 3
36 P to Kt 3	P to B 3 [9]		60 R to R 5	R to R 2
37 Kt to Q 3	B to K sq		61 R to Kt 8, ch	R to Kt 2
38 Kt to B 4	P to Kt 4		Drawn game.	

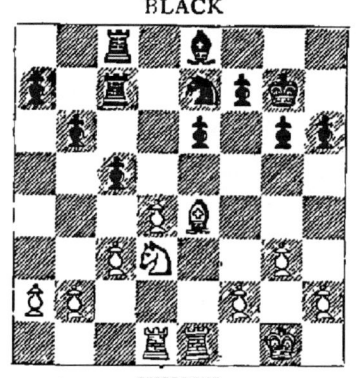

White to make his 30th move.

NOTES BY H. N. PILLSBURY

[1] Not as good as 5. P to K 5, K Kt to Q 2 ; 6. B × B, Q × B ; 7 Q to Q 2, &c.

[2] Q × B was superior.

[3] White has much the freer position, and something more energetic seems needed here to keep his advantage. 10. Q to K 2, followed by Q R to Q sq, seems superior to the text.

[4] True to the teaching of the 'Vienna' school. White by this move offers a draw. Either Q to B 2 or Q 2 were developing and kept the advantage of position with White.

[5] Were White desirous of a fight, P to K Kt 3 first, followed by Q to Q 2, was the correct idea.

[6] Black here makes a bid for something more than a draw, with which his opponent apparently would be satisfied.

[7] To prevent Kt to B 4 and Q 6.

[8] This and the next move place the Rook out of play ; it stood better at Q Kt sq.

AUGUST 16

[9] The only good move, but it serves to equalise matters.

[10] Black appears to have now fully as good a game as White, as the Knight against Bishop compensates for the weakness of Pawns on the Queen's side. The line of play now initiated seems unnecessary and hazardous; either P to K 4 or K to B 2 seems safer.

[11] Although Black has won a Pawn and at the same time kept his King sufficiently defended, yet the position will admit of no more than a draw, owing to the threatening attitude of White's Pieces.

[12] Necessary to prevent the check at K 4 with the Bishop on the 61st move. A draw is now the legitimate result of a well-played ending.

AUGUST 17.

This day sees Steinitz at his best. His game *v.* Bardeleben is a gem of the first water (afterwards awarded first prize for sound brilliancy), and the final picture is a *chef-d'œuvre* of an old master. The weather is very hot, which may have caused Tchigorin listlessly to draw against Bird, letting Pillsbury up level with $8\frac{1}{2}$. Bardeleben also loses his prominent position to $7\frac{1}{2}$, Lasker again by drawing only reached $7\frac{1}{2}$; other prominent scores being Schiffers $6\frac{1}{2}$, Bird and Walbrodt 6, Steinitz and Teichmann $5\frac{1}{2}$, Tarrasch 5. This finishes the second week, and on Monday the Minor or Amateur Tournament commences.

B. Vergani *v.* E. Schiffers.

	WHITE	BLACK		WHITE	BLACK
1	P to K 4	P to K 3	20	K to B sq	Q Kt to B 3
2	P to Q 4	P to Q 4	21	B × Kt	B P × B
3	P × P [1]	P × P	22	Kt to B 3 [8]	P × Kt
4	Kt to K B 3	Kt to K B 3	23	R × R	Kt × R
5	B to Q 3	B to Q 3 [2]	24	P × P	Q to K B 2
6	Castles	Castles	25	K to Kt 2	B to Kt sq
7	B to K 3 [3]	B to K Kt 5 [4]	26	Q to K 2	Kt to Kt 2
8	Q Kt to Q 2	Q Kt to Q 2	27	P to K B 4	P × P
9	P to B 3	P to B 3	28	Q to Kt 4	P to B 6, ch
10	Q to B 2 [5]	Q to B 2	29	K to Kt sq	K to R 2
11	P to K R 3	B × Kt	30	K to R sq	Q to Kt 3
12	Kt × B	Q R to K sq	31	R to Kt sq	Q × Q
13	Q R to K sq	Kt to K 5 [6]	32	R × Q	R to K sq
14	B to B sq	P to K B 4	33	B to K 3	Kt to B 4
15	R to K 2	P to K R 3	34	K to Kt sq	Kt × B
16	K R to K sq	P to K Kt 4 [7]	35	P × Kt	R × P
17	Kt to Q 2	B to R 7, ch	36	K to B 2	R to K 7, ch
18	K to B sq	B to B 5	37	K × P	R × P
19	K to Kt sq	B to R 7, ch		White resigns.	

Photo., Bradshaw, Hastings

AUGUST 17

Notes by I. Gunsberg.

[1] This old-fashioned continuation is after all safest, as it leaves White the initiative of the first move, and he can proceed in a quiet way; whereas in the more showy continuation of 3. Q Kt to B 3, Black has often been known to obtain a dangerous preponderance on the Queen's side.

[2] We prefer B to K 2 for the second player in every opening where it is impossible to play B to Q B 4.

[3] The Bishop is not strongly posted on K 3.

[4] As a rule it is not good to pin the King's Knight, unless one is assured of the co-operation of the Queen's Knight either on K 4 or Q 5. If Black, however, had played P to B 3 and Q to B 2, then there would have been some object in pinning the King's Knight.

[5] White proceeds in the usual manner of development, but his game would be all the better if B to K 3 had not been played. It is strange that so many players should neglect the favourable opportunity which they have in this opening of converting the game into Queen's side play by resorting to P to Q Kt 3 and P to B 4, instead of playing P to B 3 and Q to B 2.

[6] This is a distinct gain for Black, and the direct result of the move of B to K 3, without which it would not only have been impossible for Black to plant his Knight on K 5, but it would perhaps have been feasible for White to play Kt to K 5.

[7] Black vigorously utilises the gain of time to develop an incisive attack.

[8] White breaks down under the pressure of attack. Black was threatening Kt to R 4, and Kt to Kt 6, mate. If White had played 22. P to K Kt 4, Kt × P; 23. P × Kt, Q to Kt 6, wins. Or if 22. P to Kt 4, Kt × P; 23. K to Kt 2, Kt × P, wins.

W. Steinitz v. C. von Bardeleben.

	WHITE	BLACK
1	P to K 4	P to K 4
2	Kt to K B 3	Kt to Q B 3
3	B to B 4	B to B 4
4	P to B 3	Kt to B 3
5	P to Q 4	P × P
6	P × P	B to Kt 5, ch
7	Kt to B 3 [1]	P to Q 4 [2]
8	P × P	K Kt × P
9	Castles	B to K 3 [3]
10	B to K Kt 5	B to K 2
11	B × Kt	Q B × B
12	Kt × B	Q × Kt
13	B × B	Kt × B

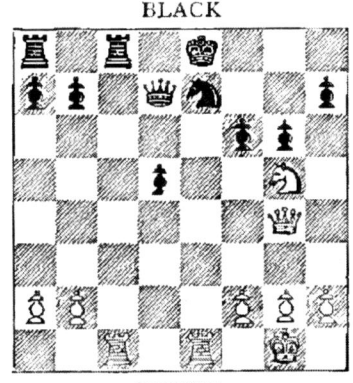

White to make his 22nd move.

	WHITE	BLACK		WHITE	BLACK
14	R to K sq (!)[4]	P to K B 3	21	Kt to Kt 5, ch	K to K sq
15	Q to K 2	Q to Q 2	22	R × Kt, ch (!!)[7]	K to B sq [8]
16	Q R to B sq	P to B 3 [5]	23	R to B 7, ch	K to Kt sq
17	P to Q 5 [6]	P × P	24	R to Kt 7, ch	K to R sq
18	Kt to Q 4	K to B 2	25	R × P, ch (!)[9]	Resigns.[10]
19	Kt to K 6	K R to Q B sq			
20	Q to Kt 4	P to Kt 3			

NOTES BY DR. TARRASCH.

[1] This move is mentioned by Greco, and Steinitz has again recommended it in his 'Modern Chess Instructor'; this variation was also played by him against Schlechter in this Tournament.

[2] Schlechter here played Kt × K P, which is the correct move, following it up . 8. Castles, B × Kt ; 9. P × B, P to Q 4 ; 10. B to R 3 (Steinitz's new move, on which the whole variation depends), B to K 3; 11. B to Kt 5, Kt to Q 3, with an equal game.

[3] If Kt (or B) × Kt ; 10. P × Kt, B × P, White gets a dangerous attack by 11 B × P, ch, K × B ; 12. Q to Kt 3, ch, &c

[4] The point of all the exchanges, as by this move White obtains command of the board, prevents Black from Castling, and initiates a most powerful attack on the King.

[5] It would have been preferable to play the K to B 2, as White had then nothing better than 17. Q × Kt, ch, Q × Q ; 18. R × Q, ch, K × R ; 19. R × P, ch, followed by R × Q Kt P, and Black has still a prospect of a draw.

[6] A nice sacrifice of a Pawn, making way for the Knight to powerfully strengthen the attack.

[7] Here begins a grand combination. (See diagram.)

[8] The position is most interesting, all the White Pieces being *en prise*. If K × R, then follows 23. R to K sq, ch, K to Q 3 , 24. Q to Q Kt 4, ch, K to B 2 ; 25. Kt to K 6, ch, K to Kt sq ; 26. Q to K B 4, ch, and wins.

[9] The checks by the Rook are delightful, as Black cannot take with King or he loses his Queen with a check, nor can he take with Queen or he is mated

[[10] For now if K to Kt sq, Mr. Steinitz (at the time) demonstrated the following brilliant and remarkable mate in ten moves:—

26	R to Kt 7, ch	K to R sq (or if K to B sq ; 27. Kt to R 7, ch, &c.)	30	Q to Kt 7, ch	K to K sq
27	Q to R 4, ch	K × R	31	Q to Kt 8, ch	K to K 2
			32	Q to B 7, ch	K to Q sq
28	Q to R 7, ch	K to B sq	33	Q to B 8, ch	Q to K sq
29	Q to R 8, ch	K to K 2	34	Kt to B 7, ch	K to Q 2
			35	Q to Q 6, mate.	ED.]

AUGUST 17

J. H. BLACKBURNE v. A. BURN.

	WHITE	BLACK		WHITE	BLACK
1	P to K 4	P to K 3	27	Kt × B P	Q to Kt 5
2	Kt to Q B 3	P to Q 4	28	Q to Q 2	Q × K P
3	P to Q 4	Kt to K B 3			
4	B to K Kt 5	P × P [1]			
5	Kt × P [2]	B to K 2			
6	Kt × Kt, ch	B × Kt			
7	B × B	Q × B			
8	Kt to B 3	Castles			
9	B to Q 3	P to B 4			
10	P to B 3	P × P			
11	Kt × P	P to K 4 [3]			
12	Kt to Kt 5	Kt to B 3			
13	Castles [4]	B to K 3			
14	Q to R 4	Q R to Q sq			
15	K R to Q sq	Q to Kt 4			
16	B to B sq	B to Kt 5			
17	R to Q 3	R × R			
18	B × R	B to B 6	29	Q to Q 6, ch	K to B 2
19	B to B sq	P to Q R 3	30	B × Kt, ch	Q × B [6]
20	Kt to Q 6	Kt to Q sq	31	Q to B 7, ch	K to Kt 3
21	Q to B 2	P to B 4	32	Q to Kt 3, ch	K × Kt
22	K to R sq	B to B 3	33	R to K B sq, ch	K to K 5
23	R to Q sq	Kt to K 3	34	R to K sq, ch	K to Q 4
24	P to B 3	R to B 3	35	Q to Q 3, ch	K to B 4
25	B to B 4	P to K 5 [5]	36	Q to Q 4, ch	K to Kt 4
26	P × P	K to B sq	37	Q to Kt 4, mate.	

White to make his 29th move.

NOTES BY E. SCHIFFERS.

[1] The usual move here is B to K 2.

[2] After 5. B × Kt, Black would probably have retaken with the Pawn, as in the game Marco v. Burn.

[3] The Queen's Bishop is now free and the game equalised.

[4] A good continuation also was Kt to Q B 7, R to Kt sq; Kt to Q 5, &c.

[5] Apparently Black cannot save the Pawn.

[6] After 30. ... R × B, would follow 31. Q to B 7, ch, 32. Q × P, ch 33. R to K B sq, ch, and wins.

W. H. K. POLLOCK v. D. JANOWSKI.

	WHITE	BLACK		WHITE	BLACK
1	P to K 4	P to K 4	3	P to B 3	Kt to B 3 [1]
2	Kt to K B 3	Kt to Q B 3	4	P to Q 4	K Kt × P

	WHITE	BLACK		WHITE	BLACK
5	P to Q 5	Kt to Q Kt sq	27	P to B 3	Q to K 7
6	B to Q 3	Kt to B 4	28	R to Kt 3	P to K Kt 4
7	Kt × P	Kt × B, ch	29	R to Q 4	P to R 5
8	Kt × Kt	B to K 2	30	B to B 2	Kt to R 4
9	Castles	P to Q 3	31	R to K 4	Q to Q 7
10	P to Q B 4 [2]	Castles [3]	32	R × Kt P [8]	Q to B 8, ch
11	Kt to B 3 [4]	B to K B 4 (!) [5]	33	K to R 2	Q to B 8
12	Q to B 3 [6]	B to Kt 3	34	B to Kt sq	Kt to Kt 6
13	B to K B 4	Kt to Q 2	35	R to K Kt 4	K to Kt 3
14	K R to K sq	B to B 3	36	R × B P	P to B 4
15	Q R to B sq	B × Kt	37	R to Q 4	Kt to K 7
16	R × B	Q to B 3	38	B to K 3	P to B 5 [9]
17	Q to K 3	P to K R 3	39	R to K 4 (!) [10]	
18	B to Kt 3	Q R to K sq [7]			Q to Q Kt 8 (!) [11]
19	Q × R	R × Q	40	R to K 6, ch	K to R 4
20	R × R, ch	K to R 2	41	B to B 2	Kt to Kt 6
21	R to K 3	Q to Q 5	42	B to K sq	Kt to B 8, ch
22	P to K R 3	P to K R 4	43	K to Kt sq	Kt to K 6
23	Kt to K sq	B to K 5	44	K to R 2	Kt to B 8, ch
24	Kt to B 3	B × Kt	45	K to Kt sq	Kt to K 6
25	R × B	Kt to B 3	46	K to R 2	
26	K R to Q 3	Q to K 5		Drawn game.	

NOTES BY C. VON BARDELEBEN.

[1] I prefer the usual defence, P to Q 4.

[2] White would have a very good game if he played 10. Q to B 3 in order to prevent Black developing his Queen's Bishop.

[3] B to B 4 would be better.

[4] Now again White should have played Q to B 3.

[5] After this move has been made, the game is equalised.

[6] Too late (!)

[7] White threatened to play 19. Q to K 7, and therefore Black rightly gives two Rooks for the Queen.

[8] This looks very dangerous, but the attack of Black is not so strong as it seems to be

[9] If Black takes the Rook with the Knight, the White Pawns become very strong, and Black would have no better chance than after the line adopted.

[10] Very cleverly played Of course now Black cannot capture the Bishop because of 40. R to K 6, ch, and mate on the next move

[11] The only way to defend the King against the threatening 40. R to K 6, ch, K to R 4 ; 41. R to R 7, mate.

AUGUST 17

A. Walbrodt v. C. Schlechter.

	WHITE	BLACK		WHITE	BLACK
1	P to K 4	P to K 4	24	R to Q sq	K R to K sq
2	Kt to K B 3	Kt to K B 3	25	K to Q 2	Kt to R 3
3	Kt to B 3	Kt to B 3	26	R to Q Kt sq [6]	
4	P to Q 4	B to Kt 5 [1]			P to Kt 3
5	P to Q 5	Kt to K 2	27	Kt to Q 4	R to K 4 [7]
6	Kt × P	Kt × K P	28	R to K R sq [8]	R to Kt 4
7	Q to Q 4	B × Kt, ch	29	P to Kt 3	K to Kt 2
8	P × B	Kt to K B 3	30	B to K 2	R (Kt 4) to K 3
9	P to Q B 4	P to Q 3	31	B to Q 3	R to Kt 4
10	Kt to B 3	Kt to Kt 3	32	R (R sq) to R 4	
11	B to Kt 2 [2]	Q to K 2, ch			R (Kt 4) to K 4
12	B to K 2	B to B 4	33	Kt to B 3	R (K 4) to K 2
13	Castles Q R	Q to K 5	34	P to Kt 4	P to R 3
14	Q to Q 2	Q to B 5 [3]	35	R to R sq	K to R sq
15	B × Kt	Q × Q, ch	36	Kt to R 2	K to Kt 2
16	R × Q	P × B	37	R to K Kt sq	Kt to Kt sq
17	Kt to Q 4	B to Q 2	38	Kt to B 3 [9]	P to R 3
18	P to K R 4	Castles K R [4]	39	Kt to Q 4	K to R sq
19	P to R 5	Kt to K 2	40	R to Q Kt sq [10]	
20	R to R 4	K to R sq			R to K 4
21	R to B 4	Kt to Kt sq	41	Kt to B 3	R (K 4) to K 2
22	B to Q 3 [5]	Q R to K sq	42	R to K Kt sq	K to Kt 2
23	Kt to B 3	R to K 2	43	R to Q Kt sq	K to R sq
			44	K to B 3	K to Kt 2
			45	K to Q 4	R to K 4
			46	K to B 3	R (K 4) to K 2
			47	R to K Kt sq	K to R sq [11]
			48	R to Q Kt sq	K to Kt 2
			49	K to Q 2	K to R sq
			50	R to Kt 3	K to Kt 2
			51	K to B 3	K to R sq
			52	R to R 3	B to B sq
			53	R to Kt 3	B to Q 2
			54	R to Kt sq	K to Kt 2
			55	R to K R sq	K to R sq
			56	K to Q 2	K to Kt 2
			57	Kt to Q 4	R to K 4

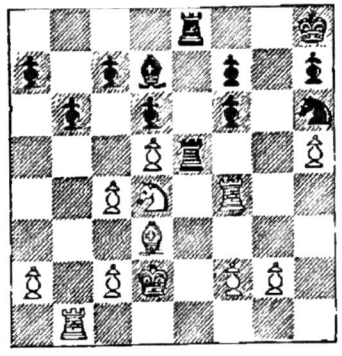

White to make his 28th move.

Drawn game.

Notes by J. H. Blackburne.

[1] P × P, turning it into a 'Scotch,' is considered best
[2] B to K 2 or Q 3 looks stronger.

[3] The position already has a drawish appearance.

[4] This is risky; White, however, has scarcely sufficient force left to do any serious damage.

[5] Better to have got rid of the adverse Bishop by B to Kt 4, afterwards planting the Knight on K B 5.

[6] If R × P, then Kt to Kt 5, recovering the Pawn with the better position.

[7] Here Black gives a chance. Kt to Kt sq or K to Kt 2, defending the Pawn, ought to have been played.

[8] A more enterprising player would have ventured upon R × B P, in which case the following variation would probably have occurred—28. R × B P, R × R P; 29. P to K B 3, R to R 7; 30. K to B 3, K to Kt 2; 31. R to B 4, and White has the superior game, because if Black now plays R × P, White replies with R to K R sq.

[9] Here again he misses his opportunity. P to R 6, ch, gives many chances of winning; for example—38. P to R 6, ch, K × P; 39. Kt to B 3, K to Kt 2; 40. P to Kt 5, P to K B 4 (best); 41. Kt to Q 4, R to K 4; 42. R to R 4, and White has the advantage. Black, instead of 38. K × P, might also play Kt × P or K to R sq, but in either case White obtains the better position.

[10] B to B 5 would be more to the purpose.

[11] Both players wait for the mistake, which never comes; hence the result—a draw.

Dr. Tarrasch v. R. Teichmann.

	WHITE	BLACK
1	P to K 4	P to K 4
2	Kt to K B 3	Kt to Q B 3
3	B to Kt 5	P to Q R 3
4	B to R 4	Kt to K B 3
5	P to Q 3	P to Q 3
6	P to Q B 3	B to K 2 [1]
7	Q Kt to Q 2	Castles
8	Kt to B sq	P to Q Kt 4
9	B to Kt 3 [2]	P to Q 4
10	Q to K 2	P × P
11	P × P	B to Q B 4
12	Kt to Kt 3	Q to K 2
13	Castles [3]	Q Kt to R 4
14	B to B 2	Kt to B 5
15	P to Q R 4 [4]	R to Kt sq
16	P × P	P × P
17	P to Q Kt 3	Kt to Q 3
18	B to Kt 5	P to K R 3
19	B to K 3	B to Kt 3 [5]
20	B × B	R × B
21	Q to K 3	R to B 3 [6]
22	P to K R 3	Kt to Kt 2 [7]
23	K R to Q B sq	
		R to K sq
24	B to Q 3	Kt to Q 3

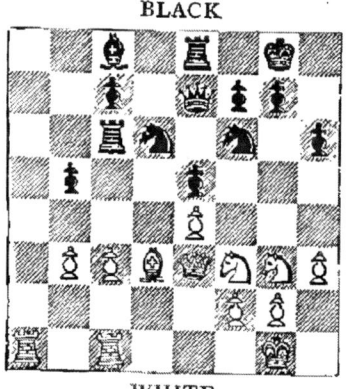

White to make his 25th move.

	WHITE	BLACK
25	R to R 5 [8]	R to R 3 [9]
26	K R to R sq [10]	
		R × R
27	R × R	Q to Q 2
28	P to B 4 [11]	P to B 3
29	R to R 7	B to Kt 2
30	Q to K 2	P × P
31	P × P	P to B 4
32	Q to Q Kt 2	Q to B sq
33	Kt × P	Q to Kt sq
34	Q to R sq [12]	Kt to B sq

	WHITE	BLACK
35	R × B	Q × R
36	Kt to Kt 4	Kt × Kt
37	P × Kt	P to B 3
38	Kt to B 5	Q to Q 2
39	B to B 2	Q to Q B 2
40	Q to R 3	Kt to Kt 3
41	P to K Kt 3	R to R sq
42	Q to Kt 2	K to B sq
43	Q to Kt 3	Kt to Q 2
44	Kt to K 3	
	White resigns.[13]	

NOTES BY H. N. PILLSBURY.

[1] A well-known form of the Lopez attack has developed. Many masters, notably Tchigorin, prefer to develop this Bishop at K Kt 2.

[2] Steinitz and others would prefer B to B 2 at once.

[3] Generally the first player in previous games in this opening has preferred to Castle Queen's Rook, and prosecute the attack upon the adverse King by advancing his Pawns; but the Black Pawns would advance upon the Queen's side too rapidly in this position, therefore Dr Tarrasch abandons this idea.

[4] The opened file proves of great service to White later on.

[5] Inasmuch as the King's Pawn needs more protection soon, Black might have tried here Kt to Q 2, being then prepared to support it by P to K B 3.

[6] The movement of the Rook only loses time, and leads to the direct loss of a Pawn later on. Moreover, Kt to Q 2 was always correct to prevent the Queen's entrance at B 5.

[7] Also loss of time.

[8] This move might have won a clear Pawn.

[9] An error: R to Kt 3; 26. Q to B 5, B to Kt 2 would have saved the Pawn.

[10] Unaccountable, except perhaps on account of time-pressure: 26 R × P, Kt × R; 27. B × Kt, &c., would have won the Pawn clear.

[11] Also here Q to B 5 would win a Pawn.

[12] A tremendous error which loses the exchange; R to R 5 still left White with the superior game.

[13] White here exceeded his time, and thereupon resigned. Black should win, however, being soon able to enter the 8th row with combined Queen and Rook and form a mating position, from which White could only escape by decisive loss of material.

H. N. Pillsbury v. J. Mason.

	WHITE	BLACK		WHITE	BLACK
1	P to Q 4	P to Q 4	19	Kt to K 5	P to B 4 [5]
2	P to Q B 4	P to K 3	20	R × P	R × R
3	Kt to Q B 3	Kt to K B 3	21	R × R	Kt to Q 2
4	B to Kt 5	B to K 2	22	R to B 6	Kt to Kt sq [6]
5	Kt to B 3	P to Q Kt 3	23	R × Q	Kt × Q
6	P to K 3	B to Kt 2	24	Kt to B 6	P to K Kt 3
7	R to B sq	P × P [1]	25	Kt × P	R to R sq
8	B × P	Q Kt to Q 2	26	Kt to B 6	K to Kt 2 [7]
9	Castles	Castles	27	P to Q R 3	R to Q B sq
10	Q to K 2	Kt to Q 4	28	P to K Kt 4	Kt to B 2
11	B × B	Q × B	29	Kt to K 7	R to Q Kt sq
12	Kt × Kt	P × Kt	30	R to Q 7	Kt to K 3
13	B to Kt 5	Q to Q 3 [2]	31	Kt × Q P	R to Q B sq
14	R to B 2	P to Q B 3	32	Kt × P	R to B 7
15	B to Q 3	Kt to B 3 [3]	33	P to Kt 4	Kt to Kt 4
16	K R to Q B sq	Q R to B sq	34	P to Q R 4	Kt to K 5
17	B to R 6 [4]	B × B	35	P to R 5	Kt × P
18	Q × B	R to B 2	36	P to R 6	Resigns. [8]

Notes by R. Teichmann.

[1] If he intended to take this Pawn he might have waited till White had developed his B to Q 3, then gaining a move; though White would most likely have exchanged himself next move.

[2] He cannot push the P to B 4 on account of B × Kt; winning a Pawn.

[3] But I do not understand why he did not now play P to Q B 4, which seems to give him at least an even game. After the text move the Pawn is fixed and irretrievably weak.

[4] Taking immediate advantage of the omission, the Black Bishop's Pawn is doomed now.

[5] Seeing now that he cannot play K R to B sq on account of 17. Kt × P, R × Kt; 18. Q × R, ch (!), he prefers to lose the Pawn another way.

[6] There is no more to be said about the remainder of the game; he has to submit to the loss of several more Pawns, and might as well have resigned at once.

[7] A little trap: if 17. R × P, R to Q B sq; 18. R to Q 6, Kt to Kt 5, winning a Piece, but White is not in a hurry.

[8] It is evident that White Queen's Rook's Pawn will cost a Piece, and nothing in the way of disaster can happen to White's King except by the greatest kindness on White's part, such as 36. ... Kt to R 6, ch; 37. K to R sq, Kt to Kt 4; 38. P to R 7, Kt to B 6.

H. E. Bird v. M. Tchigorin.

	WHITE	BLACK		WHITE	BLACK
1	P to K 4	P to K 4	19	B to Q 3	B to Kt 2
2	Kt to K B 3	Kt to Q B 3	20	Kt to Q sq	P to R 3
3	B to B 4	B to B 4	21	Kt to K 3	P to Q B 4
4	P to Q Kt 4	B × Kt P	22	Kt to B 5	Q to B 3
5	P to B 3	B to R 4	23	B to K 4	B × B
6	Q to Kt 3	Q to B 3 [1]	24	Q × B	Q R to K sq
7	Castles	B to Kt 3	25	K to Kt 2	R to K 3
8	P to Q 4	P × P	26	Q to K Kt 4	K R to K sq
9	P to K 5	Q to Kt 3	27	R to B 2	Q to Kt 3
10	P × P	Kt × Q P	28	Q to B 3	P to K R 4
11	Kt × Kt	B × Kt	29	Q R to K 2	P to B 5
12	Kt to B 3	Kt to R 3	30	Kt to R 4	Q to Q 6
13	B to K 3 [2]	B × P	31	Q to Q B 6	B to B 3 [4]
14	B × Kt [3]	Q × B	32	R × R	R × R
15	P to Kt 3	Castles	33	R × R	P × R
16	K R to K sq	P to Q 3	34	Q to K 8, ch	K to R 2
17	Q R to B sq	P to Q B 3	35	Q × R P, ch	
18	Q to Kt sq	P to Q Kt 4		Drawn game.	

NOTES BY A. ALBIN.

[1] Many are of opinion that this defence is very bizarre, but of course much depends upon the lines of attack adopted by White. We find that Herr Tchigorin now plays his Black Bishop to Q Kt 3, and that he did not play K Kt to R 3 like his opponent Mr. Steinitz in his cable match. These being two essential points in this defence it is not easy to find the right continuation for the attack.

[2] B to R 3 would have been stronger, and if P to Q B 4, then 14. Kt to Kt 5, with a strong attack.

[3] White's resources are at an end and Black should win this game

[4] A weak move which allows a forced draw. The winning move is, I think, P to Q 4 (!).

[The latter part of this game was rapidly played. Mr. Bird's trap was ingenious, and he is unequalled at the lightning style.—ED.]

G. Marco v. A. Albin.

	WHITE	BLACK		WHITE	BLACK
1	P to K 4	P to K 3	6	B to Q 3	Castles
2	P to Q 4	P to Q 4	7	Castles	B to Kt 5
3	Kt to Q B 3	B to Kt 5 [1]	8	Q B to Kt 5	Kt to B 3
4	P × P	P × P	9	Kt to K 2	P to K R 3
5	Kt to K B 3	Kt to K B 3	10	B to R 4	B × Kt

WHITE	BLACK
11 P × B	P to K Kt 4
12 B to Kt 3	Q to Q 2
13 P to B 3	B to Q 3
14 B × B	Q × B
15 Kt to Kt 3	Kt to K 2
16 B to B 2	Q to B 5
17 Q to Q 3	Kt to Kt 3
18 Q R to K sq	P to K R 4 [2]
19 R to K 5 [3]	Kt to R 5
20 R to K 3	K to Kt 2
21 Kt × P, ch	Kt × Kt
22 Q to R 7, ch	K to B 3
23 Q × Kt	R to K R sq
24 Q to Kt 4	Resigns. [4]

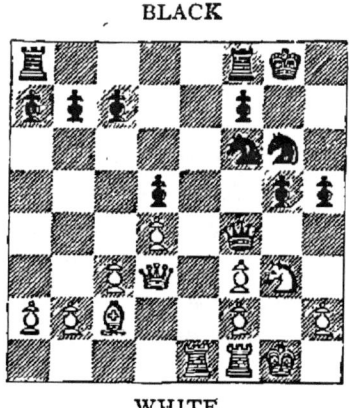

BLACK

WHITE

White to make his 19th move.

NOTES BY E. SCHIFFERS.

[1] This move is justly condemned by theory; it would not be advantageous to exchange the Bishop for the Queen's Knight, and still less so to retreat

[2] After 18. ... Kt to R 5, would follow 19. R to K 3, threatening Kt to B 5.

[3] A pretty but unsound sacrifice; Black might have played 19. ... Kt × R; 20. P × R, Q × P, and White would simply have lost the exchange. (See diagram.)

[4] Black inadvertently touched the Pawn at K B 3, which compelled the loss of the Queen.

[This was one of the questions which came before the Committee, but they decided that, although the touching may have been unintentional, Herr Marco was quite within his rights, if not even bound, to insist on the Pawn being taken, especially as the touching of it was probably an outcome of mental workings, for its capture with the Knight was at first sight very strong.—ED.]

J. MIESES v. E. LASKER.

WHITE	BLACK	WHITE	BLACK
1 P to K 4	P to K 4	10 Castles	R to Kt sq [3]
2 Kt to K B 3	Kt to Q B 3	11 R to K sq [4]	Kt to R 3
3 P to Q 4	P × P	12 Kt to Q 2	Castles
4 Kt × P	Kt to K B 3	13 Kt to B 3	P to B 3 [5]
5 Kt × Kt	Kt P × Kt	14 B × Kt	B × B
6 P to K 5	Q to K 2	15 Q to B 4, ch	K to R sq
7 Q to K 2	Kt to Kt sq [1]	16 P to Q Kt 3	B to K Kt 2
8 P to K Kt 3	P to K Kt 3 [2]	17 P to K 6 [6]	P to Q 4 [7]
9 B to Kt 2	B to K Kt 2	18 Q × B P	R to Q sq

AUGUST 17

	WHITE	BLACK
19	Q R to Q sq	R to Kt 3

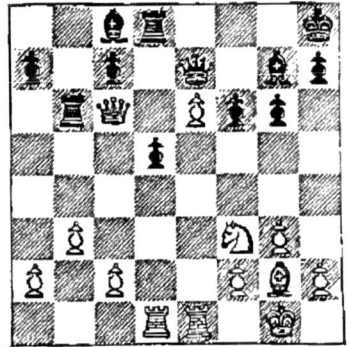

White to make his 20th move.

	WHITE	BLACK
20	Q to R 4 [8]	P to Q B 4
21	Q to R 4	R × K P
22	B to R 3	R to K 7
23	B × B	R × B
24	K to Kt 2	P to Q 5
25	Q to B 4	P to K B 4
26	R × R	Q × R
27	R to K sq (!) [9]	
		Q to R 3 [10]
28	Kt to Kt 5	Q to B 3, ch
29	Q to B 3 [11]	Q to Q 2 [12]
30	P to K R 4	P to Q B 5 [13]
31	P × P	R × P
32	Q to R 8, ch	R to B sq
33	R to K 7 [14]	R × Q
34	R × Q	P to K R 3
35	Kt to K 6	B to K 4
36	P to K B 4 [15]	R to K sq
37	R to Q 8 [16]	R × R
38	Kt × R	B to B 2
39	Kt to B 6	B to Kt 3
40	K to B 3	K to Kt 2
41	K to K 2	P to Kt 4
42	P to R 5 [17]	P × P
43	P × P	K to B 3
44	K to Q 3	B to B 2
45	Kt × R P	B × P
46	P to R 4	B to B 2
47	Kt to B 6	K to Kt 4
48	Kt × P [18]	K × P
49	Kt × P	K to Kt 4
50	K to K 4	P to R 4
51	Kt to Kt 7 [19]	P to R 5
52	K to B 3 [20]	B to Kt 3
53	P to B 4	K to B 3
54	Kt to K 8, ch	K to K 2
55	Kt to Kt 7	K to B 3
56	Kt to R 5, ch	K to K 4
	Drawn game.	

NOTES BY DR. TARRASCH.

[1] The usual move Kt to Q 4 is far better; from Knight's square the Knight comes into the game with difficulty and into unfavourable positions.

[2] The right move here was P to B 3.

[3] It would be very dangerous to take the King's Pawn. Black would have a very difficult game after B × P; 11. R to K sq, P to B 3; 12. Q to Q sq, K to B sq; 13. P to K B 4, B to Q 5, ch; 14. K to R sq.

[4] White has already a strong, well-developed game.

[5] White is now much better equipped than five moves ago.

[6] Very well played. If Black captures the Pawn, then Kt to Q 4 follows with advantage to White.

[7] Black sacrifices the Bishop's Pawn in order, later on, to successfully attack the King's Pawn; he might nevertheless have come off badly.

[8] Up to this point Mieses has led the assault adequately, but now he loses the opportunity of winning the game by an elegant sacrifice of the Queen. Instead of drawing back the Queen he ought to have simply played 20. Kt to Q 4, and if R × Q ; 21. Kt × R, Q to K sq ; 22. Kt × R, Q × Kt ; 23. P to K 7, Q to K sq ; 24 R × P, B to Q 2 ; 25. R × B, and Black has lost. On the other hand, 21. Q × R was threatened, to be followed by Kt to B 6 on similar lines. If 20 ... B to Kt 2, then follows, 21. Q × B, R × Q ; 22. Kt to B 6, Q to K sq ; 23. Kt × R, Q × Kt ; 24. P to K 7, Q to K sq , 25. B × P, R to Kt sq ; 26 B to B 6, Q × B ; 27. R to Q 8, ch, Q to K sq ; 28 R × R, and wins ; if in this variation 23. . . R to Kt sq ; 24. Kt to B 7, ch, K to Kt sq ; 25. P to K 7, K × Kt (?) ; 26. B × P, ch. In the other replies also White gets a decided advantage ; the text move, however, allows Black some freedom.

[9] White has now carried out his plans and obtained the entire command of the King's file, for should Black displace his Queen by Q × Q B P, then White would with 28 R to K 7 obtain a decided advantage ; the following elegant termination might have come about : 28.. . R to K Kt sq ; 29. Kt to Kt 5, P to K R 3 ; 30. Kt to B 7, ch, K to R 2 ; 31. Q × P, ch, B × Q ; 32. Kt to Kt 5, ch, K to R sq ; 33. R to R 7, mate.

[10] Now R to K 7 would simply be answered by B to B 3

[11] If White covers the check in any other way, Black opposes with R to K sq

[12] After the exchange of the Queen, White would also have an advantage on account of the possession of the King's file, and the better position of the Pawns.

[13] R to K sq would not be good on account of R × R, ch, followed by Q to Q 5.

[14] Again very masterly and surprisingly well played. Hereby White forces the exchange of the Queens and gets a better end game.

[15] Why White does not take the Queen's Pawn is difficult to understand. The text move makes the win more difficult, as it enables Black to dissolve the King's side later on.

[16] This is now the best , 37. Kt × P, B × Kt ; 38 R × B, R to K 7, ch ; 39. K to B 3, R × P ; 40. R to Q 8, ch, K to Kt 2 ; 41. R to Q 7, ch, and 42. R × P, would probably not be sufficient for a win.

[17] The consequences of White's 36th move show themselves now ; whilst White stands better on the Queen's side, Black gets a little chance on the King's side.

[18] White had here for the last time a chance to win, namely, by P to R 5. The game might then have proceeded as follows :—

WHITE	BLACK	WHITE	BLACK
48 P to R 5	K × P	53 Kt × P	K to B 5 (else White stops the Pawns with K to K 3 or K to K 4, followed by Kt to B 3)
49 P to R 6	B to Kt 3		
50 P to R 7	B × P		
51 Kt × B	K to Kt 5		
52 Kt to B 6	P to R 4	54 Kt to K 6, ch	K to K 4

AUGUST 17

	WHITE	BLACK		WHITE	BLACK
55	Kt to Kt 5	K to B 5	59	P to B 6	P to R 5
56	Kt to R 3, ch	K to Kt 6	60	P to B 7	P to R 6
57	P to B 4	K × Kt	61	P to B 8 (Q)	P to R 7
58	P to B 5	P to B 5	62	Q to B 2, ch	K to Kt 6
59	P to B 6	P to B 6	63	Q to Q sq	K to Kt 2
60	P to B 7	P to B 7	64	Q to K 2, ch	K to Kt 8 (or else Q to K B sq follows)
61	P to B 8(Q),ch	K to Kt 7			
62	Q to Kt 8, ch		65	K to K 3	P to B 5, ch
	or if—		66	K × P	P to R 8 (Q)
58		K to Kt 7	67	K to Kt 3, and wins.

[19] White thinks to win with this move, which threatens Kt × P or Kt to K 6, ch, but has overlooked the advance of the Pawn. No other move either could now win the game.

[20] After Knight checks and Kt × B White could no longer stop the Pawn.

I. GUNSBERG v. S. TINSLEY.

	WHITE	BLACK		WHITE	BLACK
1	P to K 4	P to Q 4	18	B × Kt	Kt × B
2	P × P	K Kt to B 3 [1]	19	Kt × B	B to Kt 2
3	P to Q 4 [2]	Kt × P	20	P to Q R 4 [7]	Q to B 3
4	P to Q B 4	Kt to K B 3	21	P to B 3	Kt to Kt 5 [8]
5	K Kt to B 3	P to B 3	22	B × P, ch	K to R sq
6	B to K 2 [3]	P to K 3	23	Kt to K 4 [9]	R × R
7	Castles	B to Q 3	24	R × R	Kt to K 6
8	P to Q Kt 3	Castles	25	Q to Q 3	Kt × R
9	B to Kt 2	Q Kt to Q 2	26	P to Q Kt 4	Kt to Kt 7
10	Q Kt to Q 2	Q to B 2	27	Q to Q 4	Q × P
11	R to Q B sq [4]	B to B 5 [5]	28	Q to K 5	Q to Q B 8, ch
12	P to K Kt 3	B to R 3	29	K to Kt 2	K × B
13	B to Q 3	R to Q sq	30	Q to R 5, ch	K to Kt sq
14	Q to B 2	P to B 4 [6]	31	Kt to Kt 5	Q to B 7, ch
15	Q R to Q sq	P to Q Kt 3	32	K to Kt sq	Q to Kt 3
16	P × P	B × Kt		White resigns.	
17	P × P	P × P			

NOTES BY J. MASON.

[1] Whether this or 2. Q × P, the time expended in retreat before inferior force is about the same; but the latter affords more variety of proceeding, and is therefore usually preferred.

[2] Though if White now chooses to rely upon the Pawn a question arises: Is it worth it? For instance, 3. P to Q B 4, P to B 3; 4. P × P, Kt × P; 5. Kt to K B 3, P to K 4; 6. P to Q 3, B to Q B 4, and Black will have a first-rate development, somewhat similar to that in the Two Knights' Defence, as compensation.

[3] An effort might well be made to post this Bishop at Q 3 directly. The opening appears to be conducted in a more or less mechanical or

perfunctory sort of way by both parties. Black blocks in his Queen's Bishop unnecessarily, and White retorts with a fianchetto, the use of which must be perfectly problematical, compared with that of other well-tried formations at his disposal

[4] Worse than useless, as matters fall out. Anyway, the Rook could hardly do good on this file, except in the event of subsequent P to Q 5, or something like that, not likely in the circumstances. But the reply may have been overlooked. 11 Q to B 2, leaving the Rook free to move otherwise, would be stronger.

[5] This is well played, if only to get round to defend his own King. And in driving it that way White weakens his position.

[6] Also good. Black improves from move to move, and when his Queen's Bishop takes the field, comes nearly level with his opponent

[7] To prevent 20. P to Q Kt 4 apparently, but the King should have been attended to by 20. P to B 3, seeing it to be almost certain that the Black Queen would take the diagonal, menacing instant mate. From this point White has indeed a difficult game.

[8] Meaning the exchange, if nothing more.

[9] On principle, as the saying is, 23. B to K 4 could be no worse. A Rook is lost and another Piece—the Bishop, to wit—in a desperate effort; and what might be an easily and well-prolonged contest comes to a surprisingly sudden end.

This concludes the first fortnight and the lesser half of the Tournament; the next round will be the middle one. The final scores and positions now begin to be guessed at, so it will be interesting to compare the present totals with those at the end of last week.

Steinitz	$4\frac{1}{2}$	$5\frac{1}{2}$	Burn	$2\frac{1}{2}$ $3\frac{1}{2}$
Tchigorin	4	$8\frac{1}{2}$	Pollock	2 $4\frac{1}{2}$
Bardeleben	4	$7\frac{1}{2}$	Schlechter	2 $4\frac{1}{2}$
Pillsbury	$3\frac{1}{2}$	$8\frac{1}{2}$	Gunsberg	2 $4\frac{1}{2}$
Schiffers	$3\frac{1}{2}$	$6\frac{1}{2}$	Blackburne	2 4
Lasker	3	$7\frac{1}{2}$	Janowski	2 $3\frac{1}{2}$
Tinsley	3	4	Albin	2 3
Mieses	3	$3\frac{1}{2}$	Tarrasch	$1\frac{1}{2}$ 5
Bird	$2\frac{1}{2}$	6	Mason	$1\frac{1}{2}$ 4
Walbrodt	$2\frac{1}{2}$	6	Marco	$1\frac{1}{2}$ 4
Teichmann	$2\frac{1}{2}$	$5\frac{1}{2}$	Vergani	— 1
Maximum				5 10

It will be seen that while this was Steinitz's fatal week, Tchigorin and Lasker both made their $4\frac{1}{2}$, and Pillsbury won all his games. Seeing, too, that this young master's only loss was on the first day to Tchigorin who is abreast, the end is already foreshadowed.

Photo., Bradshaw, Hastings

E. Lasker

AUGUST 19.

The play of the 19th is chiefly characterised by the shortness of the games and the disasters to the Black forces. Six games are finished before the first adjournment, and the Black men only score one and a half out of the eleven. Lasker is again first to win. The Schiffers v. Steinitz game is well worthy of attention and is a good example of the veteran's style.

On this day also the Committee, finding that applause, even if slight, was liable to be misunderstood by our foreign competitors, and in any case was annoying to the players, put up a notice asking visitors to refrain, and the directors of play and stewards had strict instructions to enforce the notice.

E. Lasker v. I. Gunsberg.

	WHITE	BLACK
1	P to K 4	P to K 3
2	P to Q 4	P to Q 4
3	Kt to Q B 3	Kt to K B 3
4	P to K 5	K Kt to Q 2
5	P to K B 4	P to Q B 4
6	P × P	B × P [1]
7	Q to Kt 4	Castles
8	B to Q 3	P to K B 4
9	Q to R 3	Kt to Q B 3
10	P to K Kt 4	Q to K 2
11	P × P	Kt to Kt 5
12	Kt to B 3 [2]	P × P
13	P to Q R 3 [3]	Kt × B
14	P × Kt	Kt to B 3
15	Q to Kt 2	P to Q 5 [4]
16	Kt to K 2	Kt to R 4 [5]
17	R to K Kt sq	P to Q R 4 [6]
18	Q to R 3	Q to K sq
19	R to Kt 5	P to R 3
20	R × Kt	Q to Kt 3

White to make his 12th move

	WHITE	BLACK
21	B to Q 2	B to Q 2
22	K to B 2	B to K sq
23	R to R 4	B to K 2
24	R to K Kt sq	B × R, ch [7]
25	Q × B	Q to R 3

WHITE	BLACK	WHITE	BLACK
26 K Kt × P	K to R 2	29 Kt to Kt 5, ch	K to Kt 3
27 B to B 3	Q × P	30 P to K 6	P to R 4
28 Kt to K 6	R to K Kt sq	31 Kt to B 7, ch	Resigns.

NOTES BY H. N. PILLSBURY.

[1] Kt to Q B 3 is far superior.

[2] White avoids wisely the complications arising from 12. P × P, Kt × B, ch; 13. P × Kt, Kt × K P; 14. P × Kt, B × P, &c., as Black appears to obtain too strong an attack for the sacrificed Piece. (See diagram.)

[3] 13. B × P, R × B; 14. Q × R, Kt to K B sq, followed by Kt × P, ch, would have given Black a winning superiority.

[4] R to Q sq, followed soon by Kt to K sq, would be better. The text loses at least a Pawn.

[5] It would be better to retreat this Knight to K sq. It is loosely placed at R 4.

[6] P to K Kt 3 was absolutely necessary to save the Knight.

[7] Black recovers the exchange for his lost Piece, but it is not enough.

S. TINSLEY v. B. VERGANI.

	WHITE	BLACK
1	P to Q 4	P to Q 4
2	P to Q B 4	P to K 3
3	Kt to Q B 3	Kt to K B 3
4	Kt to B 3	Kt to Q B 3 [1]
5	P to K 3	B to K 2
6	B to K 2	Castles
7	Castles	P to Q Kt 3
8	Kt to K 5	B to Kt 2 [2]
9	P to B 4	Kt to Q Kt sq
10	P × P	Kt × P [3]
11	B to Q 3	Kt to K B 3
12	Q to K 2	B to Q 3 [4]
13	R to Q sq	P to B 3
14	B to Q 2	Q to K 2
15	Q R to Q B sq	Q Kt to Q 2
16	Q to B 3	Kt to Q 4
17	Kt × Q Kt	Q × Kt
18	P to K 4 [5]	Kt to K 2
19	P to K 5	B to B 2
20	B to K 3	Kt to Q 4
21	Kt × Kt	B P × Kt
22	P to B 5	P × P

BLACK

WHITE

White to make his 18th move.

	WHITE	BLACK
23	B × P	Q to K 2 [6]
24	Q to Kt 3	B to Q sq
25	B to R 6	P to B 3
26	P to K 6	R to K sq
27	B to B 4	P to Kt 3 [7]
28	B × P	K to R sq
29	B × R	Q × B

AUGUST 19

	WHITE	BLACK		WHITE	BLACK
30	B to R 6	Q to Kt 3	38	R × P	K to Kt sq
31	Q × Q	P × Q	39	R to Q B sq	K to B 2
32	B to B 8	P to Q Kt	40	K R to B 7	B to K 3
33	B to B 5	B to B 2	41	R (R 7) to Kt 7	
34	B to K 7	B to Q sq			P to B 4
35	B × B	R × B	42	R × P	R × P
36	R to B 7	B to B sq	43	R (Kt 5) to Kt 7	
37	P to K 7	R to K sq			Resigns.

NOTES BY R. TEICHMANN.

[1] This is against the elementary rules, to obstruct the Queen's Bishop's Pawn with the Knight in close games. The move can only be good when a break in the centre with P to K 4 is feasible.

[2] Thereby trying to rectify the mistake pointed out in Note 1.

[3] Here P × P would be better to prevent an advance of the White King's Pawn.

[4] White has not taken proper advantage of Black's feeble development, and Black would now have at least equalised the game with P to Q B 4. I cannot see the object of the text move.

[5] Initiating a powerful attack. The advance of this Pawn is mostly decisive in close games, and it is therefore necessary to re-take with the Pawn when an exchange takes place on Q 4.

[6] There was no defence against the double threat B to Kt 5 and B to R 6.

[7] A blunder; but his game is hopeless anyhow.

E. SCHIFFERS v. W. STEINITZ.

	WHITE	BLACK		WHITE	BLACK
1	P to K 4	P to K 4	17	P to K Kt 3	P to B 5
2	K Kt to B 3	Q Kt to B 3			
3	Q Kt to B 3	K Kt to B 3			
4	B to Kt 5	B to Kt 5			
5	Kt to Q 5 [1]	Kt × Kt			
6	P × Kt	P to K 5			
7	P × Kt	Q P × P			
8	B to K 2	P × Kt			
9	B × P	Castles			
10	Castles	B to Q 3 [2]			
11	P to Q 4	P to K B 4			
12	P to Q B 4 [3]	B to K 2 [4]			
13	P to Q 5 [5]	P to B 4			
14	B to Q 2	B to Q 3			
15	Q R to B sq	Q to B 3			
16	B to B 3	Q to R 3			

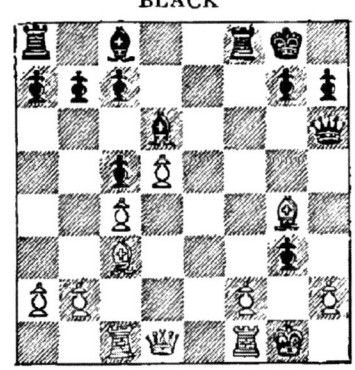

White to make his 19th move.

WHITE	BLACK	WHITE	BLACK
18 B to K Kt 4 [6]	P × P	37 K to B 3	B to K 5, ch
19 R P × P	B × P	38 K to B 2	B to Kt 8
20 P × B	R × R, ch	39 B to Q 6	B × P
21 Q × R	B × B	40 B × K B P	B × P
22 Q to B 4	Q × Q	41 P to Q 6	K to K 3
23 P × Q	R to Q sq	42 K to K 3	B × P
24 B to K 5	R to Q 2	43 K to Q 2	B to Kt 4
25 K to B 2	K to B 2	44 K to B 3	B to B 3
26 R to K Kt sq	P to K R 4	45 K to B 4	P to Kt 3
27 K to Kt 3	K to Kt 3	46 B to Kt 3	B to Q 4, ch
28 P to Q Kt 3	K to B 4	47 K to B 3	P to Kt 4
29 R to K sq	R to K 2	48 K to Q 3	P to Q R 4
30 B to B 3	R × R	49 K to K 3	P to Q R 5
31 B × R	P to K Kt 3	50 K to Q 3	P to R 6
32 B to B 3	B to Q 8	51 K to B 2	P to Kt 5
33 B to K 5	P to K Kt 4	52 B to K 5	P to Kt 6, ch
34 B × P	P × P, ch	53 K to B 3	P to Kt 7
35 K to B 2	B to B 7		White resigns.
36 B to Kt 8	P to R 3		

NOTES BY A. ALBIN

[1] Not good in this position; only when Black has played P to Q R 3 and the White Bishop is on Q R 4 sq. The ex-champion, Mr. Steinitz, has refuted this variation in the Ruy Lopez in his match with Zukertort, and we have now a complete analysis, which shows that the game is lost for White. Dr. Tarrasch has played it against Albin, and won on this analysis after twenty moves.

[2] Dr Tarrasch played here at once P to K B 4, which is stronger

[3] That seems to be the best.

[4] The consequence of Black not playing (immediately after B to Q 3) Q to R 5, in order to weaken the King's flank Pawns, which is the principal idea in this opening. (See the game Albin v. Tarrasch, Aug. 20.)

[5] Instead of this he should play P to Q Kt 4 (!) and B to Kt 2, the only way for a counter-attack.

[6] A blunder which loses at once. Mr. Steinitz played this ending very finely.

J. H. BLACKBURNE v. C. VON BARDELEBEN.

WHITE	BLACK	WHITE	BLACK
1 P to Q 4	P to Q 4	6 B to K 2	Castles
2 P to Q B 4	P to K 3	7 Castles	Q Kt to Q 2
3 Kt to Q B 3	P to Q B 3 [1]	8 Q to B 2	P × P [2]
4 P to K 3	B to Q 3	9 B × P	P to K 4
5 Kt to B 3	Kt to B 3	10 R to Q sq	P × P

	WHITE	BLACK
11	Kt × P	Kt to K 4
12	B to K 2	Q to B 2
13	P to K R 3	Kt to Kt 3
14	B to Q 2	Q to K 2
15	B to K sq	Kt to R 5
16	Kt to B 3	B to K B 4
17	Q to R 4	Kt × Kt, ch
18	B × Kt	Q to K 4
19	P to K Kt 3	B × P [3]
20	Kt to K 2	B to Q B 4
21	Q to R 4 [4]	B to K 3
22	B to B 3	Q to B 4
23	K to Kt 2	B to Q 4
24	R × B [5]	P × R [6]
25	P to K Kt 4	Q to K 3
26	Kt to B 4	Q to Q 3
27	R to R sq	K R to Q sq
28	P to Kt 5	P to Q 5

BLACK

WHITE

White to make his 24th move.

	WHITE	BLACK
29	P × Kt	P to K R 3
30	P × Q P	Resigns.[7]

NOTES BY E. SCHIFFERS.

[1] A good move which renders Queen's Pawn secure, and makes it possible to play P to K 4 eventually.

[2] Probably Black did not wish to isolate the Queen's Pawn; still, P to K 4 would have been better.

[3] White has now lost a Pawn, but obtains a strong attacking position, which is still further enhanced by the open King's Rook's file.

[4] Black threatened B × P, &c.

[5] Blackburne has played this game throughout in his best style.

[6] After Kt × R, evidently would follow 25. P to K 4, and White wins.

[7] [Herr Bardeleben's sealed move was B × P, and he sent word in the interval that he resigned, so as to save his opponent waiting about.—ED.]

A. BURN v. W. H. K. POLLOCK.

	WHITE	BLACK		WHITE	BLACK
1	P to Q 4	P to Q B 4 [1]	9	B P × P	Kt to B 3
2	P to Q 5 [2]	P to K Kt 3	10	Kt to B 3	Castles
3	P to K 4	B to Kt 2	11	Q to B 2	R to K sq
4	P to K B 4	Kt to Q R 3 [3]	12	B to Q 2	B to Q 2
5	Kt to K B 3	Kt to B 2	13	Q R to K sq	P to Q Kt 4 [4]
6	P to Q B 4	P to Q 3	14	Q to Kt sq [5]	P to Kt 5 [6]
7	B to Q 3	P to K 3	15	Kt to Q sq	P to Q R 4
8	Castles	P × P	16	Kt to B 2	Kt to Kt 4 [7]

WHITE	BLACK	WHITE	BLACK
17 B to B sq	R to Q B sq [8]	28 Kt to Q 3	Q to Kt 3
18 Kt to Q 2	Kt to Q 5	29 P to K 5	Kt to B sq
19 Kt to B 4	B to Kt 4	30 P to B 5 [10]	Q P × P
20 B to Q 2	R to R sq	31 P to Q 6	K to R sq
21 Q to Q sq	R to R 2	32 P to B 6 [11]	B to R 3
22 P to Q Kt 3	P to R 5	33 R × P	B to K 6, ch
23 B to K 3	P × P	34 K to R sq	K R to R sq
24 B × Kt	P × B	35 R to K 7	K R to R 4
25 P × P	B × Kt	36 R × P	Q × P
26 B × B	R to R 7	37 R to K Kt 7	P to R 4
27 Q to B 3 [9]	Kt to Q 2	38 Q to Kt 7	Resigns.

NOTES BY J. H. BLACKBURNE.

[1] A favourite defence of Pollock's, and one which he occasionally plays in tournaments, but it is of doubtful merit

[2] P to K 4, turning it into an old form of the 'Sicilian,' may also be played.

[3] If B × Kt, then Q to R 4, ch, and Q × B.

[4] A good move if properly followed up

[5] This, or P to Q Kt 3, appears the only move to avoid the loss of a Pawn.

[6] Instead of this, he certainly ought to have played P to B 5, followed by P to Kt 5 and P to Q R 4. His only hope was in breaking through with the Pawns on the Queen's side

[7] B to Kt 4, threatening P to B 5, was more forcing.

[8] Losing too much time with this Rook; rather have gone on with the P to R 5.

[9] Q × P would be answered by Kt to Kt 5, followed by Kt × Kt; then Q to Kt 3 and B to Q 5, winning.

[10] A very fine move, to which there is no satisfactory reply.

[11] P × P was equally good.

D. JANOWSKI v. A. WALBRODT

WHITE	BLACK	WHITE	BLACK
1 P to K 4	P to K 4	11 B to K R 4	P to Kt 4
2 Kt to K B 3	Kt to Q B 3	12 B to Kt 3	K to B sq [4]
3 B to Kt 5	P to Q R 3	13 B to Q 5	Q to K 2
4 B to R 4	Kt to B 3	14 Q to Q 2	Q R to K sq
5 Kt to B 3	P to Q 3	15 Q R to K sq	Kt to Q sq
6 Castles [1]	B to Q 2 [2]	16 B to Kt 3	B to K Kt 5
7 P to Q 4	P to Q Kt 4	17 Q to K 3	P to Q B 3
8 P × P [3]	P × P	18 R to Q sq	B to B 2 [5]
9 B to Kt 3	B to Q 3	19 P to Q R 4	Kt to Q 2
10 B to Kt 5	P to R 3	20 P × P	R P × P

AUGUST 19

	WHITE	BLACK		WHITE	BLACK
21	Q to R 7	B × Kt	41	P to Kt 3	Kt to Kt 3 [9]
22	P × B	Kt to B 4	42	R to R 6	K to B 3
23	B to R 2	K to Kt 2 [6]	43	P to Q B 4	P × P
24	R to Q 2	Kt (Q sq) to K 3	44	P × P	P to B 4
25	B × Kt	Kt × B	45	Kt to K 3 [10]	K to Kt 2
26	K R to Q sq	B to Kt sq [7]	46	B × P, ch	B × B
27	Q × Q	R × Q	47	R × Kt	R to K B 5
28	R to Q 7	K R to K sq	48	R to Kt 7, ch	K to Kt 3
29	K to Kt 2	Kt to Q 5	49	Kt to Q 5	R to B sq
30	R × R	R × R	50	R to Kt 6, ch	K to B 2
31	R to Q 2	P to B 3	51	R to Q B 6	B to Q 5
32	Kt to Q sq	Kt to K 3	52	R to B 7, ch	K to K 3 [11]
33	Kt to K 3	K to Kt 3	53	R to K R 7	P to R 5
34	Kt to K B 5	R to Q R 2	54	P to B 4 [12]	P × P
35	P to Q B 3	R to K B 2	55	K to B 3	K to K 4
36	P to K R 4	B to B 2	56	R to R 5, ch	K to Q 3
37	R to Q sq	Kt to B 4 [8]	57	R × P	R to Q Kt sq
38	R to K R sq	P to R 4	58	R to R 6, ch	K to K 4
39	P × P	P × P	59	R to R 5, ch	K to Q 3
40	R to R sq	Kt to R 5	60	Kt × P	R to Kt 5
			61	R to Q 5, ch	K to B 3
			62	Kt to K 6	R × P
			63	Kt × B, ch	P × Kt
			64	K to B 4	R to B 7
			65	P to B 3	R to B 5
			66	K to K 5	R to B 6
			67	P to B 4	P to Q 6
			68	K to Q 4	R to R 6
			69	K to K 3	P to Q 7, ch
			70	K × P	R to K B 6
			71	P to B 5	R to K R 6
			72	R to Q 3	R to R 7, ch
			73	K to K 3	R to R 5
			74	P to K 5	K to B 4
			75	P to K 6	Resigns.

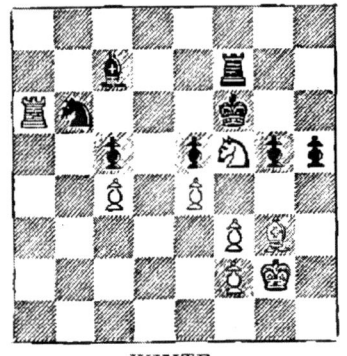

White to make his 45th move.

NOTES BY H. N. PILLSBURY.

[1] Premature; P to Q 4 is more usual and better.

[2] For Black could obtain a very good counter-attack at once by P to Q Kt 4; 7. B to Kt 3, B to Kt 5, threatening Kt to Q 5, &c.

[3] Of course forced, for if 8. B to Kt 3, Kt × Q P; 9. Kt × Kt, P × Kt; 10. Q × P, P to Q B 4 and 5, winning the Bishop.

[4] Black's plan of counter-attack with the Pawns seems to be quite correct, and the King is well placed here.

⁵ Black plays too timidly; either Kt to R 4 or Kt to K 3 was perfectly safe and more attacking. White could not afford Q to Kt 6 in either case.

⁶ Something more attacking is needed all along here. Perhaps P to R 4; 24. P to R 3, Kt to K 3 and B 5 would be stronger than the text.

⁷ Why not Kt to Q 5?

⁸ Black should by all means have dislodged the adverse Knight by Kt to Kt 2, and he had then rather the best of it, owing to the imprisoned White Bishop. White from this stage outplays him at all points, and never offers him another opportunity for so doing.

⁹ If Kt × P, White answers R to Q B sq, with a winning game.

¹⁰ Winning a Pawn and the game (see diagram).

¹¹ If K to Kt 3; 53. Kt to K 7, ch, K to B 3; 54. Kt to B 5, winning a second Pawn in a few moves.

¹² With this and the entrance of the King on the next move, the result of the game becomes only a question of time.

E. Schlechter v. Dr. Tarrasch.

	WHITE	BLACK
1	P to K 4	P to K 4
2	Kt to K B 3	Kt to Q B 3
3	Kt to B 3	Kt to B 3
4	B to Kt 5	P to Q R 3
5	B × Kt	Q P × B
6	Kt × P	Kt × P
7	Kt × Kt	Q to Q 5
8	Castles	Q × K Kt
9	R to K sq	B to K 3
10	P to Q 4	Q to K B 4 ¹
11	B to Kt 5	P to R 3
12	Q to Q 3 (!)	K to Q 2 ²
13	B to R 4	R to K sq
14	R to K 3	B to Q 3
15	Q R to K sq	Q to Q Kt 4
16	Kt × B	P × Kt
17	Q to R 3	P to Q R 4
18	P to Q B 3	Q to Kt 3
19	B to Kt 3	Q to B 2
20	P to Q B 4 ³	B × P
21	R × R	R × R
22	R × R	K × R
23	B × P	Q to Q 2
24	Q to K 3, ch	B to K 3
25	B to B 5	P to B 3

White to make his 20th move.

	WHITE	BLACK
26	P to Q R 3	K to B 2
27	Q to Kt 3	B to Q 4
28	P to R 3	Q to K 3
29	P to B 3	Q to K 6, ch
30	Q to B 2	Q to Kt 6
31	K to R 2	P to Q Kt 3
32	B to Q 6	B to K 3
33	Q to Q 2	P to R 4
34	B to B 7	P to Q R 5
35	B to Kt 3	P to Q Kt 4

AUGUST 19

WHITE	BLACK		WHITE	BLACK
36 B to K sq	B to B 4		45 K to Q 2	K to Kt 6
37 Q to K B 2	Q to B 7		46 P to B 4	B to Kt 5
38 Q × Q	B × Q [4]		47 K to B sq	K to R 7
39 K to Kt sq	K to K 3		48 B to Kt 4	P to Kt 3
40 K to B 2	K to Q 4		49 K to B 2	B to B 4, ch
41 K to K 3	K to B 5		50 K to B 3	B to K 5
42 P to K Kt 3	B to Q 6		51 P to B 5	P × P
43 B to B 3	B to B 8		52 B to K 7	
44 P to R 4	B to R 6		Drawn game.	

NOTES BY C. VON BARDELEBEN.

[1] This move is better than Q to Q 4, for the latter move would be followed by 11. B to Kt 5 (!), and if P to B 3 (?); 12. B × P.

[2] This is somewhat dangerous. Black ought to have played Q to R 4; 13. B to R 4, Q to R 4; of course he cannot play 12 ... P × B because of 13. Kt to Q 6, ch, winning the Queen.

[3] This sacrifice leads to a clear draw. If White prepared the advance of the Queen's Bishop's Pawn by 20. P to Kt 3, he would have a good attack; the continuation might be then P to Q Kt 4, 21. R to Q B sq, R to Q sq; 22 P to Q B 4, P × P; 23 P × P, P to Q B 4; 24 P to Q 5, B to B 4; 25. R (B sq) to K sq (!), with an excellent game. (See diagram.)

[4] After the exchange of the Queens there is not the slightest doubt that the result of the struggle will be a draw.

R. TEICHMANN v. H. N. PILLSBURY.

WHITE	BLACK		WHITE	BLACK
1 P to K 4	P to K 4		16 Q × Kt	Kt to B 4 (!)
2 Kt to K B 3	Kt to Q B 3		17 Q to B 3	Kt to Q 5
3 B to Kt 5	P to K Kt 3 [1]		18 Kt × Kt	Q × Kt, ch
4 P to Q 4	P × P		19 K to Kt 2	Q to Kt 5
5 Kt × P	B to Kt 2		20 P to K 5 [7]	Q × P
6 B to K 3	Kt to K B 3		21 B to B 4 [8]	Q × P, ch
7 Kt to Q B 3	Castles		22 R to B 2	Q to B 4
8 P to K B 3 [2]	Kt to K 2 [3]		23 Q to K 3	Q to R 6, ch
9 Castles	P to Q B 3		24 K to Kt sq	B to K 3
10 B to Q 3	P to Q 4		25 B to K 2 [9]	Q to R 3
11 Kt (Q 4) to K 2 [4]			26 R to B 4	Q to Kt 4
	P × P		27 B to Q 3	Q R to Q sq
12 P × P [5]	Kt to Kt 5		28 Q to B 3 [10]	B × K P
13 Q to Q 2	Q to Q 3 [6]		29 P to K R 4	B to Q 5, ch
14 P to K Kt 3	Q to K 4		30 K to R 2 [11]	Q to Q R 4
15 Q R to K sq	Kt × B		White resigns.	

NOTES BY S. TINSLEY.

[1] The well-informed chess editor of the 'Times Democrat' (New Orleans) says of this opening that 'if not actually the invention of Mr. A. P. Barnes, of New York, it was at least first brought into prominent notice by him in the Canadian "Spectator," July 1880, and subsequently in an analytical article of some length and importance in "Brentano's Monthly," vol. i. 1881, p. 73. It is somewhat singular that the "Handbuch" wholly overlooks this fact in its last edition, as well we believe as the actual merits of the defence, which, by the way, is highly esteemed and was almost persistently adopted by Pillsbury at the Hastings Meeting.'

[2] The double object of preventing Kt to K Kt 5 presently, and the exchange of Knight for Bishop is thus accomplished, but at the expense of a very weak centre of Pawns

[3] Preventing an inopportune exchange by White, who might possibly have taken the Piece earlier without much harm. Black is also now ready to assail the weak central position by P to Q 4, &c.

[4] Supposing now P to K 5 instead —an obvious move—then 11 ... Kt (B 3) to K sq; 12. P to B 4, P to Q B 4, with a fine attack.

[5] Allowing the very evil, Kt to Kt 5, which was previously guarded against. B × P was probably a lesser evil; Kt × P clearly loses his Queen's Knight's Pawn.

[6] Attention may be directed to the series of very forcible moves by which Black wins this game. This is one. He gains time by a threat of immediate mate, which can only be defended by White compromising his King's position.

[7] As there appears no means of saving the valuable Pawn this is the best course.

[8] The game is almost hopeless, as another Pawn must go at once, and this is the best chance.

[9] It would be bad to open the file by B × B. Also his King's Pawn is weak when the attack comes. B to B sq seems better.

[10] Presumably a trap, but Black's reply demonstrates that the Pawn may safely be taken. The whole game, in fact, seems to show that one player sees a little clearer and further than the other, and is mercilessly exact

[11] R × B is answered effectively by Q to Q B 4.

J. MASON v. H. E. BIRD.

WHITE	BLACK	WHITE	BLACK
1 P to K 4	P to K 3	8 B to Q 3	P to Q B 4 [2]
2 P to Q 4	P to Q 4	9 P × P	Kt to B 3
3 Kt to Q B 3	Kt to K B 3	10 Kt to B 3	P to K R 4 [3]
4 B to K Kt 5	B to K 2	11 Q to Kt 3	P to R 5
5 B × Kt	B × B	12 Q to Kt 4	B × P
6 P to K 5	B to K 2	13 Castles K R	B to Q 2
7 Q to Kt 4	K to B sq [1]	14 P to Q R 3	K to Kt sq

AUGUST 19

	WHITE	BLACK
15	Q R to K sq [4]	B to K 2 [5]
16	Kt to K 2	R to R 3 [6]
17	Kt (K 2) to Q 4 [7]	R to B sq
18	P to B 3	K to R sq
19	R to K 2	P to R 3 (?)
20	K R to K sq	Kt to R 4
21	K to R sq	Kt to B 3 [8]
22	Kt × Kt	R × Kt [9]
23	Kt to Q 4	R to B sq
24	P to K B 4 [10]	P to K Kt 3
25	Q to R 3 [11]	B to B 4
26	Kt to B 3 [12]	K to Kt 2
27	Kt to Kt 5 [13]	B to K 2 [14]
28	Kt to B 3	Q to Kt 3
29	Q to Kt 4	Q B to Kt 4 [15]
30	B × B	Q × B [16]
31	Kt to Q 4	Q to Q 2
32	P to B 5 [17]	K P × P
33	P to K 6 (!)	P × P

White to make his 32nd move.

	WHITE	BLACK
34	Kt × B P, ch	K to R 2
35	Kt × R	R to B 5
36	Q × K P	Q × Q
37	R × Q	B to B sq
38	Kt to B 7	Resigns.

NOTES BY DR. TARRASCH.

[1] The King's move—quite *à la Bird*—is disadvantageous for Black. He might have Castled without hesitation.

[2] First P to Q Kt 3 and then P to Q B 4 would be very good, in order that he might capture with the Pawn, after Q P × P.

[3] The advance of the Rook's Pawn has no great value; the Rook cannot be developed advantageously *via* K R 3.

[4] White has a far better developed game.

[5] To keep the Knight out of his K Kt 4.

[6] The Rook can get into play nowhere.

[7] White should play P to Q B 4, in order to open the file and bring the strength of both Rooks there where Black can only oppose one; instead of this he moves to and fro without any clear plan.

[8] 'Risum teneatis, amice?'

[9] In consequence of the faulty move with the Rook's Pawn, Black does not dare take the Knight with Pawn, which would have considerably strengthened the centre.

[10] At last a little life gets into the game; this threatens P to B 5.

[11] To continue with P to K Kt 4, without the Pawn being taken *en passant*.

[12] Black ought rather to have guarded the Rook with K to Kt 2, and White in his turn should now play P to K Kt 4, as his plan might be stopped later on.

[13] Threatening again P to K Kt 4, for after R P × P *en passant* there follows Q × R, ch, and Kt × B P, ch.

[14] Against this nothing can be said. The Knight must go back, and, as Herr Marco used to say, the attack could not be forced through if Black did not dig his own grave.

[15] The decisive mistake.

[16] It was rather better to take with the Pawn. Now at last the decisive advance of the King's Bishop's Pawn is possible.

[17] A beautiful final combination.

M. Tchigorin v. G. Marco.

WHITE	BLACK		WHITE	BLACK
1 P to K 4	P to K 3		13 P to Q R 4	Kt to Kt 3
2 Q to K 2	P to K 4[1]		14 P to R 5	B × P, ch
3 P to K Kt 3	Kt to Q B 3		15 R × B	Kt × R
4 B to Kt 2	B to B 4[2]		16 Q × Kt	P to Q 4
5 P to Q B 3	Kt to B 3		17 Kt to K 3[5]	P to B 3
6 Kt to B 3	P to Q 3		18 Q to R 2	B to K 3
7 P to Q 3	Castles		19 Kt to B sq	P to K R 3
8 Q Kt to Q 2	Kt to K Kt 5[3]		20 B to K 3	R to B 3
9 Castles	P to B 4		21 Q to Q B 2	B to Kt 5
10 P to Kt 4	B to Kt 3		22 Kt (B 3) to Q 2	P to Q 5[6]
11 Kt to B 4	P × P		23 P × P	P × P
12 P × P	Kt to K 2[4]		24 Q to B 4, ch	K to R 2
			25 B × Q P	R to Q 3
			26 B to B 3	R to Q 6
			27 R to K sq	Q to Q 2
			28 R to K 3	R to Q sq
			29 P to K 5	R × R
			30 Kt × R	B to K 3
			31 Q to B 5	Q to Q 6
			32 B to K 4	Q to K 7
			33 Kt (Q 2) to B sq	R to Q 2
			34 B to R sq	Q to R 7
			35 Q to B 3	P to R 4
			36 B to Q Kt 2	R to K B 2
			37 Q to B 2	Resigns.

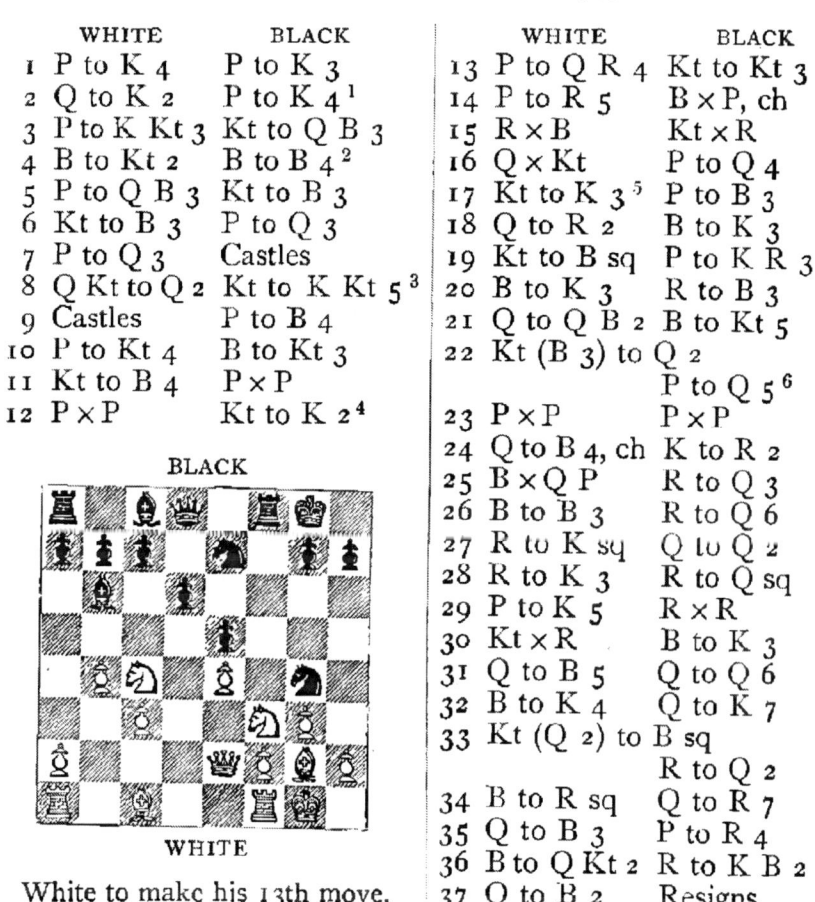

BLACK

WHITE

White to make his 13th move.

Notes by R. Teichmann.

[1] I do not think that this is loss of time; the position of the White Queen at K 2 is, to say the least, no advantage for White.

[2] Here I prefer Kt to B 3, B to K 2, and P to Q 4, with a view of pushing the Q P to Q 5, if White does not take it.

[3] This counter-attack is a little premature; P to Q R 3 first would have been better.

[4] It is very curious that in this position Black has already almost a hopeless game (see diagram). He can do nothing against the threatened P to Q R 4, after which he would have to move the Queen's Rook's Pawn and allow White to isolate the Queen's Pawn.

[5] Best. Of course if P × P, then Q to R 2, ch, and Kt to K sq, with a very good game.

[6] Having now got a game which seems to afford good chances of a prolonged fight, he throws it away at once by this blunder, which cost a valuable Pawn. The Black position falls to pieces after this.

A. ALBIN v. J. MIESES.

	WHITE	BLACK		WHITE	BLACK
1	P to K 4	P to K 4	14	Kt × P	P to B 4 [3]
2	Kt to K B 3	Kt to Q B 3	15	Kt to Q 5	Q to B 2
3	B to Kt 5	P to Q R 3	16	Kt to K B 3	P to B 3
4	B to R 4	P to Q 3	17	Kt to B 3	B × Kt
5	B × Kt [1]	P × B	18	P × B	Q × P
6	P to Q 3	P to Kt 3	19	Q to Q 3	Castles
7	Kt to Q B 3	B to K Kt 2	20	Kt to R 4	B to K 3
8	Q to K 2	Kt to K 2 (!)	21	Kt × P	B to B 5
9	P to K R 3	P to K B 4	22	Q to B 3	Q R to Q Kt sq
10	B to Kt 5	P to B 5	23	K to Q 2	Q R to Kt 7
11	Castles Q R	P to R 3	24	R to Q B sq	B to Kt 6
12	B × Kt	Q × B	25	Q to Q sq	R to Kt sq
13	P to Q 4 [2]	P × P	26	Kt × P	B × P
			27	Q to Kt 4, ch	K to B sq
			28	Q to B 5, ch	K to K sq
			29	Q to Kt 6, ch	K to Q 2
			30	Q to Kt 7, ch	K to B sq
			31	K to K 3	B to Kt 6 (??) [4]
			32	R to R sq	P to Q R 4
			33	R × Q	B × R
			34	R to Q sq	R(Kt sq) to Kt 2
			35	Q to B 8, ch	K to B 2
			36	Q × P, ch	K to Kt 3
			37	Kt to Q 3	R to Kt 4
			38	Kt to K 5	P to R 5
			39	Q × P, ch	K to R 2
			40	R to Q 6	R to R 4
			41	R to Q 7	Resigns.

BLACK

WHITE

White to make his 15th move.

NOTES BY C. VON BARDELEBEN.

[1] The usual move; 5. P to Q 4 is better.

[2] This move is not good, because it opens the diagonal to the hostile King's Bishop.

[3] Black plays too hastily to get an attack. The advantage of the two Bishops would yield the second player a superior game if he adopted a line of play to slowly and gradually improve his position. The proper move would be : B to Q 2 ; 15. Q to B 3, Castles K R, to be followed by Q to B 2 and P to B 4 (see diagram)

[4] Black need not have lost the game if he had not made such a blunder.

This middle round completes the full half of the Tournament, and leaves each player with ten games to play.

The totals to date are now :—

Tchigorin	$9\frac{1}{2}$	Mason		5
Pillsbury	$9\frac{1}{2}$	Tinsley		5
Lasker	$8\frac{1}{2}$	Blackburne		5
Bardeleben	$7\frac{1}{2}$	Pollock		$4\frac{1}{2}$
Schiffers	$6\frac{1}{2}$	Burn		$4\frac{1}{2}$
Steinitz	$6\frac{1}{2}$	Janowski		$4\frac{1}{2}$
Bird	6	Gunsberg		4
Walbrodt	6	Marco		4
Teichmann	$5\frac{1}{2}$	Albin		4
Tarrasch	$5\frac{1}{2}$	Mieses		$3\frac{1}{2}$
Schlechter	5	Vergani		1

AUGUST 20.

AGAIN a most exciting day. Lasker meets Pillsbury, and a fine game results. Tchigorin has a desperate and brilliant struggle with Walbrodt, considering one move nearly an hour, and, although he only draws, he again heads the score on account of Pillsbury's loss. Vergani scores his first win, and it is pleasing to see the visitors crowding round him to shake hands.

E. LASKER v. H. N. PILLSBURY.

	WHITE	BLACK		WHITE	BLACK
1	P to K 4	P to K 4	25	Q × R P	Q to Kt 2
2	Kt to K B 3	Kt to Q B 3	26	Q to R 4	P to B 3 [8]
3	B to Kt 5	P to K Kt 3 [1]	27	Q to K 4	Q to Q 2
4	P to Q 4	P × P	28	P to Q R 4	P to K 4
5	Kt × P	B to Kt 2	29	P to R 3	R to Kt 5 (?) [9]
6	Kt × Kt [2]	Kt P × Kt [3]	30	Q to K sq	P to K 5
7	B to Q B 4	Kt to K 2	31	P to R 5	P to Q 4
8	Kt to B 3 [4]	P to Q 3	32	P to R 6	Q to K 2 (?) [10]
9	Castles	B to K 3			
10	B to Kt 3	Castles			
11	B to K 3	P to Q B 4			
12	B × B [5]	P × B			
13	Q to Q 2	R to Kt sq			
14	Q R to Kt sq	Kt to B 3			
15	P to Q Kt 3	Q to R 5			
16	P to B 3	Kt to Q 5			
17	Kt to K 2	B to K 4			
18	P to K B 4 (?) [6]				
		Kt × Kt, ch			
19	Q × Kt	B × P			
20	B × B	R × B			
21	R × R	Q × R			
22	R to K B sq	Q to K 4			
23	Q to R 6 [7]	Q to Q 5, ch			
24	K to R sq	Q × P			

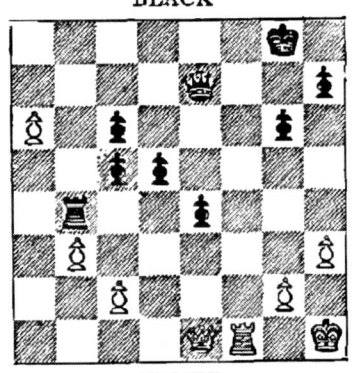

BLACK

WHITE

White to make his 33rd move.

33 Q to Kt 3 (!) [11]
            P to K 6 [12]

WHITE	BLACK		WHITE	BLACK
34 R to R sq	Q to B 3		38 Q to Q 6	R to Kt 2
35 R to K sq	P to Q 5 [13]		39 Q × P (B 6)	P to K 7
36 P to R 7	Q to Q sq		40 Q × R	Resigns.
37 R to R sq	Q to R sq			

NOTES BY DR. TARRASCH.

[1] This defence is not worse than others.

[2] Lasker ever strives after simplifying the games.

[3] Q P × Kt would be safer, and following this up with an exchange of Queens would probably end in a draw.

[4] To prevent P to Q 4.

[5] It would be better to meet the threatening move, P to B 5, with Q to K 2. Black in the actual game obtains a good position through his strong centre and the open King's Bishop's file.

[6] A great mistake. Lasker overlooked that after Kt × Kt, ch; 19 Q × Kt, B × P, 20 R × B, R × R; 21. P to Kt 3, Black could save the Piece with Q to Kt 5, or he could also play 21. R to Kt 5. 18. P to Kt 3 should have been played, after which the games were about equal; but after the gain of a Pawn Black ought to have won.

[7] The only chance.

[8] To prevent Q to Q 7.

[9] So far Pillsbury played the game splendidly, but now he begins to experiment, and finally loses a won game by careless play. The simple move R to K sq, in combination with the advancing centre, must have won with certainty, as the analyses of the two players have shown. It is very often dangerous to move a Rook away from the first line.

[10] Black entirely underestimates the threatening danger, or else he would have retired with his Rook instead of pressing on his own centre.

[11] White cuts off the retreat of the Black Rook.

[12] One more offensive instead of defensive move. The Rook ought to have retired at least to Kt 3, and P to R 7 would not have led to a win—namely, R to Kt 3; 34 P to R 7 (?), Q × P; 35. Q to Q 6, R to Kt sq; 36. Q to K 6, ch, K to Kt 2 (!); but after 34 R to R sq, Black could have stopped the dangerous Pawn with Q to R 2, and after 35. Q to Q 6, P to K 6 (not R × P, on account of 36. R to K B sq, Q to R sq; 37. Q to K 6, ch, followed by R to B 7); 36. Q × P (B 5) (?), P to K 7, and R × R P, and so finally have won the Pawn. But with 36. R to K B sq (!), R to Kt sq; 37. Q to K 6, ch, K to Kt 2; 38. Q × K P, White would still remain with an advantage, as the Queen's Rook's Pawn could not be taken on account of Q to K 5, ch, and Black's King is without defence.

[13] The game is lost, chiefly through the unfavourable position of the Rook. After P to K 7 there followed 36. P to R 7, Q to B 8, ch; 37. K to R 2; or after Q to B 7, White wins with 36. Q × K P, Q × Q; 37. R × Q, R to Kt sq; 38. P to R 7, R to R sq; 39. R to K 7, Q Kt 7, and Q Kt 8.

AUGUST 20

A. Albin v. Dr. Tarrasch.

	WHITE	BLACK		WHITE	BLACK
1	P to K 4	P to K 4	13	P to Q 4	Q to R 5
2	Kt to K B 3	Kt to K B 3	14	P to Kt 3	Q to B 3
3	Kt to Q B 3	Kt to Q B 3	15	P to K R 3	P to K R 4
4	B to Kt 5	B to Kt 5	16	K to Kt 2	P to R 5
5	Kt to Q 5	Kt × Kt	17	K R to Kt sq[4]	P × P
6	P × Kt	P to K 5	18	P × P	P to B 5
7	P × Kt	Q P × P	19	B × P[5]	P to K Kt 4
8	B to K 2[1]	P × Kt	20	B × B	Q × B, ch
9	B × P	Castles	21	K to R 2	P × B
10	Castles	P to K B 4	22	K R to K B sq	
11	P to Q B 3[2]	B to Q 3			Q to K 7, ch
12	Q to Kt 3, ch[3]		23	K to Kt sq	B × P
		K to R sq		White resigns.	

Notes by J. H. Blackburne.

[1] B to B 4 is better.

[2] This only drives the Bishop to a stronger position. P to Q 4 at once is certainly better.

[3] A useless check; the Queen is completely out of play for the rest of the game. P to Q 4 was the correct move.

[4] White is now in difficulties, but this move makes matters worse. Q to B 2, preventing the threatened move of Q to Kt 3, seems to be the only move.

[5] This loses a Piece, but P × P is not much better, as in the latter case Q to R 5 wins easily.

M. Tchigorin v. A. Walbrodt.

	WHITE	BLACK		WHITE	BLACK
1	P to K 4	P to K 4	15	B to Q 2	Q R to K sq
2	P to K B 4	P to Q 4	16	Q R to Q sq	R to K 4
3	Kt to K B 3	Q P × P	17	K to R sq	K R to K sq
4	Kt × P	B to Q 3[1]	18	Kt × B	Q × Kt
5	P to Q 4	P × P en passant	19	Q to Kt 3	Q to B 4
6	B × P	Kt to K B 3	20	B to R 6[5]	K R to K 2
7	Castles	Castles	21	P to B 4	Kt to K 6
8	Kt to Q B 3	Q Kt to Q 2	22	B to K 4[6]	Kt × Q R
9	Kt × Kt	Q × Kt	23	R × Kt	Q to Q 3 (!)[7]
10	Q to B 3[2]	R to Kt sq (!)[3]	24	R × Q	P × R
11	P to B 5	P to Q Kt 3	25	B to K 3[8]	R × B
12	B to K Kt 5	B to Kt 2	26	B to B 2	R × P
13	Q to R 3	Kt to Q 4	27	P to K R 3	R to B 3
14	Kt to K 4[4]	P to K B 3	28	K to R 2	R to K 4

WHITE	BLACK		WHITE	BLACK
29 Q to Q 3	P to K R 3 [9]		33 P to Q R 4	P to Q Kt 4
30 P to Q Kt 4 [10]	P to R 3		34 P to R 5	K to K sq
31 Q to Kt 3, ch	K to B sq		35 P to R 4	R to B 5
32 B to Kt 3	R to K 2		36 Q to Q sq	P to Q 4
			37 B to B 2	K to B 2
			38 P to Kt 4	K to Kt sq [11]
			39 P to Kt 5	R P × P
			40 R P × P	P × P
			41 Q to R 5	R to B 5
			42 K to Kt 3	P to Q 5
			43 Q × P	R to B 6, ch
			44 K to Kt 4	R to Q 2
			45 Q to Kt 6	K to B sq
			46 B to R 4	P to Q 6
			47 Q to K 6	R to K B 2
			48 Q to Q 6, ch	K to Kt sq
			49 B to K 7	P to Q 7
			50 Q to Kt 8, ch	
			Drawn game.	

Black to make his 38th move.

NOTES BY C. VON BARDELEBEN.

[1] The best move. Disadvantageous would be B to K 3, because of 5. Q to K 2.

[2] I prefer 10. P to B 5.

[3] In order to allow P to Q Kt 3.

[4] Preferable would be 14 Kt × Kt, B × Kt ; 15. Q R to K sq.

[5] The attack introduced by this move proves disadvantageous, but in any case White's position would be precarious.

[6] This move looks brilliant, but really is bad, giving the second player the superior game. Better would be 22. B × Kt, R × B ; 23. Q to B 2.

[7] Very well played. The first player had probably overlooked this move, when he played 22. B to K 4.

[8] White is obliged to give up a Piece.

[9] R to K sq would be better.

[10] Both players overlooked that White could win a Pawn by 30. B to Kt 3, R to K sq ; 31. B × P (if 31. ... R to Q sq, then 32. Q to Kt 3, ch).

[11] Here Black misses an opportunity to get the superior game. He should have played 38. ... R (K 2) to K 5 ; 39. P to Kt 5, R to Kt 5 ; 40. P × R P, P × P ; 41. Q to K 2, R (B 5) to K 5 ; and if 42. Q to B 2, then P to Q 5 ; 43. Q to B 7, ch, R to K 2 (see diagram).

AUGUST 20

J. Mason v. W. H. K. Pollock.

	WHITE	BLACK
1	P to K 4	P to K 4
2	Kt to K B 3	Kt to Q B 3
3	B to Kt 5	P to Q 3
4	Kt to B 3	B to Q 2 [1]
5	P to Q 3 [2]	Kt to B 3
6	B to Kt 5	B to K 2
7	Q to Q 2	P to K R 3
8	B to K 3	P to R 3 [3]
9	B to R 4	P to Q Kt 4
10	B to Kt 3	Kt to Q R 4
11	Castles	Kt × B
12	R P × Kt	P to B 3
13	Kt to K 2	Kt to R 2
14	Kt to Kt 3	Kt to Kt 4
15	Kt to K sq	P to B 3
16	P to K B 4	Kt to B 2
17	P to B 5	P to Q 4
18	Q to K 2	P to Q 5
19	B to Q 2	Castles [4]
20	Kt to B 3	K to R 2
21	Kt to R 4	Kt to R sq
22	Kt to R 5	R to K Kt sq
23	K to R sq	Q to K sq
24	Kt to Kt 3	Q to B 2
25	Q to Kt 4	B to K B sq
26	Kt to Kt 6	B to B sq [5]

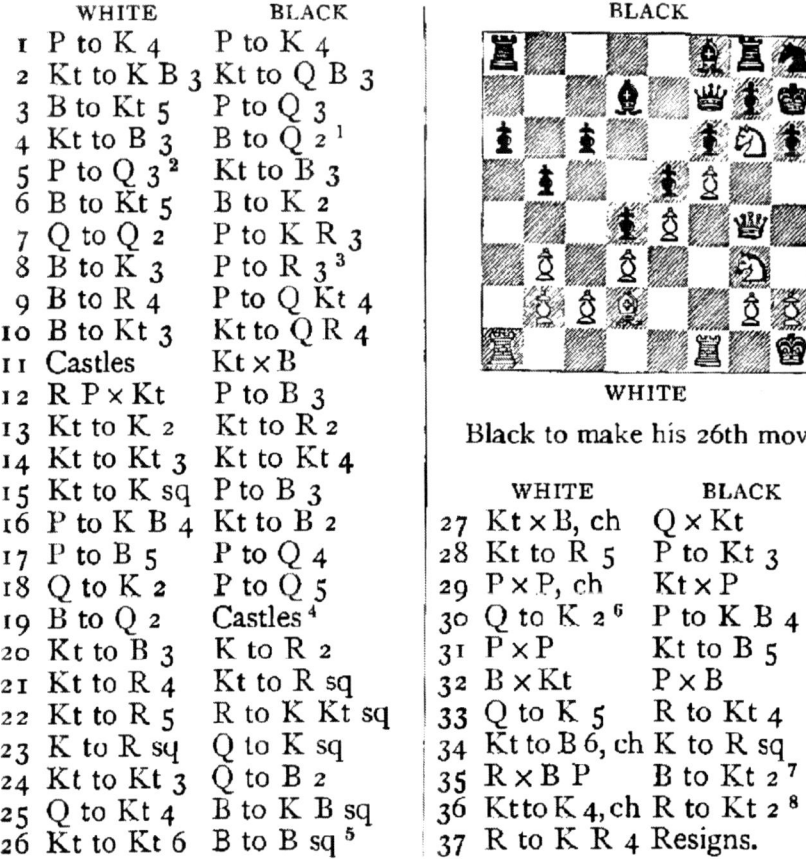

Black to make his 26th move

	WHITE	BLACK
27	Kt × B, ch	Q × Kt
28	Kt to R 5	P to Kt 3
29	P × P, ch	Kt × P
30	Q to K 2 [6]	P to K B 4
31	P × P	Kt to B 5
32	B × Kt	P × B
33	Q to K 5	R to Kt 4
34	Kt to B 6, ch	K to R sq
35	R × B P	B to Kt 2 [7]
36	Kt to K 4, ch	R to Kt 2 [8]
37	R to K R 4	Resigns.

Notes by E. Schiffers.

[1] This move seems futile, as the doubling of Pawns on the Bishop's file is not dangerous for Black. The correct move is 4. ... Kt to B 3, and after 5. P to Q 4, Kt to Q 2 (Tchigorin's defence).

[2] The natural continuation here would be Castling, in conjunction with P to Q 4.

[3] Here Black might advantageously play Kt to Kt 5, in order to exchange the Knight for the Bishop at K 3.

[4] A very dangerous Castling position; Black ought to have made earlier preparation to move P to B 4, in order to ease his game, which is extremely hampered at present.

[5] Clearly, if Kt × Kt, then 27. P × P, ch, and Black loses the Bishop at Q 2.

[6] If 30. Kt × P, ch, then Q × Kt.

[7] The Bishop is in sad straits.

[8] After Q to K Kt 2, would follow 37. Kt × R, Q × Q; 38. Kt to B 7, ch, and 39. Kt × Q.

R. Teichmann v. J. H. Blackburne.

	WHITE	BLACK		WHITE	BLACK
1	P to Q 4	P to Q 4	37	Q to K 2	K to R sq
2	P to Q B 4	P × P	38	P to K Kt 4	B to Q B sq
3	Kt to K B 3	Kt to K B 3	39	B to Q 3	K to Kt sq
4	P to K 3	P to K 3	40	R to R 3	P to Kt 3
5	B × P	Q Kt to Q 2	41	R to K 3	B to Q B 4
6	Kt to B 3	B to K 2	42	R to K 4	Q to B sq
7	Castles	Castles	43	P to Kt 4	B to Q 3
8	P to Q Kt 3 [1]	P to Q Kt 3	44	B to B 4	R to K sq
9	B to Kt 2	B to Kt 2	45	P to K Kt 5 [7]	B to K B 4 [8]
10	Kt to K 2 [2]	Kt to K 5	46	R to K 3	P × P
11	Kt to Kt 3	Q Kt to B 3			
12	B to Q 3	Kt × Kt			
13	R P × Kt	Q to Q 4			
14	R to B sq	Q R to B sq			
15	B to B 4	Q to K 5			
16	B to Q 3	Q to Q 4			
17	B to B 4	Q to K R 4			
18	Kt to K 5	Q to Kt 4			
19	B to K 2	P to B 4 [3]			
20	B to K B 3	B to R 3			
21	R to K sq	B to Q 3			
22	Kt to B 4	B to Kt sq			
23	Kt to Q 2 [4]	P × P			
24	R × R	R × R			
25	P × P	Kt to Q 4			
26	B to K 4	Kt to B 3 [5]			
27	B to K B 3	Q to Kt 3			
28	Kt to K 4	Kt × Kt			
29	B × Kt	Q to Kt 4			
30	R to K 3	B to Q 3			
31	P to Q 5	P to K 4			
32	B to Q 3	B to Kt 2			
33	B to B 4	R to Q sq			
34	Q to K sq	P to B 3			
35	P to R 4	Q to Kt 3 [6]			
36	B to B 3	Q to K sq			

BLACK

White to make his 47th move.

47	P to Kt 4 [9]	B to Q 2
48	B × P	R × B (!)
49	R × R	Q to B 5 [10]
50	R to K 8, ch	K to Kt 2
51	R to K 7, ch	K to R 3
52	Q to K 4	Q to R 7, ch
53	K to B sq	Q to R 6, ch
54	K to K sq	B × P, ch
55	K to Q sq	B × Kt P, ch
56	B to K 2 [11]	Q to Q Kt 6, ch

White resigns.[12]

NOTES BY DR. TARRASCH.

[1] This is not the correct method of development; P to K 4 followed by B to K 3 was preferable.

[2] Without any special tendency, better was Q to K 2, or B to Q 3, followed by P to K 4.

AUGUST 20

[3] In this game a great many moves are made without any special effect. Black has obtained an equal game long ago.

[4] No clear plan can be perceived in White's play.

[5] Nor is there much of a plan in Black's game; this is perhaps the most tedious game that was played at Hastings.

[6] Both players have a great deal of patience.

[7] Now at last it begins to get more interesting. White has arranged his Pieces with some definite object, and with this move he succeeds in breaking through.

[8] After P to B 4 White might have sacrificed for the King's Pawn with success.

[9] A great mistake, which gives Black an opportunity for a beautiful combination by which he decides the game in his favour. With the simple move 47. B × P White had an advantage; for instance, if B × P, 48. P to Q 6, ch, B to K 3; 49. P to Q 7, R to K 2; 50. B to Q B 7 and wins; again, if 47. ... B × B; 48. R × B, R × R; 49. P to Q 6, ch, with an advantage for White; or again, if 47. ... R × B; 48. R · R, Q to B 3; 49. R to K 8, ch, K to Kt 2; 50. P to Kt 5, or P to Kt 3.

[10] The decisive move; if the Rook moves from K 5, then Q to R 7, ch, and Q to R 8 is threatened.

[11] After K to B sq there comes Q to Q R 6, ch, and B to K B 4 wins the Queen.

[12] The Queen is lost after 57. Q to Q B 2, by Q × P, ch; 58. K to B sq, B to R 6, ch; 59. K to Kt sq; or after 57. K to B sq, by Q to R 6, ch; 58. K to Q sq, Q to R 8, ch; 59. K to B 2, B to K B 4.

C. Schlechter v. A. Burn.

	WHITE	BLACK
1	P to K 4	P to K 3
2	P to Q 4	P to Q 4
3	Kt to Q B 3	Kt to K B 3
4	P × P [1]	P × P
5	Q B to Kt 5	P to Q B 3
6	Kt to K B 3	B to Q 3
7	B to Q 3	Castles
8	Castles	R to K sq
9	Q to Q 2	B to K 3
10	Kt to K 2	Q Kt to Q 2
11	Kt to Kt 3	Q to B 2
12	Q R to K sq	P to K R 3
13	B × Kt	Kt × B
14	P to Q B 3	B to K Kt 5
15	R × R	R × R
16	R to K sq	Q B × Kt
17	R × R, ch	Kt × R
18	P × B	Kt to K B 3

	WHITE	BLACK
19	Q to K 2	P to K Kt 3
20	Q to B sq	Q to Q 2
21	Q to Kt 2	K to B sq

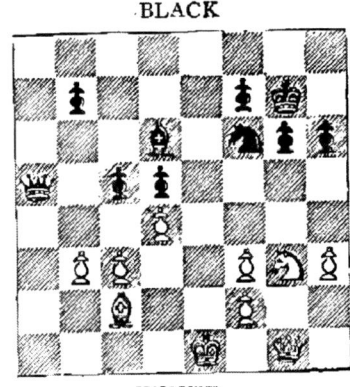

White to make his 33rd move.

WHITE	BLACK	WHITE	BLACK
22 Kt to K 2	Kt to K R 4	31 P × P	P to Q B 4
23 Q to Kt 4	Q to B 2	32 Kt to Kt 3	Q to R 4
24 P to K R 3	K to Kt 2	33 Kt to B 5, ch	K to B sq
25 K to B sq	Kt to K B 3	34 Kt × B	Q × P, ch
26 Q to Kt sq	Q to Q R 4	35 K to B sq	Q × B
27 B to Kt sq²	Q to Kt 4	36 P × P	P to Q 5 ³
28 P to Kt 3	P to Q R 4	37 Q to Kt 3	Q × P
29 B to B 2	P to R 5	38 Q to B 4	K to Kt 2 ⁴
30 K to K sq	P × P	39 Q × Kt, ch	Resigns.

NOTES BY R. TEICHMANN.

¹ Leading to a drawn position. This variation has been played so often that it is entirely exhausted, and affords no chance for either player to try for a win.

² The manœuvres of the White King and Queen have enabled Black to begin an attack on the weak Queen's side Pawns, which he conducts with great energy. White ought now to have played P to R 3, and if Q to Kt 3, then P to Kt 4, followed by K to Kt 2, in order to bring the Queen over to the Queen's wing again.

³ Q × P at once would have been much better; White could not then have taken the Knight's Pawn on account of Q to Kt 4, ch, and if 27. Q to Kt 3, then Q to Q 5 (!), followed by Kt to R 4 and B 5, winning.

⁴ A blunder, which loses at once. Q to Kt 4 would still have given him good drawing chances: e.g., 38. ... Q to Kt 4; 39. Q × P, Q to B 8, ch; 40. K to Kt 2, Kt to R 4; 41. Q to R 8, ch, K to K 2; 42. Q to K 5, ch, K to Q 2; 43. Kt × B or Kt P, Kt to B 5, ch; 44. K to R 2, Q to B 8 (!), forcing the draw.

C. VON BARDELEBEN v. D. JANOWSKI.

WHITE	BLACK
1 P to Q 4	P to Q 4
2 P to Q B 4	P to K 3
3 Kt to Q B 3	Kt to K B 3
4 B to B 4	B to K 2 ¹
5 P to K 3	Castles
6 Kt to B 3	P to B 4
7 P × B P	B × P
8 B to Q 3	Kt to B 3
9 Castles	B to K 2 ²
10 R to B sq	P × P
11 B × P	Q to R 4 ³
12 Kt to Q Kt 5	P to Q R 3
13 B to B 7 ⁴	P to Q Kt 3

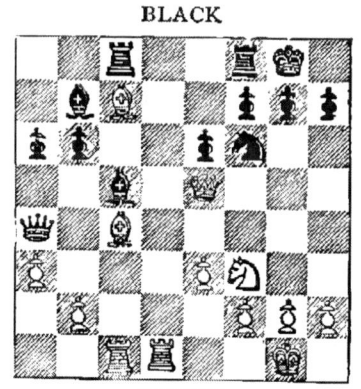

White to make his 19th move.

WHITE	BLACK	WHITE	BLACK
14 Q Kt to Q 4	Kt × Kt	38 Q to K 8, ch	K to R 2
15 Q × Kt	B to B 4	39 R to Q 4	Q to Kt 8, ch
16 Q to K 5	B to Kt 2	40 K to Kt 2	Q to Kt 2, ch
17 K R to Q sq	Q R to B sq	41 P to K 4	Q to K 2
18 P to Q R 3	Q to R 5	42 Q × Q	R × Q
19 P to Q Kt 3 [5]	Q to B 3 [6]	43 K to B 3 [11]	R to Kt 2
20 B to Q 6	B × B	44 R to Q 5	R to Kt 6, ch
21 R × B	Q to B 2	45 K to B 4	R to Kt 7
22 Q R to Q sq	B × Kt [7]	46 P to B 3	R × P
23 P × B	P to Q Kt 4	47 R × P	R to K Kt 7
24 B to Q 3	K to R sq	48 R to Q 5 [12]	P to R 4
25 Q to Q 4	K R to Q sq	49 P to R 5	R to Q R 7
26 B to K 4	Kt to Q 4 [8]	50 K to Kt 3	R to R 6
27 R × R, ch	R × R	51 P to K 5	P × P
28 P to B 4	P to B 3 [9]	52 R × P	K to R 3
29 P to B 5	R to K sq	53 R to Kt 5	K to Kt 4
30 B × Kt [10]	P × B	54 P to B 6, ch	K × P
31 Q × Q P	P to R 3	55 R × P	P to Kt 4
32 P to Q R 4	P × P	56 R to R 6, ch	K to B 4
33 P × P	Q to B 7	57 P to R 6	P to Kt 5
34 R to Q 4	R to Q B sq	58 R to R 5, ch	K to Kt 3
35 Q to K 6	P to Q R 4	59 K × P	R × P
36 Q to Q 7	R to B sq		Drawn game.
37 R to K Kt 4	R to B 2		

NOTES BY I. GUNSBERG.

[1] There is no particular reason why Black should not play B to Q 3.

[2] There are certain positions in the openings which by their very nature indicate the treatment which they require. The move of B to B 4 by White is objectionable solely on the ground that it gives Black a leverage to help him to play P to K 4, but Black, in his last two moves, makes no preparation, such as R to K sq, to attain that object.

[3] The move of Q to R 4, which is sometimes good, is not to be commended in a case like this, where the further movements of the Queen, such as Q to K R 4, may be curtailed by the swarm of White's minor Pieces. Black need not have feared the exchange of Queens; the White Bishop on K B 4 has played there in order to be a thorn in Black's Queen's side. Why then not get rid of it by Kt to K R 4, and reduce the game to its level of deserved nothingness?

[4] Whereas now White, by excellent play, places with his Bishop Black's Queen out of activity, and weakens the Queen's wing.

[5] If 19. P to Q Kt 4, B to K 2; 20. B × K P, P × B, 21. Q × P, ch, K to R sq (best); 22. Q × B, Kt to Q 4, with advantage. If again, 19. P to Q Kt 4, B to K 2; 20. B × Kt P, R × B wins.

⁶ If Q × R P ; 20 R to R sq.

⁷ Black gains nothing by this exchange. P to Q Kt 4 would have been my selection.

⁸ It would have been better to exchange off at once rather than place the Knight in a position where it remains pinned.

⁹ R to Q 2 would have prevented the loss of a Pawn, and got rid of the pinning of the Knight

¹⁰ If 30. P × P, Kt to B 6 ; 31. R to K sq, R × P, &c.

¹¹ P to B 3 was better ; it consolidates White's Pawn position, giving him time to manœuvre with his King and Rook. The failure to adopt this move has helped to bring about the draw.

¹² If White plays R to R 8 instead, then Black is prepared to advance his King's Rook's Pawn, which would quite counteract the intended advance of White Queen's Rook's Pawn.

B. Vergani v. I. Gunsberg.

	WHITE	BLACK		WHITE	BLACK
1	P to K 4	P to K 4	15	Kt to Q Kt 5	P to Q B 3 (?) ³
2	K Kt to B 3	Q Kt to B 3	16	Kt to Q 6	Q × R P
3	B to B 4	B to B 4	17	Kt to K Kt 5	P to K R 3 ⁴
4	P to B 3	Kt to B 3	18	Kt (Q 6) × B P ⁵	
5	P to Q 3	Castles			P × Kt
6	B to K 3	B × B ¹	19	Kt × Kt P	R × R, ch
7	P × B	P to Q 4	20	Q × R (¹) ⁶	B to K 3
8	P × P	Kt × P	21	Kt × B	Kt to B 5 ⁷
9	P to K 4 ²	Kt to K 6	22	Kt × Kt	P × Kt
10	Q to K 2	Kt × B	23	Q to K 2	Q to R 4
11	P × Kt	Q to Q 3	24	P to K 5	R to K sq
12	Castles	Kt to K 2	25	P to K 6	Q to K B 4
13	Kt to R 3	Kt to Kt 3	26	R to K sq	P to K Kt 3
14	Q R to Q sq	Q to R 3	27	Q to K 4	Q to B 3 ⁸
			28	Q to K 5 (?) ⁹	K to Kt 2 (?) ¹⁰
			29	Q to Q 4	P to R 3
			30	K to B 2	R to Q sq
			31	Q × Q, ch	K × Q
			32	P to K 7	R to K sq
			33	K to B 3	R × P ¹¹
			34	R × R, ch	K × R
			35	K × P	K to B 3
			36	P to R 4	P to R 4
			37	P to B 5	K to K 3
			38	K to Kt 5	K to B 2
			39	P to K Kt 4	K to Kt 2
			40	P to R 5	P × P
			41	P × P	K to R 2
			42	P to R 6	Resigns.

BLACK

WHITE

White to make his 18th move.

AUGUST 20

NOTES BY C. VON BARDELEBEN.

[1] The usual move is B to Kt 3.

[2] I prefer 9. Q to K 2.

[3] A mistake which costs the game, because the Black Queen, after the move P to Q B 3, is out of play. Black ought to play Q to Q B 3. [Probably played as a trap.—ED.]

[4] If P to B 3, then 18. Kt × R P, K × Kt ; 19. Q to R 5, ch.

[5] The sacrifice is sound ; 18. Kt (Kt 5) × P would not be so good as 18. Kt (Q 6) × B P, on account of B to K 3 , 19. Q to R 5, B × Kt ; 20. Kt × B, R × Kt ; 21. R × R, K × R ; 22. R to B sq, ch, K to Kt sq ; 23. Q × Kt, &c. (see diagram).

[6] If 20. R × R (?), then Kt to B 5.

[7] This move is forced, for White threatened 22. R to Q 7.

[8] If Q × Q, then 28. R × Q, P to K Kt 4 , 29. K to B 2, K to Kt 2 ; 30. P to R 4, P × P ; 31. R × P, R × P ; 32 R × P, and White wins.

[9] A mistake ; the right move was 28. K to B 2.

[10] Black does not take advantage of his opponent's mistake. He ought to play Q × Q ; 29. R × Q, K to Kt 2 ; 30. R to K 4, P to K Kt 4 ; 31. P to R 4, P × P ; 32. R × P, R × P ; 33. R × P, R to K 7 ; 34. P to Q Kt 4, R to Q B 7 ; 35. R to R 3, P to Kt 3, followed by P to R 4. By this line of play Black would be able to draw.

[11] Black's game is lost. If P to K Kt 4, then 34. P to R 4.

W. STEINITZ v. J. MIESES.

	WHITE	BLACK		WHITE	BLACK
1	P to Q 4	P to Q 4	17	B × Q	B to Kt 5
2	P to Q B 4	P × P	18	B × P	B × Kt
3	P to K 3[1]	P to K 4	19	P × B	B × P
4	Kt to Q B 3	P × P	20	P to Q B 4	K R to Q B sq[5]
5	P × P	Kt to K B 3	21	B × P	B × B P
6	B × P.	B to K 2	22	B to Q sq	Q R to Kt sq
7	Kt to B 3	Castles	23	B to Q 4	B to Kt 6
8	Castles	P to Q Kt 3	24	B to K 2	R to Kt 5
9	Kt to K 5	B to Kt 2	25	B × R P	R to R sq
10	Q to Kt 3	Q to K sq	26	B × Kt	P × B
11	R to K sq[2]	Kt to B 3[3]	27	B to Kt 5	B × P[6]
12	Kt × Kt	Q × Kt	28	B to Q 3	R to Q sq
13	P to Q 5	Q to B 4	29	R to K 3	R (Kt 5) to Q 5
14	P to Q R 3[4]	P to Q R 3	30	B to K 2	B to Q 8
15	P to Q R 4[4]	Q to Kt 5	31	B to B sq	B to B 7
16	B to K B 4	Q × Q		Drawn game.	

NOTES BY H. N. PILLSBURY.

[1] 3. Kt to K B 3 is considered the strongest continuation in the Gambit accepted. [As introduced by Blackburne.—ED.]

² Threatening 12. B × P, ch, R × B; 13. Kt × R, Q × Kt; 14. R × B, &c.

³ This and Black's 12th move fully equalise the position.

⁴ These two moves are clear loss of time, and B to K B 4 at once was the correct play.

⁵ The foregoing exchanges and this move force a draw. White makes a futile effort to avoid this result, but there is nothing left in the position to play for.

⁶ A certain draw now.

E. Schiffers v. G. Marco.

	WHITE	BLACK		WHITE	BLACK
1	P to K 4	P to K 4	20	Kt × Kt, ch	Kt × Kt
2	Kt to K B 3	P to Q 3	21	Kt to Kt 3	K to Kt 2
3	P to Q 4	Kt to Q 2	22	R to Q 3	B to Q 3
4	P × P¹	P × P	23	Q R to Q sq	B to B 2
5	B to Q B 4	B to Q 3	24	P to Kt 4	P to Kt 3
6	Castles	K Kt to B 3	25	P × P	P × P
7	Kt to B 3	P to K R 3²	26	Q to B 3	Q to R 3
8	Q to K 2	P to B 3	27	Q to Q 2	R to R sq
9	P to Q R 4	Castles	28	P to K B 3	R (K 3) to K sq
10	R to Q sq	Q to B 2	29	Q to B 3	Q to Kt 4
11	P to R 3	R to K sq³	30	Q to Kt 3	R to Q sq⁶
12	Kt to R 4	Kt to Kt 3⁴	31	P to Q B 4	Q to R 3
13	B to Kt 3	B to K 3	32	P to B 5	Q to Kt 2
14	B × B	R × B	33	Q to R 3	P to Q Kt 4
15	Kt to B 5	B to B sq	34	Q to B 3	Q to B sq
16	B to K 3	K to R 2	35	Q to B sq	R × R
17	P to R 5⁵	Q Kt to Q 2	36	R × R	Q to K 3
18	Q to B 4	P to K Kt 3		Drawn game.	
19	Kt to Q 5	Q to B sq			

Notes by I. Gunsberg.

¹ With this move White relieves Black of the disadvantage attendant on any close defence, whatever the opening may be, by P to Q 3 being played, shutting in the King's Bishop.

² A hardly necessary precaution.

³ The Rook makes room for the Knight, to play to B sq, then to Kt 3. After Kt to B sq, P to K Kt 4 would deserve consideration.

⁴ Kt to B sq was better; the Knight has no prospect on Q Kt 3.

⁵ There seems to be a want of purpose in the game. White's move of 10. R to Q sq was an unprofitable one, and with the text move White forces the Knight into a better position.

⁶ Although both players handle their forces with care, yet neither of them have succeeded in gaining any advantage. White threatened by R to Q 7 to obtain a winning attack. Black's move of R to Q sq,

AUGUST 20

however, prevents this at the right moment. After this the game soon drifts into an unpromising blocked position, resulting in a draw being agreed upon.

S. Tinsley v. H. E. Bird.

	WHITE	BLACK
1	P to Q 4	P to Q 4
2	P to Q B 4	P to K 3
3	Kt to K B 3	P to Q B 3
4	P to K 3	Q Kt to Q 2
5	Kt to Q B 3	B to Q 3
6	B to Q 3	P to K B 4
7	P × P	B P × P
8	B to Q 2	P to Q R 3
9	R to Q B sq	Kt to K R 3 [1]
10	Q to Kt 3 [2]	Q to K 2
11	P to K Kt 3	Kt to B 2
12	P to K R 4	Castles
13	P to R 5	P to Q Kt 4
14	P to R 6 [3]	P to Kt 3 [4]
15	Kt to K R 4	Kt to B 3
16	P to B 4	B to Q 2
17	B to K 2	P to Kt 5
18	Kt to R 4	Kt to K 5 [5]
19	Kt to Kt 6	Kt × Kt P
20	R to R 3	Kt × B
21	K × Kt	B to Kt 4, ch
22	K to B 2	Q R to Kt sq
23	Kt to R 4	Kt × R P [6]
24	Q R to K R sq	Q to K sq
25	Kt to B 5	Kt to Kt 5, ch
26	K to K sq	B to B 5
27	Q to B 2	B × Kt
28	P to Kt 3	B to Kt 4 [7]
29	Q × B	R to Q B sq
30	Q × Kt P	Kt to B 3
31	P to Q R 4	B to Q 6
32	Kt to B 3	B to K 5
33	K to B 2	R to B 7
34	R to Q B sq	R × R
35	B × R	B × Kt
36	K × B	R to B 2
37	R to R 2	R to Q B 2
38	B to R 3	Kt to B 5
39	Q to Kt 6	Q to Q B sq
40	Q to Kt 4	K to Kt 2
41	P to R 5	P to R 3
42	Q to Kt 6	P to Kt 4
43	P × P	Kt × P, ch
44	K to Kt 3	R to B 3
45	Q to R 7, ch	Q to B 2, ch
46	Q × Q, ch	R × Q
47	B to B 5	Kt to K 5, ch
48	K to B 3	Kt × B
49	R to Q B 2	K to B 3
50	R × Kt	R to Kt 2 (?) [8]

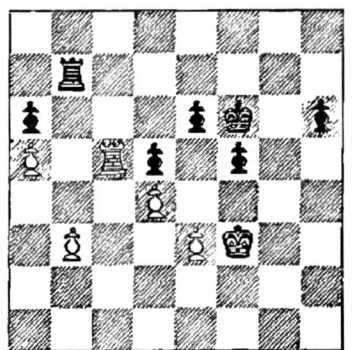

White to make his 51st move.

51	R to B 6	R × P
52	R × R P	R to Kt sq
53	K to B 4	R to Kt 5
54	K to B 3	P to R 4
55	R to R 8	R to R 5
56	P to R 6	P to R 5
57	P to R 7	K to Kt 2
58	R to K 8	R × R P
59	R × K P	R to R 8
60	R to K 5	R to K Kt 8
61	K to B 2	R to Kt 4

WHITE	BLACK	WHITE	BLACK
62 R×Q P	P to R 6	67 R to K 2 (?)[9]	K to Kt 4
63 R to B 5	R to Kt 7, ch	68 R to K R 2	R×R
64 K to B 3	R to Kt 8	69 K×R	P to B 5
65 R to B 2	R to R 8	70 P×P, ch	
66 K to Kt 3	K to B 3	Drawn game.	

NOTES BY E. SCHIFFERS.

[1] I prefer Kt to K B 3.

[2] Q to Q Kt 3 is rarely good in this opening.

[3] An attack of little promise, and which only results in a weak Pawn at K R 6

[4] If Kt × P, then 15. Kt × K P, &c. ; 14. ... P × P, would evidently not be good.

[5] Black has now the better game.

[6] Black is already two Pawns ahead ; the weakness of the moves P to K R 5 and P to K R 6 now becomes apparent.

[7] Apparently, Black could have won another Pawn by B × P.

[8] Black should have exchanged Rooks and must then win by force : e.g. 50. ... R × R ; 51. P × R, P to K 4 ; 52. P to Q Kt 4, K to K 3 ; 53 P to Kt 5, K to Q 2 and wins, having two passed Pawns. Or 51. ... K to K 2 ; 52. K to B 4, P to R 4 ; 53. P to Kt 4, P to R 5 ; 54. P to Kt 5, K to Q 2, &c. ; or else 53. K to Kt 5, P to K 4, and wins.

[9] 67. R to K R 2 immediately [as pointed out by Mr. Tinsley at the conclusion of the game.—ED.] gave White a good chance of winning. After R to R 2, R anywhere ; 68. K to B 2, and wins the Pawn at R 3. Black evidently could not exchange Rooks with the King at B 3 ; 67. ... R × R ; 68. K × R, K to Kt 4 ; 69. K × P, P to B 5 ; 70. P to K 4, and wins.

Photo., Bradshaw, Hastings

J. H. Blackburne

AUGUST 21.

To-day (21st) Tchigorin and Steinitz are to meet, and the play of the round must prove entertaining and important to the score. The leader, Tchigorin, loses a curious and fine game to Steinitz. Blackburne plays another Bishop's Gambit on Pillsbury and draws; and Lasker, though meeting with a stubborn resistance, wins, and thus heads the score again with $10\frac{1}{2}$, Tchigorin and Pillsbury being 10, whilst no one else is more than 8—a gap which continues to the end of the Tournament. This round is very rich in good games.

J. H. Blackburne v. H. N. Pillsbury.

	WHITE	BLACK		WHITE	BLACK
1	P to K 4	P to K 4	23	R to R 3	R to Q B sq
2	P to K B 4	P × P [1]	24	R to Q 3	R to B 3
3	B to B 4	P to Q 4	25	K to B sq	K to B sq
4	B × P	Kt to K B 3	26	K to K sq	K to K 2
5	Kt to Q B 3	B to Q Kt 5	27	K to Q sq	P to B 4
6	Kt to B 3	Castles	28	P to B 3	P to K Kt 4
7	Castles	B × Kt [2]	29	K to B 2	P to Kt 5
8	Q P × B	P to B 3	30	P to Kt 3	P to K Kt 4
9	B to B 4	Q × Q	31	P to Q R 4	K to K 3
10	R × Q	Kt × P	32	Kt to Kt 3	K to K 4
11	Q B × P	Kt to Q 2	33	R to K 3, ch	Kt to K 5
12	R to Q 4 [3]	Q Kt to B 3	34	Kt to Q 2	R to R 3
13	R to K sq	B to B 4	35	R to K 2	K to Q 4
14	B to Q 3 [4]	K R to K sq	36	Kt × Kt	P × Kt
15	B to K 5	P to B 4	37	R to Q 2, ch	K to K 4
16	R to R 4	B to Kt 3	38	R to K 2	P to R 4 ([1])
17	Q B × Kt	Kt × B	39	P to Kt 5	R to K B 3
18	R × R, ch	Kt × R	40	K to Kt 3	R to B 6
19	P to Q Kt 4	P × P	41	K to B 2	P to K 6 [5]
20	B × B	R P × B	42	K to Q 3	K to Q 4
21	P × P	Kt to Q 3	43	R × P	R × R, ch
22	Kt to Q 2	P to R 3	44	K × R	K to B 5

White to make his 39th move.

WHITE	BLACK
45 K to K 4	K to Kt 6
46 K to B 5	K × R P
47 K × P (Kt 4)	K to Kt 6
48 P to R 4	P × P
49 P × P	P to R 5
50 P to R 5	P to R 6
51 P to R 6	P to R 7
52 P to R 7	P Queens
53 P Queens	Q × P
54 Q to K 8	Q to Q B 2
55 K to B 3	K to Kt 4
56 Q to K 4, ch	K × P
57 Q to Kt sq, ch	K to R 3
58 Q to R 2, ch	Q to R 4
59 Q to K 6, ch	Q to Kt 3
60 Q to R 2, ch	K to Kt 4
61 Q to Kt 3, ch	K to B 3
62 Q to K 6, ch	K to B 2
63 Q to K 7, ch	K to Kt sq
64 K to K 2	K to R 2
65 K to Q sq	Q to Q Kt 8, ch
66 K to Q 2	Q to Kt 7, ch
67 K to Q sq	K to R 3
68 Q to Q 6, ch	P to Kt 3
69 Q to Q 5	P to Kt 4
70 Q to R 8, ch	K to Kt 3
71 Q to Q 8, ch	K to B 4
72 Q to K 7, ch	K to B 5
73 Q to K 6, ch	K to Kt 5
74 Q to Q 6, ch	K to R 4
75 Q to B 7, ch	K to R 5
76 Q to R 7, ch	
Drawn game.	

NOTES BY A. ALBIN.

[1] To accept the King's Gambit is at all events better than to decline; we have seen the contrary in the game Blackburne v. Schlechter in the last Leipsic Tournament. The defence has more resources than the attack.

[2] Mr. Pillsbury plays here to simplify the game because his famous opponent is dangerous.

[3] R to K sq at once is preferable. I don't see how Black can save the game. If Q Kt to B 3, then 13. B to Q 3, B to B 4 (if K Kt to B 4, then 14 B to Q 6), 14. Kt to R 4, and wins. Or if K Kt to B 3, then 13. B to Q 6, R to Q sq; 14. B to K 7, R to K sq (if 13. R to K sq, then 14 Kt to K 5, R × R, ch; 15. R × R); 15. Kt to Kt 5 (!). Again, if K Kt to B 4, then 13. B to Q 6, R to Q sq; 14. B to Q 7, R to K sq; 15. Kt to K 5, and wins.

[4] Kt to R 5 is superior; Black must play P to Q B 4 to prevent the loss of two Knights against one Rook; and even then White has more chances for a win For instance, if 14. Kt. to R 5, P to Q B 4; 15. Kt × B (!), White would get four Pawns on the Queen's side and keep two Bishops. Only one defence is possible, and that consists as

reply to Kt to R 5, P to K Kt 3. And even then White gets the better game after Kt × B (better than P to K Kt 4).

⁵ R to B 8 seems to give more winning chances.

A. Burn v. H. E. Bird.

	WHITE	BLACK
1	P to Q 4	P to K B 4
2	P to Q B 4	P to K 3
3	P to K 3	Kt to K B 3
4	Kt to K B 3¹	P to Q Kt 3
5	B to K 2	B to Kt 2
6	Castles	Kt to Q B 3
7	Kt to Q B 3	B to Q Kt 5 ²
8	B to Q 2	Castles
9	Q to Q B 2	B × Kt
10	B × B	Kt to K 5
11	B to K sq	P to Q 3
12	Q R to Q sq	Q to B 3
13	Kt to Q 2³	Kt to K 2
14	P to K B 3	Kt to Kt 4
15	B to B 2	Q to R 3
16	K R to K sq	Kt to Kt 3
17	B to Q 3	P to B 3
18	P to B 5	Kt P × P
19	P × P	P to Q 4
20	Kt to Kt 3	B to B sq
21	Kt to Q 4	B to Q 2
22	R to K 2⁴	Q to R 4
23	Q to Q R 4	P to K 4
24	Kt × Q B P	P to K 5 ⁵
25	B to Kt 5	P × P
26	R to Q 2	P × P

White to make his 25th move.

	WHITE	BLACK
27	B to K 2	Kt to R 6, ch
28	K × P	Q to Kt 4, ch
29	B to Kt 3	P to B 5
30	R × P	Kt to R 5, ch
31	K to R sq	B × Kt
32	Q × B	Q to K 2
33	R to Q 7	P × B ⁶
34	B to B 4, ch	K to R sq
35	R × Q	Kt to B 7, ch
36	K to Kt sq	Kt to R 6, ch
	Drawn game.	

Notes by H. N. Pillsbury.

¹ 4. B to Q 3 and 5. Kt to K 2, as between Steinitz and Albin, seems a better development.

² A favourite idea of Mr. Bird is to exchange the Black Bishop for White Queen's Knight.

³ The main objection to this form of opening for Black has always been that at some point White by advancing P to Q 5 could block the adverse Bishop out, or else in some way take advantage of Black King's third square. This point seems to have now arrived, and the advance of the Pawn would seem difficult to answer satisfactorily. If, for instance, Black answers P × P ; 14. P × P, Kt to K 2 ; 15. B to B 4, with the better game (White could not attempt to win two

Pieces for a Rook, however, by 15. Q × P, B × P ; 16. R × B, &c., on account of K R to Q B sq ; 17. Q to Kt 7, Q R to Kt sq, and Black would win). If Black play 13. Kt to Q sq, then 14. Kt to Q 4 ; and if P × P (P to K 4 (?) ; 15. Kt × P, Q × Kt ; 16. B to Q 3, and should win), 15. P × P, B × P ; 16. Kt × P, Q × Kt ; 17. R × B, with the better game.

[4] This seems a move to not much purpose. Perhaps 22. P to B 4, Kt to K 5 ; 23. B × Kt, B P × B ; 24. B to Kt 3, threatening to continue Q to R 4, &c., would be more aggressive.

[5] Of course, if R to Q B sq, then Kt to K 7, ch, &c. The attack which Black now obtains is very beautiful, and almost wins (see diagram).

[6] All very fine chess indeed, but there appears to be no more than a draw, a just ending to a most interesting game.

D. JANOWSKI v. G. MARCO.

	WHITE	BLACK		WHITE	BLACK
1	P to K 4	P to K 4	15	K R to Q sq	Kt to K 3 [5]
2	Kt to K B 3	Kt to Q B 3	16	B × Kt	K × B
3	B to Kt 5	P to Q R 3	17	Kt to Q 5, ch	K to Kt 2
4	B to R 4	Kt to B 3	18	Kt to Kt 6	R to Q Kt sq
5	Kt to B 3	P to Q 3	19	Kt × B	Q R × Kt
6	Castles	P to K Kt 3 [1]	20	B × Kt	P × B [6]
7	P to Q 4	P to Q Kt 4	21	P to Q R 4	P to R 3 [7]
8	P × P	P × P	22	P × P	P × P
9	Q × Q	Kt × Q	23	R to R 7	K to B 3 [8]
10	B to Kt 3 [2]	B to Q 3	24	R (Q sq) to R sq	
11	B to R 6 [3]	Kt to Kt 5			P to Kt 4
12	B to Q 2 [4]	Castles	25	R to Kt 7	R to Q Kt sq
13	P to K R 3	Kt to K B 3	26	R × R	R × R
14	B to Kt 5	K to Kt 2	27	K to K B sq	P to R 4 [9]
			28	P to Kt 4	P × P
			29	P × P	K to Kt 3
			30	K to Kt 2	R to K B sq [10]
			31	Kt to K sq	R to B 5
			32	P to K B 3	R to B sq
			33	Kt to Q 3	P to B 4 [11]
			34	R to R 6	R to Q sq
			35	P to Q Kt 3	K to B 3 [12]
			36	R to Q B 6	B to K 2
			37	K to B sq	R to Q 3
			38	R to B 7 [13]	R to Q 5
			39	Kt × B P	B × Kt
			40	R × B	R to Q 8, ch
			41	K to K 2	R to Q B 8
			42	P to Q B 3	R to B 7, ch

BLACK

WHITE

White to make his 21st move.

AUGUST 21

WHITE	BLACK		WHITE	BLACK
43 K to Q 3	R to B 7		51 K to B sq	R to Kt 8, ch
44 K to K 3	R to B 7		52 K to Kt 2	R to Kt 7, ch
45 P to Kt 4	R to B 8		53 K to R 3	R to Kt 8
46 K to Q 2	R to B 8		54 K to Kt 2	R to Kt 7, ch
47 R × Kt P [14]	R × P		55 K to Kt 3	R to Kt 8
48 R to B 5	R to B 5		56 K to B 4	R to Kt 8
49 P to Kt 5	R × Kt P		57 R to Kt 5	Resigns.
50 P to Kt 6	R to Kt 7, ch			

NOTES BY DR TARRASCH.

[1] Carelessly played. The Bishop does not get to Kt 2. B to Q 2 or B to K 2 was better.

[2] Now not only is P to K Kt 3 rendered useless, and therefore loss of time, but the King's side is disarranged also.

[3] B to Kt 5 was better and would have won a Pawn at once, for if Black defended the Knight with B to K 2, then he lost the King's Pawn, and if he moved the Knight away, then he lost the King's Bishop's Pawn with B × Kt and B × K B P.

[4] Here also B to Kt 5 was stronger in order to threaten B × Kt and B × B P, as well as P to K R 3. After 12. ... P to K B 3, 13 B to Q 2, Black was in a worse position than he is after the text moves, which allow the retreat of the Knight to K B 3.

[5] The decisive mistake, with B to K 3 he might have averted any direct disadvantage, even if White should have the better game.

[6] Black has his Pawns in such a bad position that his game must collapse (see diagram).

[7] Black should not permit White the possession of the Queen's Rook's file, but play either R to Q R sq or P to Kt 5.

[8] Here also R to Q R sq was preferable.

[9] Black stands so badly that he can undertake nothing, but nevertheless he offers his opponent as many difficulties as he can.

[10] Threatening R to B 5.

[11] Black ought under no circumstances to make this move, which deprives the Bishop of its support.

[12] After P to B 5 follows 36. P × P, P × P; 37 Kt to Kt 2, P to B 6, 38. Kt to B 4, with win of a Pawn.

[13] Of course not R × P, on account of R × Kt.

[14] The two passed Pawns make a certain win for White.

C. SCHLECHTER v. J. MIESES.

WHITE	BLACK		WHITE	BLACK
1 P to K 4	P to K 4		5 P to Q 4	B to Q 2
2 Kt to K B 3	Kt to Q B 3		6 Castles	P to Q Kt 4
3 B to Kt 5	P to Q R 3		7 B to Kt 3	Kt × P
4 B to R 4	P to Q 3		8 Kt × Kt	P × Kt

204 THE HASTINGS CHESS TOURNAMENT

	WHITE	BLACK
9	P to Q B 3	P × P
10	Q to R 5 [1]	Q to K 2
11	Kt × P	Kt to B 3
12	Q to B 3	B to B 3
13	Kt to Q 5	B × Kt
14	P × B	Q to Q 2
15	P to Q R 4	R to Q Kt sq
16	P × P	P × P
17	B to Kt 5	B to K 2
18	B to B 2	Q to Kt 4
19	Q × Q	Kt × Q
20	K R to K sq	P to B 3
21	B to Q 2	P to Kt 3
22	R to R 7	K to Q 2
23	B to R 5	B to Q sq
24	P to B 4	R to K sq
25	R to Q B sq (!)	
		Kt to K 6
26	B × B P	K to B sq [2]

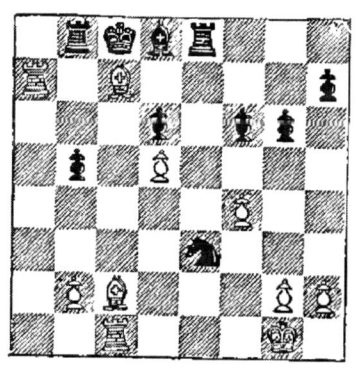

BLACK

WHITE

White to make his 27th move.

	WHITE	BLACK
27	B to Q 3 [3]	Kt to B 5
28	B × Kt	B × B
29	R × B, ch	K × R
30	B × P, ch	K to Q sq
31	B × R	K × B
32	R to B 2	R to Kt 5
33	K to B 2 [4]	R × B P, ch
34	K to K 3	R to Q Kt 5
35	K to Q 3	P to B 4
36	R to K 2, ch	K to Q 2
37	K to B 3	R to K R 5
38	P to K Kt 3	R to K Kt 5
39	P to Kt 4	P to R 4
40	R to K 6	P to Kt 4
41	R to B 6	P to B 5
42	P × P	P × P
43	R to B 7, ch	K to K sq
44	R to B 5	R to R 5
45	K to B 4	R × P
46	R × B P	K to Q sq
47	R to B 7	R to R 5, ch
48	K to Kt 5	R to Q 5
49	K to B 6	R × Kt P
50	R to K R 7	R to K R 5
51	K × P	K to B sq
52	R to R 8, ch	K to Kt 2
53	K to Q 7	R to R 8
54	P to Q 6	P to R 5
55	R to R 7	P to R 6
56	K to K 8, ch	K to R 3 [5]
57	P to Q 7	R to K sq, ch
58	K to B 8	R to B 8, ch
59	K to K sq	R to K sq, ch
60	R to K 2	

Drawn game.

NOTES BY E. SCHIFFERS.

[1] If 10. Q to Q 5, then B to K 3; 11. Q to B 6, ch, B to Q 2; 12. Q to Q 5, and draws.

[2] After B × B would follow 27. B to B 5, ch, K to K 2 (!); 28. R (B sq) × B, ch, K to B sq; 29. R to B 7, ch, K to Kt sq; 30. R to Kt 7, ch, K to R sq; 31. R × P, ch, K to Kt sq; 32. B to K 6, ch, and wins.

AUGUST 21

[3] If 27. B × R, then B to Kt 3 (!).
[4] After 33 P to K Kt 3, would follow 33. ... R to Q 5.
[5] Not K to B 3, on account of the reply Q to R 8, ch, presently.

R. Teichmann v. I Gunsberg.

	WHITE	BLACK		WHITE	BLACK
1	P to K 4	P to K 4	22	R to Kt 2	Kt to Q 3
2	Kt to Q B 3	Kt to Q B 3 [1]	23	P to K R 4	Kt to B 2
3	B to B 4	Kt to B 3	24	P × P [10]	R P × P
4	P to Q 3 [2]	B to B 4 [3]	25	R (Kt 2) to B 2	
5	P to B 4	P to Q 3			R to Kt 3 [11]
6	Kt to B 3	P to K R 3 [4]	26	Kt to R 2	K to Kt 2
7	Kt to Q R 4	B to Kt 3	27	R to K sq	R to K R sq
8	Kt × B	R P × Kt [5]	28	Kt to B sq	R to R 5
9	Castles	Castles	29	R to Kt 2	R (Kt 3) to R 3
10	P × P [6]	P × P	30	Q to B 3	K to Kt sq
11	Q to K sq	Kt to K sq	31	Q to B 5	R to R 8, ch
12	Q to Kt 3	Q to Q 3	32	K to B 2	Q × Q, ch
13	P to Q R 3	P to Q Kt 4	33	K P × Q	R (R 3) to R 5
14	B to Kt 3 [7]	R to R 3	34	B to Q 3	Kt to Q 5
15	B to K 3	K to R 2	35	B to B 3	P to B 4
16	R to B 2 [8]	B to K 3	36	B × Kt	B P × B
			37	Kt to Q 2	R × R
			38	K × R	R to R 8, ch
			39	Kt to B sq [12]	K to Kt 2
			40	K to B 2	Kt to R 3
			41	K to K 2	Kt to Kt sq
			42	K to B 2	K to B 2
			43	R to R 2	R × R, ch
			44	Kt × R	K to K 2 [13]
			45	Kt to B sq	K to Q 2
			46	Kt to Q 2	Kt to K 2
			47	Kt to K 4	Kt to Q 4
			48	K to K 2	K to K 2
			49	P to Q B 3	P to Q Kt 3
			50	K to Q 2	Kt to K 6
			51	Kt to B 2	K to Q 2
			52	P to Kt 3	Kt to Q 4
			53	P to B 4	Kt to B 6
			54	K to B 2	K to B 3
			55	Kt to R sq [14]	P × P
			56	Kt P × P	P to Kt 4
			57	K to Kt 3	P to K 5
			58	P × P, ch	K × P

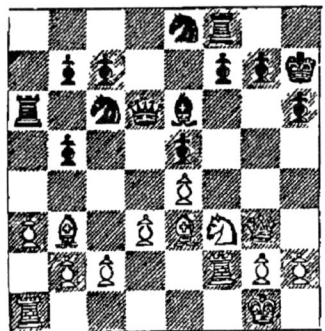

BLACK

WHITE

White to make his 17th move.

17	B × B	Q × B
18	Q R to K B sq	
		P to K B 3
19	Q to R 4 [9]	R to Kt sq
20	P to K Kt 4	P to Kt 4
21	Q to Kt 3	Q R to R sq

WHITE	BLACK	WHITE	BLACK
59 K to B 2	P to K 6 [15]	68 Kt to Q 6	K to B 7
60 Kt to Kt 3	K to R 5	69 Kt to Kt 5	K to Kt 6
61 Kt to K 4	Kt to Q 4	70 Kt to Q 6	K to Kt 7
62 Kt to B 5, ch	K × P	71 Kt to K 4	Kt to K 4
63 Kt to K 6	Kt to Kt 5, ch	72 Kt × B P	K to B 7
64 K to Q sq	Kt to B 3	73 Kt to K 4	Kt × Q P
65 Kt to B 7	Kt to K 4	74 P to B 6	Kt to B 5, ch
66 K to K 2	K to Kt 6	75 K to B 3	P to K 7
67 Kt to Kt 5	Kt to B 3		White resigns.[16]

NOTES BY S. TINSLEY.

[1] At the very outset some considerable difficulty is experienced in dealing with a game of such proportions as this within reasonable limits. The difficulty is the greater because the particular variations on both sides are comparatively rare. Here it may be concluded that Black has a somewhat superior move in Kt to K B 3, if one may trust the testimony of general practice recently. The superiority is, however, not easily defined

[2] To prevent Kt × K P, 5. Kt × Kt (B × P, ch, is poor), P to Q 4, &c., regaining the Piece with a good game. But the necessity, if such it be, of P to Q 3 here leaves White with very little attacking chances for some time.

[3] This feature of all Vienna games and Steinitz Gambits is not, I think, commendable, especially when the Black Bishop, as here, is played to B 4. In fact White's troubles, later, may largely be traced to the open position thus obtained. He has four courses now that are possible alternatives Kt to K B 3; B to K 3; Kt to R 4, to dispose of the White Bishop; or P to Q R 3 to preserve his own. The course adopted is, in fact, rather too risky for general practice.

[4] Kt to K Kt 5 leads to no enduring attack, being answered by Q to K 2 (not R to B sq, because Black can then probably play Kt × R P safely).

[5] In spite of the open file now obtained the loss of the powerful Bishop is serious, and on both sides one is almost disposed to wish players would preserve the Piece by such a much-despised move as P to R 3!

[6] But for the powerful reply P to Q 4 White might well play here P to B 5. The text move further opens Black's game.

[7] Of course White loses the Piece at once, if B × P, by Q to B 4, ch.

[8] It is impossible to follow the game in detail; but for a time it will be found that White obtains a most excellent game, if not a winning position

[9] A very tempting trap. White threatens to win the exchange by Kt to Kt 5, ch. It may be that the true line of attack is by Kt to K R 4 or even P to K R 4. But the whole series of moves now forthcoming show on the one hand subtle and dangerous attack such as could only be met by a splendidly handled defence.

AUGUST 21

[10] I suggest instead K to B 2, followed by R to R sq, &c., piling up the attack on the weak Rook's Pawn. The objection to the line of play adopted is that it prematurely opens the Rook's file for the opponent. It, in fact, ultimately lost the game.

[11] White threatened probably 26. Kt × P, ch, and if P × Kt ; 27. R to B 6, winning the Queen or mating afterwards by Q to R 3, ch, followed by Q to R 6.

[12] The Rook must not be allowed to get to B 8 or Kt 8 on the Queen's side.

[13] From this point the game assumes the form of an end game requiring the greatest nicety of handling. The objects underlying the play are not very obscure

[14] Supposing now 55. Kt to K 4, Kt × Kt ; 56. P × Kt, P × P. 57. P × P, K to B 4 ; 58. K to Kt 3, P to Q 6 ; 59 K to B 3, P to Q 7 ; 60. K × P, K × P, and Black has the position to win easily.

[15] The winning stroke. The rest is comparatively easy.

[16] I happened to see a good deal of this ending as it was being played at Hastings. It occupied two or three sittings. It charmed me then ; I am still more struck in going over it in the complete form. I fear it has been impossible to do justice to either side. In many respects it is a grand game for both men to have played. But, taking all the circumstances into account, I doubt whether Mr. Gunsberg's conduct of this game, and especially of the ending, can be easily surpassed.

J. Mason v. B. Vergani.

	WHITE	BLACK		WHITE	BLACK
1	P to K 4	P to K 4	19	Castles Q R	Q to K 2
2	Kt to K B 3	Kt to Q B 3	20	Q R to Kt sq	P to B 4 [5]
3	B to B 4	B to B 4	21	P × P	P × P
4	Kt to B 3	Kt to B 3	22	Kt to Kt 5	R to R sq
5	P to Q 3	P to Q 3	23	R to Q sq [6]	P to B 3 [7]
6	Kt to K 2	B to K 3	24	P to K B 3	Q R to Q sq
7	Kt to Kt 3 [1]	B × B	25	K to Kt sq	B to Kt 3
8	P × B	Kt to K 2	26	K R to K sq	R to R 3
9	Q to K 2	Castles	27	P to K Kt 3	B to B 2
10	B to Kt 5	Kt to K sq	28	Q to Q 3	Q to B 3
11	B × Kt [2]	Q × B	29	Q to Kt 3	B to Kt 3 [8]
12	Kt to B 5	Q to B 3	30	P to B 5 (!)	P × P
13	P to K R 4	P to K Kt 3	31	R × R	B × R
14	Kt to R 6, ch	K to Kt 2	32	Q × P, ch [9]	Q to K 2
15	Kt to Kt 4	Q to B 5	33	Q to B 8	R to B 3 [10]
16	Kt to Kt 5 [3]	Kt to B 3	34	R to Q sq	R to Q 3
17	Kt × Kt	Q × Kt	35	R × R	Q × R
18	Kt to B 3	P to K R 4 [4]	36	Q × B	Q × Q

BLACK

White to make his 30th move.

	WHITE	BLACK
37	Kt to K 6, ch	K to B 3
38	Kt × Q	P to K 5
39	P × P	P × P
40	K to B sq	K to B 4
41	K to Q 2	K to Kt 5
42	K to K 3	K × P
43	Kt to K 6	K × P
44	Kt to B 4	K to Kt 5
45	Kt × P [11]	K × Kt
46	K × P	K to Kt 3
47	K to K 5	K to B 2
48	K to Q 6	K to K sq
49	K × P (B 6)	K to Q sq
50	K × P	K to B 2
51	P to B 4	K to Q 2
52	K to Kt 5	K to B 2
53	K to R 6	K to Kt sq
54	P to B 5	K to R sq
55	P to Kt 4	K to Kt sq
56	P to Kt 5	K to R sq
57	P to B 6	K to Kt sq
58	P to B 7, ch	Resigns.

NOTES BY DR. TARRASCH.

[1] Usually in similar positions the Bishop is played to Kt 3; one can also leave it very well at B 4: one gets the open Queen's file, K B 5 is ready for the Knight, and the Pawn at B 4 has its effect; therefore Black ought not to exchange the Bishops.

[2] If White does not exchange, Black can force the Bishop at Kt 5 back to Q 2 by P to B 3, and then advance the Pawn to B 4.

[3] White now threatens to win the Queen by advancing Pawn to K Kt 3.

[4] White threatened to continue the attack with P to K Kt 4 and 5, followed by P to R 5, and therefore P to K R 3 ought to be played, in order to draw away the Queen after P to K Kt 4, and then to play P to K R 4 in answer to P to Kt 5, or P to Kt 4 in answer to P to R 5. The text move denudes the King unnecessarily, and provides White with a target for his shots.

[5] This second weakening is the consequence of the first; Black wishes to prevent P to K Kt 4.

[6] In order to advance the King's Bishop's Pawn. The position of Black's King is certainly very bare, but the attack against it is temporarily at a standstill; the contest shifts towards the centre, till at last at the extreme Queen's side it is decisively finished.

[7] Again an unnecessary weakening.

[8] The decisively wrong move. (See diagram.)

[9] Now at last Black's position is broken.

[10] Black has no saving move.

[11] The simplest way to victory. The rest is silence.

M. Tchigorin v. W Steinitz.

	WHITE	BLACK		WHITE	BLACK
1	P to K 4	P to K 4	25	P to Q R 3	P to Q B 4
2	K Kt to B 3	Q Kt to B 3	26	P to B 3	K to B 3
3	B to B 4	B to B 4	27	K R to Q sq	R to Q R sq [4]
4	P to Q Kt 4	B × Kt P	28	K to B 2	R to R 5
5	P to B 3	B to R 4	29	K to K 3	P to K R 4 [5]
6	Castles	P to Q 3	30	K to Q 2	P to Kt 5
7	P to Q 4	P × P	31	P × P	R × P
8	P × P	K Kt to B 3	32	K R to Q Kt sq	
9	P to K 5	P × P			R × R [6]
10	B to R 3	B to K 3 [1]	33	R × R	P to Q Kt 4
11	B to Kt 5 [2]	Q to Q 4	34	R to Q R sq	P to Kt 5
12	Q to R 4	Castles Q R	35	K to B 2	K to Q 4
13	B × Kt	P × B	36	R to Q sq, ch	K to B 5
14	B to B 5	B to Kt 3	37	R to Q 8	B to Q 4
15	Q to R 6, ch[3]	K to Kt sq	38	P to K R 4	K to Q 5
16	Kt × P	Kt to Q 2	39	R to Q Kt 8	B to K 3
17	Q Kt to B 3	Kt × B	40	R to Kt 7	P to Kt 3
18	Q to K 2	Q to Q 3	41	R to Kt 5	P to Kt 6, ch
19	P × Kt	Q × P	42	K to Kt 2	P to B 5
20	Kt to R 4	Q to Q Kt 4	43	R to Kt 4	K to Q 6
21	Q × Q	P × Q	44	R to Kt 6	P to B 6, ch
22	Kt × B	R P × Kt	45	K to Kt sq	K to K 6 [7]
23	Kt to B 6, ch	K to Kt 2		White resigns.	
24	Kt × R, ch	R × Kt			

Notes by E. Lasker.

[1] So far everything is book. It has always been the opinion that Black, although two Pawns ahead, will not be able to develop his Pieces, as Castling King's side is prevented, and the King dare not occupy the centre any length of time Black seemed to believe that he may get his King safely Castled to the Queen's side, but this game does not corroborate such an opinion, in spite of the success which attended that manœuvre in this instance.

[2] Tchigorin's favourite post for the Bishop in the Evans' Gambit.

[3] White ultimately wins the exchange by this manœuvre, but at an enormous expense. It would have been better to leave things as they were, and to continue simply with 15. Kt × P If then 15. ... Kt to Q 2; 16. Kt × Q B P must win the exchange in favourable position; and if 15. ... Kt to K 5; 16. B × B, B P × B; 17 Q × R P will equalise the material forces. with the position to White's advantage.

[4] A Rook being very well qualified to support advancing Pawns and to check the approach of the hostile King, it is judicious play to avoid its exchange for the present.

[5] Advancing these Pawns, which constitute the only weakness in Black's camp, protects them against any possible attack of the Rooks or King.

[6] Now it is just as well to simplify, two united passed Pawns with the support of the King and Bishop being more than a match for King and Rook. Black need only take care to leave the passed Pawns as much as possible on the colour not dominated by the Bishop—i.e. on black squares.

[7] Thr atening B to B 5, ch ; 45. P to K Kt 4 would be answered by K × P. White is therefore perfectly helpless.

A. ALBIN v. E. SCHIFFERS.

	WHITE	BLACK		WHITE	BLACK
1	P to K 4	P to Q B 4	18	Q to Q Kt 4 [5]	P to Q B 4
2	Kt to K B 3	P to K 3 [1]	19	Q to K 4 [6]	P to Q B 5
3	Kt to Q B 3	Kt to Q B 3	20	Q × Q	P × Q
4	P to Q 4	P × P	21	R to K sq, ch	K to Q sq
5	Kt × P	Kt to B 3	22	B × B P [7]	B to B 3
6	B to K 3	B to Kt 5	23	R × B P	P × B
7	B to Q 3 [2]	P to Q 4	24	R × Kt P	P to K R 4
8	P × P	Kt × P	25	P to K B 4	R to K sq
9	Kt × Kt	P × Kt	26	R to Q sq, ch	K to B sq
10	B to Q 2	Q to R 4	27	R to Q 6	B to K 5
11	Castles [3]	Kt × Kt	28	R to Q 4	P to R 4
12	P × Kt	B × P	29	R × P, ch	K to Kt sq
13	Q to B 3	B to Q 2 [4]	30	R to B 5	R to R 3
14	B × B	Q × B	31	R to Kt 5, ch	K to R sq
15	Q R to Kt sq	Q to B 3	32	P to B 3	P to Q R 5
16	Q to K 4	Q to Kt 4	33	R × P [8]	P to Q R 6
17	R to Kt 7	Q to Q 4	34	R (Kt 7) to Kt 5	
					B to Q 6
			35	R to R 5	R to K 8, ch
			36	K to B 2	R to K 7, ch
			37	K to B 3	R × R P
			38	K to K 3	B to B 8
			39	K to Q 4	K to R 2
			40	P to Q B 4 [9]	R to Q B 7 [10]
			41	R to R 7, ch	K to Kt 3
			42	R to Q Kt 5, ch	
					K to B 3
			43	R to R 6, ch	K to Q 2
			44	R to Q 5, ch	K to B 2
			45	R × R	P to R 7
			46	R to B 5, ch	K to Kt 2
			47	R to R 3	R to Q 7, ch

BLACK

White to make his 18th move.

	WHITE	BLACK		WHITE	BLACK
48	K to K 5	R × P	55	R (B 5) to B 7	
49	P to R 4	K to Kt 3			R to Q 7, ch
50	R to Kt 5, ch	K to B 3	56	K to B 3	R to R 7
51	R to R 6, ch	K to B 2	57	P to R 5	K to B 4
52	K to Q 4	R to K B 7	58	R to B 5, ch	K to Kt 3
53	R to R 7, ch	K to B 3	59	R (B 5) to R 5	
54	R to K B 5	K to Kt 3			Resigns.

NOTES BY R. TEICHMANN.

[1] This way of playing the Sicilian defence is rather old-fashioned, the usual continuation nowadays being the 'King's Fianchetto,' leaving the King's Pawn unmoved.

[2] Here I prefer 7. Kt × Kt, Kt P × Kt ; 8. P to K 5, Kt to Q 4 (best) ; 9. B to Q 2, with a splendid development.

[3] Giving up a Pawn for an ingenious attack Kt × Kt would obviously have led to a drawn position.

[4] It is evident that Castling would lose a Piece by B × B, threatening B × P, ch, if Queen retakes.

[5] 18. R to Q sq appears to be a much stronger continuation of the attack. Black could then neither exchange Queens nor Castle, and if 18. ... P to K B 4 ; 19. Q to Q Kt 4, P to Q B 4 ; 20. Q to Kt 2 ('), and if now B to B 3 ; 21. R × Kt P, with a winning game.

[6] If now Q to Kt 2, Black simply Castles and is out of danger, threatening besides B to B 3.

[7] A risky course ; but with a Pawn behind in the end game this seems to be his best chance of obtaining a draw. He wins nearly all the Black Pawns.

[8] This is a decisive mistake. P to Q R 3 would have given him very good chances of drawing at least.

[9] The play hereabouts is extremely interesting and very difficult for both sides.

[10] This, however, is a very bad mistake which loses a whole Rook. With R × R he ought to have won. The remainder is plain sailing for White.

E. LASKER v. S. TINSLEY.

	WHITE	BLACK		WHITE	BLACK
1	P to K 4	P to K 3	9	Q to K 2	B to Kt 2
2	P to Q 4	P to Q 4	10	R to Q sq [3]	R to K sq
3	Kt to Q B 3	P × P [1]	11	P to Q B 4	P to Q R 4 [4]
4	Kt × P	Kt to K B 3	12	Kt to B 3	Q to B sq
5	B to Q 3	B to K 2	13	B to K B 4	B to Q 3
6	Kt to K B 3	Q Kt to Q 2	14	B to K 5 [5]	B × Kt [6]
7	Castles	Castles	15	P × B	B × B [7]
8	P to B 3	P to Q Kt 3 [2]	16	P × B	Kt to R 4

WHITE	BLACK	WHITE	BLACK
17 B × P, ch	K to R sq [8]	23 B × Kt	P to B 3
18 B to K 4	P to Q B 3	24 P to B 4	Kt to B 2
19 P to K B 4	Kt × B P [9]	25 Kt to K 4	P to Kt 5 [10]
20 Q to Q 2	Kt to R 6, ch	26 B × P	P to B 4
21 K to R sq	P to K Kt 4	27 Q to B 3, ch	Resigns.[11]
22 B to Kt 2	Kt × K P		

NOTES BY H. N. PILLSBURY.

[1] This variation of the 'French' appears to give White too much freedom of action, and is therefore hardly commendable.

[2] A better plan to free his game would be 8. P to Q Kt 4.

[3] A powerful move, for Black can only advance the Bishop's Pawn now under the penalty of an isolated Pawn

[4] Simply a lost move; Q to B sq at once, followed soon by P to B 4, was the only correct course. Moreover, the Queen's Rook's Pawn should be posted at the third to prevent the entrance of adverse Pieces at Kt 5.

[5] With this White acquires a commanding superiority in position.

[6] Very bad indeed, as White can eventually form a strong attack with his Rooks through the Knight's file, Kt to B sq seems better.

[7] This is fatal, losing at least a Pawn, and totally disrupting Black's position on the King's side Kt to B sq might still be played.

[8] Obviously if K × B; 18. Q to Q 3, ch, &c.

[9] Losing a Piece in a few moves, but, after P to Kt 3; 20. Q to B 3, Kt to Kt sq; 21. Kt to Kt 5 or R to Q 6, Black's game was equally lost.

[10] Black attempts to regain the Piece, but it is useless.

[11] For if P to K 4; 28. Q to R 3, ch, K to Kt sq; 29. B × P, &c.

A. WALBRODT v. C. VON BARDELEBEN.

WHITE	BLACK	WHITE	BLACK
1 P to K 4	P to K 4	13 Kt to Kt 3	P to K B 4
2 K Kt to B 3	Q Kt to B 3	14 P to B 3	B to Q 2
3 B to Kt 5	P to Q R 3	15 Q to B 2	Kt to Q sq [4]
4 B to R 4	Kt to B 3	16 B to Kt 5	Q to B 2
5 Castles	Kt × P	17 Q to Q 3	P to B 5 [5]
6 B × Kt [1]	Q P × B	18 Q × B	P × Kt
7 Q to K 2	Kt to Kt 4 [2]	19 R P × P	Q to Kt 3
8 P to Q 4	Kt to K 3	20 Q to Q 2 [6]	Kt to K 3
9 P × P	B to B 4 [3]	21 B to K 3	Kt to B 4
10 R to Q sq	Q to K 2	22 Q to K 2	K to R sq
11 Kt to B 3	Castles	23 Q to B 4	Black abandoned the game.[7]
12 Kt to K 4	B to Kt 3		

AUGUST 21

Notes by E. Schiffers.

[1] P to Q 4 is usual here, but the text move is not to be found fault with.

[2] He should play Kt to B 3. Kt to Q B 4 followed by Kt to K 3 is to be found in the books.

[3] Kt to Q 5 ; 10. Kt × Kt, Q × Kt is better, and if 11. R to Q sq, B to K Kt 5.

[4] Black is in perplexity, he begins to feel the pressure of the adverse Knights, but P to B 5 was better here.

[5] If the natural move, B to K 3, then 18. B × Kt, R × B ; 19. Q × R, R × Q ; 20. R × R, ch, Q to B sq ; 21. R × Q, ch, and wins.

[6] Here he could also very well play :

WHITE	BLACK	WHITE	BLACK
20 B × Kt (and if R × B)		24 R to Q 7, ch	K to K sq (!)
21 Q × R	R × Q	25 R to K sq (and if Q × Kt P)	
22 R × R, ch	K to B 2	26 Kt to Q 4	B × Kt
23 P to K 6, ch	K to K 2 (!) (if	27 P × B	Q to Kt 3
K × P; 24. R to K sq, ch, &c.)		28 R × B P and wins.	

[7] If Q to K 3, there might follow 24. Q × Q, Kt × Q ; 25. B × B, and White must eventually win. Or if Kt to K 4 ; 24. B × B, B P × B ; 25. Kt to R 4, Q to Kt 5 ; 26. R to Q 4. Or if Kt to K 3 ; 24. B × B, B P × B ; 25. R to Q 6 ; and 26. Kt to Q 4, &c.

W. H. K. Pollock v. Dr. Tarrasch.

	WHITE	BLACK
1	P to K 4	P to K 3
2	P to K 5 [1]	P to K B 3 [2]
3	P to Q 4	P to Q B 4
4	B to Q 3	P to B 4 [3]
5	P to K Kt 4 (!) [4]	P × Q P
6	P × P	Q to R 4, ch
7	P to B 3	Q × K P, ch
8	Kt to K 2	Kt to Q B 3 [5]
9	Castles	B to B 4
10	R to K sq	Q to B 3
11	Q Kt to Q 2 [6]	K P × P
12	P × P	B to K 2
13	Kt to K B 3	K to Q sq [7]
14	B to K Kt 5	Q to B 2
15	B × B, ch	K Kt × B
16	Q to Q 2	P to K R 3
17	Kt to K 5	Kt × Kt
18	P × Kt	P to Q Kt 3 [8]
19	Kt to B 4	B to Kt 2
20	B to Kt 5	Kt to B 3

White to make his 21st move.

	WHITE	BLACK
21	P to K 6	Q to K 2 [9]
22	Kt to Kt 6	Q to Kt 4, ch
23	Q × Q, ch	P × Q
24	Kt × R	Kt to Q 5
25	P to K 7, ch	Resigns.

Notes by C von Bardeleben.

[1] This continuation was first adopted by Steinitz against Winawer in the Vienna Tournament, 1882. I do not think it quite sound.

[2] The simple move P to Q 4 seems to be the best answer to the irregular second move of White.

[3] I prefer P to K Kt 3.

[4] An excellent move.

[5] I prefer K P × P, 9. P × P, Q to B 3; 10. Q Kt to B 3, Kt to K 2, though in any case Black's position would be precarious.

[6] White plays with great energy and sound judgment.

[7] If Q to Kt 3, ch, then 14. K to R sq, Kt to B 3; 15. Kt to B 4, Q to B 2; 16. Kt to Kt 5, Q to B sq; 17. B × P and White will win.

[8] P to K Kt 4 would be better in order to prevent the next move of White.

[9] Suicide, but the game is beyond all remedy. If Q to K sq, then 22. Q to B 3, R to K Kt sq; 23. P × P or Q R to Q sq, and White wins easily.

Counting adjourned games as complete, the various scores are now :—

Lasker	$10\frac{1}{2}$	Blackburne	$6\frac{1}{2}$
Tchigorin	10	Janowski	6
Pillsbury	10	Teichmann	$5\frac{1}{2}$
Bardeleben	8	Tinsley	$5\frac{1}{2}$
Steinitz	8	Pollock	$5\frac{1}{2}$
Walbrodt	$7\frac{1}{2}$	Burn	5
Schiffers	7	Albin	5
Bird	7	Gunsberg	5
Mason	7	Marco	$4\frac{1}{2}$
Tarrasch	$6\frac{1}{2}$	Mieses	$4\frac{1}{2}$
Schlechter	$6\frac{1}{2}$	Vergani	2

AUGUST 22.

THE bye day, August 22, has arrived with its full programme. In the morning we all drive to visit Mr. Farmer Atkinson (former M.P.), and to lunch with him at his pretty place at Ore (near Hastings), where we are most hospitably treated by our jovial host, shown numerous curiosities, well fed, and sent back to the afternoon Problem-solving Tournament, where we find Messrs. Studd and Schwann patiently waiting for us as we are late. We get ready as quickly as possible, and about forty solvers enjoy the intellectual meal. The three problems prove to be very fine, and the whole affair is exceedingly well arranged by its promoters, who deserve the very best thanks of the Committee.

The competition is held in the large room of the Tournament, and the intending solvers having settled themselves in various ways, mostly at the tables that on other days are used for the games, are each supplied by Mr. Studd with a handsomely got up double sheet. The first page is a frontispiece in red and gold; page two contains the three problems with their inscriptions; page three is for the solutions, and bears the instructions. 'These must include all variations, but in case of possible duals one continuation given will be sufficient. The problems must be solved from the diagram only.' The fourth page is left blank, but can be used for the solutions if necessary. The managers sit at a large table on the platform overlooking the room and attend to the solvers. It is also explained that the problems are guaranteed by their authors not to have been published, and that they have been most carefully examined; but that should any problem be cooked, the cook would be taken. Every try is examined with praiseworthy care before it is returned to the solvers.

Mieses is first to give in solutions, but proves not to be quite correct, and others keep popping up to the platform only to return discomforted, or to try again. Marco is after all first to be correct—time, 1 hr. 35 min.; Schlechter second, in 1 hr. 40 min.; and Mieses third, in 1 hr. 55 min.

PROBLEMS SET IN THE SOLUTION TOURNEY OF THE HASTINGS INTERNATIONAL TOURNAMENT.

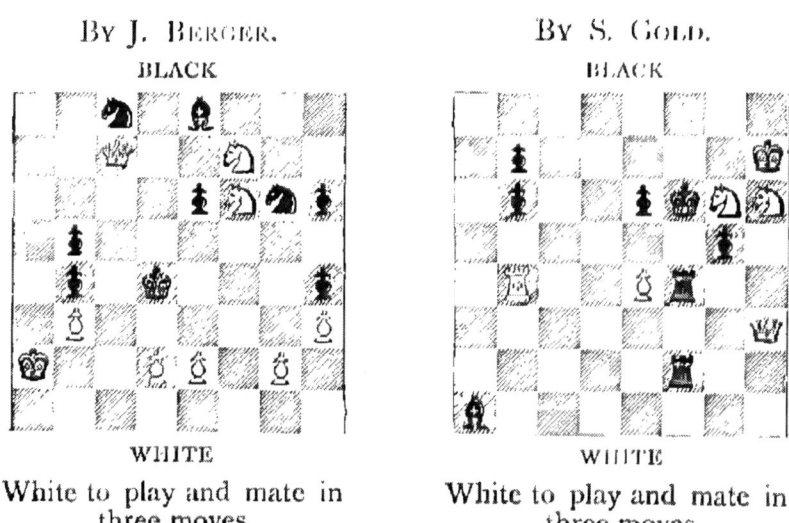

By J. Berger.

White to play and mate in three moves.

By S. Gold.

White to play and mate in three moves.

By D. P.

White to play and mate in four moves.

Mr. Studd now kindly presents his prizes to the successful competitors, and we go home to prepare for the Banquet in the evening.

AUGUST 22

THE BANQUET.

On Thursday, August 22, the masters and press were entertained at a Banquet at the Queen's Hotel. The menu, which was served with the usual excellence of the establishment, was as follows:—

Tortue Claire.

Saumon et Concombre.   Sauce Mousseline.

Filets de Soles Frites.

Petites Bouchees de Homard.

Poulet Sauté à la Chasseur.

Aloyau de Bœuf.

D'Agneau Roti, Sauce Menthe.

Légumes de Saison.

Caneton d'Aylesbury.

Pouding St. Clair aux abricots.

Compôte de Fruits.   Gelee au Marasquin.

Tarte de Pommes.   Custard.

Bavaroise au Chocolat.

Pouding Glacé Nesselrode.

Dessert.

The usual toasts were honoured, and some capital speeches made. Of the competitors, Mr. Lasker in the course of his speech spoke in favour of tournaments, and told us that he had taken up his residence in England and considered it his second fatherland. Mr. Steinitz told us that our Tournament would create a new era in chess. Herr Tchigorin chiefly thanked the Committee for kindly treatment, and took the opportunity of announcing the coming St. Petersburg Tournament. Dr. Tarrasch said that the excuse of some for doing badly was a good one, viz., that the lovely town was too charming and attractive, and a number of enchanting causes rendered them too happy. Mr. Bird spoke of the Tournament as unique.

AUGUST 23.

THERE are two great features of this day—the notably increased attendance, and the large number of sacrificed Pieces, which seem to be flying about in reckless profusion.

Pillsbury defending an Evans' is the first to win, avoiding one of Bird's neat little traps. Steinitz and Burn are both terribly pressed for time as they approach the thirty moves, and the excitement round the board is intense. The director is wondering if he must get a telescope to see if the hands on either or both of the clocks have passed the hour.

W. STEINITZ v. A. BURN.

	WHITE	BLACK
1	P to Q 4	P to Q 4
2	P to Q B 4	P to K 3
3	Kt to Q B 3	Kt to K B 3
4	Kt to B 3	B to K 2
5	B to B 4	Castles
6	P to K 3	P to Q B 4
7	Q P × P	B × P
8	P × P	P × P [1]
9	B to Q 3	Kt to B 3
10	Castles	B to K 3
11	R to Q B sq	R to Q B sq
12	B to Kt sq	Q to R 4 [2]
13	Kt to Q 2	B to K 2
14	Kt to Q Kt 3	Q to Q sq
15	Q to Q 3	Q to Q 2
16	K R to Q sq	K R to Q sq
17	Q to K 2	Q to K sq
18	Kt to Kt 5	B to K Kt 5
19	P to B 3	B to K 3
20	B to B 7	R to Q 2
21	B to Kt 3	K R to Q sq
22	P to Q R 3	K to R sq
23	B to K sq	Kt to Q 2

	WHITE	BLACK
24	B to B 3	Kt to Kt 3
25	Q to Q 3	Q to Kt sq
26	Kt to R 5 [3]	P to Q 5 [4]

White to make his 27th move.

27	Kt × Kt [5]	P × Kt
28	Kt × Q P	P to Q B 4
29	Q to R 6 [6]	P × Kt
30	Q B × P	R × R

Photo., Bradshaw, Hastings.

W Steinitz

AUGUST 23

	WHITE	BLACK		WHITE	BLACK
31	R × R	R to Q B sq	44	K to K 3	K to K sq
32	R to B 3 [7]	R × R	45	K to Q 3	K to Q sq
33	P × R	Q to Q Kt sq	46	P to B 5	K to B 2
34	Q to Q 3	P to K B 4	47	K to B 4	P to Q R 3
35	P to Kt 4	Kt to B 5	48	P to Q 5	B to B sq
36	P × P	Kt × R P	49	P to Q B 6	B to K 2
37	P × B	Q × B, ch	50	K to Kt 3	K to Q 3
38	Q × Q	Kt × Q	51	K to R 4	B to Q sq
39	K to B 2	K to Kt sq	52	K to Kt 3	P to Kt 4
40	P to Q B 4	Kt to R 6	53	P × P *en passant*	
41	P to B 5	Kt to Kt 4			P × P
42	P to B 4	Kt × B [8]	54	P to R 3	
43	P × Kt	K to B sq		Drawn game.[9]	

NOTES BY I. GUNSBERG.

[1] There is not much harm in this isolated Pawn. Black, however, could prevent it by altering his tactics, and let such moves as P to Q Kt 3 and B to Kt 2 precede the advance of the Queen's Bishop's Pawn, which causes the isolated Pawn.

[2] This is one of those routine moves in this opening which, in this particular instance, has no merits to recommend it.

[3] Now we get a first glimpse of all this subtle manœuvring. White under the guise of attacking the isolated Queen's Pawn has placed his Pieces favourably for a King's side attack. The move is peculiarly characteristic of Mr Steinitz's play. He does not depend on success in one direction, but his attacks are formed with a view to their bearing on all sides of the board. If Black replies to this excellent move, which engages the Queen's side with Kt × Kt, then B × Kt, threatening to follow up with B × Kt once more, would be bad for Black. The only other move left to defend the White Queen's Knight's Pawn would be R to Q 2, but this move would create weaknesses of a different kind by blocking Black's Pieces.

[4] This, perhaps, was the least expected of Black's replies. A move of this kind, however, under difficulties and pressure of time limit, as this assuredly must have been, is often very useful; it serves the purpose of defence better than the more cautious move, such as R to Q 2 would have been. Very often it is well worth while taking such risks. The position is extremely interesting, and capable of treatment in many different ways.

[5] Black has verily attained his object of creating a dangerous complication. 27. Kt × Q P would have avoided the necessity of giving up a Piece.

[6] His only resource is to try for another Pawn; with six Pawns to three, White should be able to hold his own, but it is a poor outcome of the fine position which he had previous to his 27th move.

[7] It seems that White is not even going to have the satisfaction of

getting a second Pawn, for if he now plays 32. R × R, Q × R ; 33. Q × P, Q to B 8, ch ; 34. K to B 2, Q to Q 7, ch ; 35. K to Kt 3, Q to K 8, ch ; 36. K to B 4, B to Q 3, ch, and Black wins.

[8] This exchange was not well advised, it unites White's Pawns therefore lessens Black's chances of winning.

[9] The position is a most peculiar one, and White deserves great credit for the uphill fight. Of course, K × P is impossible, as then one of the two Pawns would be bound to go in. The White King stops the Queen's Rook's Pawn and the White Pawn stops the Queen's Knight's Pawn.

E. SCHIFFERS v. D. JANOWSKI.

	WHITE	BLACK
1	P to K 4	P to K 4
2	Kt to K B 3	Kt to Q B 3
3	B to Kt 5	P to Q R 3
4	B to R 4	P to Q 3
5	Castles	B to Q 2
6	P to B 3	P to K Kt 3
7	P to Q 4	B to Kt 2
8	B to Kt 3	Kt to B 3
9	R to K sq	Castles
10	Q Kt to Q 2	Q to K 2
11	Kt to B 4	Q R to Q sq
12	Kt to K 3 [1]	P × P
13	P × P	Q × P
14	P to K R 3 [2]	B to B sq [3]
15	P to Kt 4	Q to K sq
16	Kt to B 5	P × Kt [4]
17	R × Q	Q R × R
18	P to Kt 5	Kt to K 5
19	B to K B 4	K to R sq
20	P to K R 4	P to B 3
21	K to Kt 2	Kt to K 2
22	P to R 5	P × P
23	Kt × P	Kt × Kt
24	B × Kt	P to R 3
25	B to K B 4	Kt to B 3
26	Q to Q 2	K to R 2
27	R to K sq [5]	Kt × P [6]
28	B to B 7 [7]	R × R
29	B to Kt 6, ch	K to Kt sq
30	Q × R	B to K 3 [8]
31	P to B 3 [9]	R to B 3
32	Q to R 5 [10]	B to B 2 [11]

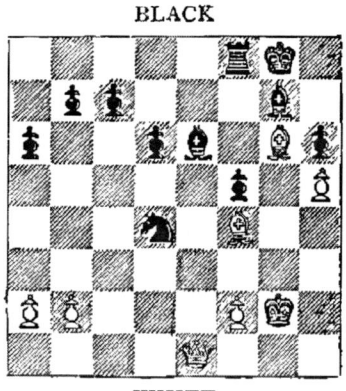

WHITE

White to make his 31st move.

	WHITE	BLACK
33	B × B, ch [12]	R × B
34	Q to Q 5	P to Kt 3 [13]
35	Q to R 8, ch	K to R 2
36	Q to K 8 [14]	R to B 3
37	Q to Q 7	Kt to K 3
38	B to Q 2	P to B 4
39	Q × P	Kt to Q 5 [15]
40	Q to Q 7	P to K B 5 [16]
41	Q to Kt 4 [17]	R to K 3 [18]
42	Q × P [19]	R to K 7, ch
43	K to B sq	R to K 4
44	Q to B 7	R to K 3
45	P to B 4	R to K B 3
46	Q to Kt 7	P to R 4 [20]
47	K to Kt 2	R to K 3
48	B to B 3	R to K B 3
49	Q to K 4, ch	K to R sq

AUGUST 23

WHITE	BLACK		WHITE	BLACK
50 K to Kt 3	R to K 3		62 Q to Q 7	R to K 6 (?) [21]
51 Q to R 8, ch	K to R 2		63 B × Kt	P × B
52 K to Kt 4	R to B 3		64 P to B 5	R to K 5, ch
53 Q to Kt 7	K to R sq		65 K to B 3	R to K 6, ch
54 Q to Q 7	R to B sq		66 K to B 4 [22]	R to K 8
55 Q to Q B 7	R to B 3		67 P to Kt 3	R to B 8, ch
56 Q to Kt 8, ch	K to R 2		68 K to K 4	R to K 8, ch
57 P to Q R 3	R to K 3		69 K to Q 5	K to Kt sq
58 Q to Kt 7	R to Q 3		70 K to B 6	R to K 6
59 Q to K 4, ch	K to R sq		71 Q to Q 5, ch	K to R 2
60 Q to K 8, ch	K to R 2		72 K × P	R to K 4
61 Q to K 7	R to K 3		73 Q to B 7	Resigns.[23]

NOTES BY DR. TARRASCH.

[1] White has treated the opening very carefully and correctly, and he now makes a promising sacrifice of a Pawn.

[2] White, of course, is playing to win the Queen, and wishes to deprive her of the square at Kt 4 ; he threatens now to effect his intention with 15. B to B 2, Q to B 5 ; 16. Kt to B sq ; or if 15. . . . Q to K 2, then 16. Kt to B 5 ; or if 15. . . . Q to K sq ; 16. Kt to Q 5, B to K 3 ; 17. Kt × Kt, ch, followed by P to Q 5, winning a Piece. But this threat can be frustrated, and therefore it seems to me better to move at once 14. B to B 2, with perhaps the following continuation : Q to B 5 ; 15. Kt to B sq, Q to Kt 5 ; 16. P to K R 3, Q to R 4 , 17. B to Kt 5, whereupon Black, in order not to lose his Queen by Kt to Kt 3 has nothing better than to sacrifice a Piece for two Pawns by B × P ; 18. Kt to Kt 3, Q to Kt 5 ; 19 P × B, Q × R P ; and then Black is at a disadvantage.

[3] This simple move opens a safe square to the Queen.

[4] The sacrifice of the Queen is not forced ; the Queen could move without hesitation to Q 2 ; White would continue then probably with Kt × B and Q B to Kt 5. Evidently Black thought to get a better game through the sacrifice of the Queen, and, indeed, White has for a long time a very difficult game, the more so as Rook, Knight, and Pawn form about an equivalent for the Queen. And certainly one cannot help recognising that Black has greater chances of success after the Queen's sacrifice than before. The startling idea of the Queen's sacrifice is a proof of a deep conception and understanding of the position.

[5] If White protects the Queen's Pawn by an advance, his chances become still less, as his King's Bishop is cut off, and Black gets a point at K 4 for the support of his Pieces.

[6] This was not the strongest , it was better to play R × R and B × P (not Kt × P on account of White's Q to K 7). The simple move B to Q 2 was also good (in order to re-take with the Bishop after 28. R × R).

⁷ By this brilliant play White brings his Bishop to a good square and robs the Black Rook of the King's file.

⁸ Black must close the King's file, as one consequence of the position of the Bishops is that White threatens him with immediate loss with Q to K 7 and B × R P. But the actual move made is a grievous mistake, which at one stroke destroys all Black's chances for a win as now the Pawns of the Queen's side are not sufficiently protected. The correct move was Kt to K 3, after which Black has a better prospect of winning than White, for if White withdraws the attacked Bishop for instance to Q 2, then the Queen's Pawn will advance, and if, instead, the Queen protects the Bishop, then Black will exchange, and then move K to R sq (to avoid Q to Q B 4, ch), and has an unassailable position, as well as the prospect of gradually utilising the passed Pawn (see diagram).

⁹ White would entice Black to play B to Q 4, which would be a mistake, on account of Q to K 7.

¹⁰ White attacks at the right place, the game must be decided on the Queen's side, and here White must try to get a passed Pawn, and therefore seeks if possible to win the Knight's Pawn, on which hangs the Rook's Pawn. 32. Q to Q 2 would not have been so good, for then might follow B to Q 4 ; 33. B × R P, B × P, ch, and the King has no favourable square, for after 34 K to B 2, R to K 3 follows, and after 34 K to Kt 3 there follows P to B 5, ch ; 35. B × P, R × B (!), when White loses his Queen by the King's Bishop's move whichever way he takes the Rook

¹¹ Black has no better move.

¹² Q × Q B P was much stronger, because White wins the Knight's Pawn after the exchange on Kt 6, also the Rook's Pawn, or, in case the former advances to Kt 4, the Rook's Pawn by Q to Q B 8, ch, and was then sure to get a passed Pawn on the Queen's side, and considering the totally helpless position of Black's Pawns would win others.

¹³ Kt to B 3 is no help on account of 35. Q to K 6.

¹⁴ This only leads finally to the win of the Queen's Pawn, after which Black can again protect his Pawns. It was simpler and better to take the Rook's Pawn, and then through the advance of the Queen's wing Pawns to create a passed Pawn on the Queen's Rook file.

¹⁵ One sees now that Black's position is again completely secured.

¹⁶ Absolutely necessary, or else White's Bishop moves over this square to K 5.

¹⁷ Still stronger was 41. Q to Q Kt 7, P to R 4 ; 42. Q to K 4, ch, and B × B P, as the Bishop could then attack the Knight's Pawn, the key of Black's position, from behind.

¹⁸ Black could without risk protect the Bishop's Pawn with Kt to K 3. If then White played B to K sq and R 4, Black could reply with Kt to Kt 4. The loss of the King's Rook's Pawn was of no importance.

¹⁹ B × P was preferable, for then the Bishop was in a better position, and could attack opportunely the Knight's Pawn from Q B 7. The loss of White's Knight's Pawn was not to be feared. 42. B × P,

AUGUST 28

R to K 7, ch , 43. K to R 3 (or B sq), R × P (?) ; 44. Q to Kt 6, ch, K to R sq , 45 B × R P, B × B ; 46. Q × B, ch, K to Kt sq , 47. Q to Kt 6, ch, and P to R 6.

[20] In spite of the win of the King's Bishop's Pawn, one can see no way which should lead White to victory.

[21] This is simple suicide. If the Rook kept the 3rd rank, it is not clear how White could win ; at any rate so far White has not shown that he had found the way of doing so , now victory is easy.

[22] More precise was K to B 2, for then the Rook could not prevent the advance of the King's Bishop's Pawn ; after Black's K to Kt sq, White could play Q to Q 8, ch, and Q × Kt P.

[23] The whole end game is very interesting, difficult, and instructive.

S. TINSLEY v. C. SCHLECHTER

	WHITE	BLACK		WHITE	BLACK
1	P to Q 4	P to Q 4	20	P to K R 3	K R to K sq
2	P to Q B 4	P to K 3	21	K to B 2	B to B 4
3	Kt to Q B 3	Kt to K B 3	22	B to K 3 [4]	P to K R 4
4	P to K Kt 3 [1]	P × P	23	B to B 5 (?)	P to R 5
5	Q to R 4, ch	B to Q 2	24	P to K Kt 4	B to K 5
6	Q × B P	B to B 3	25	R to Q 4	B × B
7	P to B 3	B to K 2	26	K × B	P to Kt 3 [5]
8	B to Kt 2	Castles	27	R to B 3	P to B 4
9	P to K 3 [2]	Q Kt to Q 2	28	R to R 4	Kt × Q P
10	K Kt to K 2	P to K 4	29	Kt × Kt	R × Kt
11	Castles	P × P	30	R to K B sq	R to Q 6
12	Kt × P	Kt to K 4	31	P to B 5 [6]	R to Kt 6, ch
13	Q to K 2	B to B 4	32	K to R 2	R to K 7, ch
14	R to Q sq	Q to K 2	33	K to R sq	R × P, ch
15	P to B 4	B × Kt	34	K to Kt sq	R to Kt 6, ch
16	P × B	Kt to Kt 3	35	K to R sq	Kt to K 4
17	P to Q 5	Q × Q [3]	36	P to Kt 5	Kt to B 6
18	Kt × Q	Q R to Q sq	37	R × Kt	R × R
19	Kt to B 3	B to Q 2		White resigns.	

NOTES BY J MASON.

[1] The 'King's Fianchetto' is seldom made use of by the first player in the Queen's Pawn's Opening It is not considered sufficiently aggressive.

[2] Now P to K 4 looks perfectly safe. And it would prevent Black partly taking over the attack by advancing his King's Pawn a little further on

[3] As will be seen, the young Austrian representative is somewhat the better prepared for the semi-ending consequent upon the disappearance of the Queens.

224 THE HASTINGS CHESS TOURNAMENT

[4] Yet White's position is pretty strong The isolation of the Pawn does not count for much ; or, if it does, it is fairly offset by the superior influence of his Bishops. The play, however, is shy, if not dull, and ill suited to Mr. Tinsley's ingenious style It is hard to see the good of 23. B to B 5, for instance. Why not 23. B × P, if the Bishop is to move at all? The Piece could hardly be imprisoned to capture—if P to Kt 3 ; 24. Kt to Kt 5, &c.—and the Pawn would be worth having.

[5] With the better game. White Bishop and Rook come in for awkward handling ; while, to say nothing of Pawn, &c., the King himself is not free from peril.

[6] There is really nothing good now, but this invitation to the Knight is the more speedily fatal.

E. LASKER v. R. TEICHMANN.

	WHITE	BLACK		WHITE	BLACK
1	P to Q 4	P to Q 4	14	Kt × P [8]	P × Kt
2	Kt to K B 3	Kt to K B 3	15	B × P, ch	K to R sq
3	P to Q B 4	P × P [1]	16	Q R to B sq	R to B sq [9]
4	P to K 3	P to K 3	17	Q to Kt 4 [10]	Q to K sq
5	B × P	B to K 2 [2]	18	B × Kt	R × B (!)
6	Castles	Castles	19	Q × R	Kt × B
7	Kt to B 3	P to Q Kt 3 [3]	20	Q to B 5	Kt to B sq
8	Q to K 2	B to Kt 2	21	Kt to Q 5	B × Kt [11]
9	P to K 4 (!)	P to Q B 4 [4]	22	R × B	B to B 4
10	R to Q sq	P × P	23	Q R to Q sq	Q to K 2 [12]
11	Kt × P	Q to B sq	24	P to K Kt 3	P to Q R 4
12	P to K 5 [5]	K Kt to Q 2 [6]	25	K to Kt 2	K to Kt sq
13	B to B 4	R to Q sq [7]	26	Q to K 4	R to B sq
			27	P to K B 4	P to Kt 3 [13]
			28	P to K R 3	Q to K B 2
			29	P to Q Kt 3	Q to K 3
			30	P to K Kt 4	R to B 2
			31	K R to Q 2	R to K 2
			32	R to K 2	R to K B 2 [14]
			33	R to K B sq	Q to B sq
			34	P to B 5	Q to Kt 2
			35	Q × Q	R × Q
			36	K to B 3	P × P [15]
			37	P × P	K to B 2
			38	R to Q sq	K to K 2
			39	R to K Kt 2	K to B 2
			40	K to K 4	R to B 2
			41	R to Q 3	R to B sq

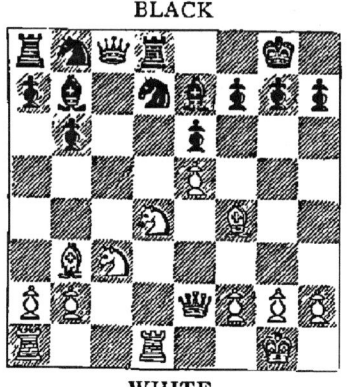

BLACK

WHITE

White to make his 14th move.

AUGUST 23

	WHITE	BLACK		WHITE	BLACK
42	P to K R 4	R to B 3	45	R to Kt 7	R to Q sq
43	R (Q 3) to Kt 3		46	R (Kt 2) to Kt 7	
		R to B sq			R to Q 5, ch
44	R to Kt 7, ch	K to K sq	47	K to B 3	Resigns.

NOTES BY W. STEINITZ.

[1] Since White usually develops the King's Bishop in some manner with the view of Castling on the King's side, Black, by this early capture, deprives himself of the chance of gaining a move.

[2] P to B 4, followed by Kt to B 3, threatening the isolation of the Queen's Pawn, is superior, for the reason alone that Black has not wasted a move with his Bishop in case White exchanges Pawns.

[3] Opposed to the principles laid down in the 'Modern Chess Instructor.' The two wing Pawns on either side ought to be kept unmoved as long as possible.

[4] The long postponement of this advance, which becomes generally necessary in this opening, makes already a strong difference in favour of White's position.

[5] White has formed his battle order faultlessly, and has obtained a great superiority of development and disposition of forces, which might have been more firmly established by B to B 4 at this juncture, while the next move opens a good counter-resource for the adversary.

[6] Rather than allow himself to be so closely crowded he should have ventured on a promising investment of a Pawn, which was likely to return a capital game; perhaps thus :—

12		Kt to Q 4	17	Q to K 4 (or K to R sq)	
13	B × Kt	P × B			R × Kt
14	Q to B 3	R to Q sq	18	R × R	Kt to Kt 5
15	Kt to B 5	B to B sq	19	Kt to K 3	Kt × R
16	Q Kt × P	Kt to B 3	20	Kt × Kt	Q to B 3, and
	And it				wins.

[7] His Queen is still more uncomfortably choked up by this move. Kt to Q B 4 gave him more time for shaping his defence and for development. If White answered P to Q Kt 4, then the same Knight to R 3, and afterwards to B 2, would fairly secure the Queen's wing.

[8] The sacrifice is not sound, and, moreover, uncalled for, as there was hardly any good answer to 14 Q R to B sq. Black was then a little too late with 14. ... Kt to Q B 4, on account of 15. P to Q Kt 4, Kt to R 3, 16. B × Kt, Kt × B (or 16. ... B × B; 17. P to Kt 5, followed by Kt to K 4); 17. Kt to K 4, Q to Kt sq (if Q to Q 2; 18. Kt to B 5, &c.), 18. P to Q R 3, with a fine game.

[9] A fine move, which seems to have been overlooked by White in his sacrificing plan.

[10] If 17. Kt to Q 5, Q to K sq; 18. Kt to B 7, Q to Kt 3; 19. Q B to Kt 3, Kt to B 4; 20. P to Q R 3, Kt to B 3, with material advantage and a well-balanced position in all directions.

[11] Misjudged. 21. ... B to B 4 was the right play. White could not displace the Bishop by 22. P to Q Kt 4 on account of the rejoinder B × Kt, winning a Pawn. Nor was 22. Kt to B 7 of any use, as Black would answer Q to B 3.

[12] Black seems over-anxious not to allow the adverse Rooks to double on his second file; but this could do no harm, and he ought to have brought out Kt to K 3, which could have been well followed up by Q to Kt 3.

[13] Very compromising in many ways. Sooner or later the opponent will force the Bishop's Pawn on, supported by the King's Knight's Pawn, and thus obtain two combined passed Pawns in the centre; whereas if the Pawn were kept at Kt 2, White must have been content with one passed Pawn for a long time. Moreover, if he had now played the clearly much stronger 27. ... Q to Q B 2, White could hardly venture on 28. P to B 5, on account of the rejoinder 28. ... B to K 2, opening the file for Queen and Rook, and also threatening B to Kt 4.

[14] Indecision marks Black's defence. The Rook stood much better where he was, and White's King's Pawn should have been once more attacked by 32. ... Kt to Q 2, when, after 33. R (Q sq) to K sq, B to Kt 5 , 34 P to B 5, P × P; 35. P × P, Q to B 2, Black would gain important time at least, since, in reply to 36. P to K 5, he would check with the Queen at Kt 2, followed by Kt to B 3.

[15] Only adding another important open file for one of the Rooks without affording the least relief to himself. The game is practically decided for White, though it still requires fine ending play, to which, however, Mr. Lasker is more than equal.

A. ALBIN *v.* J. MASON.

	WHITE	BLACK		WHITE	BLACK
1	P to K 4	P to K 4	17	Kt to K 2	P to K B 4
2	Kt to K B 3	Kt to Q B 3	18	Kt to Kt 3	Kt × Kt
3	B to Kt 5	Kt to B 3	19	R P × Kt	B to B 3
4	Castles	B to K 2	20	R to R sq	P to K Kt 3
5	P to Q 4 [1]	Kt × K P [2]	21	R to R 3	Q R to K sq
6	P to Q 5 [3]	Kt to Kt sq [4]	22	Q R to K R sq	
7	Kt × P	Castles			R to K 2
8	B to Q 3	Kt to K B 3	23	B to B 3	B × B
9	P to Q B 4	P to Q 3	24	Q × B	P to Kt 3
10	Kt to K B 3	B to Kt 5	25	R to R 6	R to Kt 2
11	Q to B 2 [5]	Kt to R 3	26	P to Kt 3	R to K sq
12	B to Q 2	Kt to B 4	27	P to Q Kt 4	Q to K 2
13	Kt to B 3	B × Kt	28	Q to R 3	Q to K 7
14	P × B	Kt × B	29	P to B 5 (!)	Q to Q 7 [6]
15	Q × Kt	Q to Q 2	30	Q × P	Q × Kt P
16	K to Kt 2	Kt to R 4	31	P × Kt P	P × P

AUGUST 23

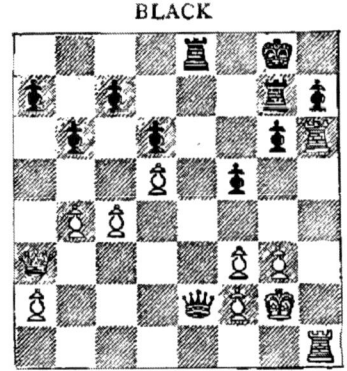

BLACK

WHITE
White to make his 29th move.

WHITE	BLACK
32 Q to R 6	R to Q B 2
33 Q to Q 3	Q to Kt 7
34 Q to Kt sq	R to K 7

WHITE	BLACK
35 Q × Q	R × Q
36 P to R 4	R (B 2) to B 7
37 R to K B sq	R to Q 7
38 R (R 6) to R sq	
	R × Q P
39 R to Q sq	R to R 4 [7]
40 R × P	R × R P
41 R to Q 8, ch	K to Kt 2
42 R to Q 7, ch	K to B 3
43 R (R sq) × P	R (R 4) to R 7
44 R (R 7) to B 7, ch	
	K to K 3
45 K to R 3	R × P
46 R (B 7) to K 7, ch	
	K to B 3
47 R to B 7, ch	K to K 3
Drawn game.	

NOTES BY C. VON BARDELEBEN.

[1] The books recommend 5. Kt to B 3, and there is no doubt that this move gives the first player better chances than 5. P to Q 4; for Black has nothing better to play than P to Q 3, whereupon follows 6. P to Q 4, B to Q 2; 7. R to K sq (!), and Black has a cramped game. If he Castles, then 8. B × Kt, B × B; 9. P × P, P × P; 10. Q × Q, Q R × Q; 11. Kt × P, B × P; 12. Kt × B, Kt × Kt; 13. Kt to Q 3 (!), P to K B 4; 14. P to K B 3, B to B 4, ch; 15. Kt × B, Kt × Kt; 16. B to Kt 5, and wins.

[2] I prefer P × P; 6. P to K 5, Kt to K 5; 7. Kt × P, Castles.

[3] The usual move is 6. Q to K 2.

[4] The simplest way to equalise the game is : Kt to Q 3; 7. B to R 4, P to K 5; 8. P × Kt, P × Kt; 9. P × P, ch, B × P; 10. B × B, ch, Q × B; 11. Q × P, Castles.

[5] Preferable would be 11. P to Q R 3, and if 11. ... Kt to R 3, then 12. P to Q Kt 4.

[6] If Black played Kt P × P; 30. P × P, P × P, White would answer with Q × R P, and have a somewhat better game.

[7] If R (Q Kt 7) to Q 7, then 40. R × R, R × R; 41. R to Q Kt sq.

C. VON BARDELEBEN v. M. TCHIGORIN.

WHITE	BLACK
1 P to Q 4	P to Q 4
2 Kt to K B 3	B to Kt 5
3 P to K 3 [1]	P to K 3

WHITE	BLACK
4 B to K 2	Kt to Q 2
5 P to Q Kt 3	K Kt to B 3
6 B to Kt 2	B to Q 3

WHITE	BLACK	WHITE	BLACK
7 Q Kt to Q 2	P to B 3 [2]	20 R × R	Q × P, ch
8 Kt to K 5 [3]	B × B	21 K to R sq	R × R
9 Q × B	Castles	22 Q Kt to B 3 [10]	
10 P to K B 4 [4]	R to B sq		Q × P
11 Castles K R	P to B 4	23 Kt × Kt	Kt × Kt
12 Q R to B sq [5]	P × P [6]	24 Q × P	Kt to B 3
13 P × P	Q to R 4	25 Kt to Kt 5	Q to B 2 [11]
14 Kt to Q 3	B to R 6	26 Kt × B P [12]	Q × Kt
15 B × B	Q × B	27 Q to K 5	Q to Q 2
16 P to B 4	P to Q Kt 3	28 R to K sq	Q to Q 4, ch
17 P to K Kt 4 [7]	Q to Q 3 [8]	29 Q × Q	P × Q
18 Kt to K 5	P × P	30 R to K 7	R to B 8, ch
19 R × P	P to Q Kt 4 [9]	White resigns.	

NOTES BY H. N. PILLSBURY.

[1] The more aggressive 3. P to B 4 is mostly preferred.

[2] This move might at any rate be reserved, and the sequel shows that at least one move is lost, since four moves later it is advanced to the fourth. Castling at once seems preferable.

[3] The 'Stonewall' formation which White obtains now is not very powerful without the aid of the King's Bishop at Q 3 for attacking purposes. After 8. Castles, Castles; 9. P to B 4, Q to K 2; 10. R to K sq, White evidently did not like Black's rejoinder of P to K 4, but continue, 11. P × K P, Kt × P; 12. Kt × Kt, B × B; 13. Kt × Q B P, winning at least a Pawn. Or should Black in the foregoing continue 10. R to K sq, then 11 Q to B 2, P to K 4; 12. P × K P, Kt × P; 13. Kt × Kt, B × Kt; 14. Q B × B, Q × B; 15. B × B, Kt × B; 16. Kt to B 3, with a good game, as Black will either have to submit to an isolated Queen's Pawn, or allow White to gain time to develop his Rooks on the Queen's file. All other variations in the foregoing appear to yield White at least an equal position.

[4] P to K 4 here seems quite feasible for White.

[5] If White intended to attack the King by the means of R to B 3 and R 3, as is usual in 'Stonewall' variation, it would be better to continue P to B 3 here.

[6] Q to R 4 at once seems superior.

[7] White's Queen's Pawn is the weak spot in his position, and Black threatens anyhow Q to Q 3. There was no necessity for such a suicidal move as the text, however, and it would seem that 17. P to Q Kt 4 (threatening P to Q B 5), P × P; 18. Kt × P, Q to R 5; 19. Kt to Q 6, R × R; 20. R × R, Kt to Q 4; 21. Q to Kt 2 would give White a slight advantage.

[8] Winning at least a Pawn.

[9] This White apparently overlooked.

[10] Desperate, but there is nothing to be done.

[11] Black can safely take the Knight's Pawn with Queen, for it

AUGUST 28

26. R to K Kt sq, then Q to Q 5 ; or if 26. Kt × B P, Q to K 5, ch ;
27. K to Kt sq, R to B 7, winning easily.

[12] Of course a final error, overlooking that if Q × Kt ; 27. P to Kt 5, Q to Q 2, retaining the Piece, but his game was lost anyway.

H. E. BIRD v. H. N. PILLSBURY.

	WHITE	BLACK
1	P to K 4	P to K 4
2	K Kt to B 3	Q Kt to B 3
3	B to B 4	B to B 4
4	P to Q Kt 4	B × Kt P
5	P to B 3	B to Q 3 [1]
6	P to Q 4	Kt to B 3
7	Kt to Kt 5 [2]	Castles
8	Kt × K B P [3]	R × Kt
9	B × R, ch	K × B
10	P to K B 4	P × Q P (!)
11	P to K 5	B to K 2
12	P × Kt	B × P [4]
13	Castles	P to Q 4
14	Kt to Q 2	P × P
15	Kt to B 3	K to Kt sq
16	R to Kt sq	P to Q Kt 3
17	B to K 3	B to Kt 5
18	Q to R 4	B × Kt
19	R × B	Q to Q 3
20	R to Q sq	R to Q sq
21	R to R 3	P to Q 5
22	B to B sq	Q to K 3
23	Q to B 2	P to Q 6 (!) [5]
24	R(R 3) × Q P	Kt to Q 5
25	P to B 5	Q to K 5
26	B to R 3 [6]	P to B 4 (!)
27	Q to K B 2	Kt to K 7, ch

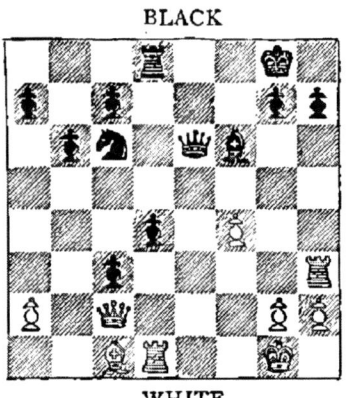

Black to make his 23rd move.

	WHITE	BLACK
28	K to B sq	R × R
29	R × R	Q × R
30	Q × Kt	Q × P, ch
31	K to K sq	Q to Kt 8, ch
32	K to B 2	B to Q 5, ch
33	K to Kt 3	Q to Kt 3, ch
34	K to R 3	P to K R 4
35	P to Kt 3	Q to Kt 5, ch
36	Q × Q	P × Q, ch
37	K × P	B to K 6
38	K to B 3	B to R 3
	White resigns.	

NOTES BY E. SCHIFFERS.

[1] A defence adopted formerly by Kieseritzky and Mayet ; it has not been practised for a long time by strong players, which circumstance partly explains the success attending Mr. Pillsbury's revival of it at Hastings.

[2] Weak ; he ought to have played 7. Castles, with the continuation R to K sq, Q Kt to K Kt 3 (*via* Q 2 and K B sq), &c.

[3] Anderssen, in a game with Kieseritzky, continued : 8. P to K B 4,

P×BP; 9. P to K 5, B×P; 10. P×B, Kt×P; 11. B to Q Kt 3, P to K R 3; 12. Kt to K R 3, P to K Kt 4; 13. Castles, P to Q 3; by which Black obtains four Pawns in exchange for the Bishop.

[4] Black has now three Pawns to compensate for the exchange, and his position is unembarrassed.

[5] A move which leads to a speedy victory. (See diagram.)

[6] Just before the end, Mr. Bird has a joke in his well-known style; if 26. ... Kt×Q, White mates in four.

G. Marco v. Dr. Tarrasch.

	WHITE	BLACK		WHITE	BLACK
1	P to K 4	P to K 4	18	P to R 5	P to B 4 [7]
2	Kt to K B 3	Kt to Q B 3	19	K P×P	P to K 5
3	B to Kt 5	P to Q R 3	20	Kt to Kt 5	R×P
4	B to R 4	Kt to B 3	21	Kt (Q 2)×K P	
5	Castles	P to Q 3			B×Kt
6	B×Kt, ch [1]	P×B	22	Kt×B [8]	B×P, ch [9]
7	P to Q 4	Kt to Q 2 [2]	23	K×B	Q to R 5, ch
8	P×P [3]	P×P	24	K to Kt sq	R to R 4
9	B to Kt 5	P to B 3	25	P to B 3 [10]	R to K B sq
10	B to K 3	B to Q 3	26	B to Kt 5 [11]	Q to R 7, ch
11	Q to Q 3	R to Q Kt sq	27	K to B 2	Kt to K 4
12	Q Kt to Q 2	Kt to Kt 3 [4]	28	K to K 3	R×B
13	P to B 4	Q to K 2	29	Kt×R	Q to B 5, ch
14	Q to B 2	P to Q B 4	30	K to K 2	Q×Kt
15	P to Q Kt 4 [5]		31	R to B 2	Kt×K R P [12]
		Kt to Q 2	32	P×Kt	Q to K 4, ch
16	P to Kt 5	Castles [6]	33	Q to K 4	Q×R
17	P to Q R 4	B to Kt 2	34	Q to K 6, ch	K to R sq
			35	Q to K 7	R to Q Kt sq
			36	R to Kt 2	R to K Kt sq
			37	R to Kt 5	Q to R 7, ch
			38	K to K 3	Q×B P
			39	P×P	Q to Q 5, ch
			40	K to K 2	R to Q Kt sq
			41	K to B sq [13]	

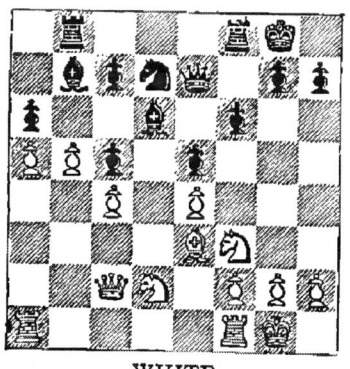

BLACK

WHITE

Black to make his 18th move.

Black announced mate in 5 moves by

		R to Kt 8, ch
42	K to Kt 2	R to Kt 8, ch
43	K to R 3	R to R 8, ch
44	K to Kt 3	Q to R 5, ch
45	K to Kt 2	Q to R 7, mate

AUGUST 23

NOTES BY S. TINSLEY.

¹ Bearing in mind one essential principle of all close games—viz. the importance of keeping the opposing forces shut up—it can scarcely be advisable thus early to exchange, opening at once a file for the Queen's side Rook, &c. The usual P to Q 4 is obviously superior at this point Or White may even play P to Q 3, followed perhaps by P to Q B 3 (to preserve the King's Bishop). Q Kt to Q 2, Q to K 2, and R to K sq are also occasionally adopted here.

² Dr. Tarrasch's patent. It looks awkward, and so it is.

³ Still further opening up the game for Black. Kt to B 3 is clearly the correct course, and would develop White's game, leaving Black to get his Pieces free as best he can.

⁴ R × P would lose the exchange, as White replies Kt to Kt 3 at once

⁵ This move is deceptive At first sight good, because, of course, the Pawn cannot be taken safely; but on examination the effect will be found to be to enable Black to dispose of his doubled Pawn and gain still further liberty, leaving the Queen's side Pawns (White) isolated. He might have aimed at getting a Kt to Q 5 by (1) Q R to Q sq; (2) Kt to Q Kt sq; (3) Kt to B 3, and afterwards to K 2 or Q 5, as needed by the circumstances of the time.

⁶ 16. . . P × P; 17 P × P, R × P, would give White a strong passed Pawn on the Queen's Rook's file.

⁷ Students of Dr. Tarrasch's play will be struck with the effective simplicity of his moves when the critical time arrives. So here. The whole scene changes in a moment, and the game is all in Black's hands. Every Piece, too, is in its right place The position is worthy of special note. (See diagram.)

⁸ 22. Q × B, R × Kt (¹); 23. Q × Q, B × Q; 24. B × R, B × B, and Black has gained two Pieces for the Rook.

⁹ The sacrifice appears to be of questionable merit, though it yields at a critical period an immediate attack.

¹⁰ We suggest for White now P to K B 4 instead, and we imagine White has a valid defence against all immediate attacks. The variations are somewhat obvious Here is one: 25. P to B 4, Kt to K 4; 26 P × Kt, Q to R 7, ch; 27. K to B 2, R to K B sq, ch; 28. Kt to B 6, ch, &c.

¹¹ Apparently to prevent the attack by 26. . . . Q to R 7, ch, 27. K to B 2, R × P, ch; 28. K × R, R to B 4, ch, &c.

¹² This remarkably fine move soon leads to a final breakdown of the defences. It is safe to say that few besides Dr. Tarrasch would have discovered this way to a conclusion.

¹³ It is fair to point out (I was looking on at the time) that Herr Marco was inclined to resign at this period, but in the general interests of competitors played to the end like a man. A curious game, very interesting. White, in spite of a poor opening, might, I think, have done better. The game produces a not easily defined impression that there was 'a way out of it' after the sacrifice at move 22.

J. Mieses v. A. Walbrodt.

	WHITE	BLACK		WHITE	BLACK
1	P to K 4	P to K 4	21	K R to K 3	Kt to K 4
2	Kt to Q B 3	Kt to Q B 3	22	P to R 3	P to B 4 [6]
3	B to B 4	P to Q 3	23	R to K B sq	Kt to B 2
4	P to Q 3	P to K Kt 3 [1]	24	Q to B 4	Q R to K sq
5	K Kt to K 2	B to Kt 2	25	P to Kt 3	Q to B 6
6	Castles [2]	Kt to R 4	26	K to R sq	R × R
7	B to Q 5	Kt to K 2	27	Q × R	Kt to K 4
8	P to B 4	Castles	28	K to R 2	Q × Kt P
9	P to Q R 3	Q Kt to B 3	29	Q to Kt 5	Q × Q P
10	Kt to Kt 3	Kt × B	30	R to B 2	Kt to B 2
11	Kt × Kt	P × P	31	Q to K 7	Q to Q 5
12	B × P	B to K 3 [3]	32	R to B sq	Q to K 4
13	Q to B sq [4]	B × Kt	33	Q × Kt P	P to B 5
14	P × B	Kt to K 2	34	Kt to K 4	R to K sq
15	B to R 6 [5]	Kt × P	35	R to K sq	P to B 6, ch
16	P to B 4	Kt to Kt 3	36	K to Kt sq	Q to Q 5, ch
17	Q to B 4	P to K B 4	37	K to B sq	Q × P, ch
18	Q R to K sq	B × B	38	K to B 2	Q to B 7, ch
19	Q × B	Q to B 3	39	K × P	R × Kt
20	R to B 3	Kt to Q 2		White resigns.	

Notes by R. Teichmann.

[1] This treatment of the defence in the Vienna game cannot be recommended. White must, after opening the King's Bishop's file by P to K B 4, get a very strong attack on the weak Black King's Bishop's Pawn.

[2] He ought to have played P to Q R 3 in order to preserve the King's Bishop.

[3] If B × P; 13. B to R 6 (!), B to Kt 2 (best); 14. B × B, and White has good prospects of a strong attack.

[4] Kt to B 3 appears to be much better.

[5] Unintelligible. I do not see the slightest prospect of a compensating attack for the loss of this valuable Pawn.

[6] Black has played very well, and has established an absolutely unassailable position; winning can now only be a question of time.

I. Gunsberg v. W. H. K. Pollock.

	WHITE	BLACK		WHITE	BLACK
1	P to K 4	P to K 4	5	K Kt to K 2 [1]	P to Q 4
2	Q Kt to B 3	K Kt to B 3	6	P × P [2]	P to B 3
3	P to K Kt 3	B to B 4	7	P × P	Kt × P
4	B to Kt 2	Castles	8	P to Q 3	B to K Kt 5

AUGUST .23

	WHITE	BLACK		WHITE	BLACK
9	P to B 3 [3]	B to K 3	20	B × Kt	P × B
10	P to Q R 3 [4]	B to Q Kt 3	21	Kt × P	Kt to Q 5
11	B to Q 2	P to Q R 4	22	Q to K 3 [7]	R to R 3
12	Q to B sq	R to B sq	23	Q R to B sq [8]	Q to Kt 4
13	Kt to Q sq	Kt to Q 4	24	K R to K sq [9]	Q × Kt P
14	Kt to B 2	P to B 4	25	Kt to K 2	Kt × Kt, ch
15	Castles	P to B 5 (!)	26	Q × Kt	B to R 6
16	K to R sq	P × P	27	Q to B sq [10]	R to Kt 3
17	P × P [5]	R to B 4	28	P to B 5	B × B
18	P to Q B 4 [6]	R to R 4, ch	29	Q × B	Q × Q, mate
19	K to Kt sq	Kt to B 5 (!)			

NOTES BY A. ALBIN.

[1] Kt to R 4 is the usual and best move in this position.

[2] Kt × P is better.

[3] P to R 3 is more correct, in order not to open the file for the Black Bishop.

[4] Why not Kt to K 4?

[5] Kt × P, followed by Kt to K 4 and R to K Kt sq, was the only way to obtain any chances.

[6] P to K Kt 4 seems to be stronger; if Q to R 5, ch, K to Kt sq, followed eventually by B to Kt 5.

[7] K R to K sq, to make room for the King, and to disengage finally the Knight, was preferable.

[8] Why not K R to K sq?

[9] Too late; White is helpless.

[10] Black has played the whole game in a masterly manner.

B. VERGANI v. J. H BLACKBURNE.

	WHITE	BLACK		WHITE	BLACK
1	P to K 4	P to Q 4	16	Q to Kt sq [3]	Q to K B 2
2	P × P	P to Q B 3 [1]	17	P to Q B 3	Kt to B 3
3	P × P	Kt × P	18	P to K B 4	B to K 2 [4]
4	Kt to K B 3	P to K 4	19	P × P [5]	Kt × P
5	P to Q 3	P to B 4	20	P to Q 4 [6]	Kt to B 5
6	Kt to B 3	Kt to B 3	21	Q to Q 3	B to B 3
7	B to Kt 5	B to K 2	22	Kt to B 3	P to K Kt 3
8	P to K Kt 3	P to K R 3	23	Kt to Q 2 [7]	Q to Q 2
9	B × Kt	B × B	24	P to Kt 3	Kt to Kt 7 [8]
10	Q to Q 2	B to K 3	25	Q to K 2 [9]	Kt × Kt
11	B to Kt 2	Castles [2]	26	Q R × Kt	R × P
12	Castles K R	Q to K 2	27	Kt to B 3	K R to Q B sq
13	Kt to Q sq	K R to Q sq	28	R to Q 2	K to R 2
14	Q to B sq	Q R to B sq	29	K R to Q sq	B to Kt sq
15	Kt to K sq	Kt to Q 5	30	Kt to K 5	Q to Q B 2

White to make his 25th move.

WHITE	BLACK
31 Q to Kt 5	B to Kt 4
32 R to Q 3	R × R
33 Q × R	B to B 3
34 Kt to B 3	R to Q sq
35 Q to K 3	B to Q 4
36 K to B sq	Q to Q 3
37 Q to K 2	R to Q 2
38 Kt to Kt sq	R to K 2
39 Q to Q 3	B × B, ch
40 K × B	Q to Q 4, ch
41 K to B 2 [10]	P to B 5
42 P × P	R to K 5
43 Kt to K 2	B to R 5, ch
44 K to Kt sq	Q to K 3
45 R to Q 2 [11]	R to K 6
46 Q to B 4	Q to Kt 5, ch
47 K to R sq	Q to B 6, ch
48 K to Kt sq	B to B 7, ch
	White resigns.

NOTES BY H. N. PILLSBURY.

[1] Black sacrifices a Pawn for the purpose of obtaining a quick development, expecting to bewilder his less experienced opponent. He obtains no sufficient compensation, however, during the opening.

[2] In view of the style of dashing tactics which Black has adopted, one would expect here Q to Q 2, and if 12. Castles K R, then Castles Q R, followed by P to K Kt 4. It seems equally as good as the text.

[3] White's tactics seem forced, and in the next few moves he drives back the enemy and brings out his Pieces again.

[4] P × P, and if 19. R × P, P to K Kt 4 seems preferable.

[5] White could have won a second Pawn by B × Kt and P × P without serious danger.

[6] And there was no objection to B × P.

[7] White has held his one Pawn thus far, and brought out the imprisoned Queen, but here he fails to foresee the combination which his opponent is preparing. 23. P to Kt 3, Kt to Q 3; 24. Kt to B 2 was straightforward and correct, and the Pawns on the Queen's side could then be speedily advanced.

[8] The initiatory move of a clever plan by which Black regains his Pawn.

[9] If 25. Kt × Kt, R × P; 26. Q to K 2 (best), B × P, ch; 27. K to R sq, R to B 7, regaining the Piece with a Pawn ahead. (See diagram.)

[10] White has well stood his ground to this point, but here goes wrong; 41. Kt to B 3 was perfectly safe and correct. If in answer Black should attempt to force matters by B to Kt 4, then 42. Q to B 4, and if Q × Q; 43. Kt × B, ch, P × Kt; 44. P × Q, and White should win.

[11] The losing move. 45. Kt to Kt 3, would have still given White a fair game, if in answer R to K 6, then 46. Q to B 4. After this error there is no saving White's game.

Photo., Bradshaw, Hastings

AUGUST 24

The excitement does not abate, and when Walbrodt *v.* Pillsbury seems to be a block sort of game, great attention is given to it; will it be a draw? Presently Lasker is seen to be uncomfortable with Albin. In the end both these draw, and let Tchigorin up level with Lasker, with Pillsbury half a point behind with $11\frac{1}{2}$. This ends the third week, and sees the beginning of Lasker's bad scoring for the end of the Tournament. The other chief scores are now Steinitz and Walbrodt 9, Bardeleben $8\frac{1}{2}$.

A. ALBIN *v.* E. LASKER.

	WHITE	BLACK		WHITE	BLACK
1	P to K 4	P to Q B 4	25	Q to Kt 4	Q to B 2
2	Kt to K B 3	Kt to Q B 3	26	P to R 3	B to R 3 [6]
3	P to Q 4	P × P	27	Q to K B 4	B × B
4	Kt × P	P to K Kt 3	28	Q × B	K to B sq
5	Kt × Kt [1]	Q P × Kt	29	R to K 3	Q to Q 2
6	Q to B 3	Kt to B 3	30	R to Kt 3	B to Kt 6
7	P to K R 3	B to K 3 [2]	31	P to R 5	B to Q 4
8	Kt to B 3	B to Kt 2	32	K to R 2	Q to K 3
9	B to Q 3	Kt to Q 2	33	P to R 6	P to B 3 [7]
10	Q to Kt 3	Q to Kt 3	34	Q × Kt P	Q to B 2
11	B to K 2	P to K R 4	35	Q × Q	K × Q
12	P to K R 4	Kt to K 4	36	Kt × B	R × P, ch
13	Castles	Kt to Kt 5	37	K to Kt 2	P × Kt
14	B × Kt	P × B	38	R to K B 3	K to K 3
15	P to K 5	B to B 4 [3]	39	P × P	P × P [8]
16	R to K sq	B × B P	40	R to Q Kt 3	R to R 2
17	Q × P	B to B 4	41	K to Kt 3	P to Q 5 [9]
18	Q to Kt 3	Q to Kt 5	42	K to B 4	R to Q B 2
19	B to Kt 5 [4]	Q × Kt P	43	K to K 4	R to B 6 [10]
20	Q R to Q sq	Q to Kt 5	44	R × P [11]	P to Q 6
21	Q to K 3	Q to Kt 3 [5]	45	K to K 3	R × P
22	Q to B 4	R to Q sq	46	P to B 4	P to Q 7, ch
23	R × R, ch	Q × R	47	K × P	R to K Kt 6
24	P to Kt 4	B to K 3		Drawn game.	

NOTES BY I. GUNSBERG.

[1] The exchange leads to nothing.

[2] Black has conducted the whole game in rather an original way, as indicated by this odd move of the Bishop, to which, however, no objection can be made. On the contrary, should White endeavour to Castle on the Queen's side, then the Bishop on K 3, in conjunction with the Bishop on K Kt 2, and the Queen on R 4, would prove very troublesome to White.

[3] Prevents Kt to K 4, and brings the Bishop into good play.

[4] It was a choice of evils. White could have played 19. P to B 4, but that move would rather expose his King in a dangerous manner, for Black would reply Q to Kt 3, ch ; 20. K to R sq, Castles Q R, with a strong game, as R × P, ch, would be threatened among other things.

[5] Black wishes at once to get out of the way of R to Q 4.

[6] Again Black does right in seeking to disestablish the Bishop which bears so strongly on his King's Pawn.

[7] White's play here required very great delicacy of treatment, and Black's last move showed that he elected with excellent judgment to simplify the game, rather than expose himself to the risk which he ran if White had been given time to play Kt to K 2, and Kt to B 4.

[8] Better than R × P if the object was to play for a safe draw, but for winning purposes we should have given the preference to R × P.

[9] The advance of this Pawn seems premature. Black might have tried R to Q B 2 first, followed perhaps by P to Q Kt 3, so as to make his Rook available to assist in forcing on the Pawn.

[10] Black perhaps put undue reliance on this move.

[11] Well played again. R × R would have lost.

C. VON BARDELEBEN v. DR. TARRASCH.

	WHITE	BLACK
1	P to K 4	P to K 4
2	Kt to K B 3	Kt to Q B 3
3	B to Kt 5	P to Q R 3
4	B to R 4	Kt to B 3
5	Castles	P to Q 3 [1]
6	Kt to B 3 [2]	P to Q Kt 4
7	B to Kt 3	B to Kt 5
8	Kt to K 2 [3]	B × Kt
9	P × B	Q to Q 2
10	P to Q R 4	Q to R 6 [4]
11	P × P	P to K R 4
12	R to K sq [5]	Kt to K Kt 5
13	P × Kt	K R P × P
14	B × P, ch [6]	K × B
15	R to R 3	Q × P, ch

Black to make his 16th move.

AUGUST 24

	WHITE	BLACK		WHITE	BLACK
16	K to B sq	P×P [7]	29	Kt to R 4	Kt to Kt sq
17	R to K Kt 3	R to K R 3	30	Kt to Kt 6	Kt to B 3
18	P to Q 3	R to B 3 [8]	31	Q to B 5	Kt to Kt sq
19	B to K 3	B to K 2	32	Q×Q, ch [11]	K×Q
20	R to Kt 2	Q to R 5	33	R to K B sq	B to K 2
21	Kt to Kt 3	R to B 6	34	Kt×B	K×Kt
22	K to K 2 [9]	Q to B 3	35	R (Kt 2) to Kt sq	
23	Kt to B 5	R to K R 6			K to Q 2
24	K to Q 2	R to K R 2	36	R to Q R sq	R×R
25	Q×P	B to B sq	37	R×R	Kt to K 2
26	Q to B 3 [10]	K to K sq	38	R to R 7	R to R 7
27	R (K sq) to K Kt sq		39	K to K 2	Kt to B 3
		Q to B 2	40	R to R sq	K to K 3
28	Q to Kt 4	Kt to K 2		Drawn game.	

NOTES BY E. LASKER.

[1] This defence leaves Black with a somewhat cramped position, if White continues with 6. P to Q 4, B to Q 2 ; 7. P×P, P×P ; 8. Kt to B 3, B to Q 3 ; 9. B to K Kt 5, Kt to K 2 ; 10. B to Kt 3.

[2] A mistake. White having Castled ought to immediately open the centre by P to Q 4. Now he comes into difficulties.

[3] It is hard to see how he could prevent the threatened Kt to Q 5 in any other way. The alternative would have been : 8. P to K R 3, B to R 4 ; 9. P to Kt 4, B to Kt 3. (It is remarkable that in this position the sacrifice of Knight against two Pawns is bad. If 9. ... Kt×Kt P ; 10. P×Kt, B×P ; 11. B to Q 5 (?), Kt to Q 5 ; 12. Kt× K P, B×Q ; 13. B×P, ch, K to K 2 ; 14. Kt to Q 5, mate.) 10. P to Q 3, Kt to Q R 4 ; whereupon Black appears to have slightly the better position.

[4] A splendid and profound combination. Its idea is illustrated by the two following moves of Black. Had White seen it, he probably would have played 10. P to Q B 3, Q to R 6 ; 11. Kt to Kt 3, P to K R 4 ; 12. P to Q 4, with a good game, as the sacrifice 12. ... Kt to Kt 5 ; 13. P×Kt, P×P, would fail on account of 14. R to K sq.

[5] He must provide (in view of the threatened Kt to K Kt 5) an escape for his King. Suppose instead 12. P×Kt, Kt to Kt 5 ; 13. P× Kt, P×P ; 14. R to K sq, Q×P, ch ; 15. K to B sq, Q to R 6, ch ; 16. K to Kt sq, Q to R 8, mate.

[6] The only possible means to avert disaster. Kt to Kt 3 instead would not answer that purpose, as the consequence would be : 14. Kt to Kt 3, Kt to Q 5 ; 15. R to K 3, Q×P, ch ; 16. K to B sq, Q to R 8, ch ; 17. Kt×Q, R×Kt, ch ; 18. K to K 2, R×Q ; 19. R×P, R to Kt sq ; 20. B to R 4, Kt to B 6 ; winning in such or similar manner in any variation White may choose.

[7] It is here that Black misses his chance. The move actually made is elegant, but not sufficiently strong. He should have taken

advantage of the momentary dislocation of the White Pieces in the following manner: 16. ... Kt to Q 5. This threatens Kt to B 6. White has, therefore, only two alternatives: 17. Kt × Kt, Q to R 8, ch; 18. K to K 2, Q × K P, ch, 19. R to K 3, Q × Kt, 20. P × P, B to K 2; 21. R to R sq, B to Kt 4; 22. R × R, R × R, 23. P to Q B 3, Q to Q 4; and the result of the game cannot be doubtful, as White must lose the exchange at the very least. Or White may continue at his 17th turn: 17. Kt to Kt sq, B to K 2; 18. Q × P, B to R 5; 19. Kt to R 3 (19. Q to Kt 2 would lose on account of Q × Q, ch, 20. K × Q, Kt × P, &c.), 19. ... Q R to K B sq, whereupon White has no sufficient defence. Suppose, for instance, 20. P × P, Q to R 8, ch, 21. Kt to Kt sq, K to Kt sq.

[8] Here R to R 8 suggests itself. If, then, 19. Kt to Kt sq, R to B 3; 20. R to Kt 2, Q to R 5, 21. Q × P, Q × Q; 22. R × Q, Kt to Kt 5; winning either Bishop's Pawn or Queen's Pawn. But 19. P to Q B 3, threatening Q to Kt 3, ch, would have been a sufficient reply.

[9] All these manœuvres are excellent. White brings his King into safety on the Queen's side, and will soon be able to assume the attack against the opened King's side of Black. Black's extra Pawn at Kt 5 is of no permanent value, being indefensible in the long run.

[10] Now it is White who has, without a doubt, the better game. It would have been advisable to double the Rooks on the King's Knight's file, and afterwards to proceed with R to Kt 3 and B 3. Black seems to have no defence against this manœuvre. Suppose, for instance, 26. R (K sq) to K Kt sq, R to Q R 7; 27. R to Kt 3, R × P; 28. R to B 3, K to K sq; 29. B to Kt 5, Q to Kt 3; 30. Kt × Kt P, ch, and mates in a few more moves.

[11] After this exchange of Queens the draw becomes the natural and legitimate result.

A. WALBRODT v. H. N. PILLSBURY.

	WHITE	BLACK		WHITE	BLACK
1	P to K 4	P to K 4	15	B × B	Kt × B
2	Kt to K B 3	Kt to Q B 3	16	Kt to B 4	Q to Q 3
3	B to Kt 5	P to K Kt 3	17	Kt × Kt	P × Kt [4]
4	P to Q 3 [1]	B to Kt 2	18	Q to Q 2	R to K B 4
5	Kt to B 3	K Kt to K 2	19	Q R to K sq	P to Q R 4 [5]
6	Castles	Castles	20	R to K 4	P to Kt 3
7	B to Q 2	Kt to Q 5	21	K R to K sq	R to K sq
8	Kt × Kt	P × Kt	22	P to Q R 4 [6]	P to K R 4
9	Kt to K 2	P to Q 4 [2]	23	P to Q Kt 3	Q to Q 4
10	P × P	Kt × P	24	Q to K 2	K to B 2
11	Q to B sq	P to Q B 4	25	Q to Q 2	K to Kt 2
12	B to Q B 4	B to K 3	26	Q to K 2	
13	B to R 6	Kt to B 2 [3]		Drawn game.	
14	Q B × B	K × B			

AUGUST 24

NOTES BY DR. TARRASCH.

[1] White treats the opening so carefully and defensively that Black gets the better game in a few moves.

[2] Still better was P to K R 3, in order to prevent the threatened exchange of the Bishop at Kt 2, by Q to B sq and B to R 6

[3] The minor Pieces are exchanged so early that a draw—and quite a commonplace draw—becomes already probable.

[4] The backward position of the King's Pawn gives Black's game a little weakness, which, however, can easily be defended, considering Black's good position in general.

[5] What is the use of this?

[6] And why this?

W. H. K. POLLOCK v. H. E. BIRD.

	WHITE	BLACK		WHITE	BLACK
1	P to K 4	P to K 4	11	P to B 4 (!)	B to K Kt 5
2	Q Kt to B 3	K Kt to B 3	12	P × P	B × Kt [1]
3	P to B 4	P to Q 4	13	P × B	Kt to B 6
4	B P × P	Kt × P	14	Q to K sq	Kt × Q P
5	Kt to K B 3	B to K 2 [1]	15	K to R sq	Kt to B 5 [5]
6	P to Q 4	Castles	16	B to B 4, ch	K to R sq
7	B to Q 3	P to K B 4	17	Q to K 4	Q to Q 3 [6]
8	P × P en passant		18	Q × Kt P	Kt to Q B 3
		B to Q Kt 5 [3]	19	Q × R, ch	R to B sq
9	Castles	B × Kt	20	B × Kt (!)	Q to B 3
10	P × B	R × P [3]	21	B to K 5	Resigns.

NOTES BY C. VON BARDELEBEN.

[1] The usual move is better, B to Q Kt 5.

[2] This sacrifice is not sound. The right move was Kt × P.

[3] Better would be Kt × K B P.

[4] If Q × P, then 13. Q to K 2, Kt to Q 3; 14 P to B 4, and White has the better game.

[5] A mistake, which costs the game. In order to prevent 16. B to K Kt 5, Black should have played 15 ... R to B sq, but White would in any case have the superior game with his two Bishops and the open King's Knight's file.

[6] Now Black's game is hopeless. If Kt to Kt 3, then 18 B to K Kt 5, winning the exchange.

J. H. BLACKBURNE v. G. MARCO.

	WHITE	BLACK		WHITE	BLACK
1	P to K 4	P to K 4	4	Kt × P	B to Q 3 [1]
2	P to K B 4	P to Q 4	5	P to Q 4 [2]	P × P en passant
3	Kt to K B 3	P × K P	6	Kt × Q P [3]	Kt to K B 3

WHITE	BLACK	WHITE	BLACK
7 B to K 2	Castles	21 R to K Kt 5	Q to Q 3
8 Castles	Kt to B 3	22 R to Kt 3	K to R sq (!)
9 Kt to B 3	Kt to Q 5	23 B to Kt 5	Q to K 4
10 B to B 3 [4]	R to K sq (!)	24 P to K R 4 (?) [7]	
11 B to Q 2	P to B 3 [5]		P to K R 3
12 K to R sq	B to K B 4	25 B to B sq	Kt to R 4
13 B to K sq	Q to B 2	26 R to Kt 4	R to B 3
14 B to B 2 [6]	Kt × B	27 B to B 4	Q × P
15 Q × Kt	B × Kt	28 P to Kt 3 (?)	Q × P
16 P × B	B × P	29 Q to K 3	Q to Q 4, ch
17 B to R 4	B to K 4 (!)	30 R to B 3	R to K 3
18 Q R to B sq	B × Kt	31 Q to B 2	Kt to B 3
19 R × B	R to K 3	White resigns.	
20 R to B 5	R to Q sq		

NOTES BY E. SCHIFFERS.

[1] Here the attack Kt to Q B 3 is possible, as first pointed out by Beaune; it is apparently irregular. The best continuation to 4. ... Kt to Q B 3 is 5. B to Q Kt 5, Kt to K B 3; 6. P to Q 4 [6. Kt × Kt, P × Kt, 7 B × P, ch, B to Q 2; 8. B × B, ch (8. B × R (?), B to K Kt 5); Q × B, with a good game in exchange for the sacrifice of the Pawn].

[2] A probable continuation might be 5. B to Q B 4, and if B × Kt, then Q to K R 5.

[3] After 6. B · P, B × Kt; 7. P × B, White has a weak isolated Pawn on K 5, without any compensating attack.

[4] 10 B to K 3 would have been better; after 10. ... Kt to K B 4 might follow for instance, 11. B to K B 2, and after 10. ... Kt × B, ch; 11. Q × Kt, R to K sq; 12. P to K R 3; or 11. .. Kt to K Kt 5; 12. P to K R 3, &c.

[5] Black deliberately prepares an attack upon the King's Bishop's Pawn.

[6] B to K Kt 3 was no better; White now loses the Pawn

[7] This move, in conjunction with 28 P to K Kt 3, effects the shutting up of the Rook on K Kt 4.

A. BURN v. J. MIESES.

WHITE	BLACK	WHITE	BLACK
1 P to Q 4	P to Q 4	8 Castles	Castles
2 Kt to K B 3	Kt to K B 3	9 B to B 4	P to Q Kt 3 [2]
3 P to Q B 4	P × P [1]	10 P to Q 5 [3]	Kt to K sq
4 P to K 3	P to K 3	11 R to K sq [4]	B to Kt 2 [5]
5 B × P	P to B 4	12 P × P	P × P
6 Kt to Q B 3	P × P	13 Q × Q	B × Q
7 P × P	B to K 2	14 R × P	K to R sq

AUGUST 24

WHITE	BLACK		WHITE	BLACK
15 Q R to K sq	Kt to K B 3		19 Kt × B	R × Kt
16 B to Q 6	R to K Kt sq		20 R × Kt [6]	K × R
17 Kt to K 5	P to Kt 3		21 B to K 7, ch	Resigns.
18 Kt to B 7, ch	K to Kt 2			

NOTES BY J. H. BLACKBURNE.

[1] An inferior defence, the capture of this Pawn is the source of all Black's subsequent troubles. P to K 3 is the correct move.

[2] An error, P to Q R 3 seems to be the only move at this juncture.

[3] Well played and strong, taking immediate advantage of Black's last move.

[4] Pressing the attack with great vigour, better than P × P at once.

[5] Fatal, but Black's game is hopelessly gone.

[6] White plays this ending with great accuracy, quite in his old form.

D. JANOWSKI v. I. GUNSBERG.

WHITE	BLACK
1 P to K 4	P to K 4
2 K Kt to B 3	Q Kt to B 3
3 B to Kt 5	P to K Kt 3
4 Kt to B 3 [1]	B to Kt 2
5 Castles	K Kt to K 2
6 P to Q R 3 [2]	Castles
7 B to B 4	P to Q 3
8 P to Q 3	P to K R 3
9 Kt to K sq	K to R 2
10 P to B 4	P to B 4 [3]
11 P × K P	Kt × P
12 B to R 2	P × P
13 R × R	Q × R
14 P × P [4]	B to Kt 5
15 Kt to K 2	Q to B 3
16 Kt to Q 3	R to K B sq
17 Q to K sq	Kt × Kt
18 P × Kt	Kt to B 3
19 Kt to B 3	Kt to Q 5
20 Kt to Q 5 [5]	Kt to K 7, ch
21 Q × Kt	B × Q
22 Kt × Q, ch	B × Kt [6]
23 B to K 3	B × Q P
24 R to Q B sq	P to B 4
25 R to Q sq	P to B 5
26 B to Kt sq	B × B

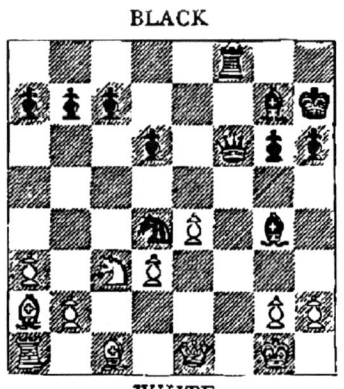

White to make his 20th move.

WHITE	BLACK
27 R × B	R to K sq
28 K to B 2	R × P
29 K to B 3	R to K 4
30 R to Q sq	R to B 4, ch
31 K to K 4	R to K 4, ch
32 K to B 3	P to Q 4
33 P to K Kt 4	R to K 2
34 B to Q 4	B × B
35 R × B	R to Q 2
36 K to B 4	K to Kt 2
37 K to K 5	K to B 2

WHITE	BLACK	WHITE	BLACK
38 R×QP	R×R	46 P to Kt 3	P to R 4
39 K×R	K to B 3	47 P to Kt 4	P to R 5
40 P to K R 4	P to K R 4	48 K to B 3	K to Kt 4
41 P×P	P×P	49 K to Kt 3	K to B 4
42 K×P	K to B 4	50 K to R 4	K to K 5
43 K to Q 4	K to Kt 5	51 K×P	K to Q 6
44 K to K 4	K×P	52 K to Kt 5	K to B 6
45 K to B 4	P to Kt 4		White resigns.

NOTES BY R. TEICHMANN.

[1] White treats this opening in a novel way, which I cannot approve of. The best line of play against this defence to the Ruy Lopez, which has been so undeservedly successful in the Tournament, is P to Q B 3 and P to Q 4, maintaining the centre and hampering the development of the black Pieces.

[2] With this move he wants to prevent the exchange of the King's Bishop, but there is no time for such slow manœuvres in the opening. Black meanwhile develops his game most favourably.

[3] This move gives Black a decisive advantage.

[4] White is already in a very bad position. If here 14. Kt × P, Black would also win. e.g. 14. ... Kt to Kt 5; 15. Kt to B 3, P to Q 4; 16 Kt to Kt 3, B to Q 5, ch; 17 Kt × B, Q to B 7, ch; 18. K to R sq, Q × Kt, winning at least a Pawn with a very good position

[5] There is nothing else. He has no move to prevent the dangerous Kt to B 7 (if B to Kt sq, then Kt to Kt 6, winning a Piece). [For if 20. B to Kt sq, Kt to Kt 6, 21 R to R 2, Kt × B; 22. Q × Kt, Q to B 7, ch, &c.—ED.] (See diagram.)

[6] Black has now an easily won end game.

C. SCHLECHTER v B VERGANI.

WHITE	BLACK	WHITE	BLACK
1 P to K 4	P to K 4	14 B to Kt 2	B to B sq
2 Kt to K B 3	Kt to Q B 3	15 Q to B 3	P to Q Kt 3
3 B to Kt 5	Kt to K B 3	16 Q R to Q sq	R to K 3 [6]
4 Castles	P to Q 3 [1]	17 P to K R 4	Q R to K sq
5 P to Q 4	P×P	18 P to R 5	Kt to K 4 [7]
6 Kt×P	B to Q 2	19 Q to R 3	P to Kt 3
7 Kt to B 3	B to K 2	20 P×P	B P×P
8 K Kt to K 2 [2]	Castles	21 Kt to Q 4	R (K 3) to K 2
9 Kt to Kt 3	Kt to K 4	22 Q×Q	R×Q
10 B×B [3]	Q×B	23 Kt to Q 5	B to Kt 2 [8]
11 P to Kt 3 [4]	Q R to Q sq	24 Kt×Kt, ch	B×Kt
12 Kt to B 5 [5]	Kt to Kt 3	25 Kt to Kt 5	Kt to B 6, ch [9]
13 R to K sq	K R to K sq	26 P×Kt	B×B

AUGUST 24

	WHITE	BLACK		WHITE	BLACK
27	Kt × R P	R to B 2	40	K to Kt 2	K to Kt 4
28	Kt to Kt 5	R to K 4 (¹)	41	R to Q 6 ¹¹	R × B P
29	R to Q 5	P to B 3 ¹⁰	42	R to K 6	K to B 5
30	R × R	B × R	43	R × K Kt P	K × K P
31	Kt to R 3	R × P	44	R to R 6	P to B 4
32	Kt to B 4	P to K R 4	45	R × P	R × P
33	Kt × B	P × Kt	46	R to R 4, ch	K to Q 6
34	R to Q sq	K to B 2	47	R to Q B 4	R to B 7
35	R to Q 7, ch	K to K 3	48	R to Kt 4	R to B 6
36	R to Q Kt 7	P to Q Kt 4	49	R to Kt 5	K to Q 5
37	R to K Kt 7	K to B 3	50	R to Kt 4, ch	P to K 5
38	R to Q 7	R to Q B 6		White resigns.¹²	
39	R to Q 2	P to Kt 5			

NOTES BY S. TINSLEY.

[1] It is sufficient to say of this variation of the Spanish game that, while it is being universally practised, the doctors are disagreeing about it. Who shall then decide?

[2] It is White's intention to go for a King's side attack by P to Q Kt 3 and B to Kt 2 presently. Otherwise, B to K 3 now or P to K B 4, or even P to K R 3, seems to offer better alternatives. Or he might safely play Kt × Kt at once, which, as the sequel shows, would have been much better.

[3] A leading principle of the Ruy Lopez and other close openings is that the Black forces must be kept closely confined as long as possible. Hence the exchange here is not good. More reasonable is B to K 2, followed soon by P to B 4.

[4] Apparently P to K B 4 is not played, because that would leave the King's Pawn somewhat isolated and subject to attack later. This method of developing the Bishop has often led to interesting games. Mr. Locock, we believe, has frequently played it with effect.

[5] The excellence of such a position is well known. But White's Knight, being unsupported by other Pieces, is not well placed at so early a stage. There are possibilities of Black retaliating with Kt × K P presently.

[6] To prevent the possibility of 17. Kt to R 7, ch, P × Kt; 18 Q × Kt, &c.

[7] The failure to keep the Knight out of this good commanding square is an important feature of this game; and we believe P to K B 4 earlier was really much better than the line of play adopted by White.

[8] The objection to capturing the Knight is that White's Knight would afterwards find a comfortable place at K 6 and remain there undisturbed.

[9] Black's Pawns are on black squares, and hence the importance of disposing of the Black Bishop by this judicious exchange.

[10] Black's 38th and 39th moves are full of force, and indeed the ending is played perfectly from this point.

[11] It is bad to abandon the Pawn thus; but the Black King is evidently coming to B 5, &c., and has P to R 5 and other good moves to 'wait' with.

[12] A good straightforward game, on Black's part especially. If Signor Vergani's reputation at Hastings rested on this game alone, it would be very high.

R. Teichmann *v.* W. Steinitz.

	WHITE	BLACK
1	P to K 4	P to K 4
2	Kt to K B 3	Kt to Q B 3
3	B to Kt 5	P to Q R 3
4	B to R 4	P to Q 3
5	P to Q 4	B to Q 2
6	P to B 3 [1]	K Kt to K 2
7	B to Kt 3 (!)	P to K R 3
8	B to K 3	P to K Kt 3 [2]
9	Q Kt to Q 2	B to Kt 2
10	Kt to B sq	Kt to R 4
11	B to B 2	Kt to B 5
12	B to Kt 3	B to K 3
13	B to B sq	P to Q Kt 4
14	Kt to K 3	P × P
15	Kt × P	Kt × Kt
16	B × Kt	B × B
17	Kt × B	Castles
18	Castles	Q to B sq
19	Q to Q 2	K to R 2
20	Q R to K sq	P to Q R 4
21	B to Q 4 (!)	P to K B 3
22	P to K B 4	R to Q sq
23	Q to K 2	P to Q B 4
24	B to B 2	P to R 5
25	Kt to B sq	Q to B 3
26	Kt to Q 3	K R to K sq
27	Q to B 3	P to R 6
28	P to Q Kt 3	Kt to Kt sq
29	B to Kt 3	B to B sq
30	P to K R 4	R to R 2
31	R to K 2	P to K B 4
32	K R to K sq	P × P [3]
33	R × P	R × R
34	R × R	Q to Q 2
35	P to K R 5	Q to B 4
36	P × P, ch	K × P
37	B to R 4	P to R 4

BLACK

White to make his 38th move.

WHITE

38	Q to K 2 [4]	K to R 2
39	Kt to B 2	B to Kt 2
40	B to Kt 5	Q to B 2
41	Q to B 3	P to Q 4
42	R to K 2	P to Q 5
43	P × P	B × P
44	Q to Q 3, ch	Q to Kt 3
45	Q × P	R to K Kt 2 (!)
46	Q to K 8	Q × Q
47	R × Q	P to B 5 [5]
48	P × P	R to Kt 2
49	K to B sq	R to Kt 8, ch

Drawn game

AUGUST 24

Notes by C. von Bardeleben.

[1] Black threatened P to Q Kt 4; 7. B to Kt 3, Kt × P; 8. Kt × Kt, P × Kt; and if 9. Q × P (?), then P to Q B 4; 10. Q to K 3, P to B 5.

[2] This move weakens the King's side; it would be preferable to play Kt to Kt 3, and B to K 2.

[3] This continuation would be safer: 32. ... Q R to K 2; 33. P × P, Q × Q; 34. R × R, ch, R × R; 35. R × R, ch, Kt × R; 36. P × P, ch, K × P; 37. P × Q, Kt to B 4; 38. B to B 2, B to K 2. White's best move would have been, perhaps, 33. P to K 5 instead of 33. P × P, in order to get a passed Pawn.

[4] Here White misses an excellent opportunity of getting a brilliant attack; he should have played:—

	WHITE	BLACK		WHITE	BLACK
38	Kt to K 5, ch	P × Kt	43	R to K 6, ch	K to Kt 2
39	R × P	Q to Kt 8, ch	44	Q × P; or—	
40	K to R 2	Kt to B 3	38		K to R 2
41	P to B 5, ch	K to B 2	39	Kt to B 6	R to K Kt 2
42	B × Kt	K × B	40	Kt to Q 8,	

threatening Kt to K 6 and Kt to Kt 5, ch.

[5] A fine combination, which secures the second player a draw.

J. Mason v. E. Schiffers.

	WHITE	BLACK		WHITE	BLACK
1	P to K 4	P to K 4	22	K R to K sq[3]	Kt to Q B 3
2	Kt to K B 3	Kt to Q B 3	23	B to Q sq[4]	Kt to B 4
3	B to Kt 5	P to Q R 3	24	Kt to B sq	P to Q R 4
4	B to R 4	Kt to B 3	25	P to Q R 4	K R to K sq
5	Kt to B 3	B to B 4	26	B to B 2	P to Q 5[5]
6	P to Q 3[1]	P to Q 3	27	Kt to Kt 3	Q R to Q sq
7	B to K 3	B to Q Kt 5			
8	Castles	B to Kt 5			
9	Kt to K 2	Castles			
10	P to B 3	B to Q R 4			
11	Kt to Kt 3	Kt to K 2			
12	P to K R 3	B to K 3			
13	B to B 2	Kt to Kt 3			
14	Kt to B 5[2]	P to Q 4			
15	Kt to Q 2	Q to Q 2			
16	Q to B 3	B × Kt			
17	Q × B	Q × Q			
18	P × Q	Kt to K 2			
19	P to K Kt 4	Kt to Q 2			
20	Kt to Kt 3	B to Kt 3			
21	B × B	P × B			

BLACK

WHITE

White to make his 30th move.

WHITE	BLACK	WHITE	BLACK
28 Kt × Kt	P × Kt	44 P to R 5 [9]	R × R P
29 K R to Q sq [6]	P to K 5 [7]	45 K to Q 4	R to B 2
30 P × K P	P to Q B 5	46 B × P [10]	R to R 5
31 P to B 3 [8]	P to Q 6	47 R to Kt 8, ch	Kt × R
32 B to Kt sq	R to K 4	48 R × Kt, ch	K to K 2
33 B to R 2	R to B 4	49 R to Kt 7, ch	K to Q 3
34 K to B 2	R to Kt sq	50 R × R	K × R [11]
35 R to Q 2	P to Q Kt 4	51 K × P	P to R 3
36 P × P	R (Kt sq) × P	52 P to B 4	K to Q 3
37 K to K 3	K to B sq	53 K to Q 4	K to K 2
38 P to R 4	P to B 3	54 P to K 5	R to R 8
39 P to Kt 5	P to R 5	55 B to K 2	R to R 7
40 P × P	P × P	56 K to K 3	R to R 6
41 R to K Kt sq	P to R 6	57 K to Q 4	R to R 7
42 P × P	R to R 4		
43 R (Q 2) to K Kt 2		Drawn game.	
	Kt to K 2		

NOTES BY H. N. PILLSBURY.

[1] Kt × P is the usual and correct procedure in positions of this kind, followed by P to Q 4

[2] Hardly well-judged; in the exchanges which shortly ensue Black obtains the superior ending owing to the strength of his centre Pawns.

[3] White should get rid of his doubled Pawn here by P to K B 4.

[4] The next three moves of White seem to indicate no definite plan; 23. P to Q 4 (and if then P to K 5; 24. P to B 3) seems more to the purpose

[5] Black obtains some superiority of position by this move.

[6] Had White foreseen the scheme of his opponent he could have easily prevented it either by P to K B 3 or Q R to Q sq. The text is very inferior to either.

[7] A very clever plot, and the sequel shows that the Pawn is well invested.

[8] Obviously if P × P, Kt × P, winning at least the exchange

[9] White can secure a draw here by K to Q 4, forcing Kt to B 3 (ch).

[10] An error which should have cost White the game. R to Q Kt 2 would leave him with a very good game.

[11] In the excitement of the exchange of Pieces, Black overlooked that P to Q 7 would win at once. After this the result can only be a draw

M. TCHIGORIN v S. TINSLEY.

WHITE	BLACK	WHITE	BLACK
1 P to K 4	P to K 3	4 Kt to R 3	Kt to Q B 3
2 Q to K 2	P to Q Kt 3 [1]	5 P to Q 3	Q to K 2 [2]
3 Kt to Q B 3	B to Kt 2	6 B to K 3	Castles

AUGUST 24

WHITE	BLACK	WHITE	BLACK
7 P to B 3[3]	Kt to B 3	24 R to B 5	P to K B 3
8 Castles	P to Q 4	25 Q to K 4	Q to B 4
9 B to B 2	P to Q 5	26 P to Q 6 ([1])	B × P
10 Kt to Q Kt sq	P to K 4	27 Q to R 8, ch	Kt to Kt sq
11 B to K sq	Q to K 3	28 R × B P	K R to B sq
12 P to Q Kt 3	P to K R 3	29 Q R to K B sq	
13 P to Kt 3	P to K Kt 4[4]		R × R
14 P to K B 4	P to Kt 5	30 R × R	P to B 3[7]
15 P × P	Q Kt × P	31 B to K 4	Kt to Q 2
16 Kt to B 4	Q to Q 3[5]	32 B to B 5	R to K 4
17 B to Kt 2	P to K R 4	33 B × Kt, ch	K × B
18 K to Kt 2	P to Q R 4	34 Q to Kt 7, ch	B to B 2
19 K R to B sq	B to K 2	35 B to B 4	Q to K 2
20 B to Q 2	B to B 3	36 B × R	Q × B
21 Q R to K sq	K Kt to Q 2	37 R to B 7, ch	K to Q sq
22 Kt to Q 5[6]	B × Kt	38 R to B 8, ch	K to K 2
23 P × B	Q R to K sq	39 Q to B 8	Resigns.

NOTES BY DR. TARRASCH.

[1] Stronger is B to K 2 or P to Q B 4.

[2] The whole game needs very little comment. Both players open in an original manner, and after a rather long fight for position Tchigorin gets an opportunity for attack. Black loses the game not through any particular mistake, but from White's stronger play in general.

[3] In order to retire the Bishop to B 2 after Black's P to Q 4.

[4] This is not good, as now the advance of White's Bishop's Pawn and the opening of the Bishop's file gain importance.

[5] White has now a much better game.

[6] The beginning of a decisive attack.

[7] Black's position is broken up and will soon be entirely destroyed. The position of White's Queen is peculiar, and also the absolutely safe position of White's King, though only protected by the Knight. It is also worthy of note that Tchigorin took, from the 31st to the 39th move, no less than fifty-six minutes, but each move is of greatest accuracy and precision.

[This game, which was adjourned at the curious position at the 31st move, caused much interesting discussion in the interval as to whether White's Queen would get out without loss, and the opinions expressed amongst the spectators as to the chances of the game were remarkably varied —ED.]

AUGUST 26.

THE three leaders all win to-day, Pillsbury especially playing very finely. But Tinsley with a clever attack knocks Bardeleben out of the first six, and Pollock with the exchange behind draws against Walbrodt, and pulls him down behind Steinitz, who wins against the very poor defence of Albin. Tarrasch treats us to another pretty finish. Bird and Janowski enliven us with a little lightning chess.

The Ladies' Tournament commenced this morning at 10 A.M., with twenty entries.

H. E. BIRD v. D. JANOWSKI.

	WHITE	BLACK
1	P to K B 4	P to Q 4
2	P to K 3	Kt to K B 3
3	Kt to K B 3	P to B 4 [1]
4	B to Kt 5, ch	Kt to B 3
5	B × Kt, ch	P × B
6	Kt to K 5	Q to B 2
7	Castles [2]	P to K 3
8	P to Q Kt 3	B to R 3 [3]
9	P to Q 3	R to Q sq
10	Q to B 3	B to Kt 2
11	B to Kt 2	B to K 2
12	Q to Kt 3	Castles
13	Kt to Q 2	Kt to K sq
14	Q Kt to B 3	P to B 3
15	Kt to Kt 4	Kt to Q 3
16	Kt to R 4 [4]	B to B sq
17	Q R to K sq [5]	Kt to B 4
18	Kt × Kt	P × Kt
19	Kt to B 2	B to Q 3
20	Q to B 3	Q R to K sq
21	Kt to R sq	R to B 2
22	Kt to Kt 3	K R to K 2
23	R to K 2	Q to Q 2

BLACK

WHITE

White to make his 16th move.

	WHITE	BLACK
24	K R to K sq	Q to K 3
25	Kt to R 5	Q to B 2
26	Kt to Kt 3 [6]	B to B 2
27	B to R 3 (?)	B to R 4
28	R to Q sq	B to Kt 5 [7]
29	B to Kt 2	P to Kt 3
30	P to B 3 [8]	B to R 4
31	P to K R 4	P to R 4

Photo, Bradshaw, Hastings.

H E Bird

AUGUST 26

	WHITE	BLACK
32	K to B 2	B to Kt 3
33	P to B 4	P to R 4
34	P to R 4 [9]	R to Kt 2
35	B to B 3	B to K 3
36	Kt to B sq	K to Kt 2
37	Q to Kt 3	Q to K 2
38	R to Kt 2	B to Kt sq [10]
39	R to K sq	Q to K 3
40	R (Kt 2) to K 2	
		B to Q sq [11]
41	Kt to Q 2	R (Kt 2) to K 2
42	K to B sq	B to Q B 2
43	Q to B 2	Q to Q 3
44	Q to B 3	P × P [12]
45	Q P × P	Q to Q 6
46	P to K 4	Q × Q, ch
47	P × Q	B × K B P
48	P × P	R × R
49	R × R	R × R
50	K × R [13]	P × P
51	B × R P	B to K 3
52	Kt to B sq	B to B sq
53	B to Q 2	B to Q 3
54	P to K B 4	B to R 3
55	B to K 3	B to B 2
56	K to B 3	B to Kt 3
57	Kt to Kt 3	K to Kt 3
58	Kt to K 2	K to B 2
59	B to Q 2	B to B 2
60	K to K 3	B to Kt 3
61	K to Q 3	B to B 2
62	B to K 3	B to Q 3
63	K to B 3	B to B 2
64	B × P	B to R 4, ch
65	P to Kt 4	B to B 2
66	B to K 3	B to B sq
67	P to R 5	B to R 3
68	Kt to B sq	K to K 3
69	Kt to Q 3	B to Q 3
70	B to B 5	B to Kt sq
71	K to Q 4	K to Q 2
72	B to Kt 6	B to Kt 2
73	Kt to B 5, ch	K to B sq
74	K to K 3	B to Q 3
75	Kt × B	K × Kt
76	P to Kt 5	B to Kt 5
77	K to B 2	B to K 2
78	B to Q 4	P to B 4
79	P to R 6, ch	K to Kt 3
80	B to B 3	K to R 2
81	B to Q 2	B to Q 3
82	K to K 2	B to B 2
83	K to Q 3	B to Q sq
84	K to B 2	B to B 2
85	K to Kt 3	B to Q 3
86	K to R 4	B to B 2

BLACK

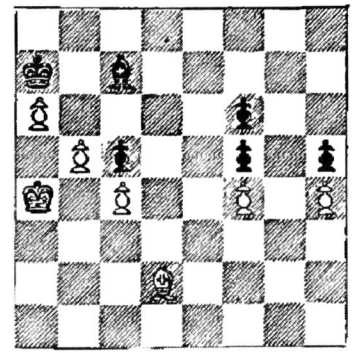

WHITE

White to make his 87th move.

87	B to K 3	B to Q 3
88	K to Kt 3	K to Kt 3
89	K to B 2	K to R 2
90	K to Q 3	B to K 2
91	K to K 2	B to Q 3
92	K to B 3	B to K 2
93	B to Q 2	B to Q sq
94	B to B 3	K to Kt sq
95	K to K 2	K to R 2
96	K to Q 3	K to Kt sq
97	K to B 2	K to R 2
98	K to Kt 3	B to B 2
99	B to Q 2	B to Q 3
100	K to R 4	B to B 2

Drawn game.[14]

NOTES BY A. ALBIN.

[1] The development of the White Bishop in this opening is the most difficult point, and for that reason Black should not play P to Q B 4; instead of that P to K 3 or any other move would be much better, and if White then plays B to Q Kt 5, ch, then P to Q B 3 in reply.

[2] White gets now the better position.

[3] Superfluous. B to Kt 2 at once is the proper move.

[4] P to K B 5 is stronger; if then P × P; 17. Kt to R 6, ch, K to R sq; 18. Kt × P, R to K Kt sq; 19. Q Kt to R 4, P to Kt 3; 20. Kt × B, and wins; or if P to K 4, then 17 Q Kt × P, P × Kt; 18. P to B 6, B × P [if P × P, then Knight takes, giving disc. ch, followed by B × P(!)]; 19. R × B, R × R, 20. Kt × R, ch, K to R sq; 21 B × P, and wins. (See diagram.)

[5] Even in this position there is time for P to K B 5. Black cannot take the Pawn; if P × P, then Kt to R 6, ch, with a strong attack; if P to K 4, there follows Kt × K P, P × Kt, B × P, and wins.

[6] White gets no more chances.

[7] Without judgment. B to Kt 3 was the right move.

[8] I would prefer at once P to K R 4, and if possible P to R 5.

[9] Very bad. The Pawns on the Queen's side begin to get very weak now.

[10] Why not P to Q 5?

[11] R (Kt 2) to K 2 followed by P to Q 5 seem to be stronger.

[12] Too late now.

[13] This exchange of all the Pieces simplifies matters

[14] [We have now reached the position we had fourteen moves ago (see diagram); after this the players made a similar set of moves and again reached the same position, drawing the game at the 115th move The whole game took six hours and ten minutes, whereas the time limit allowed anything short of sixteen hours. Speed is very desirable in its place, but it seems a pity that the player with the winning force should not have taken a little time and trouble to find the proper continuation. In the position of the diagram the quickest win is by P to Kt 6, ch, followed by K to Kt 5 or B to R 5, ch, accordingly —ED]

G. MARCO v. C. SCHLECHTER.

	WHITE	BLACK		WHITE	BLACK
1	P to K 4	P to K 4	8	B × Q	B to K 2
2	Kt to K B 3	Kt to K B 3	9	Kt to B 3	B to K 3
3	Kt × P	P to Q 3	10	Castles Q R	Kt to B 3
4	Kt to K B 3	Kt × P	11	P to Q 4	P to Q 4
5	Q to K 2 [1]	Q to K 2	12	B to K B 4	Castles Q R
6	P to Q 3	Kt to K B 3	13	Kt to K Kt 5	B to Q 3
7	B to Kt 5	Q × Q, ch [2]	14	Kt × B	P × Kt

AUGUST 26

WHITE	BLACK		WHITE	BLACK
15 B × B [3]	P × B		19 K R to Q 2	P to Q R 3
16 B to B 3	K R to K sq		20 P to K R 4	P to K Kt 3
17 K R to K sq	R to K 2			Drawn game. [4]
18 R to K 2	Q R to K sq			

NOTES BY I GUNSBERG.

[1] This leads to a perfectly even game on both sides, and is therefore inferior to 5 P to Q 4, or to Kt to B 3. If White has any reason to dread the variations arising from P to Q 4, which we do not believe is the case, then he may content himself with P to Q 3, Kt to B 3, 6. P to Q 4. For if Black then replies, as he must do sooner or later, with P to Q 4, White has the position of the normal variation of the French defence

[2] Pillsbury played here Kt to B 3 against Lasker, the game resulting in draw. B to K 3 may likewise be played, provided Black cares for struggling against the draw.

[3] It did seem worth while to exchange for the purpose of weakening the King's Pawn. White, however, has no means of making anything more out of the position. If he had retired his Bishop, Black could have taken it off, or played P to K 4. If he had played B to K Kt 5, Black would have replied P to K R 3.

[4] White had intended to play P to K Kt 4, so as to endeavour to dislodge the Knight, by P to Kt 5, and bring his Bishop to bear on the King's Pawn, and it would certainly have been worth while to carry out that intention, as the Black King's Pawn cannot move without leaving the Queen's Pawn unprotected.

J. MIESES v. R. TEICHMANN.

WHITE	BLACK		WHITE	BLACK
1 P to K 4	P to K 4		17 R to K sq	P to K 5
2 Kt to K B 3	Kt to Q B 3		18 Kt to R 3	Q to B 2
3 P to Q 4	P × P		19 P to Q Kt 4	B × B P
4 Kt × P	Kt to K B 3 [1]		20 B × Kt	P × B
5 Kt × Kt	Kt P × Kt		21 Kt × B	Q × Kt
6 P to K 5 [2]	Q to K 2		22 Q × P	B to R 3 (!)
7 Q to K 2	Kt to Q 4		23 Q R to Q sq	P to R 3
8 P to Q B 4 [3]	B to R 3		24 B to B sq	Q to B 7 (D)
9 P to Q Kt 3 [4]	Castles Q R		25 B to Q 3 (?)	P × B (!)
10 B to Kt 2	Kt to Kt 3		26 R × R, ch	R × R
11 P to K Kt 3	R to K sq		27 Q × R, ch	K to Kt 2
12 K B to R 3	P to K B 3		28 Q to K sq	B to B 8
13 Castles	P × P [5]		29 P to Kt 5 [6]	R P × P [7]
14 P to Q R 4	K to Kt sq		30 P to R 6, ch	K to R 2
15 P to R 5	Kt to Q 4		31 R × B	P to Q 7
16 Q to Q 2	Kt to B 3		32 Q to K 3, ch	P to B 4

BLACK

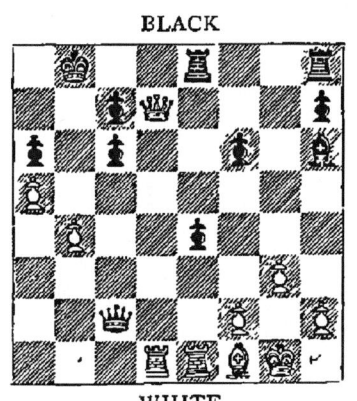

WHITE

White to make his 25th move.

WHITE	BLACK
33 R × Q	P to Q 8 (Q), ch
34 K to Kt 2	Q × R
35 Q to K 6	P to K B 4
36 P to K Kt 4	Q to K 5, ch
37 Q × Q	P × Q
38 K to B sq	K × P
39 P to K R 4	P to Kt 5
40 K to K 2	K to R 4
41 P to Kt 5	P to Kt 6
42 K to Q 2	K to Kt 5
43 P to R 5	K to R 6
44 P to Kt 6	P × P
45 P × P	P to Kt 7
46 P to Kt 7	P to Kt 8 (Q)
47 P to Kt 8 (Q)	Q to Q 6, ch
48 K to K sq	Q to Kt 8, ch
49 K to Q 2	Q to Q 6, ch
50 K to K sq	P to B 5
51 Q to Q B 8	K to Kt 7
52 Q × P	K to B 7
53 P to B 4	P to K 6
	White resigns.

NOTES BY E. SCHIFFERS.

[1] E. Schmidt's defence.

[2] This move is recommended by Steinitz in his 'Modern Chess Instructor.' L. Paulsen here played 6 Kt to Q B 3. 6. Q B to K 3 is also good.

[3] A good continuation here is 8. P to K B 4.

[4] The same continuation occurred in the last game of the match between Blackburne and Zukertort; Black won. Steinitz recommends 9. P to K B 4. In a game by correspondence between Chardin, of Samara (White), and Schiffers, of St. Petersburg (Black), the following continuation took place: 9. P to K B 4, Q to Q Kt 5, ch ; 10. K to Q sq (¹), B to Q B 4 ; 11. Kt to Q R 3 (11. Q to K 4 would have been stronger), Q × Kt (?) (11. . . Kt to Q Kt 3, with a good attack, would have been better) ; 12. P × Q, Kt to Q B 6, ch ; 13. K to Q B 2, Kt × Q ; 14. B × Kt, Q R to Kt sq ; 15. B to Q Kt 2, Castles ; 16. Q R to Q sq, P to Q 4 ; 17 K R to K sq, K R to Q sq (?), and White won. Black ought to have played 17. . . P × P ; 18. P to Q R 4 (!), B to K B 7 ; 19. R to K B sq, R × B, ch ; 20. K × R, P to Q B 6, ch ; 21. K to B 2 (¹), B × B ; 22. R × B, B × R, ch ; 23. K × B, R to Kt sq ; 24. R to Q B 2, and a draw ensues.

[5] The consequence of White having omitted to play P to K B 4.

[6] Why not 29. R × P, Q × R ; 30. Q × R to draw? White needlessly gives up his Pawns ; he eventually lost the game only through this.

[7] If Q B P × P, then 30. Q to K 4, ch, and takes the P at Q 3.

[A lively Pawn ending follows.—ED.]

AUGUST 26

I Gunsberg v. J. Mason.

WHITE	BLACK	WHITE	BLACK
1 P to K 4	P to K 4	14 Q R to Q sq [5]	P to B 3
2 Kt to K B 3	Kt to Q B 3	15 Kt × Kt, ch	P × Kt
3 P to Q 4	P × P	16 B to R 4	Q to K 2 [6]
4 B to Q B 4	B to B 4	17 Q × Kt	Q to K 3
5 Castles	P to Q 3	18 Q to B 3	Q × P [7]
6 P to B 3	P × P [1]	19 K R to K sq	Q to Kt 3
7 Q to Kt 3	Q to Q 2 [2]	20 B × P	B to Q Kt 5
8 Q × B P	Kt to B 3	21 Q × B	Q × B
9 B to K Kt 5	Q to K 2	22 R × P	P to Q R 4
10 Q to Kt 3	Castles	23 Q to Q 2	B to K 3
11 Kt to B 3	Kt to Q R 4	24 Kt to Kt 5	K R to Q sq
		25 Kt to K 4	Q to R 5
		26 Q to Q 4	R × R [8]
		27 Kt to B 6, ch	Q × Kt
		28 Q × Q	Q R to Q sq
		29 Q to Kt 5, ch	K to B sq
		30 Q × P	R to Q 8
		31 P to K R 3	R × R, ch
		32 Q × R	R to Q 2
		33 Q to K 5	K to Kt sq
		34 P to K Kt 4	P to Kt 4
		35 P to B 4	R to Q 8, ch
		36 K to B 2	R to Q 6
		37 P to B 5	B to Q 4
		38 P to B 6	P to R 3
		39 K to K 2	B to B 5
		40 Q to K 8, ch	K to R 2
		41 Q to K 4, ch	Resigns.[9]

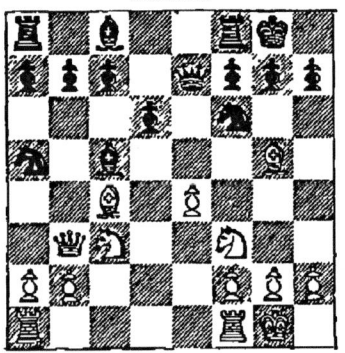

BLACK

WHITE

White to make his 12th move.

12 Q to B 2 [3]	Kt × B [4]
13 Kt to Q 5	Q to Q sq

Notes by R. Teichmann.

[1] Allowing White to get up a very strong attack; the well-known book move, B to K Kt 5, secures a decided advantage for Black.

[2] Q to K 2 would be still worse, on account of 8. Kt × P, Kt to B 3; 9. B to K Kt 5, and Black is hopeless.

[3] Very well played.

[4] This is courting disaster; B to K 3 seems to be a valid defence.

[5] Much stronger than taking the Knight at once; he threatens now P to K 5.

[6] He had nothing else against the threatened P to K 5

[7] Bold enough, but what can Black do?

[8] If he does not give up the Queen, his only alternative is K to B sq, when 27. P to K Kt 3 wins at least the exchange, for if R × R; 28. Q to R 8, ch, K to K 2; 29 Q × R, Q moves; 30. Kt × R

[9] Because after Q × R White wins easily.

B. Vergani v M. Tchigorin.

	WHITE	BLACK
1	P to K 4	P to K 4
2	Kt to K B 3	Kt to Q B 3
3	B to B 4	Kt to B 3
4	P to Q 3	B to B 4
5	Castles [1]	P to Q 3
6	B to K 3	B × B [2]
7	P × B	Kt to Q R 4
8	B to Kt 3	P to B 3
9	Q to K 2 [3]	Castles
10	Q Kt to Q 2	Q to K 2
11	P to B 3 [4]	Kt × B
12	Kt × Kt [5]	P to Q 4
13	P × P	Kt × P
14	K Kt to Q 2 [6]	Q to Kt 4
15	Q R to K sq	B to Kt 5
16	Q to B 2	P to K B 4
17	K to R sq [7]	Q to Kt 3
18	Kt to B sq	P to B 5
19	P to K 4	Kt to K 6
20	R to Kt sq	Q to R 4
21	Kt to B 3 [8]	Kt × P
22	Kt × P	B to R 6
23	R × Kt	B × R, ch
24	Q × B	Q × Kt
25	Q to B 3	Q R to K sq
26	P to Q 4	Q to K 3

Black to make his 21st move.

	WHITE	BLACK
27	P to K 5	R to K 2
28	R to Kt sq	P to K R 3
29	P to Kt 3 [9]	P to K Kt 4
30	Kt to Q 3	R to Kt 2
31	P to K R 3	K to R sq
32	Kt to B 5	Q to B 4
33	Kt to K 4	P to K R 4
34	Kt to B 6	P to Kt 5
35	P × P	P × P
36	Q to K 4 [10]	R × Kt

White resigns.

NOTES BY J. H. BLACKBURNE.

[1] It is better not to Castle too early in this opening. B to K 3 or Kt to B 3 is preferable.

[2] This is now considered stronger than retiring B to Kt 3.

[3] Kt to B 3, with the idea of reaching K Kt 3, *via* K 2, is the right line of play.

[4] Bad play; this Pawn ought not to be moved. Kt to R 4 could have been played with safety; for instance, 11. Kt to R 4, Kt × B; 12. R P × Kt, Kt × P; 13. Kt × Kt, P to Q 4; 14. Kt to B 6, ch, P × Kt; 15. Q to R 5, and White recovers the Pawn with a good game. Black could also, instead of 13. P to Q 4, play P to K B 4, in which case White takes the Bishop's Pawn with Knight, followed by Kt to Kt 3, remaining with Knight against Bishop.

[5] Again bad play. P × Kt was the proper continuation.

[6] White has already a weak position, and this move does not

AUGUST 26

improve it. He certainly ought to prevent P to K B 4 as long as possible, therefore P to Q B 4, followed by P to K 4, would have been the correct course.

[7] A useless move. The position is desperate, and therefore something must be attempted. P to K 4 leads to some lively variations, for suppose 17. P to K 4, P × P; 18. Kt × P, R × Q; 19. Kt × Q, R × Q Kt P; 20. R × P, and White can make some fight

[8] This loses the 'exchange' at least. Kt to B sq instead would undoubtedly prolong the game. (See diagram.)

[9] This is a wasted move; no use trying to save a useless Pawn in a position of this kind. His only chance was Kt to Q 3 at once.

[10] All other moves are equally fatal, for R × P would still have been answered by R × Kt.

W. Steinitz v. A. Albin.

	WHITE	BLACK		WHITE	BLACK
1	P to Q 4	P to K B 4	15	P × P	P to R 4
2	P to Q B 4	P to K 3	16	Q to Q 4	P × P
3	Q Kt to B 3	B to Kt 5 [1]	17	Q × P	B to Q 2
4	P to K 3	Kt to K B 3	18	B × Kt	P × B
5	B to Q 3	Castles	19	Q × K P	Q to B 3
6	K Kt to K 2	P to Q 3 [2]	20	Q to Q 4	Q to B 2
7	Castles	P to K 4 [3]	21	P to K 4	R to K Kt 3
8	Kt to Q 5	Kt × Kt	22	P to K 5	B to Kt 4
9	P × Kt	Kt to Q 2 [4]	23	P to Q R 4	B to R 3
10	Q to R 4	Q to R 5	24	R to R 3	R to Q sq
11	Q × B	R to B 3 [5]	25	P to K 6	Q to K sq
12	Kt to Kt 3	Kt to B 4	26	Kt to B 5	P to B 3
13	R to Q sq	R to R 3	27	R to K Kt 3 [6]	Resigns.
14	P to K R 3	Kt to K 5			

Notes by Dr. Tarrasch.

[1] The Dutch game can scarcely be defended (compare the game Steinitz v. Tarrasch). After B to Kt 5 the Bishop is not in a good position, and an exchange against the Knight is usually prejudicial to Black. On K 2, however, the Bishop has no future.

[2] To follow with P to K 4. This move has this disadvantage, that it cuts off the King's Bishop from the King's side. Black does not perceive this in time.

[3] At least B × Kt should have been played before this.

[4] The exposed Bishop should retire to R 4.

[5] White wins the Bishop, and the game is of course decided. Black still makes a desperate attack.

[6] After R × P there follows 28. R × R, R × Q; 29. R × P, ch, K to R sq; 30. R × R, and wins.

E. Schiffers v. E. Lasker.

	WHITE	BLACK
1	P to K 4	P to K 4
2	Kt to K B 3	Kt to Q B 3
3	Kt to Q B 3	P to K Kt 3
4	P to Q 4	P × P
5	Kt × P	B to Kt 2
6	B to K 3	P to Q 3
7	B to Q Kt 5	B to Q 2
8	Q to Q 2	Kt to B 3
9	P to K B 3	P to Q R 3
10	B to K 2	Castles
11	Castles Q R	P to Q Kt 4
12	P to K Kt 4	P to Kt 5
13	Kt to Q 5 [1]	K Kt × Kt
14	P × Kt	Kt × Kt
15	B × Kt	R to K sq
16	B × B	K × B
17	B to Q 3	Q to B 3
18	K R to B sq	Q to Q 5
19	B to K 2 [2]	Q × Q, ch
20	R × Q	B to Kt 4
21	B × B [3]	P × B
22	K to Kt sq	R to R 4
23	P to B 3	P × P
24	P × P	R to K 6
25	K to Kt 2	R to R 5 [4]
26	P to K B 4	R to Q B 5
27	R to Q 4	R (K 6) × P
28	R to Q 2	R to K 6
29	R to Q B sq	R (K 6) to K 5
30	R × R	R × R [5]
31	R to Q B 2	R × P

BLACK

White to make his 26th move.

	WHITE	BLACK
32	R × P	R × P
33	R to Kt 7	P to Kt 5
34	K to Kt 3	R to Q 5
35	R × P	R × P
36	P to R 4	K to B 3
37	R to Kt 7	K to K 3
38	K to Kt 4	R to Q 7
39	K to Kt 5	R × P [6]
40	P to R 5	P to R 4
41	P to R 6	R to R 7
42	R to B 7	P to R 5
43	R to B 4	P to R 6
44	K to Kt 6	P to Kt 4
45	P to R 7	R × P

White resigns.

Notes by H. N. Pillsbury.

[1] The exchange of so many Pieces, which Black is now enabled to effect, leaves him with the preferable ending position. Kt to Kt sq instead would have enabled White to continue the attack by P to K R 4 and R 5, and was far superior.

[2] An error of judgment, which Black takes advantage of with masterly skill. B to K 4 was the only correct move, and the position then remained even.

[3] It was fatal to open the adverse Rook's file. 21. R to K B 2,

AUGUST 26

R to K 4 ; 22. P to Q B 4, P × P (*en passant*) ; 23. P × P, still gave fair prospects of a draw.

⁴ This Rook enters powerfully, the White Pawns soon becoming indefensible. (See diagram)

⁵ With the win of the Pawn and exchange of one Rook the position simplifies, Black being bound to win a second Pawn at least.

⁶ Of course, whenever the remaining Pawn becomes dangerous Black will simply take it off. The remainder of the game plays itself

S. Tinsley *v.* C. von Bardeleben.

	WHITE	BLACK		WHITE	BLACK
1	P to Q 4	P to Q 4	13	B to Q 3	Kt to Q B 3 [3]
2	P to Q B 4	P to K 3	14	R to Q B sq	P to B 5
3	Kt to Q B 3	Kt to K B 3	15	B to Q Kt sq	P to Q Kt 4
4	P to K 3	B to K 2	16	P to Q R 3	P to Kt 5
5	P to K B 4 [1]	P to Q Kt 3	17	P × P	Kt × P
6	Kt to B 3	B to Kt 2	18	Q to B 3	R to Kt sq
7	B to K 2	Q Kt to Q 2	19	Q R to K sq [4]	B to R sq (?) [5]
8	Castles	Castles	20	B to B sq	Kt to K sq (?) [6]
9	Kt to K 5	P to Q B 4	21	Q to R 3	Kt to B 3 [7]
10	P × Q P	K P × P	22	P to K Kt 4	Q to B sq (?) [8]
11	B to Q Kt 5 [2]	Kt to Q Kt sq	23	B to B 5	Resigns.
12	B to Q 2	P to Q R 3			

Notes by E. Schiffers.

¹ This move is better made in conjunction with P to Q B 3 (Stonewall) than P to Q B 4.

² Loss of time; P to B 5 or P × P would have been better. The exchange of the Bishop for the Knight could only be advantageous to Black, who would thus be delivered from an attacking Piece.

³ Better to have played P to B 5 at once, as the Bishop could not then advantageously move to Q Kt sq.

⁴ In order to make room for the Bishop at Q B sq (!).

⁵ An ill-chosen post for the Bishop ; better to have placed him at B sq.

⁶ A bad move in an already bad position.

⁷ If P to Kt 3, then 22. P to B 5, with a strong attack. The Bishop at R sq is virtually dead.

⁸ A move which immediately loses the game; Kt to K 5 would have been comparatively better, although White can then win a Pawn

[Herr Bardeleben was about this time far from well.—Ed.]

A. Walbrodt *v.* W. H. K. Pollock.

	WHITE	BLACK		WHITE	BLACK
1	P to K 4	P to K 4	21	B to Kt 5	Q to Q 2
2	Q Kt to B 3	Q Kt to B 3	22	P × P	Kt × P
3	B to B 4	Kt to B 3	23	Q to Q B 4	B to Kt 3
4	P to Q 3	B to Kt 5 [1]	24	Kt to K 4	Q to Q 4 [6]
5	Kt to K 2 [2]	P to Q 3	25	Kt to B 6, ch	R × Kt
6	Castles	B to Kt 5	26	Q × Q, ch	P × Q
7	P to B 3	B to K 3	27	B × R	Kt to K 6
8	B to Q Kt 5 [3]	Castles	28	R to Q B sq	R to K sq
9	B × Kt	P × B	29	P to B 3	P to K 5
10	K to R sq	P to Q 4	30	R to B 4	P to B 4
11	P to Q R 3	B to Q B 4	31	P to Q Kt 4	B to B 2
12	Q to K sq	Kt to K sq	32	R to K B 2	Kt to Kt 5
13	P to B 4	P to B 3	33	R (B 2) to B sq	
14	P to B 5	B to B 2			Kt × R P
15	Q to R 4	Kt to Q 3	34	R (K B sq) to K sq	
16	R to B 3	P × P			Kt to Kt 5
17	P × P	P to Kt 4	35	B to R 4	P to K 6
18	P × P *en p.* [4]	Q B × P	36	P × P	Kt to B 7, ch
19	B to R 6	R to B 2	37	K to Kt sq	
20	Q R to K B sq	P to B 4 [5]		Drawn game. [7]	

Notes by R. Teichmann.

[1] Avoiding the complications arising from B to B 4, after which White may turn into the King's Gambit declined with P to K B 4.

[2] This development of the Knight appears a little unnatural; I prefer Kt to K B 3.

[3] This I cannot approve of B to Kt 3 is much better, as Black then cannot exchange the Bishops without allowing one of the White Knights to enter at K B 5.

[4] Necessary, because if Q to R 6, then Kt × P.

[5] Too aggressive Kt to K sq would have given him a safe position, with good prospects of taking advantage of the weakness in White's game (Pawn at K 4).

[6] Very ingenious. By the sacrifice of the exchange he frees himself from all difficulties, and gets even winning chances.

[7] It is curious to agree to a draw in this position, which certainly would admit of much play We think Black has slightly the best of it, but after a careful analysis of the position I have come to the conclusion that he has not enough to win

AUGUST 26

Dr. Tarrasch v. J. H. Blackburne.

	WHITE	BLACK
1	P to K 4	P to K 3
2	P to Q 4	P to Q 4
3	Kt to Q B 3	P × P
4	Kt × P	Kt to Q 2
5	Kt to K B 3	K Kt to B 3
6	B to Q 3	P to B 4 [1]
7	Castles	P × P
8	Kt × Kt, ch	Kt × Kt
9	Kt × P	B to B 4 [2]
10	Kt to B 3	Q to B 2 [3]
11	Q to K 2	B to Q 2
12	Kt to K 5	B to Q 3
13	P to K B 4	Castles K R
14	B to Q 2	Q R to Q sq [4]
15	K to R sq	B to B sq
16	R to B 3	P to K Kt 3 [5]
17	P to B 4 [6]	B × Kt [7]
18	P × B	Kt to Q 2
19	B to B 3	Kt to B 4
20	B to B 2	B to Q 2
21	P to Q Kt 3 [8]	K to Kt 2
22	Q to K 3	R to K R sq

	WHITE	BLACK
23	Q R to K B sq	
		B to K sq
24	B to K sq	Q to K 2
25	R to B 6	P to K R 3
26	B to R 4	P to K Kt 4

BLACK

White to make his 27th move.

| 27 | R × R P (!) [9] | P × B |
| 28 | R × R | Resigns. |

NOTES BY C. VON BARDELEBEN.

[1] I prefer Kt × Kt ; 7. B × Kt, Kt to B 3.
[2] Better would be B to K 2, to be followed by Castles.
[3] I should have Castled, and if 11. B to K Kt 5, then B to Kt 3.
[4] If Q to Kt 3, ch ; 15. B to K 3 (!), then if Q × P (?) ; 16. Kt to B 4, Q to Kt 5 ; 17. Q R to Kt sq, and White wins a Piece.
[5] White threatens 17. R to R 3, followed by 18. Kt to Kt 4.
[6] A very fine move, which prepares for the nineteenth move of White ; if at once B to B 3, Black would reply Kt to Q 4.
[7] This exchange opens White's game, and gives him a good opportunity of an attack against the Black King's side ; preferable is P to Kt 3, to be followed by B to Kt 2.
[8] To prevent Kt to R 5.
[9] Very pretty ; if Black play R × R ; 28. B × P, wins.

H. N. Pillsbury v. A. Burn.

	WHITE	BLACK
1	P to Q 4	P to Q 4
2	P to Q B 4	P to K 3
3	Kt to Q B 3	Kt to K B 3

	WHITE	BLACK
4	B to K Kt 5 [1]	B to K 2
5	P to K 3	Castles
6	Kt to K B 3	P to Q Kt 3

	WHITE	BLACK		WHITE	BLACK
7	R to Q B sq	B to Q Kt 2	18	Q to B 4	Q R to B sq
8	P × P	Kt × P [2]	19	P to K 5 [5]	P to Q B 4 [6]
9	B × B	Q × B	20	B × P, ch	K × B
10	Kt × Kt	B × Kt	21	Kt to Kt 5, ch	
11	B to Q 3	R to Q B sq [3]			K to Kt sq
12	P to K 4	B to Kt 2	22	R to R 3 [7]	Q to K sq
13	Castles	Kt to Q 2	23	Q to R 4	K to B sq
14	Q to K 2	P to Q R 3 [4]	24	Kt to R 7, ch	K to Kt sq
15	R to Q B 3	P to Q B 3	25	Kt to B 6, ch	K to B sq
16	K R to Q B sq		26	Kt × Q	K × Kt
		P to Q Kt 4	27	Q to Kt 5	P × P
17	Q to K 3	R to B 2	28	R to R 8, ch	Resigns.[8]

NOTES BY J MASON.

[1] As to the entire advisability of this, opinions differ. The early exchange or subsequent retreat is thought not to be generally favourable by many good players. Perhaps, on principle, 4. Kt to B 3 should have preference; the Bishop to be disposed as later circumstances may require.

[2] To keep the diagonal open; a troublesome undertaking. 8. P × P, with a 'majority on the Queen's side' view, and power of later Kt to K 5 (if necessary), would probably prove stronger. There is nearly always great danger to be apprehended from the adverse Bishop at Q 3 in this class of position.

[3] The check might be fairly ventured. But 11. B × P would be bad; for the Bishop could be so shut in as to have no good escape.

[4] Mr. Burn should have played P to Q B 4 now. There was nothing to be feared from, e.g. 15. B to R 6, B × B; 16. Q × B, Kt to B 3; 17. P × P, R × P; 18 R × R, Q × R; 19. Q to Kt 7, Q to Q B sq, &c. Even a move or two further on, P to Q B 4 would be the better play. The complications, deliberately courted, as it were, hereabouts, are not at all to the advantage of the defence.

[5] What may be called the self-evident intent of this is most unaccountably ignored by his opponent. The conclusion is reached by Mr Pillsbury in about the most forcible manner possible.

[6] Further support or protection of the King is imperative—19. Kt to B sq seems best. After this unfortunate oversight, Black's is really a hopeless case. Nevertheless the ending is very instructive.

[7] Meaning mate in four—23. R to R 8, ch, 24 Q to R 4, ch, &c. Hence the reply, making way for the King. The attack is altogether overwhelming.

[8] For 29. R × Kt, ch, K × R; 30. R × R, R to K sq; 31. R × B, &c., and White has a Queen too much.

Photo., Bradshaw, Hastings

Carl Schlechter

AUGUST 27.

THE interest in the three leaders deepens; Lasker and Bardeleben have not been looking well, and most are beginning to feel the strain of so severe a contest.

Mason is playing the draw producing Giuoco, against Lasker; Albin is playing a French against Tchigorin, and evidently putting his shoulder to the wheel. Pillsbury has played P to Q 4, but his opponent (Bardeleben) is late, and presently a note arrives to say he is not well and will not come, so giving the only forfeited game in the Tournament at a rather unfortunate time. Reckoning Lasker's game as a draw, the leaders will now be equal.

C. SCHLECHTER v. E. SCHIFFERS.

	WHITE	BLACK		WHITE	BLACK
1	P to K 4	P to K 4	21	B × Kt	P × B
2	Kt to K B 3	Kt to Q B 3	22	Q to Q 3	Kt to Kt 2
3	B to Kt 5	P to Q R 3	23	Kt to B 3	B to K 2
4	B to R 4	Kt to B 3	24	B to K 3	Castles
5	Castles	Kt × P	25	Kt to Q 4	Q to Q 2
6	P to Q 4	P to Q Kt 4			
7	B to Kt 3	P to Q 4			
8	P to Q R 4	R to Q Kt sq			
9	R P × P	R P × P			
10	P × P	Kt to K 2 [1]			
11	P to B 3	Q B to Kt 5			
12	B to K 3	P to Q B 3			
13	B to B 2	Q Kt to B 4			
14	B to R 7	R to B sq			
15	P to R 3	B × Kt			
16	Q × B	Kt to R 5			
17	Q to K 2	Kt to Q B 4			
18	P to Q Kt 4	Kt to K 3			
19	P to K B 4	P to Kt 3			
20	Kt to Q 2	Kt to K B 4			

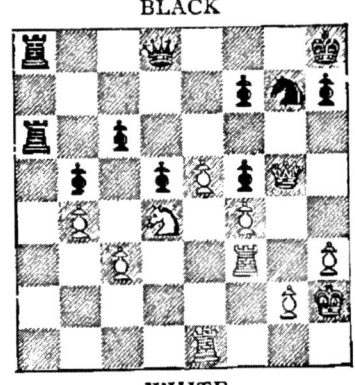

White to make his 37th move.

WHITE	BLACK	WHITE	BLACK
26 Kt to Kt 3	R to R sq	39 R × Kt	K to Kt 2
27 B to B 5	K to R sq	40 R to B 6	R to Q B sq
28 B × B	Q × B	41 P to K 6	P × P
29 Kt to Q 4	Q to Q 2	42 R (K sq) × P	P to Q 5
30 Kt to Kt 3	R to K Kt sq [2]	43 P × P	R to R 5
31 Kt to Q 4	K R to K sq	44 R to K 7, ch	K to Kt sq
32 K to R 2	R to K B sq	45 R (B 6) to B 7 (!) [5]	
33 Q to Kt 3	R to R 5 [3]		R × P
34 Q to Kt 5	K R to R sq	46 R to Kt 7, ch	K to B sq
35 Q R to K sq	Q R to R 3	47 R (K 7) to B 7, ch	
36 R to B 3	Q to Q sq [4]		K to K sq
37 Kt × K B P	Q × Q	48 R × P	Resigns.
38 P × Q	Kt × Kt		

NOTES BY C. VON BARDELEBEN.

[1] I prefer B to K 3 here.

[2] Q to K 2 would be better.

[3] Black's position is not good, and it is very difficult, perhaps impossible, to find a sufficient defence. If, for instance, R × R, 34. R × R, R to K Kt sq, then White plays 35. R to R 6, R to Q B sq; 36. Q to Kt 5, and 37. Q to B 6, winning the Queen's Bishop's Pawn.

[4] Black is forced to give up a Pawn. If he played R to K Kt sq, White would answer 37. Q to B 6, threatening 38. R to Kt 3; 39. R × Kt; 40. Kt × K B P, and by this line of play obtain a decisive advantage. (See diagram.)

[5] White plays the ending very well.

R. Teichmann v. S. Tinsley.

WHITE	BLACK
1 P to K 4	P to K 3
2 P to Q 4	P to Q 4
3 Kt to Q B 3	P × P [1]
4 Kt × P	Kt to K B 3
5 B to Q 3	B to K 2
6 Kt to K B 3	Q Kt to Q 2
7 Castles	Castles
8 Kt × Kt, ch	B × Kt
9 Q to K 2	R to K sq
10 Kt to K 5 [2]	P to K Kt 3 [3]
11 P to K B 4 [4]	P to Q B 4
12 P to Q B 3 [5]	P × P
13 P × P	Kt to K B sq [6]
14 B to K 3	B to Q 2

BLACK

WHITE

White to make his 26th move.

AUGUST 27

	WHITE	BLACK		WHITE	BLACK
15	R to B 2	R to B sq	27	Q to B 3	Q to K 2
16	B to K 4 [7]	P to Q Kt 3	28	P to Q 5	P × P
17	Q R to K B sq	R to K 2 [8]	29	R × P	R to K sq
18	P to K Kt 4 [9]	B to Kt 2	30	B to Q 2	Kt to K 3
19	B to B 2 [10]	P to K B 3	31	B to B 3	B × B
20	Kt × B	Q × Kt	32	P × B	Q × P [14]
21	B to Kt 3 [11]	K to R sq	33	R to K 5 (¹)	Kt to B 2 (¹)
22	P to K R 4	P to B 4	34	Q to K 3	R to K B sq [15]
23	R to Q sq	P × P	35	P to B 5	Q to B 3 [16]
24	Q × P	P to K R 4 [12]	36	P × P	R × P
25	Q to K 2	B to B 3	37	R × P, ch	K to Kt 2
26	R to Kt 2 [13]	R to Kt 2	38	Q to R 6, mate.	

Notes by Dr. Tarrasch.

[1] This move is bad, because Black gives up the hold in the centre. Black could only equalise the game by a further advance of the King's Pawn, and White can easily prevent this.

[2] To prevent P to K 4. Compare the similar game of Dr. Tarrasch v. Blackburne.

[3] To prevent the possible sacrifice of the Bishop at R 7; also to guard his diagonal.

[4] Still better was first P to Q B 3, as then the advance of the Queen's Bishop's Pawn would lead to its loss.

[5] Whilst now Kt × Kt would be replied to with B × P, ch. White permits the Queen's Pawn to be isolated

[6] Kt to Kt 3 and Q 4 was better.

[7] This would have been much stronger in the preceding move, as then no favourable cover for the Knight's Pawn existed.

[8] Black's position is very cramped, the Pieces hampering one another.

[9] White vigorously proceeds with the attack.

[10] Simpler and perhaps better would have been to play P to Kt 5; and to take the Pawn if P to K B 4, in this way keeping the Knight in its dominating position, whilst now it must be exchanged; or he might have played 19. P to B 5, K P × P, 20 P × P, B × Kt; 21. P × B, R × P; 22 B to Q 4; or if 20. ... P × P, 21 B × P, B × B, 22. R × B, with a strong attack, but it is true with a comparatively free play for Black

[11] With 21. P to B 5, K P × P; 22. P × P, White could have shut in the Bishop; and if 22 ... Q R to K sq, have continued with Q to B 4, ch.

[12] Black has with his last moves prevented the threatening attack by P to R 5, but his game has now new weak points at Kt 3 and R 4.

[13] White lays an extraordinarily fine trap. If Black takes the Rook's Pawn, the following continuation may then ensue · 26. P to Q 5, P × P; 27. R × Q P, Q to K sq; 28. B to Q 4, ch, K to R 2; 29. Q to

K 4 (!!) (threatening R × R P, mate), R × Q ; 30. R × P, ch, P × R ; or 27. B to Kt 8, ch, K to R 3 ; 28. B to Kt 7, mate. (See diagram.)

[14] At last Black takes the offered Pawn ; he can do it quite safely.

[15] This is a mistake which is fatal at once. Black should have exchanged the Rooks and played after 35. P × R, K to R 2 ; or after 35. Q × R, Q to K 2. Now a pretty termination comes about.

[16] P to K Kt 4 does not help on account of 36. R to K 4 (!).

J. Mason v. E. Lasker.

	WHITE	BLACK		WHITE	BLACK
1	P to K 4	P to K 4	34	R (B 5) to B 2	Q to Kt 5 [6]
2	Kt to K B 3	Kt to Q B 3	35	Kt to Kt 3 [7]	P to Q R 4
3	B to B 4	B to B 4	36	R to R sq	Kt to Q B 4
4	P to Q 3	Kt to B 3	37	Q to B sq	K R to Q sq
5	Kt to B 3	P to Q 3	38	Kt to B 5	Q to Kt 4
6	B to K 3 [1]	B × B	39	P to K Kt 4 [8]	Kt to K 3
7	P × B	Kt to Q R 4	40	Q to K 3	Kt to B 5
8	B to Kt 3	P to B 3	41	R to Q 2	P to B 4
9	Castles	Kt × B	42	Q to B 2	P to B 5 [9]
10	R P × Kt	Castles	43	Q P × P	R × R
11	Q to K sq	Kt to K sq	44	Q × R	R × Q
12	Q to Kt 3	P to B 3	45	P × Q	R × B P
13	Kt to K R 4	B to K 3	46	R to Q Kt sq [10]	
14	R to B 2 [2]	Q to Kt 3			Kt to R 6
15	Q R to K B sq		47	Kt to K 3	R to B 4
		Q R to Q sq	48	K to Kt 2	Kt to B 5, ch
16	K to R sq [3]	R to Q 2 [4]	49	K to B 3	P to K R 4
17	Kt to B 5	K to R sq			
18	Kt to Q R 4	Q to B 2			
19	Q to R 4	P to Q Kt 3			
20	Kt to B 3	Q to Q sq			
21	Q to Kt 3	Kt to B 2			
22	Kt to K R 4	R to K sq [5]			
23	Q to B 3	B to B 2			
24	Kt to B 5	B to K 3			
25	Q to Kt 3	B × Kt			
26	R × B	Kt to K 3			
27	Q to B 2	Kt to Kt 4			
28	Q to K sq	P to Q 4			
29	Q to R 4	P to Q 5			
30	P × P	R × P			
31	Kt to K 2	R to Q 2			
32	Q to B 2	Kt to K 3			
33	Q to K 3	Q to K 2			

BLACK

WHITE

White to make his 50th move.

50	P to Q Kt 4 [11]	R × P
51	P × Q R P	P × P, ch

AUGUST 27

	WHITE	BLACK		WHITE	BLACK
52	K × P	P × P	68	P × P	P × P
53	Kt to B 4 [12]	Kt to K 3 [13]	69	K to R 5	R to Kt 2
54	P to R 4	Kt to Q 5	70	R to R 8, ch	K to B 2
55	R to Q R sq	Kt to B 3	71	R to R 7, ch	K to Kt sq
56	K to B 5	R to Kt 5	72	R to R 5	P to B 5
57	Kt × R P	Kt × Kt	73	R × P	P to B 6 [16]
58	R × Kt	R × Kt P	74	R to K B 5 [17]	R to K B 2
59	K to Kt 6	R to K Kt 7, ch	75	R to Kt 5, ch	K to B sq
60	K to R 5	K to R 2	76	R to Kt sq	R to K Kt 2 [18]
61	R to R 7	R to K 7	77	R to K B sq	R to Kt 6
62	R to Kt 7	K to Kt sq [14]	78	K to R 6	K to B 2
63	K to Kt 6	R to Kt 7, ch	79	P to R 5	K to B 3
64	K to R 5	P to Kt 3, ch	80	K to R 7	K to B 4
65	K to R 6	R to Kt 5	81	P to R 6	K to B 5
66	R to Kt 7, ch	K to B sq	82	K to R 8	
67	R to Q R 7 [15]	P to B 4		Drawn game.	

Notes by S. Tinsley.

[1] The opening is commonplace and dull, and it seems a pity nothing better can be suggested for White here. The move made, B to K 3, is too common, and it is obvious Black can take the Piece without danger (as here), doubling White's Pawn; or he may allow White to capture the Bishop and double his Pawns. Again he may safely retire to Kt 3.

[2] On general principles Q R to Q sq seems to have its points; but White is naturally anxious to keep hold of the Queen's Rook's file.

[3] Apparently waiting, and to avoid a 'pin.'

[4] Not P to Q 4, to which White replies Q × K P (!).

[5] Again, not P to K Kt 4, to which the reply is Q × Kt P; 23. P × Q, R × R, ch, &c.

[6] It is here that the game, after exemplary patience and skill on both sides, begins to assume interesting features, and it should be observed how tenaciously Herr Lasker sticks to this small advantage on the Queen's side.

[7] Kt to Q B sq, with a view to P to Q B 3, would be bad in the end, the reply being Kt to B 4 with a treble attack on the Queen's Pawn.

[8] The first really poor move, giving Black an opening of which he promptly avails himself—the 'hole' at B 5.

[9] At last the attack by Black begins to tell. If Kt P × P, Black gets in by Q × Kt P.

[10] He could do nothing by 46 R to Q sq, P to R 3, &c., because of the mating position left at home.

[11] Most ingenious. If P × P, the Rook is shut out for the time, and White has the Rook's file open as well as the Queen's file, with slight attacking chances.

[12] Defending his own Pawn and threatening to win Black's by

R to Q R sq. It was this consideration which compelled Black to exchange at the 51st move, in spite of its bringing the White King more forward, for he must have his Knight available for the Queen's side.

[13] Clever, and prepared by his 51. He can play his Kt to Q B 4 if necessary, attacking the now undefended King's Pawn and afterwards go to Kt 2. If 52. K to B 5, Kt to Q 5, ch, closing the files long enough to avoid the threatening mate after 53. K to Kt 6.

[14] Not R × P, for then White draws at least by R × P, ch, the position being a stalemate if White K × R.

[15] R × P leaves a mate on the move !

[16] Black cannot win by R to K 2, on account of K to Kt 6, threatening mate

[17] A simple retreat to K sq would have left Black nothing except a drawn position.

[18] Playing instantaneously, Herr Lasker missed the win which to his score was so important. The Rook is won in two moves by R to R 7, ch, followed by R to Kt 2, ch. The game affords many examples of Mr Mason's splendid defensive powers in difficult situations

M. Tchigorin v. A. Albin.

	WHITE	BLACK		WHITE	BLACK
1	P to K 4	P to K 3	24	B to Q 2	B to B 2
2	Q to K 2	Q Kt to B 3	25	B to K B 3	K to Q 2
3	K Kt to B 3	P to K 4 [1]	26	Kt to Kt 4	Kt × Kt
4	P to K Kt 3	B to B 4	27	P × Kt	Kt to R sq
5	P to B 3	B to Kt 3	28	K to Kt 2	Q R to R sq
6	P to Q 3	P to Q 4	29	K R to Q Kt sq	
7	B to Kt 2	P to Q 5			K R to Q Kt sq
8	Castles	B to K Kt 5	30	B to Q sq	P to Kt 3
9	Kt to R 3	P to Q R 3	31	P to Q Kt 5 [3]	R P × P
10	Kt to B 4	B to R 2	32	B P × P	P × P
11	P to K R 3	B × Kt	33	R × P	Kt to B 2
12	B × B	P to K R 3	34	R to Kt 2	Kt to Q 3
13	Kt to Q 2	Kt to B 3	35	B to Kt 3	P to Kt 4 [4]
14	P to B 4	P to K Kt 4	36	R(Kt2)to R2	P × P
15	B to Kt 2	R to K Kt sq	37	B × R P, ch	K to K 2
16	P to Q R 3	Kt to K 2	38	R to B sq	B to R 4 [5]
17	Kt to B 3	Kt to Kt 3	39	B × B	R × B
18	Kt to R 2	Q to Q 2 [2]	40	R to B 7, ch	K to B 3
19	Q to B 3	Q to K 3	41	R to K R 7	R(Kt sq) to R sq
20	Q to B 5	P to B 3	42	R to B 2	R × B
21	Q × Q	P × Q	43	R (B 2) to B 7 [6]	
22	P to Q Kt 4	Q R to B sq			R to K Kt sq
23	P to Q R 4	B to Kt sq	44	R × P, ch	R to Kt 3

AUGUST 27

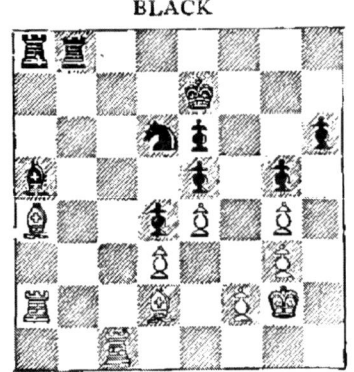

BLACK

WHITE

White to make his 39th move.

WHITE	BLACK
45 R(R6) to R 7	R to R 6
46 R to Q 2	R to Q R 3
47 K to B sq	R to Kt sq
48 R to R 6, ch	R to Kt 3
49 R (R 6) to R 7	
	R to Kt sq
50 R to R 6, ch	R to Kt 3
51 R (R 6) to R 7	
	R to R 8, ch
52 K to Kt 2	R to R 3
53 K to R 3	R to R 8
54 K to R 2	R to R 3
55 K to Kt 2	R to Q Kt 3
56 R to Q R 7	R to K Kt sq
57 R to R 6, ch	R to K Kt 3
58 R (R 6) to R 7	
	R to K Kt sq

Drawn game.[7]

NOTES BY H. N. PILLSBURY.

[1] Bringing about an open game, with the White Queen indifferently placed.

[2] The position appears slightly in Black's favour; in block positions of this nature Knights are generally better than Bishops for attacking purposes. Black might here have avoided the exchange of Queens by Q to K 2, and Castling Q R.

[3] White is playing to win, while his opponent is willing to draw. In attempting to force matters White presently gets into some difficulty.

[4] A good move, and putting White on the defensive, as he cannot advance the Pawn, or it would be lost, Black being able to attack it four times, by R to R 3, K R to Q R sq, Kt to Kt 2, &c.

[5] Another fine move, and the draw which White is now compelled to force is all that is left. (See diagram.)

[6] Very neat; Black's King is so surrounded by his own Pawns that he cannot utilise his extra Piece.

[7] A fine game, with a most instructive ending.

DR. TARRASCH v. H. E. BIRD.

WHITE	BLACK	WHITE	BLACK
1 P to K 4	P to Q B 4	8 Q to Q 2	B to Q 2
2 Kt to K B 3	Kt to Q B 3	9 Castles K R	Kt to B 3
3 Kt to B 3	P to K Kt 3	10 P to K R 3	Q to B sq [2]
4 P to Q 4	P × P	11 P to B 4	K to B sq [3]
5 Kt × P	B to Kt 2	12 Q R to Q sq	P to R 5
6 B to K 3	P to K R 4 [1]	13 Kt × Kt	B × Kt
7 B to K 2	P to Q 3	14 P to K 5	P × P

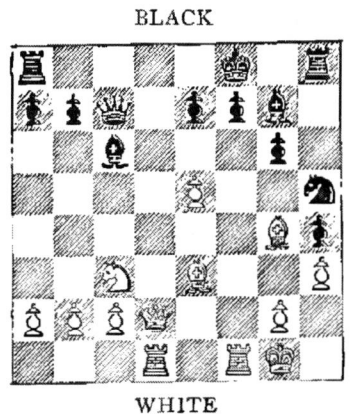

BLACK

WHITE

White to make his 17th move.

	WHITE	BLACK
15	P × P	Kt to R 4
16	B to Kt 4	Q to B 2
17	Q to B 2	B to K sq
18	Kt to Q 5 [4]	Q × K P
19	Kt × P	B to K B 3 [5]
20	Kt to Q 5	B to Kt 2
21	B to B 5, ch	K to Kt sq
22	Kt to K 7, ch	K to R 2
23	R to Q 5 [6]	Kt to Kt 6
24	R × Q	B × R
25	R to K sq	B × P
26	B to Q 4	B × B
27	Q × B	P to B 4
28	Kt × Kt P [7]	Resigns.

NOTES BY I. GUNSBERG.

[1] As it is White's object to advance his King's Bishop's Pawn, Black stands a chance of getting his King's Rook's Pawn isolated and weakened through this advance.

[2] As a matter of course Black aims at a King's side attack, and P to K R 4 was intended to facilitate that operation. We, however, think that the proper continuation of the Sicilian must be on the Queen's side, by such moves as R to B sq, and Q to R 4, &c., the idea being also to utilise the Black King's Bishop for an attack in the same direction crossways.

[3] With what object is not clear. He exposes himself to the coming advance by means of which White will be able to free his King's Bishop's file for the action of the Rook against the Black King.

[4] A fine and subtle move by which White obtains a winning attack.

[5] His only possible reply against White's threat of Kt × P, ch, or B to Q B 5.

[6] It is quite a pleasure to see the way in which Dr. Tarrasch scientifically dissects his opponent. The move hardly admits of a satisfactory reply, for if the Queen moves away, R × Kt, ch, follows.

[7] Neat again. If B × Kt, R to K 7 wins.

A. WALBRODT v. G. MARCO.

	WHITE	BLACK		WHITE	BLACK
1	P to K 4	P to K 4	7	Q to K 2	Kt to Q 4
2	Kt to K B 3	Kt to Q B 3	8	P to Q B 4 [1]	Q to Kt 5, ch
3	P to Q 4	P × P	9	Kt to Q 2 [2]	Kt to B 5
4	Kt × P	Kt to B 3	10	Q to K 4	Kt to K 3
5	Kt × Kt	Kt P × Kt	11	P to B 4	B to Kt 2
6	P to K 5	Q to K 2	12	P to Q R 3	Q to Kt 3

AUGUST 27

	WHITE	BLACK
13	Kt to B 3	P to Q B 4
14	Q to Q 3	Kt to Q 5
15	Kt × Kt	P × Kt
16	P to Q Kt 4	P to Q B 4
17	R to Q Kt sq	Q to B 3 [3]
18	P × P	B × P
19	B to Kt 2	Castles K R
20	B × P	B × B
21	Q × B	P to B 3
22	B to Q 3	P × P
23	P × P	Q R to K sq [4]
24	R to Kt 2	P to Q 3
25	Q × R P	R × P, ch
26	K to Q sq	B to B sq
27	Q to Kt 6	Q to R 5, ch
28	Q to Kt 3	Q to R 2
29	K to B sq	R to Q R 4
30	R to R 2	B to B 4
31	B × B	Q R × B
32	R to Q sq	R to Kt sq
33	Q to Q 3	R to Q B 4
34	R to Q B 2	R (Kt sq) to Q B sq
35	Q to Q Kt 3	R to Kt sq
36	Q to Q 3	R to Kt 3
37	Q to K 3	R to K 4
38	Q to K B 3	Q to Kt sq
39	R to Q 3	R to Kt 8, ch
40	K to Q 2	R (Kt 8) to K 8
41	R to Q 5	R to K sq
42	R to Q Kt 5	Q to R 2
43	R to Kt 3	Q to Q 5, ch

	WHITE	BLACK
44	R to Q 3	Q to R 8
45	R (Q 3) to B 3	R (K 8) to K 5 [5]
46	R to B sq	Q to Kt 7, ch
47	R (B sq) to B 2	Q to Kt 3
48	R to B sq	Q to Q 5, ch
49	K to B 2	R to K 7, ch
50	K to Kt sq	R to Kt sq, ch
51	K to R sq	R (Kt sq) to Kt 7 [6]

BLACK

WHITE

White to make his 52nd move.

52	Q to R 8, ch	K to B 2
53	R to B 3, ch	K to Kt 3
54	R to Kt 3, ch	K to R 3
55	R to R 3, ch	K to Kt 3
56	R to Kt 3, ch	K to R 3
57	R to R 3, ch	K to Kt 3
58	R to Kt 3, ch	

Drawn game.

NOTES BY E. SCHIFFERS.

[1] Up to the present the moves are the same as in the game Mieses *v.* Teichmann; the latter here played B to R 3.

[2] 9. K to Q sq is preferable.

[3] I do not understand why Black does not here take the Pawn at his Kt 5.

[4] Q × K Kt P would not have been good, on account of 24. R to K Kt sq, threatening P to K 6.

[5] Much better would have been R to K B 8, which, after 46. Q to Q 5, ch, K to R sq, would at least lead to winning the Queen's Rook's Pawn.

[6] Black's continuation only leads to a draw. After this move, White forces a perpetual check. With other moves, instead of 51. ... R to Kt 7, White would exchange Queens. This exchange made now would give Black a mate in two moves.

W. H. K. Pollock *v.* J. Mieses.

	WHITE	BLACK
1	P to K 4	P to K 4
2	Kt to K B 3	Kt to Q B 3
3	B to Kt 5	P to Q R 3
4	B × Kt	Q P × B
5	Castles [1]	B to K Kt 5
6	P to K R 3	P to K R 4
7	P to Q 3	B to Q B 4 [2]
8	P × B	P × P
9	Kt to Kt 5	P to Kt 6
10	Q to B 3	P × P, ch
11	R × P	Kt to B 3
12	Kt to B 3	Q to K 2
13	Kt to R 3	B × R, ch
14	K × B [3]	Kt to R 4
15	B to K Kt 5	P to B 3
16	B to K 3	P to K Kt 4 (!)
17	R to K B sq	Castles Q R
18	K to K sq	Kt to B 5
19	Kt to B 2	K to Kt sq
20	P to K Kt 3 [4]	Kt to K 3
21	Kt to Kt 4	Q to Kt 5
22	Q × P	Kt to Q 5
23	Kt × K P [5]	Kt × P, ch
24	K to Q 2	Kt × B
25	K × Kt	Q to Q 5, ch
26	K to Q 2	K R to K sq
27	Kt × P, ch [6]	P × Kt
28	Q × Q	R × Q
29	K to K 3	P to B 4
30	Kt to K 2	R to Q 2
31	R to B 5	K R to Q sq
32	Kt to B sq	P to B 5 (!) [7]
33	P × P	R to Q 8
34	Kt to Kt 3	R to K 8, ch
35	K to B 3	R to Q 6, ch

White to make his 33rd move.

	WHITE	BLACK
36	K to B 2	R to Q Kt 8
37	R × P	R × P, ch
38	K to K sq	R × R P
39	Kt to B sq	R to K 6, ch
40	K to Q sq	R to K Kt 7
41	R to Q R 5	R (K 6) × Kt P
42	R × P	R to K R 6
43	Kt to K 2	R to R 8, ch
44	K to Q 2	R (R 8) to R 7
45	K to Q 3	R × Kt
46	K to Q 4	K to Kt 2
47	R to K 6	R to Q 7, ch
48	K to B 5	R to Q 3
49	R × R	P × R, ch
50	K × P	R to Q 7, ch
51	K to B 5	K to B 2
52	P to K 5	R to Q 8
53	P to K 6	R to Q 7
54	K to Kt 5	R to K 7

White resigns.

AUGUST 27

Notes by C. von Bardeleben.

[1] Better is 5. P to Q 3, or P to Q 4.

[2] I prefer Q to B 3; if White then plays 8. P × B, Black answers with P × P; 9. Kt to Kt 5, Q to R 3; 10. Kt to R 3, Q to R 5; 11. K to R 2, P × Kt; 12. P to K Kt 3, Q to R 2, being a Pawn ahead; or 9. B to Kt 5, Q to Kt 3; 10. Kt × P [if 10. Kt to R 2 (?), then Q to R 4 (!)], Q × B; 11. P to K B 4, P × P *en passant*; 12. Kt × P, Q to R 3, having the better position.

[3] This brings the King into a bad position. Better would be 14. Kt × B, Kt to R 4; 15 B to K 3, Q to R 5; 16. Kt to K 2.

[4] A weak move, which drives the hostile Knight to a very good square. White should have played 20. K to Q 2, in order to bring his King to Q B sq.

[5] If 23. K to Q 2, K R to B sq.

[6] Better would be 27. R to B 5.

[7] Very well calculated. (See diagram.)

J. H. Blackburne *v.* I. Gunsberg.

	WHITE	BLACK
1	P to K 4	P to K 4
2	P to K B 4	P × P
3	B to B 4	P to Q 4
4	B × P	Q to R 5, ch
5	K to B sq	P to K Kt 4
6	Q to B 3 [1]	P to Q B 3
7	Q to B 3	P to B 3
8	Kt to B 3 [2]	Q to R 3
9	P to Q 4	Kt to K 2
10	B to B 4	Kt to Q 2
11	P to Q R 4 [3]	B to Kt 2
12	Kt to R 3 [4]	P to K B 4 (!) [5]
13	P to R 4 [6]	Kt to B 3 (!)
14	Kt × P	Kt × P
15	Q to Q 3 [7]	Kt to Kt 6, ch [8]
16	K to Kt sq	Kt × R
17	B × P	Q × P
18	Q to K 3	Kt to Kt 6 (!!) [9]
19	B × Kt	Q × P [10]
20	Q × Q	B × Q, ch
21	K to R 2	B × P
22	R to Q sq (!) [11]	
		R to B sq
23	B to Q 6	B to B 3
24	Kt to R 3	P to B 5 [12]

White to make his 19th move.

	WHITE	BLACK
25	Kt × P	B to Kt 5
26	R to Q 3	R to Q sq [13]
27	P to Kt 3	B to Kt 4 [14]
28	Kt to K 6 [15]	B × Kt
29	B × B	R to B 3
30	B × Kt	R to R 3, ch
31	K to Kt 2	B × B
32	R to K 3	B × Kt
	White resigns.	

Notes by Dr. Tarrasch.

[1] Played against Englisch in the Paris Tournament of 1878. The idea lies in the succeeding moves

[2] Instead of this White could by B × Kt, followed by Q × K B P, win a Pawn, this would nevertheless not be advantageous for him, as his game would be undeveloped, and his Queen exposed to various assaults. But by the move made the Queen stands badly, as it occupies the natural outlet of the Queen's Knight The consequence of this is that the attack is not of much value.

[3] In order soon to drive the Knight back to Q 2 if it should play to Kt 3.

[4] Here the Knight is very badly placed, in consequence of hampering the Rook.

[5] On P to K 5, Kt to Q Kt 3 and Q 4 would follow.

[6] White tries to maintain the attack The attack and counter-attack are highly interesting. After B P × P, advantage would result for White, but Black had to carry out some interesting manœuvres.

[7] If White exchanges the Knights, the advantage to Black is evident. White therefore sacrifices the exchange.

[8] Kt × Kt would be bad on account of B × P.

[9] By this charming move Black secures his advantage, and at the same time spoils the intended assault by R to K sq. (See diagram.)

[10] Simple, yet unexpected

[11] Cleverly played; Black cannot now take the Knight on account of B to B 7, ch, and R to Q 8, ch

[12] With this the Queen's side is relieved and the game practically finished.

[13] Threatening R × B and B to K 4.

[14] Now threatening R × B and R × Kt.

[15] Other moves also are equally futile

A. Burn v B. Vergani.

	WHITE	BLACK		WHITE	BLACK
1	P to K 4	P to K 4	14	B × Kt	Q to K B sq
2	Kt to K B 3	Kt to Q B 3	15	Q to Kt 4, ch	K to B 3
3	B to Kt 5	Kt to K B 3	16	P to Q B 4	Q to R 3
4	Kt to Q B 3	P to Q 3 [1]	17	P × P, ch	K × P
5	Castles	P to K Kt 3 [2]	18	Q to Q 7, ch	K to R 3
6	R to K sq	B to Q 2	19	P to K Kt 3	R to K Kt sq
7	P to Q 4	Kt × Q P [3]	20	Q R to Q sq	Q to K B sq
8	Kt × Kt	P × Kt	21	R to K 4	K to R 2
9	Q × P	B × B	22	Q R to K sq	R to B sq
10	Kt × B	P to Q R 3 [4]	23	Q to R 4, ch	K to Kt sq
11	P to K 5	P × Kt	24	Q to R 5	P to Q B 3
12	P × P, ch [5]	K to Q 2	25	R to R 4	R to K sq
13	B to Kt 5	B × P [6]	26	R to Q B sq	R to B sq

AUGUST 27

WHITE	BLACK	WHITE	BLACK
27 P to Q Kt 4	B to K 2	30 P × P	K to Q sq
28 B to Q 4	P to Q B 4	31 Q × P	Resigns.[7]
29 Q to R 7, ch	K to B 2		

NOTES BY R. TEICHMANN.

[1] Why not simply B to Kt 5, which gives Black a very good game?

[2] There is no time now for the Fianchetto, B to K 2 and Castles being necessary.

[3] This unfavourable exchange is forced.

[4] His game is already hopeless; there is no satisfactory defence against P to K 5.

[5] Stronger than P × Kt, ch, after which the position of the Black King looks pretty safe at Q 2.

[6] Best under the circumstances. If B to Kt 2; 14. R to K 7, ch, K to B sq; 15. B × Kt, B × B; 16. Q to Kt 4, ch, winning the Queen.

[7] A somewhat easy victory. Some of the masters had a much harder task with the Signor Vergani.

D. JANOWSKI v. W. STEINITZ.

	WHITE	BLACK
1	P to K 4	P to K 4
2	Kt to K B 3	Kt to Q B 3
3	B to Kt 5	P to Q R 3
4	B to R 4	P to Q 3
5	Castles	K Kt to K 2
6	B to Kt 3 [1]	Kt to R 4
7	P to Q 4 [2]	P × P
8	Kt × P	P to Q B 4
9	Kt to B 5	Kt × Kt [3]
10	P × Kt	Kt × B [4]
11	R to K sq, ch	B to K 2
12	P to B 6	P × P
13	R P × Kt	P to Q 4 [5]
14	Q to R 5	Q to Q 3
15	Kt to B 3	B to K 3
16	Kt to Kt 5 [6]	Q to B 3
17	R × B	Q × Kt
18	B to R 6	K to Q sq
19	Q × B P	R to K sq
20	Q R to K sq	Q to Q 2

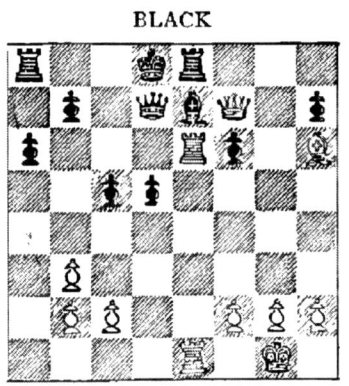

White to make his 21st move.

	WHITE	BLACK
21	B to Kt 7 (!)	R to Q B sq
22	B × P	B × B
23	Q × B, ch	K to B 2
24	Q to K 5, ch	Resigns.

NOTES BY H. N. PILLSBURY.

[1] New but not true ; either P to Q 4 or P to Q 3 was the correct move

[2] This and the following move should have cost White a Piece and the game.

[3] Evidently a grave error ; for after B × Kt ; if 10 P × B, P to B 5 wins a clear Piece, and White obtains nothing for it.

[4] Obviously if now P to B 5 ; 11. Q to K 2, ch, winning a Pawn.

[5] B to K 3 seems preferable, followed soon by Q to Q 2.

[6] Very pretty, winning by force ; after this Black has no resource.

At the end of this day the excitement is intense, for several unexpected events have happened and affected the score seriously.

Whilst Pillsbury has had a bloodless victory against his most dangerous remaining opponent, Tchigorin and Steinitz have both failed to win, and from the adjourned position it looks very doubtful whether Lasker can do so either. There are only four more rounds, and the leaders are still in a bunch.

The scores, including the results of unfinished games, are :—

Lasker	$13\frac{1}{2}$	Teichmann	8
Tchigorin	$13\frac{1}{2}$	Gunsberg	8
Pillsbury	$13\frac{1}{2}$	Janowski	$7\frac{1}{2}$
Steinitz	10	Bird	$7\frac{1}{2}$
Tarrasch	10	Burn	$7\frac{1}{2}$
Walbrodt	10	Blackburne	$7\frac{1}{2}$
Schlechter	9	Marco	$6\frac{1}{2}$
Bardeleben	$8\frac{1}{2}$	Albin	$6\frac{1}{2}$
Schiffers	$8\frac{1}{2}$	Tinsley	$6\frac{1}{2}$
Mason	$8\frac{1}{2}$	Mieses	$5\frac{1}{2}$
Pollock	8	Vergani	3

Photo., Bradshaw, Hastings

J. Mieses.

AUGUST 28.

EVERYONE is on the alert. Schlechter who has only lost one is to play Pillsbury; Tchigorin is trying his hand at Mieses' Scotch, and Lasker has Vergani.

At the end of the day Lasker has 14, and his adjourned Mason game. Tchigorin is 14, and Pillsbury 13½. Walbrodt has lost another, whilst Schiffers, Gunsberg, Blackburne, and Teichmann are pulling up.

J. MIESES v. M. TCHIGORIN.

	WHITE	BLACK
1	P to K 4	P to K 4
2	Kt to K B 3	Kt to Q B 3
3	P to Q 4	P × P
4	Kt × P	Q to R 5
5	Kt to Kt 5	Q × K P, ch
6	B to K 2 [1]	B to Kt 5, ch
7	B to Q 2	K to Q sq
8	Castles	B × B
9	Kt × B [2]	Q to K B 5
10	P to K Kt 3 [3]	Q to R 3
11	Kt to B 4	K Kt to K 2
12	Q to Q 3	P to Q R 3
13	Kt to Q 4	Kt × Kt
14	Q × Kt	Kt to B 3
15	Q to B 3	R to K sq
16	B to B 3	Q to B 3 [4]
17	Q × Q	P × Q
18	B to Q 5	R to K 2
19	K R to K sq	P to Q 3
20	R × R	K × R
21	R to K sq, ch	K to B sq
22	B to K 4	B to K 3
23	Kt to K 3	K to Kt 2
24	Kt to Q 5	B × Kt
25	B × B	Kt to Kt 5

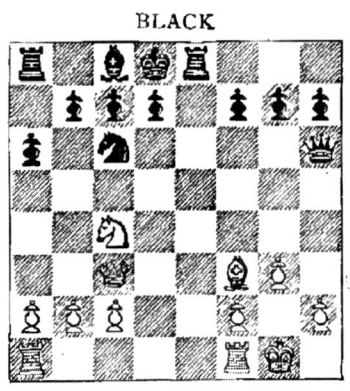

Black to make his 16th move.

	WHITE	BLACK
26	B to Kt 3	K to B sq
27	R to K 4	Kt to B 3
28	R to K R 4	K to Kt 2
29	R to Kt 4, ch	K to R sq
30	R to B 4 [5]	Kt to K 4 [6]
31	R × P	K to Kt 2
32	R to B 4	R to K sq
33	K to Kt 2	P to Q B 3
34	R to K 4	P to Q 4
35	R to K sq	R to K 3

WHITE	BLACK	WHITE	BLACK
36 P to K B 4	Kt to Kt 5	45 P × P	K to B -
37 R × R	P × R	46 K to B 4	P to R 3
38 P to B 3	P to B 4	47 P to R 3	P to Q R 4
39 P to K R 3	Kt to K 6, ch	48 P to Kt 3	Kt to K sq
40 K to B 2	Kt to B 4	49 P to Kt 4	B P × P
41 P to Kt 4	Kt to Q 3	50 B P × P	P × P
42 K to K 3	P to Kt 3	51 P × P	Kt to B 2
43 P to B 5	P × P	52 B to B 6	K to K 3
44 B × P	P × P		Drawn game.

Notes by E Schiffers

[1] In my opinion, after 6. B to K 3, White obtains a much better chance of a successful attack.

[2] Blackburne playing against Steinitz took here with the Queen and then moved Kt to Q B 3, which better pleases me.

[3] The moves up to the present stage are the same as in a correspondence game between London and Vienna (White). Here Vienna continued 10. P to Q B 4, to which Black replied with Kt to K B 3.

[4] Indispensable; White threatened B × Kt, Kt P × B; Kt to K 5, &c. After the exchange of Queens, Black will find it difficult to turn to account the extra doubled Pawn. (See diagram.)

[5] Evidently White cannot take King's Bishop's Pawn

[6] If Black defends the Pawn at K B 3, then a draw ensues (R to Kt 4, ch, &c.).

I. Gunsberg v. A. Albin.

WHITE	BLACK
1 P to K 4	P to K 3
2 P to Q 4	P to Q 4
3 P × P [1]	P × P
4 Kt to K B 3	B to Q 3
5 Kt to B 3	P to Q B 3
6 B to Q 3	B to K Kt 5
7 Q to K 2, ch	Kt to K 2
8 B to Q 2	Kt to Q 2
9 Castles Q R [2]	Q to B 2 [3]
10 P to K R 3	B to R 4
11 P to K Kt 4	B to Kt 3
12 B × B	R P × B
13 Kt to K Kt 5	Kt to K B sq [4]
14 Q R to K sq	Q to Q 2 [5]
15 Kt to R 4 [6]	P to B 3
16 Kt to B 5 [7]	B × Kt
17 P × B	Kt to R 2 [8]

White to make his 16th move.

WHITE	BLACK
18 Kt to K 6	K to B 2
19 Kt × P [9]	Kt to K B sq

AUGUST 28

WHITE	BLACK		WHITE	BLACK
20 P to Kt 5	R to R 2		32 Q to K 4, ch	K to Kt sq
21 P × P	K × P		33 R to Q 6	Q to K 2
22 B to B 3, ch	K to B 2 [10]		34 Q × Q P	Q to K 6, ch
23 Q to K 5	Kt to B 4		35 Q × Q	R × Q
24 Q to B 6, ch	K to Kt sq		36 B to K 5	Kt to B 4
25 Kt to K 6	Kt × Kt		37 R to K 6	Kt to Kt 2
26 R × Kt	P to Q 5		38 R to Kt 6	K to R 2
27 R to Q sq	R to K B sq		39 R × Kt, ch [12]	R × R
28 Q to K 5	R × P		40 B × R	K × B
29 R × P, ch	K to R 2 [11]		41 R to Q 7, ch	K to Kt 3
30 R to K 6	R to B 2		42 R × P	Resigns.
31 P to B 4	Kt to Kt 2			

NOTES BY S. TINSLEY.

[1] Modern practice avoids this old variation. Let me point out to a novice one simple and yet important objection to it. Black's Queen's Bishop is a source of anxiety to him in all French defences and in many other close games. The text move opens the file, and gives that Piece the freedom of action it could never otherwise obtain till late in the game.

[2] Of course the object is to risk a little for immediate attack on the Black King, when Castling Queen's side is adopted so early. And, be it observed, Black cannot do much at this point.

[3] If now Black Castles King's Rook, then B × P, ch, would easily prove advantageous, owing to the position of Black's Queen's Bishop. Supposing, Castles; 10. B × P, ch, K × B, 11. Kt to Kt 5, ch, K moves; 12. Q × B, &c.

[4] Black would like to Castle Queen's Rook also; but then follows Kt × B P. Black has already a most uncomfortable position.

[5] Hoping to force off Queens. Thus 14. ... Q to Q 2; 15. ... P to B 3; 16. Kt to K 6, Kt × Kt; 17. Q × Kt, Q × Q, 18. R × Q, K to Q 2, &c.

[6] The initiation of one of the prettiest combinations of the Tournament. By the aid of diagram the play can be easily followed from this point.

[7] Forcible as well as pretty; because if the Knight is not taken, one will in any case go to K 6 with effect.

[8] Of course P × Kt is unsound, the reply being B × P, and the Piece is regained with much advantage of material and position.

[9] It requires the light thrown upon the game by the after-play to prove that this is sound.

[10] One of the best features of the position. If 22. ... P to Q 5; 23. B × P, ch, Q × B; 24. Q × Kt, mate.

[11] If 29. ... Kt to Kt 2; 30. R × Kt, ch, Q × R; 31. Q to K 6, ch, winning the Rook at R 6.

[12] There has been elegance and brilliancy enough. The simple

and forcible style is the best, even though not quite artistic, whatever that may mean. Black had a wretched position throughout, after move seven or eight, and had no opening for his well-known powers. White took full advantage of the opportunities, and the result is a very entertaining game.

B. Vergani v. E. Lasker.

	WHITE	BLACK		WHITE	BLACK
1	P to K 4	P to K 4	19	P to Q Kt 3	P to Q Kt 4
2	Kt to K B 3	Kt to Q B 3	20	R to K 2 [2]	P to Q R 4
3	B to Kt 5	P to Q R 3	21	Q R to K sq	P to R 5
4	B to R 4	Kt to B 3	22	P to Kt 4 [3]	B to B 5
5	Castles	Kt × P	23	R to Kt 2	P to R 6
6	R to K sq [1]	Kt to B 4	24	R to Kt sq	Q to Q 2
7	B × Kt	Q P × B	25	Kt to Q 2	B × R P [4]
8	Kt × P	B to K 2	26	R to R sq	B to B 5
9	P to Q 4	Kt to K 3	27	K R to Kt sq	P to R 7
10	P to B 3	Castles	28	R to Kt 2	R to R 6
11	P to K B 4	P to K Kt 3	29	R (Kt 2) × P [5]	
12	B to K 3	B to Q 3			R × R
13	Kt to Q 2	Kt to Kt 2	30	R × R	B × R
14	Kt to K 4	B to K B 4	31	Kt (Q 2) to K 4	
15	Kt to Kt 3	B to K 3			Q to B 2
16	Q to K 2	R to K sq	32	Kt × K B P	Q × Kt
17	Q to K B 2	P to B 3	33	Q × B, ch	Q to K 3
18	Kt to B 3	B to Q 4		White resigns.	

Notes by J. Mason.

[1] Allowing immediate retreat Kt to B 4. Hence 6 P to Q 4 is usually preferred. White has to part with his Bishop for one Knight or the other; and the defence becomes simplified, if not strengthened, accordingly.

[2] This doubling of the Rooks turns out of little use. It would perhaps be more to the purpose to take steps to dislodge one of the hostile Bishops, as an extension of the idea involved in P to Kt 3. From the moment he is compelled to the further advance of his Knight's Pawn, Signor Vergani's position becomes one of increasing difficulty.

[3] Apparently based upon a serious miscalculation, or else a downright blunder.

[4] Of course. This gift of a Pawn is virtually a gift of the game.

[5] Expediting a foregone conclusion. The explanation seems to be that White overlooked now that his opponent could support the Bishop, and at the same time obviate the danger from the attack of the Knight upon King and Queen.

W. Steinitz v. S. Tinsley.

	WHITE	BLACK
1	P to Q 4	K Kt to B 3
2	P to Q B 4	P to Q B 4 [1]
3	P to Q 5	P to Q 3
4	Q Kt to B 3	P to K Kt 3
5	P to K 4	B to Kt 2
6	B to Q 3 [2]	Castles
7	K Kt to K 2	Q Kt to Q 2
8	Kt to B 4	Kt to K 4
9	B to K 2	P to Q Kt 3
10	P to K R 4	P to K R 4
11	P to K B 3	Q R to Kt sq
12	Kt to R 3	P to R 3
13	P to R 4	R to K sq
14	Kt to B 2	P to K 3
15	B to Kt 5	P × P
16	Kt × P	B to K 3
17	Kt to K 3	Q to Q 2
18	Kt to R 3 [3]	Kt to B 3
19	B to B 4	B × Kt
20	R × B	Kt to Q 5
21	B to Q 3	R to Kt 2
22	K to B 2	Kt to K 3
23	B to Kt 3	B to R 3
24	Kt to Q 5	Kt × Kt
25	B P × Kt	Kt to B 5 [4]
26	B × Kt	B × B
27	B × P	B to K 4
28	B × R	B to Q 5, ch

Black to make his 25th move.

	WHITE	BLACK
29	K to B sq	Q × B
30	Q to Kt 3	R to R sq
31	R to Kt sq	Q to R 3, ch
32	Q to Kt 5	Q × P
33	Q × Q	R × Q
34	P to B 4	R to Kt 5
35	P to Q Kt 3	P to B 5
36	K to K 2	K to Kt 2 [5]
37	K to Q 2	B to B 3
38	R to K 3	P to B 6, ch
39	K to B 2	B to Q 5
40	R to K 2	R to Kt 4 [6]
41	P to Q Kt 4	P to B 4
42	K to Q 3	Resigns.

NOTES BY R. TEICHMANN.

[1] An original way of meeting the Queen's Gambit, but certainly not a good one. The player who in a close game can push his Queen's Pawn to Q 5 and maintain it there has, as a rule, the better game.

[2] Certainly P to K B 4, with a view of forcing P to K 5 sooner or later, was the right course here.

[3] All this seems somewhat inconsistent and without a preconceived plan.

[4] So far Black has done very well, and obtained the superior position, which he could have improved with Kt to B 2 (see diagram), preparing an advance of the Queen's side Pawns. The text move is an oversight which loses the exchange and a Pawn.

[5] B to B 4 seems to give him a much better chance, threatening P × P and R × P, ch.

[6] Concluding the game with another blunder. After this the Rook or Bishop is lost.

C. von Bardeleben v. E. Schiffers.

	WHITE	BLACK
1	P to K 4	P to Q B 4
2	Kt to Q B 3	Kt to Q B 3
3	P to K Kt 3	P to Q 3
4	B to Kt 2	P to K 4 [1]
5	K Kt to K 2	P to B 4
6	P to Q 3	Kt to B 3
7	Castles	P × P [2]
8	P × P	B to K 2
9	Kt to Q 5	Castles
10	P to Q B 3	B to K 3
11	P to K R 3	Q to Q 2
12	K to R 2	Q R to K sq
13	B to K 3	B to Q sq
14	Kt × Kt, ch	B × Kt
15	Q to Q 2	R to Q sq
16	P to Kt 3	P to Q Kt 4 [3]
17	P to Q Kt 4	P × P
18	P × P	B to B 5
19	K R to B sq	Q to K B 2
20	P to Q R 4	P to Q R 3
21	P × P	P × P
22	R to R 3	B to K 2 [4]
23	B to Kt 6	R to Kt sq
24	R to K B 3	Q to K 3
25	R × R, ch	B × R
26	B to R 5	Q to B 2
27	Kt to B 3	Kt to Q 5
28	Q to K 3	B to K 2
29	R to Q sq	R to K B sq
30	P to B 4	Kt to Kt 6
31	B to B 7 [5]	P × P
32	P × P	Q × P, ch
33	Q × Q	R × Q
34	B × P	B × B
35	R × B [6]	R to B 7
36	K to Kt 3	R to B 7
37	Kt to Q 5	Kt to B 8
38	P to K 5 [7]	Kt to K 7, ch

White to make his 38th move.

	WHITE	BLACK
39	K to Kt 4 [8]	P to R 4, ch
40	K to Kt 5 [9]	Kt to Kt 6
41	Kt to K 3	R to K 7
42	K to B 4	P to R 5
43	B to Q 5, ch	B × B
44	R × B [10]	R to B 7, ch
45	K to Kt 4	Kt to K 7
46	R × P	R to B 5, ch
47	K to Kt 5	R to B 6
48	R to Kt 8, ch	K to B 2
49	Kt to B 5	R × P
50	R to Kt 6 [11]	R to Kt 6, ch [12]
51	K × P	R to Kt 8 [13]
52	K to R 3	Kt to B 5 ch
53	K to R 2	R to Kt 7, ch
54	K to R sq	R to K 7
55	R to Kt 7, ch	K to Kt 3
56	Kt to K 7, ch	K to Kt 4
57	Kt to B 6	P to Kt 3
58	R to Kt 5	K to Kt 5
59	R to B 5 [14]	R to Q 7
60	K to Kt sq [15]	R to Q 6
61	P to K 6 [16]	

Drawn game.[17]

AUGUST 28

NOTES BY DR. TARRASCH.

¹ Recommended by Anderssen.

² This exchange is advantageous for White, who gets the open Queen's file, and altogether freer scope. This game offers few interesting points either in the opening or in the middle game. A strenuous fight for the better position. As every move comes, each player has several other moves in consideration besides the actual one in the text. The game is easily understood even without any annotations.

³ To play P to Q Kt 5, and then establish the Knight at Q 5 later on.

⁴ Threatens P to Q 4, and eventually Bishop takes Queen's Knight's Pawn.

⁵ Strong also was P to K B 5 and P to K Kt 4, introducing a Pawn attack on the King's side.

⁶ After a weary fight, the position seems now clear, and White has an advantage, for he has a strong passed Pawn and the Black Queen's Knight's Pawn is also threatened.

⁷ One would now think that White's better position was decisive, but Schiffers finds a clever way of spoiling White's victory.

⁸ K to R 4 was preferable.

⁹ Of course the Pawn cannot be taken on account of Kt to Kt 6, ch, and R × B.

¹⁰ White now wins the Knight's Pawn, whilst the Rook's Pawn is also threatened, but still he cannot enforce the victory.

¹¹ Here was still a chance, though a very weak one, for White to win, namely 50. P to K 6, ch, K × P; 51. R to K 8, ch, K to Q 4 (!), 52. R × Kt.

¹² Black's counter-move to the threat of P to K 6, ch, is most clever.

¹³ Now threatening Kt to B 5 and P to Kt 4, mate.

¹⁴ Black threatens to win by K to Kt 6.

¹⁵ Again Black threatens to win by K to Kt 6, and if R to B 3, ch, Kt to Q 6. Now White could frustrate the attack after K to Kt 6; 61. R to B 3, ch, Kt to Q 6, by 62. K to B sq, or by giving up the exchange.

¹⁶ Black again threatens K to Kt 6, but is again frustrated on account of R to K Kt 5, ch.

¹⁷ A drawn game ought to look like this one. Both players have during seven hours made the greatest exertions to win, but attack and counter-attack have been baffled by the correct defence, and the board is nearly empty after R to Q 8, ch, and Kt × K P.

W. H. K. POLLOCK v J. H. BLACKBURNE.

	WHITE	BLACK		WHITE	BLACK
1	P to K 4	P to K 4	6	B × B	P × P
2	Kt to K B 3	P to Q 3	7	Kt to B 3	P to Q B 3
3	P to Q 4	B to Kt 5	8	Castles	K Kt to B 3
4	P × P	Kt to Q 2¹	9	Q to K 2	Q to B 2
5	B to K 2²	B × Kt	10	Q to B 4³	Kt to Kt 3

	WHITE	BLACK
11	Q to Kt 3	B to K 2
12	P to Q R 4	Castles K R
13	B to K 3	Q Kt to Q 2
14	Q R to Q sq[4]	Kt to B 4
15	Q to B 4	Kt to K 3
16	Kt to K 2	K R to Q sq
17	Kt to Kt 3	P to K Kt 3
18	B to K 2	P to K R 4
19	P to K B 3	Kt to B 5
20	B × Kt[5]	P × B
21	Kt to R sq	Q to Kt 3, ch
22	Kt to B 2	R × R
23	B × R	B to B 4[6]

BLACK

WHITE

White to make his 24th move.

	WHITE	BLACK
24	P to Q Kt 4[7]	B × Kt, ch
25	R × B	R to Q sq
26	Q to B sq	R to Q 7[8]
27	P to Kt 3	P × P
28	P × P	Q to Q 5
29	P to B 3	Q to K 6
30	P to Q B 4	Q to Q 5
31	B to K 2	R to R 7
32	K to R 2	R × P
33	P to Kt 5	R to R 8
34	Q to Kt 2	R to R 7
35	Q to B sq	Kt to Q 2[9]
36	R to Kt 2	Kt to B 4
37	Q to B 2	Q × Q
38	R × Q	Kt to Q 6
39	R to Kt 2	Kt to K 8
40	P × P	P × P
41	R to B 2	Kt × P, ch
42	K to Kt 2	Kt to Q 5
43	B to Q sq	R to R 8[10]
44	R to Q 2	P to Q B 4
45	K to B 2	P to R 4[11]
46	K to K 3	K to B sq
47	K to B 4	P to B 3
48	P to K 5	K to K 2
49	K to K 4	P × P
50	K × P	R to R 6
51	R to Q Kt 2	Kt to B 3, ch
52	K to B 4	Kt to Kt 5
53	R to Q 2	R to Q 6
54	R × R	Kt × R, ch
55	K to Kt 5	Kt to K 4
56	B to Kt 3	K to B 2
57	B to Q sq	K to Kt 2
58	B to Kt 3	Kt to B 2, ch
59	K to B 4	K to B 3
60	K to K 4	K to K 3
61	B to Q sq	Kt to Q 3, ch
62	K to B 4	K to B 3
63	B to Kt 3	P to Kt 4, ch
64	K to B 3	K to K 4
65	K to K 3	Kt to K 5
66	P to Kt 4	P to K R 5
67	B to B 2	Kt to B 3
68	B to Q sq	P to R 6
69	K to B 3	K to Q 5

White resigns.

NOTES BY H. N. PILLSBURY.

[1] The sacrifice of a Pawn so early in the game, merely to secure a slightly quicker development, should not be sound.

[2] 5. P × P, B × P ; 6. B to K 2 was perfectly safe, with a Pawn plus.

AUGUST 28

[3] This attack is premature and results in loss of valuable time. 10. B to K 3 was the correct developing move.

[4] K R to Q sq was the proper move, more especially after having commenced a Pawn advance upon the Queen's wing.

[5] This capture involves White in grave difficulties; he should have moved K R to K sq.

[6] After Q × P; 24. Kt to Q 3, Q to Kt 3 (ch); 25. K to R sq, Q to B 2; 26. P to Q B 3, White obtains a good counter-attack for the lost Pawn.

[7] There appears to have been no necessity for this, and Black could have safely replied, Q × P; 25. Q × Q, B × Q; 26. Kt to Q 3, B to Q 7, with a fine game. White could still have obtained a fair game by 24. P to B 3, Q R to Q sq; 25. B to Kt 3, R to Q 2; 26. P to K Kt 3, &c.

[8] Black plays for a deep game; he could simply win the Queen's wing Pawns, and his opponent could obtain no counter-attack to compensate for their loss.

[9] With the entrance of the Knight Black soon wins a second Pawn, after which the result is merely a question of time.

[10] R × R would have saved time; the two Pawns plus would have settled matters in a shorter time.

[11] P to B 3 at once, followed by K to B 2 and to K 3 would have shortened matters also.

A. Walbrodt v. A. Burn.

	WHITE	BLACK
1	P to K 4	P to K 3
2	P to Q 4	P to Q 4
3	Kt to Q B 3	Kt to K B 3
4	B to Q 3 [1]	P to Q B 4 (!) [2]
5	P × Q P	K P × P [3]
6	P × B P	B × P
7	Kt to K B 3	Castles
8	Castles	Kt to Q B 3
9	B to K Kt 5	B to K 3
10	Q to Q 2	R to K sq
11	Q to K B 4 [4]	B to K 2
12	Kt to Q Kt 5	R to Q B sq
13	Q R to Q sq [5]	Kt to Q Kt 5 (!)
14	B × Kt	Kt × B
15	P × Kt	P × B (!) [6]
16	Q Kt to Q 4	K to R sq
17	K R to K sq	Q to Q 3
18	Q to R 6 [7]	R to K Kt sq
19	Kt to R 4	R to Kt 4
20	Kt × B	P × Kt
21	P to K B 4	R to Kt 2 [8]
22	P to Q 4	R to B 7

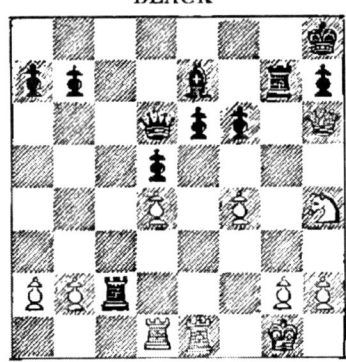

BLACK

WHITE

White to make his 23rd move.

23	R to Q B sq [9]	Q to Kt 5 (!)
24	Q to R 5 [10]	Q to Q 7
25	Kt to B 3	Q × P, mate

Notes by C. von Bardeleben.

[1] A dull continuation. I prefer the usual moves 4. B to Kt 5, or 4. P to K 5.

[2] The right answer.

[3] I believe that still better would be B P × P; the game might proceed then in the following way :—6. B to Kt 5, ch, B to Q 2; 7. Q × P (!) (if 7. P × P (?) then B × B; 8. Kt × B, Q to R 4, ch, or 8. P × P, ch, K × P; 9. Kt × B, Q to R 4, ch, winning a Piece), B × B; 8. Kt × B, P to Q R 3 (!); 9. Kt to Q B 3, Kt to B 3; or, 7. B × B, ch, Q × B; 8. Q × P, Kt to B 3, and Black has in both cases the better development.

[4] The attack introduced by this and the following move is not sound. White should have played 11. Q R to Q sq.

[5] At this juncture 13. P to Q B 3 was absolutely necessary to prevent the following move of Black

[6] Very well played. Black, after having exchanged the hostile King's Bishop, runs the risk of weakening his Pawns on the King's side to obtain thus attacking prospects.

[7] This square is very unfavourable for the Queen. Better would be 10. Q × Q

[8] Of course not Q × P, because of 22. Kt to Kt 6, ch, winning the Queen.

[9] This proves to be fatal at once, but the White game is no longer to be saved (see diagram). If, for instance, 23 Q to R 5, then, R × P; 24. P to R 4, Q × P; 25. R to K B sq, Q to K 6, ch; 26. K to R sq, R to Kt sq; or, 25 Q to K 8, ch (?), R to Kt sq; 26. Q × B, K R × P, ch (!); 27. Kt × R, Q to B 7, ch; 28. K to R sq, Q × Kt, mate. If White defends the Queen's Knight's Pawn with 23. R to Kt sq, Black answers Q to Kt 3.

[10] He should have played 24. Kt to B 3, but only to prolong the struggle. Black has played the attack very cleverly.

Dr. Tarrasch v. D. Janowski.

	WHITE	BLACK		WHITE	BLACK
1	P to Q 4	P to Q 4	12	Kt to Q Kt 5	Kt to K sq
2	P to Q B 4	P to K 3	13	B to K 3	P to Q R 3
3	Kt to Q B 3	Kt to K B 3	14	Kt to B 3	Kt to B 3 [5]
4	B to Kt 5	B to K 2	15	Q to K 2	P to Q Kt 4
5	Kt to B 3	Castles	16	B to Kt 3	B to Kt 2
6	R to B sq [1]	P × P	17	K R to Q sq	Kt to Q Kt 5
7	P to K 3 [2]	P to Q B 4	18	Kt to K 5	Q R to B sq
8	B × P	P × P	19	P to K R 3	Q Kt to Q 4
9	P × P	Kt to B 3	20	Kt × Kt	Kt × Kt
10	Castles	Q to R 4 [3]	21	R × R	R × R
11	B to B 4 [4]	R to Q sq	22	Q to R 5	P to Kt 3

AUGUST 28

WHITE	BLACK	WHITE	BLACK
23 Q to B 3	P to B 4 [6]	26 B to R 6, ch	K to Kt sq
24 Q to Kt 3	K to Kt 2	27 Kt × P	B to B 3
25 P to K R 4	Q to Q sq [7]	28 Kt to K 5, ch	Resigns.

NOTES BY J. H. BLACKBURNE.

[1] Perhaps it is better to play the King's Pawn before this move.

[2] P to K 4 could also be played, and would have led to a more open game.

[3] Q to Kt 3 is more attacking and appears stronger.

[4] This Bishop ought to have retired to K 3 at once.

[5] B to B 3, bringing one more Piece to bear on the weak Queen's Pawn, would have given Black a good game.

[6] This loses; P to B 3 might probably have saved the game.

[7] An unaccountable blunder; the game, however, could not be saved.

H. N. PILLSBURY v. C. SCHLECHTER.

WHITE	BLACK
1 P to Q 4	P to Q 4
2 P to Q B 4	P to K 3
3 Q Kt to B 3	K Kt to B 3
4 B to Kt 5	B to K 2
5 Kt to B 3	Q Kt to Q 2
6 P to K 3	P to Q Kt 3
7 R to B sq [1]	B to Kt 2
8 P × P	P × P
9 B to Q 3	Castles
10 Castles	P to B 4
11 B to Q Kt sq [2]	Kt to K 5 [3]
12 B to B 4	Kt × Kt
13 R × Kt	P to B 5
14 Kt to K 5	P to B 4 [4]
15 K to R sq	Kt × Kt
16 B × Kt	B to Q 3
17 P to B 4	B to B sq [5]
18 Q to R 5	P to Q R 3
19 R to K B 3	R to R 2
20 R to K R 3	P to Kt 3
21 Q to R 6	B × B
22 B P × B	R to K Kt 2
23 R to K B 3	P to Q Kt 4
24 R to Q B sq	Q to K 2 [6]

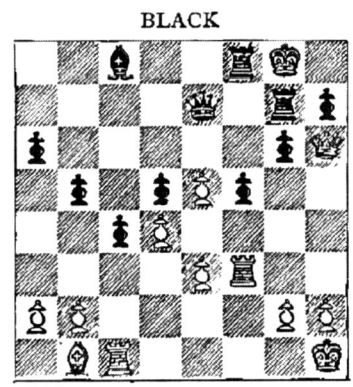

White to make his 25th move.

WHITE	BLACK
25 Q R to K B sq	R (B sq) to B 2
26 P to K R 4	B to K 3
27 P to K Kt 4 [7]	Q to Q 2 [8]
28 P × P	P × P
29 Q to R 5	R to Kt 3
30 B × P	B × B
31 R × B	R × R
32 R × R	P to Kt 5
33 Q to B 3	P to B 6

	WHITE	BLACK
34	P × P	P × P
35	R to B 8, ch	K to Kt 2
36	R to Q Kt 8	Q to K 2
37	Q to B 4	P to K R 4
38	P to K 6 [9]	R × P
39	R to Q B 8	R to K 5 [10]
40	R to B 7	R × Q
41	R × Q, ch	R to B 2
42	R to K 5	P to B 7
43	R to Kt 5, ch	K to R 3
44	R to Kt sq	R to Q Kt 2

White resigns.

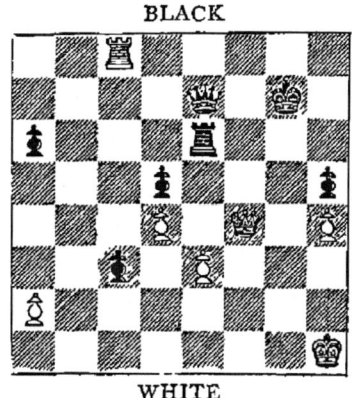

Black to make his 39th move.

NOTES BY W. STEINITZ.

[1] White's game has been modelled chiefly after Steinitz's favourite attack. Here, however, 7. P × P is preferable, for if 7. ... P × P; 8. B to Kt 5, B to Kt 2 ; 9. Kt to K 5, with a strong attack.

[2] As often shown in my annotations in similar positions, it is absolutely injurious to White's game to allow three well-supportable Pawns against two to be established on the Queen's side. The prospect of a King's side attack on which White speculates is quite unreliable in comparison to the disadvantage on the Queen's side to which he is subjected At any rate, Pawns ought to be exchanged first, and thus Black's centre weakened.

[3] It was better to make sure of his superiority on the Queen's side by P to B 5 at once

[4] He had sufficient force on the King's side to ignore any hostile attack in that direction, and systematic operations on the other wing, commencing with P to Q Kt 4, were most in order.

[5] The combination of this with the next five moves, more especially with the two closely following, is full of high ingenuity, which, however, is wasted on an imaginary danger. For all purposes of defence it was only necessary to advance P to K Kt 3 at the right time, and then to play R to B 2, followed by B to K B sq eventually. The Queen's wing was still the proper point of attack to which he should have directed his attention more promptly.

[6] For aggressive purposes on the Queen's side, the Queen was better placed at B 2.

[7] This rash attack and Black's timid reply were only to be accounted for as results of time pressure on both sides.

[8] There was not the slightest danger in capturing the Pawn with a Pawn ahead, while this loses one.

[9] A fatal miscalculation R to Q B 8 led to a most probable draw, for if 38. ... R to Kt 5 ; 39. Q to B 6, ch, &c.

[10] Black seizes his opportunity with scientific exactitude. (See diagram.)

AUGUST 28

H. E. Bird v. R. Teichmann.

	WHITE	BLACK
1	P to K B 4	P to Q 4
2	P to K 3	P to K Kt 3 [1]
3	Kt to K B 3	B to Kt 2
4	Kt to Q B 3	Kt to K B 3
5	P to Q 4	P to Q Kt 3
6	Kt to K 5	B to Kt 2
7	B to K 2	Q Kt to Q 2
8	B to Kt 5	Castles
9	Castles	Kt to Kt sq (!)
10	B to Q 2	P to Q R 3
11	B to K 2	P to Q B 4
12	B to K sq	Kt to B 3
13	B to R 4	P to K 3
14	Kt to Kt 4	P × P
15	P × P	Kt to Kt sq [2]
16	Q to K sq	Q Kt to Q 2
17	B to Q 3	Q to B 2
18	Kt to K 5	Q R to Q B sq
19	R to Q sq	P to Q Kt 4
20	Kt to K 2	Kt to K 5
21	Kt to Kt 3	P to K B 4
22	P to Q B 3	Q Kt × Kt
23	B P × Kt	B to R 3
24	Kt × Kt [3]	Q P × Kt
25	B to B 2	B to Q 4
26	B to Kt 3	P to Kt 4
27	B to K B 2	Q to K B 2
28	Q to K 2	Q to Kt 3
29	P to K R 3	R to Q B 2
30	P to K Kt 3	P to K B 5
31	Q to Kt 4	P to K 6

	WHITE	BLACK
32	B to K sq	R to Q B 5 (!) [4]

White to make his 33rd move.

	WHITE	BLACK
33	K to R 2	Q to K 5
34	R to K Kt sq	P to B 6
35	Q × Q	B × Q
36	B × R	P × B
37	B to B 2	P × B
38	K R to B sq	P to Kt 5
39	R × P	B to K 6
40	R to K sq	B × R
41	R × B	B × P, ch (!)
42	K to Kt sq	B to R 7, ch
43	K to B sq	P to Kt 6
44	R to Kt 4, ch	K to R sq
45	P to Q Kt 3	P to Kt 7, ch
46	K to B 2	B to Kt 8, ch

White resigns.

NOTES BY E. SCHIFFERS.

[1] A good continuation, preventing P to Q Kt 3, B to Q Kt 2, and B to Q 3, as generally played by Bird, and which gives White many chances of attack.

[2] Curious, but practical manœuvres of the Knight.

[3] Black has now obtained a strong passed Pawn.

[4] After this move, Black's Pawns rush forward with irresistible force.

G. Marco v. J. Mason.

	WHITE	BLACK
1	P to K 4	P to K Kt 3
2	P to Q 4	P to Q 3
3	P to Q B 3	B to Kt 2 [1]
4	B to K 3	P to K 4
5	P × P [2]	B × P
6	Kt to B 3	Kt to Q B 3
7	B to Q B 4 [3]	Q to K 2
8	Q Kt to Q 2	B to Kt 2
9	Castles	Kt to B 3
10	B to Q 4	Castles
11	R to K sq	Kt · B
12	Kt × Kt [4]	P to B 4
13	Kt to B 2	B to K 3
14	B to Q 5	B × B
15	P × B	Q to Q 2
16	Kt to K 3	K R to K sq
17	Kt (Q 2) to B 4 [5]	
		P to Q Kt 4
18	Kt to Q 2	Kt to K 5
19	Kt (Q 2) to B sq	
		P to Q R 4
20	Q to B 2	P to R 5
21	P to Q R 3	P to B 5 [6]
22	Kt × P	P × Kt
23	R × Kt	R × R
24	Q × R	Q to Kt 4
25	R to Kt sq	R to K sq
26	Q to B 3	Q to Kt 6 [7]
27	Q to Q sq	Q to Kt 4
28	Kt to K 3	B to R 3
29	Kt to B 2	R to K 4
30	Kt to Kt 4	Q to K sq
31	K to B sq	R to R 4
32	Q to K 2 [8]	Q × Q, ch
33	K × Q	R × R P
34	K to B 3	R to R 4
35	P to Kt 4	R to K 4
36	Kt to B 6	R to K sq
37	R to Q sq	B to Kt 2
38	Kt to R 4	R to Q B sq
39	R to K sq	R to B 4

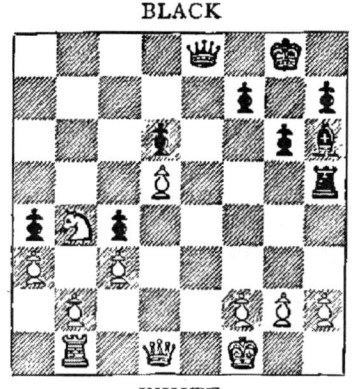

White to make his 32nd move.

	WHITE	BLACK
40	R to K 8, ch	B to B sq
41	Kt to B 6	K to Kt 2
42	Kt to Kt 4 [9]	R to R 4
43	R to B 8	P to R 4
44	R × P	P × P, ch
45	K × P	P to B 4, ch
46	K to B 4	K to B 3
47	R to B 8	B to R 3, ch
48	K to B 3	P to Kt 4
49	R to Q 8	P to Kt 5, ch
50	K to Kt 3	B to B 8
51	R × P, ch	K to Kt 4
52	Kt to Q 3	P to B 5, ch
53	K to Kt 2	P to B 6, ch
54	K to Kt sq [10]	B to Q 7
55	P to B 4	R to R sq
56	P to B 5	R to Q Kt sq
57	R to Kt 6	R to K R sq
58	R to K 6	B to B 5
59	Kt × B	K × Kt
60	P to Q 6	P to Kt 6
61	P × P, ch	K × P
62	R to Kt 6, ch	K to B 5
63	P to Q 7	K to K 6
64	R to K 6, ch	K to B 5
65	R to K 8	Resigns.

AUGUST 28

Notes by H. N. Pillsbury.

[1] Perhaps this is the least objectionable of the Fianchetto openings, but most modern masters prefer to meet the open game face to face. One example being, that the French defence was adopted only once by the first five prize winners, as second players.

[2] The usual development of B to Q 3, Kt to K 2, Kt to Q 2, &c., is considered preferable by most players.

[3] Black should not have left the Bishop to be taken, nor should White fail to take advantage of the omission. After 7 Kt x B, Kt x Kt; 8. B to K 2, &c., with a timely advance of P to K B 4. Black's weakness upon the King's wing was bound to make itself evident sooner or later.

[4] P x Kt, so as to make use of the open file with the Queen's Rook, might also be considered here.

[5] Black has obtained a very good position, and this move enables him to obtain a strong attack with his Queen's wing Pawns; P to Q B 4 was the correct play.

[6] An error, P to K B 4 first (threatening P to Q B 5, Kt to B 4 and to Q 6) was quite strong, and if in answer, 22. P to B 3, Kt to B 3, left Black with a fine game.

[7] B to R 3 would have at least regained the lost Pawn e.g. B to R 3; 27 Kt to K 3, B x Kt; 28 P x B, Q to B 4; 29 R to K sq, R to K 4, &c., or if 27. Kt to Kt 3, R to K 4; 28. Kt to K 4, P to B 4, 29. Kt x Q P, Q x Kt P; 30 Q to Q sq, Q x Q B P, &c.

[8] White can well afford the sacrifice of the Rook's Pawn, and, owing to the isolation of the Black Pawns on the Queen's wing, this seems the shortest route to victory. (See diagram.)

[9] Winning a Pawn, as he threatens R to R 8.

[10] White avoids complications, but there was nothing to fear from K to Kt 3; if in answer R to R sq, then 55 R to K 6, R to K R sq; 56. R to K 5, ch, winning easily. After this point, however, winning is merely a question of a few moves, anyhow.

AUGUST 29.

Thursday, August 29, is the last bye day, and it is the Carnival week at Hastings. The masters are supplied with tickets for the various entertainments, and some enjoy the fun, whilst others rest for the final struggle for position, as no one game is too easy and every opponent must be respected. There are some adjourned games to play off, and the players and others enter the room smothered with *confetti*, for a miniature battle of Hastings is raging outside, and the carpet and furniture inside the room soon give abundant evidence of the tempting festivities.

AUGUST 30.

On this day Tarrasch meets Lasker, and a sturdy fight ensues, a draw seeming likely; Steinitz, too, has a severe tussle with Marco. At the end of the day Tchigorin leads again with 15, Lasker and Pillsbury are 14½, Steinitz and Tarrasch (still to meet) 12, Walbrodt, Teichmann, and Schlechter 10, Bardeleben and Schiffers 9½ with an adjourned game between them.

A. Walbrodt v. A. Albin.

	WHITE	BLACK		WHITE	BLACK
1	P to K 4	P to K 3	26	P to Q Kt 3	P × P
2	P to Q 4	P to Q 4	27	Q × P	Q to Kt 4
3	Kt to Q B 3	Kt to K B 3	28	Q to Q 3	Q to R 4
4	B to K Kt 5	B to K 2	29	Q to Q 2	Kt to Kt 5
5	P to K 5	K Kt to Q 2	30	P to K Kt 4 [5]	Q to B 4
6	B × B	Q × B	31	Q to B 3	Q to Kt 4
7	Q to Kt 4 [1]	Castles	32	R to Kt 2	R to R 6
8	P to K B 4	P to K B 4	33	P × P	Kt × R P (?)
9	Q to R 3	P to Q R 3			
10	Kt to B 3	P to Q B 4			
11	Castles	Kt to Q B 3			
12	K to Kt sq	P to Q Kt 4 [2]			
13	P × P	Kt × P			
14	Kt to Q 4	Kt × Kt			
15	R × Kt	P to Kt 5			
16	Kt to Q sq [3]	Kt to K 5			
17	Q to K 3	B to Q 2			
18	B to Q 3	Kt to B 4			
19	P to K R 3	B to Kt 4 [4]			
20	B × B	P × B			
21	R × Kt P	K R to Kt sq			
22	P to Q B 3	Kt to R 3			
23	R to Q 4	P to Kt 5			
24	K R to K sq	Q to Q B 2			
25	R to K 2	Q to R 4			

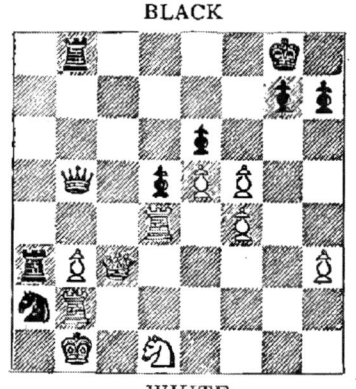

BLACK

WHITE

White to make his 34th move.

34 Q to Q 3 [6]   R to Q B sq (!) [7]

Photo., Brodshaw, Hastings

WHITE	BLACK	WHITE	BLACK
35 R to B 2	R × P, ch	40 K to R 2	Q to R 4, ch
36 Kt to Kt 2	Kt to B 6, ch	41 Q to R 3	R to R 8, ch
37 K to B sq	R × Kt [8]	42 K × R	Q × Q, ch
38 R × R	Kt to K 7, ch	43 K to Kt sq	Kt × R
39 K to Kt sq	R to B 8, ch		White resigns.

NOTES BY R. TEICHMANN.

[1] I do not believe in this move, whether played in this or other variations of the French defence; the attack of the second player on the Queen's side is as a rule stronger than White's direct King's side attack.

[2] Black inaugurates at once a powerful attack on the Queen's side, whilst White's attack is not sufficiently prepared yet.

[3] If R × P then Kt to K 5, followed by Kt to B 7, wins the exchange.

[4] This sacrifice of a Pawn, although leading to a strong attack, does not appear to be quite correct. Simply 19. ... Kt × B, followed by K R to Q B sq, B to Kt 4, and P to Q R 4, would have yielded a lasting attack without loss of material.

[5] There is really nothing threatened on the Queen's side now, and he is quite right in pursuing his attack on the other wing.

[6] An unaccountable mistake. Black's last move was an error, and now 34. R × Kt, R × P, ch; 35. Q × R (!), Q × Q, ch; 36. R to Kt 2 would have given White a won game (see diagram).

[7] Ingenious and decisive; after this unexpected stroke the White position is beyond remedy.

[8] Black finishes the game with great vigour and elegance.

W. H. K. POLLOCK v. M. TCHIGORIN.

WHITE	BLACK
1 P to K 4	P to K 4
2 Kt to K B 3	Kt to Q B 3
3 B to B 4	B to B 4
4 P to Q Kt 4	B × Kt P
5 P to B 3	B to R 4
6 P to Q 4	P × P
7 Castles	P to Q 3
8 P × P	B to Kt 3
9 Kt to B 3	Kt to R 4
10 B to K Kt 5	P to K B 3
11 B to R 4 [1]	Kt to K 2
12 R to K sq [2]	B to Kt 5
13 P to K 5 [3]	Q P × P
14 Q P × P	Q × Q
15 Q R × Q	Kt × B
16 P × P	P × P

White to make his 21st move.

	WHITE	BLACK		WHITE	BLACK
17	B × P [4]	K to B 2	30	B to R 3	R to K B 4
18	B × Kt	B × Kt	31	K R to B 7	R to Kt 4, ch
19	P × B	B to R 4	32	K to R 3	B to B 3
20	R to Q 7	Kt to Kt 3 [5]	33	P to B 4	R to R 4, ch
21	R × P	K R to Q B sq	34	K to Kt 2	K to B 4, ch
22	R × P	B × Kt	35	K to R sq	Kt to B 6
23	B to R 3, ch	K to B 3	36	R to Kt 5, ch	K to K 3
24	K R to K 7	R to Kt sq, ch	37	P to B 5, ch	R × P
25	K to B sq	Q R to Q sq	38	R to B 6, ch	K to Q 2
26	R to B 7, ch	K to Kt 3	39	R to Q 6, ch	K to B 2
27	K to Kt 2	Kt to B 5	40	R to Kt sq	R to K R 4
28	B to B 5	R to Q 4		White resigns.	
29	B to B 8	Kt to Q 7			

NOTES BY C. VON BARDELEBEN.

[1] I prefer 11. B to B 4.

[2] A weak move. White should have played 12. Q to K 2, and if Black answers B to Kt 5 ; 13. Q R to Q sq ; by this line of play White would prepare the advance of the King's Pawn better than by 12. R to K sq.

[3] This proves to be disadvantageous

[4] If 17. Kt to Q 5, then Castles Q R ; 18. Kt × Kt, ch, K to Kt sq, and Black has the better game.

[5] An excellent move, which practically decides the game in Black's favour. (See diagram)

J. H. BLACKBURNE v. J. MASON.

	WHITE	BLACK		WHITE	BLACK
1	P to K 4	P to K 4	18	R × B	R × R
2	Kt to K B 3	Kt to Q B 3	19	Q × R	K Kt to K 2
3	B to B 4	B to B 4	20	R to K sq	Castles [3]
4	P to Q Kt 4	B × P	21	Kt to Kt 5	Q to B 3
5	P to B 3	B to R 4	22	Kt to K 6 [4]	R to B 2
6	P to Q 4	P × P	23	P to R 3	P to K R 3
7	Castles	P × P	24	Kt × B P	Kt to Kt 3
8	P to K 5 [1]	P to Q 4 [2]	25	R to K 8, ch [5]	K to R 2
9	P × P en p.	Q × P	26	Kt to K 6	Q to B 4
10	Q to Kt 3	B to K 3	27	P to B 3	Q Kt to K 4
11	B × B	P × B	28	Q to K 2	R to B 3
12	R to Q sq	Q to Kt 5	29	Kt to B 5	R to B 3
13	Q × P, ch	Q to K 2	30	Kt to K 4	Kt to B 5 [6]
14	Q to Kt 3	P to B 7	31	Q to K 3 [7]	Q to Kt 3 [8]
15	Q × B P	R to Q sq	32	Q × Kt	Q × R
16	Q Kt to Q 2	Q to B 2	33	Kt to Q 6	Kt to Kt 3
17	B to R 3	B × Kt	34	Q to Q 2	Q to K 4

AUGUST 30

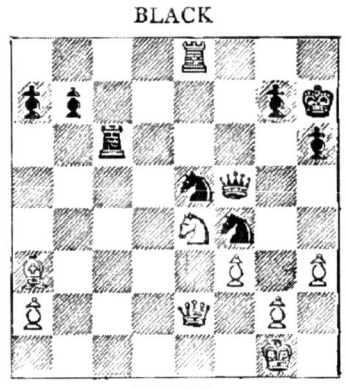

White to make his 31st move.

	WHITE	BLACK
35	Kt to K 4	Q to Q Kt 4
36	B to Kt 2	R to B 2
37	K to R 2	R to Q 2
38	Q to B sq	Q to K 7
39	B to B 3	Kt to R 5
40	Q to Kt 2	Kt × P, ch
41	K to Kt 3	Q × Kt
42	P × Kt	Q to Kt 3, ch
43	K to R 2	R to Q 8
44	Q to K B 2	Q to Q 6
45	B to Kt 4	R to Q B 8
46	Q to R 4	Q to B 7, ch
47	K to Kt 3	R to Kt 8, ch

White resigns.

NOTES BY E. SCHIFFERS.

[1] The best continuation here, as is well known, is Q to Kt 3 (!).

[2] A good move pointed out by Zukertort. The 'Handbuch' gives also 8. K Kt to K 2.

[3] White has lost the attack, and has not regained the Pawn; 'the peculiarity of this opening,' as Hoffer remarked.

[4] If 22. R to K 6, then might follow Q to K B 4 (Q to Q R 8, ch, R to K sq); 23. B × Kt (23. R × Kt, Kt × R, and if 24. B × Kt, Q to Kt 8, ch, &c.), R to K sq, and afterwards R × B or P to K R 3.

[5] White succeeds in regaining the Gambit Pawn. We think that by careful defensive play White could obtain a draw.

[6] Taking advantage now of the retirement of White's Rook from the game, Black obtains the attack, winning the exchange.

[7] Other moves are not better; if Q to Q 2, then Kt to B 5, or if Q to K B 2, then Q to Kt 3, threatening Kt × P, ch. (See diagram.)

[8] Still stronger would have been Kt × Kt P, and if 32. K × Kt, then Q to Kt 3, ch; 33. K to R sq, Q × R, and if then 34. P to K B 4, R to K 3; 35. P × Kt, R × P, &c. 31. R to Q B 7 would also win.

A. BURN v. R. TEICHMANN.

	WHITE	BLACK		WHITE	BLACK
1	P to Q 4	P to Q 4	8	P to Q Kt 4	P to K 4
2	P to Q B 4	P to K 3	9	P × P [4]	Kt × K P
3	Kt to Q B 3	Kt to K B 3	10	Kt × Kt [5]	B × Kt
4	Kt to K B 3	P to Q B 3 [1]	11	B to Kt 2	Q to K 2
5	P to K 3 [2]	B to Q 3	12	B to K 2 [6]	Castles
6	B to Q 3	Q Kt to Q 2	13	Q to B 2	B to Q 2
7	P to B 5 [3]	B to B 2	14	Castles	Q R to K sq

WHITE	BLACK
15 Q R to Q sq	B to Kt sq [7]
16 Kt to Kt sq	Kt to K 5
17 Kt to Q 2	P to K B 4
18 B to Q 4	Kt to Kt 4 [8]
19 B to Q 3	P to B 5
20 K to R sq	Q to B 2
21 Kt to K B 3 [9]	Kt × Kt
22 P × Kt	Q to R 4 [10]
23 R to Kt sq	R to B 2 [11]
24 Q to K 2	B to K 4
25 B to B 2 [12]	R to B 3
26 B × B [13]	and Black

announced mate in 4 moves (see diagram).

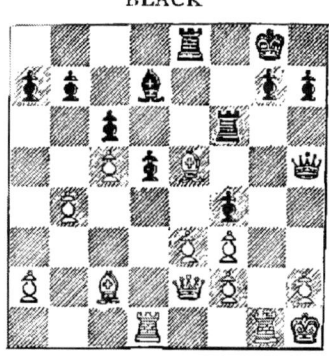

Position at the end.

NOTES BY DR. TARRASCH.

[1] This move in the Queen's Gambit chiefly cramps the Queen's side. Preferable is B to K 2, and, as soon as possible, P to Q B 4.

[2] I prefer B to B 4 or Kt 5.

[3] In regard to this advance, compare the game Burn v. Tarrasch (Round 9, August 16). One may make this advance and then continue with P to Q Kt 4, P to Q R 4, P to Kt 5, P to R 5, and P to R 6. Hereby one usually gets an advantage on the Queen's side, but one must remember that Black will advance in the centre with his King's Pawns and then readily proceeds to an attack on the King's side. Against this attack one must be armed, and the advance of P to Q B 5 should only be made after the proper development of the Pieces.

[4] This move is not suitable to the combination commenced with P to B 5, as the Pawn at B 5, in case the White Pawns advance, will become too weak. White should therefore play B from Q 3 to K 2, where he ought to have gone at once when the advance of the Queen's Bishop's Pawn was planned.

[5] B to K 2 was better, followed eventually by Kt to Q 4, or at once Kt to Q 4.

[6] White has now not the slightest advantage from his chain of Pawns on the Queen's side; Black's Pawns and Pieces are much better placed, and White's King's side is constantly threatened with an attack.

[7] To make room for the Queen.

[8] To prepare the way for P to B 5.

[9] White is very cramped, but this move ruins his game.

[10] It is now difficult to defend the King's Rook's Pawn.

[11] Not Q × B P, ch ; 24. R to Kt 2, B to R 6, because of 25. B × R P, ch, &c. The King's Knight's Pawn must be defended.

[12] Better to exchange the Bishops at once.

[13] He evidently overlooks the highly elegant termination of a game played by Black with great energy and skill.

AUGUST 30

D. JANOWSKI v. C. SCHLECHTER.

	WHITE	BLACK
1	P to Q 4	P to Q 4
2	P to Q B 4	P to K 3
3	Kt to Q B 3	Kt to K B 3
4	B to Kt 5 [1]	Q Kt to Q 2 [2]
5	P × P	P × P
6	P to K 3 [3]	B to K 2
7	Kt to B 3	Castles
8	B to Q 3	P to B 3
9	Castles	R to K sq
10	R to B sq	Kt to K 5
11	B to K B 4 [4]	Kt × Kt
12	P × Kt [5]	Kt to B sq [6]
13	R to Kt sq	B to Q 3
14	B × B	Q × B
15	Kt to K 5	P to B 3
16	Kt to B 3	R to K 2 [7]
17	P to B 4	P × P [8]
18	B × P, ch	B to K 3
19	Q to Kt 3	K to R sq
20	Kt to Q 2	B × B
21	Kt × B	Q to Q 4
22	K R to Q B sq [9]	
		Q R to K sq
23	Q to R 3	Kt to Kt 3
24	Q to Q 6 [10]	R to Q sq
25	Q to Kt 3	P to K B 4
26	Q to Kt 5	Q R to K sq [11]
27	P to K R 4	P to B 5 [12]

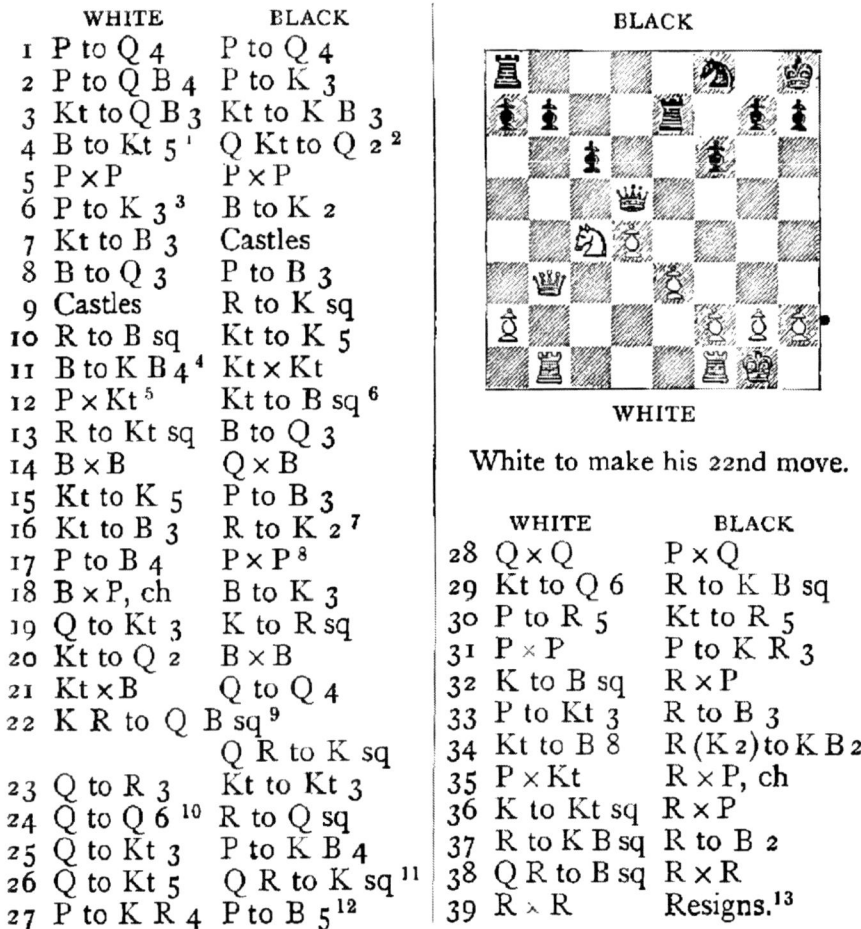

White to make his 22nd move.

	WHITE	BLACK
28	Q × Q	P × Q
29	Kt to Q 6	R to K B sq
30	P to R 5	Kt to R 5
31	P × P	P to K R 3
32	K to B sq	R × P
33	P to Kt 3	R to B 3
34	Kt to B 8	R (K 2) to K B 2
35	P × Kt	R × P, ch
36	K to Kt sq	R × P
37	R to K B sq	R to B 2
38	Q R to B sq	R × R
39	R × R	Resigns. [13]

NOTES BY S. TINSLEY.

[1] Several authorities agree in commending the playing of this Bishop out to the King's side (he may go to B 4 or Kt 5) at an early stage of the Queen's Pawn game. Personally I have usually retained the Piece for Queen's side defence, &c., but his scope is limited in that case after P to K 3.

[2] This move, it will be seen, constitutes a neat trap.

[3] Supposing now 6. Kt × P, then the intention evidently is Kt × Kt; 7. B × Q, B to Kt 5, ch, and wins. But as 6. Kt × P is impracticable, it was scarcely good to capture the Pawn and open the diagonal for Black's Bishop.

[4] This also is a good deal in the nature of a trap. By it Kt × Q P is threatened at once. It will be observed Black could not retake the Piece except on penalty of losing his Queen by B to B 7.

⁵ White has already a shade of advantage—possibly more; but it is not easy to find a manifestly superior move to that chosen by Herr Schlechter at this point.

⁶ Usually in the Queen's Pawn defence, this excellent move may be commended when feasible.

⁷ It is evident that Black's Queen's Knight's Pawn is a source of anxiety and weakness as well as a hindrance to development in this variation, especially with the file open for White's Queen's Rook. Hence the whole line of play adopted by Black is scarcely worthy of imitation, and the old style of P to Q Kt 3, &c., would certainly in this case have been better.

⁸ The capture, again, gives White just what he desires, viz. the open game. There seems no objection to B to K 3 now.

⁹ A strong supporting move. But now Q to R 3, with the double threat Q × R and Kt to Kt 6, seems almost unanswerable. If the reply is K R to K sq, then Kt to Q 6. (See diagram.)

¹⁰ Q × R P is obviously unsound, the reply being P to Q Kt 4, winning the Knight.

¹¹ The threat was Kt to K 5, and if Kt × Kt, Q × R.

¹² It was evidently anticipated that this move, which first lost a Pawn, and ultimately a Piece, would at least equalise the game. The defence, however, is excellent, and the last few moves deserve special notice.

¹³ White threatens, among other things of a disagreeable nature, Kt to K 7, R to B 8, and Kt to Kt 6, with a mating position.

I. Gunsberg v. C. von Bardeleben.

	WHITE	BLACK
1	P to K 4	P to K 4
2	P to K B 4	P to Q 4
3	K P × P	P to K 5
4	Q to K 2 ¹	Kt to K B 3
5	Kt to Q B 3	B to Q 3
6	Kt × P	Castles
7	Kt × Kt, ch	Q × Kt
8	Q to B 3	B to K B 4
9	P to Q 3	B to Kt 5, ch
10	K to Q sq	Kt to Q 2
11	P to B 3 ²	B × B P ³
12	P × B	Q × P
13	R to Kt sq	Kt to B 4
14	Q to B 2 ⁴	Kt × P
15	Q to Kt 3	Q R to Q sq
16	B × Kt	B × B
17	R to Kt 2	R × P

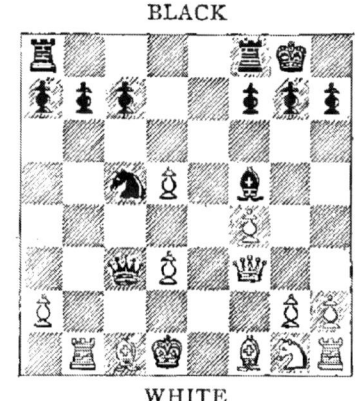

White to make his 14th move.

WHITE	BLACK
18 R to Q 2	R to K sq (!)

White resigns.

AUGUST 30

NOTES BY R. TEICHMANN.

[1] I prefer the following variation, which was played by Dr. Tarrasch against Walbrodt in the Leipsic Tournament, 1894:—4. Kt to Q B 3, Kt to K B 3; 5. P to Q 3, B to Q Kt 5; 6. P × P, Kt × P; 7. Q to Q 4, B × Kt; 8. P × B, Castles; 9. B to K 2, regaining the Pawn with a good game.

[2] White has a very difficult defence; of course if P to K Kt 4, then Q to R 5. With the text move White tries to force his game; it would have been better to prepare the move with Kt to K 2.

[3] A bold and ingenious sacrifice, which, if not quite correct on analysis, gives him certainly a most embarrassing attack.

[4] This defence is unintelligible, the more so as the Queen has to play again next move. The position after Black's sacrifice is extremely difficult and interesting; the best defence appears to be, Kt to K 2, but even then Black maintains an overwhelming attack, always getting a compensation in Pawns or position for the sacrificed Piece: e.g. 14. Kt to K 2, Q to R 4, best (if Q × P, ch; 15. Q × Q, Kt × Q; 16. B to K 3, Kt to B 7, ch; 17. B × Kt, B × R; 18. Kt to B 3, and White has the best of it); 15. Kt to Q 4, Q × P; 16. Kt × B, Q × R; 17. Q to B 2, Kt × P; 18. Q to B 2, Kt to B 7, ch; 19. Q × Kt, Q × Kt.

J. MIESES v. B. VERGANI.

	WHITE	BLACK
1	P to K 4	P to K 4
2	Kt to Q B 3	Kt to Q B 3
3	P to K Kt 3	B to B 4
4	B to Kt 2	P to Q 3
5	Kt to R 4	B to Kt 3 [1]
6	Kt to K 2	B to Kt 5 [2]
7	P to K B 3	B to Q 2
8	Kt × B	R P × Kt
9	P to Q 3	K Kt to K 2
10	P to K B 4	B to Kt 5 [3]
11	P to K R 3	B × Kt
12	Q × B	Kt to Kt 3 [4]
13	P to B 5	Kt to B sq
14	Castles	Kt to Q 2
15	P to B 3	Castles
16	P to B 6 [5]	P × P [6]
17	B to R 6	K to R sq
18	B × R	Q × B
19	B to B 3	Q to Kt 2
20	B to Kt 4	R to Q sq [7]
21	Q to B 3	Q Kt to Kt sq
22	K to R 2	R to Kt sq

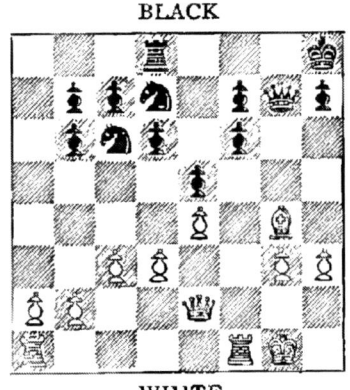

White to make his 21st move.

	WHITE	BLACK
23	R to K Kt sq	Kt to B sq
24	Q R to K B sq	
		Q Kt to Q 2
25	B × Kt	Kt × B
26	Q to B 5	R to Q sq
27	P to K Kt 4	Q to Kt 3
28	P to Kt 5	Q × Q

	WHITE	BLACK		WHITE	BLACK
29	R × Q	R to K B sq [8]	43	R × P	K to K sq
30	P × P	Kt to B 4	44	R to R 8, ch	K to Q 2
31	R to R 5	Kt to Q 2	45	R to R 8	P to B 4
32	R to R 6	R to K Kt sq	46	P × P	Kt P × P
33	R × R, ch	K × R	47	R × P	P to B 5
34	K to Kt 3 [9]	Kt to B 4	48	R to R 7	Kt to Q 5, ch [13]
35	K to Kt 4	Kt × Q P	49	P × Kt	P to B 6
36	K to B 5	Kt to B 5 [10]	50	R × P, ch	K to B 3
37	R to R 4	Kt to K 3 [11]	51	R to B 8	K to Kt 2
38	R to Kt 4, ch	K to B sq	52	P to B 7	P to B 7
39	P to Kt 4	P to Kt 4	53	R to B 8	K × R
40	R to K Kt sq	P to Kt 3	54	P Queens	K to Q 2
41	R to Q R sq	P to R 3	55	Q to B 7, ch	K to Q sq
42	P to Q R 4 [12]	P × P	56	Q to B 4	Resigns.

NOTES BY I. GUNSBERG.

[1] K Kt to K 2 is not amiss here, as Kt × B need hardly be dreaded

[2] As White intends to take Black's King's Bishop with his Queen's Knight, this move has no point. For with a Black King's Bishop off the board, White can safely play P to K B 3.

[3] Black would have done better to preserve this Bishop. B to Kt 5 again is useless, P to K B 4 was permissible.

[4] P × P was best. Anything to prevent the solid phalanx threatened by P to B 5. P × P would somewhat loosen White's position.

[5] A bold and enterprising idea.

[6] A difficult position. If Kt × P, B to Kt 5 would probably have followed. We should almost have preferred this way of defence, for if Black then plays Kt to K 2, White must get rid of his Queen's Bishop by B × Kt, in order to continue the attack, and this Bishop off the board would have been a point in Black's favour.

[7] If Kt to B sq, the King's Bishop's Pawn could not have been successfully defended

[8] Black defends himself with considerable ability. If he had played P × P, White would have replied R × B P, getting his two Rooks into play.

[9] A rather bold course White might have prevented the loss of a Pawn by P to Q Kt 4, and it is not apparent that Black could do anything to prevent White bringing his King into the game, as the Black King cannot move

[10] Of course White's endeavour is directed towards checking with the Rook, playing R to Kt 7, thus gaining either the Rook's Pawn or the King's Bishop's Pawn. As Black has hardly any favourable prospect of preventing this, he might just as well have tried his luck with Kt × P.

[11] If P to K R 4—

38	R × Kt	P × R	40	K to Kt 5	P to R 5
39	K × P	K to R 2	41	K to R 5	P to Kt 4

AUGUST 30

	WHITE	BLACK		WHITE	BLACK
42	K to Kt 5	P to B 4	45	K to Kt 5	K to Kt sq
43	P to Kt 4	P to Kt 3	46	K × P, and White will win.	
44	K to R 5	P to B 5			

Of course Black may vary his tactics on the Queen's side, but so may also White. The foregoing should only serve as a useful example underlying this end game, how to gain the opposition. Should Black at any time attempt to play P to B 3 and P to Q 4, White must play his K to B 5, then he would be in a position to play P to K 5, and P to K 6. Black could not have played Kt to Kt 3 with any advantage, as after R to Kt 4, White would come on with his King's Rook's Pawn.

[12] No doubt the quickest way to bring matters to a crisis. White might, however, have gone after the King's Rook's Pawn by R to K Kt sq, R to Kt 4, and R to R 4.

[13] Better to have a futile idea than no ideas at all.

G. Marco v. W. Steinitz.

	WHITE	BLACK		WHITE	BLACK
1	P to K 4	P to K 4	28	P × R	R to Kt sq [5]
2	K Kt to B 3	Q Kt to B 3	29	Kt to B 4	R × P
3	B to Kt 5	P to Q R 3	30	B to Kt 3 [6]	R to Kt 4
4	B to R 4	P to Q 3	31	Q to B 6	B to B sq (!)
5	Castles	Kt to K 2 [1]	32	Q × R P	Q to Kt 4
6	P to B 3	P to K Kt 3	33	R to K B sq	Kt × Kt
7	P to Q 4	B to Q 2	34	B × Kt	Q × K P, ch
8	B to K 3	B to Kt 2	35	K to R sq	R to K B 4
9	P × P	P × P			
10	Q Kt to Q 2	Castles			
11	R to K sq	Kt to B sq			
12	B to B 5	R to K sq			
13	Kt to B sq	P to Q Kt 3			
14	B to R 3	Kt (B sq) to R 2			
15	Q to Q 3	Q B to B sq			
16	Q to K 2	B to Kt 2			
17	Kt to K 3	P to Q Kt 4			
18	B to B 2	P to Kt 5 [2]			
19	B × P	Kt × B			
20	P × Kt	Kt to Kt 4			
21	Q to B 4 [3]	Kt to Q 3			
22	Q to Kt 3	Kt × P			
23	Q R to Q sq	Kt to Q 3			
24	Kt to Q 5 [4]	P to K 5			
25	Kt to Q 2	B × Kt			
26	Q × B	P to K 6 (!)			
27	R × P	R × R			

White to make his 36th move.

36	R to R sq (?) [7]	
		B to Q 3 (!)
37	B to B sq [8]	B × P

White resigns.

NOTES BY C. VON BARDELEBEN.

[1] I prefer Kt to B 3 here.
[2] Black being very cramped rightly sacrifices a Pawn in order to get an easier game.
[3] A weak move, which loses at once the gained Pawn. Better would be 21 Kt to B 4, to plant the Knight at R 5.
[4] 24 Kt to Q 2 would be better.
[5] If B × P, then 29 Kt to B 4.
[6] With 30. Kt × Kt, P × Kt ; 31. Q × P, Q × Q ; 32. R × Q, R × P, 33. B to Kt 3, the game would have ended in a draw. The move 30 B to Kt 3 is somewhat dangerous.
[7] A very weak move, after which the game of the first player becomes hopeless. Black has in any case the better game, but White could escape with a draw, perhaps, if he played 36 R × R, P × R ; 37. P to K R 3, B to B 4 ; 38. K to R 2, Q to Kt 8, ch ; 39. K to Kt 3, Q to B 7, ch ; 40. K to R 2, B to Q 3, ch ; 41. K to R sq, Q to K 8, ch , 42 B to B sq, Q to Kt 6 ; 43. K to Kt sq, &c.
[8] White cannot save the game ; if 37. P to K R 3, then Q to Kt 6, and Black wins.

H. E. BIRD v. E SCHIFFERS.

	WHITE	BLACK		WHITE	BLACK
1	P to K 4	P to K 4	25	B × Kt	P × B
2	Kt to K B 3	Kt to Q B 3	26	Castles K R	B to K 2
3	B to B 4	Kt to B 3	27	Kt to Q 2 [5]	R to Q sq
4	Kt to Kt 5	P to Q 4	28	Kt to B 4	B to B 3
5	P × P	Kt to R 4	29	Q R to B sq	Q × P
6	B to Kt 5, ch	P to B 3	30	Q × Q	R × Q
7	P × P	P × P	31	Kt × P	B × B P
8	Q to B 3	Q to B 2 [1]	32	Kt to B 4	R to K sq
9	B to K 2 [2]	B to Q 3	33	R to B 2	B to B 3
10	Kt to B 3	Castles	34	P to R 5 [6]	P to B 6
11	P to Q 3	R to Kt sq	35	Kt to K 3 [7]	P × P
12	P to K R 4 [3]	B to K Kt 5	36	K × P	P to B 5
13	Q to K 3	B × B	37	Kt to Kt 4	P to B 6, ch
14	Q × B	P to B 4	38	K to R 3 [8]	B to Q 5
15	K Kt to K 4	Kt × Kt	39	K R to Q B sq	R to K 7 [9]
16	Kt × Kt [4]	P to B 4	40	K to Kt 3 [10]	B to Kt 7
17	Kt to Kt 5	Q to Q 2	41	R × B	R × R
18	P to Q Kt 3	Kt to B 3	42	R × P	R(Kt 7)to Q 7 [11]
19	P to Q B 3	Q R to K sq	43	R to R 5 [12]	R to Q 4
20	B to K 3	P to Q R 4	44	R to R 8, ch	K to R 2
21	Q to B 3	Kt to K 2	45	R to R 7	R to K B 4
22	Q to R 3	Kt to Q 4	46	P to Kt 4	R to Q 5
23	B to Q 2	P to R 3	47	Kt to K 3	R to Kt 4, ch
24	Kt to K 4	Kt to B 5			

AUGUST 30

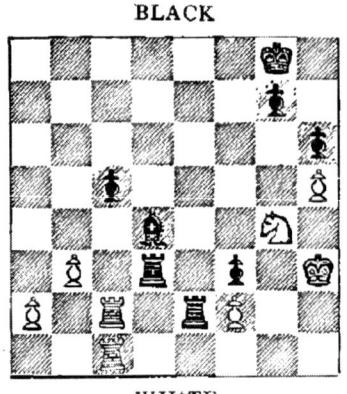

White to make his 40th move.

WHITE	BLACK
48 K × P	R × Kt P [13]
49 P to R 3	R to K R 5
50 K to K 2	R (R 5) × P
51 R to Q 7	R to K R 5
52 R to Q 3	R to Q R 5
53 R to B 3	R to Kt 8
54 Kt to B 4	P to R 4
55 Kt to Kt 2	R to K 5, ch
56 K to Q 2	R (Kt 8) to K 8
57 K to Q 3	R to K B 5
58 R to B 2	R to B 6, ch
59 K to Q 4	R × R P
60 Kt to B 4	R to K B 6

White resigns.

NOTES BY W. STEINITZ.

[1] If 8. ... P to K 5 (?); 9. Kt × K P, Q to K 2 (or 9. ... P × B; 10. Kt × Kt, ch, followed by Q × R); 10. B to Q 3, B to Kt 5; 11. Q to B 4, maintaining his Pawns.

[2] Mr. Cheshire of Hastings informs me that he originated the combination of White's last two moves in games played by him about 1883, some of which were at the time published. The last move seems preferable to 9. B to R 4, which in theory and practice has been commonly adopted before.

[3] The advance of this Pawn only weakens the King's side and otherwise serves no good purpose. Also it happens, this very Pawn becomes subsequently detached from this wing, being compelled to advance further, and its loss decides the game for the opponent.

[4] Strategical considerations pointed unanimously to P × Kt as the superior and even compulsory move. It should have been foreseen that the Queen's Bishop's Pawn would have to be advanced, and subsequently the Queen's Pawn would become weak; furthermore there was the open Queen's file for White, and Black's King's Bishop's Pawn was practically stopped. There was also a supported foothold provided for White's Knight at Q 5, and a long diagonal was opened for his Queen on the other wing. Not a single plea of correspondingly equal value could be advanced for the move adopted.

[5] The Knight has returned from his solitary wanderings on the other wing, but is now actually in the way of necessities of the defence of White's Queen's Pawn.

[6] Compare note 3.

[7] White's game breaks up after this. A much better defence was 35. P × P, R × P; 36. Kt to K 3, B to Q 5; 37. K to Kt 2, R to B 5; 38. R to Q sq or K R sq, with very fair drawing prospects.

[8] Loss of time. Compare his move after next.

[9] Black's play is remarkably clever, and the gain of the exchange

which on the next move becomes apparent is already forced. (See diagram.)

[10] If 40. R × R, P × R, dis. ch, followed by R to Q 8.

[11] Perhaps the safest in combination with the next move, though 42. ... R × R P; 43. R to B 8, ch, K to R 2; 44. Kt to K 5, R to Q 4; 45. Kt to Kt 6, R × P, was equally good, as Black's King would escape from the checks *via* Kt sq and B 2.

[12] In view of White having been reluctant to capture the Pawn, his best chance was now to advance the Knight's Pawn. If he could then push the other Pawn to R 4 without being compelled to exchange Rooks he would make sure of a draw at least.

[13] A part of the plan formed on the forty-second move; all this is acute play. The key to White's position on the Queen's side is captured, and since the King's Rook's Pawn cannot escape either, the game is virtually over already.

[We believe that the combination of the eighth and ninth moves is a complete answer to the Two Knights' Defence. White apparently maintains the Pawn with perfect safety and with patience soon gets attacking chances. It would be interesting to see it thrashed out by our great masters.—ED.]

H. N. Pillsbury *v.* S. Tinsley.

	WHITE	BLACK		WHITE	BLACK
1	P to Q 4	P to Q 4	23	K to R sq	Q × Q B P
2	P to Q B 4	P to K 3	24	Kt × R	R × Kt
3	Kt to Q B 3	Kt to K B 3	25	P to Q Kt 4	Q × P [6]
4	B to Kt 5	P to B 3 [1]	26	B × P	Kt to B 3
5	P to K 3	Q Kt to Q 2	27	B to Kt 6	R to K B sq
6	Kt to B 3	B to Q 3	28	R to Q Kt sq	Q to Q 3
7	B to Q 3	P to K R 3	29	Q R to Q sq	Kt to Q 4
8	B to R 4	Castles			
9	Castles	R to K sq [2]			
10	P to K 4	P × K P			
11	Kt × P	B to K 2			
12	Q to K 2	Kt × Kt			
13	B × B	Q × B			
14	Q × Kt	P to K B 4 [3]			
15	Q to K 3	Kt to B 3			
16	Q R to K sq	Q to K B sq			
17	Kt to K 5	B to Q 2			
18	P to K B 4	Q R to Q sq			
19	P to B 5	B to B sq			
20	Kt to B 4 [4]	Kt to Kt 5			
21	Q to K 2	Q to B 3 [5]			
22	Kt to Q 6	Q × P, ch			

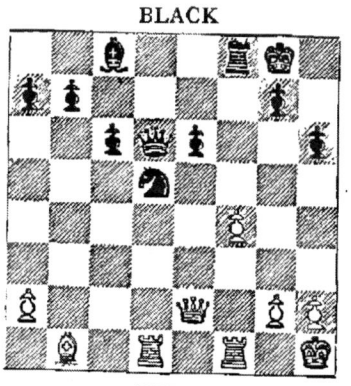

BLACK

WHITE

Black to make his 30th move.

AUGUST 30

	WHITE	BLACK		WHITE	BLACK
30	B to Kt sq	B to Q 2 [7]	51	Q to Q 6, ch	K to Kt 4
31	Q to K 4	R to B 3	52	R × B	Q × R [11]
32	P to K Kt 4	P to B 4	53	Q × Q	Kt × Q
33	Q to R 7, ch	K to B sq	54	R to B 5, ch	K to Kt 3
34	B to Kt 6	R × B [8]	55	R × P	Kt to B 6
35	Q × R	B to B 3	56	R to Q R 5	K to B 3
36	K to Kt sq	P to B 5	57	K to Kt 3	P to Kt 3
37	Q to K 4	P to B 6	58	K to B 4	Kt to K 7, ch
38	P to B 5	P to K 4	59	K to K 3	Kt to B 6
39	Q to Q B 4	K to K 2	60	K to Q 3	Kt to Q 8
40	R to B 2	P to Q Kt 4	61	K to K 2	Kt to B 6, ch
41	Q to K 4	Kt to B 5 [9]	62	K to B 3	P to Q R 3
42	P to B 6, ch [10]	Q × P	63	P to K R 4	P to R 4
43	Q to Kt 4, ch	K to B 2	64	R × P, ch	K to K 4
44	Q × B P	Q to Kt 3	65	R × P	P × P, ch
45	P to K R 3	Q to K 5	66	K × P	Kt × P
46	K to R 2	P to Kt 5	67	R to Q Kt 6	K to Q 5
47	Q to B 2	K to K 3	68	P to R 5	K to B 4
48	Q to B 5	B to Q 4	69	R to Kt 8	Kt to B 6
49	Q to B 8, ch	K to K 2	70	P to R 6	Kt to Q 4
50	Q to B 7, ch	K to B 3	71	K to Kt 5	Resigns.

NOTES BY R. TEICHMANN.

[1] This is a little inferior to the usual development with P to Q B 4. It allows White later on to advance his King's Pawn, thus opening the game.

[2] If here P × P; 10 B × P, P to K 4; 11. P to Q 5, with the better position.

[3] There was no occasion for weakening the King's Pawn. Kt to K B 3 was the natural move, followed by the same development as in the actual game.

[4] Overlooking most likely the loss of the Queen's Pawn. After 19. P to K R 3 Black would have a very uncomfortable position.

[5] R × P at once was preferable. If then 22. Kt to Q 6, R × Kt, 23. P × R, Q × P, and Black has two Pawns for the exchange with a safe game

[6] Q to B sq might be taken into consideration, but with the text move Black gets winning chances for the end game.

[7] And now he misses the chance to force a favourable end game with Kt to B 6. White had nothing better than to exchange Queens, because after 31. Q to B 2 (?), Kt × R, 32 R × Kt (best), Q × P, 33. Q to R 7, ch, K to B 2; 34. B to Kt 6, ch (if Q to Kt 6, ch, K to K 2; 35. Q × P, ch (?), R to B 2, winning), K to B 3; 35. B to Q 3, and Black must win, as White cannot win the Bishop e.g. 36. R to B sq, ch, K to K 2; 37. R × R, K × R, mate being now threatened on Q B sq

[8] This second sacrifice of the exchange is quite unnecessary, and throws his chance away; with R × P he could, in my opinion, still have drawn: e.g. R × P; 35. Q to R 8, ch, K to K 2; 36. Q × P, ch, K to Q sq; 37. Q to R 7 (best; Black threatens B to B 3), B to B 3 (of course not Kt to K 6 (?) on account of Q × B, ch (!), winning); 38. B to K 4, R × R, ch; 39. R × R, Kt to K 2 (!); 40. B × B (has White anything better?), Q × B, ch; 41. K to Kt sq, Q to Q 4, and I do not see how White can win, perpetual check and advances of passed Pawns being threatened.

[9] There is no choice; White threatened to double his Rooks on the King's file.

[10] If 42. R × Q, K to R 6, ch; 43. K to B sq, B × Q; 44. R to K 6, ch, K to Q 2, and Black would still have good chances of drawing.

[11] Obviously if Kt × R, mate in two or loss of the Queen follows.

Dr. Tarrasch v. E. Lasker.

	WHITE	BLACK		WHITE	BLACK
1	P to K 4	P to K 4	27	Kt to B 3	B to Q B 3
2	Kt to K B 3	Kt to Q B 3	28	R to B 2	B × K P
3	B to Kt 5	Kt to B 3	29	R × P	R to Q sq [8]
4	Castles	Kt × P	30	Kt (Kt 3) to K 4	
5	P to Q 4	Kt to Q 3			B (B 3) × Kt
6	B × Kt	Q P × B	31	Kt × B	B × Kt P
7	P × P	Kt to B 4	32	P to Kt 4	P to B 4
8	Q × Q	K × Q	33	K to Kt 2	P to B 5
9	Kt to B 3 [1]	P to K R 3	34	R to B 2	B to Q 5
10	B to Q 2	B to K 3	35	R to Q 2	K to Kt 4
11	Kt to K 2	P to Q B 4	36	Kt to B 3, ch	K to Kt 5
12	B to B 3 [2]	P to K Kt 4	37	Kt to K 2	B to B 3
13	Kt to Q 2 [3]	K to Q 2			
14	P to K B 4	K to B 3			
15	R to B 2	R to K Kt sq [4]			
16	P × P	P × P			
17	Kt to K 4	R to Q sq			
18	Kt (K 2) to Kt 3				
		Kt to Q 5			
19	B to Q 2 [5]	Kt × P			
20	R to Q B sq	Kt to Q 5			
21	B × P	R to Q 4			
22	B to K 3	B to Kt 2			
23	B × Kt [6]	R × B			
24	R × P, ch	K to Kt 3			
25	R (B 2) to B 2	R to Q 4 [7]			
26	R × R	B × R			

White to make his 41st move.

AUGUST 30

	WHITE	BLACK		WHITE	BLACK
38	R × R	B × R	44	P to K R 4	B to Q 5
39	K to B 3	P to B 6	45	P to R 5	P to Kt 4
40	K to K 4	K to B 5	46	P to R 6	P to Kt 5
41	K to B 5 [9]	K to Q 6 [10]	47	P to Kt 6	P to R 4
42	Kt × P	K × Kt	48	P to Kt 7	P to R 5
43	P to Kt 5	B to Kt 3	49	P Queens	Resigns.

NOTES BY H N. PILLSBURY.

[1] R to Q sq, ch, seems feasible; it would prevent the King from reaching the post at Q B 3, which it frequently attains in this variation of the opening.

[2] 12 Kt to B 4, B to B 5 ; 13. K R to Q sq, K to B sq ; 14. P to Q Kt 3, B to Kt 4 ; 15. P to Q B 4, B to B 3 ; 16 Kt to Q 5, &c., seems a good variation for White, and perhaps better than the text.

[3] R to Q sq, ch, first would have kept the Black King out of the position at B 3.

[4] Preventing White from continuing P to K Kt 4, which he would now meet with P × P.

[5] It might be safer to play R to Q B sq before the text move

[6] This does not seem to turn out very well, mainly because Black retains both Bishops. 23. P to Q Kt 4, and if B × P ; 24. Kt × P, K to Kt 3 ; 25. Kt (Kt 3) to K 4, &c., seems to clear the way for White's Pawns on the King's side to advance ; for if P to Q B 3, then 26. Kt × B, P × Kt , 27. Kt to B 6, B × Kt , 28. R × B, and should win. Should Black instead continue 23 P to Kt 3, then 24 P × P, P × P , and the B × Kt, &c., continuation would have given White a powerful attack with both Rooks in fine play.

[7] By this fine manœuvre Black eventually regains the Pawn with the better game. Should White now continue R × P, B × K P, and the Rook is in trouble.

[8] Forcing the win of one of the Pawns.

[9] White should have taken the Pawn first, and a drawn game would have resulted.

[10] Black throws away the game, which seems to be won by P to B 7.

42	P to Kt 5	B × P	49	P to Kt 6	
43	K × B	K to Q 6		(or 49 Kt to B sq, K × Kt ;	
44	Kt to B sq, ch	K to Q 7		50. P to Kt 6, P to R 6, &c.,	
45	Kt to Kt 3, ch	K to Q 8		Black should win)	
46	K to B 5 (best)				P × Kt
		P to R 4	50	P to Kt 7	P to Kt 7
47	P to Q R 4	P to Kt 4	51	P Queens	P to B 8 (Q), and
48	P × P	P to R 5			should win.

In both these variations the Pawn at the seventh square can be forced to Queen shortly.

[Mr. Lasker pointed out this win immediately on the conclusion of the game. The position will well repay study.—ED.]

AUGUST 31.

EVERYONE is at fever heat. Will Tchigorin maintain his lead, or will it be Lasker, or perhaps Pillsbury? All have at least one stiff game left, and Steinitz is to meet Tarrasch. It is very soon reported that Tchigorin, the leader, is on the brink of a precipice, and great is the rush to see him fall or save himself. Later on Blackburne is making a good fight against Lasker, then he seems to be winning and is adopting steady tactics rather than risk a loss by complications, whilst Pillsbury is steadily improving his position in spite of the excitement around him. The date is notable also in being disastrous to the White forces, which only score 2½ out of 11. Schiffers much strengthens his position by beating Walbrodt, whilst Bardeleben and Teichmann draw, all four of these being in the running for prizes. Marco plays a very fine ending to day. At the commencement of the day Tchigorin is 15, Pillsbury and Lasker 14½, Steinitz and Tarrasch 12, Schlechter, Schiffers, Bardeleben, and Teichmann 10, with two more games each to play.

C. VON BARDELEBEN v. R. TEICHMANN.

	WHITE	BLACK		WHITE	BLACK
1	P to Q 4	P to Q 4	16	Q to B 2 [3]	Kt to K 2
2	P to Q B 4	P to K 3	17	P to Q Kt 4	B to Q 3
3	Kt to Q B 3	Kt to K B 3	18	Kt to Q 4	Q to Q 2
4	B to B 4	P to Q B 4	19	B × B [1]	Q × B
5	P × B P [1]	B × P	20	Q to K 2	Q to K 4
6	P to K 3	Kt to B 3	21	B to R 6	Q to Kt sq
7	Kt to K B 3	Castles	22	B × B	Q × B
8	B to K 2	P to Q Kt 3	23	Kt to R 2	Kt to K 5
9	P × P	P × P	24	R × R	R × R
10	Castles	B to Kt 2 [2]	25	R to B sq	R × R
11	Q to R 4	Q to Q 2	26	Kt × R	Q to B 2
12	P to Q R 3	Q R to Q B sq	27	Q to B 2	Q × Q
13	Q R to Q B sq	K R to Q sq	28	Kt × Q	K to B sq
14	K R to Q sq	P to K R 3	29	K to B sq	K to K sq
15	B to Q 3	Q to K 3	30	K to K 2	K to Q 2 [5]
				Drawn game.	

Photo., Bradshaw, Hastings

E. v. Bardeleben

AUGUST 31

NOTES BY DR TARRASCH.

[1] P to K 3 is stronger. By the text move White helps Black over the difficulties of the opening.

[2] Black has already an equal game.

[3] Threatening B to B 5.

[4] The game becomes a draw without any exciting features.

[5] The game might easily have been played further, as it is clear that either of the players might have been able to win or to lose it.

J. MIESES v. G. MARCO.

	WHITE	BLACK
1	P to K 4	P to K 4
2	Kt to K B 3	Kt to Q B 3
3	P to Q 4	P × P
4	Kt × P	Kt to B 3
5	Kt × Kt	Kt P × Kt
6	P to K 5	Q to K 2 [1]
7	Q to K 2	Kt to Q 4
8	P to Q Kt 3 [2]	P to Q R 4 (!)
9	B to Kt 2	P to R 5
10	Kt to Q 2	P × P
11	R P × P	R × R
12	B × R	Q to R 6
13	Q to Q sq [3]	B to Kt 5
14	B to Q 4	B to B 6
15	B × B	Kt × B
16	Kt to B 4	Q to R 2
17	Q to B sq	Castles
18	B to Q 3	P to Q 4
19	P × P en p.	R to K sq, ch
20	Kt to K 3	Kt to Q 4
21	Castles	Kt × Kt
22	P × Kt	R × P
23	K to R sq	P × P
24	R to B 4 [4]	Q to K 2
25	R to B sq	P to Kt 3
26	Q to R sq	B to Kt 2
27	Q to Q 4	P to Q B 4
28	Q to K B 4	K to Kt 2
29	P to Q Kt 4	R to K 8
30	P × P	R × R, ch
31	Q × R	P × P
32	P to R 3	Q to K 6

White to make his 24th move

	WHITE	BLACK
33	K to R 2	Q to Q 7
34	Q to Q R sq, ch	
		K to R 3
35	Q to K B sq	P to B 4
36	B to K 2	B to K 5
37	B to Q 3	K to Kt 4
38	K to R sq	B to R sq
39	Q to K Kt sq	P to R 4
40	B to B sq	Q to K 8
41	K to R 2	Q to K 4, ch
42	K to R sq	Q to Q 5
43	K to R 2	Q to K B 5
44	Q to Kt sq	P to R 5
45	B to K 2	Q to Kt 6
46	Q to K B sq	Q × R P, ch
47	K to Kt sq	Q to K 6, ch
48	K to R sq	Q to K Kt 6
49	B to B 3	B × B

WHITE	BLACK	WHITE	BLACK
50 P×B	P to R 6	53 K×P	K to B 4
51 Q to K 2	Q to Kt 7, ch	54 K to B 2	P to Kt 4
52 Q×Q, ch	P×Q, ch		White resigns.

NOTES BY A. ALBIN.

[1] Not good. Kt to Q 4 is the usual move.

[2] He should play P to Q B 4 (if Q to Kt 4, ch, then 9. Q to Q 2, Kt to B 4; 10. Q×Q, B×Q, ch; 11. B to Q 2, B×B, ch; 12. Kt×B, Kt to Kt 3; 13. Kt to B 3), with the better game; and if instead of check with the Queen, Kt to Kt 3, then White would get a better development of his game.

[3] This trouble with the defence is the consequence of his 8th move.

[4] Black is a Pawn ahead and must win. (See diagram.)

I. GUNSBERG v. H. E. BIRD.

WHITE	BLACK
1 P to K 4	P to K 3
2 P to Q 4	P to Q 4
3 Q Kt to B 3	K Kt to B 3
4 B to K Kt 5	B to K 2
5 B×Kt	B×B
6 P to K 5	B to K 2
7 Q to Kt 4	K to B sq [1]
8 P to K B 4	P to Q B 4
9 P×P	Kt to B 3
10 Kt to B 3	Q to R 4
11 Kt to Q 2 [2]	Q to Kt 5
12 Castles	Kt×P
13 Q to Kt 3	Kt to B 3
14 Kt to Kt 3	Kt to R 4
15 Kt to Q 4	Q×B P
16 P to B 5	B to B 3
17 Q Kt to Kt 5	P to K 4
18 Kt to Kt 3	Kt×Kt, ch
19 Q×Kt	P to Q 5
20 P to Kt 4	P to Q R 3
21 Kt to R 3	P to K R 4 [3]
22 B to B 4	P×P
23 B×B P	R to R 6 [4]
24 Q to Q 5	Q×Q
25 B×Q	B×P
26 B×P	R to R 2
27 B to Kt 2	R to R 3
28 Q R to B sq	B to Kt 4, ch

White to make his 22nd move.

WHITE	BLACK
29 K to Kt sq	B to B 5
30 Kt to B 4	R to K B 3 [5]
31 P to Kt 3	P to Q 6 [6]
32 P to B 3	P to Q 7, ch
33 K to Kt 2	B to Q 6
34 Kt×Q P	B×R [7]
35 Kt×B	R to Q 2
36 P to B 4	R to Q 8
37 K to R 3	P to K 5
38 P to B 5	P to K 6 [8]
39 Kt×P	R×R
40 P to B 6	R×R P
41 B to Q 5	B to Q 3, ch
	White resigns.

AUGUST 31

NOTES BY H. N. PILLSBURY.

[1] The foregoing line of play is the invention of J. W. Showalter, of New York At this point Black has several moves; P to K Kt 3 is weakening. B to K B sq, while somewhat backward, is perfectly safe. Castling is also safe, but requires correct afterplay In the match Showalter v. Albin, New York City, occurred the following · 7. Castles ; 8 B to Q 3, P to K B 4 ; 9. Q to R 3, P to B 4 ; 10 P × P, Kt to Q 2 ; 11 P to B 4, Kt × B P ; 12. Castles, P to Q Kt 4, &c The text move also appears perfectly safe.

[2] Losing a Pawn. Castling is safe and correct.

[3] With this powerful move Black forces the entrance of the Rook and Queen's Bishop, and, with a Pawn behind, White has little to do but await developments, his game being virtually lost. (See diagram.)

[4] Correctly forcing the exchange of Queens.

[5] White threatened Kt × P.

[6] The winning move , Black's Bishops become all-powerful.

[7] White offers up only the exchange, for if 34 B × Kt ; 35 R × R, ch, P × R ; 36. R to Q sq, regaining the Piece.

[8] The advance of the Pawn settles matters, and White's remaining moves are merely desperate attempts to save an untenable game.

B. VERGANI v. H. N. PILLSBURY.

	WHITE	BLACK
1	P to K 4	P to K 4
2	Kt to K B 3	Kt to Q B 3
3	B to B 4	B to B 4
4	P to B 3	Kt to B 3
5	P to Q 3	Castles
6	Q Kt to Q 2	P to Q 4
7	P × P	Kt × P
8	Kt to K 4	B to K 2
9	Castles	P to K R 3
10	P to K R 3	B to K 3
11	B to Kt 3	P to B 4
12	Kt to Kt 3	Q to Q 2
13	K to R 2 (?)[1]	B to Q 3
14	R to K sq	Q R to K sq
15	B to Q 2	Q to B 2
16	Q to K 2	Kt to B 5 ([1])
17	B × B [2]	Kt × B ([1])
18	Kt to Kt sq	P to K 5
19	K to R sq	Kt to B 4
20	P × P	B × Kt
21	P × B	Kt × P [3]
22	Q to K 3	Kt to K 4
23	P to Kt 3	Kt to Q 6 [4]

BLACK

WHITE

White to make his 24th move.

	WHITE	BLACK
24	K to R 2	Kt × R
25	B × Kt	P to Q Kt 3
26	Q to B sq	Q to Q 4
27	Q to B 2	R to Q sq
28	P to B 4	Q to Q 6
29	R to B sq	P to B 4

	WHITE	BLACK		WHITE	BLACK
30	Kt to B 3	Q × Q	39	R to Q B 2	Kt to K 6
31	R × Q	R to Q 8	40	R to Kt 2	Kt to B 8
32	B to B 2	R to K sq	41	R to Q B 2	Kt × P, ch
33	P to K R 4 [5]	Kt to B 3	42	K to R 2	Kt to B 8, ch
34	B to Kt sq	Kt to Kt 5, ch	43	K to R sq	P to K Kt 4
35	K to R sq [6]	K to B 2	44	P × P	P × P
36	R to Kt 2 [7]	P to Q R 4	45	R to B 3	P to Kt 5
37	R to Q B 2	R to K 5	46	Kt to R 2	R (K 5) to K 8
38	R to Kt 2	K to B 3		White resigns.	

NOTES BY E. SCHIFFERS

[1] In consequence of White's excessively languid style of play in this 'Giuoco Pianissimo,' Black had already obtained a superiority in position, but this move still further damages White's game.

[2] Evidently the Knight could not be taken.

[3] White's game is now hopeless

[4] In Morphy's style.

[5] White has scarcely any moves; by this move the Black Knight is invited to K Kt 5

[6] Throughout all the game the White King is unable to make a final choice of one of two squares on the Rook's file

[7] The Rook now begins to dance about.

W. STEINITZ *v* DR. TARRASCH.

	WHITE	BLACK		WHITE	BLACK
1	P to Q 4	P to K B 4	20	Q to B 7 [4]	P to Q 3
2	P to Q B 4	P to K 3	21	Q × Q	B × Q
3	Q Kt to B 3	B to Kt 5	22	P to Q R 4 (!)	B to Q sq [5]
4	P to K 3	Kt to K B 3	23	Kt to K 2	P to Q R 3
5	B to Q 3	Castles	24	Kt to Q B sq	Kt to K 2
6	Kt to K 2 [1]	P to Q Kt 3	25	Kt to Kt 3	K to Kt 2
7	Castles	B to Kt 2	26	R to K B sq	Kt to B sq (!)
8	P to B 3	Kt to B 3	27	Kt to Q 2	B to K 2
9	P to K 4	P × P	28	B to K 2	B to Q sq
10	P × P	P to K 4	29	B to K Kt 4	P to Q Kt 4 [6]
11	Kt to Q 5	B to K 2 [2]	30	B to K 6	B to K B 3
12	Kt × Kt, ch	R × Kt	31	P to R 5 [7]	P to K Kt 4 (!)
13	R × R	B × R	32	P to K R 4 [8]	P × P
14	P to Q 5 (!)	Kt to K 2	33	B to R 6, ch	K to Kt 3
15	Kt to Kt 3	P to K Kt 3	34	B to Kt 4	Kt to K 2
16	P to B 5 (!)	K to R sq [3]	35	B to K 3	R to K B sq
17	B to K 3	Kt to Kt sq	36	R to Q B sq	B to B sq
18	Q to Q B sq	Q to K 2	37	B to K 2	P to R 6 (!)
19	P × P	B P × P	38	P to K Kt 3	P to R 4

AUGUST 31

	WHITE	BLACK		WHITE	BLACK
39	R to B 7	R to K Kt sq	49	K to Kt sq	P to R 7, ch
40	K to R 2	R to K B sq	50	K to B sq	Kt x B, ch
41	B to Q sq [9]	Kt to Kt sq	51	K to K 2	B x R
42	R to B 6	B to K 2	52	K x Kt	P to Kt 5 [12]
43	Kt to B 3	Kt to B 3	53	Kt to B 3	B to Q sq
44	Kt to R 4, ch	K to B 2	54	Kt x P	B x P
45	B to B 3	B to Kt 5 [10]	55	B to B 3	K to Kt 3
			56	B to K 2	B to Kt 3, ch
			57	K to Q 2	B to B 7 [13]
			58	Kt to B sq	P to R 4
			59	B to Kt 5	B to R 6 (¹)
			60	K to K 2	B x Kt, ch
			61	K x Q B	B x P
			62	K to Kt 2	B to K 8
			63	B to K 8, ch	K to Kt 4
			64	K to B 3	P to K R 5
			65	B to Q 7	P to R 5
			66	B x P	P to R 6
			67	B to Q 7	P to R 7
			68	K to Kt 2	B to Kt 6
			69	B to K 8	K to B 5
			70	B to R 5	K to K 6
46	B to R sq	B to Q 2	71	P to Kt 3	B to B 5
47	R to B 7	R to B sq (¹)	72	B to Kt 6	K to Q 6
48	R x R [11]	Kt to Kt 5, ch		White resigns.	

White to make his 46th move.

NOTES BY J. MASON.

[1] Regarding the opening, so far, with his first move Dr Tarrasch starts on a line of defence which has latterly incurred some critical condemnation. On the other hand, Mr. Steinitz does not adhere very closely to any of the approved forms of attack; especially in taking this post with his Knight, apparently intending P to K 4, and an open game. However, this being the first contest between these great players, it may be assumed that the strategy of each was adjusted partly on the *do ut des* principle; in order that issue might be the sooner joined, and a decisive result eventually recorded

[2] What should be the effect of Kt x Kt can be only vaguely surmised; but it seems feasible, considering that White leaves a Pawn *en prise*.

[3] But here the Pawn is no good gift! Because of 17. Q to Kt 3, threatening check, and winning a Piece in consequence.

[4] The advantage, if any, is with White. Yet to make an appreciable impression is very difficult His best chance is in exchanging Queens, relying upon the then remains of his superior position to produce a winning ending.

⁵ The precarious nature of the defence may be inferred from the manœuvres, more or less forced, all along here.

⁶ Getting the Pawn out of attack and keeping the adverse Knight out from B 4, whence he might do much harm

⁷ Probably it would be better to defer this in favour of advancing the King's Knight's and Rook's Pawns; opening the King's Rook's file, or getting in with R to B 7—a fatal move in the circumstances

⁸ An attempt at the foregoing, i.e. to get in R to B 7. But the momentary delay makes all the difference. There is risk now, where there was none before—a Pawn's a Pawn for a' that!

⁹ The Pawn should be got rid of, it is really so very dangerous. White would, perhaps, have a little the best of it then; whereas, as it happens, he soon finds himself fighting a losing battle

¹⁰ Taking the lead, which is maintained to the end. White's unsupported Bishop is in jeopardy.

¹¹ Most of White's play hereabouts is forced; absolutely or to avoid something worse.

¹² Important - to prevent the backing up of the Rook's Pawn.

¹³ Winning soon resolves itself into a question of time. Even reduced to Bishops of opposite colours, with a passed Pawn on each side, Black's way should be fairly certain. It comes to this at move 60, when the manner of winning is much less difficult than it is interesting.

E. SCHIFFERS *v.* A. WALBRODT.

	WHITE	BLACK
1	P to K 4	P to K 4
2	Kt to K B 3	Kt to Q B 3
3	B to Kt 5	P to Q R 3
4	B to R 4	Kt to B 3
5	P to Q 3	P to Q 3
6	P to B 3	B to Q 2
7	Castles	B to K 2 ¹
8	R to K sq	Castles
9	Q Kt to Q 2	Kt to K sq
10	P to Q 4	B to B 3 ²
11	Kt to B sq	Q to K 2
12	Kt to K 3	P to R 3 ³
13	P to Q 5	Kt to Kt sq
14	B × B	Q × B ⁴
15	Kt to B 5	K to R 2
16	P to K R 3	R to R sq ⁵
17	Kt to R 2	Q to Q sq ⁶
18	R to K 3 ⁷	P to K Kt 3
19	Kt to Kt 3	Kt to Q 2
20	Kt to Kt 4	B to Kt 2

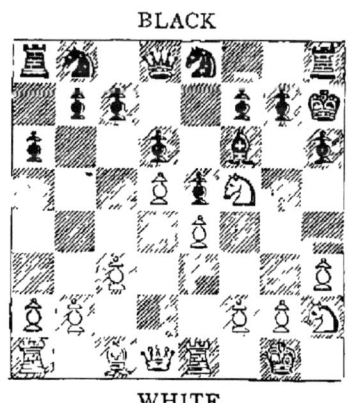

BLACK

WHITE

White to make his 18th move

	WHITE	BLACK
21	R to K sq	Q to R 5 ⁸
22	Kt to R 2	R to K B sq
23	Kt to B 3	Q to K 2
24	Q to B 2 ⁹	R to B sq
25	B to K 3	P to Q B 3

AUGUST 31

	WHITE	BLACK		WHITE	BLACK
26	Q R to Q sq	Q Kt to B 3	36	K Kt × K B P	R to R sq
27	P × P [10]	P × P	37	B to K 3	R × P
28	P to Q Kt 4 [11]	Kt to Q 2	38	Q to Kt sq	R to R 6
29	Q to Q 3	Q to K 3 [12]	39	B × P [14]	Q to B 3
30	Q × R P	Kt to Kt sq	40	Q to B sq [15]	R to R 7
31	Q to R 4	P to K B 4	41	B × B	Kt × B
32	P × P	P × P	42	R × Q P	Kt to K 3 [16]
33	Q to B 2	K to Kt sq	43	R × Q Kt	Kt to B 5
34	B to R 7	Kt to Q 2 [13]	44	Q to Q sq	K to R sq
35	K Kt to Q 4	Q to B 2	45	Q to Q 6	Resigns.

Notes by I. Gunsberg

[1] I myself prefer to develop the King's Bishop on K Kt 2, whenever I am compelled to play P to Q 3 for Black.

[2] With one move Black hopelessly blocks his King's Knight and his King's Bishop's Pawn. It is almost certain that he will sooner or later have to play P to K Kt 3 to get a more comfortable square for his Bishop. There was no great danger in P × P, 11 P × P, P to B 4. When playing B to K 2 with P on Q 3, P to K B 4 is Black's only hope of developing his game. If White replies to this with 12. Q to Kt 3, ch, K to R sq, White hardly dare take the Queen's Knight's Pawn.

[3] This move does not strengthen Black's position; P × P was again advisable.

[4] He takes with the Queen in order to provide for Kt to B 5.

[5] Black with this move unfolds the object he had in view when playing P to K R 3. He shows himself by the contemplation of such a manœuvre to have great resource in what may be described as heavy manœuvring in close positions.

[6] Played for the purpose of enabling Black to play B to Kt 4 if necessary, also to get out his Queen's Knight. White obviously contemplates in some form or other to be able to take the King's Rook's Pawn.

[7] The position hardly gives sufficient promise for this Rook to be brought into play. Q to Kt 4 was probably best, or perhaps, 18 Kt to Kt 4. There was a very enticing move in 18. Q to R 5, but Black would simply have replied with P to K Kt 3 with advantage to himself, as White could not save the Knight. (See diagram.)

[8] It is highly interesting to see how Black, by excellent tactics, gets rid of his difficulties and actually obtains the better game. Of course the Black Queen can only be displaced from R 5 by two moves of White, so that when the Queen is compelled to retire to K 2, Black would have gained time and likewise made room for his Queen's Rook to come into play.

[9] White is actually reduced to take measures to stop Black's aggression, which was threatened by P to K B 4.

[10] White had no better means of avoiding the pressure on the centre which Black could bring to bear.

[11] Likewise intended to prevent the advance in the centre by P to Q 4, for then White would play with advantage B to B 5.

[12] Played with the obvious intention of giving up the Queen's Rook's Pawn for the sake of the King's side attack which Black would gain afterwards, by his being at last able to play P to K B 4.

[13] Of course Black's object was R to R sq; at the same time, however, White's threat of Kt to Q 4 was rather obvious, and should have been forestalled.

[14] White has obtained the best of the struggle, mainly owing, however, to the fact that his neglect of his Queen's side was too risky.

[15] Another excellent move, which still leaves matters in suspense. It defends the Bishop and gains further time by attacking the Black Rook. Black could hardly reply with B × B, as 41. Kt × B, ch, K to R 2; 42. Kt to Kt 4 would be followed by 43. Q × R. Black must submit to the inevitable by moving his Rook.

[16] The game has now resolved itself into a rout. Black cannot defend his Knight with Q to Q sq, as then 43. Kt × Kt, K × Kt; 44. Q to R 6, ch, with forced mate.

S. Tinsley v. W. H. K. Pollock.

	WHITE	BLACK		WHITE	BLACK
1	P to Q 4	P to K B 4	25	P × B	Q × P
2	P to Q B 4	P to K 3	26	R to B 2	P to R 3
3	P to K Kt 3	Kt to K B 3	27	K to B sq	R to R 8, ch
4	B to Kt 2	B to Kt 5, ch [1]	28	K to Kt 2	P to Q Kt 4
5	Kt to B 3	Castles	29	Q to Kt 4	K to R 2
6	Q to Kt 3	P to Q B 4	30	B to K 2	Kt to Q 3
7	P to K 3	Kt to Q B 3	31	B to B 3	R to R 5
8	P to Q R 3	P × P [2]	32	Q to Kt sq	R to Q B 5
9	P × B	P × Kt	33	R to Q 2	Kt to K 5
10	P × P	Kt to K 4			
11	Kt to B 3	Kt to Q 6, ch			
12	K to K 2	Kt × B, ch			
13	K R × Kt [3]	P to Q Kt 3			
14	Kt to Q 4	Kt to K 5			
15	K R to Q sq	Q to Kt 4			
16	P to K R 4	Q to Kt 3 [4]			
17	B to B 3	B to Kt 2			
18	Kt to Q Kt 5	P to Q 4			
19	P × P	P × P			
20	R × R P	R × R			
21	Kt × R	K to R sq			
22	P to Kt 5	Q to K B 3			
23	R to Q B sq	R to Q R sq			
24	Kt to B 6	B × Kt			

BLACK

WHITE

White to make his 36th move.

AUGUST 31

	WHITE	BLACK		WHITE	BLACK
34	R to Q 3	R to B 4	44	P to K B 4	Q to B 3 [7]
35	P to R 5	K to Kt sq [5]	45	Q to K 8, ch	K to R 2
36	Q to R 2	K to R sq	46	B to K 6	Q × B
37	Q to R 5	K to R 2	47	Q × Q	P to Kt 6
38	Q to Q 8	Kt × Q B P	48	Q to Q Kt 6	Kt to K 5
39	Q to K B 8	Q to B sq	49	Q to Kt 6, ch	K to Kt sq
40	Q to B 7	P to Kt 5	50	R × Q P	R to B 7, ch
41	P to Kt 4	P × P [6]	51	K to B 3	R to Q 7
42	Q to Kt 6, ch	K to R sq	52	Q × Kt	Resigns.
43	B × Kt P	Q to Q sq			

NOTES BY R. TEICHMANN.

[1] In this variation the Black King's Bishop cannot be well used otherwise; it seems therefore best to exchange it for the White Knight, a course which in other variations cannot be recommended.

[2] B × Kt, ch, followed by Q to K 2, seems to be preferable.

[3] White has now a very good development.

[4] Q to B 3 would have been much better.

[5] With a view to taking the Bishop's Pawn, which he could not do before, on account of Kt × Q B P, R × Kt (!), R × R, Q × P, ch, drawing at least. But he ought to have played the K to R sq instead, after which I find no satisfactory defence for White.

[6] There was no necessity for taking this Pawn, but even taking it ought not to result in any disadvantage.

[7] A blunder, which loses the game at once. Black could have drawn the game easily if he simply kept the Queen on the last row; whenever White threatened mate with B to B 5, then K or Q to Kt sq.

E. LASKER v. J. H. BLACKBURNE.

	WHITE	BLACK
1	P to K 4	P to K 4
2	Kt to K B 3	Kt to Q B 3
3	B to Kt 5	P to Q 3
4	P to Q 4	B to Q 2
5	Kt to B 3	P × P
6	Kt × P	Kt × Kt
7	Q × Kt [1]	B × B
8	Kt × B	Kt to K 2 (!) [2]
9	Castles	Kt to B 3
10	Q to B 3 [3]	P to Q R 3
11	Kt to R 3 [4]	Q to B 3 (!) [5]
12	Q to Q Kt 3	Castles [6]
13	P to Q B 4 [7]	R to K sq
14	R to K sq	Q to Kt 3

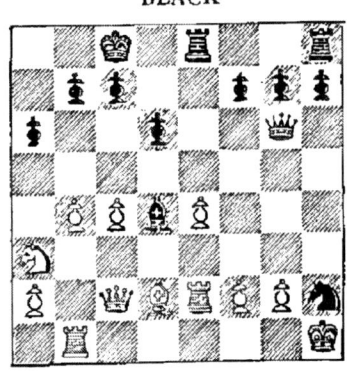

White to make his 21st move.

316   THE HASTINGS CHESS TOURNAMENT

WHITE	BLACK
15 B to Q 2 [8]	B to K 2 [9]
16 Q to B 2	B to B 3
17 Q R to Kt sq	B to Q 5 [10]
18 P to Q Kt 4	Kt to K 4
19 R to K 2 [11]	Kt to B 6, ch
20 K to R sq	Kt × P [12]
21 B to B 4 [13]	Kt to Kt 5 [14]
22 B to Kt 3	B to K 4 [15]
23 Q to Q 3	B × B [16]
24 Q × B	Kt to B 3 [17]
25 Q to R 3, ch	K to Kt sq
26 P to B 3	Kt to R 4 [18]
27 R to Q 2	R to K 4
28 K to Kt sq	Kt to B 5 [19]
29 Q to R 4	Kt to K 3 [20]
30 R to Q 5	Kt to Kt 4
31 Q to Kt 3	R × R
32 B P × R	P to K R 4 [21]
33 P to Kt 5	P to R 5
34 Q to Kt 4 [22]	P × P
35 Kt × P	P to R 6
36 R to Kt 2	P × P [23]
37 R × P	Kt to R 6, ch
38 K to B sq	Q to B 3 [24]

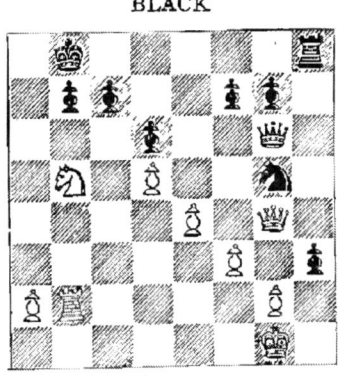

Black to make his 36th move.

WHITE	BLACK
39 P to K 5 [25]	P × P
40 R to R 2	P to K 5 [26]
41 R × Kt	Q to R 8, ch
42 K to Kt 2	P × P, ch
43 K to Kt 3 (?) [27]	
	Q to K 4, ch
44 K × P	Q × P, ch [28]

White resigns.

NOTES BY DR. TARRASCH.

[1] B × B, ch, ought to have been played first, and White would have got a good game, whilst now the Queen's Knight gets displaced.

[2] Through repeated exchanges Black has now freed his cramped position.

[3] White wishes to prevent the development of the King's Bishop, but he does not attain this object, and deprives his Knight of its best square ; Q to K 3 would have been better.

[4] After Kt to Q 4 the same counter-move would follow.

[5] Well played ; Black does not mind having his Pawns doubled, in order to relieve the pressure on the King's Knight's Pawn. White ought on his part to exchange rather than move his Queen away ; his chances of attack are about nil.

[6] Black is now better developed and soon proceeds to attack.

[7] This weakens Queen's 4th, but other moves give no better result for White.

[8] White gives up the Pawn either willingly or forced ; if he strengthens it with P to B 3, Black attacks it again with P to B 4.

[9] Black could easily take the Pawn ; after R × P ; 16. R × R, Q × R ; 17. R to K sq, Q to B 4 ; 18. R to K 8, ch, and White gets an attack which no sooner begins than it is ended..

AUGUST 31

[10] Black has played admirably with the King's Bishop, which now occupies a threatening position

[11] A mistake which ought at once to lead to a definite solution; the Rook stands here unguarded. R to Q Kt 3 was a powerful defensive move.

[12] Black does not make the best use of his opportunities (see diagram); he might have decided the game here with—

WHITE	BLACK	WHITE	BLACK
20	Q to R 4	23 B × B	Kt × P
21 P to R 3	Kt to Kt 8 (!)	24 P × Kt	Q × P, ch
22 P to Kt 4	Q × P, ch	25 K to Kt sq	R to K 3
23 K × Kt	Q × P, ch	26 B to B 4	R to Kt 3, ch
24 K to B sq	Q to R 6, ch	27 B to Kt 3	R to R 3
25 K to Kt sq	R to K 3, &c.	Again if—	
Or if –		21 B to B 4	B to K 4
22 R to K sq	Kt × P	22 B × B	R × B
23 P × Kt	Q × P, ch	23 P to R 3 (after P × Kt mate follows in 3 moves)	
24 K to Kt sq	R to K 3		Kt to Q 5, and wins the Rook.
Or if—			
22 R to K 3	B × R		

[13] After K × Kt, Queen checks at R 4 and takes the Rook.

[14] Threatening R × P.

[15] Here, for the second time, Black could finish and even gain the brilliancy prize by—

22	Q to R 4, ch	24 R to Q 2	B × P, ch
23 K to Kt sq	R to K 3 (threatening R to R 3)	25 B × B (if R × B, R to R 3; 26. K to B sq, Kt to K 6, winning the Queen)	
24 R (K 2) to K sq (the Rook must make room for the King, as after B to B 4, R to R 3 follows)			R to R 3
		26 K to B sq	R to B 3 (threatening Kt to K 6, ch, and at the same time Q to R 8, ch, which is followed by R × B, ch), and wins.
	B × P, ch		
25 B × B	R to R 3		
26 K to B sq	R to B 3, and wins; or if—		

[16] And here Black has a third opportunity of winning with—

23	Q to R 4, ch	28 Kt × Kt	Q to R 8, ch, followed by Q × R, or if—
24 K to Kt sq	R to K 3		
25 B × B	Kt × B	25 R to K sq	R to R 3
26 Q to K 3 (Q to B 2, Kt to B 6, ch)		26 K to B sq	B × B
	R to R 3	27 Q × B	Kt to R 7, ch
27 Q to R 3, ch	Q × Q, followed by R × P, and Black has two Pawns more; or—	28 K to Kt sq	Kt to B 6, ch, and mates accordingly; or if—
		25 R to B 2	R to R 3
27 P to B 3	Kt × Q B P	26 K to B sq	Q to R 8, ch, followed by Q × Kt P, and a winning attack.

[17] R × P cannot be played on account of 25. R × R, Q × R; 26 P to B 3.

[18] Here R to K 4 at once was decisive; the only counter-move was P to Kt 4, and then followed P to K R 4 and K R to R 3.

[19] A stronger attack would come from Q to Kt 4 (threatening the Rook and also the Knight by Q to K 6, ch), continuing with 29. R to K B 2 (!), Kt to B 5; 30. Q to R 2 (if Q to Q 7, R to Q sq, and Kt to R 6, ch), Q to B 3, followed by R to R 4, or 30. ... R to K 3, followed by R to R 3.

[20] Now the Knight is driven back, and the dangerous threat of R to R 4 is obviated by White.

[21] The advance of this Pawn renews the attack.

[22] The only square on which the Queen does not get lost through the Knight checking

[23] White brings his Rook to the King's side; Black could have prevented this, by attacking the Rook with 36 . Q to B 3 The Rook could not be played indifferently on account of P to R 7, ch, and Q to R 8, ch. After 37. R to Kt sq comes P × P, with much greater strength, for example, 38 K × P, Kt × P; 39 Q × Kt, R to R 7, ch. But if White instead of withdrawing the Rook played 37. Q to Q 7, then the King's side would be weakened by the removal of the Queen, and then follows—

WHITE	BLACK	WHITE	BLACK
	R to Q B sq	40 K × P	Kt to R 5, ch
38 R to Q B 2	P × P	41 K to Kt sq	(K to Kt 3, Q to
39 Kt × P	Kt × P, ch	B 6, ch)	
40 K × P	Kt to K 8, ch		Q to Kt 4, ch
	followed by Kt to B 7; or—	42 K to B 2	Q to Q 7, ch,
39 R × P	Kt × P, ch		with mate in a few moves.

In the last variation, if 38. R to K B 2, Q to B 5 (threatening Q to Kt 6, followed by P × P or P to R 7, or perhaps Q to K 6, ch), with decisive effect (See diagram)

[24] Q to R 3 was better (threatening Q to B 8, ch, and Kt to B 5, ch), 39 P to B 4, Kt × P; 40. R to Kt sq, Q to R 7, &c.; or if 39 R to Q B 2, Q to K 6; 40 Q × P, Q × P, ch; 41. K to K sq, Q × P, ch; 42. K to Q 2, Q × P, ch, &c.

[25] To deprive the Queen of the capture of the King's Bishop's Pawn. After Q × K P there could come Q × Kt P.

[26] R to R 5 would have been a great mistake on account of R × Kt. Black now sacrifices the Knight, being sure of getting his opponent's Knight; but this would have been very difficult if White had played 41 Q × P, and if Q to R 8, ch; 42. Q to K sq, threatening R × Kt.

[27] Or he might have played 43. Q × P, Q to Kt 2, ch; 44. K to Kt 3, R × R, ch; 45. K × R, Q × Kt; 46. Q × P

[28] Black can now exchange Rooks and take the Knight or force the attack with R to K sq.

AUGUST 31

A. Albin v. A. Burn.

	WHITE	BLACK
1	P to K 4	P to K 3
2	P to Q 4	P to Q 4
3	P to K 5 [1]	P to Q B 4
4	P to Q B 3	Kt to Q B 3
5	P to K B 4 [2]	P × P [3]
6	P × P	Q to Kt 3
7	Kt to K B 3	Kt to R 3 [4]
8	B to Q 3 (!)	B to Q 2
9	B to B 2	Kt to Q Kt 5
10	Castles	R to B sq
11	B to R 4	Kt to B 4
12	B × B, ch	K × B
13	Kt to B 3	R to B 5
14	Kt to R 4	Q to R 3
15	P to Q Kt 3	R to B 3
16	P to K Kt 4 [5]	Kt to B 7 [6]
17	P × Kt	Kt × R
18	R to B 2	P to Q Kt 4
19	P × P, ch	P × P
20	Kt to B 5, ch	B × Kt
21	P × B	R × P
22	B to K 3	Kt × P
23	P × Kt	R to B 3
24	P to Kt 4 [7]	R to B 5
25	Q to Kt sq	Q to R 6
26	B to Q 2	P to Kt 3
27	Kt to K sq	K R to Q B sq
28	Kt to Q 3	P to Q R 4 (!)

White to make his 24th move.

	WHITE	BLACK
29	R to B 3 [8]	P × P [9]
30	Kt to B 5, ch	K R × Kt
31	R × Q	P × R
32	Q to Kt 3	R to R 5
33	Q to R 2	K to B 3 (!) [10]
34	K to Kt 2	K R to B 5
35	K to Kt 3	P to Kt 5
36	K to Kt 4	K to Kt 4 (!)
37	K to Kt 5	R to R 3
38	P to K R 4	K to R 5 (!)
39	Q to R sq	R (R 3) to B 3
40	B to K 3	P to Kt 6

White resigns.[11]

Notes by C. von Bardeleben.

[1] This line of play leads to an interesting game, but is not so sound as 3. Q Kt to B 3.

[2] At this juncture the only good move is 5. Kt to B 3, recommended by the late German master, Louis Paulsen. After 5. P to K B 4, Black gets a great advantage of position.

[3] This is not the best way to take advantage of White's weak fifth move. Black should have played 5. ... Q to Kt 3; 6. Kt to B 3, B to Q 2 (!) (this move must be made at once to prevent 7. B to Q 3, because it is Black's intention to bring his King's Knight to K B 4, and thus to attack the White Queen's Pawn); 7. B to K 2, Kt to R 3; 8. P × P, B × P; 9. P to Q Kt 4, B to B 7, ch; 10. K to B sq, B to K 6;

or, 8. Castles, P × P; 9. P × P, Kt × Q P (!); 10. Kt × Kt, Kt to B 4, with an excellent game

⁴ Better would be B to Q 2, in order to prevent 8. B to Q 3.

⁵ This move looks very dangerous, but is good enough if correctly continued.

⁶ This sacrifice is of very doubtful value; preferable would be Kt to R 3.

⁷ Here White misses a good opportunity of getting a violent attack. If he played 24 P to B 5, whereupon Black has probably no better answer than P × P, upon which follows, 25. Q × P, ch, K to B sq; 26. P to K 6, with an excellent game. (See diagram)

⁸ If 29 P × P, then P to Kt 5 (!), and the Black Queen's Knight's Pawn cannot be taken off because of 30 ... R to B 8, ch.

⁹ A brilliant combination, which turns the game in favour of Black by sacrificing the Queen.

¹⁰ Black manœuvres very cleverly with his King, compare the 36th and 38th move of Black.

¹¹ White can do nothing else, anything is indifferent; for instance, 41. K to B 6, and then follows P to Kt 7; 42. Q to Q sq, ch, R to B 7, 43. Q to Q 4, ch, K to Kt 6; 44 Q to Q 3, ch, K to R 7, or 42 Q to R 2, R to Kt 5; 43 Q to Kt sq, K to Kt 4 (threatening P to R 7); 44. Q to Q 3, ch, R (B 3) to B 5, and Black wins

M. TCHIGORIN v. D. JANOWSKI.

	WHITE	BLACK
1	P to K 4	P to K 4
2	Kt to Q B 3	Kt to K B 3
3	P to Q 3 ¹	P to Q 4
4	P × P	Kt × P
5	Q to K 2 ²	Kt to Q B 3
6	B to Q 2	B to K 2
7	Castles	Castles
8	Q to B 3 ³	B to K 3
9	K Kt to K 2	P to B 4 ⁴
10	Q to R 3	Q to Q 3
11	Kt × Kt	Q × Kt
12	Kt to B 3	Q to R 4
13	P to Q R 3 ⁵	B × P ⁶
14	Kt to Kt sq ⁷	
		B × P, ch
15	K × B	Q to R 7, ch
16	K to B sq	Kt to Q 5

White resigns.⁸

BLACK

White to make his 14th move.

NOTES BY R. TEICHMANN.

¹ Shutting his King's Bishop in, and allowing the second player the initiative.

² An unfavourable place for the Queen in open games. He ought to have developed his King's side Pieces as quickly as possible.

³ P to K Kt 3 and B to Kt 2 were imperative now.

⁴ Black has now a splendid development, whilst all the White Pieces are most unfavourably placed

⁵ We know that 'Interdum dormitat Homerus,' but this is too feeble, and really playing for self-mate The only way to avoid immediate disaster was Kt to Kt sq, giving up a Pawn , but even then he could not have held out very long.

⁶ Obvious enough   If 14. P × B, Q × P, ch ; 15. K to Kt sq, Kt to Kt 5, and mate cannot be averted

⁷ Overlooking the forced mate   But if, for instance, 14. B to K sq, B to Kt 5 ; 15. K to Kt sq, P to Q Kt 4 ; followed by B × Kt , 17. B × B, P to Kt 5, and Black must win.

⁸ It was certainly very hard on Tchigorin, that he had such a day of chess-blindness so near to the end of the Tournament, when he was leading and the first prize seemed a certainty for him, but such are the *vicissitudines belli*.

J. MASON *v.* C. SCHLECHTER.

	WHITE	BLACK		WHITE	BLACK
1	P to K 3	P to Q 4	21	R to Q Kt 3	Q to R 3
2	P to Q B 4	P to K 3	22	R to Q R 3	Q to Kt 2
3	Kt to K B 3	Kt to K B 3	23	R to Q Kt 3	R to B 2 ⁵
4	P to Q Kt 3 ¹	P to Q Kt 3	24	P to Q B 5	Kt to K sq
5	B to Kt 2	B to Kt 2	25	Kt (Q 2) to	B 4
6	B to K 2	B to K 2			Q to Q 4
7	Castles	Castles	26	P × P	P × P
8	Kt to K 5	Q Kt to Q 2	27	R to K sq ⁶	B × Kt
9	P to B 4	P to B 4	28	Kt × B	R (Q sq)to B sq⁷
10	P to Q 4 ²	P × B P	29	R × P	R to B 7
11	Kt P × P	Kt to K 5	30	Q to K 4	Q to R 4
12	B to K B 3	P × P	31	R to Kt 3	Q to Q 7
13	P × P	Q to B 2	32	Kt to Q 3	Q × P, ch
14	Q to K 2	Kt to Q 3	33	K to B sq	Q to R 6, ch
15	Kt to Q 2	B × B	34	K to Kt sq	Q to Kt 6, ch,⁸
16	R × B ³	Q R to B sq	35	K to B sq	Kt to B 3
17	R to Q B sq	K R to Q sq	36	Q to R sq	Kt × P
18	R to K R 3	Kt to B sq	37	R to K 2	R × R ⁹
19	P to Kt 4 ⁴	B to B 3	38	K × R	R to B 7, ch
20	R to K B 3	Q to Kt 2	39	K moves	Kt to K 6, mate.

NOTES BY E SCHIFFERS.

¹ I would draw attention to the fine unbroken line extending from White's Queen's Rook's Pawn to Black's King's Bishop's Pawn.

² After this, two holes are formed at once, at K 3 and at K 4.

³ The game becomes quite even.

⁴ White's King is left too much exposed by this move.

⁵ Black decided to allow White to play P to Q B 5.

⁶ If White takes the Queen's Knight's Pawn, then Black captures the Queen's Pawn.

⁷ White's game cannot now be saved; Black first skilfully occupied the Queen's Bishop's file, and has now taken possession of the seventh rank.

⁸ The reserve cavalry finally completes White's destruction.

⁹ 'The great drawing master,' as Schlechter was jokingly called, showed that he could occasionally mate too.

It can well be believed that the misfortunes of the other two leaders, following on Pillsbury's loss to Schlechter, did not decrease the excitement. Pillsbury, who had apparently thrown away his chance, has now become first again, leading by half a point. At no time during the Tournament has more than a whole point separated the first and third, reckoning the adjourned games; but in the early stages it was of course felt that time might work changes.

The following is the score at the close of the day:—

Pillsbury	15½	Mason		9½
Tchigorin	15	Burn		9½
Lasker	14½	Janowski		9½
Tarrasch	12*	Gunsberg		9
Steinitz	12*	Bird		8½
Schlechter	11	Marco		8½
Schiffers	11	Pollock		8
Bardeleben	10½	Albin		7½
Teichmann	10½	Tinsley		7½
Walbrodt	10	Mieses		7
Blackburne	9½	Vergani		3

* And their adjourned game.

SEPTEMBER 2

THE LAST ROUND.

THE pairing for this was obviously known, for it was the only one left, and it was entered on with not a single prize determined yet, or in any way certain. The three leaders all had dangerous opponents of the first rank. As the day goes on the first two leaders seem likely to draw, whilst Lasker has made a brilliant sacrifice which wins. Schiffers and Bardeleben are progressing all right, whilst Teichmann looks like drawing. Pillsbury presently wins his game brilliantly and secures first prize; it is impossible to prevent the onlookers from applauding, and the cheers ring for him in true British style

At the end of the day Tchigorin v. Schlechter, and Teichmann v. Mason stood adjourned, whilst Steinitz v. Tarrasch finished their adjourned game, settling the fourth and fifth prizes; but even then the second, third, and seventh prizes were all undetermined.

H. E. Bird v. J. Mieses.

	WHITE	BLACK
1	P to K 4	P to K 4
2	Kt to K B 3	Kt to Q B 3
3	B to B 4	B to K 2
4	P to Q 4	P × P [1]
5	Kt × P [2]	Kt to B 3
6	Kt × Kt [3]	Q P × Kt
7	B to Q 3 [4]	B to K 3
8	Castles	Q to Q 2 (!) [5]
9	Q to K sq [6]	Castles Q R
10	Q to R 5	K to Kt sq
11	B to K 3	P to Q Kt 3
12	Q to K sq	Kt to Kt 5
13	Kt to Q 2	B to Q 3
14	Kt to B 3	P to K B 4 [7]

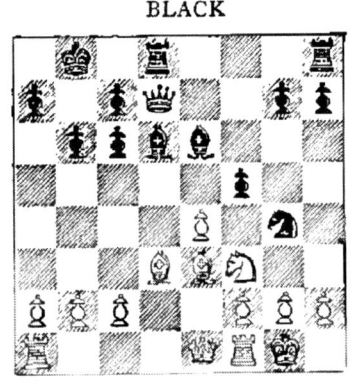

White to make his 15th move.

WHITE	BLACK	WHITE	BLACK
15 P to K R 3	P to K R 4	45 K × R	P to Q R 5
16 B to K Kt 5	Q R to K sq	46 P to Kt 4	P × P
17 Q to B 3	B to B 2	47 P × P	K to Kt 5
18 Kt to Q 4 [8]	B to B 4	48 K to B 3	P to R 6
19 Kt × K B P	P to Kt 3	49 P to Kt 5	Kt to Q 4
20 Kt to R 4	Kt to K 4	50 P to K 4	Kt to K 2
21 B to K 2	B to Q 5	51 K to B 4	K to Kt 6
22 Q to K Kt 3	B to B 5	52 K to K 5	P to B 4
23 B × B	Kt × B	53 K to B 6	Kt to Kt sq, ch
24 P to Q B 3	B to B 4	54 K to B 7	P to B 5
25 P to Kt 3	Kt to Q 7	55 K × Kt	P to B 6
26 K R to Q sq	Kt × K P	56 P to Kt 6	P to B 7
27 R × Q	Kt × Q	57 K to B 7	K to Kt 7
28 P to Kt 4	Kt to K 7, ch	58 R to R sq	P to R 7
29 K to B sq	B to Q 3	59 P to Kt 7	R P Queens
30 B to K 3	Kt × P	60 R × Q	K × R
31 B to Q 4	B × P	61 P Queens	P Queens
32 B × R	R × B	62 Q to Q R 8, ch	
33 P to R 3	B to B 4		K to Kt 2
34 Kt × P	R to K sq	63 Q to Kt 7, ch	K to R 3
35 P to Q R 4	R to K 7	64 P to K 5	Q to K B 5, ch
36 R to B 7	R to Q 7	65 K to K 6	Q to R 3, ch
37 Kt to K 5	K to Kt 2	66 K to B 5	Q to R 4, ch
38 P to R 5	P × P	67 K to B 4	Q to R 7, ch
39 Kt to B 4	R to B 7	68 K to B 5	Q to R 4, ch
40 Kt × P, ch	K to Kt 3	69 K to B 6	Q to R 3, ch
41 Kt to B 4, ch [9]	K to Kt 4 (!)	70 K to B 2	Q to R 2, ch
42 Kt to K 3	B × Kt	71 K to K 6	Q to Kt 3, ch
43 P × B	P to R 4 [10]	72 K to Q 7	Q to Kt 2, ch
44 R to B 2	R × R	Drawn game.	

NOTES BY C. VON BARDELEBEN.

[1] The usual move is P to Q 3 ; P × P is not good.

[2] White fails to take advantage of the weak fourth move of Black ; he should have played 5. P to B 3, P × P, 6 Q to Q 5, or 5. .... Kt to B 3 ; 6. P to K 5, Kt to K 5, 7. B to Q 5, Kt to B 4 , 8 P × P, and would have obtained the better game.

[3] By this line of play White gets no attacking chances. An interesting and more promising continuation would be 6. Castles, and, if then 6 . Kt × P, White would be enabled to establish a brilliant attack by 7. Kt to B 5, P to K Kt 3 (if 7. .... Castles (?) ; 8 Q to Kt 4, Kt to Kt 4 ; 9. Kt × B, ch, winning a Piece) ; 8. B × P, ch (!), K × B , 9. Q to Q 5, ch, K to B 3 ; 10. Kt to R 6 (!), and Black cannot save the King's Knight because of 11. Kt to Kt 4, ch, K to Kt 2 ; 12. B to

R 6, mate; if Black plays instead of 9. . . . K to B 3, 9. . . . K to K sq, White may proceed with 10. Kt to Kt 7, ch, K to B sq; 11. B to R 6, Kt to B 3; 12. Kt to R 5, ch, K to K sq; 13. Kt to Kt 7, ch, drawing by perpetual check, or with 10. Kt × B, Kt to B 3 (!) (10. . . . Q × Kt [?]; 11. R to K sq); 11. Kt × Kt, Kt × Q; 12. Kt × Q, K × Q; 13. P to Q B 4, &c.

[4] This move loses too much time. Better would be 7. Q × Q, ch, B × Q; 8. Castles.

[5] This and the following move yield the second player the superior game.

[6] An unsound and useless diversion of the Queen. Better would be the simple development of Pieces by 9. Kt to B 3, Castles Q R; 10. B to K 3.

[7] Black plays too hastily for attack, and thus throws away his advantage of position. The right move was P to B 3; if then 15. P to K R 3, he answers P to K R 4, and White cannot take the Knight because of 15. . . . P × P; 16. Kt to Q 4, B to R 7, ch; 17. K to R sq, Q to B 2; 18. Kt × B, B to Kt 6, ch; 19. K to Kt sq, R to R 8, ch (!); 20. K × R, Q to R 4, ch; or 18. P to K Kt 3, Q to R 4.

[8] Preferable would be 18. P × P.

[9] Better would be 41. Kt to Kt 3, but the ending is very difficult, and Black has, in any case, some chance for a draw.

[10] In spite of the loss of the exchange Black has now at least an even game.

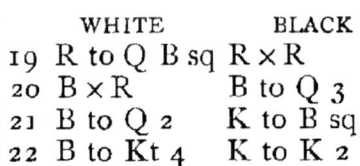

H. N. Pillsbury v. I. Gunsberg.

	WHITE	BLACK		WHITE	BLACK
1	P to Q 4	P to Q 4	19	R to Q B sq	R × R
2	P to Q B 4	P to Q B 3	20	B × R	B to Q 3
3	P to K 3	P to K Kt 3	21	B to Q 2	K to B sq
4	Kt to Q B 3	B to Kt 2 [1]	22	B to Kt 4	K to K 2
5	Kt to B 3	Kt to B 3			
6	B to Q 3	Castles			
7	Kt to K 5	P × P			
8	B × B P	Kt to Q 4			
9	P to B 4	B to K 3			
10	Q to Kt 3 [2]	P to Q Kt 4			
11	B × Kt	B × B			
12	Kt × B	Q × Kt			
13	Q × Q	P × Q			
14	Kt to Q 3 [3]	Kt to Q 2			
15	B to Q 2	K R to B sq			
16	K to K 2	P to K 3			
17	K R to Q B sq				
		B to B sq			
18	R × R	R × R			

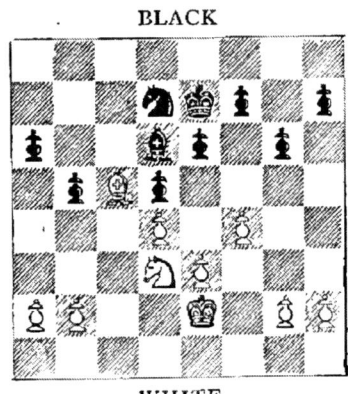

BLACK

WHITE

White to make his 24th move.

	WHITE	BLACK		WHITE	BLACK
23	B to B 5	P to Q R 3 [4]	32	P to K 4 [10]	P × P
24	P to Q Kt 4	P to B 3	33	P to Q 5, ch	K to Q 3
25	P to K Kt 4	B × B [5]	34	K to K 3	P to Kt 5 [11]
26	Kt P × B	Kt to Kt sq [6]	35	K × P	P to R 5
27	P to B 5 [7]	P to Kt 4	36	K to Q 4	P to R 4
28	Kt to Kt 4	P to Q R 4	37	P × P	P to R 6
29	P to B 6 [8]	K to Q 3	38	K to B 4	P to B 4
30	P × P [9]	Kt × P	39	P to R 6	P to B 5
31	Kt × Kt	K × Kt	40	P to R 7	Resigns.

NOTES BY E. LASKER.

[1] Black chooses a peculiar, but not altogether sound, manner of development. The objection to this mode of bringing the Bishop out is that it costs two moves, brings the Bishop on a line which is blocked, and allows the first player possibilities of a King's side attack beginning with P to K R 4.

[2] So far White has treated the opening to perfection; but here 10. B to Q 3, soon to be followed by P to K R 4, seems preferable.

[3] He must now try to reserve his Knight for the ending, as the abundance of obstructions leaves little scope to the Bishops and Rooks.

[4] Almost obviously 23. ... P to Q R 4 would have been better, and would have reduced White's chance for a win to zero. For instance: 23. ... P to Q R 4; 24. P to Q Kt 4, P × P; 25. B × P, B × B; 26. Kt × B, K to Q 3; 27. P to Kt 4, P to B 3; soon to be followed by P to K 4.

[5] And here 25. ... Kt × B; 26. Kt P × Kt, B to B 2, would have left the game perfectly even, a Bishop being so much more suitable to stop advancing Pawns than a Knight.

[6] His best continuation was 26 ... P to Q R 4, when the following play would have been possible. 27. P to B 5, P to Kt 4, 28. P to B 6, Kt to Kt 3, 29. Kt to B 5, P × P, 30. P × P, K to Q 3; 31. Kt to Kt 7, ch, K × P; 32. Kt × P, ch, K to B 2; and Black has, if anything, the better chance, as he threatens Kt to B 5 and Q 3.

[7] White's play from here unto the end is of the highest order. If this Pawn is taken, 27 ... Kt P × P; 28. P × P, P × P; then 29. Kt to B 4 follows, which would ensure to White the advantage of two united passed centre Pawns. If, on the other hand, 27 .. K P × P; 28. P × P, P to Kt 4; 29. Kt to Kt 4, would lead to the same result.

[8] Threatening, of course, P to B 7.

[9] If now 30. ... P × Kt, then 31. P to K 7, K × P; 32. P to B 7.

[10] The key to this remarkable combination. Whether the offered Pawn is taken or not, White will always win with his two united passed Pawns, e.g.:—32. . K to Q 3; 33. P × P, K to K 2; 34. K to K 3, K to Q 3; 35. K to K 4, K to K 2; 36. K to B 5, P to Kt 5; 37. P to Q 6, ch, and wins.

SEPTEMBER 2

[11] 34. ... P to B 4 would find its reply in 35. P × P, P to Q Kt 5 ; 36. P to B 6, P to R 5 ; 37. P to B 7, K to K 2 ; 38. P to Q 6, ch, K to B sq ; 39. P to Q 7, K to K 2 ; 40. P to B 8, Queens, &c.

Dr. Tarrasch v. B. Vergani.

	WHITE	BLACK
1	P to K 4	P to K 4
2	Kt to Q B 3	Kt to Q B 3 [1]
3	P to K Kt 3 [2]	P to Q 3
4	B to Kt 2	P to K Kt 3 [3]
5	P to Q 3	B to Kt 2
6	B to K 3	B to K 3
7	K Kt to K 2	K Kt to K 2
8	Kt to Q 5	Castles
9	Q to Q 2	Q to Q 2
10	P to Q B 3	Kt to Q sq
11	P to K R 4	P to K R 4 [4]
12	Kt × Kt, ch	Q × Kt
13	P to Q 4	K to R 2
14	Castles K R	P to K B 3 [5]
15	P to K B 4	P to K B 4
16	B P × P	Q P × P
17	B to Kt 5	B to B 3 [6]
18	B × B	Q × B
19	Q P × P	Q × K P
20	P × P	B × P
21	Kt to B 4	Kt to B 3
22	Q R to K sq	Q to B 4, ch
23	Q to K 3 [7]	Q × Q, ch
24	R × Q	K R to K sq
25	K R to K sq	B to Q 2 [8]
26	B to K 4	R to K Kt sq
27	Kt × R P [9]	K to R 3
28	Kt to B 6	R to Kt 2
29	Kt × B	R × Kt
30	B × Kt	P × B
31	R to K 7	R to Q 7
32	R (K sq) to K 2	Q R to Q sq [10]
33	K to B 2	R (Q 7) to Q 2
34	P to K Kt 4	R to B sq, ch

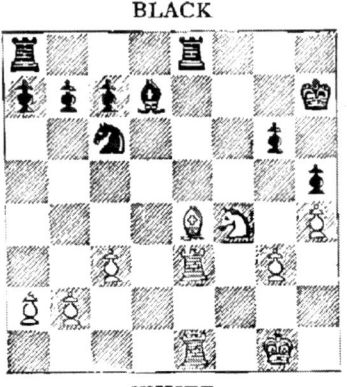

Black to make his 26th move

	WHITE	BLACK
35	K to Kt 3	R to B 2
36	R × R (B 7)	R × R
37	R to K 6	K to R 2
38	R × B P	K to Kt 2
39	R to R 6	P to B 4
40	R to Q B 6	R to Q 2
41	R × B P	R to K B 2
42	R to R 5	R to B 2
43	P to B 4	R × P
44	R × P, ch	K to Kt sq
45	P to Kt 3	R to Q 5
46	P to R 4	R to Q 3
47	P to Kt 4	R to Q 5
48	R to R 8, ch	K to Kt 2
49	P to Q Kt 5	R to Q 6, ch
50	K to B 4	R to Q 5, ch
51	K to B 3	R to Q 6, ch
52	K to K 4	R to K R 6
53	P to Kt 6	R × P
54	K to B 4	Resigns.

Notes by S. Tinsley.

[1] See notes on game Teichmann *v.* Gunsberg, Round XIII, August 21. By playing Kt to K B 3 instead, Black can at once proceed with P to Q 4, &c., getting an early open game if he so desires.

[2] Personal preferences stand for little; nevertheless, I confess a preference for this method of development. But it is hardly strong, and for some time at least yields no attack.

[3] He might, instead, venture on P to K B 4, followed by Kt to B 3 and B to K 2. There is already a lack of freedom, and White can develop at leisure.

[4] There certainly would be danger in allowing P to R 5. But herein lies a serious objection to Black's development (P to K Kt 3).

[5] Signor Vergani appears to have had some idea when playing 10... Kt to Q sq, to bring that Piece into play *via* K 3; and now Kt to B 2 appears to be the object. There is a want of firmness of purpose about the game here, and it comes out next move when the Pawn is played to the fourth square.

[6] The exchange offered is an error. There is every reason for retaining the Bishop for defence, &c.

[7] Dr Tarrasch's argument is that he will be left with the rather superior ending after the exchange, and so it turns out, owing to the position of Black's Knight, necessitating the loss or doubling of a Pawn. But the game lacks interest to some extent on that account.

[8] An ingenious defence, preventing 25 B × Kt, B × B, 26. R to K 7, ch, followed by R × P. But now comes the collapse, for it is little else.

[9] It will be found that Black cannot escape without loss (see diagram), and I can see no better defence than that actually made.

[10] A slightly better course was, perhaps, R × R. White is left with the best position and a Pawn to the good, and little more need be said, except that Dr. Tarrasch's play shines by contrast with a rather indifferent defence.

A. Walbrodt *v.* W. Steinitz.

	WHITE	BLACK		WHITE	BLACK
1	P to K 4	P to K 4	11	Kt × P	Kt × Kt
2	K Kt to B 3	Q Kt to B 3	12	Q × Kt	B × B
3	B to Kt 5	P to Q R 3	13	Q × B	P to Q 4 [5]
4	B to R 4	P to Q 3 [1]	14	P × P	Q × P
5	Castles	Kt to B 3 [2]	15	B to B 4	P to B 3
6	P to B 3	B to Q 2 [3]	16	R to K 5	Q to Q 6
7	P to Q 4	B to K 2	17	R to Q sq	Q to Kt 3
8	R to K sq	Castles	18	Kt to K 3	B to B sq
9	Q Kt to Q 2	R to K sq	19	Q to Kt 3	P to Kt 4
10	Kt to B sq	P × P [4]	20	P to K R 3	Kt to K 5 [6]

SEPTEMBER 2

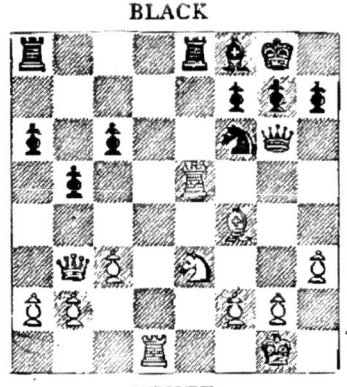

Black to make his 20th move.

	WHITE	BLACK
21	Q to B 2	R × R
22	B × R	R to K sq
23	B to B 4	Q to R 3 [7]
24	B to B 7	B to B 4
25	R to Q 8 [8]	R × R
26	B × R	Q to K 3 [9]
27	Q to Q 3	P to B 4 [10]
28	P to Q Kt 3 [11]	P to B 5 [12]
29	Kt to Q sq	Kt × K B P
30	Kt × Kt	Q to K 8, ch
31	K to R 2	B × Kt [13]
32	P to K R 4	P to K R 4
	White resigns.	

NOTES BY I. GUNSBERG.

[1] In the game Lasker v. Steinitz, we have given our opinion about this defence, and the fact that Black is successful in this instance does not induce us to alter our views. His success may be attributed to a vigorous effort at a counter-attack, such as we think the second player in the Ruy Lopez is bound to make whenever he resorts to the close defence of P to Q 3 or P to K Kt 3.

[2] This move is, we think, preferable to the move of Kt to K 2, played by Steinitz against Lasker, as Black can Castle one move earlier.

[3] If Black had taken the King's Pawn, White need not necessarily have played for its recovery at once by B × Kt, ch, followed by Q to R 4. He could have played with greater advantage 7. P to Q 4.

[4] Elsewhere, in expressing our disbelief in the efficacy of the manœuvre of the Queen's Knight, we expressed our opinion that at the time when this Knight plays to B sq, then Black should adopt a vigorous policy beginning with P × P, and not wait till White has completed his tardy developing moves. The success achieved by Black in this instance fully bears out our views.

[5] Black is fortunate in having obtained the opportunity, which he seizes at the right moment, to free his Bishop, always so inconveniently blocked in as a result of the P to Q 3 defence.

[6] With this excellent move Black succeeds in counteracting the effect produced by White's vigorous handling of his Rooks.

[7] Black cleverly utilises the awkward position of White's Queen's Bishop, in order to get up an attack on White's King's Bishop's Pawn.

[8] The only other way to prevent Kt × B P, which was threatened, was by Kt to Kt 4, but that hardly forms a lasting remedy, as the Knight would be subject to attack by Black's Pawns.

[9] This move keeps up the attack, Kt × B P being again threatened.

[10] More vigorous play, and again threatening Kt × B P, followed by P to B 5.

[11] Black's intention to play P to B 5 was so obvious that it is surprising White did not play B to B 7 to prevent that.

[12] Though Black might have played Kt × K B P at once, yet this move is better still, as it forces the game.

[13] And mate soon follows. The way Black obtained the mastery over White is very instructive, and there is a pretty neatness about the last few moves which, combined with Black's virile handling of the opening after White's move of Kt to B sq, makes this game a most refreshing and at the same time eloquent contrast to the game produced by the strategy of concentrating towards the rear, employed by Steinitz in his game against Lasker played with the same opening.

W. H. K. Pollock *v.* E. Schiffers.

	WHITE	BLACK		WHITE	BLACK
1	P to K 4	P to K 4	23	R to K B sq	R × P
2	Kt to K B 3	Q Kt to B 3	24	R to K Kt 5	P to Kt 3
3	B to B 4	Kt to B 3	25	R to B 8, ch	K to Q 2
4	P to Q 4	P × P	26	R to B 7, ch	K to Q 3
5	Kt to Kt 5	P to Q 4	27	R × R P	R to Kt 8, ch
6	P × P	Kt to Q R 4 [1]	28	K to B 2	R × P, ch
7	Q × P [2]	Kt × B	29	K to Kt 3	P to Kt 4 [7]
8	Q × Q Kt	Q × P	30	R × K Kt P	R to Kt 6
9	Q to K 2, ch [3]	B to K 3	31	K to B 4	R to B 5, ch
10	Castles K R	Castles Q R	32	K to Kt 5	R × P
11	Kt × B	Q × Kt	33	R (Kt 6) to Kt 7	
12	Q × Q, ch	P × Q [4]			R to K 4, ch
13	Kt to B 3	B to Q Kt 5	34	K to R 6	R to R 5, ch
14	B to K Kt 5	B × Kt	35	K to Kt 6	R × R
15	P × B	R to Q 4	36	R × R	P to Kt 5
16	B to K 3	K R to Q sq [5]	37	P to Kt 4	P to Kt 6
17	P to Q B 4	R to Q R 4	38	R to R 3	R to Q Kt 4
18	P to Q R 4	R to Q 3	39	R to Q 3, ch	K to K 2
19	K R to Q Kt sq		40	R to Q sq	P to Kt 7
		Kt to Kt 5	41	R to Q Kt sq	P to R 4
20	R to Q Kt 5 [6]	R × P	42	P to K R 4	P to R 5
21	Q R to Q Kt sq		43	P to R 5	P to R 6
		Kt × B	44	P to R 6	P to R 7
22	P × Kt	R to Q Kt 3		White resigns.	

Notes by Dr. Tarrasch

[1] The usual move here is Kt to K 4
[2] The game is about equal for the two players
[3] The exchange of Queens was preferable
[4] After a dozen moves the players have reached the end game,

SEPTEMBER 2

Black, being in possession of the open Queen's file, has a slight advantage and makes the best use of it.

[5] Now the superiority of Black's game is evident.

[6] Even without this blunder White cannot prevent some loss.

[7] Now follows the race of the Pawns and White arrives too late. The final moves need no comment; besides which the whole game is easily understood.

J. H. Blackburne v. S. Tinsley.

	WHITE	BLACK
1	P to K 4	P to K 3
2	Kt to Q B 3	P to Q 4
3	P to Q 4	P × P [1]
4	Kt × P	Kt to K B 3
5	B to Q 3	Kt to B 3
6	P to Q B 3	B to K 2
7	Kt to B 3	Castles
8	Q to B 2	P to K R 3
9	Castles	Kt to Q 4
10	B to Q 2	P to B 4 [2]
11	Kt to Kt 3	B to Kt 4
12	K R to K sq	B × B
13	Q × B	B to Q 2
14	Q R to Q sq	Q to B 3
15	B to B 2	Q R to Q sq
16	P to B 4 (!) [3]	K Kt to K 2
17	P to Kt 4 (!)	B to B sq
18	Q to B 3	Kt to Kt 3 [4]
19	Kt to R 5	Q to B 2
20	P to Q 5 (!)	P × P [5]

White to make his 20th move.

	WHITE	BLACK
21	P × P	Kt to Kt sq
22	P to Q 6 (!)	P × P
23	B to Kt 3	P to Q 4
24	R × P	Resigns.

Notes by C. von Bardeleben.

[1] A deviation from the usual line of play, which is not to be recommended.

[2] Weakening the King's Pawn. Better would be P to Q Kt 3, to be followed by B to Kt 2.

[3] The attack introduced by this and the following move proves very strong. The whole game is very well played by Mr. Blackburne.

[4] This move increases the difficulties of Black, but whatever he plays he has a cramped game.

[5] Black's game is hopeless. If Q Kt to K 2, then 21. P × P, B × P; 22. R × B, and White wins.

A. Burn v. E. Lasker.

	WHITE	BLACK
1	P to Q 4	P to Q 4
2	P to Q B 4	P to K 3
3	Kt to K B 3	Kt to K B 3
4	Kt to B 3	P to B 4
5	P to K 3 [1]	Kt to B 3
6	B P × P	K P × P
7	B to Q 3	P to Q R 3
8	P × P	B × P
9	Castles	Castles
10	B to Q 2	R to K sq
11	R to B sq	B to R 2
12	Kt to K 2 [2]	B to Kt 5
13	B to B 3 [3]	Kt to K 5
14	Kt to Kt 3	Kt × P [4]
15	R × Kt	R × P
16	Kt to B 5 [5]	R × Kt [6]
17	P × R	B × Kt
18	B × B	Q to Kt 4, ch

BLACK

White to make his 15th move.

WHITE	BLACK
19 B to Kt 4	P to K R 4
20 Q to Q 2	B to K 6
White resigns.	

Notes by H. N. Pillsbury.

[1] In a game between Blackburne and Showalter the former here continued B to K Kt 5.

[2] It would be better to prevent the pinning by P to K R 3; Black has much the freer position of Pieces, fully compensating for the isolated Pawn.

[3] Kt to Kt 3 at once was the correct move, and would have prevented the formation of the attack which ensues.

[4] This pretty sacrifice leads to fine complications, but there appears to be a flaw in it.

[5] Why not simply B to K 2? If in answer 16. . . Q to Kt 3; then 17. Kt to Q 4, or if 16. . . B × Kt; 17. B × B, Q to Kt 3; 18. Q to K B sq. White appears to retain at least the exchange ahead in all variations.

[6] Black now demolishes the opposing position with a few well-chosen, timely strokes.

[After 16. B to K 2, Q to Kt 3; 17. Kt to Q 4, R × Kt may have deterred White.—Ed.]

D. Janowski v. A. Albin.

	WHITE	BLACK		WHITE	BLACK
1	P to Q 4	P to K B 4 [1]	4	P to K 3	Kt to K B 3
2	P to Q B 4	P to K 3	5	B to Q 3 [3]	Castles
3	Kt to Q B 3	B to Kt 5 [2]	6	Kt to B 3 [4]	P to Q 3

SEPTEMBER 2

WHITE	BLACK		WHITE	BLACK
7 Q to Kt 3	P to Q B 4 [5]		11 Q to B 2	P to K 4 [6]
8 Castles	Kt to B 3		12 B × P [7]	P to K 5
9 R to Q sq	B × Kt		13 B × B [8]	P × Kt
10 P × B	Q to K 2		14 K B to R 3	Kt to K 5 [9]
			15 P to K Kt 3	Q R to Q sq
			16 Q R to Kt sq	P to Q Kt 3
			17 B to B sq	Q R to K sq
			18 B to Q 3	Q to Q 2 [10]
			19 K to R sq	Q to R 6
			20 B to B sq	Q to R 4
			21 P to K R 3	Kt to Kt 4
			22 K to R 2	R to K 5
			23 Q to R 4 [11]	Kt × R P
			24 Q × Kt [12]	Kt × B P, ch
			25 K to Kt sq	Kt to R 3, ch
			26 B × Kt	Q × B
			27 Q R to Kt 2	Q × P, ch
			28 K to B sq	R to R 5, and wins.

Black to make his 11th move.

NOTES BY S. TINSLEY.

[1] Dealing with general principles, it may be said that Black plays for King's side attack by adopting this somewhat risky advance at so early a stage. If the attack proves unsuccessful, the King's Pawn and centre generally are left weak for the middle and end game play.

[2] Probably inferior in most cases. Here Kt to B 3 first is excellent.

[3] A far superior line of play about this point is P to K Kt 3, as Kt to K 5 (Black) is very easily defended by Q to Q 3 or Kt 3. Then Kt to K 2 and B to Kt 2 can follow as convenient.

[4] P to K Kt 3 was still advisable. It was, in fact, imperative to prevent any chance of P to B 5 by Black.

[5] A very ingenious reply to a poor move. If 8. P × P, P × P, and there is an immediate attack on the Bishop. That White's seventh move is not good is proved by his eleventh move, which see.

[6] Herr Albin's genius is well displayed in this striking position. The play should be followed carefully from this point (see diagram).

[7] It is pretty clear Black has now all the attack. It is also evident that White did not see the pretty *coup* in store for him, and even if he had noticed it, the remedy is not easy to seek. By the advance of the centre Pawn Black, in fact, has thus early a fine game.

[8] Black's 12. P to K 5 is splendidly conceived, and B × P seems the natural reply. But it proves insufficient, as is observed by the *Standard* correspondent, who suggests the following variations:—13. Kt to R 4. If 13... P to K Kt 4, then 14. B × B, R × B; 15. Kt to B 5, &c. The most difficult variation ensues from 13.... Kt to Kt 5. The continuation then would be: 14. B × B, R × P; 15. Kt to B 5,

Q to B 3 ; 16. Q × P, R × B ; 17. Q × Kt, Q × Kt ; 18. Q × Q, R × Q,
and White could make a fight of it ; or if 14. . . . R × B ; 15. P to B 3,
Kt × P ; 16 Q × P, Q × Q ; 17. P × Q, Kt to Kt 5, &c. There are a
number of interesting variations emanating if any of the above moves
are changed

[9] Again the play is fine, for if the obvious P × P, then Kt to Kt 4
with a telling attack.

[10] If now 19. B × Kt, then R × B ; 20. Q to R 6, and wins easily.

[11] It is too dangerous to leave the position wholly at Black's
mercy ; but the point is, there is now little to be done.

[12] Herr Albin, who was pardonably proud of this game, explained
after that he intended, if 24. B × Kt, R to B 3, and the game is over
because Q × B, ch, and mate by R to R 3 cannot be avoided. It is
one more of the very pretty ideas underlying this charming little
partie.

C. Schlechter *v.* M Tchigorin.

	WHITE	BLACK		WHITE	BLACK
1	P to K 4	P to K 4	28	K to K 2	R to K R sq
2	Kt to K B 3	Kt to Q B 3	29	P to Q Kt 4	Q R to K Kt sq
3	B to Kt 5	P to Q R 3	30	R to K Kt sq	P to Kt 5 [6]
4	B to R 4	Kt to B 3	31	P to K B 4	Kt to Q sq [7]
5	Castles	P to Q 3	32	P to B 5 [8]	Kt to B 2
6	P to Q 4	Kt to Q 2 [1]	33	Kt to B 2	Kt to Q 3
7	Kt to B 3	B to K 2	34	B to B 5	Kt to Kt 3
8	Kt to K 2 [2]	Castles	35	Kt to Q sq [9]	Kt to B sq
9	P to B 3	B to B 3	36	Kt to K 3	K to B 2
10	Kt to Kt 3	Kt to K 2	37	Kt to Q 5	P to B 3
11	B to Kt 3 [3]	Kt to K Kt 3	38	Kt to B 7	Kt × K P
12	B to K 3	R to K sq	39	Q R to Q sq	Kt × B
13	Q to Q 2	Kt (Q 2) to B sq	40	P × Kt	R to Q sq
14	P × P [4]	P × P	41	Kt to K 6	R × R
15	Q × Q	B × Q	42	R × R	K to K 2
16	Kt to Kt 5	B × Kt	43	P to R 4 [10]	P × P *en passant*
17	B × B	B to K 3	44	R to R sq	K to B 2
18	Kt to K 2 [5]	B × B	45	R × P	Kt to K 2
19	P × B	Kt to K 3	46	P to K Kt 4	P to R 5
20	B to K 3	Q R to Q sq	47	P to B 4	Kt to Kt 3 [11]
21	K R to Q sq	P to K B 3	48	P × Kt	K × Kt
22	P to B 3	K to B 2	49	P to Kt 7	R to K Kt sq
23	K to B 2	K to K 2	50	R × P	R × P
24	P to Kt 3	Kt (Kt 3) to B	51	K to K 3	K to B 2
25	K to K sq	Kt to Q 2 [sq	52	P to Kt 4	K to Kt 3 [12]
26	Kt to B sq	P to K Kt 4	53	R to R 8	P to B 4
27	Kt to Q 3	P to K R 4	54	P × P, ch	K × P

SEPTEMBER 2

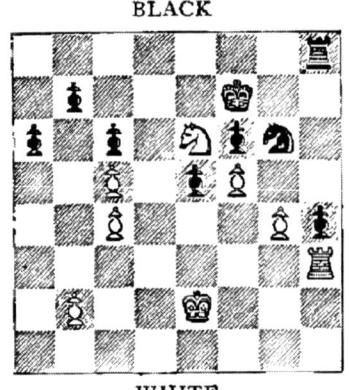

White to make his 48th move.

WHITE	BLACK
55 R to R 5, ch	K to K 3
56 R to R 6, ch	K to Q 2
57 P to Kt 5 [13]	R P × P
58 P × P	P × P
59 K to K 4	R to K 2
60 R to Q Kt 6	K to B 2
61 R × P (Kt 5)	K to B 3
62 R to R 5	R to K sq
63 R to R 7	R to K 3 [14]
64 R to R 5 [15]	R to K 2
65 R to R sq	K × P
66 R to B sq, ch	K to Q 3 [16]
67 R to Q sq, ch	K to B 2
68 R to B sq, ch	K to Q 2
69 R to Q sq, ch	K to B sq
70 R to Q 5 [17]	K to B 2
71 R to B 5, ch	K to Q 3
72 R to Kt 5	K to B 3
73 R to Kt sq	P to Kt 4
74 R to B sq, ch	K to Kt 3
75 R to Q Kt sq	R to K sq [18]
76 R to Kt 2	K to B 4
77 R to B 2, ch	K to Kt 5
78 R to Kt 2, ch	K to B 5
White resigns.	

NOTES BY W. STEINITZ.

[1] The idea of blocking the Bishop with the Knight by development on the part of the first player, and by retreat (as here) for the second player, was first brought out by Steinitz, and, singularly enough, each time in a game against Blackburne. The development occurred in a match in 1876, and the retreat in a 'Three Knights' Game' in the London Tournament of 1883. In this opening the main object of the retreat is to avoid the necessity of exchanging centre Pawns, and thus to keep White King's Knight inactive. The judgment about the efficacy of this scheme involves the question whether the Black King's Knight should be brought out previously at B 3 or at K 2.

[2] It is always worth while to obtain two Bishops against Knight and Bishop early. Kt to Q 5, with the view of exchanging, followed by R to K sq, was therefore stronger

[3] B to B 2 is generally preferable in such positions, as it gives more freedom to the Queen's Knight's Pawn, which it may be useful to advance in some contingencies. 11. Kt to R 5, and if Kt to K Kt 3; 12. B × Kt, B × B; 13. Kt × B, ch, Q × Kt; 14. P × P, Kt × P; 15. Kt to Q 7, with the better game, was also worth trying for.

[4] More lively and promising was 14. Kt to Kt 5, Kt to K 3; 15. Kt × Kt, B × Kt; 16. B × B, R × B; 17. P to B 3, &c. Dry dulness reigns in this game for a long time after the exchanges, which are the natural outcome of this, were effected.

[5] Neumann and Winawer have first shown that the Knight is

more often stronger than the Bishop when a Pawn is doubled in the camp of the latter. It was, therefore, all the more objectionable to allow his Pawns to be doubled here, as the adversary had still both Knights on the board. B to B 2, retaining the two Bishops, was best

[6] Life and spirit has been infused by Mr. Tchigorin into an apparently barren position, which did not seem capable of such interesting attacking development.

[7] P × P would have either effected the isolation of White's King's Pawn, or given Black two Pawns to one on the King's wing, which being supported by heavier Pieces was rather stronger than White's similar constellation in the centre.

[8] 32. Kt to B 5, Kt to B 2; 33. Q R to Q sq, Kt to Q 3; 34. Kt × Kt, K × Kt, 35. B to B 5 led to equalisation, and White could expect no more.

[9] Again an easy draw could have been secured by 34. B × Kt, ch, or Knight at Kt 6, followed by P to Q Kt 3. This and the next movements of the Knight imperil his game, the root of his central position, his King's Pawn, being left without good support.

[10] White was bound to stop the advance of the adverse King's Rook's Pawn, which would also make room for the Black Rook attacking the King's Bishop's Pawn later on by R to R 4.

[11] A fine move. Black threatens Kt to B sq in case White refuses to exchange at once. (See diagram.)

[12] Threatening R to R 2

[13] White's defence, after the loss of the Pawn, has developed remarkable resources of resistance up to this point, where his tenacity breaks down. K to Q 3 would have made it at least extremely difficult for Black to win, and opened various prospects of a draw

[14] The manner in which Black gains the move, and consequently the Pawn, is an instructive lesson for students.

[15] In a similar way if 64. K to B 5, R to K sq; 65 K to K 4, R to K 2, &c

[16] This might have caused prolongation. The precise way of winning, as pointed out by Mr. Tchigorin, was 66, . . . K to Kt 5; 67. R to Kt sq, ch, K to B 6, 68. R to B sq, ch (or 68. R to Kt 5 or Kt 6, K to B 5, &c.), K to Kt 7; 69 R to B 5, K to Kt 6, and will give support for his Pawn with the King at Kt 5 or B 5 in a few moves.

[17] If White had now played R to Kt sq, Black could not win except by entering on a war with his King downward again, and adopting the process shown in the last note

[18] A fine ending, typical of its kind.

R Teichmann *v.* J. Mason.

WHITE	BLACK	WHITE	BLACK
1 P to Q 4	P to Q 4	4 B to B 4	B to Q 3 [1]
2 P to Q B 4	P to K 3	5 B to Kt 3	P to Q Kt 3 [2]
3 Kt to Q B 3	Kt to K B 3	6 P to K 3	B to Kt 2

SEPTEMBER 2

	WHITE	BLACK
7	P × P	Kt × P
8	Kt to B 3	Kt × Kt [3]
9	P × Kt	Kt to Q 2
10	B to Q 3	P to K R 3
11	Q to K 2	Q to K 2
12	B to B 2	Castles
13	B to K R 4	Q to K sq [4]
14	Kt to Q 2	P to K B 4
15	P to K B 4	Q R to B sq
16	Castles	P to Q B 4
17	B to Q Kt 3	B to Q 4
18	Q R to B sq	B × B
19	P × B	B to K 2
20	B × B	Q × B [5]
21	Q to Q 3	Q to Q 3
22	P to K R 3	Kt to B 3
23	Kt to B 4	Q to Q 4
24	Kt to Q 2	K R to Q sq
25	K R to Q sq	R to B 2
26	P to Q B 4	Q to Q 3
27	Kt to B 3	Kt to K 5
28	Kt to K 5	Q to K 2
29	Q to K 2	P × P
30	P × P	Q to R 5
31	Q to K 3	Q to Kt 6 [6]
32	Q × Q	Kt × Q
33	K to B 2	Kt to K 5, ch
34	K to K 3	Kt to B 3 [7]
35	K to B 3	Kt to Q 2
36	R to Q 3	Kt × Kt
37	B P × Kt	P to Q Kt 4
38	K to K 3	P × P [8]
39	P × P	K to B 2
40	R to R 3	P to K Kt 4
41	R to R 6	R to Q Kt sq
42	R to B 2	R to Kt 6, ch
43	K to K 2	R to Kt 6
44	K to B 2	R to Q 6

	WHITE	BLACK
45	R to Q 6	P to B 5
46	P to B 5	P to K R 4
47	P to B 6 [9]	K to K 2
48	K to K 2	R to Q Kt 6
49	K to B sq	P to Kt 5
50	P × P	P × P

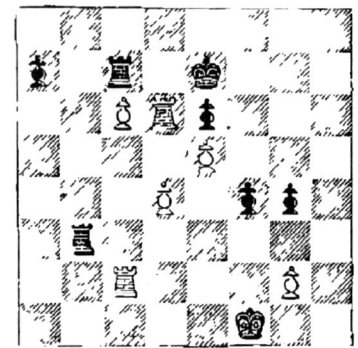

White to make his 51st move.

	WHITE	BLACK
51	P to Q 5	P × P
52	R to K Kt 6	R to Kt 3
53	R to B 5	R to B sq
54	K to K 2	P to Q R 3
55	K to Q 3	R to Kt 4
56	K to Q 4	R × R
57	K × R	P to B 6
58	P × P	P × P
59	R to B 6	P to B 7
60	R × P	K to K 3
61	R to B 6, ch	K × P
62	R to Q 6	P to R 4
63	R × P, ch	K to K 3
64	R to Q 4	K to K 2
65	R to K 4, ch	K to B 2 [10]
66	K to Kt 6	R to Kt sq, ch
67	K × P	Resigns.

NOTES BY E. SCHIFFERS.

[1] Stronger would have been B to Q Kt 5, and if 5 Q to Kt 3, then Kt to B 3, threatening Kt × P (Q × B, Kt to B 7, ch). Black, after

⁴ ... B to Q Kt 5, threatens Kt to K 5, when an opportunity presents itself

² And now B to Q Kt 5 might have been played.

³ A premature exchange ; Black only unites White's Pawns in the centre.

⁴ It is evident that P to Kt 4 would only disturb Black's Castling position, and further White's purpose. If 13. ... Kt to B 3, then 14. Q to Q 3, &c.

⁵ Black, apparently, endeavours all along to simplify the play ; the game is perfectly even at present.

⁶ Instead of this move, Black might have attempted to get up an attack by means of P to Kt 4, and R to Kt 2 or R 2.

⁷ And now P to Kt 4 might have been played.

⁸ Black gratuitously assists White in obtaining a passed Pawn.

⁹ The passed Pawn is now so strong that Black will hardly be able to draw

¹⁰ After 65. K to Q sq, would follow 66. K to Q 6, and White wins easily

G. Marco v. C. von Bardeleben.

	WHITE	BLACK		WHITE	BLACK
1	P to K 4	P to K Kt 3 [1]	26	Q × Q	B × Q [4]
2	P to Q 4	B to Kt 2	27	K Kt to K 2	R to R sq
3	P to Q B 3	P to Q 3	28	Kt to Kt 5	B × Kt
4	B to K 3	Kt to Q 2	29	B × B	P to R 3
5	B to Q B 4	K Kt to B 3	30	B to Q 3	Kt to Q 2
6	Kt to Q 2	P to K 4	31	Kt to Q 4	Kt to K 4
7	P to Q 5 [2]	Castles	32	Kt to K 6, ch	K to B 3
8	P to K R 4	Kt to Kt 3	33	B to K 2	R to R 7
9	B to K 2	Kt to K sq	34	R to Q 2	R to R 6
10	P to R 5	P to K B 4 [3]	35	Kt × Q B P	Kt × P
11	P × Kt P	P × Kt P	36	R to Q 3	R to R 8, ch
12	P to B 3	P to B 5	37	R to Q sq	R × R, ch
13	B to B 2	B to B 3	38	K × R	Kt to R 7 [5]
14	P to K Kt 3	P × P	39	Kt to K 6	P to B 6
15	B × P	Kt to Kt 2	40	B to Q 3	P to B 7
16	Q to B 2	Kt to R 4	41	Kt × B	K × Kt
17	B to B 2	Kt to K B 5	42	P to B 4	K to B 3
18	Castles	K to Kt 2	43	P to Kt 4	P Queens
19	B to K 3	R to R sq	44	B × Q	Kt × B
20	R × R	Q × R	45	K to K 2	Kt to Kt 6, ch
21	B × Kt	P × B	46	K to B 3	Kt to R 4
22	Kt to Kt 3	B to Q 2	47	P to B 5	P × P
23	B to Q 3	Q to R 4	48	P × P	K to K 4
24	Kt to Q 4	Q to K 4	49	P to B 6	P × P
25	Q to Kt 2	Q to Kt 4	50	P × P	K to Q 3

SEPTEMBER 2

WHITE	BLACK		WHITE	BLACK
51 K to Kt 4	K × P		54 K to Kt 5	Kt × P, ch
52 K to Kt 5	K to Q 3		55 K to B 4	Kt to B 6
53 K × P	Kt to Kt 6			White resigns.

NOTES BY R. TEICHMANN.

[1] This was the last game in the Tournament, and Herr von Bardeleben had to win the game if he wanted to be amongst the prize winners. He adopted, therefore, an opening which is but little analysed and allows of complications.

[2] A very bad move, especially after he has developed the B to B 4.

[3] Quite right; the attack of the first player need not be feared with all his Pieces blocked in.

[4] Black has by far the best of the end game; his Rook is able to take possession of the open file and the White King's Bishop's Pawn is very weak.

[5] Having conducted the whole end game with great skill and accuracy, Herr von Bardeleben reaps now the benefit of his superior strategy. White has to give up a Piece for the passed Pawn.

A game played by the winner of the Minor Tournament, Herr MAROCZY (Black) against Rev. J. OWEN (White), who tied with him in his section.

WHITE	BLACK		WHITE	BLACK
1 K Kt to B 3	P to K Kt 3		21 Kt to Kt 5	Castles
2 P to Q 4	B to Kt 2		22 K to R 2	Q to Kt 3
3 P to K 3 [1]	P to Q 3 [2]		23 P to R 3	Kt to Q B 4
4 B to Q 3	P to K 4		24 B to B 2	P to Kt 6
5 P to B 3	B to Kt 5 [3]		25 B to K 4 [6]	Kt to B 4
6 P to K R 3	B × Kt			
7 Q × B	P to Q B 3			
8 Kt to R 3	Kt to Q 2			
9 Kt to B 4 [4]	Q to B 2			
10 P to Q 5 [5]	Kt to B 4			
11 B to B 2	Kt to K 2			
12 P to K 4	P × P			
13 P × P	Kt to Q 2			
14 B to Kt 3	P to Q Kt 4			
15 Kt to K 3	P to B 4			
16 Q to K 2	R to Q Kt sq			
17 Castles	P to B 5			
18 Kt to B 2	P to Q R 4			
19 Kt to R 3	Q to B 4			
20 P to B 4	P to Kt 5			

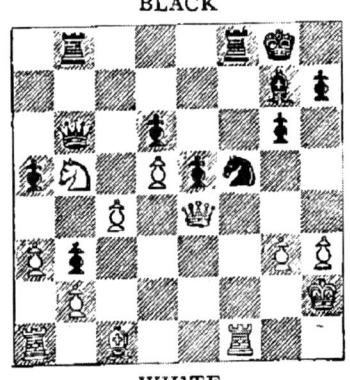

BLACK

WHITE

Black to make his 28th move.

WHITE	BLACK	WHITE	BLACK
26 P to Kt 4 [7]	P × P *en p.*, ch	35 K to R 3	B to B 5 [10]
27 P × P	Kt × B [8]	36 Q to B 8, ch	K to Kt 2
28 Q × Kt	Kt × P	37 Q to B 7, ch	K to R 3
29 K × Kt	R × R	38 Q × R	R to Q 7
30 B to K 3	R × R	39 Kt × P [11]	K to R 4
31 B × Q	R × B	40 Q to Kt sq	R to Q 6, ch
32 P to K R 4	B to R 3	41 K to Kt 2	R to Kt 6, ch
33 K to Kt 2	R to R 7	White resigns.	
34 Q to Kt 4 [9]	R × P, ch		

NOTES BY I. GUNSBERG.

[1] Against this defence we should be inclined to play 3 P to K 4.

[2] Rightly taking advantage of White's passive move and preparing to play P to K 4.

[3] As a rule Black does not gain much through the capture of this Knight, though in the present instance Black has some prospect of embarrassing the White Queen after re-taking his Bishop by playing P to K B 4 later on. For that purpose Black would have done better to have also made the preparatory move of 7. Q to B sq instead of P to Q B 3.

[4] This Knight passes a most unfortunate existence for the whole of this game. He has no prospects of developing on B 4. His proper place should have been B 2, to strengthen the centre, and to enable White to stop the coming advance of the King's Bishop's Pawn by playing such moves as P to K 4 and P to K Kt 4, &c.

[5] This only results in Black's favour by allowing him freer scope on the Queen's side.

[6] How splendidly Black has developed his game on both wings may be seen from the position. Black threatened P to B 6, but the text move is hardly calculated to improve White's defence. B to Kt sq would have been better. The worst of White's position is that he cannot play P to B 3, as that would create a weak spot on his King's Knight's file.

[7] When in difficulties it is right to make a counter-demonstration, even though it is a bad one, for the onus of proving it to be bad is thrown on the other side; but Black in this instance takes advantage of his opportunity in a masterly manner.

[8] With the obvious intention of sacrificing a Piece, he enters on a very long-headed combination, in which he gives up his Queen for two Rooks.

[9] Owing to Black's admirable disposition of his forces it would have been quite useless for White to have attempted to defend the Knight's Pawn by Q to K 2 or Q to Kt sq. White therefore adopts the right course by endeavouring to bring his Queen and Knight into Black's game. On second consideration we think, nevertheless, that there was a good deal of play in 34. Q to Kt sq, threatening Kt to B 3.

[10] Played with great courage and intrepidity. Of course, Black

SEPTEMBER 2

saw that White threatened his Rook by a series of checks; but he deliberately submits to it, and steers with a great deal of confidence into a mating combination.

[11] This was fatal, but Black's last move was such a fine one that White had not much choice of moves left. Black's object was two-fold—first, to get the White Knight away so that it should not be able to stop the Black Knight's Pawn from Queening by playing Kt to B 3; secondly, to compel the White Queen to play to Kt sq, where she could be captured by R to Q 6, ch, followed by R to Kt 6, ch. But 39 Kt to B 3, R to Q 6, ch; 40 K to Kt 2, R × Kt; 41. P to B 5 gives White a faint prospect of being able to draw. But with Kt × P, Black wins speedily with a clever move of K to R 4. The game on the whole is exceedingly well played by Black.

CONSULTATION GAME.

The following is a consultation game played between Messrs. Blackburne and Pillsbury (White) and Messrs. Tchigorin and Schiffers (Black), on Thursday, August 15; it is a very fine specimen of chess, and will well repay study:—

QUEEN'S GAMBIT DECLINED.

	WHITE	BLACK		WHITE	BLACK
1	P to Q 4	P to Q 4	25	B × Kt	R × B
2	P to Q B 4	Kt to Q B 3	26	B × R P	P to Kt 3
3	Kt to K B 3	B to K Kt 5	27	B to Q 3	Kt to K 2
4	P × P	B × Kt	28	R to R 3	Q R to K B sq
5	Kt P × B	Q × P	29	R to Kt 2	Kt to Q 4
6	P to K 3	P to K 3	30	B to B 4	R (B sq) to B 4
7	Kt to Q B 3	B to Kt 5	31	B × Kt	P × B
8	B to Q 2	B × Kt	32	R to Kt 5	R × Kt P
9	P × B	K Kt to K 2	33	R × Q P	R to Kt 7
10	P to K 4	Q to K R 4	34	P to K 6	R (B 5) × B P
11	R to Q Kt sq	R to Q Kt sq	35	R to Q 8, ch	K to R 2
12	B to K 2	Castles	36	R × R P, ch	K to Kt 3
13	R to Kt 5	P to K B 4	37	R to Kt 4, ch	K to B 3
14	P to K B 4	Q to R 5	38	R × R	R × R
15	P to K 5	P to Q R 3	39	P to Q 5	R to Q B 7
16	R to Q Kt sq	Kt to Q 4	40	R to B 8, ch	K to K 2
17	B to B 4	Q to R 6	41	R to B 7, ch	K to Q sq
18	B to K B sq	Q to Kt 5	42	R to Q 7, ch	K to B sq
19	Q × Q	P × Q	43	R × K Kt P	K to Q sq
20	R to K Kt sq	P to K R 4	44	R to Kt 3	R × R P
21	P to K R 3	Kt × P	45	R to Kt 8, ch	K to K 2
22	P × P	P to R 5	46	R to Q B 8	R to R 2
23	P to Kt 5	Kt to K 2	47	K to K 2	P to B 4
24	R to K R sq	Kt (K 2) to Kt 3	48	K to Q 3, and White wins	

AWARDING THE PRIZES.

The prizes were presented by Mrs. Sayer-Milward on Tuesday afternoon, September 3, at a ceremony held in the Tournament-room. In the unavoidable absence of both president and vice-president, Mr. Cole, chairman of Committees, took the chair, and in a well-chosen speech congratulated the masters.

Mrs Sayer-Milward, who was well received, expressed her pleasure in responding to the invitation. She and her husband had both taken great interest in the Tournament, and she was sure many persons who had not witnessed the games had enjoyed reading the reports in the papers. She was pleased to be able to give away the prizes. (Applause.)

The prize list was as follows:—

    1st. H. N. Pillsbury, America, 150*l.*
    2nd. M. Tchigorin, Russia, 115*l.*
    3rd. E. Lasker, England, 85*l.*
    4th. Dr. Tarrasch, Germany, 60*l.*
    5th. W. Steinitz, America, 40*l.*
    6th. E. Schiffers, Russia, 30*l.*
    7th. { C. von Bardeleben, Germany, 15*l.* 5*s.*
         { R. Teichmann, England, 14*l.* 15*s.*

CONSOLATION MONEY.

C. Schlechter, Austria, 13*l.*
J. H. Blackburne, England, 10*l.* 10*s.*
A. Walbrodt, Germany, 7*l.*
A. Burn, England, 9*l.*
D. Janowski, France, 9*l.*
J. Mason, England, 8*l.*
H. E. Bird, England, 5*l.*
I. Gunsberg, England, 7*l.* 10*s.*
A. Albin, America, 7*l.*
G. Marco, Austria, 7*l.*
W. H. K. Pollock, Canada, 6*l.* 10*s.*
S. Tinsley, England, 7*l.*
J. Mieses, Germany, 6*l.* 10*s.*
B. Vergani, Italy, 2*l.*

THE RESULTS

THE FULL SCORE.

Names of Players	Country Represented	Total
ALBIN, A.	America	8½
BARDELEBEN, C. VON	Germany	11½
BIRD, H. E.	England	9
BLACKBURNE, J. H.	England	10½
BURN, A.	England	9½
GUNSBERG, I.	England	9
JANOWSKI, D.	France	15½
LASKER, E.	England	8½
MARCO, G.	Austria	9½
MASON, J.	England	7½
MIESES, J.	Germany	16½
PILLSBURY, H. N.	America	8
POLLOCK, W. H. K.	Canada	12
SCHIFFERS, E.	Russia	11
SCHLECHTER, C.	Austria	13
STEINITZ, W.	America	14
TARRASCH, Dr.	Germany	16
TCHIGORIN, M.	Russia	11½
TEICHMANN, R.	England	7½
TINSLEY, S.	England	3
VERGANI, B.	Italy	10
WALBRODT, A.	Germany	

N. W. Van Lennep (Holland) was reserve man.

There was a tie for seventh place between Bardeleben and Teichmann, so that they were given half consolation money as well as the half prize. Each non-prize winner received 1*l*. for every win, and in the event of his winning a game from the first, second, or third prize winner, he received 2*l* instead of 1*l*. For a draw against a prize winner, 10*s*. was given. Tchigorin also received a handsome ring, presented by Mr. J. Cooke, of Knockgraffon, and 'The Theory and Practice of Chess' (in four octavo volumes), by Carlo Salvioli, to the player who won most Evans' Gambits (accepted), also an enlarged photograph, given by Mr. Bradshaw, of Hastings, as the first winner of seven games. A special prize of 5*l*., given by the Committee to the non-prize winner who made the highest score (including drawn games) against the seven prize winners, was taken by Schlechter, and Mr Cole kindly gave each competitor a copy of his work on 'The Antiquities of Hastings.'

On the motion of Mr. Pillsbury, seconded by Mr. Lasker, a vote of thanks was accorded Mrs. Sayer-Milward for distributing the prizes.

In addition to these the Solution Tourney prizes to Messrs. Marco, Schlechter, and Mieses had already been given, and the Brilliancy prizes of 5*l* and 3*l*. were not at that time awarded, but eventually fell to Messrs. Steinitz and Tarrasch.

The prizes for the Amateur Tournament and Ladies' Tournament were given separately.

Various speeches concluded the meeting.

Report of the Sub-committee for the Hastings International Chess Tournament Brilliancy Prizes.

Having been appointed by the Committee to adjudicate on the games for this competition, we have to report that thirteen games were submitted on behalf of various of the players, all of them having some happy stroke of brilliancy, and most of them showing masterly strategy and combinations. From this wealth of chess gems we select as prize winners:—

First.—W Steinitz for his victory over C. von Bardeleben, in which the whole of the play was extremely artistic and beautiful, as well as brilliant

Second.—Dr Tarrasch for his masterly and well-fought game with A. Walbrodt, in which the terminal combination was most brilliant and unexpected.

Approximate, and worthy of high commendation, are the fine games, I Gunsberg against J. Mason, A Albin against D. Janowski, and H N. Pillsbury against D. Janowski.

John G. Colborne,
C. D. Locock,
F. W. Womersley.

BIOGRAPHIES.

PILLSBURY, HARRY N., twenty-two at the time of the Tournament, was born on December 5, 1872, at Somerville, Mass., U.S.A. He was educated for a commercial career, and did not make a study of the game till five years ago.

Mr. Pillsbury is decidedly pleasant and unassuming in manner, and a perfect type of an American and a tremendous smoker. He is remarkably self composed, and sits at the chess-table in a comfortable style and with a self-confident look on his face.

His style of play is energetic, free from fads, and correct; whilst looking carefully after his defences, he is always pressing forward for chances of a win, which he is very quick to detect. The openings are thoroughly known, and his fearless middle game manœuvring is superb.

His chief successes are:—

In 1890 he beat Steinitz, receiving Pawn and move.
In 1890 „ „ H. N. Stone by 5 to 2.
In 1893 „ „ Walbrodt.
In 1893 „ „ Schottlander.
1893. First prize, New York City C.C.
1895. First prize, Hastings.

TCHIGORIN, MICHAEL I., forty-four at the time of the Tournament, was born on October 31, 1850. He was educated at Gatchino, near St. Petersburg, and entered the Government Administration.

In his younger days chess was to him an amusement only, and it was not till he was nearly thirty years of age that we find him coming to the front, when, in 1880, he beat Schiffers his teacher, who was then the acknowledged champion of Russia, as also others of Russian chess fame. He founded the St. Petersburg Chess Club, and has worthily shone as its president.

His style of play is quite of 'the old school,' brilliantly attacking and ever towards the King, perhaps best described by the simple word beautiful. He is probably the greatest master of the King's side attack and rarely plays dull games. His chief energy is thrown into the middle game rather than the opening, which he sometimes conducts with too much indifference. His analytical ability is of the very highest order, and blindfold play does not come amiss.

In difficult positions Tchigorin gets very excited, and at times seems quite fierce, sitting at the board with his black hair brushed back, splendid bright eyes, and flushed face looking as if he could see right through the table. When calm, however, he is decidedly handsome, and calculated to beget confidence.

We have spelt this expert's name as he spells it himself when using English characters.

His chief successes are :—

1881. Divided third prize at Berlin with Winawer, following Blackburne and Zukertort.

1883 Fourth prize at London (Grand Tournament).

1889 Divided first and second prizes at New York.

1895. Second prize at Hastings.

In 1893 he played a drawn match with Tarrasch, and in 1890 with Gunsberg.

LASKER, EMANUEL, twenty-six at the time of the Tournament, was born on December 24, 1868, at Berlinchen, Prussia, but has now definitely adopted England as his 'second fatherland.'

His chess dates from his boyhood, and was first learnt from Dr. Lasker, his brother. It is noticeable that he entered straight into the Haupt Tournament at Breslau in 1889.

The impression one gets of him is that of a modest and intelligent gentleman, with evident culture, but frail and delicate in health.

At simultaneous chess he is very rapid and successful, beating down his opponents with relentless accuracy, often winning, as in his match games, in the opening, to which he gives a great amount of attention.

Lasker, unlike many experts, has first-class business qualities.

His chief successes are :—

1889. First prize at a smaller Tournament, Berlin, without a lost game, at the age of twenty.

1889. First prize at Breslau (G.C.A.) and mastership.

1889. Second prize at Amsterdam.

1891. First prize at London (B.C.A.).

1893. First prize at New York, with an absolutely clean score of thirteen.

1895. Third prize at Hastings.

In matches he has beaten Bardeleben, Mieses, Bird, Miniati, Englisch, Blackburne, and Showalter, only losing four games in the series, two of them being to Bird

In 1892 he won the Quintangular match arranged by that generous patron Sir George Newnes. The results were: Lasker 6½, Blackburne 6, Mason 4, Gunsberg 2½, and Bird 1.

On May 26, 1894, he won the championship of the world by scoring his tenth win against Steinitz's five (four drawn) On October 19, in the same year, he was taken suddenly ill with typhoid fever, when he was carefully attended by Dr. B Lasker, his brother, who came over from Berlin for the purpose. This illness, after some delays, prevented him playing his promised return match with Steinitz. Doubtless he will, however, now soon give Steinitz an opportunity for revenge.

Like his great rival, he takes chess and life generally in a very serious way, and there seems to be but little fun in either of their natures. If this means that humour is inimical to chess, so much the worse for the latter. On the other hand, however, there is Dr. Tarrasch, who has plenty of true humour in his nature, and Pillsbury and others are not wanting in that element.

TARRASCH, SIEGBERT, M D, thirty-three at the time of the Tournament, was born on March 5, 1862, at Breslau, where he commenced his education.

He is a man of the highest educational attainments, and not being able to devote so much time and attention to the game as devotees would like to see him do, his performances have been a little irregular, and at times he has completely disappeared from the chess world.

He enjoyed a considerable reputation in the game whilst at college and university, in spite of the pressure of his other studies, taking first place indoors and frequenting chess resorts, where he played successfully with the habitués. It is said also that he was fond of correspondence and blindfold play.

Visitors to the Congress will remember him as a neat, well-dressed, sprightly gentleman of very engaging manners, and always with a fresh flower in his button-hole. Certainly a favourite with the onlookers, his board was generally well patronised whoever was his opponent.

Journalistic work has occupied a considerable amount of his time, and his annotations are very far above the average; those in this book were supplied in German, so that some may have lost a little of their pristine beauty in the process of translation.

His chief successes are :—

1884. First prize and title of master at Nuremberg (Minor Tournament).

1885. Divided second and other prizes at Hamburg ; near the end of the Tournament he led by a clear point.

1887 Divided fifth and sixth prizes at Frankfort.

1889. First prize at Breslau.

1890. First prize at Manchester.

1892. First prize at Dresden.

1894. First prize at Leipsic.

1895. Fourth prize at Hastings.

He played a drawn match with Tchigorin in 1893, maintaining the lead in the early part.

STEINITZ, WILHELM, fifty-nine at the time of the Tournament, was born on May 17, 1836, at Prague, Bohemia.

Educated in Vienna, he soon made a chess name for himself, and was sent to the London Tournament in 1862 as the representative of Austria. At that time he adopted this country, but deserted us in 1883, becoming an American citizen.

His style of play is firm and tenacious, aiming at accurate positioning and steady crushing rather than at brilliant attacks or rapid finishes. Opponents are always treated with due respect, in that he invariably does his best , should his *vis-à-vis* be weak the crush quickly produces a smash, but skittle play is unknown to him.

On the other hand he has a way of treating the openings with all sorts of eccentricities, perhaps owing to an over-desire to experiment, or arising from self-reliance ; but some of his ventures must be very trying to an opponent who may scarcely feel flattered by being met with an apparently weak manœuvre at the commencement of the game.

Mr. Steinitz stands high also as a theoretician and as a writer ; he has a powerful pen, and when he chooses can use expressive English. He evidently strives to be fair to friends and foes alike, but appears sometimes to fail to see that after all he is much like many others in this respect. Possessed of a fine intellect, and extremely fond of the game, he is apt to lose sight of all other considerations, people and business alike. Chess is his very life and soul, the one thing for which he lives.

In appearance he is peculiar and striking . fine and large head with prominent forehead, grey hair and ruddy beard, rather portly, suffering from a slight lameness which naturally increases with years; he now walks with a stick. He is said to be a good swimmer, he has at any rate plenty of buoyancy of nature, and can be entertaining and affable.

Before entering the Tournament some important conditions were made in the various chess columns of the press, and the Committee feared the entry might be lost, but were pleased to find that he eventually joined in the ordinary way, accepting the same conditions as the other competitors.

There is one curious fact, that, whilst he is shortsighted, his writing is remarkably thin and small, being peculiarly difficult to read.

With such a grand list of successes the veteran should be able to rest on his laurels, at peace with all, using his ready pen and his great experience in advancing chess in all its branches, and enjoying the just fruits of his gigantic achievements.

His chief successes are —

1862. Sixth prize at London, following Anderssen, Paulsen, Owen, M'Donnell, and Dubois

1867. Third prize at Paris with thirteen entries, following Kolisch and Winawer.

1867 Second prize at Dundee with ten entries, following Neumann

1870. Second prize at Baden with ten entries, following Anderssen.

1872. First prize at London with eight entries.

1873. First prize at Vienna with twelve entries.

1882. Divided first and second prizes with Winawer at Vienna.

1883. Second prize at London with fourteen entries, following Zukertort This is the tournament in which the late Dr. Zukertort played so magnificently

1894. First prize at New York, followed by Albin and Hymes

1895. Fifth prize at Hastings.

Besides numerous prizes (mostly first) in handicap tournaments. It is however in match play that he chiefly shines. His victims are —

1862. Dubois by 5 to 3.	1872. Zukertort by 7 to 1.
1863. Deacon by 5 to 1.	1876. Blackburne by 7 to 0.
1863. Mongredien by 7 to 0.	1882. Martinez by 7 to 0.
1863. Blackburne by 7 to 1.	1882. Martinez by 3 to 1.
1866. Anderssen by 8 to 6.	1882. Sellman by 3 to 0.
1866 Bird by 7 to 5.	1883. Mackenzie by 3 to 1.
1867. Fraser by 3 to 1.	1883. Golmayo by 8 to 1.
1870. Blackburne by 5 to 0.	1883. Martinez by 9 to 0.

1885. Sellman by 3 to 0.
1886. Zukertort by 10 to 5.
1889. Tchigorin by 10 to 6.
1891. Gunsberg by 6 to 4.

1892. Tchigorin by 10 to 8.
Beating every one till he met Lasker in 1894.

SCHIFFERS, EMANUEL G. A., forty-five at the time of the Tournament, was born of German parents on May 4, 1850, at St. Petersburg, where he was educated, attending there the Classical Gymnasium till 1867, and, continuing his studies in the Physical and Mathematical faculty till 1871, became private tutor. In appearance he is rather formidable, tall and somewhat massive framed, with a fine crop of curly iron-grey hair surmounting a massive well-set head, an intelligent but kindly countenance, and a general appearance of stability and robust manhood. And with all this he is in manner both gentle and refined, with plenty of true wit.

Chess seems to have been taken up at about fifteen, and at twenty he played with decided success against Tschoumoff and others, whilst about 1875 he made good practice with Winawer. He came to know Tchigorin in 1873 and used to play him at the odds of a Knight, but two years later the latter attained first-class strength, and in 1880 he beat Schiffers, depriving him of his proud position as the leading player of Russia, though he may justly still claim the second place.

He has won matches against Tchigorin, Mitropolsky, Wainstein, Jankowitsch, Chardin, and Alapin, two against each of the last three. Since 1880 however he has lost two or three matches against Tchigorin, but has otherwise held his own against all comers and has won many prizes in handicaps.

BARDELEBEN, CURT VON, thirty-four at the time of the Tournament, was born at Berlin, where he was educated in the legal profession, in which he now practises.

He has always been fond of chess, though he quitted public life in 1883, coming forth again in 1887 with renewed energy.

He writes English freely, as may be seen by his annotations, but does not show much disposition to speak it. Visitors to the Tournament will remember him as a carefully dressed, delicate-looking man, with a straw hat generally poised on his head, and with a modest and gentlemanly demeanour, though of a somewhat retiring disposition.

His style of play is analytical and exact rather than intuitive, a good example of what is known as the German school of thought. In our Tournament he was the last to lose a game, and his final position probably suffered considerably from his bad health.

His chief successes are :—

1882. First prize in Berlin Minor Tournament.

1883 First prize in London Minor Tournament, not losing a game till he had secured the first place.

1883. Fifth prize at Nuremberg, twenty entries.

1887 Fourth prize at Frankfort; all the early part of the tournament he looked like capturing the coveted first position, but health giving way brought disappointment.

1888. Tie for third prize at Bradford; here again he looked like doing better.

1888. Divided first and second prizes at Leipsic, coming ahead of Mieses and Tarrasch.

1889. Tie for fourth at Breslau.

1895. Tie for seventh prize at Hastings, having led the score in the early rounds.

In 1890 he played a drawn match with Scheve; in 1891 he beat Hollander; in 1894 he beat Dr. Gottschall by 4 to 1; in 1895 he played a drawn game with Blackburne and beat Teichmann by 3 to 1.

TEICHMANN, RICHARD, twenty-six at the time of the Tournament, was born on December 24, 1868, near Altenburg, Germany, where he was educated, passing on to Berlin and Jena after distinguishing himself considerably. He came to England in 1892, and has adopted this country permanently, playing as an English representative.

He has now been a student of the game for about ten years, and appears to be still improving, so that he bids fair to be even more distinguished at chess than he is as a linguist.

He speaks English with great fluency, as he does most of the European languages, he is pleasant and gentlemanly in manners, less self-assertive than some, and bids fair to become a great favourite.

He plays the modern style, is very persistent, and, although avoiding rash dashes, can put in some brilliant variations when occasion arises.

His chief successes are :—

1891. First prize at Berlin.

1892. Fourth prize in Simpson's Handicap.

1893. First prize in Simpson's Handicap.

1893. Divided second and third prizes in 'Black and White' Masters' Tournament.

1894. Third prize at Leipsic with eighteen entries, and Tarrasch and Lipke first and second. He was at first only placed in the reserves by the Leipsic Committee.

1894. First prize in Simpson's Handicap.

1895. Divided seventh prize with Bardeleben in the Hastings Tournament.

He has not gone in much for personal matches; he however defeated Loman by 7 games to 2 draws, and in 1893, by 5 wins and 2 draws to nothing, showing that he was no mean opponent.

SCHLECHTER, CARL, twenty-one at the time of the Tournament, was born on March 2, 1874, at Vienna, where he was educated for a commercial career. He learnt chess at sixteen, and has been a serious student of the game for about three years. He is rather small in stature, with bright eyes, and a modest and almost shy manner.

His style of play is not strictly Viennese, as on occasions he can play games of the most dashing description. His memorable game with Fleissig influenced the Committee greatly in selecting him; and his game with Bardeleben in this Tournament is a very fine specimen also. When taking his flights of fancy he generally proves to be correct, showing a very fine judgment of position and of the possibilities of attacking combinations. He rarely loses a game, but is inclined to miss the just reward of his labours by lapsing into a draw. He is the chess editor of 'Allgemeine Sport Zeitung' and often contributes to other papers, having rapidly advanced into fame. Though he drew too many games he has amply justified the Committee's selection, and we shall before long be hearing of his doing great things.

His chief successes were:—

1892. First prize at Vienna (Quadrangular Tournament). A drawn match with Marco shortly after, in which ten drawn games were played in succession without a win being scored at all!

1894. Third prize at Vienna (Club Masters' Tournament), following Marco and Weiss.

1895 Special prize at Hastings for the best score against the prize winners, also second prize for problem solving. Herr Schlechter is equally good as a problem composer.

BLACKBURNE, JOSEPH H., fifty-two at the time of the Tournament, was born on December 10, 1842, at Manchester, where he was educated for a commercial career, and he writes a fine bold hand. He has always played for England, and when in his prime brought much glory to his native land.

His chess seems to have been an outgrowth of the too much despised draughts, at which, as a youth, he preferred to shine, though he was far from a mean performer at the more noble game, as at most games of skill When eighteen he drew a game on even terms with Paulsen, and was further stimulated by taking part in one of Morphy's blindfold performances. Within a month 'J. H. B.' was successfully playing ten games simultaneously blindfold, an accomplishment at which he is still without an equal and now practically without a rival, at least in this country.

The blindfold *séances* are conducted with spirit and dash, and with wonderful accuracy, often winding up with the greatest brilliancies.

Blackburne is also an adept at peripatetic simultaneous play, at which he is deservedly popular, and he occasionally gives us some fine specimens of problem composition

His style is intuitive and imaginative, with a high degree of skill in the end games—perhaps rather too impatient to get off the books and detesting a dull, plodding position.

He has a remarkable memory for all branches of the game, and is one of our greatest authorities on the historical side of the subject. He is one of those also who are ever ready to give assistance without looking for a return, a characteristic which was found of the greatest value at Hastings, where he has for the last few years resided, when the Committee were arranging the Tournament.

His chief successes are :—

1868. Third prize and British Championship at London (B.C.A.).

1870. Tie for third prize with Neumann at Baden-Baden, with Anderssen and Steinitz first and second.

1873. Tie for first prize with Steinitz at Vienna.

1874. First prize at Simpson's.

1878. Third prize at Paris (with twelve entries).

1880. Divided first three prizes with Schwarz and Englisch at Wiesbaden (with sixteen entries).

1881. First prize at Berlin (with seventeen entries), followed by Zukertort, Tchigorin, and Winawer, but not closely, for Blackburne had two games to spare, though he had started with his only loss.

1882. Sixth prize at Vienna, Steinitz, Winawer, and Mason in the first three places.

1883. Third prize at London (Grand Tournament), following Zukertort and Steinitz.

1884. Second prize at Nuremberg (with eighteen entries), following Winawer.

1885. Divided second, third, fourth, fifth, and sixth prizes at Hamburg, following Gunsberg.

1885 First prize at Hereford.

1886. First prize at London (B.C A.), followed by Burn, Gunsberg, and Taubenhaus.

1886. First prize at London (B C.A. Handicap), followed by Bird and Gunsberg.

1887. Tie for second prize at Frankfort with Weiss, headed by Mackenzie.

1887. Third prize at London (B.C.A.).

1888. Sixth prize at Bradford.

1888 Divided first and second prizes at London (B.C.A) with Gunsberg.

1889. Fourth prize at New York; he was second at the end of the first round.

1890. Second prize at Manchester, following Tarrasch.

1894. Tie for fourth prize at Leipsic.

In 1887 Blackburne won his return match with Zukertort by 5 to 1, and in 1890 he beat Lee by 7 to 2. In 1891 he beat Señor Golmayo by 5 to 3, and Señor Vasquez by 5 to 1. In 1895 he drew with Bardeleben.

Nobody but Steinitz can show such a record.

WALBRODT, CARL A., twenty-three at the time of the Tournament, was born on November 28, 1871, at Amsterdam, but, though Holland claims the honour of his birth, he is of pure German descent and resides at Berlin, where he was educated. The Walbrodt brothers are the flourishing proprietors of a stencil and pattern factory at Berlin.

As a boy at home he became famous at his favourite pastime, but did not try conclusions with the first-rates till he was eighteen or nineteen years of age, when, joining the chess club, he won the first prize in the tournament without a loss, and then tried a match with Schallop, when he lost the first three games, drew the next, and then won five and the match! Thus jumping into fame literally with one bound and only one preliminary hop His heading Blackburne and others in a tournament at nineteen years of age is a feat to be proud of and ever remembered His hand writing is peculiar, and the scores that he handed in at Hastings were rarely complete and never legible.

BIOGRAPHIES

His chief successes are :—

1892. Divided fourth and fifth prizes at Dresden (not losing a game).

1894. Tie for fourth prize at Leipsic.

In 1891 he beat Schallop by 5 to 3.

In 1891 he drew a match with Scheve.

In 1892 he beat Bardeleben by 4 to 0 (four drawn).

In 1893 he beat Delmar by 5 to 3.

BURN AMOS forty-six at the time of the Tournament, was born on December 31, 1848, at Hull, England, where he commenced his education. Later on he was apprenticed at Liverpool to a firm of merchants. He is now well-to-do and follows chess as a pastime pure and simple, and has several times been president of the Liverpool Chess Club A good deal of his time is spent in America. He commenced the game about 1865, and, making rapid progress, shortly afterwards won the first prize at the Liverpool Chess Club Handicap at Pawn and move

He is exceedingly retiring in manner and almost gives the impression of moroseness ; but a more intimate acquaintance with him shows him to be of a most kindly disposition and with a fund of dry humour.

His play is of the safe school ; it is almost peculiar to himself, and scarcely of an attacking style, though it is a curious fact that he rarely draws a game The start he made in this Tournament was certainly not up to his proper form ; in fact, it was not till the very end of the first week that he seemed to be at his ease.

His chief successes are :—

1871. Tie for first prize at London (B C.A.).

1886. Second prize at London (B C A.), after tying with Blackburne for first place , Gunsberg and Taubenhaus tying for third and fourth places.

1886. First prize at Nottingham, Schallop and Gunsberg following on.

1887. Divided first and second prizes at London with Gunsberg.

1888. Fifth prize at Bradford.

1889. First prize at Amsterdam with six wins, no losses, and two draws against Lasker and Mason.

He has little favoured personal matches, but he played a drawn match with Bird and also with Captain Mackenzie in 1886.

JANOWSKI, D , is of Polish extraction, but has been for some time a resident of Paris, and frequents the Café Regence there, a favourite resort for chess-players. He looks every whit French, and was always attired in the usual faultless style of the nation of his adoption. His manners, too, were of the highest polish and not quite suggesting the Polish His play also is of a vivacious and dashing character, always dangerous to the very best, and fighting everything to the bitter end 'While there are any Pieces left there is always a chance,' seemed to be his motto. His defeat of Tchigorin at the end of the Tournament was a very good one and most unfortunate for his opponent. Steinitz again succumbed to one of his violent onslaughts in another grand game. The veteran made one weak move, and not so very weak, after all, but it made the opportunity, which was promptly seized and successfully utilised.

He gained sixth prize at Leipsic in 1894, and played a drawn match with Mieses.

MASON, JAMES, who hails from New York, was forty-five at the time of the Tournament, and was born on November 19, 1849.

He commenced the study of the game about twenty-five years ago and quickly showed his real talent ; but Mason's chess career has contained so many disappointments, always showing what he could do but rarely doing much. He has not the strength to take the game seriously, playing as for recreation only, and is an extreme illustration of what the English players generally have been accused of—playing while the clocks are ticking and taking no heed between whiles. Frequently, by pulling himself together, he has bowled over his opponents like nine-pins, but often when a brilliant success seemed inevitable he has apparently had enough of it and takes a lower position than expected. Training in any form seems altogether foreign to his nature, and in this respect he is the exact opposite of Steinitz, who lives for chess, but in style of play he resembles him very closely, though less eccentric.

He has splendid conversational powers, makes a first-rate companion with a lively vivacious manner, and is generous to a fault. 'Begone, dull care ! you and I will never agree.'

Most of his games are of the very highest class, displaying the finest judgment and a keen insight into the intricacies of a position, subtle to a degree, and spotting the slightest weakness, however obscure in nature.

He is a good writer, using particularly fine English, and a first-class annotator also Several didactic books are the outcome of his pen, and nothing could be clearer or more instructive, showing him to be as good a teacher as he is a chessist.

His chief successes are —

1876 First prize at Philadelphia.
1876 First prize at New York.

1881. Divided fifth and sixth prizes at Berlin, after a brilliant commencement.

1882. Third prize at Vienna; he was first at the end of the first round.

1883. Tie for fifth, sixth, and seventh prizes at London; second at the end of the first round, and played a magnificent game with Zukertort (up to the time of adjournment), who was then in splendid form and came out an easy first.

1884. Third prize at Nuremberg.

1884. First prize in Simpson's Handicap.

1885. Tie for second prize at Hamburg

1886. Fifth prize at London (B C.A.).

1888. Second in Simpson's Handicap.

1888. Tie for third prize at Bradford (eighteen entries), not losing till the fifteenth (!) round

1889. Divided third, fourth, and fifth prizes at Amsterdam with Van Vliet and Gunsberg.

1889. Seventh prize at New York.

1890. Tie for fifth prize at Manchester.

1890. Tie for third prize in Simpson's Handicap.

1891. Second prize at London (B C.A).

1892. Divided second prize in 'Black and White' Tournament with Tinsley.

BIRD, H. E., sixty-five at the time of the Tournament, was born on July 14, 1830, sometimes called the 'G.O.M.' of chess, a title in which he rather rejoices We find him in the tournament of 1851, and he is still amongst us as fresh as ever. Our friend is a great talker, very entertaining, and ever ready for a game; will play matches with anybody, at any time, for any stake or no stake, all comers alike. His play is essentially lively, eccentric and tricky. His draw in this Tournament against Tchigorin was obtained by a device that few would have thought it worth while to try against such an opponent; he tried to catch Pillsbury also, but it did not come off. The win, however, against Steinitz is a good specimen of his general play, and a fine game to boot.

His profession is, or was, that of accountant, and in his early days, when he followed it closely, he bore a considerable reputation. Now he writes a good deal, and is the author of several well-known books on chess

He is a very ready and fluent speaker, and sometimes assumes an amusingly confident air. But the scoring of his games is—! and most had no scores at all at Hastings, the moves having to be obtained from other sources.

His chief successes were with the old players whose names have now become items of history, and seem to belong to the far away past, but in

1867, he scored 6 to Steinitz's 7, with several drawn games, just after the latter had beaten Anderssen for the World's Championship.

1873. He beat Wisker.

1889. First prize in Simpson's Handicap, followed by Lee and Muller.

1889. First prize at London (B C.A.).

1890. Second prize in Simpson's Handicap.

1891. First prize in Simpson's Handicap.

1891. Tie for fourth prize at London (B.C.A) with C. D. Locock.

1893. Drawn match with Jasnogrodsky.

1894. Third prize in Simpson's Handicap.

GUNSBERG, ISIDOR, forty at the time of the Tournament, was born on November 2, 1854, at Buda-Pest, Hungary.

He came to England in 1863 and has adopted this country, playing as an English representative. In his young days his play was quite of the recklessly brilliant type, but as time wore on we find a sufficiency of soundness and accuracy intermingling with his style till, in 1885, he astonishes the world by winning the Hamburg Masters' Tournament by some beautiful play ahead of Blackburne, Tarrasch, &c., carrying everything before him just about that time.

His manner is particularly pleasant, he is a very expert speaker and ready writer. He is a tremendous worker, and of late years has allowed overwork to mar his position somewhat in the chess-playing world. He is a man of indomitable energy, but is reported to lack that buoyancy of nature which is necessary to stand against adverse circumstances, though he can be wonderfully calm in exciting and difficult positions.

Though chess-writing is now his chief occupation, representing the 'Daily News' and many other papers, he still makes simultaneous play a speciality, at which he practises great quickness with decided success A friend to provincial chess, he is ever ready to lend a helping hand, and is the London expert mentioned in our Introduction.

His chief successes are:—

1885. First prize in City of London Handicap.

1885. First prize in Pursell's Handicap.

1885. First prize at Hamburg (with eighteen entries), and Blackburne, Englisch, Mason, Tarrasch, and Weiss ties for second place.

1885. First prize in B.C.A. Tournament.

1886. Tie with Taubenhaus for third and fourth prizes at London (with thirteen entries).

1887. Tie with Burn for first prize in B.C.A. Tournament.

1888. First prize at Bradford (with eighteen entries), his score was $14\frac{1}{2}$, Mackenzie following with 13, and Bardeleben and Mason tying for third place with 12.

1888. First prize in Simpson's Handicap.

1889. Third prize at New York (with twenty entries), following Tchigorin and Weiss.

1889. Divided third, fourth, and fifth prizes at Amsterdam.

1889. Second prize at London (B.C.A.).

1889. Tie for fourth prize at Breslau (with eighteen entries).

1890. Tie for fifth prize at Manchester (with twenty entries).

His principal matches are:—v. Bird in 1886, won by 5 to 1; v. Blackburne in 1887, won by 5 to 2; and later played a drawn match with Tchigorin, 9 all, scored 4 to 6 v. Steinitz; 3 to 0 v. Lee; and 3 to 2 v. Bird.

ALBIN, ADOLF, forty-seven at the time of the Tournament, was born at Bucharest, Roumania. He was educated at Vienna for a mercantile career, and filled an engagement with the German railway king, Dr. Stroussberg, till his downfall. Herr Albin, however, kept up his end of the see-saw for a few years by returning to Vienna. He now represents New York.

The goddess of chess did not make his acquaintance till he was a well-grown man, but so great was his aptitude that, never too old to learn, he quickly came to the front and, after winning several first prizes in Vienna tournaments, he entered the Masters' Tournament at Dresden in 1892, and surprised the world by giving Dr Tarrasch his only defeat in a very fine game.

His style of play is ingenious and picturesque, with a pleasing dash of rashness, perhaps deficient in book knowledge but showing a keen appreciation of the leading principles of the game.

His other chief successes are:—

1893. Second prize at New York, following Lasker; a drawn match with Hodges of New York; and a win v. Delmar.

MARCO, GEORG, from Vienna, a man of considerable stature and fine muscular appearance, so much so that he has been jokingly termed 'the strongest chess-player of the world.' He won the first prize finely in the last Amsterdam National Tournament without losing a game, and coming out ahead of Weiss, Schlechter, Englisch, &c. His general appearance is very German, with but little of the bandbox about him.

One of the chief favourites with the visitors, and apparently on good terms with the masters also, he was largely the life of the Tourney, always bubbling over with fun, and cracking jokes with any and all who could understand his language He certainly should have done better considering his record and his quite recent performance, but he did not look in earnest, and perhaps was not.

His style of game also might be called playful, delighting in comical and puzzling positions of a problematic type.

POLLOCK, W. H. K., thirty six at the time of the Tournament, was born on February 21, 1859, at Cheltenham. Educated at Somersetshire College, Bath, and Clifton College, he took his medical qualification in Ireland, 1882, where he acquired much of his chess, being a favourite at the Dublin Chess Club, especially on account of his great ability in the direction of simultaneous play. Later, he and his brother (Rev J Pollock) were well known at Bath, but we hear of him in a great variety of places in the British Isles and America. He has played in numerous tournaments with varying success Crossing the herring pond five years ago, on the occasion of the American Congress, he settled in Canada, and became the chief representative of that country, but up to the time of going to press he had not returned from England. He beat Moehl in 1891, and could probably take a better position by treating the game more seriously.

Pleasant in manners, brilliant in style, and an agreeable companion or opponent, he still lacks staying power. Many of his games are of the highest order, and the one against Weiss at the 1886 Congress has become historic. He is a good writer, and is, or was, the chess editor of several columns, and has contributed to many others. Many brilliancy prizes at various times have fallen to his lot.

TINSLEY, SAMUEL, forty eight at the time of the Tournament, was born in 1847, at Barnet, Herts, where he was educated. Unlike most of the masters he did not take up chess till he was well on in years, and even then seems not to have taken it up seriously before reaching the forties. His style is brilliant and attacking, and dealing somewhat in traps rather than safety, leading of necessity to but few draws. He is reported also to shine at the lightning style of play favoured by so many amateurs.

Of late years, like Gunsberg, he has given more attention to the journalistic side of the game. He has the honour of having written the first daily reports the London 'Times' has printed of any tournament, viz. that of Hastings. 1895, and, like some others, handicapped himself by dividing his attention between the game and journalism.

He is full of fun, and always ready with a joke even against himself

His chief successes are :—

1889. Beat Muller by 7 to 0.

1890. Divided seventh prize at Manchester with Alapin and Von Scheve.

1890. Beat Muller, 5 to 1.

1892. Divided second and third prizes with Mason in 'Black and White' Masters' Tournament.

MIESES, JACQUES, thirty at the time of the Tournament, was born on February 27, 1865, at Leipsic, where he was educated, passing to the university there, and at Berlin, natural history being his chief love.

He studied chess at an early age, and at seventeen joined one of the Berlin chess clubs, winning the first prize in the annual tournament.

The early days, however, were more given to theoretical chess and to problems, of which he is now considered one of the finest, if not the finest, solver, as well as being a good composer. He is also a good writer, and has contributed much to the literature of chess, at our own Tournament he was one of those who weakened his position by attending to press matters as well as his play. He was a friend of Dr. Tarrasch's, and, like him, sometimes seemed to be allowing the distracting beauties of the town and district to be engaging some of the attention due to the more serious work of the Congress-room.

He was a man of polished manners and evident culture, speaking English with an easy style.

His chief successes are :—

1888. Tie for second prize at Nuremberg.

1888 Third prize at Leipsic, following Bardeleben.

1889. Third prize at Breslau, following Tarrasch and Burn.

In 1894 he played a drawn match with Walbrodt and Janowski.

VERGANI, BENJAMIN, the only Italian representative who has played in these tournaments for about thirty years. His score, it is true, was not brilliant, but his play was better than the result showed, he was slightly overmatched, and with the first-rates a very little difference in strength makes all the difference in the end. He came with first-class recommendations and had won second prize in the last Italian National Tournament, besides having some reputation as a blindfold player. He was slight of figure and lame, but always with a smile, though amongst strangers whose language he could not speak. His play was of the imaginative order, but became perhaps somewhat over-cautious; there was, however, a tendency to over-elaboration ending in a breakdown, but a little more practice with the European masters would soon correct that fault. Our young friend must remember that 'Faint heart never won fair lady,' and woo the fair Caissa again with less dangerous rivals.

MAROCZY, GÉZA, first prize winner of the Minor Tournament and now a master, was twenty-five at the time of the Tournament, and was born on March 3, 1870, at Szegedin, in Hungary. He was educated at the Zurich University, where he learnt his chess, though he did not seriously study the game till two years ago, and last year he won the first prize in the club tournaments at Buda-Pest, where he is now following his profession as engineer.

His style is extremely attacking, producing some most interesting and brilliant games.

Lady THOMAS, EDITH M., of the Manor of Marston, Beds, who won the first prize of the Ladies' Major Tournament, besides being a good chessist, is an expert musician and good singer, late pupil of Sir John Goss. She lived for some years with her husband, Sir Geo. Thomas, Bart., at Constantinople, but now resides in this country, and is sometimes to be seen at the Ladies' Chess Club, London

Mrs RIDPATH, of Paris, winner of the Minor Tournament, and her husband, Mr J. Ridpath, were at one time active members of our local club, and, though addicted to travel, we understand that they may shortly be coming to reside near us again.

APPENDIX

ACCOUNTS.

UNTIL this book is published the accounts cannot be quite closed, and pressure on our space prohibits our giving the list of subscribers; but we are authorised to say that copies of properly audited accounts with the list of subscribers will be issued shortly.

We can for general information add the following figures:— Donations, including £50 from J. Watney, Esq., £50 from H. Chapman, Esq., £25 from Sir George Newnes, Bart., and £20 from W. J. Evelyn, Esq (Egypt), amounted to nearly £600. £160 9s of this was given by the Hastings Chess Club, this being made up to £327 16s. from other local sources. Then non-local subscriptions amounted to £264 0s 2d., making in all £591 16s. 2d. There were also £6 from A. E. Studd, Esq, for prizes for problem solving, £5 from Horace Chapman, Esq, and Anonymous for brilliancy prize, and £3 from W. Leuchars, Esq., for second brilliancy prize, making a cash total of £607 7s 8d, besides prizes in kind from J Cooke, Esq., and G. Bradshaw, Esq. To this must be added £105 entrance fees, £35 press subscriptions, and some gate-money, &c. Against this there is Masters' prize money, £627 10s, £25 Amateurs' Tournament, besides hire of rooms for same, the expenses of Ladies' Tournament, loss on 'The Book of the Tournament,' including purchase of subscribers' copies, expenditure for printing, postage, telegrams, &c., expenses of the various social events, and purchase or hire of necessary material, as well as furnishing, &c., apparently still leaving a small balance of something under £20. It is worthy of note that the prize money is more that the donations from all sources. This is mainly due to the economical methods of management, a hard-working Hon Secretary and Committee, rooms for the masters lent by the town authorities free, and even the handsome pictures decorating the walls lent for the purpose of the Tournament by a local friend (Mr Th. Mann)

SYSTEM OF PAIRING.

In the early days of the Hastings Chess Club the want was felt of a system for pairing players for tournaments, which will not be found to be easy if one tries by a haphazard method. We, therefore, devised a scheme which is still in use, and has always worked satisfactorily, besides being most simple in application. Since then Prof. Berger's system has been invented and come into general use, and is based on somewhat the same principle.

Our scheme is :—We number the players, which can be done by lot, having previously decided the order according to the following plan .—

No. 1 plays 2, 3, 4, 5, 1 in order,
No. 2   „   1, 2, 3, 4, 5   „
No. 3   „   5, 1, 2, 3, 4   „
No. 4   „   4, 5, 1, 2, 3   „
No. 5   „   3, 4, 5, 1, 2   „

and so on for a larger number of players, always, however, making the draw for an *odd* number of competitors. On the day on which anyone is down to play himself, he, of course, has a bye, and it can be entered so on the time-sheet. Now, if there are an even number of players, say six, each one meets the extra one on what would have been his bye day, and the pairing becomes :—

No. 1 plays 2, 3, 4, 5, 6 in order,
No. 2   „   1, 6, 3, 4, 5   „
No. 3   „   5, 1, 2, 6, 4   „
No. 4   „   6, 5, 1, 2, 3   „
No. 5   „   3, 4, 6, 1, 2   „
No. 6   „   4, 2, 5, 3, 1   „

the 6's coming in where the player's own number would naturally be placed. One distinct advantage is that a competitor starts his list at a particular place, and plays right down and then commences at the top, except for what we term the bye man

This was the system which was used in this Tournament except that, after the arrangement of the numbers, the draw made on the morning of each day decided which of the rounds were to be taken An examination of p. 12 will make this clear.

When the rounds are taken in order, by a simple calculation one can determine what opponents meet in any given round, and, of course, No. 1 need not start with No. 2 if it is preferred otherwise.

INSTRUCTIONS TO DIRECTORS OF PLAY.

Directors, who were first-class amateurs, were appointed to superintend each day, with stewards to assist them. These instructions were issued, and copies were furnished to the masters :—

1. The director on duty at either morning or evening sitting will be present at least a quarter of an hour before the time fixed for play, and his first duty will be to see that the clocks and sets are correct.

2 He will see that the clocks are set going at the time fixed for play.

APPENDIX

3. He will be present throughout the hours of play, and is bound to receive any complaints from competitors as to the infraction of the Rules and Regulations.

4. In case of an alleged infraction of the time limit, he will at once decide the fact by the state of the clock, the score of the game, and by taking any evidence of players and bystanders that he may consider necessary to form a fair judgment of the case. If the alleged infraction of the time limit be not proved to his satisfaction the game will proceed, but if proved he will at once score the game on the provisional score-sheets. He is bound to take notice of any infraction of the time limit.

5. In case of a complaint by a competitor as to an infraction of the laws of chess he will take evidence as to the facts of the case, and decide the point in dispute according to the laws in force. An appeal against his decision may be made to the Committee. If an appeal is made, the director must at once communicate with the hon. secretary, who will immediately summon a quorum of the Committee for a final decision to be made.

6. Immediately on a complaint being made as above, the director will stop the clocks of the players concerned.

7. When any game is finished, he will at once register the result on the provisional score-sheets.

8. Ten minutes before the close of play he will give notice to all players of unfinished games that such games must be adjourned, and that the player whose turn it is to move must record his next move in writing instead of making it on the board, but not before the 30th or 60th move of Black. The player who has made the last move will be called upon to record the position of the Pieces on a diagram provided, and the player who has to move will record his move on the back of the diagram and place it in an envelope, which is to be closed down. The director will write the names of the players on the envelope, and also the exact time used by each of them.

9. Before the hour fixed for resumption of play the director will see that the time by the clocks corresponds with the times stated on the envelopes. At the time fixed he will start the clocks of the players who are absent. He will open the envelopes in the presence of both players, and will make on the board the move as written down. Rule IV. is in force with regard to sealed moves, so far as it applies. Ambiguous sealed moves are to be interpreted by the opponent. An error in the diagram may be corrected from the score-sheet of the game. If either player of an adjourned game is absent his clock will be set in motion, and only after his arrival is the envelope to be opened and the move made.

10. The director may call upon competitors in an adjourned game to resume it any time when they are free, and there are two hours left for play.

11. The director will place the sealed envelopes, incomplete scores of games, and badge of office in the official box provided for the purpose, and will deliver the key to the secretary.

NOTE—In regard to Rule VII., when the score was handed to the official scorer and found correct, it was then entered on another score-sheet, the provisional score-sheet being mainly for the information of the public and not final. In Rule VIII. it was afterwards arranged that the sealed move might be entered anywhere, as the opponent might easily delay matters by being slow over the diagram. In Rule IX., with the general consent of the players, the envelopes were opened immediately the time was up.

INSTRUCTIONS TO STEWARDS.

The duty of the stewards is to look after the convenience of the visitors to the Congress, to see that the arrangements at the door and in the small chess-room are all right, to see that the lines of chairs are kept, and to give any assistance to the director of play that he may require.

OPENINGS CHOSEN.

	Number	White Won	Black Won	Drawn
Queen's side and allied openings	69	30	25	14
Ruy Lopez	43	18	12	13
French	30	16	9	5
Giuoco Piano	12	5	4	3
Vienna	12	4	6	2
Scotch	9	2	3	4
Evans'	9	1	7	1
Two Knights' Defence	7	1	5	1
Sicilian	6	3	1	2
King's Gambit Declined	5	1	3	1
Four Knights'	4	1	0	3
Petroff	4	0	2	2
Bishop's Gambit	3	0	2	1
Centre Counter	3	0	3	0
Philidor	3	1	1	1
Less favoured débuts	11	2	4	5
Total	230	85	87	58

THE INNOVATIONS.

Some of our successors will perhaps be asking wherein the Hastings Tournament differed from the preceding ones, especially as regards its method of management, so we will endeavour to indicate the chief points, some of which were new.

Starting with a considerable home guarantee before the Congress was announced, we freely invited suggestions from any and all, and as freely gave them full consideration and discussion in a small working committee, which entirely lacked merely ornamental members.

No one knew, till the morning of each day, who would meet, though the tables at which each game was to be played were arranged beforehand, avoiding unseemly scrambles and securing the maximum of fairness for the competitors. On the draw being made, ornamental cards bearing the competitors' names were put into their places, and at once acted as labels both for the seats to the players and for the players to the visitors. It was, however, after some debate, thought better to decide the first moves beforehand, and a card bearing all these particulars was displayed in the room, the names being filled in according to the draw at the opening ceremony.

There was no cancelling of scores; if a competitor retired he was to forfeit the rest of his games as they became due—in other words, no retirements were to be acknowledged. This is and can be the only fair method, for a retiring one will always be either weak or incapacitated in some way, so that he would probably or certainly lose his games. And further, a little consideration will show that in all cases more injustice is done by cancelling a score than letting it stand, especially as between those the defaulter has played.

The Committee paid (as consolation money) for wins rather than draws, which answered the purpose of encouraging players to complete their games and avoid drawn ones, much better than the replaying system sometimes adopted.

Seeing that the object of the time limit is to prevent undue protraction of games, and that so very few are completed within the first hour, when the pressure is generally most felt, the limit was not to be reckoned till a player had consumed two hours, thus just fitting the first four hours' sitting; the second sitting was three hours only, but no game could be adjourned till sixty moves, including the sealed one, had been made on each side, which of course might take eight hours, but it avoided trouble with the time limit and left very few adjourned games.

But the item which probably did most to attract so strong an entry was our announcement that we should make no official appointments outside our own Committee; it will easily be seen that amongst professionals conflicting interests arise, and perhaps sometimes unfortunate jealousies. On the other hand, it was the only one which gave rise to trouble, not so much on account of the obvious disabilities, as in reference to the brilliancy prizes. When these were given, the donors, one of whom was the vice-president, eventually selected the judges, and most naturally chose two who had acted satisfactorily for a preceding International Tournament; but when these were made known two of the competitors dissented, declining to agree to 'anyone outside our own Committee.' We were therefore on the horns of a dilemma; our announcement had been strained into a construction which, apparently, it would bear, though never intended, and we had accepted the prizes and proclaimed them. It seemed at first inevitable that we must either return the prizes or let them be given as a purely private affair, robbing them of most of their glory. After some correspondence, however, the two judges relieved us in our perplexity by retiring, and the donors consented to the altered arrangements.

SOLUTIONS TO PROBLEMS SET IN THE SOLUTION TOURNEY.

No 1. Berger.—Key: K to Kt 2, followed by 2. K to B 2, 2. Q to R 2, 2. Q to B 2, 2. Kt to Kt 5, &c., accordingly

No. 2. Gold.—Key R to Kt 2, followed by 2. Q to R 3, 2. Q to B 3, ch, &c., accordingly.

The near tries of R × P and R to Q 4 (which have been claimed by some as cooks) are both defeated by R to B 4.

No. 3. D. P.—Key. K to K 7, threatening 2. K to B 8, 3 Q to K 8 (!); 4. R to B 4, mate.

Unfortunately, No. 1 had an obscure cook which was not discovered at the time; the position as given has been amended by Mr. Studd, with the author's consent, by a slight alteration.

INDEX

Accounts, 363
Albin (biography), 359
Bardeleben (biography), 350
Biographies:—
    Albin, 359
    Bardeleben, 350
    Bird, 357
    Blackburne, 352
    Burn, 355
    Gunsberg, 358
    Janowski, 355
    Lasker, 346
    Marco, 359
    Maroczy, 362
    Mason, 356
    Mieses, 361
    Pillsbury, 345
    Pollock, 360
    Ridpath, Mrs., 362
    Schiffers, 350
    Schlechter, 352
    Steinitz, 348
    Tarrasch, 347
    Tchigorin, 345
    Teichmann, 351
    Thomas, Lady, 362
    Tinsley, 360
    Vergani, 362
    Walbrodt, 354
Bird (biography), 357
Blackburne (biography), 352
Burn (biography), 355
Consultation game, 341
Early history, 4
Gunsberg (biography), 358
Items, 2
Janowski (biography), 355
Lasker (biography), 346
Marco (biography), 359
Maroczy (biography), 362

Maroczy v. Owen, 339
Mason (biography), 356
Mieses (biography), 361
Opening day, 10
Openings, 366
    Centre Counter, 50, 169, 233
    Evans', 87, 115, 132, 141, 165, 209, 229, 291, 292
    Four Knights', 16, 19, 32, 44, 98, 100, 135, 161, 173, 178, 187, 207, 264
    French, 14, 27, 40, 55, 65, 80, 94, 98, 121, 153, 156, 159, 165, 171, 180, 182, 191, 211, 213, 246, 259, 262, 266, 276, 283, 290, 308, 319, 331
    From's, 64, 77
    Giuoco, 19, 32, 42, 54, 93, 100, 128, 130, 135, 157, 194, 207, 264, 309
    Hungarian, 149, 323
    Indian, 83, 288, 338, 339
    King's Gambits, 20, 47, 127, 187, 199, 239, 271, 296
    Petroff, 76, 98, 105, 114, 161, 187, 250
    Philidor, 70, 196, 281
    Ponziani, 82, 159
    Queen's side and allied openings, 13, 22, 24, 25, 29, 30, 34, 36, 41, 48, 55, 57, 66, 69, 72, 73, 79, 84, 86, 90, 92, 95, 96, 108, 110, 111, 118, 123, 124, 133, 139, 147, 148, 150, 151, 164, 172, 174, 175, 190, 192, 195, 197, 201, 218, 223, 224, 227, 240, 248, 255, 257, 259, 279, 284, 285, 287, 293, 295, 302, 305, 310, 314, 321, 325, 332, 336, 339, 341

Openings (*cont.*)—
  Ruy Lopez, 16, 38, 53, 60, 62, 78, 102, 107, 108, 126, 134, 140, 143, 145, 162, 176, 179, 183, 185, 189, 202, 203, 212, 220, 226, 230, 236, 238, 240, 242, 244, 245, 261, 270, 272, 273, 278, 299, 304, 312, 315, 328, 334
  Scotch, 26, 39, 58, 66, 166, 251, 253, 268, 275, 307
  Sicilian, 46, 52, 210, 235, 267, 280
  Three Knights', 24, 114, 256
  Two Knights' Defence, 32, 54, 71, 100, 135, 254, 300, 330
  Vienna, 17, 88, 104, 113, 127, 205, 232, 239, 258, 297, 320, 327
Pairings, 12, 363
Pillsbury (biography), 345
Pollock (biography), 360
Prizes, &c., 6, 8, 342
Problems, 216, 368
Regulations, 6, 364, 366
Ridpath, Mrs. (biography), 362
Rules, 8
Schiffers (biography), 350
Schlechter (biography), 352
Social, 10, 59, 138, 215, 217, 289
Solutions, 368
Steinitz (biography), 348
Tarrasch (biography), 347
Tchigorin (biography), 345
Teichmann (biography), 351
Thomas, Lady (biography), 362
Tinsley (biography), 360
Vergani (biography), 362
Walbrodt (biography), 354
Withdrawals, 8, 367

CHESS

The Modern Chess Instructor. Part I. By W. STEINITZ. Large 8°, pp. xli +193 . . $1 50

CONTENTS: Description of the Game—The Notation—Laws of the Game—Technical Terms—Chess as a Training of Mind—The Modern School and its Tendency—Relative Value of Pieces, and Principles of Play—Analysis of the Following Openings, with Illustrative Games. The Ruy Lopez; Double Ruy Lopez; Three and Four Knights' Game; The Scotch Gambit; The Two Knights' Defence; Petroff's Defence; Philidor's Defence. The Appendix contains the games of the contest between Messrs Steinitz and Tschigorin, Played at Havana in January and February, 1889, with notations by the author

This volume, by a writer who is recognized as the highest authority on its special subject (chess analysis), is the first *original* work in its department that has appeared in this country.

"This volume will be warmly welcomed by students of this fascinating game It begins at the beginning and leaves nothing unexplained"—*Rochester Herald.*

"A work which is certain to take the highest position as a students hand-book"—*Boston Weekly Post*

PART II. SECTION I.

Containing the analyses of the Ponziani Opening and of the Giuoco Piano Opening, With Illustrative Games and Notes.

Large 8°, pp. viii+64, paper, ...75

The Hastings Chess Tournament Book.

Containing the full official record of the 320 games played by the 22 competitors at this latest international Congress, annotated by a distinguished body of experts, including in their number eight prize winners. Together with biographical sketches of the 22 players with portraits and autographs of each; the rules under which the Tournament was played; and 200 diagrams of situations, etc., etc. 8°, net $1 75

Whist Nuggets. Papers about Whist and Whist-Players. Compiled by W. G. McGuckin . $1 00

PARTIAL LIST OF CONTENTS: Whist and Whist-Players, *Abraham Hayward*—Modern Whist—*London Quarterly Review*—Thirty-nine Articles of Whist, *Richard Irving Dunbar* — Rhyming Maxims, *William Pole* — The Duffer's Whist Maxims, *Cavendish* — Cards Spiritualized—Mrs. Battle's Opinions on Whist, *Charles Lamb*—Ladies' Whist, *Spectator*--A Whist Party *Philip H Welch*—A Hand at Cards, *G. W. P*,—Metternish's Whist, *Chambers Journal.*